The Exemplary Middle School
Second Edition

The Exemplary Middle School

Second Edition

Paul S. George
University of Florida

William M. Alexander
University of Florida

Harcourt Brace Jovanovich College Publishers

Fort Worth ■ Philadelphia ■ San Diego ■ New York ■ Orlando ■ Austin ■ San Antonio
Toronto ■ Montreal ■ London ■ Sydney ■ Tokyo

Editor-in-Chief: Ted Buchholz
Acquisitions Editor: Jo-Anne Weaver
Project Editor: Nancy Lombardi
Cover Design: Nick Welch
Senior Production Manager: Ken Dunaway
Text Design: Jane Tenenbaum/Impressions

ISBN: 0-15-768446
Library of Congress Catalog Card Number 92–72262
Printed in the United States of America
2   3   4   5   6   7   8   9   0   1   039   9   8   7   6   5   4   3   2   1

To Reisa and Nell, exemplary women

Preface

The *Exemplary Middle School* is a basic textbook for students in the field of middle school education. It is comprehensive in scope beginning with a discussion of the characteristics and needs of the students, describing in detail exemplary middle school practices which best meet those needs, and proceeding to a discussion of leadership and the implementation of these programs. We have prepared the book to be of substantial and specific help both to the beginner in middle school education and the practitioner seeking continued school improvement in already exemplary schools.

We have long been directly and deeply involved in the search for better education for children in the middle school years. This search has lasted throughout the twentieth century, with the junior high school developing early and becoming the dominant school between elementary and high school during the 1920 to 1960 period. Dissatisfaction with the junior high school and with the still common K8-4 plan of organization (without a school in the middle), led one of the authors and other educators to propose early in the 1960s the alternative organization now commonly called the "middle school." As explained in Chapter 2, the middle school concept has caught on widely since 1960, with some 15,000 schools now using this organization (usually, but not always, three or more years including grades 6 and 7). As researchers, consultants to school districts and faculties, and trainers of middle school personnel, we have been actively involved in the search for effective middle schools which would help achieve the long sought goal of education continuity from early childhood through adolescence, linking elementary and secondary with a dynamic program for children in the middle.

Although the middle school movement of the last three decades has encompassed some 15,000 middle school units, these schools have only begun to develop a uniformity of the characteristics educators have agreed upon as essential for effective education in the middle of a child's school career. Perhaps the early years of the middle school movement were too much of a "bandwagon" time, with many middle schools being established for social, economic, or political reasons only indirectly associated with the needs of the students. In Chapter 2, we examine the movement in detail and call attention to the remaining gap between the consensus-based characteristics of middle schools and the actual

practices—although much has been accomplished in narrowing this gap since the first edition of this textbook a decade ago. This book bridges the gap between theory and practice, aiming toward a significant increase in the number of exemplary schools and of exemplary practices in schools.

We believe that most books on the middle school published since *The Emergent Middle School* (Holt, Rinehart and Winston, 1968) have lacked an adequate balance between theory, research, and illustrative practices. In order to help our readers relate theory and research to practice, we have been eager to include many illustrations of exemplary practices and schools. Using our experience and knowledge, the recommendations of other middle school educators, and the literature on middle school education, we identified more than 100 middle schools throughout the United States, Canada, and beyond as being representative of exemplary practices. In both editions, we have asked the leaders of these schools to share materials explaining their schools, and exemplary practices therein, and have been pleased with the wealth of materials provided. We have visited and studied closely many of the schools referred to in this book. We include an appendix which, while incomplete, is a useful directory of exemplary middle schools. We regret the impossibility of including all good middle schools in this book, as well as our failure to hear from a few schools in time to include them.

The organization and content of the text are based on the characteristics of middle school students described in Chapter 1, and the definition of the middle school and its essential characteristics presented in Chapter 2. Chapter 1 summarizes the information available on this age group, and looks especially closely at a new group of students, those identified as "at risk". Chapter 2 is devoted to a history of the middle school movement and a concise explanation of the middle school concept as it has emerged. Chapter 3 is devoted to the middle school curriculum, the major domains therein, and trends in the process of curriculum development which promise to be significant in the next decade.Our concern for providing readers with specific, sometimes how-to—do-it is evident in Chapter 4, on instruction. Chapter 5 examines the nature of the student-teacher relationship at the middle level and the teacher's role in affective education, with extended examples of effective components of what have come to be called "advisor-advisee" programs. Chapter 6 illustrates another unique feature of exemplary middle schools, the interdisciplinary team, which bridges the gap between the self-contained classroom of the elementary school, and the departments of the high school. Illustrations are drawn from many new schools, and major new descriptions of exemplary teams are offered in this second edition. Chapter 7 focuses on alternative methods of grouping middle schools students, with an important new section concentrating on the issue of ability grouping and the nature of the middle school's response to that growing problem. Chapter 7 also contains a major section on "mainstreaming". In Chapter 8, we give atten-

tion to the problems of time and space (schedule and building) which we have found to be very critical in the middle school, especially since so many middle schools have inherited the buildings of predecessor organizations and sometimes maintain their schedules. We illustrate new building conceptualizations which we believe will more nearly match the middle school concept in the coming new century. We give extended attention to different instructional strategies, with major attention to large group, small group, and individualized instruction. We introduce the "reading/writing workshop" approach in this second edition, as well as "consultation and co-teaching" approaches which have become popular in recent years. Chapter 9 studies the processes of planning and evaluating middle schools, with step-by-step instructions born out of the last decade on our involvement in such activities. Chapter 10 turns to the critical matter of leadership roles in the middle school, with special attention to the process of shared decision-making so crucial to the long-term success of exemplary middle schools.

The authors consider the extensive use of up-to-date illustrative materials a unique feature of this book, and we and our readers are indebted to the educators in schools providing these examples. Readers may also find the roster of exemplary schools and the index references useful in identifying schools and practices of special interest to them. Our section at the end of each chapter on "Additional Suggestions for Further Study" provides useful additional references in the areas of theory and research. Particular attention is called to the inclusion in these lists of bibliographic information about doctoral dissertations dealing with middle school education; these studies are providing significant resources for further implementation and support for middle school theory and desired practices.

We are grateful to all the personnel of the middle and other schools in which we have worked as teachers and consultants for the stimulus given our thinking and writing about middle school education. We are also influenced by and are grateful for the challenge and other contributions of the hundreds of students in our middle school leadership courses at the University of Florida. Especially, we wish to thank again the principals and other personnel of the exemplary middle schools cited in this text for their valuable assistance.

The authors wish to provide special acknowledgment for the assistance of Mary Yonek in the preparation of the first draft of Chapter 1, to Donna Bushnell in the preparation of Chapter 5, and to Gaylon Currie for assistance in the compilation of sources from which the end-of-chapter reading suggestions are drawn. We also thank Cathi Dillard and Terri Click, of the Orange County Public Schools, for their substantial assistance in the preparation of our descriptions of the area of consultation and co-teaching methodologies. Finally, we wish to gratefully acknowledge the cheerful and determined energy and time which Reisa George devoted to the editing of the several versions through which this manuscript passed on its way to publication.

About the Authors

Paul S. George is Professor of Education, in the Department of Educational Leadership, at the University of Florida, in Gainesville, Florida. Dr. George has been involved in the study of middle school education since he became a ninth grade teacher in 1964. He has published 5 books and approximately 100 monographs, articles, and videos on the topic of middle school education. Dr. George has served as a consultant to educational groups of all kinds in forty-five states, and nine foreign countries. In the past twenty-five years, he has addressed a total audience numbering nearly 80,000 people at state, national, and international meetings, conferences, and workshops, including guest lectures at more than twenty-five universities in the United States, Canada, France, and Japan. Dr. George has also spent considerable time in the study of Japanese education, and in the investigation of organization and leadership in the corporate world, seeking insight into what those areas might offer to American education. The American Association of School Administrators (AASA) has referred to Professor George as "the foremost expert on middle schools in the country." He is married and the father of three children.

William M. Alexander is Professor Emeritus of Education at the University of Florida, Gainesville, Florida. Often called the "Father of the Middle School," Dr. Alexander has been involved in middle level education for half a century. He is a man of "firsts" in that regard. He was the senior author of the first textbook on the subject of middle school education (*The Emergent Middle School,* published by Holt, Rinehart and Winston, in 1968). He initiated the first league of middle school, the successful Florida League of Middle Schools, in 1972; he established the first program in middle school teacher education in the nation, at the University of Florida. He presented one of the first keynote addresses to the National Middle School Association, and was one of the first recipients of the prestigious Lounsbury Award, given by the NMSA. Dr. Alexander was one of the first presidents of the Association for Supervision and Curriculum Development. He is married and the father of two children and four grandchildren.

Contents

1

The Middle School Student

This book is about students and educators who learn and teach in schools in the middle of the school ladder, and the characteristics of exemplary middle school programs and experiences. This first chapter defines the characteristics and needs of students who fall into the general category of early adolescence, since the middle school focuses on programs which are congruent with those characteristics and needs. We focus on generalizations which can be safely offered about the age group, and those aspects of the age group which are most directly relevant to the organization and operation of quality middle level schools. We then examine, albeit briefly, major demographic changes which have emerged during the last decade. We conclude by emphasizing the importance of student development in decisions about individual school programs and organization.

The Early Adolescent and the School

Research and experience over the decade of the 1980s and the early 1990s (George & Anderson, 1989) indicates that there has been a close correlation between the longevity of quality middle school programs and the degree to which the members of the school staff possess what might be described as a compassionate understanding of the characteristics and needs of the learners in the school. Educators who are able to organize and open an exemplary middle school, and then maintain the school program at a high level of quality for a decade or more, point to such an understanding as one of the most important enabling factors associated with their success. During this same period, the authors have visited hundreds of middle and junior high schools; every outstanding school we have ever visited has had, among the staff, a clear understanding of the nature and needs of the students and an irrevocable commitment to meeting those needs in the school setting. Evidently, there is such a sufficiently direct connection between exemplary middle school programs and an understanding of the characteristics of the students that it is folly to proceed with any endeavor related to middle school education without first focusing firmly on the nature and needs of the developing adolescent. Hence, we begin this textbook with an examination of the student in the middle level school.

Knowledge about the Age Group

Prior to the 1980s, little attention was paid to the characteristics of students between the ages of ten and fifteen, except by parents and educators. Both of these groups seem to have sensed that there were very special differences that separated this age group from younger children and older adolescents, but there was little confirmation of this intuitive understanding available from professionals in research on human development, medicine, the criminal justice system, the church, or other areas.

> The teens, especially the earlier years, are a time of growth and change second only to infancy in sheer velocity. And yet until recently, knowledge about developmental processes in adolescents has been scattered among the disciplines and lacking in a unifying theory. Much of it has been gleaned from clinical studies that have tended to emphasize pathologies rather than normal development. (Staff, 1990, p. 3)

More than a decade ago, Lipsitz (1980) argued that "we are less informed about this stage of development than about any other among minors in America." At that point, professionals found it difficult to agree even on the proper terminology to describe the age group; such conceptual disarray continues, although some progress has been made. For some, the term "transescence" coined by Donald Eichhorn (Eichhorn, 1966) has a great deal of appeal, because of their personal acquaintance with and fondness for one of middle school education's most important pioneers. Others use the term "developing adolescent;" still others choose more informal terms like "in-between-ager." Each of the terms "later childhood," "preadolescence," "emerging adolescence," and "early adolescence" describes definite and large groups of the middle school population, but each fails to be inclusive of the total range of ages and development which fall into the middle school years. To use all of these terms in a single reference is tedious. So we ourselves are inclined to use these terms somewhat interchangeably, and mostly to talk about boys and girls, learners, or students in the middle school or of middle school age, and sometimes just to abbreviate the reference to "middle schoolers."

In the same sense that we have difficulty defining and using concepts like "fun" and "obscenity" in wholly satisfactory ways, we have difficulty coming to agreement, yet, about the dimensions of this age group, let alone the proper descriptive term. Similarly, however, most of us would agree that "we know it when we see it." Middle schoolers are involved in a stage of development that begins just prior to puberty and extends through the early stages of adolescence. It involves many changes in physical, sexual, social, emotional, moral, psychological, and intellectual dimensions.

Regardless of what we call these learners, or the exact dimensions of the developmental phase, there is a growing unanimity about the significance of this period of growing up. A variety of professional organizations devote substantial time and resources to the nature of these students and to the importance of improving schooling during these years: The National Middle School Association, American Association of School Administrators, Association for Supervision and Curriculum Development, the National Association for Secondary School Principals, and others, including the National Science Foundation, offer workshops, give journal space, and highlight many conference sessions on the early adolescent student and the implications for schooling which flow from a knowledge of those students. The National Middle School Association membership has grown from about 1,000 to over 12,000 in the last ten years, an indication of growing interest in and concern about the age group and its education. No less prestigious a group than the Carnegie Corporation has devoted impressive resources to the age group and its education. In *Turning Points*, an influential publication of the Carnegie Task Force on Education of Young Adolescents (1989, p. 20), the authors underline their convictions about the importance of this developmental period by writing that:

> Young adolescents today make fateful choices, fateful for them and for our nation. The period of life from ages 10 to 15 represents for many young people their last best chance to choose a path toward productive and fulfilling lives.

Human development research and scholarship has increasingly identified the importance of early adolescence as a unique phase of growing up. Psychologists Shave and Shave (1989) write, for example, about early adolescence "as a distinct developmental phase that is quantitatively different" from both earlier and later periods. They argue that the changes experienced during early adolescence are "developmentally unique in both the intensity and the reactivity of early adolescents to self-experiences and life situations." Human development specialists Feldman and Elliott (1990) articulate the now-prevailing view that early adolescence is a pivotal stage of life when the person is defined, by our society, as being neither adult nor child. They are, write Feldman and Elliot, "changing physically, maturing sexually, becoming increasingly able to engage in complex reasoning, and markedly expanding their knowledge of themselves and the world about them. These and many other factors foster an urge in them to gain more control over how and with whom they spend their time" (1990, p. 4). Again, from the Carnegie Council on Adolescent Development, "This is a time of immense importance in the development of the young person" (1989, p. 21).

In recent years, knowledge of this phase of human development has evolved to the point that we are not only certain about its importance, we also recognize that the experience can be vastly different from one individual to another. For girls, the tremendous changes usually happen earlier than for boys. For some youngsters of both sexes, it may be "an exceptionally stressful time in the life course;" for others, possibly the majority, the supposed tumult of the period in and of itself, the "storm and stress" may be much less significant and for some it may be virtually nonexistent (Simmons & Blyth, 1987). These middle schoolers "differ enormously in their personalities, talents, growth patterns, and coping skills, but the twelve-year-old has virtually nothing in common with the nineteen-year-old" (Staff, 1990). Early adolescents show as much variability in their backgrounds, life experiences, values, and aspirations as do adults.

Regardless of the nature of the experience itself, however, most American youth manage, somehow, to come through the critical years of this period relatively unscathed:

> With good schools, supportive families, and caring community institutions, they grow to adulthood meeting the requirement of the workplace, the commitments to families and friends, and the responsibilities of citizenship. Even under less-than-optimal conditions for healthy growth, many youngsters manage to become contributing members of society. Some achieve this feat despite threats to their well-being that were almost unknown to their parents and grandparents. (Staff, 1990)

Even though variability may be the most outstanding characteristic of the entire population of the age group, this should not be taken to imply that there are no important commonalities of experience for early adolescents as an age group. All middle school students experience many similar changes; physically, intellectually, and emotionally they are in a period of extraordinary transition. Even though the transition from child to adult is not a predictable sequence of stages, most members of the age group are influenced and react to similar stimuli—both internal and external—some endocrinological, but mostly social and psychological. Striving for independence and a sense of self, most middle schoolers undergo the common difficult task of balancing the pressures of family, friends, church, community and school, with the desire to define a value system that fits their own needs, while experiencing phenomenal changes intellectually, physically, and otherwise.

Dorman, Lipsitz, and Verner (1985) suggest the following as needs of young adolescents as a school group:

- diversity (in experiencing teaching, curriculum, and scheduling);
- self-exploration and self-definition;
- meaningful participation in school and community;
- positive social interaction with peers and adults;
- physical activity;
- competence and achievement; and
- structure and clear limits.

Other scholars of the age group identify similar lists of developmental tasks which should be substantially underway or accomplished during early adolescence. Simmons and Blyth (1987, p. 17) identify: "the need to form a new self-image; to intensify peer relationships; to establish independence; to plan for the future; and to deal with conformity versus deviance issues." Thornburg's (1980) earlier designation of seven developmental tasks remains a useful one to note as we turn to a brief identification of some major characteristics of the age group:

1. becoming aware of increased physical changes;
2. organizing knowledge and concepts into problem-solving strategies;
3. learning new social/sex roles;
4. recognizing one's identification with stereotype;
5. developing friendships with others;
6. gaining a sense of independence; and
7. developing a sense of morality and values.

Physical Characteristics

Middle school students typically range from ten to fifteen years of age. A growth spurt (accelerated rate increase in height and weight) and sexual maturation generally occur during this time period, although they often begin earlier for some and arrive later in a few individuals. Changes in body size and symmetry, and in the primary and secondary sex characteristics, mark this transitional time.

Maturation has been occurring earlier in successive generations due to several factors, including nutrition and quality of medical care; this is known as the "secular trend" (Lambert, Rothschild, Altland & Green, 1972; Coleman, 1980). With these trends combining with other social and psychological factors, sexual activity is beginning earlier, and teenage pregnancy rates have increased (Faulkenberry, Vincent, James & Johnson, 1987; National Center for Health Statistics, 1990). The incidence of adolescent AIDS and ARC (AIDS related complex) is also on the rise (National AIDS Information Clearinghouse, 1990). This secular trend and its ramifications make understanding this period critical for the middle school educator. As a result of earlier maturation, sexual relations, pregnancy, and sexually transmitted diseases are now issues of concern at the middle school, whether or not educators and parents prefer it.

Girls generally reach sexual maturity earlier than boys. Female maturity is most frequently defined as the age of menarche, about 12 years of age (Frisancho, 1981), although reproductive capability may not be reached until several months or even a year or more later. For boys, maturity is often measured as the peak of the growth spurt, at about 14 years of age (Simmons & Blyth, 1987). Thus, girls reach maturity, on the average, two years before boys. At a time when students are learning to relate to one another in social situations, the developmental lag between boys and girls can be awkward and embarrassing for those involved.

Boys of the same age are usually not of interest to girls unless they are early maturers. Instead, mature girls will often be attracted to older boys, who may have sexual knowledge and drive that can be confusing or overwhelming to a young girl. Late maturing females are sometimes tall and thin, with no evident sexual development. Being "different" can lead to extreme self-consciousness and withdrawal. Consequently, self-esteem and self-concept are closely related to physical development. Adolescent females report significantly lower self-esteem, sense of self-stability, self-image, and higher self-consciousness than do males (Simmons & Blyth, 1987).

The girl who is not yet menstruating and has no breast development may invent excuses to avoid physical exercise that requires undressing in front of other girls. Late maturing males may also suffer from feelings of inadequacy, particularly at a time when athletic prowess begins to take on added importance and early maturing boys, with more developed muscles, are at a definite advantage in most sports. The "gang shower" may be assiduously avoided by late maturing girls and boys.

This transitional period involves not only visible external physical changes, but also internal ones. Hormonal fluctuations may cause mood swings. Rapid physical development brings increased nutritional demands. Middle schoolers in the throes of such development may become alternately excitable and lethargic. In the past, many people have attributed what has been deemed the erratic behavior of middle schoolers to hormonal changes. However, recent research has shown that the physiological changes are only a portion of what contributes to the well-known emotional states and behaviors of middle school students.

Although the growth spurt and sexual maturation are biological processes, they do not occur in a vacuum. Interactions and interrelationships between biological and behavioral changes can influence the child's self-concept as he or she moves from childhood to adolescence. Individual variation in biological maturation and associated changes in size and body composition is the backdrop against which children evaluate and interpret their own growth, maturation, and social status among peers (Montemayor, Adams & Gullotta, 1990, pp. 59–60). Brooks-Gunn and Warren, investigating this relationship between hormones and affective behavior, concluded that hormonal development alone did not account for behavioral changes in adolescence. "Even if hormonal effects are demonstrated, they must be evaluated relative to contextual effects and relative to interactive effects before assuming a direct relation between hormones and behavior" (1989, p. 51).

Physical development, in which diversity is the rule rather than the exception, is of great concern to middle schoolers. Any development perceived by the student to be abnormal can cause great anxiety and influence social and emotional development. Early maturers may excel in physical activities and, as a consequence, develop increased self-confidence and feelings of competence. Conversely, late maturers may become insecure and withdrawn, feeling unable to compete with larger, more mature children. The question, "Am I normal?" is never far away from the minds of middle school learners, and physical development is a very important part of the answer.

Middle school students need frequent opportunities for physical movement, and for rest and change of activity. They also need help in diet, nutrition, personal hygiene, and coping with such physical factors as menstruation, growing beards, changing voices, and outgrowing clothes. The opportunity for personal counseling on such matters is unparalleled.

Intellectual Characteristics

Until relatively recently, middle school educators had accepted the theories and concepts of Jean Piaget without question or modification. Piaget (1977) described four stages of cognitive thought: the sensorimotor period (0–2 years); preoperational thought (2–7 years); concrete operations (7–11 years); and formal operations (11–12 years into adulthood). This Piagetan theory, especially as it applies to students from 11–15, has frequently been used as the justification for middle school program changes which place more emphasis on complex intellectual tasks, since Piaget held that formal operations began at age eleven.

Unfortunately, other research studies (e.g., Eson & Wolmsley, 1980; Miller, 1980) indicate that great numbers of students remain in the stage of concrete operations throughout their tenure in the middle school. Children in the concrete operations phase are often unable to generalize to broad contexts—that is, to hypothesize from existing facts. They may have great difficulty dealing effectively with the past in a realistically chronological way. They may be unable to reverse mental operations or consider situations which appear to be contrary to their personal observations. Teaching a class with students operating at concrete levels can be difficult, to say the least, since most middle school curricula have been designed to involve substantial amounts of hypothesizing, conceptualizing, and symbolizing. Providing diverse learning experiences, with varied instructional delivery, can help communicate the subject matter to students in either stage.

Others have suggested that since many early adolescents are not ready to move into complex operations at the age which Piaget suggests, it may be harmful to push them too hard to make the transition (see Toepfer, 1980). It may be because children are in a "plateau" period of brain growth from 12–14 years; these researchers have suggested that pushing adolescents to attain higher levels of thinking skills based on Piaget's theories may cause frustration and lower self-esteem. The experience of the authors of this text is that most middle school educators believe that their students are, in fact, far less mature in the stage of intellectual development which they have reached than was previously believed to be the case. If the observations of many classroom teachers are accurate, many students remain in the concrete stage throughout the middle school years, and far fewer have advanced to formal operations by their arrival at the middle school door than was once believed. None of this should be taken, however, as an endorsement by the authors of the idea that middle schools should be less intellectually rigorous than they now are. Quite the contrary, we believe that all middle school students deserve and require a rich, meaningful, and challenging educational experience.

Conceptual Framework

In two studies of adolescents, Adelson (1983) interviewed over 750 students in an attempt to discern the development of an adolescent's intellectual framework. He was interested in exploring the move from concrete to abstract thinking in political cognition. He concluded that between the ages of 13 and 15, adolescents experience a gradual shift in cognitive orientation. Orientations to five major topics displayed the differences between early and later adolescents. Those themes are: community, law, social principles, psychology, and understanding of the social order.

Adelson found that adolescents in the lower stages of cognitive reasoning can only think about community and its institutions in very concrete terms, not as a part of the social process. Similarly, such youth view the law as a punitive instrument of society, rather than a protective device for citizens.

The student still in the early reasoning stages is unable to extrapolate social ideals to cover a range of circumstances. For instance, "a child may aver solemnly that 'the majority rules,' yet later . . . remark that the smartest person ought to make all the decisions" (p. 160). Early adolescents also simplify human behavior. Motivations are attributed to simple emotions. Later in adolescence, students are able to recognize that a multitude of emotions and circumstances contribute to actions. Early adolescents live in the present, with less understanding of how the past affects current events.

Finally, in the beginning of adolescence, students do not comprehend how the elements of the social structure work and are interrelated. That is, the concepts of political parties, electoral processes, and government offices are only superficially understood. Only in later adolescence do students have the ability to separate the elements of the social order and to integrate them into a coherent framework.

Adelson argued that only by understanding these conceptual stages can educators alleviate both adult and adolescent frustrations in the classroom. Students may appear to be operating in one stage of reasoning, then revert to a lower stage. Confusion may result when students seem to understand complicated concepts, but can not extend those concepts to other situations. Adelson's theory illustrates how students and teachers may operate from different frameworks, and understanding this can help educators to structure activities.

Moral Development

Piaget (1977) contributed to the early work in one of the most well known theories of moral development. He assumed that cognitive and moral development progress together, that moral development is really the development of the thought process. Distinguishing between right and wrong is moral, of course; but it is primarily an intellectual task.

Furthermore, both intellectual and moral development proceed, Piaget held, through a series of discrete stages or phases. The stages of moral judgment, as elaborated by Piaget, are sequential and universal. That is, children and youth always develop through the same stages, in the same order, wherever they are in the world. They may not all reach all of the stages, but development occurs in a very orderly manner.

The first stage is moral realism, in which children judge very objectively. For example, more damage is worse, no matter what the cause. The second stage, morality of cooperation, applies to middle schoolers. In this stage, judgments about morality are made subjectively, usually according to the perceived intent. For example, a child operating in the morality of cooperation stage would consider a boy to be naughtier who breaks one cup while trying to sneak some jam out of the cupboard instead of the child who breaks fifteen cups by opening a door and accidentally knocking over the cups (Piaget's example).

Lawrence Kohlberg (1981), building on Piaget's classifications, proposed that individuals develop moral judgment by moving through a series of six stages contained within three levels (see also Rich & DeVitis, 1985; Kroger, 1989). They are:

Level One:	Preconventional
Stage 1	Punishment and Obedience: literal obedience to avoid punishment.
Stage 2	Individual Instrumental Purpose and Exchange: serving one's own or other's needs for personal benefit.
Level Two:	Conventional
Stage 3	Mutual Interpersonal Expectations, Relationships, and Conformity: the desire to please others and conform to perceived norms of "right" and "wrong."
Stage 4	Social System and Conscience Maintenance: doing one's duty to preserve the social order.
Level Three:	Postconventional and Principled
Stage 5	Prior Rights and Social Contract: commitment to *relative* social order; rules may be changed if needed.
Stage 6	Universal Ethical Principles: action determined by conscience, based on self-chosen ethical principles.

Middle level educators are most likely to see students who are thinking and acting, in terms of moral development, in Stages 1 to 4. Some middle school students will continue to demonstrate the predominance of Stage 1, where "what we can get away with" determines what is "right" to them. Near age 10, some children will begin to enter Stage 2, where what is right and wrong depends on who is involved and their relationship.

In Stage 2, relationships and their outcomes are important in moral reasoning. In the second stage, however, relationships are often limited to one-on-one situations in which what is "right" depends on the nature of the relationship. Groups are not yet important. If the other person is important to the actor or decision-maker, then one is bound to consider him or her when making decisions or acting in one way or another. If the other person is not a "central character" in the constellation of the person's relationships, then one is not bound to act with the other person's interests in mind. In other words, right is what produces pleasure for me in our relationship; wrong is whatever does not produce pleasure.

Students progress from egocentric behavior in Stage 2 to the desire to please others and win acceptance in Stage 3, where approval from groups is important. This includes not only peers but adult role models and perceived community norms as well. In Stage 3, the student becomes very sensitive to the opinions and values of groups of people that they know, care about, and interact with on a regular basis: their peers, their family, their church group, and other reference groups. Agreeing with what these groups define as good and rejecting what they define as bad becomes central.

Perhaps only a minority of students move into Stage 4 during their middle school years. Moving into Stage 4 requires an understanding of the need for social order beyond individual benefit and beyond the approval of groups which are made up of people who are known and cared for. Stage 4 is very advanced, in terms of moral development, in so far as it involves a willingness to do what is right because one knows that institutions (like schools) will cease to function effectively unless most group members voluntarily act in moral ways, following the rules and behaving for the good of the institution.

Several years ago, one of the authors spent a brief period of time at the Center for the Study of Moral Education, in the School of Education, at Harvard University, in some extended conversations with Lawrence Kohlberg on the significance of these concepts of moral development for middle school educators (George, 1980). Among the areas of agreement was that there is one very crucial point in moral development, a sort of a "go–no go" spot, and it has to do with the years students spend in middle level schools. Kohlberg argued that if students have not fully mastered Stage 3 before they move on to high school, they probably never will. That is, students who have not matured to the point where they identify with groups they care about by the time they leave middle school may never understand the ideas which support the rule of law and the importance of maintaining the social order, let alone understand the Constitution or universal principles of justice and morality which characterize the highest stages of moral development.

The special readiness of early adolescents for learning about group citizenship, in the sense of moral identification with groups which is the heart of Stage

3, holds special meaning for middle school educators. Middle school educators may be able to make important contributions to the continued moral development of early adolescents by organizing and operating middle schools so that positive group involvement, loyalty, duty, responsibility, ownership, and citizenship are emphasized. This makes advisory groups, interdisciplinary teams, long-term relationships and other aspects of middle schools even more important.

Recent research in comparative education (Duke, 1986; George, 1989) confirms our belief that early adolescents move through a period of distinctive, virtually unparalleled, readiness to learn about group citizenship. The Japanese believe that prior to the middle grades, children are too young to learn the really important lessons of group involvement, and that if the lessons have not been internalized by the time the students move on to the high school, it may be too late to do so. Consequently, Japanese educators organize and operate their middle level schools to capitalize on what they believe is the prime time in life to learn concepts like duty, responsibility, loyalty, involvement, and commitment. In Japanese junior high schools, perhaps the most academic schools in the world, almost ten hours a week are devoted to learning to be an important member of an important group. Homerooms, clubs, school duties, and other components of the school experience are designed to teach the concepts of group citizenship which are related to the third stage of moral development.

Psychosocial Characteristics

The cognitive and intellectual skills that make their appearance in the lives of many middle schoolers not only influence the manner in which they are able to deal with academically oriented abstractions and situations; these same skills also provide the early adolescent with new abilities to use in examining their sense of self and their relationships with their families, friends, and school teachers.

> Evidence reveals that, among early adolescents, the cognitive shift from concrete thought to abstract reasoning is accompanied by a shift from concrete self-definition to abstract self-portraiture that describes their psychological interior. As they become aware of their different "selves," many teenagers become troubled by the inconsistencies. Older adolescents, once they have traversed this difficult stage, no longer experience so much internal conflict. (Staff, 1990)

Middle school students become increasingly aware of their own selves and of relationships with others. Indeed, human beings may be more aware of others during this period than during any other time of life. Not only are "Who am I?" and "Am I normal?" persistent questions, but also "Who do you think I am?" dominates much reflection and many relationships. Furthermore, the evidence suggests that the movement into adolescence is one toward greater independence and greater need for freedom from the total authority of adults, including parents and teachers.

This change does not happen overnight, but gradually and incrementally the early adolescent becomes more self-directing. In the process, the youth may turn increasingly to the peer group for approval and encouragement, and away from the former authority. Parents and teachers, once omnipotent in a child's life, may be shocked, hurt, and even angry when their omnipotence is challenged by the emergence of a new sense of identity and independence.

> The task of adolescents is to move through these developmental stages from differentiation to the integration of these multiple self-concepts toward a clear and consolidated sense of the true self. This realistic and internalized sense of self will form the basis for further identity development. Failure to chart these waters successfully may result in a number of potential psychological risks. (Staff, 1990)

Erikson's Theory of Identity and Identity Crisis

Erik Erikson's psychosocial theories were among the earliest work to generate much research and commentary about adolescent psychosocial development. Erikson (1963) theorized that individuals progress through eight stages of development. Each stage affects the next; unsuccessful resolution of a stage may negatively effect ego development later on in life. The stages which most affect middle schoolers are Stage Four, Industry versus Inferiority, and Stage Five, Crisis of Identity versus Role Confusion.

In Stage Four (ages six or seven through ages eleven or twelve), the early adolescent is attempting to develop a sense of competence and achievement. Inability to complete relevant tasks successfully may lead to a negative self-concept and the child may "consider himself doomed to mediocrity or inadequacy" (Erikson, 1963, p. 260). Proficiencies at various tasks in this phase set the stage for positive self-esteem and continued success. Middle school educators need to provide the opportunity for realization of social, physical, and academic goals.

Stage Five is the Identity versus Role Confusion phase (ages eleven or twelve through eighteen). Many middle schoolers may function in the lower range of this stage. The need for independence and peer acceptance increases in this stage; students are looking for a "sense of self." Early adolescents in this stage look for role models and heroes and attempt to integrate those ideals into their own value system.

Middle school educators must recognize that this is a confusing time for students. While Erikson's work has been criticized for being practicably unclear and sexually and culturally biased (see Kroger, 1989), it continues to be one of the fundamental theories for adolescent identity formation. Affective education, built on a realization of the importance of identity development, can play a supportive role in assisting students in defining their changing sense of self and relationships with others.

Self-Esteem

Cotton's (1985) comprehensive review of the literature of the development of self-esteem points out the importance of the transition into early adolescence. As in all such major transitions in life, early adolescence is a sensitive and vulnerable time for self-esteem. The transition almost always brings lower self-esteem as the person grapples with the turbulence and confusion of major growth experiences. But, when these experiences are completed successfully, self-esteem is likely to return to a more positive position.

Because of the emergent nature of identity development and the parallel formation of moral reasoning, middle school students are known for their vacillating self-esteem. Middle school teachers know the unpredictable nature of students, in this regard, often from one day to the next. The desire to fit in—please peers as well as parents—while attempting to incorporate the values of the community, local church, family, and friends can be exhausting as well as confusing for the middle schooler. Television serves as a conveyor of values and beliefs, as well as images of success and beauty, and can have both positive and negative influences on adolescent viewers and their sense of self-esteem (Greeson & Williams, 1986; Luker & Johnston, 1988). Not looking, sounding, or acting "right" can have negative effects on adolescent self-esteem.

Self-consciousness is at its peak in early adolescence and decreases thereafter (de Rosenroll, 1987), but the student with poor self-esteem may not see self-consciousness as a stage. The lonely adolescent, seeking ways either to become part of the group or to dull rejection, may turn to alcohol or other drugs (Mijuskovic, 1988).

Much of the research on dropouts and at-risk youth shows that these students feel alienated in the school environment, and report negative perceptions of themselves in relation to the school (Mills, Dunham & Alpert, 1988). Low self-esteem has far reaching implications. Affective education—teaching about emotions, feelings, relationships—is critical in the middle school. Students at the middle level are in need of a program that recognizes and accommodates the changing nature of the adolescent's psychological and social development.

A growing number of students are being identified as disadvantaged and learning disabled. The job of learning correct social behavior may be complicated for all early adolescents, and especially difficult for disaffected youth (Jackson, 1987). The effective middle school prioritizes affective education for all students with extra emphasis on students who may have started out with a deficit.

Tierno (1983) stated that "the programs developed by many, if not most, middle schools stress cognitive considerations over the social-emotional concerns of their students" (p. 579). Unfortunately, the pressure to raise standardized test scores and "make the grade" have relegated social skill development to a low priority for many educators. Educators assume that such skills are part of the implicit curriculum; in point of fact, they need to be *taught*. Defining the sense of self, independence, and changing relationships with others are areas that need to be explored within the school program.

"Individualism is a cornerstone of American ideology" (Oliner, 1986). However, egocentrism is often overdeveloped to the exclusion of others. That is, middle schoolers need guidance in developing social skills and learning how to interact appropriately with other children and adults. Oliner said, "In order to restore personal and social balance, appropriate self-interest needs to be augmented by a sense of community responsibility. The schools also have a legitimate role to play in cultivating a sense of community" (1986, p. 390).

Parent-child relationships can also benefit from attention to the psychosocial aspects of development as a part of middle school education. Social learning theory asserts that conflict between parents and adolescents stems from a lack of positive interactions and a lack of problem-solving skills (Hall, 1987). The deficient skills can be taught to the student and the youth will, ideally, generalize those skills to use at home.

"Parents and teachers must continuously modify their expectations and relationships as the adolescent swings between childlike and adult behaviors" (Newman, 1985, p. 642). Schoolwide commitment to affective education can help ease the tensions while early adolescents develop appropriate social skills.

A study by Streitmatter and Pate (1989) asserted that there is a relationship between levels of psychosocial maturity and stereotypical thinking. Programs for developing social skills that involve differing value systems should take into account the developmental status of the students. Middle schoolers may be in very different stages of both development and readiness to consider or adopt information that conflicts with their own value system.

Allan and Dyck (1984) recommended developing a guidance curriculum that draws inspiration from the rites of passage in other cultures. Students need to be made aware of both emotional and physical changes that they will be experiencing in adolescence; using the format of a rite of passage can ease the transition. Students learn about what to expect, discuss real life problems they experience, and construct their own developmental task to help them through difficult situations.

Peer Pressure

Young people can also be remarkably clannish. . . . It is important to understand . . . such intolerance as a defense against a sense of identity confusion. For adolescents . . . help one another temporarily through much discomfort by forming cliques and by stereotyping themselves, their ideals, and their enemies. (Erikson, 1963, p. 262)

In the past, many theorists asserted that peer pressure is responsible for adolescent deviance. Drug and alcohol abuse, sexual experimentation, and other undesirable behaviors have been blamed on the influence of peer pressure. Recently, however, educators and adolescent psychologists have begun to hypothesize that peer influence is only one part of what makes adolescents behave the way they do.

Peer pressure is a reality, but is not the ultimate controller of an adolescent's actions. "Adolescents do generate their own norms and rules, but this process does not and can not develop in isolation from the institutional context of the communities in which they live and learn" (Ianni, 1989, p. 679). Scheidlinger (1984) suggested that the adolescent peer group is "better characterized by notions of growth and adaptation than those of turmoil and conflict" (p. 393). The peer group is infrequently responsible for negative behavior, but instead often acts as a sounding board.

Oetting and Beauvais (1987) related their own peer cluster theory to adolescent drug use and discount the use of the concept of peer pressure. Peer cluster theory connects drug use and other deviant behaviors to the behavior of the adolescent himself, rather than attributing actions and influence to other persons.

Peer pressure implies a passive acceptance of a barely resistible power. From the dynamic viewpoint of peer clusters, every member of a peer cluster is seen as an active, participating agent in shaping the norms and behaviors of that cluster. From the outside, it may look like peer pressure is leading to conformity, especially if a parent or counselor wants to believe in the innocence of a particular child. What is actually occurring is a considerable amount of behavior norming, with each youth moving toward a commonly defined set of behaviors (p. 206).

However, this is not to say that the peer cluster is not a factor in undesirable behavior. In fact, according to Oetting and Beauvais, "any treatment or prevention program [for drug abuse] that does not ultimately lead to changes in peer associations may be doomed to failure" (p. 212).

Peer relations allow the early adolescent to redefine sense of self in terms of what is normal in everyday life. Relationships with peers first, and then adults, begin to be reciprocal rather than "unilaterally controlled" by adults (Schwartz, Merten & Bursik, 1987). Early adolescents look to peers for reinforcement and comfort; adults need to allow room for individual growth and diversity of relationships. Learning to relate to others is one of the primary lessons a school can teach. "Excessive attention to individual achievement and success has obscured one of the fundamental missions of schools, which is to produce people capable of living with some degree of responsibility and care for one another" (Oliner, 1986, p. 404). Peer groups are a natural extension of the acquisition of social skills.

The At-Risk Middle School Student

Unfortunately for us all, one significant trend to emerge since the first edition of this textbook in 1981 is that there are ever-growing numbers of middle school learners, across all social groups, who are not successfully negotiating the twists and turns in the course of human developmental challenges, who emerge from this period increasingly unlikely ever to reach their full potential. These students move through adolescence at the same time they face "demands, expectations, risks, and temptations that seem both more numerous and more complicated than they were only a generation ago" (Staff, 1990, p. 5). All Americans struggle with the high rate of divorce, economies regularly disrupted by distant wars, the declining influence of organized religion, radically increased personal freedom, and what President Carter called a "cultural malaise." But only early adolescents must develop their sense of self and their personal momentum for their future in such a milieu. The "good news" may be that there are not even more youth placed at risk by the challenge of development during such trying times.

> The "bad news" is that millions of today's early adolescents personally endure increasing poverty, continuing racial prejudice, parental unemployment, family disruption, and community disintegration. (Kozol, 1991)
>
> They are regularly exposed to life-limiting opportunities (e.g., easy availability of drugs and alcohol, social glorification of sexual promiscuity) which may forever limit their options. For them, simultaneously denied the guidance and support they require, such obstacles can "permanently impair physical and emotional health, destroy motivation and ability to succeed in school and jobs, and damage personal relationships and the chance to become an effective parent." (Staff, 1990)

As the Carnegie Council on Adolescent Development points out:

> Unfortunately, by age 15, substantial numbers of American youth are at risk of reaching adulthood unable to meet adequately the requirements of the work place, the commitments of relationships in families and with friends, and the responsibilities of participation in a democratic society. These youth are among the estimated 7 million young people—one in four adolescents—who are extremely vulnerable to multiple high-risk behaviors and school failure. Another 7 million may be at moderate risk, but remain a cause for serious concern. (1989, p. 8)

Substantial portions of such children appear to be members of minority cultures, and the number of at-risk minority youth appearing in American middle level schools far exceeds the representation of those students in schools and classrooms of years past. Each year, the demographic makeup of the typical middle school becomes, in the opinion of many practitioners, skewed more and more in the direction of minority culture youth who, because of their life situation, enter the school increasingly at risk.

> By the year 2020, because of higher birth rates among minority populations and patterns of immigration, nearly half of all school-age children will be non-white. Continuing to allow minority youth to face extraordinary risks of failure is a direct threat to our national standard of living and democratic foundations. (Carnegie, 1989, p. 27)

And again:

> The spector of a divided society—one affluent the other poor—looms ominously on the American horizon. Inherent in this scenario is the potential for serious conflict between generations, among races and ethnic groups, and between the economically disenfranchised and middle- and upper-income groups. It is a disturbing scenario which must not occur. (Carnegie, 1989, p. 32)

Sharon Fritz, principal of Milbrae, California's Taylor Middle School, described it well in terms of the professional experience of middle school educators during this period:

> Ten years ago this school population of 550 was predominantly Caucasian, college bound, and conservative. Twenty teachers primarily lectured to seventh and eighth grade students almost every period. Discipline problems consisted of students being sent to the office for not having a pencil, forgetting a book, or talking without raising their hands. One out of ten were ESL, primarily native speakers of Chinese or Japanese.
>
> Today the school population consists of 650 students who speak 22 different languages. One out of four is enrolled in our ESL program. . . . Last week we identified close to 100 students who we feel are academically in need of support. We allocate a large portion of our money to provide a homework center for our kids after school. If someone had told us ten years ago that this is the way it would be, we would have laughed.
>
> We are very proud of our kids and each other. But we are also grappling with the following realities which did not exist ten years ago:
>> Multiple languages in each classroom
>> More and more single-parent homes (many of our kids live with their grandparents or various other relatives)
>> More disparity between the haves and the have nots . . . more have nots
>> Greater numbers of parents who have no parenting skills
>> Latch key children
>
> (Fritz, personal communication, March, 1991)

Of course, the staff at Taylor Middle, and thousands of other middle level schools, have every right to be proud of their students and of their professional efforts to serve those students. At Taylor Middle, for example, the commitment to the students' welfare has, if anything, become more positive and constant during this period of time, staff development has been continuous, state department reviews have resulted in numerous commendations including a designation as a "California Distinguished School", interdisciplinary units are being taught. Many middle school educators seem to feel, however, that events may be outpacing their efforts to keep up, especially with the demographic changes that the student population continues to present.

Feldman and Elliot (1990) argue that, among other initiatives which must occur, is a dramatically expanded research effort to learn more about minority youth, especially African-American and Hispanic early adolescents. Little is known about the normal development of minority adolescents, especially those who come from socioeconomically advantaged settings. Why we know so little and how this scarcity of knowledge can be corrected are important issues to be confronted by human development scholars, educators, and the society as a whole. Recent research studies, however, do support the contention that at-risk students profit from direct training interventions designed to increase their academic achievement motivation, self-efficacy, persistence, confidence, responsibility, and citizenship (Hughes & Martray, 1991).

A few such programs based on the characteristics of at-risk young adolescents have demonstrated admirable early progress. The Accelerated Schools Project, at Stanford University, has caught national attention. Accelerated schools focus on: high expectations on the part of parents, teachers, and students; specific deadlines as to when students are to meet certain requirements; stimulating and relevant instructional programs; and a fundamental shared decision-making process. Perhaps the most common feature of Accelerated Schools, all of which may be different in some ways, is the insistence that all children in the schools be brought to a certain level of competence by specific deadlines and should adhere to a core of curricular, instructional, and organizational practices (Hopfenberg, Levin, Meister & Rogers, 1990).

The Middle School Efficacy Program (Syropoulos, 1990), implemented in the sixth grade of the middle schools of Detroit, Michigan, is particularly promising, we think. The program is intended to improve academic achievement through the development of positive attitudes toward self and learning. Specifically, the Middle School Efficacy Program focuses on six modules of instruction which replace the traditional language arts program in favor of units that deal with personal motivation, taking moderate academic risks, envisioning positive personal futures, setting realistic goals, and working cooperatively with others. The results so far are very positive, with experimental groups exceeding control groups in the areas of absenteeism, citizenship, school attitudes, and, importantly, in reading and mathematics.

Effective Parenting Information for Children (EPIC), a national non-profit organization, focuses on coordinating parent education with school-based efforts for at-risk and other students. New middle school programs focus on three areas: self-concept and self-esteem; rules, rights, and responsibilities; and decision-making and problem-solving. Participation in the program appears to provoke positive changes in parents' self-confidence in dealing with their children, and improvements in the school-day behavior of students, their self-concepts, and other important variables related to the school success of at-risk youth.[1]

The Program for Disadvantaged Youth, of the Edna McConnell Clark Foundation (Mizell & Gonzalez, 1991), is an initiative focused on five urban school

---

[1]For more information on EPIC, contact the national office at 1300 Elmwood Avenue, Room 319, State University College at Buffalo, Buffalo, NY 14222.

systems (Baltimore, Louisville, Milwaukee, Oakland, and San Diego) and the reform of their middle level schools. The objectives of the program include: completion of the middle grades curriculum by all students on time; exhibition of mastery of higher order thinking, reasoning, and comprehension skills; more positive attitudes toward self and school; and increased clarity about options for high school and beyond. A total of 12 middle schools are attempting to implement new programs focused on these outcomes. The Foundation is working to establish strong interschool networks to make positive changes permanent.

In a somewhat similar framework, the College Board (Council on College-Level Services, 1991) has developed an initiative aimed at fostering improved articulation between middle and high schools so that "greater numbers of diverse students . . . pursue a more challenging curriculum in high school." The new program hopes to induce more poor and minority group students, who make up large proportions of at-risk students, to enroll in Advanced Placement courses, and to engage middle and high school educators in exploring new methods for preparing these students for doing so. The initiative proposes that curriculum plans focus on the development of Individual Instructional Plans for all students, with new diagnostic assessment procedures, groups of mentors, and other components aimed at the goals of the initiative.

Individual school districts, perhaps by the hundreds, are deeply involved in their own drop-out prevention programs for at-risk youth of middle school age. The Syracuse Stay In School Partnership Project (Meyer, Harootunian & Williams, 1991) is a good example of a collaborative effort involving a school district, a university, and the state Department of Education. In this project, students identified as at-risk are not pulled out for intervention. Instructional innovations are aimed at these students as they remain in the regular classroom, thus avoiding the worst effects of further isolating a group of students already alienated from school. Staff development activities help teachers develop a greater repertoire of instructional strategies. Teachers form peer support groups around at-risk students so that the students develop positive interaction patterns (friendships). Peer tutoring programs and an after-school diet and nutrition activity are in the planning stages (Meyer, Harootunian & Williams, 1991).

Broward County, Florida has received both funding and recognition for its "Model School Adjustment Program", implemented in 1985 at Driftwood Middle School and disseminated to three other middle schools in that district. Students enter the program in sixth grade, and by 1990, 340 sixth graders had been served. The program includes a *required* ten week parent education component, as well as extensive tutoring and counseling services. Results reported have been significantly positive.

Many individual schools, now perhaps several thousand, within districts where little concentrated efforts are underway, are developing their own efforts to deal with the at-risk situations which confront them more each year. Exciting efforts, known to the authors, are underway at Fairport Middle School (in

Dayton, Ohio), at Benicia Middle School (in Benicia, California), and at Southwest Junior High School (in Palm Bay, Florida). At Westwood Middle School in Gainesville, Florida, for example, at-risk students are invited to school a week early for an "Orientation Camp," called the "Roundup." It is an on-campus experience that gives at-risk students "extra tools" to increase their chances of making a successful adjustment to middle school. "It provides an opportunity for the staff's first personal experiences with these students to be positive ones. The program is structured around activities designed to enhance self-esteem, ease concern about the transition to a new school or grade, develop study habits and skills, and communication skills; these are interpreted as characteristics which differentiate the at-risk student from the regular student at Westwood. Other programs at Westwood supplement the Roundup: peer facilitator groups, a mentoring program, and special grants. The school has also responded to an initiative from a church in the neighborhood of many of the students in the school's at-risk population; church volunteers meet weekly with interested students to help them complete particularly challenging and important class assignments like science projects, important papers, and so on. Educators at Larsen Middle School (Elgin, Illinois) have developed a short term intensive program for bringing students who appear to be falling "through the cracks" back up to successful levels of performance. Rogers Middle School, in Fort Lauderdale, Florida, offers a "RAP" program for over-aged seventh grade students aimed at moving them on to the ninth grade on time, by helping them complete both the seventh and eighth grade curricula in a one-year program. Ysleta Middle School, in El Paso, Texas, has organized STAR (Students and Teachers Achieving Results), a three-teacher interdisciplinary team effort which involves parents and the community as an integral part of the program. Mechanicsburg Area Intermediate School (Pennsylvania) has established a mentor program which is a low-cost, high-return effort to pair at-risk students with volunteer adult mentors who help their charges negotiate the academic world more successfully.

Similarly, the staff at Sandburg Middle School (in Anoka, Minnesota) offer a program called PASS (Parents, Administrators, Students, and Staff) which focuses on getting at-risk students and at least one of their parents to come to school for a two-session evening workshop. The workshop is designed to involve student and parent(s) in "contracting" for school improvement. Session one focuses on (1) identifying the problems at school, (2) getting organized at school and at home, and (3) developing a realistic action plan to which both make a commitment. The second session (at which attendance has always been 100 percent) deals with testing, self-esteem, and reviewing the action plan which has been established.

At Virgo Middle School, an inner city school in Wilmington, North Carolina, the "XL" Program targets 25 seventh graders who are placed on a team of 60–90 other students, and all are expected to perform academically and socially. The program has academic and advisory aspects. Teachers on the team have dropped the traditional grading system, and use a great deal of cooperative learning and "outward bound" style experiences. Students receive group counseling once a week for ten weeks, improving their social skills, especially problem solving and conflict resolution. Evaluation of the program indicates significant gains for students in reading, mathematics, academic and social self-esteem, attendance, and referrals to the office. While we, the authors, remain apprehensive about programs which may isolate at-risk youth in unacceptable ways, efforts such as the "XL" programs seem to be working well.

For our immediate purposes, we must focus on how exemplary middle schools can profit from programs like these, based on the knowledge educators currently possess about the nature and needs of this age group, while educators and others press forward in the attempt to learn more about all aspects of this phenomenally important period of growth and development.

Focus on the Middle School Student: Summary

The foregoing section has only briefly identified some of the most salient characteristics of middle school learners, and it is hoped that interested readers will use additional sources (such as those suggested at the end of the chapter) for further information. The point of greatest significance is that the middle school must be uniquely planned, staffed, and operated to provide a program that is truly focused on the rapidly moving and changing learners in transition from childhood to adolescence. In truth, this entire book is devoted to implications of the focus on the learner, for the authors see the exemplary middle school as one with facilities, organization, curriculum plan, student services, instruction—indeed, every aspect—developed and utilized to serve the needs and characteristics of this unique student population. The chief implication of our knowledge about middle school learners is that they need a school focused sharply on their needs—the exemplary middle school—and that educators, with the help of researchers in related fields, must keep searching out these needs and the best means for their satisfaction.

ADDITIONAL SUGGESTIONS FOR FURTHER STUDY

A. Books and Monographs

Beane, J. & Lipka, R. (1986). *Self-concept, self-esteem, and the curriculum.* New York: Teachers College Press.

Cotton, N. (1985). *The development of self-esteem and self-esteem regulation.* In J. Mack & Ablon, S. (Eds.) *The development and sustaining of self-esteem in childhood.* New York: International Universities Press, pp. 122–150.

Gardner, H. (1985). *Frames of mind: The theory of multiple intelligences.* New York: Basic Books.

Gilligan, C., Lyons, N. & Hammer, T. (Eds.). *Making connections: The relational worlds of adolescent girls at Emma Willard School.* (1990) Cambridge, MA: Harvard University Press.

Johnston, J. H. (1990). *The new American family and the school.* Columbus: National Middle School Association.

NASSP's Council on Middle Level Education (1989). *Middle level education's responsibility for intellectual development.* Reston, VA: National Association of Secondary School Principals.

Stevenson, C. (1992). *Teaching ten to fourteen year olds.* New York: Longman.

B. Periodicals

Adelson, J. (1983). The growth of thought in adolescence. *Educational Horizons, 61,* 156–162.

Arth, A. A. (1990). Moving into middle school: Concerns of transescent students. *Educational Horizons, 68,* 105–106.

Connell, M. E. (1990). Click: Poets at work in the middle school. *English Journal, 79* (7), 30–32.

Hillman, S. B. (1991). What developmental psychology has to say about early adolescence. *Middle School Journal, 23* (1), 3–8.

Matthews, D. B. & Odom, B. L. (1989). Anxiety: A component of self-esteem. *Elementary School Guidance and Counseling, 24* (2), 153–59.

Mohr, P. H., et al. (1987). Moral reasoning in early adolescence: Implications for drug abuse prevention. *School Counselor, 35* (2), 120–27.

Montemayor, R., Adams, G. R. & Gullotta, T. P. (Eds.) (1990). *From childhood to adolescence: A transitional period?* Newbury Park, CA: Sage.

C. ERIC

Sparapani, E. F. & Opalewski, D. A. (Oct. 1989). *A survey of interests and opinions of middle grades youngsters.* Paper presented at the Annual Meeting of the Midwest Educational Research Association. (ERIC Document Reproduction Service No. ED 315 184)

D. Dissertations and Dissertation Abstracts

Cooper, M. A. Factors associated with middle school "at risk" students in the regular classroom. (Doctoral dissertation, Temple University, 1988). *Dissertation Abstracts International,* 49/07a, 1763.

Levine, M. E. R. A description of eight shy middle school students. (Doctoral dissertation, University of Florida, 1988). *Dissertation Abstracts International,* 49/12a, 3604.

Ketterman-Brockett, D. P. N. The classification of students experiencing school difficulty and the correlates of school success for at-risk students. (Doctoral dissertation, University of California, Riverside, 1989). *Dissertation Abstracts International,* 50/ 05a, 1255.

CHAPTER 2

The Middle School Movement and Concept

The middle school, as we know it in the last decade of the twentieth century, is a school usually including grades 6–8 or 5–8, or even just 7–8, intended to help the early adolescents of these grades make a smooth transition from elementary to high school and from childhood to adolescence. During this century, the majority of school districts in the United States have tried out first a different organization, the junior high school, many later finding it lacking for their students then, and moved toward the middle school plan. But many junior high schools (usually including grades 7–9) still exist as do elementary, intermediate, and other schools including grades 7 and 8, serving the middle grade students. This chapter is intended to sketch the development of American education at the middle level, and point to the critical steps and issues in its further development treated in this volume. We describe the meaning of the middle school concept at this point in time, as it appears in the literature and in the experiences of middle school educators and students.

Levels of Education

In beginning study of the emergence of the middle level schools, the concept of levels of education should be understood. In the thinly populated agrarian society of early America, schools were small, almost family affairs requiring little internal grouping in grades. But as the population increased and larger communities developed, some differentiation became necessary and "grammar," or elementary, schools constituted a common level sought by most parents for their children. Those who survived this school, and whose parents could afford their continuation in school, could seek admission to the prep school or academy (or finishing school for girls) or, in time, the high school. In some communities one school might embrace both elementary and high school years, or the upper schools in some might be completely independent of any elementary schools, relying on home, church, or other agency for preparation in "the three Rs." Gradually, however, with ever-increasing population and increasing school enrollments, two distinct levels of education below college (always "higher" and separate) became the common pattern.

Furthermore, the two levels had to be internally organized for efficiency. The historical evidence is not clear as to why, but the grammar or elementary school became an eight-grade school and the high school a four-grade one. There were many exceptions, with the public schools in the South frequently restricted to 11 grades usually organized on a 7–4 basis, and with many elementary schools in New England retaining grade 9. The 8–4 system was not adopted from any other country; in fact it was never adopted here by any formal national mandate. Actually, it was well in the nineteenth century before the graded school itself had become somewhat universal in the United States. And as it became the convenient way to organize a school, eight-grade elementary and four-grade high schools became common. As Briggs (1920, p. 6), writing on the development of the junior high school he had helped get started, stated:

> It seems more likely that the eight-four organization is partly an historical accident, a sort of compromise between the early contending elementary and secondary schools. The former, as is well known, existed with any number of "grades" up to twelve, and the latter, as in Europe, often ran down in preparatory work as low as in primary grades. Gradually, as the two types were combined, there resulted what we now have. Certainly, there is no evidence that at any time before the present there has been any widespread effort to consider the needs of children and the demands of the nation in such a way as logically or scientifically to determine the length of either the elementary or the secondary course.

The Junior High School

Many of the early (and even later) proponents of the separate junior high school did not think of it as an entity serving distinctly different functions than the grammar or high school. Briggs (1920, p. 54) used a survey of judges (professors of education, state superintendents, city superintendents, and junior high principals) to see what agreement existed as to certain issues, with the following list defining the percentage of judges considering each item "essential" (rather than just "desirable" or "essential or desirable"):

1. A distinct educational unit: 54.1%.
2. Separated in organization from the elementary grades: 62.3%.
3. Separated in organization from the senior high school: 41%.

As we shall see, the lack of consensus on these points was probably a major factor in the emergence of the new middle school and the decline of the junior high school.

The origin of the junior high school is usually attributed to dissatisfaction with the two-level 8–4 plan, very much like the new middle school is usually related to dissatisfaction with the junior high school and the 6–3–3 plan. A troublesome question for many middle school proponents today is whether the middle school will meet the same fate as its predecessor! But there were many other factors of a more positive nature in the development of the junior high school (Van Til, Vars & Lounsbury 1961, p. 22). These authors point to the concern of colleges for getting better-prepared students, and the related belief that earlier (than grade 9) introduction of college preparatory subjects, especially mathematics and foreign languages, was highly desirable. Also noted by these authors were the several recommendations for extending the period of secondary education (not creating an in-between school), and the source of many recommendations, namely prestigious national organizations and committees. Also important were significant research studies calling attention to the problems of students and society such as potential and actual dropouts.

The junior high school movement really spread after 1920. The increased birth rate after World War I, and other factors increasing our population, meant mounting school enrollments and overcrowded schools. One answer to crowded elementary and high schools was to move grades 7–9 into a new building (or into the old high school) and just build one new building. Also, genuine improvements in education were made in many junior high schools that could be secured by reorganization elsewhere, too. Whatever the reason, instead of the situation in 1920, when four of every five high school graduates had attended an 8–4 organization, 40 years later, in 1960, four of every five high school graduates had attended a 6–3–3 system. The junior high school had become common, but it was already coming under criticism, and another school in the middle was in the offing.

Toward a Different School in the Middle

Various individuals, including many spokespersons for schools and school districts, began expressing dissatisfaction with and possible alternatives to both the junior high school and the earlier, still continuing 8–4 elementary-high school organization. The 6–3–3 and the 8–4 plans were both considered by many as unsuitable to the needs and interests of early adolescents. The first publication with which we are familiar that voiced these dissatisfactions with the junior high in particular and recommended experimentation with different approaches for this age group was a monograph prepared by collaboration of many Florida educators under the aegis of the Florida Department of Supervision and Curriculum Development of the Florida Education Association, for ASCD publication (ASCD, 1954, 47). Note these excerpts from its concluding chapter on "Toward Better Programs for Young Adolescents:"

The prevailing type of junior high program organization is a departmentalized one. . . . This type of organization provides too abrupt a change from the self-contained classroom of the elementary school, too little relationship between the subjects and the interests and needs of young adolescents, and too little time for any teacher to carry out the varied type of program needed by young adolescents.

In most junior high schools operating on the same type of program organization as that of the senior high school, dissatisfactions are readily observable. Adjustment problems of entering pupils are acute, teachers complain of lack of time for field trip and other experiences, parents feel their children are suffering because of lack of cooperation of teachers in homework and examinations, and so forth. These problems provide an excellent beginning point for faculty and student council study. Investigation can be made of why these problems exist and what solutions are available. . . .

As these are studied and solutions explored, interest usually arises in trying something different.

These educators did not suggest creating a completely new grade organization, but they did propose and illustrate changes from departmentalization to block scheduling and "little school" arrangements (a type of team organization), and to broaden choices of exploratory subjects and activities, as well as other special interest activities, all characteristic of the middle schools to be planned later. Some type of such reorganized junior high schools were either already existing or soon to come. In Upper St. Clair, Pennsylvania, there had been a study of the schools needed by young adolescents, and the plan was for a new middle school. Donald Eichhorn, one of the founders of today's middle schools and then assistant supervising principal of the Upper St. Clair Township School district, related in his pioneer work, *The Middle School* (1966, p. 2) the letter of request of August 25, 1959, of Supervising Principal Carl R. Streams to the Pennsylvania Department of Instruction for establishment of a new grades 6–8 school, saying in part:

We are requesting that the school be composed of grades 6–7–8. The reasons why we believe that this program is desirable and educationally sound are as follows:

1. From the physical and psychological point of view it is a more natural grouping. There appears to be less of a differential in maturity between the sixth and eighth grade than between the seventh and the ninth grade.
2. The social patterns are more nearly the same in grades 6, 7, and 8 than in the conventional pattern of grades 7, 8, and 9. The social maturity of the ninth grade student more nearly parallels that of the older students. A better social program could be carried on without the ninth grade student.

3. The transition from the self-contained classroom to a departmentalized program may be more gradual.

This school, the Fort Couch Middle School (still an exemplary middle school), and the district became exemplary in the middle school movement.

Grades 6–8 units, variously called junior high, intermediate, senior or upper elementary schools, were located elsewhere even before the name "middle school" became the common one for this organization (it had been used abroad for various levels, especially the high school one). Thus, the exemplary Skokie Junior High School, in the Winnetka (Illinois) Elementary School District, as early as the 1940s had modular scheduling, interdisciplinary organization and teaching, teacher advisory groups, special interest activities ("enterprises" at Skokie), and other characteristic features of many middle schools today.

The Saginaw (Michigan) Township Community School District developed the 4–4–4 plan of organization that has been used many places in later decades. An article by George Mills (1961, p. 6) justified the plan then in operation in the Saginaw Township Community School District, adjacent to Saginaw, as follows:

> For some time the junior high school concept has been under scrutiny . . . in practice it has resulted in junior high schools becoming miniature senior high schools, with the social activities, the athletic program, and the instructional programs of the senior high school moving into the lower educational levels. . . .
>
> As we studied the 320 physical, mental, emotional and social growth characteristics and teaching implications for boys and girls, from kindergarten through the 12th grade, we concluded that there were centers of similarity in this 13 year span that merited close study. . . . These conclusions led us to establish the *primary school*, which includes kindergarten through grade 4, the *middle school* with grades 5 through 8, and the *four-year high school* with grades 9 through 12.

Meanwhile, in the early 1960s and thereafter, the middle school concept was beginning to be developed further, spoken about in educational conferences, and written about in various publications. For example, Alexander presented an interpretation of the need for and characteristics of a new school in the middle at a Junior High Conference at Cornell University in the summer of 1963, stressing certain contributions the junior high had made, and enumerating other characteristics to be sought in the new middle school needed. He suggested that as near a middle unit (grades 5–8) as possible might be best, that the grades 6–8 unit was growing in popularity, and that any "clearly defined unit should more easily have the characteristics already described as desirable, than the junior high school: (1) a well-articulated 12- to 14-year system of education; (2) preparation for, even transition to, adolescence; (3) continued general education; and (4) abundant opportunities for exploration of individualization, interests, a flexible curriculum, and emphasis on values" (Alexander, 1964). The whole matter of developing new facilities for such new schools had gone far enough in the early 1960s for the Educational Facilities Laboratories (Murphy, 1965) to publish a report describing planning done for new organizations it called middle schools (although they had various grade structures and names) under way or completed in several cities (opening dates as follows), and presenting some of the detailed plans and photos in more detail for the Amory, Mississippi, Middle School (opened, not quite finished, fall, 1963); Barrington, Illinois, Middle School (opened, 1965); Bedford Middle School, Mt. Kisko, New York (1966); Matlin Junior High School, Plainview, Long Island, New York (December, 1963); McIntosh Middle School, Sarasota, Florida (Fall, 1962); Pleasant Hill Middle School, West Jefferson Hills School District, Pleasant Hill, Pennsylvania (1965); Henderson Junior High School, Little Rock, Arkansas (1965); Kennedy Junior High, Natick, Massachusetts (April, 1965); Ardis C. Egan School, Los Altos, California (May, 1963); Giana School, Rawlon School District, Rowland Heights, California (1964); Del Mar Community Intermediate School, Reed Union School District, Tiburon, California. And so, by 1965, the middle school movement seemed firmly launched across the United States, with fact-finding surveys soon following to determine periodically how the numbers and types were progressing.

We turn next to some 25 years of rapid growth in numbers of the new school unit, increasingly called the "middle school," although even for the grades 6–8, 5–8, and 7–8 (the most common) varieties, the names "junior high," "intermediate," and others have been changed in many instances but are retained in some others. In this book, when we group all structures between elementary and secondary, we usually use the term "middle level schools" or "schools in the middle," leaving the term "middle school" to designate grades 5–8, 6–8, and others that call themselves this. We see the term "middle school" as most appropriate for *a school planned and operated as a separate school to serve the educational needs of students usually enrolled in grades 6–8 or 5–8 and 10–14 years of age, building on the elementary and leading toward the high school.*

Growth in Identity of the Middle School

As this edition of *The Exemplary Middle School* is prepared, the authors are well aware that the average American is less likely today than a decade ago to be completely uninformed as to what a middle school or level is. As middle schools have become common throughout our nation and the terms "middle school" or "middle level" are increasingly used by the media, and as children are attending schools called "middle" schools, they are no longer unknown. The middle school has taken on some of the identity its founders and faculties have wanted. But, at the same time, many practices used within these schools are not unique to this level, nor are they so different from school to school, that most lay persons and many educators do not understand middle school goals and characteristics, and may simply think of the middle school as the "new junior high." This section is intended to give some factual basis for understanding how the middle school organization has caught on; the next will deal with how the new schools are succeeding in providing the features indicated as desirable.

Middle Schools Become Widespread and Numerous

We have mentioned by name only a few of the several hundred schools that, by 1965, included by intention or accident the middle grades that characterize the middle school. The first of the surveys reported in the literature of the middle school found 499 schools in 1965–66. This study, by Cuff (1967), included schools having grades 6 and 7, and not extending below grade 4 or above grade 8. In 1967–68, Alexander, aided by a U.S. Office of Education Research grant that enabled a comprehensive survey (to be reported further below), found that by this time there were 1101 schools having at least three grades and not more than five and including grades 6 and 7 (Alexander, 1968). Ronald Kealy (1970) and Mary Compton (1976), both graduate student assistants associated with the latter survey, later conducted surveys from their own institutions using the same criteria; Kealy identified 2298 middle schools in 1969–70, more than double the number found two years earlier, and Compton, in 1974, found 3723 schools, about 3 and one-half times that in 1969. The more complete follow-up (of the 1967–68 survey) by Brooks and Edwards (1978) identified 4060 middle schools, using the same criteria—almost a four-fold increase over the decade of 1967–1978. A comprehensive twenty-year replication of Alexander's original study, plus additional questions, was done by Alexander and McEwin (1989), with their latest data for the total number of schools of the same grade group used in the previous studies, being that for 1986–87, that is, 5466. To recapitulate, these various surveys beginning with that of 1967–68 and each including only middle schools having at least three grades and no more than five, and including grades 6 and 7, showed that in twenty years (1967–68 to 1987–88) the total number of grades 5–8 and 6–8 middle schools increased about 500 percent. To the 1987–88 total of these schools one can add 2627 grades 7–8 schools, now usually considered middle schools, too, 2191 of grades 7–9, and 573 "others" (grade 5 or higher, with the highest grades 7 to 9), for a total of 10,857 middle level schools. In addition, over 5000 elementary schools in 1990 still included grades 7 and 8, middle level ones (McEwin & Alexander, 1990). Newer data show that the number of schools in the middle continued to grow into the 1990s. The marked trend toward a grades 6–8 school, and a lesser one towards 5–8, is clear.

Yet, the number of schools in the middle has greatly increased over the past three decades, with the largest percent of increase being those including grades 6–8, partially explained by the greatest loss being in the grades 7–9 junior high schools. We should turn now to see what else has happened in the middle school movement during the past 25 years.

The Rationale for the Middle School

The actual reasons why the numbers of new middle schools were growing rapidly then, and now, appear to have had little to do with an authentic attempt to meet the needs of early adolescent learners. More often, school district decision-makers were motivated to consider a new grade configuration for important reasons which, nonetheless, were far from being focused on the early adolescent as a person and a learner as we advocated.

In the South, but elsewhere as well, one of the important factors in producing hundreds of new middle schools during the 1960s and 1970s was the pressure to accommodate school district racial desegregation. In literally dozens of districts of all shapes and sizes, school planners and policy-makers made an important discovery. One could redesign a district to facilitate racial desegregation by closing the junior high school(s) and moving the ninth grade to the newly desegregated high school; then move the fifth and sixth grades out of the segregated elementary schools and create new and desegregated middle schools. The result—a plan for a dramatically more desegregated school district which would be likely to receive court approval. Hundreds of middle schools that opened in the late 1960s and 1970s were products of this effort.

A few years later, the changing demographic patterns in the Northeast and Midwest brought new challenges to managing school enrollments for planners in those districts. Buildings in some districts were far below capacity in the upper grades, to the point that high schools might have to be closed, a hitherto unheard of and undesirable option. In other districts, new growth brought a surge of new enrollment in the early grades of the elementary school, leaving crowded classrooms in those buildings. In still other districts, both things happened at once, causing simultaneous crowding in some of a district's schools and underutilization in others.

It was probably in one of these latter districts where a school planner or policy-maker first had an insight which became serendipitously beneficial to the middle school movement. Why not close the junior high school, move the ninth grade into the high school(s), and increase enrollment there by 25 percent; then move the sixth grade out of the elementary school(s) and create a new middle school program for the district? Thus, one could be conservative in terms of school district capital outlay and innovative (via the new middle school program) at the same time. This was, as time proved, an almost irresistibly attractive motive for those involved. Hundreds of middle schools were, and still are, being organized to accommodate the need to utilize more fully and equitably the school facilities in the district(s) involved.

Another wave of new middle schools emerged as a result of the educational tumult following the publication of the so-called Nation At Risk report (National Commission on Excellence in Education, 1983). Virtually every state in the nation implemented laws intended to infuse high school programs with new rigor. In many states, the ninth grade continued to be counted as a high school year; consequently, the ninth grade program became more intensely dominated by graduation requirements and other contingencies which made its presence in a middle school increasingly anomalous.

More and more, it seems, district decison-makers found it difficult to defend the presence of the ninth grade in a junior high school organization. This was especially true if there were also other pressing reasons for those students to be relocated to the high school, such as enrollment or school desegregation concerns. It was at this point that momentum for districts to reorganize into a middle school configuration took on increasing power and speed. One crucial additional factor came into play at about this time: the middle school concept was proving to be very popular in districts which had adopted it over the preceding two decades (George & Oldaker, 1985).

A school program which was *effectively* implemented appeared to produce the sorts of outcomes which pleased parents, policy-makers, and practitioners alike. Student behavior and attitudes improved, home-school relationships became closer, interethnic interaction became more positive, students enjoyed school more, teachers grew increasingly more appreciative of the opportunity to work together, and in many situations academic achievement held steady or improved slightly while these other more positive outcomes became pleasantly obvious. Presented with this sort of evidence, anecdotal though it was, the active resistance of traditional junior high school educators abated. Consequently, in the 1980s, the middle school concept became a more and more popular alternative, one which educators sought to implement for its own sake.

In general, we believe that the dominant educational rationale for the middle school, over and above the expedient reasons that prompted the appearance of hundreds of new middle schools, has been and remains that of its appropriateness, potential and increasingly actual, for middle school age students. Many good middle schools today that were initially created for purposes of expediency have become outstanding exemplars of programs fitting their students. This must be, of course, the ultimate rationale for establishing and maintaining schools at any level, but it had been submerged in prior organizations for middle grade students. In fact, there simply was no specific middle, transitional level under the two-level plans, namely 8–4 and 6–6. However much the initial reasons may have varied, it is the program goals adopted and used by the school that determine its ultimate success and contribution to the society maintaining it.

Every school usually sets up some type of mission or goal statement that may be simple and brief, or practically a volume of objective-like statements, or both. Note these simple statements from early middle schools that express this basic rationale of providing a school program specifically designed to meet the basic needs and interests of middle level students. Thus an unpublished paper dated July, 1969, from the Pearl River, New York, Middle School stated well the fundamental rationale of the middle school:

> On September 10 Pearl River's new Middle School will open its doors. The middle school is an "in-between" school: it stands between the elementary school and the senior high school. As such it is designed and equipped to serve

boys and girls who are "in-between" themselves; between childhood and young adulthood. If the middle school were merely a larger edition of the elementary school or a junior edition of the senior high school, it would fail in its purpose. It must be different from either, yet an entity in itself. Since different characteristics and needs have developed at this age, we hope to develop an educational program for these boys and girls in the program of middle school.

Similarly, a paper prepared at about the same time on the philosophy of the Aspen, Colorado, Middle School based its attention on the "Middle Schooler" described as follows:

The middle schooler is at an uninhibited age when both his individual differences and his common group characteristic are most apparent. He is noisy and shy, eager and recalcitrant, adventuresome and cautious, and the individual's emotional and intellectual development ranges from still-child to near-adult. He is eager to experiment with life, but at the same time is insecure and without experience. He needs the security of wise guidance and disciplinary boundaries around a freedom to participate and explore in a variety of relevant activities and exciting experiences which will guide him toward intrinsic and extrinsic successes and the discovery of his private self, his social self, and his environment.

A pamphlet of the Atlanta, Georgia, Public Schools, issued in the early history of the middle schools there stated that a middle school is:

. . . a school between the elementary and the high school. It is a new administrative organization, housed ideally in a building designed expressly for the purpose of providing an improved educational program for children at the middle years. The age range is from about ten to fourteen. The objectives and functions of the middle school are defined in terms of the dynamic needs, characteristics and capabilities of the emerging adolescent. (Thompson, 1971, p. 2)

Further, its "primary function" was briefly stated as: "The primary function is to help each child make an effective adjustment from childhood to adolescence." The same basic rationale of the Kent County, Maryland, Middle School was stated in a pamphlet on *The Middle School:*

The Middle School in Kent County, composed of grades five, six, seven, and eight, provides students with a gradual transition from the elementary school to the high school.

The middle school exists in its own right, free from the image of the high school and free to serve the educational needs of early adolescents, who are neither elementary nor secondary by nature.

Characterized by a "middle" growth period, these children need a school where they have room to be themselves with a curriculum which emphasizes individual needs and a staff equipped with special understanding and skills in working with early adolescents. Fifth graders, emotionally and physically different from children in grades one to four, find themselves in a more compatible grouping in the middle school organization. Eighth graders, too, are more closely related to the age group in middle school than to ninth grade students. (1971, p. 2)

In 1977, the newly-organized National Middle School Association appointed a Committee on Future Goals and Directions to set out goals for the middle school (and the Association). The Committee took this position, later adopted by the Association (p. 16):

We recognize the absence of any universal definition of the middle school and of middle school goals, and intend to reject any set of standards which prescribe specific goals. At the same time we feel that the NMSA should stand for certain priority goals, and hoped this would influence members to incorporate these goals into their own school statements:

1. Every student should be well known as a person by at least one adult in the school who accepts responsibility for his/her guidance.
2. Every student should be helped to achieve optimum mastery of the skills of continued learning together with a commitment to their use and improvement.
3. Every student should acquire a functional body of fundamental knowledge.
4. Every student should have opportunities to explore and develop interests in aesthetic, leisure, career, and other aspects of life. (p. 16)

We still accept wholeheartedly this rationale and this set of goals for a middle school, and only wish they had been fully implemented and achieved for all the millions of adults who have been through the middle level schools.

As middle schools have been made out of elementary and junior high schools, or as even new ones have inherited their faculties and students from the former organizations, their basic rationales were sometimes overlooked, or even overruled, in order "not to rock the boat" or for lack of essential personnel, facilities, and funds. But many schools were more successful, and the basic aim of providing education better suited to the age group than that of former organizations still predominates in the planning and maintenance of middle schools. A significant 1987 Report of the Superintendent's Middle Grade Task Force, *Caught in the Middle: Educational Reform for Young Adolescents in California Public Schools*, was prefaced by a Foreword from State Superintendent Bill Honig once again underlining the basic function of schools in the middle:

For too long, the middle grades have been treated as a wild card for solving facilities and enrollment problems. Now it is time to face the critical educational issues at stake in these "neglected grades."

The success of the educational reform movement depends on meeting the needs of middle grade students—both academically and socially. Failing to address these needs jeopardizes efforts for educational excellence and, more importantly, for these students' future success. (p. v)

The California report was followed, in 1988, by the development of important statewide reform efforts, centering around the concepts of several hundred "Partnership Schools" who have demonstrated "an uncommon commitment to be and become state of the art middle grades schools" and a lesser number of "Foundation Schools" who will work with 12 regional networks of Partnership Schools and whose primary mission is to assist the Partnership Schools in achieving their objectives. Each regional network has received funding from private foundations (Carnegie & Kellogg).[1] A progress report (Slater, 1990, p. 2) indicated that "reform in all areas of middle grade education in California was well under way six months into the project and was expected to continue at a vigorous rate. Most of the recommendations from *Caught in the Middle* were being implemented or were expected to be implemented in the near future by some or all of the participating schools." Curriculum revision, implementation of interdisciplinary teams, advisory programs, at-risk efforts, and linkages with other schools and businesses were among the reform efforts underway.

In Florida, three years earlier, the Speaker's (of the state House of Representatives) Task Force on Middle Childhood Education (Speaker's Task Force, 1984, p. v2) had found, according to its Executive Summary:

> . . . that between the entry into the 4th grade and exit from the 8th grade, students must accomplish a number of developmental tasks, and middle childhood programs must recognize the developmental diversity and needs of students. Careful attention, therefore, should be given to program structure, curriculum, student services and personnel. Students should master these developmental tasks during grades 4–8, if they are to enter high school at a readiness level in order to complete their high school education, and successfully enter adult society.

A program (PRIME) of special financial aid to Florida's grades 4–8, particularly grades 6–8, was subsequently recommended and legislated, with annual reviews and continuation, with changes as needed and possible. A follow-up assessment of the impact of PRIME legislation on middle level education in Florida (Irvin, 1990) indicated that the legislation has, indeed, had a measurably positive effect on the state's middle school programs. In Florida, schools organized with grades 6–8 are numerous, while those with grades 7–9 are disappearing. Advisory programs, interdisciplinary teams, common planning times, and careful articulation with elementary and high school programs are now much more frequently present in middle level schools in Florida.

In 1986, the Lilly Endowment established the Middle Grades Improvement Program (MGIP) to stimulate and support middle school improvement in the

---

[1]For more information, contact Thaddeus Dumas, Manager, Office of Middle Grades Support Services, California State Department of Education, Box 944272, Sacramento, CA 94244-2720.

state of Indiana. Districts across the state were asked to submit proposals show-ing how, with Lilly's support, they would bring about a "fundamental reworking of urban middle schools" in several areas: school-based management, instruc-tional leadership, dropout prevention, and increasing public support. Sixteen school corporations were eventually invited to participate. In 1989, again with the support and guidance of the Lilly Endowment, a Middle Grades Improve-ment Network was established; by 1991, the size of the network had increased to approximately 65 middle level schools, all intent on becoming more exemplary middle schools through mutual support and other networking activities.

Other states and many school districts have conducted similar reviews of their programs for young adolescents, with a considerable impetus from a sig-nificant and much publicized report by the Carnegie Council on Adolescent Development, *Turning Points: Preparing American Youth for the 21st Century*. Although certainly not approving the current statues of education at the middle level, the report again emphasizes the basic rationale of its schools, stated in the "Executive Summary" as follows:

> Middle grade schools—junior high, intermediate, and middle schools—are potentially society's most powerful force to recapture millions of youth adrift, and help every young person thrive during early adolescence. Yet all too often these schools exacerbate the problems of young adolescents.
>
> A volatile mismatch exists between the organization and curriculum of mid-dle grade schools and the intellectual and emotional needs of young adolescents. Caught in a vortex of changing demands, the engagement of many youth in learning diminishes, and their rates of alienation, substance abuse, absenteeism, and dropping out of school begin to rise. (1989, pp. 8–10).

And the Carnegie Task Force's "A Plan for Action" emphasizes the urgency of the need for related improvements of middle grade schools, in such state-ments as these:

> The early adolescent years are crucial in determining the future success or failure of millions of American youth. All sectors of the society must be mobi-lized to build a national consensus to make transformation of middle grade schools a reality. The Task Force calls upon all sectors that care about youth to form partnerships that will create for young adolescents a time of purposeful exploration and preparation for young adulthood.
>
> The Task Force calls upon the education sector to start changing middle grade schools now. Teachers and principals are at the center of this process. We urge superintendents and boards of education to give teachers and princi-pals the authority to make essential changes, and work collaboratively to evaluate student outcomes effectively. (p. 10)

We will note repeatedly in subsequent chapters the more specific recom-mendations made in the Carnegie report as to particular improvements needed in middle level schools to serve more fully their basic rationale. Most of these are efforts already well under way in many exemplary middle schools, but many,

many schools are still struggling to be what they can and must become in serving middle level students and, thereby, society.

Desirable Characteristics of Exemplary Middle Schools

Most of the statements cited regarding the rationale of middle schools imply or specify at least one, usually several, feature(s) to be included in the middle schools, feature(s) that are indeed regarded as desirable characteristics. Reviewing just the statements quoted thus far in this chapter, the following such characteristics were mentioned regarding early middle schools: Teaching teams, house organization, grades 6–8 plans (5–8 also), exploratory opportunities, individual-small group instruction for remedial basic skills, teacher guidance, flexible schedules and space, functional curriculum, and others. By the 1970s, considerable unanimity as to these desirable characteristics was evident, and various groups and individual authors began to compile and publish lists. This unanimity has been persistent and therefore influential. True, several persons who have written and said most about "what middle schools should be like" have been doing this for most, if not all, of the some thirty years of the movement. But we have been actuated and supported greatly by all of the developing knowledge about children of the crucial ages involved and their needs which the schools should serve. This knowledge, as we note in Chapter 1, comes from medicine, human growth and development, psychology, and other related fields.

As we review several statements of what schools in the middle should be like, variously called "desirable characteristics," "desirable features," "earmarks," and so forth, note the repetition of certain ones and the occasional omission of only a few. The year 1965 seems the first in which a survey of schools in the middle tried to summarize the somewhat unique characteristics they sought. Murphy's report of *Middle Schools: Profiles of Significant Schools* for Educational Facilities Laboratory included these two paragraphs summarizing these characteristics as she found them attempted in the schools surveyed:

> In general, the proponents of the middle school envisage a school adapted to a range of children who, rampant individualists though they are, seem to have more in common with each other than with elementary-school children as a group, or high-schoolers as a group. The school would assume that, in general, its population had some mastery of the tools of learning but was not ready for the academic specialization of high school (and its attendant college-preparation pressures). The school could concentrate, then, on provisions for individual differences, so long touted, so little effected by American education, taking particular account of the increased sophistication and knowledge of today's 10- or 11-year-olds to 14-year-olds over previous generations.
>
> As will be seen in the second part of this report, the design of the new middle schools facilitates a program that introduces fifth or sixth graders gradually to specialization, and provides all kinds of physical means to realize individual differences, on one hand, and to encourage group activities large and small on the other. The schools that enroll fifth or sixth graders usually assign

them to their own classrooms for at least a share of the time. Specialization is apt to begin with subjects like art, music, and shop. All of the schools described have provided generously for these nonacademic specialties to an extent rarely, if at all, possible in elementary schools. (p. 15)

In December, 1965, on the basis of their study of the scant relevant professional literature, and of discussion in a faculty-student seminar at the University of Florida, plus school visitations and discussions there, Alexander and Williams proposed the following "Guidelines for A Model Middle School:"

> A real middle school should be designed to serve the needs of older children, preadolescents, and early adolescents. . . . A middle school organization should make a reality of the long-held ideal of individualized instruction. . . .
> A middle school program should give high priority to the intellectual components of the curriculum. . . .
> A middle school program should place primary emphasis on skills of continued learning. . . .
> A middle school should provide a rich program of exploratory experiences. . . .
> A program of health and physical education should be designed especially for boys and girls of the middle school years. . . .
> An emphasis on values should underline all aspects of a middle school program. . . .
> The organization of middle school would facilitate most effective use of the special competencies and interests of the teaching staffs. . . . (p. 219)

These authors give more detailed proposals about the three-phase curriculum (learning skills, general studies, and personal development), and about a particular plan for organizing instruction in homeroom units (teacher guidance plan), wing unit (team planning and instruction), vertical unit (little school plan), and special learning centers.

Two surveys done in the late 1960s reported further on the characteristics actually included in the new middle schools. Alexander (1968, p. 2) surveyed a 10 percent sample (110) of the 1101 schools first determined as having a grade organization classified then as "a reorganized middle school" (including grades 6 and 7, not including grade 9, and having at least three and not more than five grades), and reached these conclusions from the findings in certain areas related to their characteristic features (summary dealt with these features: curriculum opportunities, instructional organization, individualization):

> The survey data clearly confirm the existence of a recent and current movement toward a different grade organization of the school ladder. They also indicate that the new middle school organizations in general fail to provide a program and instructional organization differing very much from those in the predecessor schools, especially in the grades 7–9 junior high school. Obviously, critical evaluation of the emerging middle schools is needed to determine what improvements they are making and can make over prior organizations.

Educational Research Service, which had been able to identify only 63 middle schools in 1965, four years later identified 70 school systems having 235 middle schools to study, and secured and reported data from 154 of them. The report included in columnar fashion information as to the schools' first year operated (many "in transition"), grades included, number of students and of staff positions, ability grouping, instructional practices, subjects taught by teams, special subjects offered, and activities. This report gives summaries of the data, but no conclusions. It was reviewed and interpreted in a *NEA Research Bulletin* (1969, p. 49) published the same month as follows:

> Every school that is called a middle school is not necessarily a middle school. The reports received from the principals of schools in the survey often reveal that in a great many of the schools the middle school concept has not yet been fully interpreted. This full implementation is hampered by such factors as financial problems, the inflexibility of instructional facilities, lack of specialized teacher preparation and/or orientation, and size of schools (too small or too large). One principal's concern was "we have no precedent to guide us. We just blaze as we go along."

The growing literature on the middle school movement during the 1970s and 1980s is replete with statements pertaining to the desirable characteristics of middle level schools. A few highlights as to their identity and status in this period can be gleaned through several significant reports briefly reviewed here in chronological order. There were various studies and reports of developments in individual states, and two national updatings (already cited Kealy, 1969–70; Compton, 1974) of the 1967–68 survey as to the number of middle schools, but the first study to go fully into characteristics again was the modified replication by Brooks and Edwards a decade after the Alexander study. As already noted, they found about four times as many schools, and they used about the same size (10 percent) for their sample. This study found that the new schools still had not implemented fully the characteristics usually cited as desirable, although continued expansion was predicted because "the factors prompting middle schools to be organized a decade or more ago still exist." Brooks and Edwards wrote this closing note:

> As some have observed, it may be that the middle school movement is like the children it serves: adolescent, growing, searching for identity, preoccupied with internal problems, yet beset with external influences. As with adolescent youth, the middle school movement must struggle to find an identity that both differentiates it from other movements and provides it with high visibility and priority in the educational and public communities as well. The need for the middle school must be communicated with clarity and persuasiveness, and the uniqueness of the middle school response to that need must be made with logic and intensity. (1978, p. 16)

The present authors believe that the turning point came in the 1970s, because progress had definitely been made towards implementation of the middle school concept by 1990.

Further listing of desirable characteristics continued through the publications of the National Middle School Association, the Association for Supervision and Curriculum Development, and the National Association of Secondary School Principals (through its Council on Middle Level Education).[2] Although there were differences among the various listings, most stressed the same matters of curriculum, instructional organization, teacher guidance, instructional methodology, and middle school orientation and articulation that had been persistent in the sources already cited. Perhaps more significant were the various surveys and other research approaches conducted and reported in the 1980s both because of their more deliberate selection of characteristics to be used in the evaluation of middle schools and the middle school movement. In 1983, Educational Research Service, Inc. reported its comprehensive compilation of a Research Brief entitled *Organization of the Middle Grades: A Summary of Research*. This report did not include any tabulation of characteristics of middle schools, but focused more on the issue of middle versus junior high schools and reviewed comparisons of many factors. Its conclusions from the research included these points: that "two-thirds of the schools called middle schools were organized as 6th through 8th grade;" that "neither the junior high nor the middle school was able to achieve the goals that educational theorists established for each;" that "the latest survey of the opinion of principals regarding middle grade organizations indicated their preference for a 6th through 8th grade organization;" and that "the quality of the school program was far more important than its grade organization."

George and Oldaker (1985, p. 19) took a different approach to the basic characteristics and effectiveness issues and queried some 160 selected potentially exemplary middle schools as to their major features and effectiveness. Their response indicated that "effective schools manifest markedly similar programs regardless of their locations or other distinguishing features." These common features included interdisciplinary team organization, a flexibly scheduled day, homebase/advisor-advisee teacher guidance program, curriculum provisions for student personal development, a favorable school learning climate, and other such critical elements, all common among these schools designated as exemplary by competent judges.

---

[2]See, for example, ASCD working Group on the Emerging Adolescent (1975). *The Middle School We Need*. Washington, DC: Association for Supervision and Curriculum Development; National Middle School Association. (1982). *This We Believe*. Columbus, OH: The Association; NASSP Council on Middle Level Education. (n.d.) An Agenda for Excellence at the Middle Level. Reston, VA: National Association of Secondary School Principals.

In 1987–88, Alexander and McEwin's (1989, pp. 84–85) survey replicated the one of 1967–68 cited earlier and added a few items to facilitate use of certain desirable characteristics regarded by them and others as "earmarks" of good middle schools. These earmarks were as follows:

1. An interdisciplinary organization with a flexibly scheduled day.
2. An adequate guidance program, including a teacher advisory plan.
3. A full-scale exploratory program.
4. Curriculum provision for such broad goals and curriculum domains as personal development, continued learning skills, and basic knowledge areas.
5. Varied and effective methodology for the age group.
6. Continued orientation and articulation for students, parents, and teachers.

Their findings led to this summary:

> In conclusion, the middle level is moving toward becoming a full partner in the new three-level system of education below the college level. Much progress has been made in the implementation of desirable characteristics, but many middle-level schools (the majority on most characteristics) have yet to provide some features they need, and probably wish, to have. We suspect that most schools at all levels have a few such gaps between desired and actual characteristics, and hope that such data as reported here for the middle level will help school leaders and supporters to improve education at every level.

During the same year, a similar-sized sample (672, Alexander and McEwin had 670) of schools and the same criteria were used by the Association for Supervision and Curriculum Development for its survey, yielding very similar results. Cawelti (1989, p. 9) reported this study's findings and conclusions as follow:

> Regardless of their organization, most U.S. schools enrolling 10- to 14-year-olds do not address all the program characteristics recommended for this age group.
>
> The middle school form of organization is far more likely to provide these program characteristics needed by the early adolescent. (This key finding might seem self-evident, but it is important to document that many school leaders *have*, in fact, responded to the essential features advocated for such an institution.)
>
> Despite the superiority of the middle school program, simply placing grades 6–8 or 5–8 in a single building does not assure that the program characteristics suggested for youth of this age will be present. Many schools with grades 6–8 continue to be more similar to than different from junior high schools.

Also published in 1989, the influential Carnegie Task Force on Education of Young Adolescents, cited earlier, made broad, forceful recommendations which encompassed the basic characteristics of middle schools we have been citing and added other critical ones involving families and communities as well:

Create small communities for learning. . . . The key elements of these communities are schools-within-schools or houses, students grouped together as teams and small group advisories that ensure that every student is known well by at least one adult.

Teach a core academic program. . . .

Ensure success for all students through elimination of tracking by achievement level, flexibility in arranging instructional time, and adequate resources (time, space, equipment, and materials) for teachers.

Empower teachers and administrators to make decisions about the experiences of middle grade students. . . .

Staff middle grade schools with teachers who are expert at teaching young adolescents who have been specially prepared for assignment to the middle grades.

Improve academic performance through fostering the health and fitness of young adolescents. . . .

Reengage families in the education of young adolescents. . . .

Connect schools with communities, which together share responsibility for each middle grade student's success. (1989, p. 9)

The Carnegie Council's report and the follow-up activities promoted by grants carefully distributed by the foundation, have stimulated new developments in virtually every state in the country. In North Carolina, for example, a state task force representing all groups involved in serving young adolescents met for an entire year and submitted recommendations for improvement, in ten key areas, to the state superintendent of schools and the State Board of Education (Middle Grades Task Force, 1991). In Florida, Carnegie monies stimulated a variety of activities including teleconferences on "full service" or multi-agency schools, accompanying program directories which should permit much more effective program dissemination and networking. (Division of Public Schools, 1991).

As this book is written, the most recently published national studies of middle grades schools are those by Epstein (1990) and MacIver (1990) of the Johns Hopkins University Center for Research on Elementary and Middle Schools. Their findings, from a large sample of all types of schools including grade 7 (about 30 different grade spans) identified the following as key practices in the middle grades, more likely to be adopted in more schools than other practices:

> interdisciplinary teams of teachers
> common planning time for teams of teachers
> flexible scheduling
> students assigned to the same homeroom or advisory teacher for all years
>   spent in the middle grades
> cooperative learning as an instructional approach
> exploratory courses and minicourses
> parental involvement in workshops on early adolescence
> parents as volunteers in the middle grades.

As to practices, grade spans, and effectiveness, these conclusions were drawn:

1. Most schools that contain grade 7 have not yet developed educational programs based on recommended practices for the middle grades. . . .

2. Some practices are more prominent in certain types of middle-grade schools than in others. . . . Overall, middle schools (6–9) and 7–8 schools use more of the practices that are recommended for middle-grade education than do other schools. . . .

3. Regardless of grade span, good practices make stronger programs. . . .

4. There is much more to be learned.

Our own studies, as cited, and our experience in the field of middle grade education cause us to agree heartily with these conclusions, and we shall shortly be dealing with the how-to's of the key practices Epstein and MacIver, and others, have identified. First, however, we wish to elaborate upon our synthesis of what we believe to be the essential components of an exemplary middle school, as revealed by the research and experience we cataloged above.

The Middle School Concept: Unique and Transitional

What is a Middle School?

In American usage, a middle school is a school in the middle of the school ladder (kindergarten through high school). In some other countries, middle school denotes a school in the middle of the entire educational structure, elementary school through college or university. In North America, the term itself was used very rarely prior to the early 1960s when educators began to use it with increasing frequency.

These new schools, or more accurately, the new concepts of a school in the middle, were conceived in part as bridges from elementary to secondary education, from the childhood level served by the elementary school to the older adolescent level served by the high school. These new schools in the middle were intended to balance more effectively the subject-centeredness of the secondary school and the child-centered focus of the elementary school. The middle school was developed to provide a more deft balance between teacher subject specialization (the hallmark of the high school) and supportive interpersonal structure (the heart of the elementary program) for students who needed both to learn effectively. A widely cited definition of the middle school first appearing in the 1968 edition of the *Emergent Middle School* is germane:

... a school providing a program planned for a range of older children, pread-olescents, and early adolescents that builds upon the elementary school program for earlier childhood and in turn is built upon by the high school's program for adolescence. (Alexander, 1968, p. 5)

The concept of the transitional school is insufficient, however, because middle school learners have unique characteristics and needs which must not be simply an extension of the program of the elementary school or an earlier introduction to the demands of the high school. An effective middle school must not only build upon the program of earlier childhood and anticipate the program of secondary education to follow, but it must be directly concerned with the here-and-now problems and interests of its own students. It must provide a program uniquely suited to their special needs. Furthermore, the middle school should not be envisioned as a passive link in the chain of education below the college and university, but as a dynamic force in improving education.

Definitions of the middle school, and the resulting philosophies, should, and generally do, give much emphasis to the role of the school in providing for continuous education progress of students. For example, leaders in one school district which adopted middle school programs more than 20 years ago expressed the following policy:

> The central goal of the middle schools in Alachua County, Florida, is to assist students in moving forward continuously at their own rates of learning without undue breaks from one level to another. In the best educational program, students should move upward on an inclined plane rather than through a series of graded steps. Thus, the middle school should take each student as he is and help him move forward successfully on a continuum of learning into the high school. (Alachua County Schools, 1972, p. 7)

Because of the dominance of the graded school organization, the definitions of any school level—elementary, middle, junior high, high school—inevitably imply a range of grades usually included. Early discussions of middle school organizations in the 1960s gave extended attention to this topic, and it remains one for consideration in most middle school conferences and planning groups. Educators generally agree that grades 6 through 8 should be included, but differences of opinion come as to whether grade 5 should be included in the middle school, and as to whether grades 7 and 8 could constitute a two-year middle school. Also, the proper place of grade 9 continues to be debated.

Our experience over the last two decades is, however, that virtually any combination of grades 5 through 9 ought to be thought of, legitimately, as a middle level school. Indeed, it may be more appropriate, in this period of the maturing middle school concept, to use the term middle level. Thus, we believe that an adequate concept of the middle, or middle level, school must view it as a bridging or transitional experience, but one that is unique and which also affects the schools above and below; as a school that is focused on the educational needs of learners who are usually in transition from childhood to adolescence; and, as a school which, therefore, generally provides a program of three to five years in the middle of the school ladder below the college and university. More briefly, we define a middle school as *a school of some three to five years between the elementary and high school focused on the educational needs of students in these in-between years and designed to promote continuous educational progress for all concerned.*

Goals of Middle School Education

Early publications regarding the emerging new school in the middle proposed or inferred its goals (Johnson, 1962). Educators hoped that a major change in education at that level would eliminate the "junior" syndrome in favor of a legitimate status as a separate level of schooling. They wanted to introduce greater opportunities for teacher subject specialization than were often encountered in more typical and smaller K–8 schools. They lobbied for more attention to the middle level in teacher education programs. They hoped for a more complete realization of the original goals of the junior high school, which they then (and we now) believed were appropriate for early adolescents: continued general education, opportunities for exploration, teacher-based guidance, a flexible curriculum, and an emphasis on values and character development.

Eichhorn's school experience and graduate study convinced him that a new organization in the middle was essential; he believed, as did many other writers of the period (e.g., Lounsbury, Vars, Moss, and others) that the junior high program, as it had evolved, would never be capable of truly providing for the unique needs of the early adolescent. He proposed an attack on what he believed to be the true cause of the problem:

> More and more professional literature is offering evidence that the junior high school concept has been seriously challenged. Usually, however, the suggested remedies take the form of treating the ills of the present structure rather than proposing an attack at the root causes of the problem. Substantiated assumptions of this study indicate that the root of the problem be attacked—through an altered school district organizational pattern—that an elementary unit of grades kindergarten through five, a middle school grouping of grades six through eight, and a high school unit of grades nine through twelve, be initiated. (1966, p. 104)

It appears, from the benefit of hindsight, however, that these writers, and others, were attempting to build on the opportunity, offered by changing circumstances, to infuse the new middle school with proper pedagogical purpose.

In some cases, whole states began to organize their legislative and bureaucratic forces to focus on improvements in middle level education. Florida, for example, passed and funded the PRIME (Progress in Middle Childhood Education) law in 1984; PRIME virtually mandated middle schools in Florida, in concept as well as grade organization. California issued *Caught in the Middle* (California State Department of Education, 1987), a comprehensive plan to implement the middle school concept in the school systems of that state.

It can be argued that, ultimately, this process has run full circle, from the expedient implementation of middle schools to meet other important district goals to the realization that the middle school concept, and the goals it seeks for early adolescents, are worthy innovations in themselves. Our own bold prediction would be that the turn of the century will find district after district implementing and improving new and existing programs aimed at facilitating the educational growth of early adolescents, based on the middle school concept, simply because it is good educational practice to do so.

There is, then, a growing consensus on the overall goals that every middle level school should achieve (Carnegie, 1989)—a consensus on the nature of the middle school concept. Each middle school, despite the specific characteristics of the students in that particular population, should, first, endeavor to reach the learning goals embedded in the academic curriculum for the age group, including appropriate knowledge, skills (e.g., critical thinking), and attitudes. Each school staff should, secondly, attempt to provide a school which enhances the personal development of each middle school learner, by enriching the curriculum with expanded age-appropriate curriculum choices and activities. All middle schools should attempt to provide regular success experiences for students, resulting in a school program that, as a minimum, does no harm to the self esteem of the students therein. Third, each and every middle school should attempt to inculcate an appropriate degree of group citizenship, group loyalty, and the perception in each student that they are an important part of important groups to which they owe loyalty, duty, and involvement.

These are the three overall goals of middle school education as we see it: academic learning, personal development, and group citizenship. How each school operates to move toward these goals, however, should depend primarily upon the characteristics of the particular group of students in each school.

The Educational Zip Code

The United States Post Office made history when it developed the concept of the zip code to help deal with the complexities of accurately delivering the mail. Virtually every American now knows that a zip code indicates a general area within which there are often as many as several hundred individual addresses, each one signifying a unique home designed, ideally, to meet the special needs of the group that lives within. Everyone also has been frustrated by having the mail go astray as a consequence of having been sent to the wrong zip code. Probably every reader has memorized his or her zip code. Not nearly so many Americans know that there are "educational zip codes" every bit as important.

We believe that American education has evolved, in the last half century, to the point where the complexities of effectively delivering instruction have produced three distinct educational "zip codes," each with common characteristics which distinguish it from the other two. There are now, we maintain, three such widely acknowledged zip codes: elementary, middle, and high school. As with our knowledge of our own personal postal zip codes, most professionals know the characteristics of their own educational zip codes, and at least some of the characteristics of an adjoining zip code. The three educational zip codes, as we think they have evolved, are depicted in Figure 2.1.

These depictions indicate the traditional components of American elementary and high school programs. These educational zip codes are familiar to all educators and virtually all citizens. It is not our purpose here to explicate or question either one. It is the middle school zip code to which we must attend.

We believe that it is possible to argue that, particularly over the last thirty years, the nature of the middle school zip code has become increasingly clearer and, simultaneously, more broadly accepted and affirmed by scholars, practitioners, and lay persons. The middle school concept itself has changed very little from its beginnings in the literature of the junior high school through the current period. The basic components of the concept as it is today are, however, far more broadly recognized, understood, accepted, and utilized than ever before, as evidenced by an uncountable number of activities and publications by professional associations, foundations, state departments of education, universities, and school districts around the nation and the world.

We believe that the components of the zip code described in these dozens of documents and practices can be characterized by two important terms: unique and transitional. All of the program components of the exemplary middle school should be different from what students receive in either the elementary school or the high school, but not so severely different that such experiences make the transition from elementary to high school more difficult than it would be without

PROGRAM	ELEMENTARY	MIDDLE	HIGH
1. STUDENT-TEACHER RELATIONSHIP	Parental	Advisor	Choice
2. TEACHER ORGANIZATION	Self-contained	Interdisciplinary Team	Department
3. CURRICULUM	Skills	Exploratory	Depth
4. SCHEDULE	Self-contained	Block	Periods
5. INSTRUCTION	Teacher-directed	Diverse	Student-directed
6. STUDENT GROUPING	Chronological	Supportive	Subject
7. BUILDING ORGANIZATION	Single Classroom	Team or House	Department
8. CO-CURRICULUM	All Participate	Broad Choice	By Ability
9. GOVERANCE	Principal and Teachers	Principal and Council	Principal and Department Heads
10. TEACHER PREPARATION	Child-oriented Generalist	Flexible Resource	Academic Specialist

FIGURE 2.1   **The Middle School Unique and Transitional**

the presence of a middle level of education. Each aspect of the middle school concept is specially tailored to the needs of the students at the middle level, not merely a thoughtless and unplanned downward extension of the high school program or an upward thrust of the elementary school. Yet, each component links the elementary and high schools together so that the process of education from kindergarten to high school is a smoother passage, a more seamless transition, than what students might have otherwise experienced. The middle school concept unifies the whole educational experience while providing a special learning opportunity for early adolescents that is uniquely tailored to their characteristics and needs. Unique and transitional; these are the key words which should be used to capsulize an understanding of which "addresses" are appropriate for the middle school zip code and which are not. The middle school concept/zip code, then, denotes a number of specific programs for virtually all schools at that level.

It would be expected, for example, that educators in all such schools would recognize the students' need for teacher guidance and provide some structured opportunity for that experience. Teachers would not act as quasi-parents (*in loco parentis*) as they would in the elementary school, nor would they leave the students on their own to seek out relationships with adults on the basis of common interests or personal preferences, much as might legitimately happen in high school. Middle school educators recognize the responsibility to act as advisors to their students. Just as there are many addresses in every postal zip code, there are many, many different ways to implement a teacher-based advisory program.

Similarly, the middle school concept is centered around a special way in which teachers and students are organized to provide and receive instruction and learning: the interdisciplinary team organization. In an interdisciplinary team organization, teachers share the same students, the same schedule, the same part of the building, and the responsibility to share in the planning of the major academic subjects which students encounter during the school day. Many experienced educators say that the interdisciplinary team is the heart of an exemplary middle school, but there are, of course, at least a dozen different ways to organize and operate an interdisciplinary team. There is, however, no substitute for the interdisciplinary team organization in a good middle school; self-contained classrooms belong in the elementary school and subject-centered, university-style academic departments belong no lower than the high school level. Many school districts are, of course, organizing and operating an interdisciplinary team organization in the ninth or tenth grades of the high school, so rigid dividing lines may be inappropriate.

The curriculum of the middle school, too, has its own unique but transitional flavor. The middle school curriculum builds on and extends the skills imparted by the elementary school, introduces the world of knowledge students will encounter in depth at the high school, and bathes it all in an exploratory, interdisciplinary light. Or, it should. It is probably fair to say that curriculum is the least changed aspect of the middle school concept, in terms of altered practices in real schools in the last century. Much of what is being taught in the last decade of this century was designed during the last decade of the previous century!

Instruction, at the middle level, needs to be a deft balance of teacher and student initiative. Very young children need a great deal of teacher direction to be successful in formal education. By the time students are 16 years old, no law compels them to learn anything from anyone ever again. Middle school students should become more independent and in charge of their own learning as each day passes. Consequently, middle school teachers may have the most difficult professional responsibilities in the world of education, while working with education's most challenging student group. Diverse instruction fits students best as they move through a period of great personal diversity.

Grouping students for instruction in the middle school is a complex process and much has been learned, in the last two decades, about how to do so more effectively. We know that chronological age or the number of years a student has been in school is no longer an adequate basis for grouping when they reach the middle level. We know that they are not entirely ready to group themselves via the subject matter choices they make. We know that many middle schoolers need a great deal more "supportive interpersonal structure" in their school environment than they often receive. There is a great deal of excitement being generated among middle school educators by new and more effective ways to group early adolescent learners.

Elementary school teachers are prepared to teach basic skills to young children; high school teachers are prepared in their subjects. Middle school teacher education must include a focus on the characteristics and needs of the learner, and must prepare teachers who can function as effective learning resources in one or more subject areas. Once again, the middle level must perform a double duty.

Elementary schools are often organized by grade level, and high school are almost always laid out according to subject specialization requirements. Exemplary middle schools are organized so that there is a "smallness within bigness" which usually focuses on the interdisciplinary team area. Teachers who share the same middle school students share the same part of the building. Often the teams are organized so that there is further "smallness within bigness" through a "house" or school-within-school organization. Here, too, much has been learned in the past decade, and we have a great deal to say about these developments in later chapters.

One of the more controversial areas of the middle school program focuses on the nature of appropriate extracurricular activities for the age group. Essentially, the belief of many middle school educators, growing more firm over the years, is that middle school programs should serve the needs of middle school learners. Extracurricular activities should not be offered primarily as entertainment for the public or merely as support for high school sports, or as the exclusive province of those students who happen to mature early. Nor should such activities be watered-down versions of high school activities for which early adolescents are too young (e.g., formal dances, sophisticated newspapers or yearbooks) or those which will be repeated again in high school.

High school activities, most middle school educators believe, should be saved for high school. Elementary school activities are almost always open to participation by all children. Many high school activities, particularly in large high schools, are often restricted to those who have the particular talent or ability called for. At the middle level, participation should be open to all who choose to become involved; the middle school is not the place to begin dividing students into those who can be successful in any activity and those who can not. The middle school program is an exploratory opportunity with few options closed to anyone who wishes to participate.

Finally, middle level schools also manifest a unique and transitional method of decision making, problem solving, and policy development. Elementary schools are often small enough to involve everyone in the formal decision-making process. High schools are so large, that academic divisions take far more responsibility, much in the way of colleges and universities. Governance, in exemplary middle schools, is a careful balance between spirited leadership and broad empowerment of all the stakeholders. Most often, a governing council of some sort, where teams have representatives who work with the school administration, is the vehicle. Shared decision making has been occurring in exemplary middle schools for decades.

Most supporters of the middle school concept, then, subscribe to certain unique but transitional common elements believed to be congruent with the goals of educating students in virtually all middle level schools; this is the middle school zip code. Advisory programs, interdisciplinary team organization, an exploratory emphasis on the curriculum combined with a core of common knowledge, flexible scheduling, active instruction, specially trained teachers, shared decision making among the professionals in the school, success experiences for all students, improved health and physical education, and reconnecting the home and community with the education of early adolescent learners; this is the canon of contemporary middle school education. National, state, and local organizations and associations affirm it (Carnegie, 1989).

Typically, middle school educators attempt to embody these principles in a school philosophy which makes their commitments clear. The School Philosophy of Wakulla County Middle School, Crawfordville, Florida, for example, has guided program development there from the opening of the school in the early 1980s to the recognition of the school as a model of exemplary programs in the 1990s. The 1989–90 version states:

The middle school is an idea designed to meet the needs of children in grades six through eight. These needs stem from the characteristics of the development of the middle school child. We believe strongly that all the programs and practices of the Wakulla County Middle School should be based on a thorough knowledge of the development of middle school children and should be focused on meeting their needs.

While congruent with the educational philosophy of all the Wakulla County Schools, K–12, this school is unique in that it should provide a learning environment for middle school students. The school should not be an elementary school nor a mini-high school, but possess unique components that will provide a smooth transition from the elementary to the high school.

The environment should be student-centered rather than subject-centered and should provide a structured, orderly environment for learning. At the same time, we recognize the critical role of a middle school in the development of the self-concept and urge the establishment of a supportive, positive emotional climate.

Curriculum and instruction should appeal to the exploratory nature of middle school students, and yet provide challenge and a foundation for future studies. We believe that mastery of the basic communication and mathematics skills is of primary importance in the middle school so that students may possess the skills they need for learning in the depth required of high school students.

Believing that successful educational endeavors must include the home as an integral part, we encourage the community to be involved in all aspects of the school program in an advisory, as well as an operational, role.

The national debate about the common characteristics of middle level schools is over, at least among active participants in the middle school movement. Now that we have established the expectation that the members of one zip code should demonstrate striking differences from those in the other two, as exemplified in the philosophy above, it may be even more important to assert that each school within a zip code should be unique, and this uniqueness (just as in the case of postal addresses) should be based on "who lives there."

In the case of the postal zip code, each specific address within the zip code is, ideally, designed and operated in light of the unique characteristics and needs of the residents. Such should also be the case within educational zip codes. Within the general set of guidelines which describe each educational zip code, each specific address should be designed and operated with the characteristics and needs of those who learn there. There should be an affirmation of the general attributes of the zip code in every address in the area, but each specific location should be unique, in ways that reflect the nature of those who are there, for whom that place is their learning homebase.

For nearly a century, the evolving middle level concept has been based on the often fervently held conviction that middle school age students, as a developmental age group, are unique in their characteristics and needs. Rarely will a meeting of any group of middle level educators pass without pointed references to the special nature of the students involved. There is some evidence that establishing and maintaining high quality middle schools depends, in several ways, on the recognition of the special qualities of these learners and the willingness to tailor programs to those needs (George & Anderson, 1989).

Just as in the case of the post office, therefore, the nature of specific school addresses should be determined by who lives there. The nature and needs of the "residents" of a particular educational place should determine the design and operation of that program. The students and their developmental needs should determine, however, more than just the general guidelines of generic middle level education. The specific needs of a single population of early adolescent learners should be the foundation upon which the unique features of any particular middle level school are constructed.

But which student development characteristics should be most carefully considered when designing the school and its program? Which features of the school program should be fine tuned to those developmental characteristics? These are subjects for extended attention in later chapters of this book, particularly when we discuss the topic of schoolwide grouping strategies. At this point, we must limit the discussion to the earnest and unencumbered assertion that there is no one right way to organize and operate all middle schools. The organization and program of every middle level school should be a function of the specific characteristics and needs, the level of development, of the student population attending the school.

Schools in the Middle—Past, Present, and Future

In this chapter we have attempted to review the establishment and development of middle level schools, noting the earlier growth of the junior high, its coming into some disfavor, and its partial replacement by the newer middle school. We strongly believe that the now more popular middle school organization will become more dominant and successful in meeting the needs of middle grades students. But, to do so, much greater progress must be made in implementation of the variously entitled "basic," "desirable," "critical," or "key" characteristics, features, earmarks, or practices, long sought and still lacking in the majority of middle level schools, even the more successful grades 6–8 middle schools. Middle schools must become, in a word, more exemplary. For this to occur, many more teachers and professional personnel must be trained or retrained for the middle school, since the majority now teaching there were trained for elementary or secondary schools. These persons need relevant knowledge and understandings of the middle school. The purpose of this book is specific provision of this knowledge, hopefully presented in readily understandable form. Our own experience and study has led us to believe that this knowledge will be especially relevant to the desirable characteristics of good middle schools, so we have at least one chapter related to each such characteristic. Our choice of significant characteristics of good middle schools—those that could make a middle school "exemplary"—and the number of the chapter treating each characteristic follow:

1. The primary focus of the middle school should be on the learners in these schools, usually about ages 10–14 and having the many unique needs and interests of early adolescents. Chapter 1 was devoted to these learners, their characteristics, needs, and interests.

2. Middle school planning should recognize as fully as possible historical factors in the development of this school and level, and its rationale and desired characteristics (the middle school concept). Chapter 2 has dealt with these matters.

3. The middle school curriculum should include provision for its three basic domains or areas: personal development, continued learning skills, and basic knowledge areas. Chapter 3 presents examples of exemplary middle school curriculum opportunities, and also of middle school curriculum planning.

4. Although no single chapter can adequately deal with how to teach, current information from theory, practice, and research as to instructional methodology should be utilized fully in every middle school and classroom. Relevant information is summarized in Chapter 4.

5. The middle school should provide an adequate guidance program, with special attention to types and plans for teacher-based guidance—Chapter 5.

6. An interdisciplinary team organization is characteristic of an effective middle school—Chapter 6.

7. Exemplary middle schools can and should utilize appropriate means of grouping students. Alternative methods are described in Chapter 7.

8. Flexible scheduling and various types of space utilization should be planned for each middle school for its maximum effectiveness. These are treated in Chapter 8.

9. Exemplary middle schools depend upon effective planning and implementation. Furthermore, middle schools, new and established, should be evaluated on the extent to which they attain goals related to the needs of the students who are their clients. Chapter 9 deals with these concerns.

10. We will repeat several times that sooner or later every middle school takes on the characteristics of its leadership. Chapter 10 deals with this most important concept, and attendant behaviors.

Conclusion

The middle school has an essential role in helping early adolescents develop physically, intellectually, morally, socially, emotionally, psychologically, perhaps even spiritually (in the sense of developing meaning and purpose in their lives). Understanding what makes the early adolescent tick is the key to middle school program development. Beane said that young adolescents are "the age group that is probably more misunderstood and disliked than any other" (1990, p. 112). But countless middle school educators including Jim Beane, would argue otherwise—we know middle schoolers to be creative, energetic, unpredictable, and lovable. Knowing, and remembering, the various characteristics, needs, and stages of development allows educators to implement the elements needed for the exemplary middle school. Let us look, in the following chapters, at the components of such middle school programs.

ADDITIONAL SUGGESTIONS FOR FURTHER STUDY

A. Books and Monographs

Lawton, E. J. (1989). *A journey through time: A chronology of middle level education resources*. Columbus, OH: National Middle School Association.

B. Periodicals

Doornek, R. (1990). A multi-cultural model: Kosciuszko middle school—Milwaukee, WI. *School Arts, 89* (8), 17–20.

George, P. S. (1988). Education 2000: Which way to the middle school? *Clearing House, 62* (1), 14–17.

Gerler, E. R., Jr., et al. (1990). Succeeding in middle school: A multimodal approach. *Elementary School Guidance and Counseling, 24* (4), 263–71.

Harrington-Lueker, D. (1990). Middle school reality falls short of the ideal. *American School Board Journal, 177* (9), 27.

Honig, B. (1988). Middle grade reform. *Social Education, 52* (2), 119–20.

Raebeck, B. S. (1990). Transformation of a middle school. *Educational Leadership, 47* (7), 18–21.

C. ERIC

Alexander, W. M. & McEwin, C. K. (1989). *Earmarks of schools in the middle: a research report*. (ERIC Document Reproduction Service No. ED 312 312)

Alexander, William M.; McEwin, C. Kenneth. (1989). *Schools in the middle: progress 1968–1988*. Schools in the Middle: A Report on Trends and Practices. Reston, VA: National Association of Secondary School Principals. (ERIC Document Reproduction Service No. ED 327 000)

Appalachia Educational Lab & Virginia Education Association. (1990). *Middle schools in the making: a lesson in restructuring. A joint study*. Charleston, WV: Appalachia

Educational Lab.; Richmond: Virginia Education Association. (ERIC Document Reproduction Service No. ED 316 958)

Dorman, G. (1987). *Improving middle-grade schools: a framework for action.* Chapel Hill, NC: North Carolina University, Center for Early Adolescence. (ERIC Document Reproduction Service No. ED 289 588)

Farrar, E. & Connolly, C. (1989). *Improving middle schools in Boston: a report on Boston compact and school district initiatives.* Buffalo: State University of New York. (ERIC Document Reproduction Service No. ED 319 842)

MacIver, D. J. (1989). *Effective practices and structures for middle grades education. Policy issues.* Charleston, WV: Appalachia Educational Lab.; Baltimore, MD: Center for Research on Elementary and Middle Schools. (ERIC Document Reproduction Service No. ED 306 668)

Shann, M. H. (1990). *Making schools more effective: Indicators for improvement.* Boston, MA: Boston Univ., Mass. School of Education. (ERIC Document Reproduction Service No. ED 327 559)

Sudderth, C. R. (March, 1989). *The social battleground of school improvement: When a troubled school is impacted by an intensive renewal program.* Paper presented at the Annual Meeting of the American Educational Research Association, San Francisco, CA. (ERIC Document Reproduction Service No. ED 310 492)

Wells, A. S. (1989). *Middle school education—the critical link in dropout prevention.* ERIC/CUE Digest No. 56. New York: ERIC Clearinghouse on Urban Education. (ERIC Document Reproduction Service No. ED 311 148)

D. Dissertations and Dissertation Abstracts

Brothers, S. J. (1985). Pupil-control ideology and middle school concept implementation in selected Oklahoma middle schools (Doctoral dissertation, Oklahoma State University, 1985). *Dissertation Abstracts International,* 47/03a, 722.

Goodwin, D. W. The status of middle school education in Indiana (Doctoral dissertation, Ball State University, 1988). *Dissertation Abstracts International,* 49/07a, 1638.

Kane, C. C. (1988). Toward an expanded middle school philosophy: an analysis of philosophy and practice in middle level education (Doctoral dissertation, Florida State University, 1988). *Dissertation Abstracts International,* 49/12a, 3652.

McCall, J. C. (1988). *The development of public middle schools in Alachua County, Florida, 1970–1987* (Doctoral dissertation, University of Florida, 1988).

3

Middle School Curriculum

A critical characteristic of the exemplary middle school is its comprehensive curriculum; that is, the program of planned learning opportunities for its students. Ideally, this should be uniquely and effectively designed to provide for the continuous progress of each child enrolled. This chapter describes briefly the processes of planning such a curriculum, alternative designs, and the nature and scope of learning opportunities in major domains of the curriculum at the middle level.

Planning an Exemplary Middle School Curriculum

Curriculum planners for the new middle school must choose whether to develop a new program for the new school or to adopt the programs of predecessor schools for the grades, ages, and levels involved, or to utilize some combination of new and old programs. The fact is that old, rather than new, programs have predominated throughout the continuing development of the middle school movement, from its origins in the 1960s through the early years of the 1990s. The first comprehensive survey of middle schools concluded that the aims of the reorganization movement, as of 1968, had not been reflected in program change:

> Aims generally stated, both in the literature and by the respondents for the schools in the sample, such as "to remedy the weaknesses of the junior high school" and "to provide a program specifically designed for this age group" are not generally reflected in the curriculum plan and instructional organization of the schools surveyed. The program of studies is generally comparable to that of these grades in predecessor organizations, with a relatively sparse offering of elective and other curriculum opportunities, especially for grades 5 and 6.

Instructional organization for grade 5 is most frequently similar to that of the elementary school, with the departmentalization pattern of the junior high school introduced even here and becoming the predominant organization in the other grades (Alexander, 1968, p. 34).

Five years later, an active participant in the middle school movement at that time, James DiVirgilio, asked, "Why the Middle School Curriculum Vacuum?" and noted this observation:

> The changes that have been made in middle schools are in such areas as clubs, athletics, socials, and general school environment . . . . Currently the practice is to continue curriculum programs as they existed in the elementary fifth and sixth grades and the junior high seventh and eighth grades and to incorporate these programs into a middle school setting. This being so, it is apparent to educators interested in middle school growth that more effort is needed in projecting and organizing a curriculum that will enhance the further develop-ment of young people of middle school age. (DiVirgilio, 1973, p. 225)

In their report of a "modified replication" a decade later of the Alexander study, Brooks and Edwards concluded that "it can be safely stated that most middle school students in those schools sampled spend their day in a disciplinary, nonteamed organizational format, the same format likely dominant in junior high schools and high schools." (Brooks & Edwards, 1978, p. 12). Recent studies of changes in the middle school movement (Alexander & McEwin, 1989) yield mixed results; they indicate significantly positive changes in the organization of teachers and students, but find that little has changed in the area of the course of study offered to youngsters at this level. In the attempt to create a new school in the middle, educators have concentrated, throughout the last several decades, primarily on organizational changes such as the interdisciplinary team and not on the content of the major curriculum areas.

James Beane, a thoughtful critic of curriculum in middle level education, has written that: "The curriculum question has been an 'absent presence' in the middle school movement" (1990). Ironically, it was Beane (1975) who issued a call for an increase in "core curriculum" designs for middle level schools fifteen years earlier. Of course, the history of middle level education would indicate that similar calls have been made throughout the last half century. There is too little exciting news, in the nineties, about the status of curriculum in the middle schools of America.

During the 1980s and early years of the 1990s, much of the impetus for and control of the curriculum planning process was drawn back to and remains at the state level. This is so, it seems, in virtually every state. Largely as a result of the "back to the basics" movement of the late 1970s and 1980s, and the edu-cational earthquake of the Nation At Risk Report of the National Commission on Excellence in Education (1983), state legislatures and departments of edu-cation initiated new curriculum and testing requirements which effectively removed local school-based educators from any important formal role in the curriculum planning process. Whatever one's opinion of the outcomes of these important movements in education, nationally, there is little doubt that, for the last decade, local educators have had less and less influence on the design and development of middle school curriculum.

The dissatisfaction with the lack of change in the curriculum for the middle school is reflected, however, in the position statements which the Board of Trustees of the National Middle School Association was considering for adoption in June, 1991 (NMSA, 1991). Of the ten statements being developed to express the strong beliefs of the group, the very first one dealt with curriculum. It stated:

> Just as a middle level school is organized to meet the needs of young adolescents, NMSA believes that middle school curriculum, instruction, and assessment should;
> - relate to the lives of students;
> - integrate knowledge;
> - focus on the process of learning; and
> - be delivered in an environment in which exploration is pervasive and which is activity-based and students can learn from failure.
>
> Each of these characteristics is a necessary facet of the middle school curriculum and contributes to learning that is dynamic and meaningful. (NMSA, 1991, p. 1)

This position statement preceded nine others from the areas of middle school identity, staffing, school and community relations, affective education, student activities, alternative schooling, student behavior, sports, and leadership. At least four of these other statements could also be thought of as a part of the school curriculum. Clearly, the status of the curriculum is on the mind's of national leaders in middle school education.

Curriculum Planning at the School Level

The ideal locus of planning for the middle school is, however, in the individual school (Lipsitz, 1984). Even when national and state legislative groups and departments of education issue mandates and requirements, the actual task of implementing such a curriculum always falls, in the long run, to the individual school staff. Although external agencies and groups may attempt to control or, more properly, to facilitate and guide school curriculum planners, it is the vision and industry of the latter that determine whether the school develops and implements a program that is unique and effective for its student body. Oftentimes, middle level educators discover that balancing the mandates from external groups with the characteristics and needs of their particular learners requires simultaneous planning and implementation. Difficult as it is to plan and operate at the same time, it can be and is being done. A handout on "Curriculum Development" from the principal of the Marshall (Minnesota) Middle School reviewed some experience in the first years of curriculum planning at this school and insightfully reported:

> Six years later we have come to the realization that curriculum work is very
> difficult. It takes cooperation and time, and it seems to be never ending. It does
> seem worth the struggle, and we are coming to terms with the total process.

When educators in individual middle schools do have the opportunity to plan
the curriculum, three levels of planning within the school are essential: schoolwide; team and other small groups; and individual faculty members and their
students and parents. For schoolwide planning, the total faculty must, of course,
make those critical decisions within their power which relate to basic goals, the
general design of the curriculum, the policies of student progress and grouping,
and faculty development and inservice education for curriculum and instructional
improvement. Especially in faculties too large for extended and interested participation in discussion of details of such matters, responsibility for their exploration
and development, and in some matters decision making and implementation, is
typically vested in some type of representative curriculum council.

The importance of this sort of shared decision-making vehicle so permeates
the life of educators and students in exemplary middle schools that we make
extensive reference to its operation at several other points in this text. Nonetheless, one of the central roles of this sort of council is, admittedly, in the
development and implementation of the school curriculum.

One model for planning at the school level is the Program Improvement
Council (PIC) recommended in the Individually Guided Education (IGE) program as assisted by the Kettering Foundation's IDEA Program. The PIC model,
developed in the early 1970s, has proven its viability by its continued presence
in exemplary middle schools more than two decades later. According to its early
definition:

> A Program Improvement Council, known as the PIC, has a membership of the
> Principal and Learning Community (team) leaders. The Council's job is to
> resolve problems affecting two or more Learning Communities and to establish
> schoolwide policies. (Reeves, 1974)

A school bulletin at the Spring Hill Middle School, High Springs, Florida,
reporting the establishment of a PIC there early in the school's history, noted
that "the primary function of the PIC is to establish communication lines
between the various teams and the administration" and suggested the following
possible contributions of the organization:

1. Discuss ways to improve the use of shared school facilities.
2. Coordinate curriculum development and inservice education.
3. Define the roles of support systems to make for their more efficient use.
4. Resolve problems involving two or more units.
5. Coordinate use of outside consultants and special staff members.
6. Present projects from teachers in their respective units when expenditure of
    funds is required.

The meetings were open to all members of the faculty, with the PIC itself representing the teams ("Learning Communities," as termed by IDEA) and the administration. We will have much to say about the Program Improvement Council in our later discussion of middle school leadership.

An early organization with a similar purpose for the Webster Transitional School, Cedarburg, Wisconsin, utilizing IGE in connection with the Wisconsin Research and Development Center, was described as follows:

> The Faculty Advisory Committee is composed of one member from each academic team, two members of the allied arts team, a member of the supportive services team, student representative (optional), and the three members of the leadership team (principal, dean of students, and instructional consultant). It meets weekly. It shares decision making with all members of the professional staff on matters related to the daily operation of the school. Emphasis is on involving the staff in policy making rather than on the diffusion of information. The committee organizes and holds inservice meetings and also general faculty meetings. (Klausmeier & Daresh, 1979)

Such councils are variously called, in addition to the terms just used, "curriculum council," "council on instruction," "steering committee," "coordinating council," and other names. Their work generally includes consideration of these essential elements of curriculum planning specified in a description of the work of the Caloosa Middle School Curriculum Council of Lee County, Florida:

1. Curriculum development, articulation, and evaluation as these relate to pupil needs and achievement.

2. Instructional strategies and all areas related to these.

3. Inservice needs and activities as related to staff and program development.

4. Instructional supplies and equipment together with budgetary recommendations to support these needs in all departmental operations.

In addition to such curriculum councils, much of the work of schoolwide curriculum development and implementation in exemplary middle schools continues to be done by academic department committees, alongside the operation of the interdisciplinary team organization. It seems that, by the beginning of the 1990s, middle school educators have learned an important lesson—that subject-oriented curriculum development and interdisciplinary team life can coexist, and contribute to the efficacy and efficiency of each other. Earlier, many educators interpreted the middle school concept to mean that the subject-oriented focus and, hence, departments, ought to be banished from the school. This was because then, and even now, the interdisciplinary team organization was a fragile and vulnerable innovation, one which could easily die off, much like a crocus poking through the spring snow can be killed by a chance freeze. Consequently, many educators believed that the success of the team organization depended on the destruction of the high school-style academic departments that had found their way into the central position of many junior high schools (and, unfortunately, remain there in many so-called middle schools).

In the 1990s, subject area curriculum planning groups and interdisciplinary teams coexist in many exemplary middle schools. In such schools, the academic department has been removed from its once all important status and been given a much less central role. In curriculum planning, however, "vertical committees" or "subject planning groups" play a critical role. Typically, such groups are composed of representatives from each interdisciplinary team. The Social Studies committee, for example, would likely be composed of the Social Studies teachers from every team in the school, plus the assistant principal for curriculum. Monthly meetings of groups like this account for much of the work of local school curriculum development and implementation. The members may occasionally meet with district-level curriculum supervisors who are in touch with the mandates from the school board, the state department of education, and the legislature. More often, they react to and possibly select from curriculum materials developed and distributed by external agencies and groups, review the established scope and sequence of the curriculum in a specific subject, examine results of standardized tests, and make plans for ordering new textbooks, materials, and equipment. There may also be a need from time to time to organize special committees or other groups to work out tentative solutions to curriculum problems that cut across teams, subjects, and even schools, such as special developments in the community, state or nation demanding curriculum recognition, for example, festivals, fairs, contests and so forth. Important decisions of such groups, however, are often brought to the schoolwide Program Improvement Council for review before they are implemented.

Plans and materials developed by such schoolwide groups are essential to the successful implementation of the individual school's role in curriculum development. It is in their deliberations, consideration of goals, content and strategies, compromises, and recommendations that each school can develop a unique but effective program related to the needs of its students and the resources of its faculty, plant, and community. But departments and curriculum councils can not succeed without the careful input of ideas and implementation of program by teacher teams and individual faculty members.

Planning by Teaching Teams and Other Small Groups

Chapter 6 of this text is completely devoted to interdisciplinary team organization, and gives much attention to the planning activities of teams. The development and the implementation of the curriculum for the students in their team are the central functions of team planning, although their successful discharge involves such matters as scheduling, budgeting, and pupil personnel decisions, as well as content and instructional strategies. We simply can not overemphasize the great importance of the cooperative planning of each team in the school and of the planning between teams accomplished in large part by the schoolwide council. Chapter 6 also gives especial consideration to the leadership role of the team leader, who is a very critical person in a very critical organization.

Planning by Individual Teachers

We describe in Chapter 6 the responsibilities of individual team members for planning as members of the team and as teachers of specific student groups and individuals, and in Chapter 4 we deal with many instructional tasks, including the planning of instruction. Here we simply note that the middle school teacher is no less responsible than teachers at any other level for detailed and effective planning. Team teaching and planning make it possible for teachers to share problems and plans, but also create the obligation for each team member to do her or his share of the individual homework required for effective teaching.

Planning by External Agencies and Groups

The curriculum plan of any school at any level, as we have said, is almost inevitably the result of planning by many groups outside the school, as well as by those inside; we have considered: state board and department of education; state committees on programs of studies, textbooks, and special curriculum areas; professional organizations; various special interest groups with materials and plans to advance their missions; and the school district curriculum organization. The latter is not fully external to the individual school, but it serves all schools in the district. The city or county curriculum council and curriculum staff can be a most effective aid to the individual school, and is certainly the first resource to be consulted in the school's own planning. Districts differ widely, of course, as to the extent of centralization, and in some large, centralized districts curriculum planning may be primarily at the district level with only immediate and sometimes relatively insignificant matters settled within the school and classroom. In some districts with a long tradition of individual school initiative and in those with little resources at the district level, planning may be almost entirely at the local school level.

The pattern which seems most promising for exemplary middle schools and their districts is one in which the district provides these types of services for individual school planning:

1. A general framework of goals for the schools of the district, with an indication of specific state and local curriculum requirements and expectations and of the areas in which local schools have the freedom to develop unique programs.

2. Consultative and coordinating assistance in curriculum planning and materials for all curriculum areas and, especially, in regard to special areas such as industrial arts, wherein the individual school may have only one faculty member.

3. The organization and maintenance of district-wide councils or leagues to give optimum opportunity for sharing and planning between schools both at the same and at different levels. Such district-wide leadership is essential to the

fulfillment of the basic transitional function of the middle school as was stated very clearly in the "Philosophy of Education" material distributed by the Goddard School of Littleton, Colorado:

> The philosophy of Goddard School is based on the premise that the middle school is an integral part of the District Six educational program and that the Goddard program must be developed so that middle school students can follow a K–12 program of study without experiencing any gaps between the elementary school and the middle school or between the middle school and the high school. All important as this function is to the middle school, it can not be achieved by the middle school alone; the active involvement of district leadership and the elementary and high schools, as well as the middle school, is essential.

The district may also organize groups of citizens for participation in curriculum decisions or assist local schools in involving parents and other citizens. The Kirkwood, Missouri Schools, for example, operate three Curriculum Policy Committees—one at the elementary, one at the middle, and a third at the high school level. These Committees, according to a flier inviting citizens to join, have these functions:

- Help to coordinate curriculum offerings between the high school, middle school, and elementary divisions
- Analyze course offerings to ensure they meet student needs
- Recommend curriculum improvements to the district administration
- Study student activity programs and make suggestions for improvement
- Involve R-7 (the district) citizens, students, and staff members in curriculum planning, selection, and evaluation

The foregoing seems a good list of the functions a school district curriculum organization should discharge provided there is full representation of local schools and ample feedback from the schools. We turn now to alternative curriculum designs to be considered in curriculum planning at the district and school levels.

Alternative Curriculum Designs—A Continuum

The curriculum plans of most middle and other schools too frequently are developed or adopted without conscious attention by the planners to the design, pattern, or framework of the curriculum. Yet it is the inflexibility of some designs that causes the many problems in the school's attempt to deal effectively with curriculum pressures, especially those of the great individual differences of learners. Careful consideration of alternative curriculum designs is needed with conscious decision to employ the most appropriate design for each major aspect of the curriculum plan. Although full treatment of principles and practices of curriculum designing is beyond the scope of this book, we do note in this section some major design models that can be considered in planning the curriculum of a middle school. Figure 3.1 presents these models as being on a continuum

Most Structure →

Least Structure →

SEPARATE SUBJECTS	CORE, BLOCK, AND INTERDISCIPLINARY	INDIVIDUAL NEEDS, INTERESTS & PROGRESS	DOMAINS AND OTHER GOAL CENTERED
Basic Decisions:	Basic Decisions:	Basic Decisions:	Basic Decisions:
What subjects? When?	What areas in core, etc., and what areas separate?	What areas to be planned on individual design basis?	How do students, parents and faculty work together in defining goals and domains?
What relative emphasis—how much time per subject?	In combined area units, what factors decide scope and sequence?	What factors determine student choices?	Which school programs should serve each goal?
What principles for selecting content within each subject?	What options for teachers as to objectives?	How can teachers plan with individual students?	How can new programs be created as needed?
What options for students?	What options for students in unit activities?	How is progress determined within each area?	How can existing programs be discontinued?
What opportunities to cross subject lines?		How can learning opportunities be created as new needs and interests arise?	

FIGURE 3.1   **Continuum of Alternate Curriculum Designs**

of structure, with the most highly structured at the left and the least structured at the right.

The Separate Subjects Design

The traditional and dominant curriculum design at all levels of education is one of disciplines, major organizations of knowledge and subjects, derived for school instruction from the disciplines. Although significant departures from the subject organization occurred in the elementary school early in this century, the secondary schools have characteristically maintained the subject pattern, departing from it most frequently only to introduce various extracurricular activities to better meet the interests and needs of adolescents. The middle schools generally have adopted the subject design for most of their program, but made many combinations with other designs. And as in the elementary school, the subjects in the middle school program of studies tend to be broad fields, such as social studies, rather than separate subjects, such as history and geography.

While fully recognizing the importance of the organized knowledge content within the broad fields and other cognitive areas, middle school planners need to avoid the stereotyped program of studies, instructional organization, and schedule of many junior high schools. Indeed, it was in part to gain flexibility for the varied population that the middle school was first espoused. Language arts, social studies, science, and mathematics are constants in all middle school curriculum plans, but their provision does not enforce on the middle school the period-per-day class in each broad field, developed and taught without attention to the other fields. Subjects and activities may well be organized separately, but in the exemplary middle school the activities are curricular, a significant part of the program and of the faculty's assignments. So are the teacher guidance responsibilities in the advisor-advisee programs described in Chapter 5. Thus, the hope—and, to some extent, the practice—is that the advantages of a knowledge-based subject organization can be used without usurping the entire curriculum.

Core, Block, and Interdisciplinary Designs

Designs that utilize subject matter within and across subject lines to focus on some other organizing center, such as personal and social problems, have long been advocated for the middle school years. Units of work including materials from social studies, language arts, fine arts and perhaps mathematics and science, have been widely used in elementary schools, including grades 6 through 8 as earlier organized in many communities and still so provided in some districts. The core program, generally including language arts, social studies, and in some instances other subject fields, was even attempted in many high schools beginning in the 1930s, and was most widely provided in a block-time program in junior high schools, especially in grades 7 and 8. Called by various terms—core, block, unified studies, basic education, and others—the core was widely seen as an improvement in the junior high school program that might meet better the needs and interests of early adolescents. Had it fully succeeded, the middle school reorganization might not have occurred in such momentous proportions, nor have been so popular or so necessary.

But the reemphasis on subject organization of the post-Sputnik era of the late 1950s and 1960s caused many junior highs to abandon any design other than a strict subject one. With the advent of the middle school as a reaction against extreme subject departmentalization in the junior high school, the opportunity again existed to use some type of core, block, or interdisciplinary design. Although interdisciplinary teaming does not automatically result in a core program or even in the teaching of interdisciplinary units, it has been regarded as desirable for the middle school because of all the reasons we explain in Chapter 6. The interdisciplinary team organization, with appropriate use of interdisciplinary units, is probably the most widespread form of core in current middle school education. Some middle schools however, maintain block time and partial self-contained programs, especially in the former elementary grades, that can follow essentially the core design as described and recommended by two of its leading proponents, John H. Lounsbury and Gordon F. Vars. The following excerpt of their description of the core component of the middle school curriculum summarizes the core design and the case for this design:

> A major portion of the common learnings should be provided through a core program, most simply described as a problem-centered block-time program. At its best, core provides students with a direct and continuing opportunity to examine in depth both personal and social problems that have meaning to them. It also provides a situation in which a teacher can know a limited number of students well enough to offer the advisement or counseling most of them need so badly during the transition years, and in the process they can learn essential human relations and communication skills.
>
> Most, but not all, of the content and skills traditionally taught in English, social studies, and science classes may be taught in core, where they become tools to be utilized in the process of inquiry. Art and music, so often relegated to a peripheral role, also become important sources and tools in an inquiry process which knows no subject matter limitations. (Lounsbury & Vars, 1978, p. 46)

We believe that the advisement function recommended for core teachers is better provided in the middle school by the advisor-advisee plan described and illustrated in Chapter 5. This plan can involve more members of the faculty, with each member presumably having fewer advisees than in the core teacher guidance pattern. We also believe there are highly significant advantages in the team arrangement regarding such matters as planning for individual students, setting schedules, and involving teachers in special areas: these could not exist in a one-teacher core pattern and might be less effective in a two- or three-teacher pattern than the usual four- or more teacher team. Nevertheless, we fully agree with the major goal of focusing material from certain related subjects on the personal and social problems that serve as the designing centers in both core and interdisciplinary units. In fact, contentwise there is no real distinction between the two.

While few middle school educators have argued that the entire curriculum design should be core, James Beane (1990) has, however, recently reintroduced a forceful case for this very concept. We summarize here a number of theses presented by Beane regarding the middle school curriculum:

1. The traditional curriculum is far from being developmentally appropriate for middle school students. It is, writes Beane, "alien to life" itself.

2. The success of the contemporary middle school movement is due, in part, to the refusal of middle school educators to challenge the deeply held subject matter loyalties of traditional secondary teachers and subject area coordinators.

3. Interdisciplinary team organization does not guarantee an interdisciplinary curriculum.

4. The advocates of a subject-centric curriculum have defeated every attempt at major modifications, and remain as politically powerful interest groups devoted to protecting their special interest at the expense of virtually any other component of the school program and experience.

5. A developmentally appropriate curriculum would be dramatically different. It would be permeated by the concepts of democracy, human dignity, peace, and justice.

6. A developmentally appropriate curriculum would be most effectively implemented through the design and teaching of interdisciplinary thematic units.

7. The middle school movement is uniquely positioned to take on the challenge of authentic curriculum change; the time for a new curriculum in the middle school is now.

We find little with which to disagree among the curriculum theses put forward by Beane. Perhaps, since major middle level organizational issues have apparently been resolved and changes effectively implemented, and the pressure to centralize all curriculum decisions at state levels has abated, now may be the time to seize the initiative and implement a developmentally appropriate curriculum.

Designs Focusing on Individual Needs, Interests, and Progress

No educator we know seriously advocates a middle school curriculum of a completely elective nature, nor is any public middle school likely to provide one. But there are two quite different influences and developments in current curriculum development that conceivably could result in an almost totally individualized curriculum offering. On the one hand, there is the likelihood of vastly increased use of various systems of individualized instruction and continuous progress now made possible through the use of computer-assisted instruction. Whether these systems are, in the language of Lounsbury and Vars, "single-sequence, variable-rate," "multiple-sequence, variable-rate," or "variable-sequence, variable-rate" approaches, they all assume a considerable variation in the rate of progress through the system by individual students, and the latter two approaches assume a variation in the scope of the curriculum as well. Since these systems are most frequently provided in skills subjects, especially reading and mathematics, the difference in student experiences is usually related to learning ability and style rather than interest. However, multiple sequences in science and social studies through computerized enrichment opportunities and other materials providing for variable progress may be based on the interest factor.

Individual interests are especially the basis of such curriculum specialties of the middle school as special interest activities, exploratory courses in the fine and applied arts and other fields, minicourses in various subject fields and outside of any field, and independent study. The greatest contribution middle school curriculum has made, many educators believe, is to provide these learning opportunities for students in the middle. We doubt if any school could long and successfully maintain a curriculum based wholly on individual needs and interests, and the need for students to experience an ethos of community throughout their middle school experience would render such a curriculum undesirable. But programs which provide for students' continuous progress are desirable indeed. These programs can not be only of the sequential learning type characterized by earlier editions of programmed instruction and various self-drilling features that have dominated skills instruction. An adequate curriculum for the middle school must offer many opportunities for individual choice and many opportunities to meet individual needs, each opportunity providing so far as possible for sequential experiences that ensure continuous progress. These many and varied opportunities must be as wide in their range as schooling can provide.

Domains and Other Goal-Centered Design Plans

We believe the ideal middle school curriculum plan would be designed around major educational goals, and that an array of learning opportunities related to each goal might best thought of as the *domain* set by the goal. Thus, we see personal development as a very major goal of the middle school, and suggest various curriculum opportunities as being most closely related thereto. Health and physical education, guidance and counseling, affective development activities and interest-exploring and developing activities and courses should be classified as within the personal development domain of the curriculum so that planning and evaluation for this goal has a clear focus and convenient base. We are gratified that many recent pronouncements on middle school curriculum redesign, such as the Carnegie Foundation's *Turning Points* (1989), echo the same conviction.

We recommend that study and planning of the middle school curriculum be based on a statement of major educational goals of the middle school, with each major goal defining a domain of related learning opportunities. Each domain may include traditional subjects or significant aspects of such subjects, interdisciplinary units or aspects thereof, and many types of activities only casually (if at all) related to the subject design. These separate but related learning opportunities are indicated by the subgoals of the domain. Our suggested design is presented in the rest of this chapter in relation to three educational goals we see as dominating the curriculum of the middle school and defining its domains:

- Personal Development
- Skills of Communication and Learning
- Major Knowledge Areas

Although there are overlappings between these goals and their domains, it is expected that any middle school can fruitfully set up and evaluate its program in relation to these broad, inclusive domains. Each school, too, can add or substitute domains if indicated by its goals, and certainly it can work out problems of overlapping and omissions by its faculty's own analysis and classification of learning opportunities.

A similar design was developed by Donald E. Eichhorn and utilized in the pioneering middle schools of the Upper St. Clair School District in Pennsylvania. Eichhorn's description presents the three domains of Learning Processes, Personal Development, and Knowledge. Eichhorn's explanation of the design provides a somewhat different classification than ours, within the domains, but his design is a useful model for analysis and planning purposes in any middle school. Both designs are based on principles Eichhorn (1972, p. 42) stated more than twenty years ago:

> The characteristics and needs of the emerging adolescent learners are central to the school program development.
>
> There are three fundamental curriculum needs. These include the acquisition of learning processes necessary for self-education; the actualization of self through self-awareness, understanding, and interaction; and the active involvement of the learner with knowledge as it relates to the various aspects of [our] heritage and contribution.

Domain of Personal Development

Exemplary middle schools provide many services and opportunities to assist their students in optimum development as unique, well adjusted, healthy personalities. Subgoals of the school program for this major goal include:

1. Offering advice and guidance and other assistance with personal, educational, social and other problems.
2. Assisting students in the development of attitudes, values, and moral judgment.

3. Providing programs for the development of physical fitness and health.
4. Assisting each student in exploring and developing worthwhile interests.

Learning opportunities for each of these subgoals are described in the following sections.

Guidance and Special Services

Exemplary middle schools may be expected to have such advisor-advisee programs as we describe in Chapter 5. This organizational plan provides for each student to have one adult to whom the student can turn for help on many types of problems; it also provides a setting in which students can learn about school services outside their own school group. The advisory group may also be expected to help students achieve some maturity in their decision making which will not only decrease reliance on others for help, but also increase selectivity in the choice of other confidants and advisors. Furthermore, the advisory relationship is an excellent basis for referrals of students to the special services available in and out of the school.

As we note in Chapter 5, the use of teacher advisors in no way reduces the need for trained school counselors, but it does make possible a more effective channeling of counseling services. In many middle schools, the school counselor works closely with the faculty teams. The following statement from the district plan for middle schools in Milwaukee describes this arrangement and explains the role of counselors:

> The prime concern of the counselors shall be in the realm of accentuating the positive development of student potential, assisting in the development of a positive self-concept, enabling students to develop effective ways of relating to others, developing their problem-solving and decision-making competencies, and fostering the career development of each student. As an integral part of the middle school educational environment, the counselors shall be a part of the teaching teams and shall work with the teams in determining the needs of the students assigned to the team and shall work with the teams to resolve situations internal to that group. (Office of the Superintendent, 1979, p. 48)

Ideally, the middle school student should have access to various other special services as needed: psychological, medical, social work, and exceptional child education. And indeed many of these services are provided. For example, the Milwaukee plan cited above proposed that at least one school psychologist and one social worker be assigned to each middle school. A school nurse and other medical services are widely available through cooperative arrangements with health departments. Special provisions for many exceptional education programs are available in the middle school or in some other facility of the district. Counselors are challenged in many situations to be so well informed about the referral services available as to use them all wisely and effectively for the students. There are also those less fortunate situations where schools simply do not have such resources, and school personnel have to investigate providers of services to be found among themselves and also in other community institutions including the home.

In the 1980s, a new service became available in middle schools in some districts—the police liaison officer. In each of the middle schools of Orlando, Florida, for example, an officer hired by the police department is assigned as a "community service." These officers, almost always young and friendly, teach an array of "law awareness" classes and are generally available and interacting positively with as many students as possible. In the 1990s, as many students lives become increasingly more "at risk" and vulnerable to abuses of various kinds, the presence of such an officer may be increasingly necessary and popular, albeit lamentably, in many exemplary middle schools.

Guidance and other special series are generally considered as being received by students without the active role associated with classroom learning. We would call attention to the fact that the aim of many, perhaps all, of the types of services involved is to help the individual become an independent problem-solver to the fullest extent possible. The involvement of the learner in problem-solving activities—whether they be in classroom learning, physical and mental health, family relationships, work outside school, or other areas—should be sought through learning opportunities to be planned and evaluated in the same way as other aspects of the curriculum.

Affective Development

A most critical of all middle school goals is considered to be that of aiding a population of ever-changing individuals in the development of desirable attitudes, values, and moral judgments. These are the aspects of personality we are grouping under the general heading of affective development. The development of interests and problem-solving skills is relevant but so important and sufficiently different that we classify and focus on these subgoals elsewhere. We accept as a good definition of the affective development area the following statement of desirable student characteristics from the Stoughton (Wisconsin) Middle School:

1. Have a positive self-image.
2. Enjoy being alive.
3. Respect the rights, views, and ideas of others.
4. Know your own strengths and weaknesses.
5. Cope with problems by practicing self-discipline.
6. Set realistic goals and put forth their best effort in all things.
7. Develop a sense of morals.
8. Be able to pursue your own interests effectively.

We like, too, a statement from the Poway Unified School District in California dealing more specifically with the values subgoal:

Every person develops a value system of his own. The core of this system contains those values held common by all Americans. Other values, however, will differ according to the racial, religious, or cultural group to which the individual belongs. The strength of America depends upon our ability to maintain the strength of the common core of universally accepted values, and yet leave room for individual values which differ from the core. It is vital that teachers provide opportunities for pupils to become aware of their own values, to examine them for consistency and worth and to compare them with values held by others. The result will be deep and understanding faith in the commonly held values of our people.

Unfortunately, statements of affective goals like these are more numerous than descriptions of successfully implemented practices; affective education is, it seems, more of a desirable goal than an achieved end. Both of the school districts cited do, however, have quite specific programs for these goals. In Poway, much responsibility for affective outcomes was given to the core-like Basic Education program of two or three hours daily, while at Stoughton the responsibility was primarily that of the Multi-Level Block (four-teacher team).

Observation of exemplary middle schools as well as the review of their materials indicates that the learning opportunities for the development of affective outcomes are best planned and evaluated in the three categories that follow.

Advisory Groups

It is the A/A or advisory or homebase group, however organized and entitled to embrace the teacher guidance function, in which most faith is placed for the values clarification and moral judgment outcomes. Here also is much opportunity for the discussion of issues in and out of school, the exercise of student initiative and responsibility in conducting the affairs of the group, and the management of behavior and discipline. Our later chapter deals fully with the operation of the advisory group program as a very significant part of the middle school curriculum.

Instructional Groups

Every team situation, class, small group, and other instructional group in the middle school is a learning opportunity for the development of effective outcomes. Students acquire attitudes toward themselves as well as teachers, classes and school, in these groups. American middle school educators, like the Japanese junior high school educator (see George, 1987), recognize that there are effective learning opportunities in virtually every middle school program: intramurals, clubs, thematic units, and so on. Agreement of the faculty on desired effective outcomes and general means of their achievement is an important step in effective use of instructional groups for these affective goals. Among the characteristics of instructional groups which seem to be seeking desirable affective as well as cognitive outcomes are these:

1. Controversial, attitudinal, and other affective-type questions and discussion are permitted, even encouraged and pursued, whenever the teacher sees the possibility of making a positive contribution to affective development.

2. The feelings and values of students are respected by the teacher and their respect by students is expected.

3. Students are consulted for assistance in planning and evaluating as appropriate, with frequent opportunity to give feedback about their feelings toward the group and the curriculum.

4. The distinctions between fact and opinion and feeling are clarified wherever useful.

5. Praise is given wherever deserved, and blame is minimized.

Individual Relationships

The most critical situation for the development of feelings and values seems to be in that of the relationships of the individual student with other individuals. The teacher who is able to be empathetic and supportive with all students is likely to help their feelings of self-worth and, thus, influence their attitudes toward school, curriculum, and the teacher. It is in the teacher-student conversations, privately and, perhaps more significantly, publicly, that feelings, values, and judgments get stimulated and even exposed. And so it is that each teacher-student contact is an opportunity for affective learning, and a potentially significant item in the curriculum had by students.

These common sense assertions are born out in recent research on students' perceptions of effective relationships with their advisors (Bushnell, 1992). While teacher advisors describe effective relationships as characterized by fairness, letting students "pass" during discussions, and creating a safe environment for the expression of feelings, students have a slightly different emphasis. The picture of the effective teacher/advisor which emerges from research with students is one of the classic empathic relationship described by Carl Rogers and other members of the "person-centered" approach to psychology. That is, each student most desires a teacher who is capable of focusing on him or her as an individual, capable of dropping what they are doing and paying attention to the student's needs at the moment. Students want accurate empathy and unconditional positive regard, in the sense that they want the advisor to understand and care about them regardless of their academic standing or deportment. The capacity of the teacher to create effective one-to-one teacher-student relationships may be more important than the curriculum they design for their advisory time or how they manage the group when it meets.

Exploration and Development of Interests

Even though the 1980s were unkind to an exploratory emphasis in the curriculum, many exemplary middle schools are generally continuing and expanding the exploratory program regarded by many educators as the most significant contribution of the junior high school—a program unfortunately contracted when pressures such as those of the post-Sputnik period came to give greater priority and time to the traditional academic subjects. Without a ninth grade and its usual dominance by the high school program of studies and the college preparatory function, the middle school may and does provide a wide variety of exploratory experiences. In some middle schools, all of these experiences are called "exploratories," but other schools differentiate the more formal ones as courses in an area often called "Unified Arts" and others as activities, and still other schools may call them all "electives." Some schools make the more formal experiences required and the others elective. Although we prefer for each school to use the classification and nomenclature best suited to its program, we think a three-way classification may be best for this description: (1) exploratory courses; (2) special interest activities; and (3) seminars and independent study.

Exploratory Courses

The characteristic exploratory courses of the junior high were Art, Music, Home Economics, and Industrial Arts, and these four in some form are prominent in middle school offerings too. These areas are frequently grouped as "Unified Arts." With Typing and perhaps a broader Business course, Drama and Speech, and even Health and Physical Education, they may be termed "Related Arts." In the 1990s, instruction in the area of Computer Science has become a common part of many exploratory programs; the state of Florida has declared this area the "fifth basic." The original intent of the exploratory program was to have relatively brief, introductory courses for beginners, with longer, more intensive courses available another year for those interested. This philosophy was stated as follows in a description of the Unified Arts program of the Marshall (Michigan) Middle School:

> At Marshall Middle School, all students, grades five through eight, are required to take courses within the Unified Arts block. The emphasis at the earlier ages is on basic orientation to tools, safety, and procedures, and, by exposing students to each subject area, students are prepared for making choices later in their middle school years where more complex courses and projects are offered. Thus, art in grades 5 and 6 is a four-weeks unit, in grade 7 five weeks, and grade 8 ten weeks. The courses in home economics, general music, crafts and woodworking follow the same general pattern. The Unified Arts approach may also be designed to promote teaming and an interdisciplinary design within these fields, although this is not commonly found in visits to middle schools around the country.

More frequently found would be the exploratory program as it exists at Wakulla Middle School in Crawfordville, Florida. There, in the fall of 1991, six separate exploratory courses were offered in different arrangements at each grade level. In the sixth grade, students spent six weeks exploring each of the six areas: health, instrumental music, industrial arts, art, home economics, and business education. The assumption is made that by the seventh grade, then, students have made some distinctions about what they like and don't like, what fits them and what they do not care to pursue. So, in the seventh grade at Wakulla Middle School, students may choose three 12-week exploratories from among the six which the school curriculum offers. Then, in the eighth grade, they may exercise further choices by narrowing their work in exploratories down to two, each for one 18-week semester. By the time they move on to the Wakulla County High School, students should have had ample time to explore a wide variety of areas.

A similar path is followed by students at the two exemplary middle schools on the post at Fort Campbell, Kentucky. Sixth graders take 6 weeks of six of these: Art, German, Home Economics, Technology Education, Communications Enrichment, Music & Drama, Spanish, and Instrumental Music. The same components are available to seventh grades for 9 weeks and to eighth graders for 18 weeks. Beginning and intermediate band are offered at both the seventh and eighth grade levels.

Another approach, illustrated by the Ballston Spa (New York) Middle School Humanities Program utilizes the time traditionally allotted to Music, Art, Industrial Arts, Home Economics, and study hall to provide a wider range of activities as follows: Block Printing, Children's TV, Clothing, Colonial Ballston, Copper Foil, Craft Design, Creative Painting, Crocheting and Knitting, Drama, Food Exploration, Graphics, Guitar, Home Decoration, Lamp or Pet Cage Construction, Musicals, Power Mechanics, TV News, Tutoring, Tutoring Projects, and Tie-Dyeing–Macrame.

At Wakulla, and at many other exemplary middle schools, the decision about how to place Band in the exploratory offerings is an important one, and sometimes a difficult one to resolve satisfactorily. Middle school educators are often firmly committed to having students examine a broad range of interests and opportunities prior to making life-shaping decisions. This commitment rises naturally from an understanding of the characteristics and needs of young adolescents. At the same time, some students reach middle school having already discovered an interest, and perhaps a talent, in instrumental music. They may also be accompanied to school by influential parents who are committed to having their child continue to progress in music, and to having the students ready to participate in the high school marching band when the time comes. This is particularly the case in areas where the marching band has long been a staple of the community experience and when expectations for contest-winning high school marching bands are extremely high. Under such circumstances, high school band directors, under pressure to produce to the level of community expectations, may, in turn, exert pressure on middle school instrumental music teachers to conform to their wishes for longer, more intense, and more exclusive instrumental music programs. When these pressures are combined, many middle school leaders find themselves under fire when they attempt to offer a curriculum that provides an exposure to instrumental music to all students and a program which also expects even students who are talented musically to explore art, technology, home economics, and foreign language. What may be best for the middle school student may not fit with what the community desires. It is at this point where educational statesmanship, public relations skills, and the art of compromise may all come into play.

Typically, all sixth grade students are expected to participate in the school's sixth grade exploratory program. Then, in many schools, after having given one year to exploration, students who are irrevocably committed to instrumental music are permitted to opt out of additional exploratory participation, and move to continuous involvement in instrumental music. In Orlando, Florida, all sixth grade students participate in a one semester introduction to the exploratory curriculum, in units lasting only 4½ weeks each. All students take exploratory music during this period. Then, after the first semester, students interested only in band may remove themselves from further exploratory experiences.

In the decade of the 1990s, few seem satisfied by such compromises. All too often, instrumental music teachers complain that they are unable to offer the specialized training that they were prepared for and their talented music students are ready to receive. Block scheduling, which permits academic teams of teachers to plan together, may force music teachers into grade level band arrangements, rather than woodwinds one period and brass another, or beginning band one period and concert band another. On the other hand, middle school curriculum leaders point out that the typical 6–8 grade middle school is "one third younger" than the former 7–9 grade junior high school, and that "business as usual" is not developmentally appropriate and will not work. Further, others argue that the traditional approach to instrumental music in the middle grades (an intensive focus on the few and the talented), when judged by the criterion of continued participation in high school, college, and adult bands, is a staggering failure. It may well be that parents of instrumental music students understand, instead, that participation in band requires the development of a considerable amount of self-discipline in the student, and that this is sufficient, in and of itself, to make the middle level band experience desirable. When association with many of the brightest, most talented, and affluent students in the school is offered as an added inducement, few parents may be able to resist.

Experience in Orlando's (Orange County) middle schools, and many others thus far, indicates that interest in instrumental music has increased considerably by the exploratory music program. But more data must be collected from more programs to be able to make a persuasive case to anxious parents and to those whose careers in instrumental music may seem to be at stake.

The exploratory areas have great potential for helping middle school students identify their own interests (and disinterests), appreciate fine and applied arts, and develop some rudimentary concepts and skills in the areas concerned. Art is an area for the student to try out his or her expressive tastes, and to learn a few approaches to appreciating others' artistic expression. Crafts provide another outlet, one that can become a significant leisure activity. Homemaking (or home economics) may be less exploratory than practical, but many individuals do find interests here for further development. Industrial arts also emphasizes the practical aspects of home living, but it too can stimulate many interests, traditionally those of boys. Music has usually emphasized performance, but the general music course is intended to develop appreciation as well. Many students have already discovered interests in musical performance, as we have discussed, and so the music program provides band and chorus opportunities. Speech and drama, less frequently provided, give still further opportunities for testing out the student's interests and abilities, and going farther as indicated. In the late 1980s, the state of North Carolina took forceful action to insure that drama and dance become part of the experience of middle schoolers there. Typing and many business courses are also more practical than exploratory, although there is definitely the opportunity for the interested student to plan career studies in this area as well as to improve typing and keyboard skills later as interested.

Career education emphasis and support have stimulated more exploratory programs in the practical arts. For example, the Practical Arts course at Noe Middle School, Louisville, Kentucky, exposes students in the sixth grade to an overview of twelve of the standard career clusters, with additional recycling possible later as students are interested. At North Marion Middle School in Ocala, Florida, students follow a "wheel" schedule in grade 6, rotating through each of the following programs for about five weeks each: Agriculture, Business Education, Construction, Graphic Communication, Home Economics, Manufacturing, Power, and Transportation. At Lake City Middle School, in Lake City, Florida, a program new in 1991 offered an exploratory television course in which, among other projects, students produced a program for the school's advisory time every Monday morning.

Because it is a magnet school, Caddo Middle, in Shreveport, Louisiana, has an unusually rich exploratory program, with what they call enrichment courses lasting from nine to thirty-six weeks. Among them are these music courses: Show Choir, Choir, Guitar Ensembles, Band, Orchestra, and Piano. Caddo Middle also offers Beginning and "Research" Typing, Research Techniques and Study Skills, two levels of theater, Natural Environment, Living Law, Exploratory Foreign Language in Spanish, French, and German (for six weeks each), Drama Literature, Debate, Creative Writing (two levels), Computer Literacy, Careers, and Art Exploration. And that is not the entire listing.

Foreign languages are not as commonly offered on an exploratory basis, except at truly unusual schools like McCulloch Middle School, in Highland Park, Texas, where three years of foreign language are available. Unfortunately, at most middle schools, if the student determines interest in a particular language by an introductory exploratory course in grade 6, there may be nothing further available until high school. Other electives, as they are frequently called, especially for eighth graders, include special science, mathematics, language arts, and social studies courses, with these most frequently being either remedial or for academically talented students (see "Seminars," below). To the extent that such courses are introductory and are followed in high school by additional related courses, they further enrich the exploratory offering.

There is some evidence that teachers of the unified arts, and their supporters are developing a new consciousness of their importance to middle school education. In the fall of 1991, for example, the New England League of Middle Schools (a uniquely robust and effective league), under the leadership of James Garvin, held its third annual Unified Arts Conference. The now highly popular conference drew several thousand participants to examine 58 concurrent workshops of interest to teachers in health, art, home economics, music, media, physical education, industrial technology, and interdisciplinary studies. As unified arts educators in other areas of the country develop an increased awareness of their special significance in middle school education, perhaps new directions in authentic interdisciplinary curriculum development might result.

Service learning, perhaps best described as an important new type of exploratory course, is growing in popularity in middle schools around the country. Early adolescents, although it may not be well known, do have a deep and abiding interest in service to others, and new opportunities to express their civic spirit within the school program are proving to be very successful on a variety of dimensions. Programs as geographically far apart as the Rocky Mountains and New York City seem equally appealing. The "HUGS" program at Challenger Middle School in Colorado Springs involves students in regular opportunities to provide a variety of services, and learn in the process. The Early Adolescent Helper Program, initiated in New York City in 1982, involves both classroom study and preparation for delivery of service, and supervised placement at sites of various kinds (senior centers, Headstart programs, latchkey programs).[1] The EAHP concentrates "primarily on inner city populations, believing that the opportunity to be service 'providers' is particularly significant for inner city youngsters, who have often seen themselves solely as recipients of service" (J. Schine, personal communication, December, 1990).

Schine, the director of the program, also notes that:

> One of the strengths of the Helper Program, we believe, lies in the opportunity it provides for heterogeneous grouping, and for students who may have experienced few successes in the school setting to become 'stars' in their community involvement roles, and thus be perceived in new ways by their peers and teachers.

---

[1]For more information contact Joan G. Schine, Graduate Center, 25 West 43 Street, New York, NY 10036-8099.

At groundbreaking Shoreham-Wading River Middle School in Shoreham, New York, new ideas continue to pour forth, and one of them is in the area of service learning (W. Pardo, personal communication, October, 1991). Since 1973, each year hundreds of middle school students do community service as a part of their middle school curriculum. Four areas are the focus: young children in nearby daycare settings, nursery schools, kindergartens, and the public library; elementary schools; centers for handicapped children; and adults in congregate living facilities. Typically part of a 6- to 10-week unit by a class or a team, the students make at least one visit each week to the site of their service project. It may also involve correspondence (e.g., to nursing homes). Between visits, the students are engaged in work focusing on the service project: speakers, films, discussions, readings, and journals. Every student in the school has been involved in service learning at SWRMS since its inception nearly two decades ago!

Special Interest Activities

Variously called "classes," "activities," "minicourses," "electives," and other terms, the learning opportunities which we are classifying as special interest activities have the following distinguishing characteristics:

1. Student participation in organizing, selecting, planning, and conducting is encouraged.

2. The activity meets much less frequently and for a shorter term than the traditional exploratory courses (although some middle schools do not differentiate between the latter and the activities, giving less time to General Music, for example, than in the usual 6- to 18-week course, and perhaps more time to the guitar activity than the typical middle school having the usual exploratory course in Music).

3. Teacher responsibility for an activity is a part of the teacher's assignment, but teachers have much freedom in proposing and planning the particular activities they guide.

4. The students' participation is voluntary and no grades are given by teachers; however, the teacher advisor does help students make choices of appropriate activities.

5. Students throughout a middle school may choose any activities so that they are not organized by grades, ability levels, or other factors toward homogeneity. In some schools, the activities are organized within teams; if the teams are heterogeneous, the activity groups are likely to be also.

Examination of the descriptions of various such activity programs indicates many interesting titles and examples. At the Rupert A. Nock Middle School in Newburyport, Massachusetts, it has been a SPARK program: "The program is based on Service, Participation, Activity, Recreation and Knowledge, and in keeping with its purpose, it will be referred to as the SPARK program." The basic principles of the program, as stated in a bulletin for parents and others, further explained and illustrated the goals and nature of this special interest activity program:

1. The SPARK program offerings are student initiated.

2. The SPARK program is established to develop a student's role as a cooperative, successful, and well-adjusted group member.

3. The SPARK program offers a natural outlet for the curiosity, interest, and talents of the students.

4. The SPARK program is to help students develop positive interests and activities for leisure time.

5. The SPARK program is a necessary creativity outlet for students to meet the adjustment needs of the transitional period between childhood and adolescence.

Separate lists of activities available for one quarter of grades 5–6 and grades 7–8 students in each of the three houses of the school showed that each student has more than forty activities from which to choose.

Similarly, for many years Walt Grebing, now principal of Broomfield Heights Middle School, (Broomfield, Colorado) has championed the place of special activities in the middle school. As principal of the Louisville (Colorado) Middle School, in the seventies and early eighties, Grebing provided a SEARCH program—Students Educational Activities in Research and Creative Hobbies, and use PALS *(Persons Assisting Louisville Middle School)* in operating the program. During one quarter, twenty-four activities were offered on Mondays, twenty-eight on Tuesdays, and twenty-three on Wednesdays. Activities open to all students in grades 5–8 included the following: Silent Study, A Bank, School Services, New Games, Liquid Embroidery, Country Carvings, Ping Pong, Crewel, Minute Mysteries, String Program, All About Horses, Indoor Games, Outdoor Games, Puppetry, Soccer, Sign Language, Creative Writing, and Guitar, with many other activities restricted to one, two or three grades. In the 1990s, as principal of neighboring Broomfield Heights, Grebing's SEEK program is still functioning effectively. One list of activities for a year's programs included 44 separate possibilities, listed alphabetically from "Adopt a Grandparent" and "Fun Fitness with the Principal", on to "Public Domain and Strategy Software for the Apple" and finishing up with "Writing Music: A Beginner's Guide." Accompanying descriptions made the options all seem attractive.

At Oak Park Middle School, Decatur, Alabama, the program has been one of minicourses of four to six week's duration, with some variation in the number of days each minicourse meets. The total listing of such activities issued by the school for one year is very comprehensive, and includes some usual exploratory courses as described above. The list may be useful to readers in indicating the range of possible special interest activities. It is to be noted that not all of these would be taught in any given school term, but that the list might "serve as a guide for students and teachers in setting up exploratory offerings in the future:"

I. ACADEMIC ACTIVITIES: Banking; World-Wide Folktales and Superstitions; Classic Books; Geometric Designs; Geometric Line Design or String Art; Geometric Mobiles; Math for Fun; Plant Collections; Reading for Pleasure; Speed Math; Small Mammal Survey of Fields and Woods.

II. ART AND CRAFT RELATED ACTIVITIES: Basic Drawing; Basket Weaving; Bottlecrafts; Bread Dough Artistry; Ceramics; Christmas Crafts in Felt; Christmas Decorations; Copper Tooling; Craftsticks; Decorative Painting; Découpage; Float Painting and Other Oddities; Flower Arranging; Flower Making; Gingham Flowers; Graphics; Handicrafts; Linoleum Block Printing; Macrame; Number Painting; Papier Mâché; Polydom; Tuilling; Rice Mosaics or Seed Mosaics; Rock Art; Scrap Art; String Art; Surform Sculpturing; Tie-Dye; Transfer Art; Water Color; Wood Carving.

III. COMMUNICATIONS: One-Act Plays; Plays and Skits; Spanish (conversational); Teen Talk.

IV. GAMES: Beginning Bridge; Advanced Bridge; Chess; Checkers; Science Games; Scrabble.

V. HOBBIES: Ghost Stories; Home Decorating; Horses, Horses, Horses; Hot Air Balloon; Model Airplanes; Model Rocketry; Movie History; Pen Pals; Photography; Small Engine Repair; Soap Box Derby; Stamp Collecting; Whittling; Lanyard Weaving; and other related crafts.

VI. MUSIC: Band (Beginning); Band (Concert); Band (Intermediate); Chorus (6th grade); Chorus (7th, 8th); Guitar; Group Singing; Music Theory (Beginning).

VII. NEEDLEWORK: Cover Your Racquet (Tennis); Crewel; Crochet; Cross Stitch; Decorate Your Denims; Embroidery for Fun; Knit and Crochet; Knitting; Macrame; Needlepoint; Patchwork Pillows; Simple Sewing Crafts and Creativity.

VIII. PERSONAL IMPROVEMENT: Bicycle Safety; Careers; Charm; Handwriting; Human Relations; Lettering (Calligraphy); Medical Self Help; Motorcycle Safety; Penmanship; Safety Sanity; Shorthand; Slimnastics; Travel; Typing.

IX. PHYSICAL ACTIVITIES: Archery; Basketball; Baton; Bowling; Camping; Cheerleading; Drills and Ceremonies; Flag Football; Junior Football; Gymnastics; Softball; Volleyball; Snorkeling; Swimming; Rhythms and Games; Tennis.

At the new Tequesta Middle School, Fort Lauderdale, Florida, 120 different mini-courses have been offered by the staff during the Activity Period. All students participate in the program, which is offered once a week for a four-week period, three times a year. Students choose a different course in October, February, and May, from one of five different general areas: arts and sciences, personal development, sports and physical fitness, crafts and hobbies, and intellectual games.

At Marie Drake Middle School in Juneau, Alaska, special activities are arranged for every Friday afternoon during the winter months, January to March. In 1991, for example, 29 activities were available in a school housing only 470 students—a wide range. Choices included BB guns, cartography, chess, computer adventure, Mathcounts, swing band, and a Tlingit language group.

Clubs, which have often disappeared with the change from junior high to middle school, may have a place here, as well as being a part of some advisory programs. At Wakulla Middle School, "exploratory clubs" meet on a special schedule every two weeks for one semester, with membership and topics changing at the semester break. Among the clubs offered at Wakulla, in the 1991–92 school year were: 4-H, aerobics, checkers, cheerleading, chorus, comic books, crafts, crotcheting, current events, Florida Future Educators, girls' basketball, girls' softball, Junior Optimist Club, "Just Say No," library aides, model making, movies, National Junior Honor Society, National Junior Art Honor Society, National Geographic Club, newspaper, running club (open to staff and students), science Olympics, small wood projects, stock market game club, student council, No Club (card games), yearbook, and Young Authors. At Caddo Middle Magnet School, Shreveport, Louisiana, there are 27 clubs including the following: Mathcounts, golf, cross stitch, "Just Say No," Pentathalon, drama, New Horizons, Peer Advocates, Louisiana Club, four foreign language clubs, separate crafts clubs for boys and girls, and others. Among these lists are many traditional clubs which harken back to the days of the junior high school; as long as they are not forced on students or teachers, and can be temporary, they may make useful contributions to students curriculum experiences.

Seminars and Independent Study

Any class can be termed a seminar, although we prefer to reserve the use of the term for an instructional group in which the students have primary responsibility for investigations and creative activities culminating in their exchange and critique of papers and other products. Such a seminar is probably most frequently organized for more able students. For example, the Esperanza Middle School in Lexington Park, Maryland assigned students identified as academically talented to one of four reading groups which rotated each nine weeks between four teachers who provide for a seminar experience. Seminar activities include film making, school newspaper, novels, and science fiction, involving approximately ninety-five students. This school also provided extensive independent study opportunities, and a peer-aide program for eighth grade students. The latter program includes guiding parents visiting the school, counseling sixth grade students about their work, presenting plays and discussions with elementary school students, and orienting incoming students to the middle school.

Independent study can be made available through any type of group instructional organization: classes, teams, seminars, and special groups. Teachers can guide students who are interested and have rudimentary study skills to do independent study projects in lieu of part or all of the regularly assigned work in regular classes. We accept the time-honored definition of independent study as developed originally in a survey of practices in secondary schools, including junior high schools, and applicable, we believe, to the middle school:

> Independent study is considered by us to be learning activity largely motivated by the learner's own aims to learn and largely rewarded in terms of its intrinsic values. Such activity . . . utilizes the services of teachers and other professional personnel primarily as resources for the learner. (Alexander, 1967, p. 12)

Independent study projects that are in lieu of regular classes or of major assignments therein may be formalized by contracts or other written agreements covering such items as prerequisites, if any; description of the project and its goals; estimate of time involved; statement of student tasks; and specifics as to teacher role, conferences, and other responsibilities. The distinguishing characteristic is the student's motivation and self-direction. Note the following statement from a bulletin on "Independent Study" from the Nock Middle School:

> To be effective, independent study must be a part of, not apart from, the regular program. Its emphasis should be on creative, meaningful research that will stretch and strengthen the minds of students. Properly conducted it will help pupils grow in self-correction, self-analysis, and self-direction.
> . . . The pupil must develop self-discipline and make generalizations and comparisons. Self-control, time management, and decision-making are not taught by lecturing or completing questions in a workbook, but by allowing the pupil the freedom to develop these traits by experiencing them.

In our experience, the opportunities for introducing successful experiences in independent study into the middle school curriculum are as great as the need to do so. Independent study offers itself as an excellent vehicle for introducing the variety into the curriculum that critics like Beane desire, and for dealing with the increasing demographic diversity which students represent in the closing years of the twentieth century. It is endorsed by advocates for the gifted and talented students. Independent study is especially attractive when considering the almost limitless possibilities offered by contemporary computer-assisted instruction. We expect to see considerably more independent study opportunities in the middle school curriculum of the year 2001.

Health and Physical Education

The dominance of physical growth and development and related characteristics in the life of the middle school child demands that the program of health and physical education be carefully planned and implemented. We see these significant aspects: health education, including sex education; physical education; and intramurals. Once again, it is important to note that concern for these factors continues to grow among many groups who examine the education of young adolescents; the Carnegie Council's (1989) recommendations in this area were particularly well stated. Of the eight recommendations the council submitted, the one dealing with health and fitness was the only area of the curriculum singled out for special attention. The Carnegie Council urged educators to consider better health and fitness as the path to improving academic performance! They wrote:

> Because of the direct link between the health of young adolescents and their success in school, the Task Force concludes that middle grade schools must accept a significant responsibility, and be provided sufficient resources, to ensure that needed health services are accessible to young adolescents and that schools become health-promoting environments. Schools need not deliver the services directly, but should make sure they are provided. Moreover, the school's role will vary with the availability of family and community resources and with community values. It is essential, however, that every middle grade school have a coordinated system to identify health problems and provide treatment or referral to outside health agencies and individuals.
>   The transformed middle grade school can meet these objectives by:
>   1. Ensuring student access to health service; and
>   2. Establishing the school as a health-promoting environment. (Carnegie Council, 1989, p. 61)

Echoing the concerns of the Carnegie Council, the National Middle School Association issued, as its first resolution of the 1989–90 school year, the following:

> WHEREAS, young adolescents experience enormous physical growth and change, and WHEREAS, research suggests that for youngsters 10–15, health and fitness are not abundant, be it RESOLVED that all involved in the education and welfare of our young adolescents promote programs and practices which sustain integrated and activity-centered programs of health and physical education, ensuring the improvement of the nourishment, hygiene, safety, and health of our emerging young teens. (National Middle School Association, 1990, p. 56)

Health Education

Although aspects of health education may be treated in physical education, science, homemaking and other classes, the great need for instruction in this area suggests separate classes with qualified instructors and adequate instructional materials needed. A school health coordinator, as envisioned by the Carnegie Council, with planning and advisory groups representing various related school areas and the parents and community, should help to develop and maintain an effective program. Typical content for the health program includes: hygiene and personal care; nutrition; drugs, alcohol, and tobacco; communicable diseases, now, of course, including AIDS education in many schools; mental health; community health services; consumer health; chronic diseases; first aid; and safety education. Such a program, built on an understanding of the characteristics and needs of early adolescence, might also include education and screening for maladies that typically make their appearance during this time of life, including epilepsy and scoliosis.

Sex education can be provided in various ways. Although its provision has been and may remain controversial in some communities, the need for emerging adolescents to understand their changing bodies and the specifics of human sexuality is critical. In the 1990s, fewer and fewer communities find such programs objectionable. Teenage pregnancies and sexual diseases have become national problems and local emergencies, and there is also the related problem of changing life styles and mores as to marriage and the family. For certain, any specific course, unit, assembly, or other approach to sex education must be carefully planned with, and sponsored by, parent representatives along with representatives of the health professions, community, and church. Concentrated programs involving medical and other community representatives—along with a definite unit in the health program and related instruction as appropriate in science, physical education, and other subjects—seem a good combination.

Physical Education

Frequent physical movement is characteristic of the middle school student. In fact, one comical definition of the typical sixth grade boy, frequently heard in workshops and conferences, is that "a sixth grader is someone who runs everywhere he goes and when he gets there, he hits something or someone." Attempts to keep these students sitting still for the greater part of the day are, one might guess, doomed to failure. School curriculum designers are wise to create the maximum opportunity for appropriate movement. The greater care given to regular body-building exercise, the better for proper direction of the growing body. The exemplary physical education program characteristically includes a program of physical movement and exercise; lifetime recreational activities; and sports activities. The instructional program aims at a balance between these aspects. For example, physical education curriculum for the middle schools of Fort Campbell, Kentucky states that:

> Physical education teachers recognize the uniqueness of the age group we teach. We feel it is important to help each child develop and maintain a suitable level of physical fitness through large group games, team sports, and movement activities. The curriculum emphasizes lead-up skills, individual sports, and intramural activities. Each child should be stimulated to participate and derive enjoyment from recreation.

The list of activities at Fort Campbell middle schools is extensive:

Physical fitness conditioning—2 weeks
Softball skills and games—2–3 weeks
Falcon football—2–3 weeks

Soccer—3 weeks
Strength training—2 weeks
Wrestling—2 weeks
Aerobics—2 weeks
Volleyball—3–4 weeks
Rhythmic activities—2 weeks
Basketball—3 weeks
Tumbling and gymnastics—2 weeks
Cheerleading—1 week
Archery—2–3 weeks
Recreation games—2 weeks
Physical fitness testing—2 weeks
Track and Field—1 week

Intramurals, Interscholastic Sports, Other Extracurricular Programs, and the Role of Competition

Middle school educators, perhaps more than any others, seem to struggle with the place of competition as a component of the middle school curriculum. These professionals are caught between an awareness of the characteristics of early adolescence which make competition a hazardous activity, and the existence of tremendous stress in American society on the importance of such rivalry. The accumulated research on competition in education (Kohn, 1986) speaks loud warnings against permitting too much such activity into the school lives of young adolescents. One experienced educator, John Winton, former principal of Shelburne Middle School in Shelburne, Vermont put it exceptionally well:

> An interesting and humbling aspect of teaching young adolescents over a period of years is that one becomes aware that making predictions about the future achievement of students is hazardous. Often we are both surprised and delighted with some of the students who had exhibited modest talents . . . make significant achievements in high school or later in life. Because we are often surprised we learn to be especially thoughtful about labeling boys and girls at a time in their lives when change and disequilibrium are so prominent. We would like our students to keep an open mind about their own potentials and to give themselves a chance to grow and mature before making a firm decision about their strengths and weaknesses. An important implication of this has to do with competition.
>
> Competition is a part of our lives. No matter what we do, individuals will find ways to be competitive. That is neither a good thing nor a bad thing so long as we are not dealing with extremes. What is commonly overlooked is that while our society seems to foster competition, it may be the most cooperative society in history. Think of how many people share our roads in automobiles, for instance. The real work of our society is done through cooperation. Competition has its place, but it should not be the dominant factor, especially in the lives of boys and girls who have yet to realize their full growth and whose assessment

of their own potentials is at best incomplete. We want adolescents to try. We wish to encourage them. . . .

Creating curriculum strategies and activities which permit all students to find some success is not soft pedagogy. It is just good sense. Those who speak in terms of letting down standards are willing to sacrifice some boys and girls in order to motivate others. That can't be part of a public school philosophy. If we train children to feel success only when they can see that others have failed, we have done them all a great disservice. Our standard should be that of the greatest possible growth for each student within the limits of his or her own abilities. All middle school students must be winners.

Middle schools reduce the competitive aspects of education for students by avoiding selective activities, by stressing participation, and through individualization. At the Shelburne Middle School we have not put a heavy emphasis on grading, our classes are almost all grouped heterogeneously, and we stress participation by making it possible for all to take part at some level in school activities. As do most middle schools, we give priority to our intramural programs although we still maintain interscholastic teams for seventh and eighth graders.

We recognize participation in activities and students receive many awards and certificates. Helping in the library, taking part in a play, being on a basketball team, or tutoring a younger student are all valued and recognized equally.

(Winton, 1989, pp. 3–4)

Although many middle schools provide interscholastic athletics, as did their junior high predecessors, this practice remains decidedly controversial, and its excesses and abuse are vigorously opposed by many educators and parents. The major basis for opposition, in the 1990s, is the continuing conviction that most children of middle school age are not yet ready to profit from participation in intensely competitive and highly selective sports activities. Most middle school educators, we believe, seek to avoid the traditional secondary school model of some athletics-dominated high schools and junior high schools. Relevant, too, is the widespread desire for the middle school to be a unique institution focused on the needs of its own population rather than modeling itself after a higher level with too little thought to the special needs of a younger group. But to us, the most significant argument is that all the students in the middle school need to have experience in sports, experience that is appropriate for their physical status and that can yield feelings of satisfaction to many children who would never make the varsity team. The possible physical damage of inappropriate activities, such as that which occurs too frequently in tackle football, must also be avoided.

The evidence against the traditional interscholastic athletics and in favor of intramurals in the middle school is impressive. Excellent reviews of the issue have been available for 15 years. One such review concluded with this comment:

Middle school people who really are concerned for what is best for their students increasingly are looking for a quiet burial for interscholastic athletic programs with their overcompetitiveness and overorganization of these youngsters. They are trying in their middle schools to offer a program of intramural sports and strong physical education programs for both boys and girls, with teachers who understand and are dedicated to the best interests of these transescents. (Romano & Timmers, 1978)

Intramurals are organized in various ways in middle schools—by grades, teams, periods, and advisory groups. At Marie Drake Middle School in Juneau, Alaska, students who participate in the interscholastic program must first have participated in an intramural program, a unique requirement insofar as we know. Where there is an interdisciplinary team organization, and we hope this continues to move toward universality in exemplary middle schools, it is a very natural outgrowth of the team life to have various types of sports contests within and between teams. The intramurals may be organized by the physical education teachers and certainly should operate under their supervision, but with much interest and support from all members of the staff.

As with the marching band, however, what may be developmentally appropriate and desirable for the curriculum, may be difficult to implement successfully. Intramural programs appear to be much easier to talk about than to implement and maintain successfully. Interscholastic athletic programs have many advocates whose salary supplements and hopes for career advancement may depend upon continuing interscholastics at the middle level, and on organizing and operating those experiences as if they were "farm clubs" for the high school varsity sports program. Interscholastic programs also have a momentum from their traditional value as entertainment for the community and the symbols of group pride they represent.

The school district of Volusia County, Florida has been particularly successful in developing a viable intramural program at the middle level. At each of the 12 middle schools in the district, it works through the interdisciplinary team organization, at each grade level. As an example, at Holly Hill Middle School in Holly Hill, Florida, (T. Huth, personal communication, January, 1991) there are three activities scheduled for each grading period: two outdoor activities, and one indoor (e.g., flag football, kickball, and war ball). Each Friday, intramurals are scheduled for two periods for each grade level, replacing one period each of regular physical education and an exploratory class. The teachers of these classes act as referees and supervisors. At the end of each grading period, the teams with the most wins play off in a "House Championship" in front of their peers. Playoffs are only scheduled at the same grade level, to avoid older students running away with all the competitions. In fact, the program is so meticulously designed that the activities for each grade level are based on appropriate "themes" (e.g., 6th grade, locomotion; 7th grade, body management; 8th grade, fitness). One of the authors witnessed such a playoff day at another Volusia County middle school, DeLand Middle, and can testify to the tremendous spirit and pride which interdisciplinary teams generated at this event.[2]

---

[2]For a detailed description of the intramural program in Volusia County, contact Mrs. Harriet McAllister, Middle School Program Consultant, Volusia County School Board, 200 North Clara Avenue, DeLand, FL 32721-2118.

At Nautilus Middle School in Dade County, Florida, a carefully planned program has also worked exceptionally well. Advisory groups and physical education classes are the twin "hearts" of the program, which features almost a dozen different activities throughout the year. Field days and "Funtastic Fridays" are used for playoffs. In Fulton County, Georgia, each of the eleven middle schools offers an intramural program four days a week, after school for ninety minutes each day. Special activity busses provide transportation for the participants. Tennis, volleyball, basketball, gymnastics, track and field, aerobics, badminton, bowling, fitness training, golf, and jogging are available. "Extramural culminating events" occur in tennis, basketball, track and field, and gymnastics. Each school sends representatives, chosen through school level intramural programs, to the countywide extramural event. The purpose of the extramural event is to "promote good will, sportsmanship, and positive interschool relationships between the students of the eleven middle schools in Fulton County."

Interscholastic sports programs are not inherently undesirable; it is the abuses to which these programs have been subject that has too often rendered them counterproductive at the middle level. We believe that it is hypothetically possible to develop interscholastic programs that are effective for this age group, although it is extremely difficult to maintain their developmental purity. In the Orange County, Florida school district, for example, the recent transition from junior high school to middle school was accompanied by a retention of interscholastic athletics, but in significantly modified and developmentally appropriate form. When the transition occurred, the interscholastic program was retained but reduced from twelve junior high sports to four in the new middle schools, one for each of the nine week quarters of the year. The sports which were retained in Orange County were deemed fit for early adolescent needs for physical, social, and affective development: soccer, volleyball, basketball, and track. All four sports were available in boy's and girl's versions. The "season" for each sport was tailored to the length of the nine week grading period, with the number of competitions reduced from more than a dozen to six or eight. Schools competed against five other schools in their "cluster" since the district has 18 middle schools; this reduced travel time, distance, and late night games during the week. Competitive standings and end-of-season tournaments were eliminated. No "most valuable players" are selected. Everyone who wishes to play is a member of the team, and every team member plays in every game. It seems to us that this is what interscholastic athletics was intended to be at the middle level, and we endorse such practices.

The staff of Burlingame Intermediate School (Burlingame, California) and its longtime principal, Bob Welch, have pioneered middle level programs for two decades. The school is also out in front of those developing healthy interscholastic programs for its students. During the 1990–91 school year, for example, instead of doing away with interscholastic basketball, the school fielded eighteen "varsity" basketball teams, and although it may have been a scheduling nightmare, we would guess that it was a wonderful experience for players and parents who would not otherwise have had it. We would also guess that the local high school basketball program will benefit substantially from the way it is operated at the middle level. The philosophy of the Burlingame Middle School regarding extra and co-curricular programs is expressed by Welch (Personal communication, March 6, 1991):

> At no point in a youngster's formal academic years is there such a burst of energy from every direction, as that which occurs in the life of an emerging adolescent. This energy needs to be directed into a wide variety of activities. These activities should be positive and inclusive.
>
> At BIS we believe that every student should be in more than one activity. There is no elitism at the school. If you go out for an activity or a team, you are automatically a member of the group or team. As an example, this year (1991) we have 18 basketball teams that play interscholastic competition. For a school of 640 students, that is a very high level of participation!

Other districts, like Yakima, Washington, have arrived at a middle ground regarding intramurals and athletics (Riemke, 1988). Yakima's Middle School interscholastic programs permit only in-district competition with a system that insures participation and prohibits cutting students from teams. If the number of students exceeds that which can be accommodated on only one team, another is created (much like Burlingame). Teams are balanced by ability as well, so that there is no varsity. Intramural programs run concurrently with interscholastic ones, but for much shorter periods of time.

Whether or not to have cheerleaders is also a controversial issue at the middle level. There seems to us to be little fault to be found with cheering enthusiastically for the team of one's choice. Indeed, school spirit and pride are extraordinarily desirable in these times. Once again, it is with the abuse of these programs where trouble enters the school door. When school leaders permit cheerleading programs to degenerate into popularity contests where only popular, upper-middle-class, fairhaired, and well-formed young girls ever qualify, the goals of such activities are subverted in unacceptable ways. One exemplary middle school may have found a solution that works, at least for them. At McCulloch Middle School in Highland Park, Texas, cheerleaders have not been eliminated, but the popularity contest has. At McCulloch, if a student wants to be a cheerleader, all that is needed is a white shirt, blue shorts, and school spirit. Consequently, in 1991, there were 140 cheerleaders at the school; not the most popular, but probably the loudest. At Cope Junior High School in Bossier City, Louisiana, a similar philosophy works well. As principal Tim Gilbert explains:

> Basically, what we did was to devise an alternative plan to popular election of cheerleaders. Each year we had ten or twelve students that felt really great about being elected and about twenty that had every insecurity they ever had reconfirmed because they hadn't been elected. We now allow any students, (not

just girls), who are in the eighth grade and academically eligible, to be a cheer-leader.

We achieve this by having rotating squads. After initial opposition by a few parents, we have gained very strong parental support. The program was so successful at raising self-esteem and increasing school spirit, that it has been used as a model for all the middle schools in our system. (T. Gilbert, personal communication, January, 1991)

In the fall of 1991, Broomfield Heights Middle School (Broomfield, Colorado) announced its athletics/intramural program to its parents, through the first of many newsletters for the year. The newsletter said:

Boulder Valley Public Schools has a middle level athletic program which takes into account the nature of the physiological and psychological needs of middle level students. *All* students are welcome and encouraged to participate in these activities regardless of their skills. Emphasis is on game play and participation for *all*.

At Broomfield Heights Middle School, a gradually shifting emphasis based on the development of the students moves from complete emphasis on intramurals in the sixth grade, to intramurals with "more coaching" in the seventh grade. In the seventh grade program, some of the intramural sports include a "culminating activity" such as extramural playoffs. Intramurals at Broomfield Heights Middle School are organized through the physical education program and often include: girls' and boys' basketball, boys' wrestling, girls' volleyball, co-ed gymnastics, girl's track, and boy's track. Eighth graders participate in intramurals, but also have an opportunity for a limited interscholastic program of boy's football, wrestling, basketball and track, and girl's softball, basketball, volleyball, and track. Even so, parents were informed that "Any eighth grader may participate in the fall sports program. Students do not need previous experience. Emphasis is on skill building, participation, and enjoyment of sports." We find such programs refreshing and realistic.

There are other so-called extracurricular issues that relate to the transitions in middle level programs. The desirability of having a school newspaper, a sophisticated yearbook, dances, and even proms, is hotly debated from school to school, district to district, and within the home between parent and the young adolescent. It is the position of many middle school educators that high school-style programs, of all sorts, should be saved for the high school. Students who experience intensely competitive athletics, sophisticated proms, and lengthy yearbooks in junior high school frequently show less interest in those programs at the high school, when such activities are most developmentally appropriate. Matching middle school curriculum and the resulting activities to the characteristics and needs of the students is the most logical way to proceed.

We recommend the work, and endorse the conclusions, of respected developmental scholars like David Elkind, author of *The Hurried Child* (1981) and

All Grown Up and No Place to Go (1984). Elkind argues that students, at this age, need time to grow up, and tremendous pressure from anxious adults to "hurry" the process is clearly counterproductive. Programs for older teens should not be simply placed earlier and watered-down for younger students. Alternatives must be found. Simply eliminating those extracurricular activities that are inappropriate is not sufficient—it is only half of the process. Many middle school educators, in the seventies and eighties, in their rush to eliminate inappropriate programs did so without replacing them with effective ones. School spirit, pride, and group citizenship suffered as a result; too many middle schools became bland, lifeless places where no "robust occasions" caught students' attention or commitment. Suitable programs which foster the healthy development of individual students and stimulate school spirit, unity, pride, and citizenship are needed. Much development remains to be done in this area.

Domain of Communication and Learning Skills

The most commonly understood goal of public schools has been the development of basic communication and learning skills. We use this compound term to refer both to specific communication skills, such as speaking and listening, and specific learning skills, such as reading. We also recognize that communications skills are usually also skills of learning, and vice versa. For convenience, the major skills areas are identified here in the following categories: (1) reading and related study skills; (2) speaking, questioning, and listening skills; (3) writing skills; (4) quantitative skills; (5) use of major learning tools; and (6) thinking skills, such as problem solving, decision making, and other higher intellectual processes.

The perennial question of what is "basic" for the middle school curriculum has not yet been satisfactorily answered and, we suspect, traditional curriculum content remains in place by default. To most critics in the seventies and early eighties, stimulated by the disclosure of declining test scores and rising school costs, the basics were the traditional "3 Rs" of reading, writing, and arithmetic. The movement to reemphasize, or at least to explain these areas more fully, also at times has brought a return of traditional educational characteristics such as increased homework and memorization and a tendency to designate any content that seems important as "basic skills." Foshay's classic analysis of the basics controversy involved a classification of the 3 Rs as "coping skills," in which he also included "emotional development, physical realization, intellectual functioning, social growth, aesthetic encounters, and spiritual awareness." In addition to these coping skills, Foshay included as basics, "citizenship, morality or character, and a valid view of self," and he warned "leave one out, and the student's ability to survive is impaired" (Foshay, 1978). We also believe that the middle school has many "basic skills" to teach—all of the goals and related opportunities cited in this chapter.

Reading and Related Study Skills

Reading, generally taught directly in the junior high school only as remedial instruction for students lacking adequate skills for the junior high textbooks, has had a much more significant place in the curriculum of the middle school. During the late 1970s, with the national clamor for better reading skills, this place became even more dominant. The emphasis on reading skills continues to influence the middle school curriculum in the nineties.

Some middle schools follow a basal reading program with a commercial reading series, using a special grouping for reading within the team arrangement or a separate schedule outside the team organization. Three-level programs are also utilized, as described below in an early curriculum description of the language arts program of two teams at the Boyce Middle School, Upper St. Clair, Pennsylvania:

> Students are placed on three reading strands—corrective, developmental, and enrichment. On each of these strands, comprehension of ideas is developed through the mastery of such subskills as main ideas, specific details, sequences, comparisons, cause and effect relationships, assessment of character traits, and predictions of outcomes. Materials appropriate to the reading level of each strand have been selected for the implementation of these objectives.
>
> In addition, a unit designed to increase the reading rate of students has been included in this instructional level. The students are also instructed in methods of adjusting rate to purpose as well as study skills.

The reading program at Boyce includes several skills that are usually designated as study skills: note taking, outlining, book reporting, library skills, dictionary skills, and reading for pleasure.

In some middle schools, the reading program is considered wholly developmental; note the description of the North Marion Middle School program in Citra, Florida:

> Based on the philosophy that everyone has reading skills which may be improved, all students participate in an individualized reading program for a minimum of nine weeks each year. This is a developmental, not a remediation, program. This program utilizes a specially equipped laboratory and a special reading teacher for each grade. Pretests lead to an individual prescription, with daily evaluations. Most laboratory time is spent in individual activities, but at least one day a week is a group experience. Post-tests are given at the end of the nine weeks and most students have two nine-week sessions each year.

Continuums of reading skills have been developed within many school districts to aid in the diagnosis of reading levels and the planning of instruction. The classification of reading skills used in the continuum for middle school years at the Poway Unified School District in California indicated the breadth of the combined reading-language arts program: word identification skills; structural analysis; word meaning; comprehension skills; types of literature; literary devices; critical evaluation; study skills; organizing information; outlining; reading rate; and reading for personal/social development. Study skills in this continuum include:

- Locating information: dictionary, encyclopedia, atlas, almanac, graphic materials, library and library aids; parts of a book, index, glossary, etc.; reference material; thesaurus
- Synthesizing
- Skimming

Recent developments in the teaching of reading and related skills reveal some substantial dissatisfaction with traditional basal approaches. Some would argue that we have produced a generation of students who have much greater skill than interest in reading. Alternative "whole language" approaches, such as the reading/writing workshop approach (Atwell, 1987), appear to offer much to restore an interest in reading and writing among young adolescents. Whether these approaches will also be totally satisfactory in skill development remains to be seen. One thing is certain, however: middle school students who can read, but refuse to, or would rather not do so, are not to be preferred to those who read less skillfully but do so voraciously.

The "whole language" approach has been implemented in many elementary and middle schools in the last decade. At the middle level, it has entered the curriculum out of general dissatisfaction with traditional approaches, and as a result of the awkward combination of elementary and junior high school language arts and English courses which results from the implementation of middle schools in many districts. Illustrative of what may be the case in many middle schools is the experience of the staff at the West Windsor–Plainsboro Middle School, in Plainsboro, New Jersey. There, implementation of the reading/writing workshop approach (Atwell, 1987) has solidified the faculty in support of whole language curriculum. As supervisor Kay Goerss (personal communication, January, 1991) described it:

> Why has this course evolved so successfully? Because the teachers believe in reading. They believe that you only become a better reader by reading. The success of our basic skills classes is even more phenomenal. We do not use skill sheets or fill-in-the-blank practice. . . . Our basic skills students read, write, discuss, and evaluate literature!
>
> But what about our traditional language arts class? Why is it separate and what do students do to make connections? The class is separate because for the time being that is the schedule we live with. Someday we will be structured in interdisciplinary teams and reading/literature will join the teamed language arts/ social studies to create a whole.

Speaking, Questioning, and Listening Skills

Although questioning rarely appears in statements of objectives and written curriculum plans, as a learning skill it is of first-rank importance. Oral questioning is a very frequent learning activity, and the quality of this learning is directly related to the quality of the questions asked. Exercises in middle school language arts classes sometimes do include question formulation and refinement, and some teachers frequently do correct poorly phrased questions; but more attention seems needed. Speaking and listening skills are much more likely than questioning skills to be stipulated in the curriculum plans and their objectives, and to be implemented in classroom situations. The following statement of "Goals in Listening" in a description of the seventh grade language arts program of Nipher Middle School (Kirkwood, Missouri) is representative of the goals and nature of instruction in listening skills:

1. The ability to follow oral directions.
2. The ability to summarize ideas and draw conclusions from group discussions.
3. The ability to evaluate the accuracy and relative importance of what is heard on radio, television, lectures, and reports.
4. The ability to distinguish between relevant and irrelevant material.
5. The ability to identify the main theme of an orally presented paragraph.

Also representative is the statement in the same material on Goals in Speaking for the sixth grade (similar goals for speaking and listening are included for each middle school year):

1. Demonstrate self confidence and poise in a variety of speaking situations.
2. Organize content for a clearly defined purpose.
3. Speak from notes or an outline.
4. Get and maintain listeners' attention.
5. Participate in group and panel discussions.
6. Give adequate oral directions.
7. Use appropriate pitch, stress, and juncture as meaning signals in spoken language.
8. Participate in skits, plays, and readings.

Despite the tendency of such lists and curriculum opportunities to over-emphasize the formal speech-making skills, the inclusion of specific instruction in speech, both conversational and formal, seems highly desirable, albeit infrequent, for middle school children. Speech and especially dramatics are of high interest appeal to many middle school students, and should have a significant place in the language arts program, both in regular classroom instruction and as optional, special interest activities.

Writing Skills

Writing, both by hand and by machine (word processing), is a highly important skill of communication, and its use for note-taking and preservation, record-keeping, and composition is significant in learning. Middle schools teach spelling to help in both reading and writing; composition in various forms; keyboard skills and, less frequently, handwriting; and ways to facilitate achievement of the communication and learning goals. The writing program is generally an important phase of the language arts program, and an excellent opportunity for students to synthesize and utilize many of their learnings in other phases of language arts such as spelling, reading, literature, and grammar. Our observation indicates wide variation in the time and attention given to writing, with perhaps too much of what time and attention are given going to formal papers and too little to systematic exercises for the development of writing skills. A checklist of writing skills developed in Marion County, Florida for grades 6–10 is specific and comprehensive:

(The student will—)
- compose grammatically correct sentences.
- organize objects and information into logical groupings and orders.
- write a paragraph expressing ideas clearly.
- write for the purpose of supplying necessary information.
- write letters and messages using commonly accepted formats.
- fill out common forms.
- spell correctly.
- punctuate correctly.
- capitalize correctly.
- write legibly.

Each of these skills appeared in Level I, II, and III lists and each was further broken down to include more specific objectives.

Writing is also taught through laboratory approaches and creative writing classes, minicourses, and activities. The laboratory approach, in which a special teacher is available to help students with acute writing problems, can be combined with the reading laboratory. For example, a creative writing minicourse described as follows was offered in the Andrews (Texas) Middle School:

> Say It With Words—An opportunity for creative writing will be provided in this unit. Poetry, short stories, and other types of writing will be attempted.

Quantitative Skills

It is difficult indeed to separate skills and knowledge in the mathematics field. For general communication purposes, one needs enough understanding of some basic mathematics terms and processes to be literate in their use. This involves mathematical knowledge. Sometimes one also needs the mental agility in quantitative relationships to solve a percentage or other commonplace problem. This involves mathematical skill. For continued learning one needs the same plus skills in using tables and other presentations of quantitative data, in interpreting graphs and pictorials using quantitative data or relationships, and in projecting such data and relationships. We have to conclude that the citizen needs both the understanding of basic mathematics concepts and the skill to handle quantitative data and problems, and that a mathematics education must include both, probably taught somewhat integrally. Thus, we are really dealing here with the mathematics program as a whole.

Only reading has equaled or surpassed mathematics in public interest and concern in recent decades. The so-called "new" mathematics movement of several decades past, stimulated by several post-Sputnik national curriculum projects such as the School Mathematics Study Group (SMSG), forced parental interest as children brought home new materials and terminology. More recently, this movement has been under reassessment and continuing modifications are being made. Probably the most pervasive development has been the use of various systems of individual progress plans and materials, many of them commercially produced but some developed at least initially within a particular school or district.

In the late 1980s, the National Council of Teachers of Mathematics (1989) examined the traditional mathematics curriculum at the middle level and found it wanting. The NCTM group recognized that many students view their experience with mathematics as either incredibly boring or so difficult that it is impenetrable and impossible. They stated forcefully:

> Mathematics is a useful, exciting, and creative area of study that can be appreciated and enjoyed by all students in grades 5–8. It helps them develop their ability to solve problems and reason logically. It offers to these curious, energetic students a way to explore and make sense of their world. However, many students view the current mathematics curriculum as irrelevant, dull, and routine. Instruction has emphasized computational facility at the expense of a broad, integrated view of mathematics and has reflected neither the vitality of the subject nor the characteristics of the students. (1989, p. 65)

Thirteen new curriculum standards comprise the new program as the NCTM would like to see it. Council publications spell out the standards in great detail. The individual curriculum standards are:

1. Mathematics as problem solving
2. Mathematics as communication
3. Mathematics as reasoning
4. Mathematical connections
5. Number and number relationships
6. Number systems and number theory

7. Computation and estimation
8. Patterns and functions
9. Algebra
10. Statistics
11. Probability
12. Geometry
13. Measurement

Many states have already begun to implement changes in state guidelines to become more congruent, to use a mathematical concept with the NCTM standards. The state of Florida, for example, has designed a set of nine standards which comprise a total of sixty-one skills. The standards are clearly built on NCTM work, and include: problem solving, estimation, mathematical computations, recognition and application of geometric concepts, measurement concepts, probability and statistics, number sense and operation sense, and knowledge of basic algebraic concepts. These standards are aimed at moving the middle school mathematics curriculum away from its mind-numbing repetition of the elementary school program.

Mathematics is a discipline with much clearer sequential aspects than other fields, and the answers to problems, and the processes to solve them are generally more precise and certain than elsewhere. Hence, it is possible to have such systematic mathematics programs as was stated in this description from the Ballston Spa (New York) Middle School:

> Our mathematics program is based on three hundred specific mathematics behavioral objectives. Each objective has been placed in one of five categories: integers, rationals, reals, sets, or measurement and geography. In all categories but one, the objectives are divided into three sections for a total of fourteen sections. Within the fourteen sections which are listed under the five categories, the objectives are arranged on the basis of difficulty and necessary prerequisites in both its own and the other sections.

In the implementation of such a program, testing on an objective yields a prescription for the student, with the student's subsequent work again tested to determine further progress. Each student has an individual record monitored by a teacher. The program is common for all students, but each progresses individually. This pattern seems very desirable in middle school mathematics.

The mathematics cumulative record card of the Kirkwood, Missouri Middle Schools shown in Table 3.1 (on pages 98–99) remains illustrative of the scope and sequence of mathematics in the middle school and also of an individualized progress system. The record has been used to show the student what topics have been included each year and how they are included, at an introductory, instructional (worked with in depth), or competency level (mastery).

During the 1990–91 school year, students at Mitchell Middle School in Mitchell, South Dakota were immersed in *Transition Mathematics*, developed

TABLE 3.1

Kirkwood Middle Schools
MATHEMATICS CUMULATIVE RECORD CARD

NAME_____

Code: ▨ Introductory Level
       ☒ Instructional Level
       ■ Competency Level

CONCEPTS:

	6	7	8
Year in School	6	7	Math 8 Algebra
School Year			
Teacher's Name			

WHOLE NUMBERS (6 | 7 | 8)
- Addition with regrouping
- Subtraction with regrouping
- Multiplication with 2-digit factors
- Division with 1-digit divisors
-      2-digit divisors
- Place Value through millions
- Rounding through millions
- Find averages
- Prime numbers
- Greatest common factor
- Least common multiple
- Word problems
- Use of properties
  - Commutative
  - Associative
  - Distributive
- Exponents

FRACTIONS / MIXED NUMBERS
- Fractions
  - Find equivalents
  - Compare and order
  - Addition (unlike denominators)
  - Subtraction (unlike denominators)
  - Multiplication
  - Division
- Mixed Numbers
  - Fractions ⟷ Mixed Numbers
  - Addition with regrouping
  - Subtraction with regrouping
  - Multiplication
  - Division
  - Work Problems
  - Exponents

DECIMALS
- Place Value through millionths
- Read and write through millionths
- Compare and order
- Round off
- Addition and subtraction
- Multiplication
- Division
- Mult. & Divide by powers of ten
- Fractions ⟷ Decimals
- Terminating and repeating
- Exponents
- Word problems
- Scientific Notation

MEASUREMENT (6 | 7 | 8)
- Telling time
- Money (making change)
- English
  - Linear: nearest 1/2"
  -     nearest 1/4"
  -     nearest 1/8"
  - Weight
  - Volume
- Metric
  - Prefixes
  - Linear: meter
  -     centimeter
  -     millimeter
  - Weight
  - Volume

GEOMETRY
- Points, lines, segments
- Rays, angles, planes
- Identify plane figures
- Symmetry
- Constructions/compass and straigntedge
- Identify and measure angles
- Parallel and perpendicular lines
- Related angles
- Polygons
  - Classification
  - Perimeter
  - Area
- Triangles
  - Congruent
    - Construction
    - Proofs
  - Similar
    - Construction
    - Calculations
    - Word problems
  - Pythagorean Theorem
    - Inscribed and circumscribed
- Circles
  - Characteristics
  - Circumference
  - Area
- Solid Figures
  - Identify
  - Volume
  - Surface Area

at the University of Chicago, and published by Scott, Foresman and Company (Usiskin, et.al., 1990). The program is designed to provide a "perfect transition" from arithmetic to algebra and geometry, while attracting more and more students to math, not weeding them out. Deb Dusseau, principal at MMS, is enthusiastic about the program because of its flexibility and its capacity to make all "kids think." *Transition Mathematics* focuses on real-world applications and problem solving, integrating ideas from algebra and geometry into arithmetic lessons.

TABLE 3.1 **continued**

NAME _____

RATIO AND PROPORTION	6	7	8
Write ratios and proportions			
Find equal ratios			
Find missing number in proportions			
Word problems			
Scale drawings			

PERCENT	6	7	8
Percent ⟷ fractions			
Percent ⟷ decimals			
Find percent of a number			
Find percent one number is of another			
Find a number when a percent of it is unknown			
Word problems			

INTEGERS	6	7	8
Number line			
Compare and order			
Addition and subtraction			
Multiplication and division			
Absolute value			
Expressions with exponents			
Word problems			

GRAPHING (read, interpret, construct)	6	7	8
Bar graph			
Line graph			
Circle graph			
Coordinate graphing			
Cartesian products			
Graphing points in all four quadrants			
Graph linear equations and pairs of equations			
Slope and slope-intercept forms of equations			

SETS	6	7	8
Sets, set notation			
Venn diagrams			

IRRATIONAL NUMBERS	6	7	8
Perfect squares			
Square roots			
Finding square roots by averaging and tables			
Pythagorean Theorem			
Word problems			

BASES OTHER THAN TEN	6	7	8
Place Value			
Convert to base ten			
Addition and subtraction			

CLOCK ARITHMETIC	6	7	8
Convert to a ten clock			
Addition and subtraction			
Multiplication and division			

PROBABILITY	6	7	8
Single event			
Compound event			
Sample spaces			
Word problems			

EXPRESSIONS: EQUATIONS	6	7	8
Missing addends			
Missing minuends			
Missing factors			
Missing dividends			
Simplify expressions			
Whole numbers			
Fractions			
Decimals			
Integers			
Grouping symbols			
Order of operations			

STANDARDIZED TEST DATA

Test	Date	Concepts	Computation	Applications

ALGEBRA PLACEMENT

Test	Date	Score	Recommended

COMMENTS:

*From Kirkwood, Missouri, Public Schools.

At Eagleview Middle School in Colorado Springs, the entire mathematics program has been revised to be more consistent with the standards of groups like NCTM and with the characteristics and needs of early adolescents as they are at Eagleview Middle. Also using *Transition Mathematics*, the new math curriculum places increased emphasis on NCTM standards, with sharp *deemphasis* on many of the following: practicing routine, one-step problems; doing fill-in-the-blank exercises; answering questions that require only a "yes" or "no" answer; developing skills out of context; memorizing rules; practicing rules with tedious and repetitive paper and pencil computations; memorizing formulas, vocabulary, and isolated facts in mathematics. A gradual phase-in of new mathematics curriculum at Eagleview Middle occurred over a three year period, from 1989 to 1992.

Using Major Learning Tools

Television is a great educational tool which schools have, to date, used only minimally. Direct instruction over educational and closed-circuit channels continues in some school districts, but it has not had the popularity early advocates predicted. Some middle school teachers arrange to utilize appropriate telecasts when scheduled during an instructional period, or by assignments to students for out-of-school viewing.

Other schools in newer buildings utilize their modern television studio facilities for producing morning announcements and other programs. For example, Lake City Middle School in Lake City, Florida, opened in 1990, offers an exploratory course in Television Production to eighth graders, who use it to produce the day's opening ceremonies, brief skits on drug prevention, and so on.

Other schools, such as the middle schools of Alachua County, Florida now use television for portions of the advisory periods. During a week-long observation of an advisory group at Westwood Middle School in December, 1990, one of the authors participated in a group which took 12 minutes each day to watch the news as it was prepared for them by Channel One from Whittle Communications. Despite initial misgivings about introducing even more television viewing into the lives of young adolescents, on this occasion it seemed to be effective. It happened to be during the Mideast war, and students were intent on learning about what was happening, especially those who knew someone who was there. The teacher/advisor followed up each telecast with effective questions which turned into excellent current events discussions. Broadcast programs by CNN and other production companies are presenting school leaders with more options, and more dilemmas. Even so, at this point, despite widespread recognition of the great potential of television in education and of the many hours spent by the average middle schooler viewing television, community home–school cooperation in this field awaits great expansion to bring about adequate usage of the resource. The use of videotapes, laser discs, and other recordings offers increased opportunities yet to be fully utilized.

Middle schools today, as all other educational institutions, have access to many learning tools of great potential for learners. Printed tools, primarily books, and all other printed publications, remain the most widely targeted learning aids, and create the entire field of reading. The past decades have brought about a potential revolution in available learning tools: video, video/disc, and computer-assisted instruction of various sorts. The media center has, indeed, become more than a repository for books, and the use of its resources and of other learning resources in the community and elsewhere have become more and more the focus of lifelong learning skills.

Middle school educators approach the acquisition and use of these tools in many ways. Newly-contructed Conkwright Middle School in Winchester, Kentucky has installed two computers in the back of each classroom. Each of these computers is connected to the school media center which is, in turn, connected to a virtual world of computer resources. Students who finish their assigned work at Conkwright can move to the computer terminals and engage in enrichment work, research, and independent study of the most desirable sorts. At Conkwright, as at most middle schools, some type of formal instruction in the use of the available learning tools is essential, and many media specialists work collaboratively with language arts and other teachers to accomplish such instruction. Academic teams of teachers may also develop their own sessions for introducing students to their textbooks, learning packets, learning stations, and other resource centers. The important principle is that there is a systematic program of instruction in the use of each major tool, with the program frequently itself individualized in terms of sequential steps for learning the use of even as basic an aid as the card catalog.

More and more middle schools do have computer terminals, now for far more than for use in research projects and experiments with computer-based instruction. Current developments in the use of microcomputers may be paralleled with more opportunities for teaching about and with computers as major tools of learning for the future. Undoubtedly, the computer makes increasingly possible readier access to great bodies of information, and citizens will increasingly need to know how to retrieve and utilize information on demand.

At Piedmont Open Middle School in Charlotte, North Carolina, a Contemporary Technology Lab was established in 1990 as a cooperative venture with Charlotte's business community, and various professional societies and universities. In the Lab, students experiment and learn using technologies currently available in the workplace. There, students may choose from fifteen different technologies, in the areas of robotics, engineering, research and design, hydraulics, and telecommunications. Principal Stephanie Counts provides an example of how students are involved there (S. Counts, personal communication, 1990):

> For example, students may choose to work with a "numerical control" computer technology program used by many woodworking and machinery companies [especially numerous in the North Carolina area]. Using this program, students can "model" or produce a pattern for a particular item. The modeling data are then sent to a device that actually cuts the material. A student could, for example, design a chair leg then send these data to an electronic wood lathe which would cut this particular design into a piece of wood.

Perhaps the best-known, and most fully-developed, example of the application of advanced technology to the operation of the middle school concept, available at the time of publication of this book, was in the program for the Saturn School of Tomorrow in St. Paul, Minnesota (Bennett & King, 1991). Saturn, as a middle level school, houses about 250 students (with 80 on a waiting list), in grades 4–8, in a renovated YMCA facility in downtown St. Paul. Students come to Saturn from all over the city as part of the city's magnet desegregation program.

The mission statement for the Saturn School is: "The Saturn School Community is an interpersonal, individualized environment in which students become empowered life-long learners prepared for the twenty-first century." Core concepts of the program include the following:

1. A Personalized Learning Program is designed for each student.
2. Learning takes place in mixed age and ability groups.
3. Saturn is a textbook-free school.
4. Technology is used as a tool to support learning.
5. Course offerings are based on student interest and needs.
6. Grades are not given; progress is measured by attainment of personal growth goals.
7. A primary goal is: Students are responsible for their own learning.
8. Instruction is focused on developing learning processes.

Among the exciting programs evolving at the Saturn School, and particularly germane to the present discussion, is the use, by students and teachers, of state-of-the-art learning technologies[3], including:

a. Integrated Learning System (ILS) for reading, math, and other topics (developed by Computer Curriculum Corporation and Jostens).

b. LEGO/logo and Logowriter systems for computer programming and robotics.

c. Videodisc systems for access to high quality video libraries and sources.

d. "Discourse System" for interactive group-based instruction. Teachers using the Discourse System may present lesson content orally as in regular large group instruction, regular hand-outs and seatwork, or through computer-controlled processes. Each teacher using the Discourse System is provided with a central control unit and each student in the class has a "low profile" (and, we presume, low cost) terminal on which they can record answers to questions prompted by the teacher at the head of the class. The teacher can simultaneously view all student responses on the teacher's "Controlcom" unit. Using this system, teachers at the Saturn school can much more closely monitor student responses, deliver positive feedback, etc. Students can be encouraged to participate more fully since they may record their answers privately; even though the teacher is working with the whole class, they can view each student's response separately.

---

[3]For more information on these and other programs contact the following: Interactive Communications Systems, Inc., 8050 North Port Washington Road, Milwaukee, WI, 53217; Computer Curriculum Corporation, 1287 Lawrence Station Road, Sunnyvale, CA, 94089-9883; Jostens Learning Corporation, 7878 North 16th Street, Suite 100, Phoenix, AZ 85020-4402; Abacus Educational Systems, 921 S.W. Washington, Suite 410, Portland, OR, 97205.

But students can work as part of a group, through their individual units, at the teacher's discretion. The system may also dramatically reduce teacher time spent on record keeping, since test correction, grading, and correcting "papers" all can take less time with "Discourse."

e. Macintosh Lab for writing, HyperCard, desktop publishing, and research papers.

f. Telephone, cable, fax, voice mail, and electronic networking.

Research and development at the Education Development Center/Technical Education Research Centers (Zorfass, Remz & Persky, 1991) in Newton, Massachusetts, recognizing the receptivity of educators at the middle level, has focused on the integration of technology into middle school programs. "Make It Happen!" is a model used to guide interdisciplinary teams of teachers through a three-year change process focused on:

1. Having teams of teachers design, implement, and evaluate a curriculum that uses computers to support inquiry-based learning.

2. Helping young adolescents expand their critical thinking abilities, cooperative learning behaviors, and positive attitudes toward learning through engaging in a computer-based inquiry curriculum.

3. Assisting principals and school-based management teams to create a supportive school context that facilitates computer integration across a school.

The "Make It Happen!" model had, by fall of 1991, been field-tested in four diverse school districts in New York, Massachusetts, and New Hampshire. At each site, a team of teachers incorporating a special education teacher and a computer teacher worked together to integrate computer use into a 6- to 8-week unit cutting across all disciplines. Students become researchers and problem solvers who also utilize the whole language skills in the process! The careful design of "Make It Happen!" and the way in which the developers have taken pains to make it congruent with important middle school components suggests to us, that this sort of program is destined for greater successes.

Whether computer-centered, electronic technology will combine with the components of the middle school concept, as in the Saturn and "Make It Happen!" models, and produce a thoroughgoing "fourth revolution" (after the revolutions of schools, written word, and printing), as some have predicted, remains to be seen. However, our prediction would be that, before the end of the 1990s, video discs, minicomputers, and other, perhaps even newer, technology will be within the common experience of most middle school learners. If the past is prologue, as with other major technical innovations such as television and pocket calculators, the use of computers by individuals will become commonplace and, therefore, the earlier instruction in their use, the better.

Problem Solving and Other Higher Intellectual Processes

At the time of the first edition of this text, research in the area of brain growth seemed to indicate a plateau in ages twelve through fourteen that was thought to influence a very slow beginning for most students in areas of critical, creative, and analytical thinkings. In the last decade, however, many middle school educators have concluded that there is little reason to restrict the middle school curriculum's inclusion of opportunities for students ready for limited problem solving, evaluation of ideas, critical thinking, and related processes. At the same time it must be recognized that most children do not become fully capable of these formal operations in the middle school. Epstein and Toepfer's (1978) review of the brain growth data and of learning programs in the middle school led them to that middle school programs must: (1) discontinue the mass introduction of novel cognitive skills to middle grade students who do not have such readiness; (2) present new cognitive information at the existing skill level of students; and (3) work to mature existing cognitive skills of middle grade learners.

To these ends and to aid the development of positive self-concepts, these authors would restructure the middle school program to include a large component of opportunities for experience and practice of skills such as "community service projects in which students learn through working with the elderly in nursing homes, with children in daycare centers, and in community and natural resources reclamation projects" (Epstein & Toepfer, 1978, p. 660).

If the recommendations of Epstein and Toepfer are taken to mean that many middle school students reach the middle grades before they are able to function effectively in Piaget's stage of formal operations and that the middle school curriculum should be designed to meet students where they are and continue their development, then we concur; if these recommendations are taken to indicate that the middle school curriculum should not include rich materials designed to encourage problem solving, decision making, and critical or creative thinking, then we strongly disagree.

Problem solving and the related processes are sought in some of the activities of the advisory group (see Chapter 5). They can also be included as objectives for some students in social studies and science programs, as well as in interdisciplinary units. Problem solving as an activity in mathematics may be developed in such ways as to emphasize correct processes rather than correct answers. Special interest activity groups, frequently involving more student initiative and management than regular instructional programs, may also give opportunities for students to work out individual and group problems.

The goal, problem solving, needs to be viewed as central in the total instructional program, grades K–12. Curriculum planning groups can plan advisory group activities, interdisciplinary units, and specific instruction in the broad knowledge areas at appropriate levels so as to provide many opportunities for developing the conceptual background and interests for the problem solving and other higher intellectual skills to be learned and practiced as intellectual maturities permit.

Domain of Major Knowledge Areas

From two-thirds to three-quarters of the instructional time in the middle school is typically allotted for instruction in the major knowledge areas of language arts, mathematics, science, and social studies. Much of this ought to be and is used by teachers for learning opportunities in the other domains, especially that of communication and learning skills. Undoubtedly, the majority of scheduled instruction in language arts, almost all of that in mathematics, and smaller portions of that in science and social studies are focused on the learner becoming more competent in the skills associated with communication and in continued learning. But the learner also needs knowledge about the environment, physical and social, and of the cultural heritage to provide a substantive base for communication and further learning. This section describes how this need for knowledge is approached in the four major areas universally included in the middle school curriculum.

Language Arts

The predominant goals and learning opportunities of the language arts program relate to the learning and communication skills just considered. In addition to learning opportunities in reading and other study skills, speaking and listening, and writing, the language arts program usually includes specific instruction in grammar and spelling. Both of these areas are almost inextricably mixed with the skills areas as we defined them, but separate study materials and time allocations do have to be made for spelling and grammar, or perhaps English usage, as little or no research support exists for teaching grammar in traditional ways! Both spelling and grammar are also taught in part through vocabularies and composition assignments of other classes such as science, social studies, and literature. For sequential development, however, research-based spelling and grammar usage guides are usually considered essential, with the teachers' and students' own lists from current instruction used as supplementary guides.

One area of the language arts program is not skills-based—literature. Unfortunately, because of the push toward the skills components, especially in a "back-to-the-basics" period, literature may be neglected or taught almost as a skills subject itself—a good way to dull student appetites for reading! Among ways of organizing the literature component in the middle school are these: use of anthologies of literary selections on a class basis; studies of a few complete pieces of literature; independent reading of many sources; study of selected readings of a particular type (e.g., poetry); use of several pieces of literature related to some central theme, from either language arts or a cross-disciplinary approach; minicourses or short units on many different types and pieces of literature, perhaps with some options for student selection of the minicourses and readings therein; and combinations of these approaches. We especially like those approaches which aim toward building student interests in continued reading, as in the reading/writing workshop approach we extol elsewhere in this text. Hence, we find provocative a listing of minicourses in the Andrews (Texas) Middle School which included the following: Independent Reading; Mythology; *The Odyssey*; Safari through the Animal World; The Sporting World; The American Dream; *The Diary of Anne Frank*; Mark Twain; With Sword and Shield; the Fifth Dimension (science fiction); Johnny Tremain; American Folktales; The Bible as Literature; Whodunit; It's a Small World; and Heroes of the Old West. Surely many students can find and further develop an interest here.

We believe that the end results of independent reading will be much more significant interest and knowledge development than will come from programs of literature focused on such topics as these gleaned from an examination of some middle school program descriptions: figures of speech; identification of literary types; interpretation of footnotes in literary selections; definition of literary terms such as *theme;* and marking of end rhyme. Important as these matters may be, students can learn about them after they become really interested in literature, just as they can learn many rules of grammar after they sense the need for rules.

Mathematics

As we noted in the earlier discussion of quantitative skills, it is difficult and probably unwise to separate the teaching of mathematical skills and concepts at the middle school level. Certainly the skills are learned more readily when the concepts are understood, and the intent of mathematics instruction is to maintain the integral relationship of concept and operation. Hence, we shall give little more space to mathematics in this section, but certainly recommend its full allocation of time in the curriculum for all of the purposes and program aspects considered earlier. We would emphasize the hope, too, that mathematics would be related to knowledge in other areas, since so many concepts in science and social studies do have mathematical relationships and frequently require use of quantitative skills; for example, the whole area of taxation involves both social studies and mathematics concepts and skills.

Science

A study of the conversion of junior high schools to middle schools (Jones, 1990) indicated that there was some confusion, in the schools involved, about the nature of the sixth grade science program and some concern for the effectiveness of science instruction in the sixth grade. The study also indicated, however, that the middle school program provided more time for science instruction than the traditional junior high school program, and that interdisciplinary units in the middle school had strong science components. The author of the study concluded that "good middle school science teaching and the middle school concept can be very compatible."

In science, as well as other areas of the curriculum, both the knowledge and the skills domains have claims. As we noted earlier, problem solving is a central objective in much science teaching. A 1990 curriculum description of the Fort Campbell, Kentucky, middle schools includes these objectives:

1. Know the four areas of science (Life Science, Earth Science, Chemical Science, and Physical Science).
2. Apply the scientific method as a means of solving problems.
3. Appreciate the value of science in everyday life.
4. Be aware of the variety of careers available in science.
5. Make intelligent decisions that relate to a broad perspective of all living things and their environment.
6. Be aware of historical achievements in science.
7. Demonstrate hands-on skills in laboratory situations.

Knowledge outcomes are generally quite specifically defined, but the curriculum and instructional plans for their attainment are much more flexible and comprehensive than the premiddle school science readers of the elementary school and general science taught without a laboratory of the junior high school. Note, for example, some of the instructional guidelines developed by the Stoughton (Wisconsin) Middle School:

1. Teachers will teach science to heterogeneous groups. . . .

2. Basic skill development will be an integral part of the science program. . . .

3. Occasional enrichment excursions will be provided for students such as photography, scuba diving, the energy crisis, energy and other subjects, in addition to the Earth Science theme.

4. Learning modes will include lecture, lab, research, small group projects, or contracts when utilizing the science program.

5. The scientific method will be emphasized in the teaching of the Environmental Science program. These are the major categories: observation, prediction, application, extrapolation, synthesis, and evaluation.

6. An attitude survey will be attached to each pre- and post-test to measure affectively the motivation of the students toward science.

7. Students' knowledge and interests will increase as the Earth Science program is implemented in the eighth grade curriculum.

8. Inter-block communication will be increased for the science program by implementing periodic meetings, in an effort to coordinate and share common ideas.

Various national curriculum development projects have influenced the development of science in the middle schools. Typical of the growing interest in ecological concerns and their relationship to science is Foundational Approaches to Science Teaching (FAST), an inquiry approach, laboratory-centered program involving research in a secondary science curriculum for students from grades 6–12. The concepts in the FAST curriculum (developed at the University of Hawaii's Curriculum Research and Development Group) range across virtually every aspect of science, focusing on ecology, physical sciences, and "relational study" where students make applications of their learning to environmental issues such as air and water quality, energy, resource depletion, and population. The FAST program has, as of 1991, reached 3,000 teachers and 650,000 students.

The New York Science, Technology, and Society Education Project (NY–STEP) is developing middle level science curriculum that attempts to get students to "think globally and act locally" on perennial issues dealing with science and society. Pilot modules include areas such as: solid waste management, land use, water resources, human health science, and futurism. In an exciting departure from tradition, the New York State middle level science syllabus and the Regents Competency Test are to be revised to reflect these dramatic changes in the science curriculum. Furthermore, the NY-STEP program has explicitly sought to encourage interdisciplinary teaming within schools by suggesting interdisciplinary connections for each activity and also suggesting for each module some long-term interdisciplinary activities for various school subjects. We believe these are important steps forward in science curriculum development for the middle schools of the future, and would hope to see similar activities in other areas of the curriculum.[4]

A new project at Stanford University, the Human Biology Middle Grades Life Science Project, integrates study in the biological and behavioral sciences with a specific focus on adolescent development. The curriculum attempts to help this age group deal with high-risk behaviors with "a solid grounding in biological sciences and its natural outgrowths into health." In late 1991, the exact packaging of the curriculum had not been decided, but the emphasis will be on active investigation using scientific methods where classrooms will be "laboratories where collaborative efforts aid the finding-out process." Educators from fifteen schools in eight states field-tested the materials during the 1991–92 school year.

For the most part, however, science in the middle school is still usually a graded, sequential ordering of units of content, with life science units seemingly most common in grade 7, earth science in either or both grades 6 and 8, and other subject matter emphases coming in any grade. Some changes have occurred. The listing of units in the 1990 science continuum of the Fort Campbell middle schools, for example, is as follows:

---

[4]For more information, contact Dr. Dennis Cheek, RM 232-M, 89 Washington Avenue, Albany, NY 12234

Grade Six: Scientific Method; Small Things; Matter and Its Changes; Geology; Human Body Systems; Ecology; Weather; Insects; Plants; Motion and Energy; Heredity.

Grade Seven: Preview of Life Science; Plants; Invertebrates; Vertebrates; Protists, Monera, and Fungi; Cells; Ecosystems.

Grade Eight: Studying the Earth; The Dynamic Earth; Composition of the Earth; Oceans; Atmospheric Forces; Studying Space.

But electives, special interest activities, and minicourses also are used to achieve science objectives. In addition to its basic science program utilizing the national project and other materials in such a sequence as described above, the Graveraet Middle School (Marquette, Michigan) has offered the following electives in science: Photography; Advanced Photography; Pebble Puppies (geologic features of Michigan's Upper Peninsula); Planting; Recreational Safety and Outdoor Education (RSOE); and Substance Abuse. The Andrews Middle School (Andrews, Texas) has used a minicourse approach in science similar to the one described earlier in language arts:

> The minicourse curriculum has injected "new life" into our science program. We still teach the basic subjects required by state law, but we do it in a much different way. Our minicourses are six-week minicourses that span the subjects from astronomy to zoology. The minicourse curriculum allows the teacher to select what courses he or she will teach. This allows the teacher to teach in areas of high interest and strengths.

Course descriptions from Andrews included the following minicourse titles:

- Anatomy (the only minicourse required of all students—twelve weeks)
- Chemistry
- Ecology
- Physical Geology
- Genetics
- History of Science
- Laboratory Techniques
- Meteorology
- Space Science
- Zoology
- Astronomy
- Psychology
- Rocks and Minerals
- Historical Geology
- Micro-Biology
- Oceanography
- Pathology
- Petroleum Science

Social Studies

As the other major knowledge areas at this level, social studies has considerable responsibility within the other domains. Values clarification exercises are frequently used in social studies periods, and social studies content can provoke consideration of many ethical and moral questions. In addition to such personal development possibilities, social studies provides the opportunities for development of many skills of communication and continued learning. For example, a comprehensive curriculum workbook developed by teachers in the Nipher and North Middle Schools (Kirkwood, Missouri) included the following in a list of skills to be taught in grade 7 social studies:

- Reading for information
- Observation
- Recall
- Classification
- Analysis
- Evaluation
- Group discussion and interaction
- Making written reports
- Using the library
- Making oral reports
- Interviewing
- Role playing
- Advanced map skills
- Decision making
- Study skills processes
- Interpreting polar projection maps
- Interpreting latitude and longitude
- Evaluating qualifications of author
- Separating relevant and unrelated ideas
- Bibliographies

Perhaps more than any other knowledge area, social studies provides the subject matter base for many interdisciplinary or core units. It is relatively easy to identify literature related to social studies themes, movements, and eras. Also, along with science, social studies provides the context for practicing and acquiring all of the skills of learning and communication we presented earlier in this chapter and illustrated in the preceding paragraph.

But social studies is more than a vehicle for teaching values, literature, and learning skills. There is a great body of knowledge indispensable to successful membership in the human society, and much of this knowledge is embodied in the various plans of social studies curriculum scope and sequence used in American middle schools. The plans we have examined indicate a considerable agreement in practice only on the content of grade 8, American history. Some illustrations of the variety of plans especially for other grades, as abstracted from curriculum materials supplied the authors, follow.

In Cobb County, Georgia, the middle schools have provided two courses in grade 6: Geography Skills and Georgia Studies (two quarters); in grade 7, the course has been "Cultures of the World" with focus on various cultural regions; and grade 8, American history, chronologically organized. The MacDonald Middle School of East Lansing, Michigan offered three basic units in grade 6: (1) people and the traits they share; (2) society and interacting groups; and (3) people and their political systems. Grade 7 is World Studies, with a content similar to that of Cobb County, plus miscellaneous units such as education for consumerism, human sexuality, and careers. Grade 8 is American history with general citizenship objectives emphasized. The grade 6 program of Alton U. Farnsworth Middle School, Guilderland, New York, listed the same three units as the MacDonald School, and also these: Social Scientists; Cities and the People Who Build Them; Societies and Interacting Groups; Economics and Their Use of Resources; and Nations and Their Changing Boundaries. The grade 7 program included four units (fifteen to twenty-three weeks) relating to state geography, history, and culture, and four units (fourteen to twenty-two weeks) on early United States history (through the formation of the U.S. government). In grade 8, the chronological organization of American history is continued and concluded. The Shelburne (Vermont) Middle School includes a somewhat diverse organization of units in grade 6: Mapping Skills; Analysis of a Newspaper; U.S. Government; Human Relations; Specific Behavior Science; and Value Clarification. Grade 7 combines study of local and distant areas: Basic Fundamentals (map study especially); Champlain Valley; Europe, Africa, and Asia; Urban Study; and Current Events. The grade 8 program is the familiar chronological study of American history.

As the nineties unfold, an increased interest in civic education is noticeable on a number of fronts. One civic education program targeted specifically for the middle grades has been developed by the Close Up Foundation, CAAP (Civic Achievement Award Program) had, by 1991, been introduced to nearly one million middle grades students. Funded by the United States Congress and many private groups, three "projects" form the basis of the program. The "Learning Project" includes essays, activity sheets, maps, and timelines. The "Research Project" requires students to gather and process information. The "Civic Project" requires students to choose an issue, identify alternative approaches for dealing with the issue, and, in some cases, under adult supervision, address the issue actively in some way. In 1989, for example, students involved in CAAP participated in hundreds of civic projects including: producing and distributing pamphlets to legislators; holding community discussions in schools; working with local fire departments to correct fire hazards in schools; cleaning up the school grounds or nearby neighborhoods; serving food at shelters for the homeless; organizing tree plantings; recycling projects; water preservation campaigns; conducting surveys on school bond issues; and many others. We are convinced that this is the sort of social studies middle schoolers need as early adolescents, and that it will develop the sort of citizen activists that the society will need in the next generation.

We ourselves believe that it is quite desirable for middle schools to have differing social studies and other programs. They are influenced by many factors which vary from state to state, community to community, and school to school: local traditions; state and district regulations; programs of the schools which precede and follow; social philosophies and values; and others. But common emphases on core values of democracy are also needed and found.

Interdisciplinary, Core, and Other Organizations of Knowledge

The knowledge domain in the middle school is not completely confined to the four major subject fields just discussed. Interdisciplinary and core teaching and scheduling arrangements facilitate combinations and interdisciplinary units that draw knowledge from various disciplines. Illustrative of the combination of language arts and social studies, CLASS (Combined Language Arts and Social Studies) was a three-period block in grade 7 at Wayside Middle School, Saginaw, Texas. The main event of one year was the Pioneer Fair, with a museum, a pictorial of Texas History, a medicine show, and an exhibit room. A description of the presentation of two units taught in the Alief (Texas) Middle School, "Free Enterprise" and "Archaeological Dig," cited "the advantages of teaching specific skills and content by involving students in interesting activities and projects which require the interrelation of many disciplines as well as organizational and social skills."

Of course, the nature of the interdisciplinary team organization lends itself to the integration of the curriculum in these ways. Some schools have, indeed, managed to make such interdisciplinary units a way of life. The population of students attending Fort Campbell's two middle schools, for example, is unique: sons and daughters of military personnel who move from one part of the world to another on a frequent basis. Student attrition from the beginning of the year to the end is, consequently, extraordinarily high. Educators there have vowed to provide the students with the most enriched curriculum possible while students are in their schools. The enriched curriculum of the interdisciplinary unit has, therefore, been a standard at Fort Campbell middle schools. Two interdisciplinary units at Wassom Middle were so good that they won the Macmillan/McGraw-Hill Business Week Award for Instructional Innovation, from among 1,300 applicants, including $1,000 checks for the teachers involved. The "Technology Awareness" unit integrated math, science, and technology, and demonstrated their application to business and everyday life. The "Vacation USA" built on traditional geography content, but branched into map skills, calculating travel costs and distances, knowledge of biomes and biological characteristics of the regions through which students "travelled." Other team units included the popular "Egg Unit" used to "enlighten students on the changes in their bodies as they mature, to develop responsibility, and explain the concept of the reproductive system."

At Wassom Middle School, "interdisciplinary units are everyday occurrences. These activities are not limited to grade level teams, but may reach across grade levels into enrichment classes, and sometimes involve schoolwide participation. The following examples from 1990–1991 indicate the variety and degree of participation in them:

6th Grade
Consumer Smarts	Team, Community Resources
Holiday and National Observance Mini-units	Team

7th Grade
Vacation, USA	Team, Library, Learning Center
Roaring Twenties	Library
Endangered Wildlife	Team, Library, Learning Center
Future	Team, Library, Learning Center

8th Grade
Civil War	Social Studies, English, Library

Enrichment
Baroque, Classical, Romantic Eras	Band, Social Studies
Create a Character	Art, Communications
Advertising	German, Communications

Schoolwide
Elections	Entire School
The Great Constitution Question	Entire School
Computer Learning Month	Entire School

At Shelburne Middle School in Shelburne, Vermont, teachers and students in grades 5–8 have been involved in integrating the curriculum for many years. A longstanding organizational strategy there involves every teacher and student in one of three truly integrated, interdisciplinary teams: technology, humanities, and communications. Each student spends twelve weeks on each team. Each team involves a third of the faculty in the development of a yearly theme. Students and teachers meet in these team arrangements two afternoons a week, for two periods each session, all year long. For years, the Shelburne effort was unique; it may still be so.

At Caddo Middle Magnet School in Shreveport, Louisiana, each grade level plans an interdisciplinary curriculum festival each year. The sixth grade teams culminate their study of the Middle Ages and Renaissance by transforming the grounds of the school into a "Renaissance Faire." Students, teachers, and administrators don costumes of the period and take part in jousts, chess, and checkers while munching on "Ogre's Toes" and "Dragon Wings." Members of the local Creative Anachronism Society are called upon to demonstrate fencing, and provide explanations of knighthood and armor. The seventh grade festival is called "Colonial Days," an attempt to capture the spirit of colonial pre-Revolutionary village life. Teachers weave together language arts and social studies to produce a more complete view of that American experience. The eighth grade does "Mardi Gras" every year, transforming the school gymnasium into the French Quarter (middle school style) of New Orleans. Decorating masks and costumes, making floats, and sampling King's cakes are all a part of the fun.

More and more teachers and administrators recognize the value, it seems, of integrating the middle school curriculum. In the summer of 1991, for example, English teachers at Tenaya Middle School (Fresno, California) met and developed a list of lessons that matched the history curriculum, deriving the list from all of the textbooks to which they had access. The teachers at Tenaya cross-referenced their resulting interdisciplinary lesson list with the district mandated yearly test, to make certain that necessary skills were practiced with the context of the lessons throughout the year. In the summer of 1989, a team of core subject and exploratory course teachers from Orange County, Florida developed what they called "The Ultimate Packet," a 70-page resource to assist teachers in their efforts to integrate curriculum at the middle level (G. Pickler, Personal communication, August 22, 1989). The "Ultimate Packet" suggests numerous ways in which middle school teams can interrelate the curriculum. As they say it in Orange County:

> Increasingly, topics are being shared, formats are being exchanged, and commonalities are being realized across our curricula. The whole child is being educated by a truly interwoven fabric of academics, exploratories, physical education, and vocational studies. The result: A whole-team approach easily supported by activities presently in place in the Orange County curricula.

The "Ultimate Packet" includes carefully detailed "skills integration charts" for each grade level, 6–8, which illustrate how the five basic subjects, unified arts, and physical education all fit together. This integration is, furthermore, illustrated for each of the four 9-week periods of the school year, so that every teacher knows what every other teacher in the grade level is responsible for teaching during that grading period. The chart shows all of critical thinking, communication, computation, and study skills which can be emphasized in each subject during each grading period. Teacher Skills Focus Charts help teachers check the appropriate skills to tie into their curriculum during each nine weeks. Team Skills Focus Charts discuss common strands of skills which can be approached through team efforts. Essential Skills materials describe the details of each of the important skills which the county seeks to reinforce through integration (e.g., critical thinking).

In Bellevue, Washington, a district noted for its pioneering middle level programs, significant steps have been taken toward true integration of the curriculum in their sixth grade programs. In Bellevue's middle schools, educators have long been committed to arranging teachers and students so that smaller groups of students and teachers can spend longer periods of time together each day. In 1987, the district made a strong move to include the interdisciplinary team organization along with their traditional priorities. The result has been what they term, at Odle Middle School, the Integrated Curriculum Block: two teachers and fifty-five to sixty heterogeneously grouped sixth grade students who pursue integrated curriculum units throughout their day and week. One such unit at Odle Middle integrated the five basic subjects in a study called "Looking Back: Family Pathways, Patterns, and Traditions" in a way that covered writing competencies, speaking, listening, problem-solving, and other skills into a content that included anthropology, geography, history, reading, geometry and measurement, and genetics and heredity.

At Marie Drake Middle School in Juneau, Alaska, the 1990–1991 school goals centered on the main target of "integration and interdisciplinary curriculum." Three themes served as the focus for schoolwide interdisciplinary efforts during the year: focus for the fall was "Healthy Lifestyles;" the winter unit was "Celebrating Our Cultural Diversity;" and spring saw "Saving Our Earth—An International Responsibility."

For the last 20 years, interdisciplinary curriculum development has been underway in the middle schools of Upper St. Clair, Pennsylvania. Begun in 1971, under the pioneering efforts of Donald Eichhorn, the district has broadened its commitment to integration of the curriculum in the early 1990s (J. Smoyer, personal communication, January, 1991). Known now in the district as IDI (Interdisciplinary Instruction), the main thrust has been an integration of the science and social studies areas, but now includes more and more attention to interdisciplinary integration of all of the academic subjects in the middle schools of the district.

Significant efforts to integrate the curriculum at the middle level are also underway in the schools of Collier County, Florida. In that district, curriculum integration involves three components: cognitive, affective, and experiential. In Collier County, the interdisciplinary team, the use of the thematic unit, and the addition of what are called experiential labs in each of the middle schools are the basic components of the process. Students are taught the concepts in "an academic setting of a core curriculum classroom. Then learning will be reinforced by completing an experiment or a hands-on activity in the vocational experiential laboratory, thus marrying the core curriculum with the vocational curriculum" (S. Pino, personal communication, March, 1991).

The staff at Shelburne Middle School (Shelburne, Vermont) has attempted to "base the development of [our] curriculum and evaluation systems" on a number of "essential behaviors for learners":

Effective learners think creatively and critically.
Effective learners communicate.
Effective learners cooperate with others.
Effective learners use appropriate resources to seek, access, and apply knowledge.
Effective learners function independently.
Effective learners take risks to succeed.
Effective learners exhibit self-confidence.
Effective learners create options and make choices.

The most ambitious effort to redesign the curriculum of the middle school in an integrated manner, known to the authors, is that being undertaken in Cross Keys Middle School in Florissant, Missouri (D. Graham, personal communication, May, 1991). Similar to the efforts of educators at Kinawa Middle School in Okemos, Michigan, middle school educators at Cross Keys Middle have been working for five years to reestablish the direction of their curriculum. The new design is thoroughly interdisciplinary; it involves active learning, accommodation of learning styles, and the infusion of service projects into the regular curriculum. After much work, the staff there described, in a booklet they called "A Place of Our Own," the direction they wish to see their curriculum take. The evolution of interdisciplinary teams and the curriculum they provide, as educators at Cross Keys Middle see it, can move through what appear to be five levels:

Level 1: Teachers cooperate with each other, sharing students and time.

Level 2: Teachers share common resources, such as materials, space, time, or money.

Level 3: Teachers agree upon a shared skill that each subject area specialist will teach through their content area. A shared skill might be locating and working with the main idea in their social studies and science texts and then in the papers of their peers in their language arts classes.

Level 4: Teachers agree upon thematic units which connect the students' learnings across disciplines. As they plan the subtopics and activities, each teacher selects those from their traditional content area curriculum that fit the themes.

Level 5: Teachers agree upon a concept which connects the students' learnings and has no content area barriers. Teachers relinquish their areas of content specialization and begin to draw objectives and activities from their wide range of human talents and experiences, both in and outside of their formal training and area of certification. Once again, they become human beings, competent and experienced in life itself, first, and in content areas only incidentally.

Educators at Cross Keys Middle School believe that curriculum developed by teachers working together, at Level 5, would be characterized by several important threads running through each unit. Such units will be centered on refreshing new "metaphors." The curriculum will be based on a few "key concepts that middle school youngsters find meaningful." Active learning is sought, and traditional objectives, skill practice, and content are secondary. A "search for meaning" which results from purposeful application of new knowledge in service to the broader community is an integral component of the desired curriculum for middle schoolers at Cross Keys Middle. We, the authors, see this work as a significant, rare, and highly desirable departure from traditional middle level curriculum development.

Interdisciplinary curriculum projects such as those described in this section are, however, becoming easier to find than was the case in the 1980s. Arnold (1990) identified almost fifty exciting departures of this sort, as well as unusual curriculum programs in social studies, language arts, science, and mathematics. His compilation of robust alternatives to the standard curriculum makes good reading for those interested in injecting life and energy into the world of the middle school curriculum. We wish to reiterate, however, the concerns of contemporary critics of the current middle school curriculum: the greatest work on making the content of the curriculum congruent with the characteristics and needs of early adolescents remains to be accomplished. It is a fertile field for research and development.[5]

Evaluating and Reporting Student Progress

No subject is more certain to secure and hold the interest of both students and teachers in the middle school than grades and report cards. Unfortunately, the predominant interest of parents and, we fear, teachers, and certainly students, is in the grades (we think the term "marks" less confusing), the report cards, and the tests forever underlying grades and reports. A discussion of the evaluation and reporting of student progress seems more logically and correctly based on the purposes of evaluation and reporting, which we suggest as the following:

1. To assist each student in maintaining optimum progress toward becoming a fully self-directed learner

2. To help parents and other student advisors in their role of assisting student progress

---

[5]For more information on the question of the appropriate curriculum for middle level learners, the entire issue of the *Middle School Journal* for November, 1991 (Volume 23) is devoted to the continuing discussion of this question. Interested readers should also turn to the October 1991 (volume 49) issue of *Educational Leadership* for a theme issue on integrating the curriculum, with much attention to the middle level.

3. To provide data on student progress through the curriculum that can serve such purposes as consultation by future teachers, use in school evaluation and use in decision making for program planning

The typical situation, revealing the struggle to improve, was summed up well by Sal DiFranco, longtime principal of MacDonald Middle School in East Lansing, Michigan:

> Since we became a middle school in 1967–68, we have had periodic community and faculty debate about report cards. What is reported on a report card conjures up emotions based on tradition, ideology, political orientation, etc.. Our present report card (we fashionably call it a progress report) includes letter grades based on a student's PROGRESS. Students are "graded" on how they progress towards objectives set for them as individuals, not on how they compare to others in terms of level of achievement. To inform parents as to how their children compare with age-mates, each spring we administer standardized achievement tests in math and reading and indicate on the first and last Progress Report the student's level of instruction. The Progress Report also includes a conduct grade and comments related to learning skills and habits and personal and social behaviors that influence student progress. (S. DiFranco, personal communication, December, 1990)

We suspect that most middle school educators have struggled, as have those at MacDonald Middle, but with lamentably little progress.

Data Sources

Before turning to sections on the respective purposes, we wish to emphasize the point that student progress is progress on all goals set for student's education; it is not just the standing on written tests, standardized or otherwise. Important as test standings are in respect to the knowledge objectives they usually test, there are also significant goals in attitudes, behavior, and social relationships that are less readily tested. An adequate program of student progress evaluation and reporting may well include data taken from most or all of the following sources, as these are relevant to educational goals:

1. Conferences—with school personnel, parents and others to secure data regarding student learning and behavior.

2. Diaries and logs—kept by students and analyzed by teachers.

3. Interviews with students—to get information about their progress.

4. Inventories of many types—for information about personality development, interests, activities outside school, use of time, study habits.

5. Observation—of individuals and of groups to determine various data about behavior and learning.

6. Performance tests—including creative work, oral reports, skills in group work, physical skills and similar items best evaluated through performance.

7. Photographs and video—for later observation of performance, appearance, behavior, and so forth.

8. Rating scales—used by teachers, peers, parents, and others to estimate student behavior on specific traits and also to evaluate any aspect of the school program.

9. Recordings—of individual voices and group discussions for later analysis.

10. Records of many types—achievement, attendance, disciplinary, health, participation in activities, time studies, cumulative.

11. Written materials—papers, notebooks, workbooks, and other materials produced by individual students.

12. Written tests—standardized, teacher made, group made: to test knowledge, skills, attitudes, and performance.

Although the last two items are outnumbered in the list, they remain in practice the predominant sources of information used in evaluating and reporting student progress. Significant improvement in this important phase of middle school education requires the use of other, more relevant data for determining progress on some goals as well as more widespread concern for goals other than those which can be adequately evaluated by pencil-and-paper student products and tests.

Assisting Student Learning

Historically, grades and reports have been powerful pressures to coerce students to study and learn, much as educators may have decried this use. As there has been increasing recognition of the importance of internal motivation and decreasing use of failure and other punitive measures, experimentation with different systems of evaluation and reporting for broader purposes has increased. Especially below the high school and college levels, with their emphasis on grades as determiners of graduation and admission to the next level, attention has been given to assisting student learning through techniques of self-evaluation and individualized instruction. Individualized progress systems, such as those underway at MacDonald Middle School, make extensive provision for checking progress at each step, and this is one of their major advantages. Immediate knowledge by the student of the quality and extent of progress at every step is probably the most powerful force toward maintaining continuous progress.

Middle school classrooms provide many opportunities for student self-evaluation. Teacher-student conversations in which teachers ask such successive questions as "How are you doing on—?" "What mistake(s) did you make?" "How will you do it now (later)?" can be effective in stimulating and guiding student self-evaluation. Progress checklists and charts are widely provided in commercially prepared instructional materials, and may also be developed by teachers to fit individual situations. Such self-checking plans may include assignment of marks or simply status of completion, and are usually completed first by students and checked by teachers or teacher aides, with teacher-student conferences held as student self-evaluations are considered to need discussion. Forms can also be supplied any day by teachers to aid student self-analysis by such questions as follow:

- How did I do today?
- Did I ask the questions I needed to?
- Did I get the answers I needed?
- Did I find out what to do next? How to do it?
- How do I feel about this class? How can I make it better?

Tests can also be effectively used for self-evaluation purposes. Test exercises to help students check up on their reading comprehension or their skill in using a book or their ability to find materials in reference books, computers, and other library resources, may be very useful to students for determining skills needing practice. When test results can be disassociated from the grading system, self-correction of tests can be a valuable experience. Checking papers by pairs with the teacher available to answer questions and suggest improvement measures can also be very helpful. Students can also maintain and use effectively in self-evaluation efforts several types of records in addition to those of tests and progress in an instructional system: student diaries and logs; time records; letters to parents reporting school experiences; lists of readings; and papers corrected by teachers. Each of these materials can be useful in the student's efforts to identify progress and make improvements where needed.

Inevitably in our graded school systems, the use of marks and evaluation is related to the question of whether students move automatically from one grade to another. From his vantage point of a half-century of observation of promotion and curriculum practices, Hollis L. Caswell (1978, p. 100) summed up the problems of evaluation for promotion purposes quite well in the following statement concerning emphasis on the basics of communication and computation:

> One of the first things we tried was to apply grade standards more vigorously, often retaining pupils two or three years in the same grade. In due course we learned that cumulative nonpromotion resulted in a situation bad for all pupils.
>
> Gradually a substantial proportion of schools reduced the use of nonpromotion, and in many cases it was practically eliminated. But we found that this did not solve the problem either. . . . Even in my day it had become clear that neither holding pupils in lower grades nor passing them automatically with their chronological age group would provide a setting in which optimum development

of the basic skills of communication and computation could be achieved. It came to be widely agreed that the problem could be solved only by designing a curriculum that varied as much in opportunities as the individual differences of the pupils to be taught.

We wholly agree that it is curriculum, and instruction, which must cope with the problems of great differences in the learners of middle school age. Evaluation and reporting systems can merely provide data which teachers, parents, and especially the students can use to make appropriate choices as to learning opportunities and instructional modes. These systems can also be used to determine the students failing to achieve minimum competencies or other standards, and thereby, if the promotion system employs such standards, the students who are and are not to be held back. We would hope that the school faculty members responsible would consider fully the data in terms of each student's own status and probable future, determining whether to promote in each case on the basis of what action would most likely assist the student to perform better.

Communicating with Parents about Student Progress

Three major questions about evaluating student progress must be answered as we consider means of communicating with parents about their children's progress: (1) What standard of comparison is used? (2) What symbols are used to denote progress? (3) What means of communication with parents are used? Although the first two of these questions have to be considered in student self-evaluation and in records and reports in general, they usually are dealt with as issues in school reports to parents. Accordingly, we deal with them in this section.

Standards of Comparison

The traditional standard of comparison of the individual is with the group, of which the average or midpoint is considered the norm. In this normative evaluation, the student's progress is spoken of as exceptionally high, above average, average, below average, very poor, or some such terms, frequently equated respectively with A, B, C, D, and E or F. In comparison of standardized test scores, the norm is the midpoint of the population used for norming, and scores may be reported in percentiles, with the fiftieth percentile representing the norm of the group. This is essentially a competitive system, and its use or nonuse usually involves debate as to whether the school should foster or restrict competition.

In criterion-referenced evaluation, there is some minimum standard set as the criterion. Thus the criterion for achievement on a test for example, may be set as 75 of a possible 100; in writing exercises, not more than 3 errors in spelling; in mathematics, 9 of 10 problems correct; and so forth. In continued learning skills and other curriculum opportunities wherein learnings are specific and sequential, this pattern of evaluation seems logical; it may not operate effectively in curriculum areas in which there are knowledges and behaviors involved that can not be tested so as to yield adequate quantitative data.

TABLE 3.2   **Kirkwood Middle Schools,* Nipher and North   Basic Skills Grade Report 19 -**

	Last Name		First Name

Grade/Team		Subject		Teacher

Student Working _____ Grade Level

GRADES		QUARTER			
		1	2	3	4
Achievement					
Effort	Behavior				
	Use of class time				
	Completion of Assignments				

1st Quarter Comments:

2nd Quarter Comments:

3rd Quarter Comments:

4th Quarter Comments:

EXPLANATION OF GRADES

Achievement	*Effort*
E —Outstanding	1 —Outstanding
S —Above Average	
M—Average	2 —Satisfactory
I —Below Average	
U —Failure	3 —Unsatisfactory

Parent Signature

---

*From Kirkwood, Missouri, Public Schools.

Other standards that are employed are effort, attendance, and progress or improvement. For example, the Kirkwood, Missouri middle schools used a dual marking system in their "Basic Skills" and "Exploratory" grade report forms, as illustrated in the accompanying form (Refer back to Table 3.2 on p. 122).

Note that "effort" requires an "outstanding," "satisfactory" or "unsatisfactory" mark on three factors—behavior, use of class time, and completion of assignments. Attendance is frequently included in reports to parents, and it is a very prominent criterion for decisions as to promotion, disciplinary action, and other critical matters. Full implementation of a philosophy emphasizing progress as the consistent aim in every goal of the school for its students, really requires that the progress of the student be evaluated; to meet this requirement, diagnostic evaluation is needed for every objective with follow-up evaluation yielding an estimate of progress. Then some criterion is still needed for judging progress—is it adequate? Frequently, marking and reporting systems make some effort to appraise progress in terms of the student's ability; the report form or the teacher's oral statement may include language such as "is working up to ability" or "is not working up to ability." The illustrative mathematics report form (Table 3.3 on page 124) from the Albert D. Lawton Intermediate School of Essex Junction, Vermont permits the teacher to mark in relation to either (or both) the students or the class, and emphasizes classwork and self-motivation.

The report sent to parents in eighteen Orange County middle schools (Table 3.4 on page 125) provides much more information than parents receive in most districts. Students are evaluated in Academic Progress, Conduct, Work and Study Skills, and Social and Personal Development, in every one of the subjects they take. This information is provided in the basic academic areas, as well as physical education, two exploratory courses, and the advisory program. The evaluation of a student's Social and Personal development is particularly interesting. Parents learn of their child's progress, in every subject, in these areas:

1. growth in self-confidence,
2. pride in work,
3. responsibility,
4. cooperation, respectfulness, and consideration,
5. response to constructive criticism,
6. observation of school and classroom rules, and
7. respect for personal and school property.

Additional comments by the teachers and advisor are also possible. Copies of these computerized reports are sent to the student's counselor and team leader, as well as to the parent. Such reports seem, to us, to provide the comprehensive data parents and educators need to make sense out of student progress or the lack thereof.

We believe that the standard for comparison used should be the one most clearly related to the goals involved, and the one that seems most likely to give

TABLE 3.3   **Sample Subject Report Form***

NAME _____ GRADE _____ SECTION _____

MATHEMATICS

This is an evaluation of the student's achievement in relation to:
        himself   _____
        his class _____
Each student's strengths and weaknesses are taken into consideration.
The grade is derived by averaging homework or tests or both.

PERIOD REPORT

I.   CLASSWORK

Seeks help when needed.				
Comes prepared to class.				
Work completed on time.				
Prepares for tests.				

II.   SELF-MOTIVATION

Effort				
Respect				
Attentiveness				
Cooperation				
Works independently				

III.   OVERALL GRADE

Teacher _____ Teacher _____ Teacher _____

COMMENTS:

_____

*From Alfred D. Lawton Intermediate School, Essex Junction, Vermont.

parents and other advisors information they need to help students make optimum progress. For instructional purposes, criterion-referenced tests are very helpful in individualizing student progress within particular areas, especially those having highly sequential material. For parent information, there may be a need for normative comparisons which are easily understood , but this need should be met only if there is also help given for understanding why students are below average and what means, if any, are available for helping them. As to

TABLE 3.4

ORANGE COUNTY PUBLIC SCHOOLS
MIDDLE SCHOOL PROGRESS REPORT
GRADING PERIOD: 1 2 3 4
(Circle One)

STUDENT NAME _____ (Last) _____ (First)

GRADE _____

SCHOOL _____

TEAM _____

I. ACADEMIC PROGRESS
Code: (1) Excellent (3) Needs Improvement
(2) Steady Progress (4) In Danger of Failing

II. CONDUCT
Code: (1) Satisfactory (3) Unsatisfactory
(2) Needs Improvement

III. WORK AND STUDY SKILLS
Code: (X) Indicates Improvement Needed
No Mark Indicates Satisfactory Progress

- Attendance
- Preparation (materials, homework, etc.)
- Class Attentiveness
- Neatness and accuracy
- Completion of work on time
- Participation in class activities
- Following directions
- Performance on tests

IV. SOCIAL AND PERSONAL DEVELOPMENT
Code: (X) Indicates Improvement Needed
No Mark Indicates Satisfactory Progress

- Growth in self-confidence
- Pride in work
- Responsibility
- Cooperation, respectfulness and consideration
- Response to constructive criticism
- Observation of school and classroom rules
- Respect for personal and school property

1/MID/118–4/28/88

Distribution: White – Parent
Yellow – Team Leader
Pink – Guidance

SUBJECT

ADVISORY PERIOD	MATHEMATICS	ENGLISH	SOCIAL STUDIES	SCIENCE	READING	PHYSICAL EDUCATION	EXPLORATORY	EXPLORATORY

COMMENTS

Advisory Period: _____
Teacher _____ Conference requested ____

Mathematics: _____
Teacher _____ Conference requested ____

English: _____
Teacher _____ Conference requested ____

Social Studies: _____
Teacher _____ Conference requested ____

Science: _____
Teacher _____ Conference requested ____

Reading: _____
Teacher _____ Conference requested ____

Physical Education: _____
Teacher _____ Conference requested ____

Exploratory: _____
Teacher _____ Conference requested ____

Exploratory: _____
Teacher _____ Conference requested ____

Parent Signature _____

(AB0172 Rev/060/003)

effort, attendance, and other such factors, we see their chief use in teacher and parent understanding of individual students and their student progress.

Symbols for Marking and Reporting

Numerical marks on the 100 percent scale were once popular in the United States and still are given in a few schools, but it is the traditional letter grades (A, B, C, D, E and/or F) that have been used most widely now at all levels, and almost universally in high school and college. The grades are variously interpreted, with some districts equating each letter to a range on the 100 percent scale (for example, A = 90–100), and others using such varied explanation of A, for example, as "Outstanding Progress," "All objectives met with excellence," or "Excellent." A single grade may be assigned to a subject, or there may be marks on each of several objectives or other items used as criteria. The accompanying report form from the Stoughton (Wisconsin) Middle School (Table 3.5) illustrates several features of middle school report forms, few of which include so many features as Stoughton's: checklist of skills and behavior items that can be checked by subject to show improvement needed; record of attendance by subject; one system of letter grades, related by definition to objectives, for academic evaluation and another system for conduct in each subject area.

The report card, revised in 1990, for Fulton County, Georgia middle schools (Table 3.6 on page 128) is a marvel of contemporary computerwork. Six forms are attached; from the fall mid-quarter report to the final spring report. Each report is recorded on the bottom cumulative page which summarizes the year. The report includes subject grades in 16 areas including exploratories, physical education/health, and academics (including foreign language). It also covers behavior comments for each of the six marking periods, and a space for "general school conduct." In reading and math "skills levels" student progress is also indicated, as O (on grade level), A (above grade level) or B (below grade level). It is also possible to indicate if the curriculum in which the student is involved has been modified for some exceptionality, to "meet the individual's needs." The report is complex but informative and, we expect, satisfactory once parents become accustomed to it.

The progress report used at Burlingame Intermediate School (Table 3.7 on page 129) during the 1991–92 year gives a substantial amount of space to several important indicators which may be contributing to less than satisfactory progress: assignments not turned in; late assignments; low test grades; books/materials not brought to class; poor class participation; inattention during instruction; ineffective use of time; needs to come in for additional help; recent improvement show; behavior unsatisfactory; effort commendable. A space also indicates whether a conference is requested by the teacher. The quarterly report cards (Table 3.8 on page 130) carry the same information.

TABLE 3.5   Comprehensive Report Form*

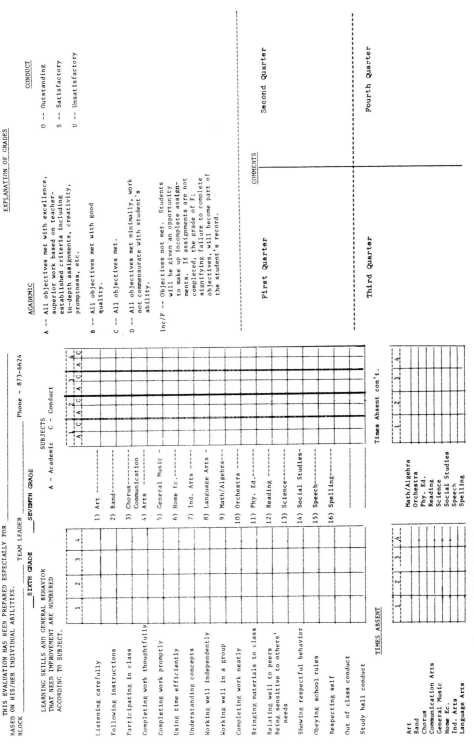

STOUGHTON MIDDLE SCHOOL
STUDENT EVALUATION

THIS EVALUATION HAS BEEN PREPARED ESPECIALLY FOR _____
BASED ON HIS/HER INDIVIDUAL ABILITIES.   TEAM LEADER _____
BLOCK _____

SIXTH GRADE   SEVENTH GRADE   Phone - 873-6624

LEARNING SKILLS AND GENERAL BEHAVIOR
THAT NEED IMPROVEMENT ARE NUMBERED
ACCORDING TO SUBJECT.

SUBJECTS
A - Academic   C - Conduct

Listening carefully
Following instructions
Participating in class
Completing work thoughtfully
Completing work promptly
Using time efficiently
Understanding concepts
Working well independently
Working well in a group
Completing work neatly
Bringing materials to class
Relating well to peers
Being sensitive to others' needs
Showing respectful behavior
Obeying school rules
Respecting self
Out of class conduct
Study hall conduct

1) Art
2) Band
3) Chorus
4) Communication Arts
5) General Music
6) Home Ec.
7) Ind. Arts
8) Language Arts
9) Math/Algebra
10) Orchestra
11) Phy. Ed.
12) Reading
13) Science
14) Social Studies
15) Speech
16) Spelling

TIMES ABSENT

Times Absent con't.

Art
Band
Chorus
Communication Arts
General Music
Home Ec.
Ind. Arts
Language Arts

Math/Algebra
Orchestra
Phy. Ed.
Reading
Science
Social Studies
Speech
Spelling

EXPLANATION OF GRADES

ACADEMIC

CONDUCT

O -- Outstanding
S -- Satisfactory
U -- Unsatisfactory

A -- All objectives met with excellence, superior work based on teacher-established criteria including in-depth assignments, creativity, promptness, etc.

B -- All objectives met with good quality.

C -- All objectives met.

D -- All objectives met minimally, work not commensurate with student's ability.

Inc/F -- Objectives not met. Students will be given an opportunity to make up incomplete assignments. If assignments are not completed, the grade of F; signifying failure to complete objectives, will become part of the student's record.

First Quarter   Second Quarter

COMMENTS

Third Quarter   Fourth Quarter

*From Stoughton, Wisconsin, Middle School.

TABLE 3.6

FULTON COUNTY MIDDLE SCHOOLS Atlanta, Georgia

RITE-WAY COMPUTER FORMS: 404-489-7715

Student Last Name   First   School Name   Middle

Home Room Teacher / Grade Level

SUBJECT AREA GRADES

BEHAVIOR COMMENTS

| | FALL | WINTER | SPRING |
| Mid-quarter | Quarter | Mid-quarter | Quarter | Mid-quarter | Quarter |

19 __ -19 __

Art
Computer
Home Ec.
Ind. Arts
Gen. Music
Band/Orch./Chorus

Phys. Ed.
Health

French
Spanish
Latin
Reading
Lang. Arts
Math.
Social Studies
Science

** MODIFIED CURRICULUM   SEE REVERSE SIDE FOR EXPLANATION
*** TALENTED AND GIFTED
SKILLS LEVEL
Reading
Math

General School Conduct

ATTENDANCE   F   W   S
Days present
Days absent
Days tardy

EXPLANATION FOR BEHAVIOR COMMENTS
No mark indicates "SATISFACTORY"
Area(s) where behavior "NEEDS IMPROVEMENT"   (2 MAX PER SUBJECT)

L. Prepare daily   Q. Follow directions   V. Improve attendance
O. Be courteous and cooperative   R. Work independently   W. Note attached or previously sent
P. Use time wisely   T. Show self-control   Y. Interact positively with peers

FALL MID-QUARTER REPORT

_____   PARENT / GUARDIAN SIGNATURE _____

FULTON COUNTY MIDDLE SCHOOLS

Name   Last   First   Middle

Home Room Teacher   Entry Date _____
                           Withdrawal Date _____
                   School Name

| Grade __ 19 __ | FALL | WINTER | SPRING |

Art
Computer
Home Ec.
Ind. Arts
Gen. Music
Band/Orch./Chorus

Phys. Ed.
Health

French
Spanish
Latin
Reading
Lang. Arts
Math.
Social Studies
Science

** MODIFIED CURRICULUM
*** TALENTED AND GIFTED
SKILLS LEVEL
Reading
Math

READING AND MATH
O- ON GRADE LEVEL
A- ABOVE GR. LEVEL
B- BELOW GR. LEVEL

GRADING SCALE
Subject Areas
A - 92 - 100
B - 83 - 91
C - 74 - 82
D - 70 - 73
F - 69 & Below

          F   W   S
Days present
Days absent
Days tardy

Next Year's Grade Assignment _____

TABLE 3.7   **Burlingame Intermediate School Process Report**

BURLINGAME INTERMEDIATE SCHOOL

PROGRESS REPORT

NAME OF STUDENT _____   GRADE _____   HOMEROOM _____   QUARTER 1 2 3 4

SUBJECT	Teacher's Initial	Current Grade	Assignments Not Turned In	Late Assignments	Low Test Grades	Books / Material Not Brought To Class	Poor Class Participation	Inattention During Instruction	Ineffective Use of Time	Needs to Come in for Additional Help	Recent Improvement Shown	Behavior Unsatisfactory	Effort Commendable	Conference Requested	COMMENTS
MATHEMATICS															
LANGUAGE ARTS															
LANGUAGE SKILLS															
SOCIAL SCIENCE															
FOREIGN LANGUAGE															
SCIENCE															
HEALTH															
PHYSICAL EDUCATION															
ART															
SHOP															
HOMEMAKING															
DRAMA															
TUTORIAL															
COMPUTER SCIENCE															
MUSIC: General															
Instrument															
JOURNALISM															
VIDEO PRODUCTIONS															
OTHER															

PLEASE NOTE THAT NOT ALL COMMENTS AND GRADES ARE ENTERED ON PROGRESS REPORT. ONLY THOSE COMMENTS THAT ARE SIGNIFICANT ARE INDICATED AT THIS TIME.

BURLINGAME INTERMEDIATE SCHOOL — PROGRESS REPORT

Student Name _____   Homeroom _____

Parent / Guardian
Signature _____

Dear Parents,
Your signature indicates receipt of your son's / daughter's progress report.
Please sign, detach this portion of the report and return to the school.

TABLE 3.8

PUPIL'S NAME		GRADE	YEAR	HOME ROOM TEACHER	BURLINGAME INTERMEDIATE SCHOOL
					ROBERT E. BEUTHEL, DISTRICT SUPERINTENDENT
					QUARTERLY REPORT

SUBJECT	TEACHER	1st QUARTER			2nd QUARTER			3rd QUARTER			4th QUARTER			FINAL
		GRADE	COMMENT CODE	TEACHER'S INITIALS	GRADE	COMMENT CODE	TEACHER'S INITIALS	GRADE	COMMENT CODE	TEACHER'S INITIALS	GRADE	COMMENT CODE	TEACHER'S INITIALS	MARK
LANGUAGE ARTS		+/−			+/−			+/−			+/−			+/−
SOCIAL SCIENCE		+/−			+/−			+/−			+/−			+/−
MATHEMATICS		+/−			+/−			+/−			+/−			+/−
SCIENCE		+/−			+/−			+/−			+/−			+/−
HEALTH		+/−			+/−			+/−			+/−			+/−
FOREIGN LANGUAGE ☐ FRENCH ☐ SPANISH		+/−			+/−			+/−			+/−			+/−
LANGUAGE SKILLS		+/−			+/−			+/−			+/−			+/−
ESL		+/−			+/−			+/−			+/−			+/−
PHYSICAL EDUCATION		+/−			+/−			+/−			+/−			+/−
EXPLORATIVES:														
ART		+/−			+/−			+/−			+/−			+/−
COMPUTER SCIENCE		+/−			+/−			+/−			+/−			+/−
CULTURAL HIGHLIGHTS		+/−			+/−			+/−			+/−			+/−
DRAMA		+/−			+/−			+/−			+/−			+/−
HOME ECONOMICS		+/−			+/−			+/−			+/−			+/−
INDUSTRIAL ARTS		+/−			+/−			+/−			+/−			+/−
JOURNALISM		+/−			+/−			+/−			+/−			+/−
MUSIC ☐ INSTRUMENTAL ☐ GENERAL		+/−			+/−			+/−			+/−			+/−
STUDY SKILLS		+/−			+/−			+/−			+/−			+/−
VIDEO PRODUCTIONS		+/−			+/−			+/−			+/−			+/−
		+/−			+/−			+/−			+/−			+/−

COMMENTS 1st QUARTER:

COMMENTS 2nd QUARTER:

COMMENTS 3rd QUARTER:

COMMENTS 4th QUARTER:

EXPLANATION OF MARKING SYSTEM

A Outstanding achievement
B Very good achievement
C Satisfactory achievement
D Poor achievement and effort
F Unsatisfactory achievement and effort
NM No mark
INC Incomplete

"PLUS" or "MINUS" signs used behind a grade indicate placement near the upper or lower limits of the specified grade.

EXPLANATION OF COMMENTS

0 · Behavior satisfactory
1 · Behavior needs improvement
2 · Behavior unsatisfactory
E · Effort commendable
K · Class participation is poor
L · Listens and follows directions
M · Student has shown recent improvement
N · Not working to capacity

P · Parent conference recommended
R · Low test grades
S · Study habits need improving
T · Absences/tardies affect school work
U · Effective use of time
W · Working below grade level
X · Books or materials not brought to class
Y · Inattention interfering with achievement
Z · Assignments not completed/late/incomp.

Not all comments are entered at each marking period. Only those comments that are particularly significant are indicated at this time.

- -

✂ DETACH HERE   **BURLINGAME INTERMEDIATE SCHOOL · QUARTERLY GRADE REPORT**

Dear Parents:
Your signature indicates receipt of your son's/daughter's report card. Please sign, detach this portion of report and return to school via your youngster. If you wish to have a telephone or personal conference with a teacher, please indicate by placing a checkmark in the box beneath your name and indicate teacher's name(s) on reverse of this form. Also, any written suggestions may be forwarded to the appropriate teacher by use of reverse of this form.

VERY TRULY YOURS,
ROBERT WELCH, PRINCIPAL

STUDENT NAME _____ HOME ROOM_____

PARENT/GUARDIAN'S
SIGNATURE **X** _____ DATE_____

CONFERENCE REQUESTED: ☐ TELEPHONE   ☐ PERSONAL
☐ PLEASE NOTE COMMENTS ON REVERSE SIDE   **1st QUARTER**

Means of Communication with Parents

The traditional and dominant means of communication with parents is the report form or card, developed by each district and even by individual schools. Great variety exists in the forms used, as the examples here indicate. Some districts use different forms for different subjects and grades. Most of the individual subject report forms from various districts using them list objectives of the subject with some indication of student strengths and weaknesses. The report forms vary especially in the use of the various symbols and in the standards of comparison as discussed earlier in this section.

Middle school educators also use a variety of plans for communicating with parents about student difficulties, before and between report cards. For example, the Progress Report (Table 3.8) from Burlingame Intermediate can be used by any teacher to report the current grade the student has earned, and a host of factors which may contribute to unsatisfactory progress, including "effort commendable." In some schools interim progress reports differ by subjects; in the middle schools in Alachua County, Florida, students receive separate progress reports in each subject, at intervals of four weeks, alternating with the nine-week report card. At College Park Middle School in Lynnwood, Washington, teachers issue progress reports as a team (see Table 3.9 on page 132), thereby reinforcing the centrality of the interdisciplinary team in the minds of parents as a part of the interim progress reporting process. Virtually all of the interim reports and regular report cards we have examined also wisely call for the return of the form accompanied by a parent signature indicating they have received and reviewed the progress report.

There still seems to be no categorical, universal answer to the question of what means of communication to use with parents to report and assist student progress, even in the 1990s with the advent of computer programs to assist in the process. There is an amazing variation in practices in reporting, regardless of grade span of the school, location, or the specific demographics of the student populations. Three principles seem especially valid and important:

1. The communication with parents should be as direct and personal as possible. This tends to be a problem with contemporary computer-generated report cards which list comments like "A pleasure to have in class" over and over again; comforting and positive, but impersonal. Consequently, middle school teachers on interdisciplinary teams have begun to rely on parent conferences for the really important problems or great success stories. Conference days set aside for this purpose are used incredibly effectively, in our opinion, when the interdisciplinary team is functioning well. The case for them is well summed up in this excerpt from the "Parent-Teacher Conference Guide" used in the Jamesville–Dewitt (New York) Middle School:

> The Middle School regularly sends you progress reports and report cards which
> summarize your child's scholastic progress. However, it's impossible to reduce
> to a few sentences, an assortment of check-marks, or any collection of letter of

TABLE 3.9 **College Place Middle School Team Progress Report**

COLLEGE PLACE MIDDLE SCHOOL TEAM PROGRESS REPORT

STUDENT_____ GRADE ____ Date _____

> Below are your child's current grades and teacher comments for ____ quarter. If you child has one Inc. or more, we strongly suggest that he/she attend STUDY CLUB until all missing work is completed. If you have any questions, please call 670-7451.

Subject	Teacher	Gr.	Comments (see below)
Science/Hea./Comp.			
English			
Math			
Social Studies			
Mastery/Enrichment			

COMMENTS:

1. Demonstrates above average effort
2. Demonstrates average effort
3. Demonstrates inconsistent effort
4. Effort has improved
5. Effort has declined
6. Plans and uses class time well
7. Shows initiative and enthusiasm for learning
8. Participates well in class activities
9. Is courteous and cooperative
10. Conduct is improving
11. Attitude is improving
12. Works beyond class requirements
13. Has the ability to do better work
14. Frequently unprepared for class
15. Misbehaves or too social in class
16. Misconduct has disturbed the class and affected student's progress
17. Needs to develop a more positive attitude
18. Needs to participate more in class activities
19. Has difficulty working independently
20. Has difficulty with tests or preparation for tests
21. More care and time should be spent on assignments
22. Does not complete assigned work
23. Works well in class, but does not do homework
24. Work is frequently turned in late
25. Needs to complete assignments in order to be eligible to take unit test(s).
26. Grade would have been higher but did not complete sufficient enrichment.
27. Is frequently tardy
28. Absences have had a negative effect on performance and achievement
29. Needs to make up assignments when absent
30. Needs to use Mastery/Enrichment time more productively
31. Makes good use of Mastery/Enrichment time
32. Attends Study Club to get help or work done
33. Should attend Study Club more often
34. Incomplete from last quarter is not made.up
35. Additional information sent home
36. Please call for a conference (670-7456)
37. Great Kid!!

_____   _____
Parent Signature   Date

number marks a unique and infinitely complex human—including your child. Telephone conversations are good, but the best base of cooperation is found in the interchange of face-to-face conferences between parents and teachers.

The Teacher Handbook of the Woodlawn Middle School (Mebane, North Carolina) classified parent conferences as: (1) impromptu—chance meeting; (2) telephone conference—quick means of contact; and (3) scheduled school conference which "is especially valuable in that it is planned in advance and the teacher has time to prepare fully for it." To help in the advance planning, the accompanying form (Table 3.10 on page 134) has been used at Woodlawn.

The staff at Burlingame Intermediate School takes parent conferencing very seriously. They believe that:

> One of the keys to an effective middle school is developing a parent community that is knowledgeable of the developmental characteristics of adolescents, understands how the essential elements of middle level education are designed to meet the needs of adolescents, and is an active partner in helping the school reach its goals. The parent education program and the parent conferencing program at BIS are key elements in providing open communications and developing an understanding of middle level education.
>
> Eleven half-days are provided for parent conferencing, after the first three progress report periods. These conferences allow teacher, parent, and student to set goals, develop procedures for maintenance or improvement of grades prior to the next report. Arena-style conferences are held in the gymnasium. All teachers are seated at tables throughout the gym with partitions to provide some degree of privacy. Parents sign-in and the administrators send the parent(s) to teachers. This allows parents to see all of their child's teachers in a relatively short period of time without elaborate scheduling problems. Arena conferencing also creates an atmosphere that allows parents to talk to other parents as they wait for a conference to talk with teachers their child may have had in a previous year.
>
> Four or five parent education sessions are also held each school year. These sessions are most often designed around developing a greater awareness of characteristics of adolescents and skills that help the parent cope with adolescents. Our school works very closely with local agencies to provide speakers and facilitators for these forums. (Welch, personal communication, March 6, 1991)

2. The report, whatever its form, should be intelligible to the parents. Since parents do not generally possess a pedagogical vocabulary and may not want to spend as much time studying explanations as the report form makers anticipate, the form must not be overly complex; explanations must be specific and clear and any follow-up conferences or other action plainly spelled out. The best guarantee of this principle lies in the development of the form; careful pilot use with representative parents to eliminate flaws and ambiguity helps greatly.

3. The ultimate purpose of the report, whether oral or written, is to increase cooperation for the student's progress. Both teacher and parent may need an occasional reminder of the purpose, for progress reports sometimes get used as

TABLE 3.10   **Parent/Teacher Conference Planning Form   Woodlawn Middle School***

DEAR _____

Your parent-teacher conference is scheduled for

Date _____ from _____ to _____

This appointment is to exchange information about

_____. Please indicate below any area(s) that you are particularly interested in discussing.

_____ Work habits	_____ Social Studies
_____ Growth as an individual	_____ Science
_____ Growth as a group member	_____ Mathematics
_____ Reading	_____ Art
_____ Writing	_____ Music
_____ Listening and Speaking	_____ Physical Education
_____ Spelling	_____ Other _____
_____ Language	

Please RETURN this prior to the conference.
If you are unable to attend at the time above, please indicate other convenient dates and times.

_____
(Parent's Signature)

TEACHER _____

(Detach here)

REMINDER: Conference to exchange information about_____

on _____from _____ to _____.

*Mebane, North Carolina

Sample Progress Letter Form

Date _____

To the parents of _____ :

We at Oaklea School believe that outstanding achievement as well as conscientious effort toward improvement should be encouraged and recognized in our students.

Your child has displayed these commendable qualities during the past four-week period and we are proud to send you this statement of merit for personal effort and achievement.

_____
Class

_____
Teacher

_____
Principal

punitive measures, or as bases for rewards extrinsic to the educational program. Positive reports are also desirable.

Much money and effort go into maintaining an evaluation and reporting system. Parents do need to know how their children are doing at school so that they can be helped at home; they can and do help in such ways as improving study conditions, offering parental encouragement and arranging for extra help at school or otherwise as teachers recommend. Parents can be helpful only as they understand their children's learning status and problems, and communication must first of all convey as accurate data as possible on this score.

Gordon Vars, longtime proponent of middle level education at Kent State University, suggests the following questions for evaluating a student progress report:

1. Does the report emphasize the broad goals of education in a democratic society? In other words, does it go beyond academics, important as they are, to include citizenship skills, acceptance of responsibility, positive attitudes?

2. Does the report reflect an awareness of the unique characteristics and needs of the age group? For example, does it contribute to wholesome self-concept development and satisfactory peer relations?

3. Does the report make proper allowance for individual differences? For example, does it report how well the student is utilizing his or her ability, as well as how his or her achievement compares with others?

4. Is the report diagnostic? That is, does it indicate specifically what the student has done and what can be done to improve?

5. Does the report "accentuate the positive?" Is the general tone positive, encouraging?

6. Is there opportunity for personal comments?

7. Is the report easily understood by parents and students? Does it speak their language or does it require a college degree to interpret?

8. Can the report be prepared without placing an undue burden on teachers?

9. Do students have appropriate input into the evaluation and reporting process?

10. Is the report designed to be used to promote student growth instead of simply judgments of past achievements? (personal communication, Fall, 1991)

Recent research on the effects of report cards and related recognition systems (MacIver, August, 1990) indicates that conventional practices may have somewhat unexpected outcomes, with at-risk students, those who have fallen behind, or those who are simply slower learners. It seems that the inclusion of handwritten comments by teachers of such students is "significantly associated with higher achievement by educationally disadvantaged students. The use of conduct grades and extensive attendance award programs are associated with lower achievement by educationally-disadvantaged students" (p. 4). The outcomes of such programs depend upon the school staff's attempts to make it possible for all students to be involved in positive ways in these programs. If such programs focus on the average and above average student, they omit the very students who most need to avoid developing "a debilitating self-image and who are more in need of a motivational boost to prompt accelerated achievement" (p. 2).

Records for Other Purposes

The same basic data used by the student in his or her self-improvement activities and by the teacher and parent in determining how to counsel and help the student serve several purposes as records. For example, the student's own cumulative record, with its compilation of test scores and other quantitative data regarding student progress as well as informative material about the student's family, health, school attendance, and other items, is important for consultation by future teacher and counselors.

Compilations of evaluative data about various populations of students become exceedingly important data sources for use in school evaluations and in program planning. Certainly the ultimate criterion of school quality is the progress its students attain, and any adequate program of school evaluation provides for consideration of such measures of student progress as available. And the first source of data for school planning committees is that of data about student achievement, behavior, and attitudes. Hence, carefully maintained records of the evaluation of each student's progress are prerequisite to the other phases of schoolwide formative and summative evaluation which must occur.

ADDITIONAL SUGGESTIONS FOR FURTHER STUDY

A. Books and Monographs

Alexander, William M. and others. (1969). *The emergent middle school, 2nd enlarged edition*. New York: Holt, Rinehart and Winston, Inc.

Curtis, Thomas E. and Bidwell, Wilma W. (1977). *Curriculum and instruction for emerging adolescents*. Reading, MA: Addison-Wesley Publishing Company.

Driscoll, K. J. (1986). *Humanities curriculum guidelines for the middle and secondary years: An inservice training document*. Philadelphia: Falmer Press.

Duffy, G. G. (Ed.). (1990). *Reading in the middle school*. Newark, DE: International Reading Association.

Frisancho, A. R. (1981). *Human adaptation: A functional interpretation*. Ann Arbor: The University of Michigan Press.

Kelly, B. J. (1990). *Physical education for the middle school.* Springfield, IL: C.C. Thomas.

Saylor, J. G., Alexander, W. & Lewis, A. (1981). *Curriculum planning for better teaching and learning.* New York: Holt, Rinehart and Winston, Inc.

Zevin, D. (1989). *Into adolescence: Choosing abstinence: A curriculum for grades 5–8.* Santa Cruz, CA: Network Publications.

B. Periodicals

Austin, R. (1988). Mathematics teaching and teachers in the year 2000. *Clearing House, 62*(1), 23–25.

Balch, (1991). What is the middle school's new role in teaching cultural literacy? *Middle School Journal, 22*(5), 38–40.

Banks, W. H., Jr. & Smith-Fee, C. (1989). Middle school PE—assertiveness training. *Journal of Physical Education, Recreation and Dance, 60*(7), 90–93.

Batesky, J. (1991). Middle school physical education curriculum: Exposure of indepth instruction? *Middle School Journal, 22*(3), 7–11.

Becker, H. J. (1990). Curriculum and instruction in middle-grade schools. *Phi Delta Kappan, 71*(6), 450–57.

Bitter, G. G. & Hatfield, M. M. (1991). Here's a math-teaching strategy that's calculated to work. *Executive Educator, 13*(1), 19–21.

Bowers, R. S. (1991). Effective models for middle school science instruction. *Middle School Journal, 22*(4), 4–9.

Fielding, E. N. (1990). Reading in the content areas: The importance of choosing appropriate level texts. *Reading, 24*(3), 179–84.

Friedler, Y. (& others). (1990). Learning scientific reasoning skills in microcomputer-based laboratories. *Journal of Research in Science Teaching, 27*(2), 173–91.

Gehrke, N. J. (1991). Explorations of teachers' development of integrative curriculums. *Journal of Curriculum and Supervision, 6*(2), 107–17.

Glass, J. C., Jr. (1991). Death, loss, and grief: Real concerns to young adolescents. *Middle School Journal, 22*(5), 15–17.

Greeson, L. E. & Williams, R. A. (1986). Social implications of music videos for youth. *Youth and Society, 18,* 177–89.

Haskvitz, A. (1989). Applied social studies: The make a difference program. *Southern Social Studies Quarterly, 15*(2), 20–26.

Haskvitz, A. (1990). Local history and the exemplary award winner: Letting students take charge. *OAH Magazine of History, 4*(3), 7–8.

Heller, P. M. (& others). (1990). Qualitative and numerical reasoning about fractions and rates by seventh- and eighth-grade students. *Journal for Research in Mathematics Education, 21*(5), 388–402.

Hoffman, R. Irene. (1988). Educational technology for elementary and middle schools. *Journal of Educational Technology Systems, 16*(4), 299–314.

Hovland, D. (1990). Middle level activities programs: Helping achieve academic success. *NASSP Bulletin, 74*(530), 15–18.

Krieger, J. (1990). Winds of revolution sweep through science education. *Chemical and Engineering News, 68*(24), 27–43.

Lounsbury, J. H. (1988). Middle level social studies: Points to ponder. *Social Education, 52*(2), 116–18.

McWhirter, A. M. (1990). Whole language in the middle school. *Reading Teacher, 43*(8), 562–65.

Peters, R. (1990). Assessing student/teacher performance and program impact on middle school curriculum. *Social Studies, 80*(4), 142–46.

Peters, R. (1990). Enhancing the global perspective of middle school students. *Southern Social Studies Quarterly, 15*(2), 35–56.

Posamentier, A. S. (1990). Geometry: A remedy for the malaise of middle school mathematics. *Mathematics Teacher, 82*(9), 678–80.

Powell, J. C. (1991). Science education: A first step in finding *the* middle school curriculum. *Middle School Journal, 22*(4), 17–22.

Roffman, D. M. (1991). AIDS education: Whose need are we meeting anyway? *Middle School Journal, 23*(1), 9–12.

Rubin, A. & Bruce, B. (1989). Alternate realizations of purpose in computer-supported writing. *Theory into Practice, 29*(4), 256–63.

Savage, R. J. (1991). A principal's perspective on social studies in the middle level school. *NASSP Bulletin, 75*(531), 53–60.

Saveland, R. (1987). A better curriculum in social studies for the middle school. *Curriculum Review, 27*(2), 16–17.

Seiter, D. M. (1988). Social studies in the middle schools. *Social Education, 52*(2), 132, 134.

Silva, C. M. & Moses, R. P. (1991). The algebra project: Making middle school mathematics count. *Journal of Negro Education, 59*(3), 375–91.

Sinatra, R. (& others). (1990). Combining visual literacy, text understanding, and writing for culturally diverse students. *Journal of Reading, 33*(8), 612–17.

Smiddie, L. (1990). Geography resources for middle school and high school teachers. *Southern Social Studies Quarterly, 15*(2), 72–80.

Talsma, G. & Hersberger, J. (1990). Star experimental geometry: Working with mathematically gifted middle school students. *Mathematics Teacher, 83*(5), 351–57.

Vancleave, J. P. (1989). Biology for every kid: 101 easy experiments that really work. *Science Activities, 26*(4), 29–37.

Vlahakis, R. (1988). The computer-infused social studies classroom. *Classroom Computer Learning, 9*(3), 58–61.

Winkler, P. (1991). Socializing the middle school science curriculum. *Middle School Journal, 22*(4), 14–16.

Zaslavsky, C. (1991). Multicultural mathematics education for the middle grades. *Arithmetic Teacher, 38*(6), 8–13.

C. ERIC

Anderson, B. T. (& others). (1989, February). *Science interests of urban seventh graders.* Paper presented at the Annual Meeting of the Eastern Educational Research Association, Savannah, GA. (ERIC Document Reproduction Service No. ED 304 314)

Berkheimer, G. D. (& others). (1990). *Using a new model of curriculum development to write a matter and molecules teaching unit* (Research Series No. 196). East Lansing, MI: Michigan State University, Inst. for Research on Teaching. (ERIC Document Reproduction Service No. ED 324 196)

Brunkhorst, B. J. (1988, April). *Student outcomes and teacher characteristics in exemplary middle and junior high science programs.* Paper presented at the Annual

Meeting of the National Association for Research in Science Teaching, Lake of the Ozarks, MO. (ERIC Document Reproduction Service No. ED 292 647)

Hodge, R. L. (1990, April). *Middle school citizenship education: a study of civic values via R. Freeman Butts' Decalogue.* Paper presented at the Annual Conference of the American Educational Research Association, Boston, MA. (ERIC Document Reproduction Service No. ED 320 837)

Johns, J. & Davis, S. J. (1990). *Integrating literature into middle school reading classrooms.* Bloomington, IN: ERIC Clearinghouse on Reading and Communication Skills. ERIC Digest. (ERIC Document Reproduction Service No. ED 316 853)

Lake, S. (1989). *Exploratory and elective courses in the middle level school* (Practitioner's Monograph #8). Sacramento, CA: California League of Middle Schools. (ERIC Document Reproduction Service No. ED 316 914)

North Carolina State Dept. of Public Instruction, Raleigh. (1987). *Preventing AIDS. Health Education Curriculum Supplement for Middle Level Schools.* Raleigh, NC: North Carolina State Dept. of Public Instruction. (ERIC Document Reproduction Service No. ED 291 702)

Podany, Z. (1990). *Software for middle school physical science.* Portland, OR: Northwest Regional Educational Lab. (ERIC Document Reproduction Service No. ED 328 444)

Smith, V. F. (& others). (1990, February). *Teaching the science in science fiction.* Paper presented at the Annual Meeting of the American Association for the Advancement of Science, New Orleans, LA. (ERIC Document Reproduction Service No. ED 328 456)

D. Dissertations and Dissertation Abstracts

Bishop, Wilma Jean, "A Study to Determine Alternative Approaches for Administering a Curriculum for Adolescents, Ages 12–14," *Dissertation Abstracts,* 39 (October 1978) 2116–A.

Cavanagh, Darol M., "A Curriculum Design Deduced from a Model of the Middle School Child," *Dissertation Abstracts,* 36 (August 1975) 679–A.

Lonsdale, Helen Coulter, "The Implications of Jean Piaget's Theory of Cognitive Development Stages for Middle/Junior High School Career Education Curriculum," *Dissertation Abstracts,* 37 (May 1977) 6928–A.

Ritz, John Michael, "Unified Arts: An Integrative Approach to Curriculum Design for the Art, Home Economics, and Industrial Arts Subject Areas in the Middle Grades," *Dissertation Abstracts,* 38 (October 1977) 1863–A.

Smith, Robert Pleas, Jr., "A Case Study in Middle School Staff and Curriculum Development and its Impact on Student Attitudes and Achievement," *Dissertation Abstracts,* 37 (April 1977) 6203–A .

Youngberg, Robert Stanley, "Perceptions of Parents' Role in Curriculum Development at the Middle and Junior High School Level," *Dissertation Abstracts,* 36 (September 1975) 1286–A.

Cox, C. A. (1989). Three studies on the effect of specially designed science courses incorporating guided inquiry, predominantly earth science activities on the affective characteristics and cognitive gains of elementary, middle school, and junior high school inservice. (Doctoral dissertation, University of South Carolina, 1989). *Dissertation Abstracts International,* 51/02a, 471.

Gunn, C. L. (1989). A health education program to impact attitudes toward body changes and development of early adolescents in grade six (Doctoral dissertation, University of Pittsburgh, 1989). *Dissertation Abstracts International*, 50/06a, 1563.

Hookstra, G. M. (1989). Middle school social studies: an examination of textbook structure, classroom interaction, and student achievement (Doctoral dissertation, Oregon State University, 1989). *Dissertation Abstracts International*, 51/05a, 1561.

Isenberg, L. E. (1988). Reconceptualizing history for schoolchildren: a computer-mediated simulation for introducing planning into the social studies curriculum (Doctoral dissertation, The University of Michigan, 1988). *Dissertation Abstracts International*, 49/08a, 2170.

Kim, H. (1989). Microcomputer-based laboratories and learning: an ethnographic study of a science classroom in an urban middle school (Doctoral dissertation, Harvard University, 1989). *Dissertation Abstracts International*, 50/08a, 2463.

Lee, O. (1989). Motivation to learn science in middle school (Doctoral dissertation, Michigan State University, 1989). *Dissertation Abstracts International*, 50/12a, 3898.

Lee, S. A. (1989). Middle school social studies textbooks in Michigan: a description of cultural and global perspectives (Doctoral dissertation, Michigan State University, 1989). *Dissertation Abstracts International*, 51/03a, 729.

White, R. M. (1989). Middle school students' perceptions toward social studies content and methodology in schools in Kentucky and Tennessee (Doctoral dissertation, Peabody College for Teachers of Vanderbilt University, 1989). *Dissertation Abstracts International*, 51/02a, 474.

Yaronczyk, A. F. (1989). An experimental study of writing collaboration at a middle school: its effects on overall writing quality, performance, apprehension, concepts and attitudes (Doctoral dissertation, Indiana University of Pennsylvania, 1989). *Dissertation Abstracts International*, 50/07a, 1931.

4

Instruction

In exemplary middle schools effective instruction is the primary goal. The design of the building, and the shape of the master schedule, even the organization of teachers and the school-wide decisions about the grouping of students; all are prerequisites for the delivery of effective instruction. Even instruction's pedagogical partner, curriculum, is, in a sense, dependent upon instruction for its effective implementation. All of this heightens the significance that should be attached to the design and conduct of instruction in middle schools. The behavior of teachers, as they plan and implement their instruction, is at once both the most obvious and the most difficult aspect of middle school education.

Characteristics of Effective Instruction in the Middle School

Teaching, at any level, can be thought of as a chain of decision making. A host of decisions are involved: decisions about who will be taught, about the curriculum to be implemented, about the instructional style to be employed. At the middle school level, educators have felt a commitment to several principles guiding the decisions about teaching. Instruction in the middle school, most educators agree, focuses on helping pupils understand themselves as unique individuals with special needs and important responsibilities. Instruction attempts to guarantee every pupil some degree of success in understanding the underlying principles and the ways of knowing in the academic disciplines. Certainly, instruction aims to promote maximum individual growth in the basic learning skills, while at the same time it permits the widest possible exploration of the world of knowledge and of the personal interests of each student. Finally, effective instruction fosters the ability to work and learn independently and cooperatively on the part of every pupil. Decisions about instruction in the exemplary middle school are strongly influenced by these commitments.

In addition to the principles that form the basis for our decision-making about instruction in the middle, there are a number of other factors that affect teaching. Research on teacher behavior and student learning styles should affect instruction. Many states have special learning objectives that elicit particular emphases in teaching, and the federal government has a steadily increasing number of guidelines and restrictions that require certain practices. The state of the art in educational technology both extends and limits what teachers may attempt. The structure of knowledge imposes its own demands, as does teachers' understanding of the process of learning and their preferences for one or another of the current explanations of the process. Long before teachers begin to instruct their pupils, many influences have been felt in the design of that instruction.

No influence is likely to be more significant than the middle school teachers themselves. The literature of middle school education is replete with references to the special characteristics desirable in persons electing to teach middle school youngsters. List after list of special talents has been drawn up, with more recent versions the result of careful research (e.g., Buckner & Brickel, 1990). Yet we believe that the qualities that distinguish a good middle school teacher from a good elementary teacher or high school teacher are probably quite limited, albeit critically important. We believe that effective middle school instruction is implemented by teachers who have the flexibility of the generalist, the expertise of the specialist and the enthusiasm of one who understands and enjoys the special nature of the middle school student.

Perhaps the most important characteristic of effective instruction at the middle school level is that it, too, carries the obligation to be both different from instruction at the elementary and high school levels, but also to bridge the gap between the two. In the elementary school, effective instructional practices are often much more likely to be teacher-directed, whereas the high school has the burden of assisting students to become self-directed and responsible for their own learning to a far greater extent than students are capable of in the elementary school. Not that student-directed instruction is impossible or unadvisable in the elementary school, but it is accurate to describe most young children as in need of a tremendous amount of teacher direction in their learning in school. It would also be foolish to claim that the average high school student is capable of sustained and satisfactory patterns of totally independent learning for prolonged periods of time. Certainly older students need guidance and direction of varying amounts throughout their latter school years, but the amount of student responsibility for their own learning should increase as each year in the public school passes.

If the emphasis of instruction in the elementary school is on a teacher-directed introduction to the world of the school and to the process of learning, and the stress at the high school level focuses on developing increasing increments of student responsibility, the middle school's obligation is to weave together these two divergent threads so that students may move from following one to pursuing the other without loss of educational momentum. Middle school teachers strive to accept students who are comfortable with almost total dependence upon the teacher for every learning experience. They act to help these students move to the place where they can survive in an academic environment much less tolerant of the personal idiosyncrasies of each learner. At the same time, the pattern of instruction in the middle school aspires to be sufficient to help students reach success in mastering the learning tasks that the curriculum of the middle grades imposes upon the learner.

The instructional strategies of the middle school are, therefore, a combination of structure, balance, and flexibility: structure, to provide the teacher directed efforts without which the basic skills of the middle school student would remain largely unextended; balance, to offer the opportunities which will teach students the skills necessary for learning on their own and the attitudes that support such learning; flexibility, to permit teachers to know when a particular instructional strategy is appropriate and when it is not, and the disposition to make the changes in style when it is necessary for the students' benefit to do so. Instruction in the middle school emanates from the purposes of the school.

Teaching methods mirror the functions of the total institution, with care needed to relate to knowledge of the characteristics of the students served. Teachers must be prepared to teach a variety of different kinds of students with a wide range of learning skills and styles. The faculty must accept the challenge to become proficient with an array of methods and techniques, choosing one or another in relation to the purposes that motivate their actions.

Middle school educators must never be committed to any one particular instructional strategy to the exclusion of any other. The literature of middle school education from the decade of the '70s seemed to argue that individualized instruction was the only approved method. The same literature, from the 1980s, argued in favor of teacher-directed, large group instruction, and individualized instruction fell from its favored position. Some might argue that cooperative learning has assumed the favored spot for the '90s. We are, however, convinced that the elevation of one particular strategy over all others is a dangerous and unproductive step to take.

Because middle school educators believe strongly in the special nature of the students they serve, it seems that the enthusiasm resulting from this commitment may have caused an overemphasis on the use of individualized instruction in middle schools in the '70s. While individualized instruction is certainly one of the most important instructional strategies to be employed in middle schools, it is just as certainly not the only such strategy to be used. Middle school and individualized instruction are not synonymous. Exactly the same thing can and must be said for direct instruction, or cooperative learning, or any other special methodology and the middle school. The tremendous effect of the research on teacher effectiveness felt in all public schools during the '80s probably brought a predictable over-reliance on teacher-directed large group instruction. Perhaps cooperative learning will experience the same fate.

The question is not, "What is the best way to teach middle school students?" It is now quite clear, from the evidence of both research and practice, that there is no one right way to teach all middle school students all the time, just like there is no one right way to organize students and teachers on interdisciplinary teams. The instructional methods chosen depend upon the objectives of instruction, the nature of the particular group of students being taught, even the grade level involved. The right question to ask about instruction in the middle school is likely to be, "What is the right method to use for these objectives with this particular group of students?"

Whatever the method may be, there are a number of perennially important factors to be considered in the selection of an instructional approach. Most important is the assurance that the method chosen does not conflict with knowledge of the characteristics and needs of the students in the middle school, and of the particular needs of students in any one school and classroom. Equally significant, however, is the requirement that the blend of instructional strategies finally designed be consistent with the obligation of the middle school to strike a balance, pedagogically, between the elementary school and the high school. In addition, the selection of teaching methods involves criteria such as: clarity of the learning task in the eyes of the learner when using a particular method; motivational power of the method; provision of immediate feedback of a method; opportunities for continuous progress provided; avoidance of excessive frustration and failure; likelihood of transfer of learning to other situations outside the classroom; and the ability to develop and preserve positive attitudes toward self, teacher, subject matter, and school in general.

A consideration of teaching methodology appropriate for middle schools might also include several other factors. First, the particular teaching method must match the instructional skill of the teacher intending to use it. Some methods are considerably more difficult to conduct effectively than others, and the expectation that all teachers will be able to use a method with equal effectiveness is bound to meet with disappointment. Second, the method chosen must not demand more of a teacher's energy than is reasonable. The phenomenon of teacher stress and burnout are too well known to ignore. Teachers in the middle school often seem, by the very nature of their tasks, to be frequently subject to considerably more stress and exhaustion than are teachers at other levels. Methods which demand even more energy and time are likely to be successfully implemented in a very few situations and for very brief periods of time. Third, methods that require a great deal of staff development time to learn will have a low priority, simply because there is so much competition for inservice education funds and, unfortunately, staff development is rarely as successful as educators would prefer. Finally, methods which, while they may be effective in producing achievement gains, conflict with the basic values and philosophy of the school and community must be examined closely prior to extensive implementation.

In Orange County, Florida, where many exemplary practices in middle school education are implemented, educators have also attempted to break new ground in specifying the sort of instruction they wish to encourage in the middle school classrooms there. A "Middle School Instructional Practices Scale" has been developed and piloted by several members of the supervisory staff (Thomas, Pickler, & Sevick, 1990). The scale includes fourteen conceptual areas based on research on teacher effectiveness over the last two decades. In each of the fourteen areas, a "From" statement represents a less desirable practice, and a "To" statement describes the ideal level of practice in that area. Then, again in each of the fourteen conceptual areas, the developers of the instrument supply concrete descriptors (not included in our description below) that will enable observes to determine the level on which the concept is practiced in a particular teacher's class or on a particular interdisciplinary team of teachers. Here are several examples of the conceptual areas:

INTRODUCTION OF FORMAL ACADEMIC DISCIPLINES AT THE APPROPRIATE LEVEL

FROM: Subject content is taught without regard to the developmental level of middle school students.

TO: Subject content is presented at a pace and degree of complexity that reflects an awareness of middle school students' developmental characteristics and needs.

PRACTICAL APPLICATION/CURRICULUM RELEVANCE

FROM: Limited opportunities are provided for students to apply skills or concepts learned in a lesson.

TO: Frequent opportunities are provided for students to apply skills and concepts to real-world situations and individual or class interests.

CONTEMPORARY INSTRUCTIONAL PRACTICES

FROM: Instructional planning and delivery consistently reflect the use of methods that are associated with the learning model of the past (single approach, passive learning, overuse of lecture, textbook driven, etc.).

TO: Instructional planning and delivery reflect the utilization of methods that are consistent with recent research on effective instruction and current district staff development efforts.

GROUPING PRACTICES (WITHIN THE TEAM)

FROM: Within the team, students are grouped according to similar ability levels at the beginning of the year, and the groups remain the same.

TO: Within the team, students are grouped and regrouped, for a variety of reasons, for varying lengths of time, and in both homogeneous and heterogeneous patterns depending on student needs and instructional goals.

Selecting instructional strategies for use in middle schools is, regardless of recent progress in districts like Orange County, not a simple or easy process. Many factors must be considered. But there are a number of methods which research and experience recommend for use with the students served by the middle school. The remainder of this chapter is a consideration of these methods, the uses they serve and the situations where they are and are not appropriate. For simplicity, the methods to be discussed are categorized in terms of the number of students usually served and the number of teachers involved in the planning of instruction.

Total Class Instruction

Research on Teacher Behavior

Teacher behavior does make a difference; but not single, discrete, separate teaching acts. What does seem to make a difference in student achievement are the teacher behaviors that tend to group together into patterns or clusters. These clusters of teacher behavior appear to be responsible for differences in learning among students exposed to different patterns. Several clusters seem consistently related to increased achievement on standardized tests: patterns of teacher expectations and role definitions; classroom management; and what might be called the direct instruction process.

In the past twenty years, research on teacher behavior has contributed mightily to our understanding of the relationship between how teachers act and the academic achievement of their students. Where for years it was not, now it is very clear that teachers do make a difference in the academic achievement of their students. What teachers do makes a difference in what learners do, and what students do in the classroom makes a difference in their learning. Research has helped us to see that it is not only the socioeconomic characteristics of the students in a school that determines the achievement within the building. In any given school, academic achievement will vary from one class to another, based, in part, on the teaching behavior exhibited in those classes (Brophy & Good, 1986).

There are some limitations in the application of the results of the research to the middle school. The research on teacher-directed instruction can, for example, be most confidently cited when dealing with basic skills, and when working in these skill areas with students who might be described as less successful, less motivated or of lower ability. Beyond these considerations, the age of the students also seems to be significant. It is also important to recall that much of the research focused on teacher behaviors that were readily measurable by low inference measures, and that perhaps much of teaching that is subtle and artistic, and therefore, difficult to observe and record, is not included in the results. Teaching is a terribly complex act, and when the object of the instruction happens to be middle school students, the difficulties and complexities seem even more important. With all of these limitations in mind, however, there do seem to be some important recommendations that can be made to teachers who have the task of teaching middle schoolers.

Total class instruction has always been, and may always be, a mainstay of middle school teaching. It remains particularly appropriate when the focus is academic achievement, in the basic skills, with less than completely successful students. It is the methodology of choice, we think, when teachers have few opportunities for effective staff development which will prepare them for more complex forms of small group and individualized instruction.

For teachers and administrators interested in raising standardized test scores in basic skills, it seems somewhat certain that teacher-directed total class instruction of a fairly traditional nature is often superior to either discovery approaches, traditional small group teaching, or individualized instruction as it is often practiced in middle schools of the '90s. In 1979, Jere Brophy summarized the effective process of total class, teacher-directed instruction; research in the '80s and '90s adds little to his conclusions at that time:

> The instruction that seems most efficient involves the teacher working with the whole class (or small groups in the early grades), presenting information in lectures/demonstrations and then following up with recitations or practice exercises in which the students get opportunities to make responses and get corrective feed back. The teacher maintains an academic focus, keeping the students involved in a lesson or engaged in seatwork, monitoring their performance, and providing individualized feedback. The pace is rapid in the sense that the class moves efficiently through the curriculum as a whole (and through the successive objectives of any given lesson), but progress from one objective to the next involves very small, easy steps. Success rates in answering teacher questions during lessons are high (about 75 percent), and success rates on assignments designed to be done independently are very high (approaching 100 percent). (Brophy, 1979, p. 34)

Classroom Management and Total Class Instruction

Teachers who are able to produce increased amounts of on-task behavior without increasing the amount of time devoted to discipline or the level of negative teacher affect are teachers who help students score higher on tests of basic skills than the students would be likely to do with some other type of teacher behavior. Apparently, this objective is easier to achieve with large group instruction than with most other forms of instruction. Task oriented but relaxed classrooms (and both aspects are equally important) are places where increased achievement is found. Large group instruction is more likely to display this binary characteristic.

Time spent on task is of the essence in increasing academic achievement, and classroom discipline efforts detract from this time. Teachers who find themselves taking significant amounts of time dealing with deviant and disruptive behavior are likely to have less time to devote to the skills to be tested. Classrooms where a great deal of pupil freedom of movement exists are classrooms where learning of basic skills is less. Socialization of pupils with each other, and of the teacher with the pupils, is also negatively correlated with pupil growth in the basic skills. Actually, within reasonable limits, the less physical movement and off-task talk the better (McDonald, 1976).

Tight control of the classroom and negative affect are not the same thing. In fact, positive affect and negative affect are not opposite ends of the same continuum of affect. That is, the elimination of negative teacher affect from the classroom does not always, or even often, mean that the more positive a teacher is, the more learning that will occur. There are, actually, many occasions when positive affect on the part of the teacher is either unrelated to increased achievement or negatively correlated such that the presence of positive affect actually produces less achievement. The use of praise is not uniformly helpful, so that when it is used it must be used very specifically and with individuals. It seems, according to the research, that classrooms with a neutral atmosphere, where neither positive nor negative affect abound, are likely to be classrooms where students spend more uninterrupted time at the tasks of learning set before them (R. Soar & D. Medley, personal communication, May, 1979).

Establishing a classroom where tasks are taken seriously by both the teacher and the students, and where time is a precious commodity is important to achievement in the basic skills. How the teacher manages the time of pupils over which he or she has control is as important as establishing a classroom where negative affect is at a minimum. Since learning is a process that takes place in time, and what a student does is essential to his learning, influencing how pupils use their time becomes a critical variable. Research has indicated a number of factors associated with uses of time in the classroom and the connection with achievement in the basic skills.

Teachers concerned with managing their classrooms to maximize the effective use of time need to know several things. A number of studies, for example, indicate that what students learn is directly related to the uses to which they put their time. That is, simply, the more time devoted to the study of a subject, the better the subject is learned. If basic skills have a priority, then more time in the school day needs to be devoted to those topics. Apparently, research does not seem to indicate that there is a point of diminishing returns; there is no apparent limit to increasing the time devoted to learning tasks. When breaks and wasted time are decreased, learning goes up. Increasing breaks will not raise productive behavior or achievement (Borg, 1979).

Although balance with other activities is important, there does seem to be quite strong research support for spending substantial amounts of student learning time in large groups in face-to-face contact with the teacher. When using a large group instructional strategy, it might be effective to devote up to two-thirds of the hour to large group teacher-directed instruction. The remaining one third of the time could then be spent in closely supervised and monitored seatwork that is directly related to the preceding large group instruction. Seatwork that is not closely monitored by the teacher actively moving around the room is negatively correlated to achievement. It is very clear that students spend more time on task when working directly with the teacher (84 percent) than when working alone in seatwork (70 percent) (Rosenshine & Stevens,1986).

Total Class Instruction: Steps in the Process

Assuming that large group teacher-directed instruction does often generate greater degrees of student on-task behavior with less need for negative teacher affect, the question remains as to what specific form this large group instruction should take. Here again, research has some important statements to make. When it comes to teaching the basic skills, in particular, there are some very definite steps to take. Rosenshine, referring to the recommended process, calls it "direct instruction" (Rosenshine & Stevens, 1986).

Direct instruction, by whatever name, may be thought of as containing a series of specific steps, beginning with the assumption of personal responsibility for student learning by the teacher. That is, teachers who feel personally responsible for whether or not their students achieve the objectives set for them, are, not surprisingly, more effective in producing higher levels of student achievement. Teachers who believe that it is up to the students to learn and that the teacher has no role or duty to motivate, inspire, or promote students' learning are less likely to act in ways that produce it. The power of teacher expectations is manifested very clearly in teaching through the direct instruction process.

The second step in effective large group instruction, following the assumption of personal responsibility by the teacher, involves a series of decisions, all made primarily by the teacher. It is the teacher, not the students, who decides what curriculum goals and objectives should be pursued. It is also the teacher who decides the materials to be used, the settings in which instruction occurs, and the time to be devoted to the process. It is the teacher who assumes the primary role in planning instruction, and students do little or no such planning.

The teacher makes a considerable effort to focus the time of both teacher and students on academic goals. Distractions, pleasant or otherwise, which draw the class away from the academic objectives at hand are discouraged. Socializing is diminished. All persons involved realize that their job is to pursue the academic objectives which have been set for them. There is no other choice.

With this mindset, the teacher then sets about to promote, through an actively directive teacher presentation, extensive coverage of the objectives that have been selected. When the teacher has arranged the class effectively, students will often be sitting with their backs to the rest of the class, while the teacher is facing the class. Having done so, the teacher begins with an overview of the lesson that ties it to previous work and which provides advance organizers to prepare the students for the skills work to come. In doing so, the teacher concentrates on the whole class, rather than a small group. Some researchers even go so far as to specify that this review and orientation should last about eight minutes. Following the introduction, the teacher should collect and check the homework, if there has been any assigned (Brophy & Good, 1986).

After the review and the checking of homework, the teacher continues the total class instruction with about a twenty-minute presentation that develops the new concepts or skills. Again, this process is highly teacher-directed, with a minimum of opportunities for student input or questions. As a part of this lesson, however, the teacher should eventually begin to ask questions and solicit student responses on the concepts or skills that have been introduced. Such questions should be of a low cognitive level, simple enough to result in a very high success rate.

The question and answer session toward the end of the lesson is very important, and the research speaks very clearly about it. Most of the questioning should be done by the teacher, and most of the answering should be done by the students. Avoiding extensive student questions and extended answers and amplifications of student questions by the teacher seem to be practices well supported by the research data. There are other surprises, though, for teachers who have been told that teacher-directed instruction is detrimental, including support for using a predictable pattern when calling on students during the re citation portion of the lesson. Random and unpredictable questioning may be counterproductive, while the structure and stability of the pattern process appears to support the anxious student. It seems important, too, when questioning, to wait at least three seconds for the student to answer (the average teacher waits one second), before interrupting with a new question or calling on a new student. It is also important to see that other students wait to be called upon, and when they do not, to remind them that everyone will get a turn and that they must wait for theirs. Focus on one student at a time, but set up the questioning session so that everyone in the class has had a chance to answer a question. Praise correct answers only, and accept questions in the form that they are asked.

The lesson, question and answer session included, should be followed by a shorter period (for example, fifteen minutes) of closely monitored seatwork. Such seatwork should be highly correlated to the lesson and should, ideally, lead to uninterrupted successful practice.

Effective total class instruction requires that the teacher set the pace at which students work, both during the lesson and while at work at their seats. Students should be held accountable for their seatwork by a teacher who spends the time during seat work walking from student to student, checking work, delivering brief praise quietly to specific individuals. Under appropriate circumstances, and with great care, homework should be assigned, homework which should take little more than fifteen minutes, but which will be collected and checked regularly. The final step is to conduct weekly and monthly reviews of the concepts and skills which are being taught.

Important Modifications

It is terribly important to stress that the same type of instruction, no matter what style or for what purposes, can not be applied equally to all types of students. Total class instruction must also be modified and adapted to take into consideration the types of students with whom one is working. The particular strategy we have been discussing, using a directive total class instructional process, seems especially appropriate when teaching the basic skills, and when teaching students who might be described as less successful, with lower academic motivation, more dependent, and anxious. Some researchers point out that these characteristics often appear with greater frequency in populations of school children from lower socioeconomic groups. Students with what has been called an external locus of control also seem to profit from the direct total class instruction (Brophy & Good, 1986).

When using total class instruction with these students, the general recommendation seems to be to follow the direct instruction model to the letter, but with some important emphases. Students who are less successful need a slower pace, with more drill and repetition, and more overlearning in small pieces. More individual monitoring is important, as is more teacher warmth, encouragement, and personalized teaching in general. Students who are anxious and dependent need less challenge, but not less than they are able to handle. They do require lower levels of criticism and of demands, and they need to know that help is always available.

Less successful students need to be gently prodded into making actual responses each time they are asked a question, but with less rigorous probing, and a greater stress on facts and on thinking operations at the lower end of the taxonomy. The oft-repeated statement that factual questions are bad and higher level questions are good is not borne out by the research on academic achievement, as far as these students are concerned. More success with lower level questions, more repetition, and more structured help of all kinds are called for (Rosenshine & Stevens, 1986).

It is also important, when working with less successful students, to be aware of teacher expectations which subtly lead to teacher behaviors associated with lower achievement in students. Teachers who expect lower ability students to learn give adequate amounts of feedback, provide equal amounts of individual attention, and are as patient with the slower students as with the higher ability pupils. It is comforting to know that such expectations are not consciously formed and that teachers, when notified of such behaviors, change immediately (Gage, 1979).

Using total class instruction with students at the other end of the continuum, those with high ability and a high record of achievement, with an internal locus of control and so forth, requires a different emphasis. Such students should be asked more difficult questions, with more rigorous probing and redirection. Incorrect answers from these pupils should be corrected. More homework should be assigned to these students, or homework of a more detailed and demanding nature. It is also possible to admit more student initiation of teacher-student interaction, and to be more flexible in response to student input generally. Less structure imposed by the teacher, and more student designed activity is desirable with higher ability, less dependent children (Walberg, 1986).

Teachers using the total class instruction model must also be prepared to modify the process further, depending upon the age or grade level of the students they teach. Generally, middle school teachers can rely on the use of more large group and whole class instruction, and less small group work, than teachers in the primary grades. Older middle school students should be able to handle more extended discussion, with slightly less drill and repetition. More cognitive challenge and higher level cognitive activity should be encouraged, along with more sustained concentration on academic activities. A more rapid pace than would be comfortable for younger students, and less individual feedback are both possible at the middle school level. Less positive affect and praise are necessary, but not to the point of having a higher level of negative affect and criticism.

In the primary grades, and in most of the middle school grades, when basic skills are the focus, and especially where the students are less successful or less academically motivated, total class instruction works well. As students mature, become more successful, and the curriculum includes more and more objectives that are beyond the basic skills, the emphasis on the use of total class instruction should lessen and the search for alternatives that permit more flexibility and more student direction of the learning process should be increased.

Brophy points out that the findings concerning the process of direct instruction do generalize to students at the middle school level, but that the most important qualification is that basic skills must be the primary goal. The instructional objective pursued seems to be the guiding factor when deciding what instructional strategy to pursue. When the focus is on basic skills in reading and math, in particular, teachers should consider the total class model. When creativity, problem solving, complex thinking, appreciation, or social and emotional education are the goals, the total class instruction process may not be the best method. It may even be that the direct instruction process is inimical to student growth in some areas other than basic skills, especially if students are older or more academically successful. Total class instruction may be inconsistent with the goals of social studies, humanities, the arts, and other essentially less cognitive and less factual areas. It may be less effective than alternatives when heterogeneous grouping is important.

Why does the total class instruction work better than individualized instruction or discovery modes, when teaching basic skills, especially to less successful students? Because using this method, under these circumstances, makes it possible to encourage higher levels of student on-task behavior with lower levels of negative teacher affect. The traditional whole class method seems easier to plan and easier to manage, leaving more time and energy for the teacher to focus on the tasks and objectives at hand. The structure provided by total class instruction apparently helps the anxious, dependent, distractible students to stay on task, and it is easier to establish standards and hold students accountable for the accomplishment of those standards. Total class instruction provides large amounts of teacher contact, and middle school students, who often measure the significance of tasks they are asked to complete by the amount of attention the teacher pays to them as they work on it, place greater significance on teacher-directed learning tasks than on those that primarily involve materials without teacher intervention. Total class instruction takes less time in changing activities, requires the training and use of fewer additional adults in the classroom, and, consequently, provides more time for instruction and less time for directions and transitions. There is more modeling and less of the elitism and labeling that sometimes occurs in rigid ability grouping within a class.

Total class instruction permits teachers to take an active role, one which allows them to, as one teacher told us, "really teach." The goals of instruction seem reachable with this process, as it does not require magical talents or hidden energy reserves to implement and continue. It is realistic and practical, and it inspires confidence in teachers which they pass on to their students. It develops a sense of community. It works.

But, as we have pointed out in the discussion above, it does not work for all objectives with all students at all grade levels. When the objectives go beyond the basic skills, or when teachers are dealing with students who possess a great deal of self-discipline and personal responsibility, there are other instructional strategies that may be preferable. Some of these strategies are effective because they build upon the characteristics of the students with whom middle school teachers work, and these same methods may be preferred because they provide a setting in which social and emotional education may occur along with the academic objectives. Under these circumstances, methods that forsake the large group teacher-directed process become more desirable.

Small Group Instruction

Small group instruction, in the discussion which follows, refers to situations in which the teacher arranges the class in groups significantly smaller than the entire class, excluding individualized instruction. The teacher, in these situations, often acts more as organizer and facilitator than direct instructor. The distinguishing characteristic of small group instruction, in our opinion, is that in this mode students often work together, rather than attending solely to the teacher or working entirely alone. In both peer teaching and group or team learning, the emphasis is on cooperative experience.

Peer Teaching

Middle school teachers are frequently aware of the need for their students to improve the skills and attitudes that they possess in working cooperatively with their peers. As in so many other ways, often the best process for attacking these attitudes and skills, with middle school students, is to do so indirectly. Peer and cross-age tutoring is one quite good method to teach both academic content and social attitudes and skills.

Respected educators have, historically, articulated the need for using more peer teaching. Nearly three decades ago, Hilda Taba wrote that the greatest untapped source of learning is in the efficient use of group relations in the classroom, and ten years later Urie Bronfenbrenner urged teachers to design two-pupil teams composed of students of differing abilities so that the students could become involved in responsible tasks on behalf of others within the classroom. (Taba, 1963; Bronfenbrenner, 1973). In a recent review of the research, Walberg (1990) confirmed the effectiveness of tutoring on the tutor and the tutee.

Wagner (1978), surveying the literature of peer teaching, identified a number of additional advantages to this instructional method, in addition to the improved human relations skills and attitudes:

1. He who teachers others, teaches himself.
2. Self-concepts of students are improved when they teach others.
3. Students who are taught by other students have an opportunity to develop a sense of warmth and recognition as a result of the attention and identification with the other student.
4. A more efficient use of human resources results when students are used to help each other.
5. Individualized instruction is more nearly possible when students are involved in teaching one another.
6. Students are more highly motivated to achieve when involved in tutoring relationships.
7. Pupils like working together.
8. Because it depends on a new kind of interaction, peer tutoring can be a focal point for eliminating some forms of discrimination.
9. Students become more active participants in their own learning.
10. Academic achievement is higher than in some other forms of instruction.

While there are many types of peer and cross-age teaching, the type that most middle school teachers are likely to be able to use involves one middle school student teaching another. Cross-age tutoring, involving the teaching of elementary school students in another school setting, is frequently impractical. That does not mean, however, that cross-age teaching is not possible within the confines of the middle school. Several methods of schoolwide grouping of students provide good settings for cross-age teaching.

Multi-age grouping of some sort, and the school-within-a-school format, seem particularly facilitative of cross-age tutoring. In schools with two, three, or four grade levels represented on one team or in one house, designing a cross-age tutoring program should be quite simple. Where teams are arranged in a school-within-a-school format, students from the higher grade level(s) can teach or tutor those from the lower grade levels. Because teams of different grade levels are located near each other in the school-within-a-school framework, moving from one team area to another is relatively easy. In schools with a conventional grade level team design, cross-age teaching is certainly not impossible, since all that is required, in most cases, is for the teachers on the teams to have the desire to do so. Under these more traditional circumstances, designing a teaching or tutoring situation in which students from the same grade level work in peer teams is just as simple as the teachers on the team wish it to be. Individual teachers who wish to arrange peer teaching situations in their own classrooms often find it relatively easy to do so. The existence of mainstreaming, following PL 94-142, provides particularly exciting opportunities for the use of peer teaching, even with single grade level classrooms.

While there are many possible models to follow when designing a peer tutoring process, it seems likely that this method, like any other, will profit from careful planning. One model known to us offers a well-structured process labeled the "Four T's of Tutoring" (Smith, 1980). Beginning with a recognition that the tutor is as much a focus of the project as the tutee, the model has, as its first step, a testing process that is used to determine the match between tutor and tutee. Tutors may, optimally, be selected so that their instructional level is just slightly higher than those that they tutor, especially in reading skills, but it is absolutely necessary that the tutor's academic level be at least equal to that of the tutee.

The second phase of the peer teaching process, as described here, is the training period. Once the tutors are selected, Smith recommends that some discussion of the characteristics of the learner and the learning situation be conducted. For example, assuming that the tutors are eighth graders and tutees are sixth graders, the discussion could develop from the following questions:

1. How have you changed since you were in the sixth grade?
2. What types of things did you do then that you think are silly now?
3. When you were in the sixth grade, how did you feel about eighth graders?
4. What types of things do you see sixth graders doing that you think are silly? Why do you suppose they do those things? Do you suppose that sixth graders think those things are silly?
5. In what ways do you act differently from sixth graders? Tenth graders?

If the tutors have a better understanding of how younger students behave, the tutoring situation should move more easily (Smith, 1980).

The preparation of the tutor should also include some discussion of effective learning and teaching, since peer teaching works best when the tutor does not exceed the tutee's learning rate, gives positive reinforcement, and helps the tutee be aware of his progress. Smith points out that such discussions do not have to be uninteresting, and that most students would welcome the opportunity to discuss questions related to learning:

1. What happens when your teacher gives you too much work?
2. How do you feel when you are asked to do something that you are almost certain that you can do, but is neither too easy or too difficult?
3. How do you feel when the teacher is uncomplimentary about your work? (Smith, 1980).

It is also important that the tutor be helped to master a simple series of steps in a teaching process. Tutors might, for example, be taught to: give an overview of the lesson, with an appropriate review; present the purpose of the lesson; present new words or terms; work through the lesson, whatever it is; and follow the lesson with a question and answer period. In essence, the tutor is presenting a teacher-directed style, but to a class of one. Instructing the tutor in the steps of a directed teaching activity should not only help the tutor do a better job with his student, but it should also help both students gain a better understanding of the process the teacher follows during those times the class is involved in whole group instruction.

According to Smith's model, just prior to the tutoring session, the teacher should teach the lesson to the tutors in very much the same way that she or he expects the tutors to present the lesson to their students. The worksheets and other materials that the tutors use during this lesson become the answer sheets for the lesson that will be presented to tutees.

The third step in the process is the actual tutoring, which should follow the training session as closely as possible. Smith recommends that the tutoring session last about thirty minutes, and be divided into three parts, approximating the parts of a teacher-directed lesson: presentation, drill or recitation, and practice. In a reading lesson, tutor and tutee might takes turns reading, followed by a worksheet or series of questions about the lesson, ending with an enjoyable application of some kind, such as a game or puzzle.

Smith uses the term "translating" to describe the fourth and final step of the peer teaching process. It is a step that involves the tutor, but it could certainly also involve the tutee. During this phase, essentially an evaluation, the tutor is asked to write answers to questions like these:

1. What skill did you teach today?
2. Describe at least one successful task accomplished by your student.
3. Did your student enjoy the tasks? Please explain.
4. How did you feel about helping your student with his or her work today?
5. Did you find any part of the lesson difficult to teach? Please explain. (Smith, 1980).

A number of benefits to the tutor accrue as a result of this experience. Students who need the skills that they were expected to learn in an earlier grade are usually more receptive to confronting their deficiencies when it is a part of a tutoring process in which they have status and responsibility. In addition, the peer teaching process provides a number of instances of meaningful repetition of skills that the tutor may need to review. Tutors also receive practice using processes of listening, speaking, reading, writing, and spelling as a part of their labors. The tutor is, of course, not the only one who is expected to improve as a result of this process.

Cooperative Learning

Cooperative learning, during the eighties, took the middle school by storm and appears, in the nineties, to be firmly fixed in the repertoire of desirable techniques for the successful middle school teacher. Perhaps because of the social nature of middle school students, perhaps because of the fascination of middle school educators for effective innovation, perhaps because of the demands of increasingly heterogeneous classrooms, middle school educators seem to feel compelled to involve their students in cooperative learning experiences. It may also be that middle school educators respect the solid research base that accompanies the claims of cooperative learning proponents.

Recent research comparing middle level education of the United States with that of Japan may shed light on the popularity of cooperative learning strategies among middle school educators (George, 1989). Many Japanese educators believe that young adolescents are at a unique point of readiness for learning about cooperation and positive group involvement. These Japanese seem convinced that there is, to use a popular phrase, a "window of opportunity" for learning group citizenship, loyalty, duty, cooperation, and so on, which opens during early adolescence and closes shortly thereafter. We tend to agree, and we suspect that the popularity of cooperative learning in middle level schools indicates that many American educators intuitively support these same assumptions about the readiness of our young adolescents to learn about group life.

The attempt to develop small group learning strategies that combine both academic inquiry and learning about the democratic process has led to the use of a number of related but somewhat different methods for use in the middle school classroom. Individual teachers have, of course, for the last two centuries, used group projects and other team learning situations to achieve a variety of objectives. Recently, however, several more clearly defined and researched models of group and team learning have made their appearance in the classroom.

These models of teaching have been most clearly cataloged and described by Joyce, Showers, and Weil (1991). These authors categorize several types of teaching methods into families of models which, in the case of cooperative learning, emphasize the social dimension of learning and teaching. Middle school and junior high school teachers have been using these methods, or portions of the methods, for many years without labeling or describing their uses for others. It is even possible, according to Joyce and his colleagues, to trace the origins of these methods to the theories of John Dewey who, as long ago as 1916, advocated the use of teaching methods that would combine both academic inquiry and democratic learning.

Organizing a class into small groups whose task is to work cooperatively while reacting to, inquiring into the nature of, and attempting to solve social problems that the teacher helps them to select is a method that teachers of older children and early adolescents have used effectively for many years. One of the earliest versions of cooperative learning was developed by Herbert Thelen. Joyce, Showers, and Weil (1991) list six steps in the application of what Thelen called the "group investigation" process:

1. The students in the group are confronted with a stimulating problem that arises naturally or is supplied by the teacher.

2. The students react to the problem and the teacher draws their attention to the diversity of their responses and reactions to the problem.

3. As the students become interested in the differences in their responses to the problem, the teacher helps them formulate a problem statement.

4. Following the formulation of a problem statement, the students organize themselves to attack and resolve the problem.

5. The students pursue the study of the problem and, at the conclusion of their study, report their results to the teacher and the rest of the class.

6. With the assistance of the teacher and the rest of the class, the investigating group evaluates the solution to the problem.

One can see immediately that even in this early version of cooperative learning the teacher plays a much different, decidedly more indirect, role than in the large group, total class instruction process. In all successful versions of cooperative learning, the teacher is careful to ensure that the students examine the process in which they are involved, that they are conscious of the methods they are using, that they are learning interpersonal and social skills involved in effective group work and that they are involved in the examination of personal meaning in the group context.

While there are many versions of cooperative learning, in the past decade, two groups of advocates have moved onto the center stage. David and Roger Johnson (1991), at the University of Minnesota, have achieved considerable recognition among middle school educators, at least in part because their approach to cooperative learning emphasizes education in cooperation itself as an integral part of the process. Robert Slavin and his colleagues at Johns Hopkins University (1988) are highly regarded, perhaps because of their long and careful attention to providing a research base from which to move toward improved practice. Both groups, it seems, have much to offer middle school educators seeking practical implementation of research-supported learning strategies.

The basic conclusion of the Johns Hopkins group, in its study of cooperative learning methods, is that all such methodologies require, for success in enhancing academic learning, two basic conditions. First, there must be a common group goal which requires collaboration in order to be achieved. Second, individuals in the group must be held accountable for their own particular contributions to the group's effort and their own achievement; the teams' success depends on the individual learning of each member. Both components are essential. In a review of research on cooperative learning, Slavin observed that when these two essentials were effectively present in the method used, results were consistently positive, not only in academic achievement, but also in such diverse but desirable outcomes as "self-esteem, intergroup relations, acceptance of academically handicapped students, attitudes toward school, and ability to work cooperatively" (Slavin, 1991a, p. 71). Little wonder, then, that such methods are popular with middle school educators.

The most extensively researched cooperative learning method appears to be the Student Team Learning (STL) process developed at Johns Hopkins. At this point, even STL appears to be taking on the characteristics of a family of methods, since four or five major versions have been developed and studied. Two STL methods are general strategies adaptable to most subjects and grades: Student Teams-Achievement Divisions (STAD), and Teams-Games-Tournaments (TGT). A third general method adapted to the STL format, Jigsaw, was originally developed by Elliot Aronson. The other methods are specifically designed for reading and mathematics programs in the intermediate grades. Slavin observes that STL programs also require, in addition to group goals and individual accountability, a sort of "equal opportunity for success" which bases the evaluation of individual learning on improvement over prior achievement, so that all group members experience an appropriate degree of challenge and are valued for their contribution by other members of the group.

In STL, if not all cooperative learning methods, students work together in groups of three, four, or five. Sometimes the students respond to a lesson presented by the teacher by making certain that all group members have mastered the lesson prior to a quiz during which group members may not help each other. In Jigsaw, students divide up the work of their group, then move off individually to work on their separate components of the group task by connecting up with members of other teams who have the same special task on which they must become expert. These "experts" then return to their base teams and teach what they have learned to the other members of their group, receiving instruction, in turn, from all of the other individual members. At the end of the process, all of the groups members have been taught what they need to know by all of the other members of the group. Students may then take quizzes or, as in social studies, present a report to the class or the teacher (Slavin, 1991a).

In other methods, somewhat complicated tournaments replace the quizzes. In Teams-Games-Tournaments (TGT), students are assigned to learning teams of four or five members. After the teacher presents the lesson, the teams study together, trying to make sure that every team member understands the lesson, since the success of the team depends upon each member functioning effectively in the slot he is assigned. At the end of a period of time (for example, a week), the teams engage in a tournament with other teams in the class. Each team member competes with students from other teams on a more or less ability-grouped basis. At the end of the tournament, winners from each competition level move up to the next highest position, competing there with those whose scores on the last set of games classifies them as on the same level. It is the spirit of competition that changes rote memorization from a dead and deadly affair into one of challenge and enthusiasm. Under these circumstances, it is also competition that begets, ironically, higher levels of cooperation.

According to one teacher known to us, the equal competition made it possible for every student to have a good chance of contributing equally to the success of the team; an example of Slavin's "equal opportunity for success." A weekly class newsletter prepared by the teacher recognized successful teams and students who contributed effectively to their teams' success. The dynamics of the process combined to produce a classroom where the objectives of small group instructional processes were quite effectively realized. For example, Geoffrey Pyne, former mathematics teacher at Mebane Middle School (Alachua, Florida) said, ". . . the students love to play the tournaments, and I believe I can honestly say that this was true for all my students. When presented as an alternative to the customary classroom methodologies in mathematics, it is accepted in a very positive manner by the students." The TGT process also allows the teacher in a school where racial issues are unusually sensitive to promote regular interaction without resorting to an unpopular seating chart, since all teams must be balanced, racially, sexually, and academically. As Pyne pointed out, the TGT process does not affect the teacher's own individual style of teaching, since it structures the way in which students work together on any objectives or content presented to the class through any chosen style or method of presentation.

The basic idea of this sort of cooperative learning is that when students learn in small, carefully structured learning groups (with group goals, equal opportunity for success, and individual accountability) they help one another learn, gain in self-esteem and feelings of individual responsibility for their learning, and increase in respect and liking for their classmates, which is increasingly important in light of the changing demographics of American middle schools. STL and other methods draw upon the group spirit that emerges from common effort, hearkening back to the experiences of each of us as we grew up and participated in team sports, music groups, and other such efforts. The exciting experience of working toward a cooperative goal, either in competition with other groups, or in comparison to some ideal goal, provides a strong motivational force that, the originators of the STL process argue, can be used by teachers to infuse classroom learning with the same urgency. Students in an STL-style classroom are involved in a learning process that provides the same kind of peer support, excitement, and camaraderie that are characteristic of team efforts elsewhere.

Recent research and development efforts at Johns Hopkins extends the cooperative learning model into the area of reading/writing in a whole language workshop-style of instruction. Student Team Reading (Stevens, 1990a) and Student Team Writing (Stevens, 1990b) seem to be promising combinations of whole language strategies and team learning. Johnson, et. al. (1991) maintain that learning to be cooperative is as important as being cooperative in order to learn. They argue, as do others (Kohn, 1991), the critical importance of developing a generation of learners who possess the social skills and propensities which will enable Americans to work together as adults with less interpersonal friction and more intergroup harmony. Like any other skill or attitude, they write, children and youth are not born with the social skills and attitudes they will need in order to be successful adults; these must be learned.

Effective interpersonal skills and attitudes must, consequently, be intentionally introduced into the school lives of early adolescents; such skills and attitudes must be taught. Cooperative learning, from this perspective, will not be fully effective unless teachers introduce these skills and attitudes prior to and throughout the whole learning cycle.

Johnson, et. al., propose five essential conditions for fully-developed cooperative learning situations. There must be "positive interdependence," and individual accountability, as with Slavin's versions. In addition, the Johnson model cites the importance of "face-to-face interaction" as the medium in which motivation, feedback, and social influence grow. They emphasize the direct instruction, modeling, coaching, and practice of interpersonal and group skills. The fifth essential quality of effective cooperative learning, as they see it, is comprised of "group processing," which is the way in which group members provide and receive feedback on "how well they are achieving their goals and maintaining effective working relationships." (Johnson, et. al., 1991, p. 1:13).

As an illustration of the essential components of cooperative learning in action, Johnson, et. al., describe an assignment from an English class in a middle level school. The students in the class are involved in writing essays on a story they have been asked to read about the experiences of a time traveler. The class is divided into groups of four students, each balanced by gender, race, achievement, and other factors which make them representative of the class. A series of instructional tasks are assigned over a period of about a week in the class:

1. A prereading discussion is held on what time travel would be like.
2. Each student writes a letter or proposal requesting funds for time travel into the future.

3. Group members read and edit each other's letters, give suggestions for improvement, and mark errors that need correcting.
4. Each student submits revised and corrected letters to the teacher, handed in with the signatures of the group members who edited them.
5. Each member reads the story and responds, tentatively to questions from the teacher.
6. Group members discuss the story and reach consensus about the teacher's questions.
7. Each student writes a composition about the meaning of the story and arguments to support their conclusions about its meaning.
8. Group members edit each other's compositions, perhaps having each member read those of two others.
9. All final compositions are submitted, along with the signatures of student editors.

In this instance, the teacher uses a point system for grading the compositions that arrives at both a group grade and individual grades for each participant. As a part of the process, the teacher instructs the students in the important cooperative skills of providing feedback on a person's work without criticizing the person; this is a skill everyone can always develop more fully. At the conclusion of the week, groups spend time processing how well they worked together and how they could improve their working relationships in the future (Johnson, et. al., 1991, pp. 1:8-9).

These and other small group instructional strategies are important for middle school educators interested in providing a balanced instructional program for the students they teach. Peer teaching, group investigations, cooperative learning—all work toward several important objectives for the middle school. Each of these methods is built, intentionally or not, on a solid grounding in the characteristics of the transescent student. Each accomplishes the objectives for which middle schools are accountable academically. And, each serves effectively in the attempt to pass on to students the social and human relations skills and attitudes that students require for effective citizenship. Middle school teachers who attempt to fashion their instructional styles without any effort to include some small group instruction will, in our opinion, serve their students less effectively than they might.

Individualized Instruction

The evidence from research cited above, testifying to the superiority of total class instruction and varieties of small group teaching, might tempt some educators to cast aside any other instructional methodologies. This would, we believe, be a mistake. While the research evidence is indeed convincing, it does not necessarily invalidate the use of methodologies that attempt to individualize instruction. Whether or not a teacher selects a method that falls within the category of individualized instruction depends upon the particular style and strengths of the teacher and, more importantly, upon the objectives that must be pursued and the students who are pursuing them.

Teachers whose classroom goals include the development of greater degrees of individual responsibility and self-discipline in learners, persistence, and personal creativity (and many other objectives that can be pursued best, if at all, with some method of individualization), should be urged to do so (Walberg, 1990). Teachers who find their preferences for and strengths in teaching expressed best through a method of individualized instruction should be encouraged to include these methods in their repertoire. All teachers, in the attempt to provide a balanced instructional program that fits every learner, must seek to develop the competencies required for individualized instruction.

The research on instruction does not tell us to do away with individualization. It suggests that on the whole, one kind of instruction is better under one set of circumstances. With the proper objectives and the correct group of students, teachers who have the skills to implement individualized instruction effectively should feel confident in doing so.

In recent years, many computer-based individualized instruction programs have become available, too many to name. Even now, however, many teachers find themselves without the resources to avail themselves of the rich opportunities that these commercial systems may provide. Too, schools and classrooms that strive to offer the balance, instructionally, that we believe to be so essential, may find it difficult to adopt a commercial system and provide the necessary time and resources to include other methods as well. For these teachers and schools, several methods of individualizing have become common responses to the need to achieve academic objectives without sacrificing the goals of increasing student self-direction and independence.

Many of the methods of individualized instruction currently popular, whether commercially produced or teacher designed, appear to follow a quasi-systematic approach to the elaboration of the learning experience. Perhaps it could not be otherwise, and some would argue that all effective instruction proceeds from the same framework, but it does seem that in the effort to individualize instruction, the systems aspects appear much more conspicuously. Each method seems to begin with an attempt to set or derive goals and objectives, followed by an assessment of some sort. This assessment, if done correctly, leads to a set of learning activities. The entire process is capped by a summative evaluation of student progress, and movement on to the next set of objectives, or back to a previous position for remediation. The various methods of individualization differ in the emphasis they give to the different parts of the system and to the packaging of the learning activities, but, for the most part, the methodology is quite similar and one method can often be used side-by-side with another.

It also seems fair to say that, with very few exceptions, most methods of individualization focus primarily on the differentiation of the pace of learning that each learner keeps, rather than on the opportunities for the learner to choose from a variety of objectives which he or she particularly prefers. Variety and choice in learning objectives are certainly not absent in the middle school, however, since the exploratory element of the middle school curriculum is one of the strongest and most popular aspects of the program in almost every middle school in the nation. But when it comes to standard academic classrooms and the objectives which remain dominant there, even though there are exceptions, individualization most frequently refers to the pace of learning rather than to the direction it takes.

We believe that one additional factor may influence a renaissance in individualized instruction in the middle level school: the growing dissatisfaction with rigid ability grouping. The move toward heterogeneous grouping brings with it the concomitant need to develop instructional strategies which can simultaneously provide challenge and success for all students. Individualized instruction, whether with a computer or a teacher as the facilitator, is likely to be much more common in the middle school classroom of the future. Some old favorites are likely to return.

Learning Centers

Learning centers are one of those old favorites; a method popular in the seventies but little utilized in the last decade, learning centers may be back in the nineties. The learning center seems to provide a popular balance between academic effort and the goals of increasing student self-direction, independence, and responsibility, as well as opportunities of heterogeneous classroom life. Learning centers, or stations as they are sometimes called, usually refer to "an area for study and activity, in or near the classroom, that has been provided for the structured exploration of a particular subject, topic, skill, or interest. It is a place for using and storing materials that relate to a special interest or curriculum area. It may be on a wall, in a corner, next to a bookcase, or on a table; but it exists somewhere in the physical space of the classroom or school" (George, et. al., 1973). It is, however, not the library or media center of the school. Learning centers frequently exhibit the following characteristics:

1. Learning centers are auto-instructional. When properly designed, they do not require the constant and continuous intervention of the teacher. Students, after consulting with the teacher, may go directly to a learning center and begin work. Consequently, a well-designed learning center will contain clear, easily-discovered objectives and plainly written directions for beginning, continuing, and completing work at the center.

2. A learning center invites each student to achieve specific objectives that are clearly communicated. The directions must specify the nature of the task and the exit behavior that is required.

3. Each learning center includes a method of recording the student's participation. The teacher may provide individual folders for each student, stored with others in an area removed from the center but convenient to both students and teacher. Students make additions to their folders whenever necessary.

4. Similarly, a learning center includes opportunities for assessment of pupil learning. Ideally, a center contains both pre-assessment and post-assessment, which students can administer to themselves or to each other without constant supervision by the teacher.

5. Each learning center involves the opportunity for student decision-making and steps towards the assumption of increased degrees of independent learning. Students should be making decisions about the management of time, use of resources, goals, evaluation of products, and other concerns.

Learning centers have a variety of uses in middle school classrooms. They can be used on a part-time basis to accomplish a wide variety of purposes. Enrichment centers, where students may go for additional work, in greater depth, on a particular topic, are effective ways to use this method, especially in heterogeneous classrooms where faster learners must be challenged. For students on the less successful end of the continuum, centers can be used for remediation or reinforcement opportunities. Centers can be particularly useful as motivational previews of coming units or themes. And, of course, learning centers can be used to bring closure to a unit that used total class instruction or small group learning as the primary instructional strategies.

For several years, at Spring Hill Middle School (High Springs, Florida), a team of teachers used learning centers as a regular part of each day's instruction. The daily master schedule provided the teachers with a thirty-minute unit of time following lunch that seemed too short to do anything difficult or complex, so the team searched for a constructive way to use the time. It was decided that this would be an excellent time of the day to encourage independent study. Student interests were surveyed and a dozen or so brightly colored, well-designed learning centers appeared on the walls of the team area. Following a conference with their advisor, each student contracted for an amount of learning centers activity, small group discussions with the counselor, or other independent learning that could be supervised by the teachers on the team. Students who had difficulties, initially, in taking hold and making the most of the opportunity met with one of the teachers and worked on the skills and attitudes necessary for effective independent study. The program, with learning centers at the heart, lasted for three years and became one of the favorite times of the day for both students and teachers.

Another effective way to introduce LCs into the classroom is in the form of a short course within another larger unit. In the average six-week unit, for example, there are usually many different activities planned, one or more of which can be learning centers involving a self-contained short course. A unit on "Comparative Government" might include a short course on "Dictatorship" offered at a learning center, with its own objectives, directions, assessments, and learning activities all relating to the subtheme of dictatorial government. Another appropriate short course for the same unit might focus on the process of "Comparing." Such centers can be a part of the unit, but separately so.

Once students have been introduced to using learning centers, know what is expected of them when using a center, and have used them on a part-time basis, additional learning centers can be introduced. They can easily become the major instructional strategy for a short unit or for a particular subject. Centers can be used, in this way, one day a week, one week during a unit, or on any other schedule that a teacher finds effective. A unit on the Civil War in American history class, for example, could be taught using learning centers as the primary instructional strategy. Such a unit might have centers on some or all of these topics: The South Before the War; The North Before the War; The Causes of the Civil War; Significant Battles of the Civil War; Music and Art of the Civil War Period; Civilians and the War; The End of the War; The Results of the War; Why the North Won the War. Individual teachers could manage such a unit in their own special ways, using the centers as the focus. Learning centers, thus, can be a supplementary strategy or the major pedagogical tool, depending upon the goals and preferences of teachers (George, et. al., 1973, p. 8).

The process of developing good learning centers follows the same steps involved in designing any good instruction, with a few modifications. Teachers must first decide what the role of the learning center will be in their instructional program: enrichment, remediation, motivation, short course, or major method. Will they be used during the whole period, the entire week, or on some other schedule? Will they be required or optional? Will they be used in one classroom, or for an interdisciplinary team unit? Many teachers recommend that the teacher new to the use of learning centers begin with using this approach for one subject or for a few hours out of the day or week. Teachers and students can, in this way, learn how to use centers effectively, with the least amount of disruption or confusion in their classes.

Once the teacher has determined the extent to which centers will be used, other steps toward implementation may be taken. Teachers and students may plan the identity of the centers. Learning activities can be designed. Assessment and evaluation plans can be drawn. One of the authors of this book lists these six steps as those necessary in constructing and implementing a center:

1. Decide, perhaps with the students, the theme or topic for the center.

2. Identify from two to five objectives that will comprise the learning goals of the center. The objectives should be precise, behavioral if possible, and range from one that all students can complete to one that only the most diligent can do. Resist the temptation to write the objectives after designing the learning activities.

3. Create at least two learning activities through which each learning objective may be accomplished.

4. Pretests and post-assessments should be developed with the objectives and learning activities that have been designed. At this point, it is appropriate to write the introduction, with its crystal clear directions. The clearer the directions, the more time the teacher will have to devote to uninterrupted helping.

5. When the essence of the center has been completed, design an attractive backdrop to appeal visually to the students. The purpose of the backdrop is to attract student attention and interest, and to have a place for the directions, signs, and signals that lead the students through the center.

6. Before students begin to work at the center, the teacher should take them on a tour of the center, answering as many questions about the center as possible. Then let them begin, in some predetermined orderly fashion. (George, 1973, p. 8)

One teacher (Doda, 1976, p. 9) used learning centers in a unit on library reference skills, with the following results:

> I have discovered that students responded, in time, with increased self-direction when using learning centers. For this particular unit, I designed fourteen learning centers, each covering one or two predetermined objectives. The glaring pretest results indicated that all but a small, select group needed instruction in all the centers. Consequently, I divided each class into half-groups of about 16 students and set up seven centers in both the classroom and our media center for almost all the students to complete. Students could work through these centers with little or no teacher help. As they completed a given center, their mastery of that center's skill was tested. Mastering a skill became a pass to another center. The children paced themselves, learning to listen to their own rhythm as learners. Those students who finished earlier than others were given a unipac, an additional individualizing tool, on the Card Catalog and the Dewey Decimal System. Meanwhile, the other students would continue with the original centers until they finished. All students found success!

Learning Activity Packages

Learning Activity Packages (LAPs) are similar in many ways to the larger more complex learning center. The basic components of each are quite alike: introduction, objectives, pre-assessment, learning activities, post-assessment and sometimes an optional extra credit or quest activity. Each is an acceptable method of individualizing instruction for teachers in classrooms that are not involved in the exclusive use of a commercial system. Each is inexpensive, relatively simple, adaptable to many uses, and interesting to students if not abused. Each is used by teachers attempting to encourage student self-direction while tackling academic tasks. But the LAP is also different in some important respects.

The LAP is also commonly known as a unipac, referring to the characteristic feature, a design intended to cover the content encompassed in a single objective. If it is well written, the LAP is like a sentence in that it should cover one complete thought, concept, or skill. Judging when one covers too much comes from experience, but one rule of thumb is that an effective LAP should involve approximately two to five hours work for the average student. Because an LAP is almost always a paper and pencil learning activity, anything longer than five hours tends to become tedious for the student; anything shorter requires too much management and design work for the teacher. One way to conceptualize the length and complexity of a typical LAP would be that if this were the only teaching method used by a teacher (which we, of course, do not recommend), thirty to thirty-five LAPs or unipacs would cover the entire school year. LAPs can be used as an effective learning activity in a class unit or as a part of a larger learning center. Suggestions for the successful use of LAPs (unipacs) include the following:

1. Begin the introduction with a brief motivational rationale telling the student why this objective needs to be completed and why it is important to the student. Follow this with an overview of the purpose and activities of the LAP. Wind up this very brief introduction with some clear, step-by-step directions for completion of the LAP, making the directions as simple as they can possibly be.

2. List the objective separately, spelling out exactly what the student will be able to do upon successful completion of the activities that will follow.

3. The pre-assessment should be brief, and if successfully completed, should lead directly to the more comprehensive post-test.

4. There should be at least five activities for each objective. The activities should present some opportunity for success and challenge for each student. Such activities should relate directly and clearly to the objective of the LAP, and most of the activities should be able to be completed by the student at his or her seat, with little or no help from the teacher.

5. The post-test should relate directly to the objectives, and may be contained in the LAP, or it may be the teacher who administers a final post-test, following the successful completion of the post-assessment in the LAP. It should be easily scored.

6. There should be a part that permits the students to evaluate the LAP.

7. Try using a different color paper for different sections of the LAP, or for different LAPs.

8. Keep consumable materials separate, or have students use their own paper for completion of the activities.

9. When designing the LAP for use in a heterogeneous class, develop the vocabulary at a level that aims at the low average students in the class. Since the LAP is designed to be a road map for individual learning trips, it should be clear to as large a number of students as possible.

10. As with learning centers, or any other method where students are expected to learn on their own, they should be given an appropriate orientation and training period to the whole process.

As with learning centers, the role of the teacher using unipacs is significantly different than that of the teacher involved in the use of large group, total class instruction. The teacher sheds the roles of presenter, demonstrator, driller, and questioner, and adopts the mantle of decision maker, planner, evaluator, facilitator, initiator, monitor, coach, and coordinator. The manner in which the teacher relates to the students in these styles of individualized instruction is much like the way in which the teacher must respond to the small group learning situation.

Excessive use of either of these strategies carries with it the same dangers that accompany a too heavy reliance on any other major instructional act. When correctly understood and used, both methods can be powerful instructional alternatives. In classrooms where more student involvement and greater personalization of the learning activity are major objectives, these modes offer attractive opportunities to teachers and students alike. This is why we predict that in the decade ahead these methods will attract more interest and use than they have in the last ten years.

Mastery Learning

Mastery learning is an attempt to individualize instruction within a systematic framework that preserves the advantages of personalizing the instruction while attempting to avoid the excesses of exclusively individualized instruction. If successful, it can be an acceptable compromise between large group teaching, small group work, and individualization (Walberg, 1990).

Advocates of the mastery learning approach make a number of very bold assumptions about teaching and learning. They claim, for example, that when using mastery learning, from 75 to 95 percent of the students in school can achieve the same level of excellence that the best students attain under traditional circumstances. These advocates also assert that mastery learning is more efficient, takes less time, and produces higher levels of motivation and better attitudes in students (Bloom, 1984).

The startling contention of mastery learning is that, if each pupil is permitted to spend the time needed to learn to the level of mastery, then progress will be almost inevitable. When students are not allowed the time they need, failure is almost automatic. Mastery learning, thus, stresses the direct relationship between time spent on task and the level of achievement, something very similar to the focus of research on teacher behavior discussed earlier in this chapter.

Mastery learning denies the inevitability of the normal curve in academic achievement. The normal curve appears when time and the quality of instruction are held constant, leaving aptitude to determine the levels of achievement reached by different students. Block, an early and prominent proponent of the mastery learning approach, maintains that when each pupil is provided with the most appropriate type of teaching and given the required amount of time to learn, that the close relationship between aptitude and achievement (and, therefore, the normal curve) will disappear (Bloom, 1984).

There are four primary variables that influence achievement and that are attacked by the mastery learning approach. First, the idea of aptitude for learning must be thought of in new terms, as the amount of time required for a person to learn a task, and not the innate ability of the student to learn at all, as in the intelligence quotient. Some students need more time and help, and may need to expend more effort, but almost all are capable of learning what the school demands. Second, the quality of instruction must be adjusted so that students are provided with learning activities that adapt to their individual learning styles. A variety of learning activities from which students can choose becomes crucial. Third, individual perseverance (and motivation) in the learning task is significant. If a student needs twenty-five hours to learn a particular skill, but is only willing to spend ten, learning will not occur. Fourth, and most important, is the time allowed for learning. An effective mastery learning strategy must find ways of altering the time frame so that individual students are able to spend the time they need. Guskey (1985) recalls the expression of these four factors in the following way:

> Degree of learning = f 1. Time allowed 2. Perseverance 3. Aptitude 4. Quality of instruction

In addition to these four primary factors, there are several other items of concern that give shape to mastery learning. One is an insistence that learners complete the necessary prerequisites before attempting to learn something new. Moving on to a new task before learning well what has been left behind is seen as a primary cause for failure in school. Mastery learning also places great significance on the role of formative and summative evaluation in facilitating learning. Formative evaluation helps to decide whether the learner should move on to a new task or return to a review of a previous or current task. Summative evaluation helps to determine, in a final way, whether the learning has been effective, and forms the basis for grading. If mastery learning is implemented, say proponents, there will be far more "As" and far fewer grades in the "D" and "F" range.

The process of implementing mastery learning, while considerably more complex than the present space permits, generally follows a series of steps (Guskey, 1985):

1. Teachers review their curriculum requirements and instructional materials to determine which content should be learned by all students and to what level of attainment.
2. Teachers specify learning objectives in the form of units of instruction with clearly specified outcomes.
3. The teacher selects the type of instruction that will be used. This may, and should, involve the use of a variety of whole class, small group, and individualized approaches to mastering the subject.

4. The teacher implements instruction as it was designed.
5. Each learning objective embedded in the instruction is matched with formative assessments, a diagnostic instrument (e.g., a quiz) used by the teacher to check on the level of learning which has been reached after the first major instructional effort. From the formative assessment, the teacher determines who has learned how much, and what major errors need to be corrected.
6. The teacher implements corrective and enrichment activities. The corrective activities are designed as remedial efforts to bring slower students to the point of mastery. Enrichment activities challenge those who initially attain mastery.
7. Finally, after however long the corrective and enrichment time lasts, the teacher administers a summative assessment to assign grades.

After a period of two decades of experimentation with mastery learning, its advocates report a number of positive results. One review of the research (Bergin, 1991) reported that for ninety-seven comparisons of average achievement scores between mastery learning and other techniques, fifty-nine comparisons indicated statistically significant results in favor of the mastery learning approach, while only three favored the alternatives. In the remaining studies, while none was statistically significant, most (twenty-eight of the thirty-four) favored the mastery learning style. Other reviews appear to support mastery learning in a similar fashion (Guskey, 1988). Recent uses of even more sophisticated statistical devices, such as meta-analysis, also indicate moderate to strong effects in favor of mastery strategies (Guskey, & Pigott, 1988). Kulik, Kulik, and Bangert-Drowns (1990) conducted a careful meta-analysis of research, concluding that mastery learning does, indeed, produce positive effects on achievement at a number of levels, including middle school, and that the positive effects are particularly strong for "weaker students in the class." One researcher concluded that mastery learning not only works, but that it works in both the regular classroom and as an effective technique for providing education for exceptional students with varying needs (Guskey, 1991).

As with any instructional approach, however, there are some unanswered questions, even among researchers and practitioners in favor of the principles of continuous progress learning (Slavin, 1989). Exactly what form of mastery learning produces positive results? Researchers would like to resolve uncertainties as to whether mastery learning works equally well with different types of educational goals and objectives. They would also like to learn the degree to which this approach is equally effective with different types of students. Others question the relationship between the presence of mastery learning and appearance of grade inflation. Still others, impressed with the promise of mastery learning, point to the need for highly specific, and widely agreed upon educational goals, a not too widespread condition in American school systems. The lack of sophisticated assessment and diagnostic tools, inadequate corrective treatment, exhausted teachers, the problems with time and content variables, and the stigma of a behavioristic-based model of teaching have been identified as challenges to the smooth operation of mastery learning strategies (Slavin, 1987).

Individual Learning Styles and Instruction

One of the most promising developments in the area of personalizing instruction is the attempt to identify the individual learning styles of learners and to adapt instruction they receive to those styles. Since middle schools are dedicated to the recognition and nurture of individual differences in learners, these relatively recent attempts to do so should continue to grow in popularity and practicality in the years ahead. Four approaches have been singled out for brief mention here.

In recent years, the work of Bernice McCarthy (1990) in the development and application of what has come to be called the 4MAT System has attracted increasing attention and support. Based on the premises that (1) learners have major learning styles linked to their preferences for the brain's hemispheric processing, and (2) teaching to these preferences or learning styles can improve teaching and learning. The 4MAT System has been implemented in long-term fashion in at least seventeen school districts. The learner's preferences for perceiving and processing the world of knowledge yield four different learning styles: the imaginative, the analytic, the common sense, and the dynamic. Teachers utilizing the 4MAT System are trained to improve instruction by using a variety of instructional strategies in a cycle of learning that appeals to each learner's preference but stretches each learner to develop more fully the other styles with which they are less comfortable.

Rita Dunn, director of the Center for the Study of Learning and Teaching Styles at St. John's University, through her writing and speaking, has become identified with an attempt to identify and utilize the individual learning styles of students in the educational process. (Dunn, 1978). Citing what they perceive to be a great need for individual student diagnosis and related prescriptions for learning, Rita and Kenneth Dunn have developed a process of analyzing each of eighteen separate elements of learning style as they conceive it to be. The general elements that comprise learning style, as described by the Dunns, include environmental, emotional, sociological, and physical components.

Once the individual learning styles of the students in the classroom have been detailed, the Dunns recommend that the teacher move to redesign the classroom to accommodate the differences. Classrooms, argue the Dunns, must be transformed from nondescript boxes into multifaceted learning environments capable of responding to and supporting the diversity of learning styles. In their text, the Dunns offer detailed and practical strategies for bringing about this classroom transformation. These suggestions are followed by a wealth of ideas for designing instruction to match the learning styles of the students: small group techniques, contracts, programmed instruction, multisensory instructional packages, "tactual" and kinesthetic resources. Case studies illustrate the ideas.

The extent to which the hopes of those who support this approach to learning styles is actually borne out in practice is the subject of somewhat acrimonious dispute (O'Neil, 1990). Advocates cite a wealth of research to support their claims for the effectiveness of matching teaching with learning styles (Dunn, 1990). Critics attack the credibility of the research and the possible conflicts of interest of research conducted by advocates (Curry, 1990).

Another area of interest, in connection with the topic of learning style, is the approach known as cognitive style mapping. Based on the assumption that each individual has an idiosyncratic approach to the process of learning, the advocates of Educational Cognitive Style attempt to identify the modes of behavior that make up an individual's cognitive style and to design a display of that style in the form of a graphic printout that is called a map. Once an educator has the information on learning style yielded by the mapping process, he or she can attempt to design instructional settings that are based on an individual's strengths. Preferences for large group, small group, and independent learning modes can be determined. Options for written, visual, or programmed materials can be exercised on the basis of an individual's cognitive style. The possibilities are as numerous as the diversity of learning styles present in the classroom (Mullally, 1977).

Mullally points out, however, that this approach to capitalizing on individual learning style (and, we believe, with all such attempts) has several limitations imposed upon it by the very nature of the quest. Specialized training, skills, and materials are required of teachers who attempt to design, implement, and manage instructional activities planned for the various cognitive styles uncovered in the class group. There is also the danger that an individual child's cognitive style, once determined by the teacher, will be assumed to remain unchanged and students may be mislabeled or permanently classified on the basis of a cognitive style that no longer exists. It is possible, however, that the seriousness of these limitations only mirrors the importance of the attempt to determine and utilize data about individual learning styles.

A third approach to the recognition and use of information concerning learning style comes from the study of psychological type. Based on the theory of the great Swiss psychologist, Carl Jung, this approach postulates that there are four basic mental processes (sensing, intuition, thinking, and feeling) used by everyone, but that each person differs to the extent that these processes are preferred and developed. Our preferences for certain processes appear at very early ages, almost as if the preferences were a part of our nature. As we grow, we are likely to rely more and more on those mental processes we prefer. Skills and interests, as well as characteristic ways of behaving toward others, develop into patterns which can be grouped into psychological types. Research in the theory of psychological type has determined that there are sixteen separate types, and that each type has a characteristic style when it comes to learning. What's more, every teacher has a preferred pattern, or type, that determines the ways in which each prefers to teach (Golay, 1982).

Students' psychological types differ in several important ways in regard to learning style, and these learning styles are directly related to effective instruction and classroom management (Lawrence, et. al., 1988). Some students prefer to be active and extroverted in their learning, often learning as they speak. Others prefer to be reflective and introverted, learning by inner analysis. Some students prefer learning directly through the senses, maintaining direct contact with the real world, while others learn quickly by leaps of intuition, by putting two ideas together to get a third. Some students make decisions about themselves and their world by rational, logical analysis; others weigh the values involved, the people concerned and how they will be affected, and use additional affective elements of decision making. Some students prefer a very planned, structured, controlled experience, while many of their classmates may respond more to flexibility and spontaneity, instead of rigid planning. All of these preferences influence the effectiveness of various instructional settings (Lawrence, et. al., 1988).

Many educators, when faced with the seemingly infinite variety of factors that determine an individual student's learning style, may grow weary at the mere thought of attempting to arrange a classroom to fit such conditions perfectly. The three approaches which are noted here seem to require almost Herculean efforts of middle school teachers already overburdened. Lawrence (1982, viii) succinctly summarized the dilemma posed by the knowledge of the existence of individual learning styles:

> Matching instruction to each learner's uniqueness is, in most situations, an unrealizable objective. Yet, to ignore individual differences in learners is foolish. Without straining to attend to uniqueness, it is possible to identify patterns in students that can serve as shortcuts to matching instruction to individuals.

What we are faced with, then, in the area of learning style, is not an insurmountable problem arising from the uniqueness of each learner, but the task of identifying patterns of style and motivation that allow us to think about smaller groups of students with relatively similar patterns. This task, we believe, seems much more likely to be accomplished than efforts based on the assumption that each individual student has an irreconcilably different learning style from every other.

The Computer and Individualization: A Comment

Some educators believe that the processes involved in the individualization of instruction will soon be drastically modified by the utilization in schools of advances in the design of personal computers and the flood of new software we have all witnessed in the last decade. Since the first edition of this text, great advances have, indeed, been made toward the development of school and classroom learning systems based on the use of computers. Our observation is, however, that the promise of computer-assisted learning has not yet been kept. In 1981, we wrote:

> The present authors, however, believe that those who predict revolutionary growth in individualized instruction via the minicomputer are likely to fall short of their hoped-for quantum leap toward a completely technologically based instructional program for the middle school. (Alexander & George, 1981, p. 247)

Such devices, we believe, will soon have a considerably greater effect on the conduct and management of instruction of all sorts, not simply because of a vastly improved capacity to store and recall information about pupil progress. We discuss some of this progress in the chapter (3) on the middle school curriculum.

The Reading/Writing Workshop Approach

It is difficult to characterize some approaches to instruction as either total class, small group, or individualized. It may even be difficult to describe some practices as purely instructional, when there is as much curriculum involved as instruction. This is probably true of mastery learning, it may be true of some applications of learning styles, and it is certainly true of what has come to be known as the Workshop Approach to instruction. Popularized at the middle level by Nancie Atwell (1987), we believe that, however it might be categorized, it promises to be an important addition to the repertoire of many middle school teachers. Limited primarily, at this point, to reading and language arts areas, the next few years may see attempts to adapt it to instruction in other areas of the curriculum.

The Workshop Approach is based on several important assumptions. First, young adolescents need time to read and write in school—regular and frequent time, as much as half a period every school day is critical. This school time is important, among other reasons, for establishing the momentum that will permit students to overcome distractions out of school that usually block their attempts to read and write in other settings. Second, young adolescents learn to enjoy reading and writing, and to improve their efforts in both areas, when they take ownership of their reading and writing. This means that students must be given extraordinary freedom in the choice of what they read. Classrooms and media centers must be equipped with high-interest reading, including dozens—if not hundreds—of paperbacks. Ownership also means that choice extends to the selection of writing topics as well. A common assignment which all students would pursue simultaneously might be valuable, but must be balanced by sufficient opportunities for individuals to choose their own vehicles for expression whether they be short stories, personal narratives, editorials, or whatever.

In observing the workshop approach in action, at Fort Clarke Middle School (Gainesville, Florida) in late May of 1991, it appeared to have a very distinct and coherent structure. Total class instruction, in many of the traditional language arts topics comes in the form of so-called mini-lessons. Students received direct instruction in punctuation, vocabulary, technique and style, and so on. The actual "workshop" time, in both reading and writing was frequent and lengthy. In reading workshops, students entered the classrooms of the language arts teachers, sat down, and immediately began to read; this happened every period in every language arts class in the sixth grade. Even in math class, when students were finished with a test or an assignment, they immediately took out a novel and began to read. The same thing happened during the period devoted to the writing workshop.

The workshop approach relies on a great deal of teacher-student, and student-student interaction focusing on their writing and reading. Teachers hold brief conferences with as many as a dozen students during a block of time. Students help each other edit their work. Group-share sessions, at the end of the workshop period, are settings for many listeners to respond to a writer's work.

The teacher's role, in the workshop approach, constantly shifts from direct instruction, to one-on-one conferences with students, to facilitating group discussions. Teachers are active, but not in the sense of making endless presentations to students. Students work a great deal on their own, but not passively filling in work sheets or other common assignments made by the teacher. Time-on-task, it seemed, was extraordinarily high.

During the week of observing the workshop approach at Fort Clarke, a number of unique experiences arose. Students, later identified as learning disabled, eagerly shared their excitement about reading. Many wrote to us about their reading and their writing (Writing to an adult in this way is a regular feature of this methodology), and we were required to respond in writing to them. This letter writing immediately established a powerfully personal relationship between student and observer; we can only guess at the bond it creates between the regular teacher and the students. Most unusual, however, was in a brief discussion in which two sixth grade boys, after hearing about our current writing project, proudly proclaimed that, when they grew up, they, too, were "going to be writers." Never before, in twenty-five years of observing middle school classes have sixth graders volunteered such a desire. When this conversation was reported to the teacher, he spontaneously turned to three girls sitting at the nearest table and asked them to tell us about their summer plans. The three girls, from different ethnic and academic backgrounds, had already made concrete plans to "get together over the summer and write."

There may be questions about the applicability of the Workshop Approach to a variety of subjects, and to special populations of students. There may also be concerns about the adequacy of instruction in specific reading skills and about reading comprehension. But there appears to be little doubt about the sheer mountain of reading and writing that students eagerly accomplish. If there is a forced choice between preparing students who can read and write well, but who really hate to do either, and taking a chance on missing a few skills but developing early adolescents who eagerly read and write, the choice is clear, we think.

The special significance of the research on teacher behavior and student learning discussed earlier in this chapter is in the ability of the results of this research to call into question those who make sweeping claims for the superiority of any single instructional strategy for all students or for all educational objectives. So long as the learning tasks we ask of our students are of radically different types, and as long as the students we serve are dramatically different in the ways in which they function in schools, no one instructional strategy will or should serve all the needs of the middle school and its students.

Consultation and Co-Teaching: Instructional Strategies for Reuniting Special Education and the Regular Middle School Classroom[1]

Two major movements are responsible for the emergence of promising practices in the education of young adolescents with specific learning disabilities. First, the continuing national emphasis on mainstreaming, attempting to find the most appropriate and most effective, as well as least restrictive, learning environment for the learning disabled student. Exceptional education teachers at the middle level, pursuing the mainstreaming mandate, continue to explore viable alternatives better suited to their students' best interests. This advocacy frequently brings them to the classroom doors of their regular education colleagues.

Second, the evolution of the middle school interdisciplinary team organization has brought together groups of regular classroom teachers who share a common group of students, instead of a single subject or discipline. In such teams, teachers often find themselves in meaningful discussions of their students; more often than not, these discussions focus on students who have special needs. In such discussions, teachers often learn a great deal about the students they teach. Commonly, this increased knowledge of students leads to a more positive feeling toward the students, more empathy with them, and an increased disposition to act on their behalf.

The team organization often brings the regular classroom teacher, it appears, to a point of far greater readiness to respond positively to the ideas and interests of exceptional education teachers who also teach some of the same students. So, there are now two groups of teachers, in many middle schools, who have a more positive view of the potential of the student with specific learning disabilities; two groups of teachers who are willing to make adjustments in the plans they

[1]Much of the first draft of this section on consultation and co-teaching was inspired by and written in collaboration with Cathi Dillard and Terri Click, staff members of the exceptional education program in Orange County Public Schools, Orlando, Florida. The authors gratefully acknowledge their assistance in preparation of the manuscript.

make and the methods they utilize, for the sake of such students. Such a critical mass of professional concern for specific students is bound to lead to attempts to change the way exceptional students are educated at the middle level. We describe, here, two efforts underway in school districts where exceptional education teachers and regular teachers on interdisciplinary teams are working together to develop new models of cooperative and collaborative effort.

Cooperative Consultation

When general education teachers on interdisciplinary teams work closely together with the exceptional education teachers, mainstreaming of SLD students can be far more effective (Robinson, 1991). Instead of scheduling such students, usually with reading or writing difficulties, directly into self-contained exceptional education classes, they are mainstreamed into as many of the classes on the interdisciplinary team as possible. The SLD teacher and the team of general education teachers consult cooperatively with each other in a problem-solving process to define a student's problems and compare the student's abilities with the demands of the educational setting. The teachers brainstorm modifications that will help the student become more successful in the regular classroom.

Usually, the teachers who are working most closely together (e.g., the exceptional education teacher and a reading teacher) commit themselves to a meeting, once a week or so, to monitor the effectiveness of their cooperative plan. Common planning times for interdisciplinary team members also makes it easier for exceptional education teachers to meet with all the student's general education teachers at once. Some students involved in this sort of program are scheduled into a Learning Strategies Class taught by the exceptional education teacher.

A "Cooperative Consultation" instructional model provides a number of benefits for middle school classrooms. Educators of different perspectives learn from each other and the general education teacher can receive support in the use of more effective instruction for the SLD students on the team. Modifications in teaching methods which result from such consultation spill over and help other students in the class, students who may not be identified as learning disabled but who may be potential drop-outs, high risk, or other less successful students. The Learning Strategies class helps the students become more effective independent learners in the regular classroom. Generally, many teachers involved in such a cooperative attempt to improve the education of exceptional students believe that their collaborative efforts are effective.

Co-Teaching

The co-teaching instructional model is a step toward even further cooperation and collaboration between the exceptional education teacher and the members of the general education interdisciplinary team. Co-teaching involves an SLD teacher and general education teacher, from the team, planning and teaching together in the same classroom; co-teaching is team teaching as it was intended to be. Typically, the general education teacher presents content material to the entire group and the SLD teacher works with *any* students needing more help. The SLD teacher also teaches the entire student group, emphasizing strategies for organizing and learning the material of the class, techniques that all middle school students can profitably use.

The SLD teacher is not labeled as an exceptional education teacher; he or she is known as the co-teacher. Likewise, the SLD students are not singled out. They are part of the total class, and use grade-appropriate textbooks and other materials, right along with the non-SLD classmates. Naturally, modifications are made in the curriculum and the materials whenever it is necessary to do so. Oral tests, extended time, and differentiated assignments and homework opportunities are among the most common modifications made for students in this very direct approach to mainstreaming.

There are several requirements for the success of the co-teaching model at the middle school level. First, the concept and the rationale must be presented clearly and straightforwardly to teams of general education teachers. Ideally, these teachers help create the design of the program and have the opportunity to volunteer for the assignment. Classes must, necessarily, be heterogeneous (comprised of about one-third SLD students from the team), and should be slightly smaller than regular general education classes on the team. Most funding formulas permit such arrangements. Finally, and perhaps most important, the exceptional education teacher and the general education teacher involved in such an effort must have some common planning time on an almost daily basis. Programs with these components will be much more likely to be effectively implemented.

Co-teaching does not, however, spring forth fully-formed like Athena from the brain of Zeus. Teachers, especially those with long histories of working alone in a subject-centered classroom, must be trained in knowing how to give assistance and support and how to receive it. Often, secondary-trained and experienced teachers have few ideas about how to work with another adult in the classroom, in anything other than an aide's role. They may even be extremely uncomfortable or anxious with another teacher in the same classroom. They need help making this adjustment.

While teams of teachers (exceptional and general education teachers) will do many things differently, the early innovators in the practice of co-teaching have emerged with a number of guidelines which can help the exceptional education teachers demonstrate their value in the partnership. At College Place Middle School in Lynwood, Washington, the exceptional education teacher works in the regular classroom in a number of ways:

1. As a resource to the regular teachers in planning lessons or units that reach all learners in concrete ways, adapting curriculum and instructional strategies.

2. To provide all students with helpful hints for remembering facts and clarifying concepts.

3. To help all students improve their strategies for learning: effective use of textbooks; using proper form; staying well-organized; having assignment calendars.

4. Modeling strategies and techniques for students.

5. Assisting the general education teacher during class by: monitoring class for on-task behavior; providing guided notes for students during lectures; working with small groups of all kinds; helping individual students read particularly difficult passages; giving oral tests.

6. As a liaison with counselors, psychologists, and special services personnel.

7. As a coordinator of parent contacts for exceptional students on the team.

8. As a peer coach for general education teachers.

9. In coordinating IEP information.

10. As a testing specialist.

11. As an unofficial counselor and advisor for students on the team.

At Scott Highlands Middle School in Apple Valley, Minnesota, general education teachers are assisted by licensed teachers or paraprofessionals who:

1. Read to or with students.
2. Assist students in notetaking.
3. Re-teach concepts from a different point of view or different mode of instruction.
4. Guide students on specific problems or assignments.
5. Read and/or interpret test questions.
6. Interpret assignment instructions.
7. Assist the classroom teacher with modification of materials and/or tests to help assure success.
8. Provide oral review for tests when necessary.
9. Monitor progress on assignments and answer questions during student seatwork.

Implementation of the Consultation and Co-Teaching Models: Experiences in One School District

In the fall of 1987, the eighteen middle level public schools of Orange County (Orlando), Florida, were reorganized, from junior high schools to the middle school concept. As a result of the lengthy and careful planning (to which we refer elsewhere) which preceded this move, district decision-makers authorized the simultaneous implementation of consultation and co-teaching practices as we have described them here. In order to allow SLD students to participate fully in the exciting new middle schools, policy-makers concluded that a different instructional model was necessary, one which departed significantly from that used in the junior high school programs.

School district planners, and especially the supervisors and teachers involved in the exceptional student education program, were excited about the possibilities of the move to middle school and what that move offered to advance the mainstreaming mandate. It was a perfect opportunity. Unfortunately, as is too often the case, so many changes accompanied the move to middle school in such a large district that the implementation of the Consultation and Co-Teaching Models may not have received the attention that was needed for fully effective implementation.

This is not to say that preparations were not made. Recommendations and guidelines were shared with school administrators throughout the year before implementation. A range of acceptable scheduling options was available, from the most traditional junior high model where little co-teaching or even consultation would occur, to the most advanced interdisciplinary team approach where co-teaching was a daily event. Staff development was held for SLD teachers. Eventually, three schools became modified pilot sites for implementing the models.

Inevitably, however, the "best laid plans" are rarely implemented perfectly; such was the case in this instance, too. Many general education teachers were not involved with the staff development efforts prior to implementation of the models. Staff development opportunities may have been insufficient to the task of preparing those who were involved. Some school principals had their attention drawn away to other seemingly more urgent priorities. The district was involved in a tumultuous reorganization affecting every school, student, and teacher in the district: new high school, new middle schools, as well as new models for instruction. It was an exciting but challenging time in Orange County.

Consequently, the district experienced a wide range of effectiveness in the implementation of consulting and co-teaching models. Terminology was different from school to school. Scheduling options ran the gamut of approved possibilities. Administrative support and understanding was firm in some schools and virtually nonexistent in others. Some general education teachers were openly enthusiastic about the possibilities; others were openly hostile to the presence of another teacher in their private classrooms. The results of the first year's experience (e.g., in suspension rates for SLD students) indicated the same variations—positive results in the schools where educators were prepared for and enthusiastic about the models, much less success in those schools where preparation and enthusiasm were absent.

Recommendations

Regular interdisciplinary team teachers and SLD teachers, working together, can provide instruction which allows all students to experience more successful learning. Teacher collaboration of this sort has enhanced the generalization of effective instructional strategies from exceptional education to the regular classroom, in Orange County and elsewhere. Success depends upon the expertise of the SLD teacher, the understanding and enthusiasm of the regular classroom teacher, and administrative support. It appears, from the Orange County experience, early in the decade of the nineties, that several recommendations are important:

1. Consultation and co-teaching models are best suited to situations where all teachers are comfortable with the middle school concept and *volunteer* to work together.

2. There may be a need, in some schools, to offer a "transition" classroom, for 6th grade students coming from fulltime SLD class settings.

3. Staff development is critical, and must precede implementation.

4. Middle school SLD students should be assigned to all teams, perhaps with the more severely disabled students on the same team. This will permit the SLD teachers to provide more concentrated support to subject area teachers and students.

5. SLD teachers, when co-teaching, should stay with the class for the entire period all five days a week.

6. SLD teachers need the same amount of planning time as their regular classroom cohorts, and whenever possible common planning time should be available for those who are co-teaching. Duty time and consultation time, for SLD teachers, needs to be synonymous.

7. Coordinators or other district level support persons must also collaborate (e.g., the exceptional education and the middle school program supervisors).

8. Administrators need as much staff development as teachers. They need to be able to articulate the program clearly to general education teachers and parents.

9. Co-teaching should be restricted to situations where the SLD teacher is experienced and certified in the fields to be taught.

10. Co-teaching should be used in areas identified by individual schools, not on a district-wide basis. One school, for example, might implement the program in 6th grade reading, another in 7th grade mathematics.

Precautions and Promises Associated With Cooperative Consultation and Co-Teaching in the Middle School

Precautions   Obviously, such interventions, alterations of teaching practices which have existed unchanged for decades, if not centuries, will not proceed without difficulty. Co-teaching, in particular, is a practice which can not be easi ly or effectively forced on a faculty. Teachers who are successful are likely to be more flexible than most, and to see their students as their clients. Effective co-teachers will be likely to view adjustments in their teaching mode as an opportunity to deliver services more effectively, rather than as an impertinent imposition upon the way things are supposed to be.

Students must be grouped carefully and correctly for the practices to work smoothly. A careful balance of SLD students and non-SLD students is required. Attempting these practices with classes comprised of primarily "low track" students will not meet with success. It may also prove difficult to schedule the common planning times which co-teaching peers require, but the temptation to go forward without that planning time should be strenuously resisted.

Promises   We (and the practitioners with whom we have worked) believe that these practices are valuable, when implemented effectively, in several ways. Most importantly, to be sure, is the assistance they may provide to the education of individual early adolescents identified as having specific learning disabilities. These students have access to the same curriculum, instruction, materials, and equipment as their non-SLD peers. The strategies used in such "co-taught" classes usually prove to be effective in assisting the learning of all students, exceptional and otherwise. Teachers of the general education subjects receive direct assistance and support in dealing with the students in their classes who need the most help in coping with the demands of the classroom. Finally, SLD students are often thrilled with the fact that they are just "one of the gang," and not sent to special education classrooms for their courses. We believe that, consequently, their motivation to succeed is likely to be increased and their self-esteem is most probably enhanced.

It seems, in the opinion of many middle school educators, that for some reason the number of students with special needs is on the rise. Simultaneously, in many states, the funding for such programs becomes more thinly spread with each passing year. The inevitability of increased mainstreaming of SLD students, if only for financial reasons, is upon us; perhaps it is overdue. Learning disabled students in a general education class, such as science, will have the opportunity to learn more than they would if they were placed in an SLD science class, when modifications are made for their specific disability. Such students will learn more, in most cases, because many middle school special education teachers are currently asked to teach in so many subject areas and grade levels that their preparations can not possibly be as thorough or their lessons as enriched, as those of the general education teacher specializing in one or two subjects. Subject matter expertise may come, at the price of exhaustion, for the LD teacher. Consultation and co-teaching models may help change this undesirable situation.

Even though SLD students may be a part of mainstream classes for longer periods of time, in consultation and co-teaching instructional models, this does not mean the SLD teacher is in danger of extinction. Rather, other teachers become more and more aware of teaching not only to those who are strong auditorially, but to those who are visual and kinesthetic learners as well, they will utilize the SLD teacher more and more frequently for ideas and methods to meet their students' particular needs.

This is why instruction via consultation and co-teaching are such valuable processes. This way of teaching features a meeting of two different spectrums; the SLD teacher and method expert; the general education teacher and subject expert. The two plan and teach together for the betterment of their students, and the results, in the years to come, may be dynamic. When the coming impact of computer-assisted instruction is factored in to the consultation and co-teaching process, educators will be far better able to prepare learning disabled students adequately without being concerned about sacrificing the needs of other learners. Perhaps the unacceptable high 50 percent dropout rate among SLD youth can be brought down to more humane levels.

Consultation and co-teaching instruction offers further important support to the middle school concept as a whole. These practices permit teachers to create the "smallness within bigness" for which the middle school concept is justifiably well-known (Carnegie, 1989). They permit educators to prize the diversity of each young adolescent without destroying the unity of the team and school. Each process strengthens the relationships between exceptional education teachers and the members of interdisciplinary teams. As middle level educators struggle for alternatives to the rigid tracking and between-class ability grouping (George, 1988), the co-teaching model offers an especially attractive option to consider. Not just for SLD students; we believe that this model holds equally great promise for reintegrating the gifted student into the regular general education classroom. No more important agendas await.

Consultation and co-teaching are not, of course, limited to only a few school districts; the practices are spreading rapidly in middle schools and elsewhere. But it may be the organization of teachers into interdisciplinary teams that encourages its use in middle schools, since teachers who previously had little experience working directly with others are now much more comfortable doing so. One example, combining co-teaching with the "reading/writing workshop approach" and with computers has been extraordinarily successful at Wayland Middle School in Wayland, Massachusetts, where co-teaching has been a K–12 venture. (Storeygard, LeBaron & Shippen, 1991). Middle school students who were not ready for a foreign language, both special education and regular students, now work in a computer lab where they use word processing to edit, revise, and otherwise improve their reading/writing skills.

Teamed Instruction

Teamwork among teachers is not, of course, limited to collaboration between general education and exceptional education teachers. Indeed, it is currently far more common to find members of the same interdisciplinary team organization trying to find ways to work together instructionally. The complexity and diversity of the attempt to instruct middle school students properly has led teams of teachers in virtually every middle school in the nation to attempt, in one way or another, to combine their talents and their efforts to bring about a more effective educational program for the students they serve. By its existence, the interdisciplinary teacher organization, as the foundation of the entire middle school program, recognizes the mandate to form team efforts to meet the needs of the students. While we have steadfastly maintained that interdisciplinary team organization and team teaching were not synonymous, and that the presence of the first does not always require or imply the presence of the second, it is hard to imagine an interdisciplinary unit that did not evolve from a team organization of at least rudimentary dimensions. It is also difficult to conceive of an interdisciplinary group of teachers who, having dealt effectively with the myriad problems that confront them regularly, did not at least discuss the possibility of coordinating their instructional efforts more closely. From this point to actual teamed instruction is a very small step, indeed.

Teams must, of course, deal with all of the team management issues that confront them, but teamed instruction is usually a much more voluntary practice, dependent upon several very important conditions. A sufficient amount of common planning time, supplementing the planning time that individual teachers need, is probably the most important of the prerequisites to teamed instruction. Many exemplary middle schools are able to provide teachers with two planning periods per day, one for the team efforts and another for the individual teacher. Teamed instruction simply requires additional planning time, and without it few teams will be able to maintain the effort for long.

A second, and perhaps no less critical, requirement for the success of teamed instruction emerges from the nature of interpersonal communication. Teaming resembles married life in several ways: when it is working well it is beautiful, and when it is not it can be horrible. Much of the work of the team on a regular basis will require interpersonal skills and attitudes of the highest caliber. An especially large supply of patience and tolerance is always in demand. Much of the success of the team will depend on how well members communicate with each other: knowing how to listen so that others will talk to you; knowing how to talk so that others will listen to you; and knowing how to solve problems in an essentially democratic fashion. Teachers who enjoy being with each other will seek opportunities to plan and teach together.

The third major component in successful teamed instruction deals with the level of proficiency among the team members in the area of planning thematic units. Since team planning is quite different from the lesson planning that individual teachers must do, it will consume large portions of teacher time if the level of skill in planning as a team is not what it should be. Team members must know how to plan for instruction as a group.

The extent to which these three factors are satisfactorily resolved will determine the amount of actual teamed instruction that will occur. Where time, predisposition, and skills are at a minimum, there will be few effective interdisciplinary thematic units offered to the students. Minimally functioning teams will find themselves consumed by the mechanics of team management and unable to find the necessary time or energy to engage in actual team teaching of the type most educators admire.

Many schools begin to investigate teamed instruction as the effort to reorganize from a departmentalized to an interdisciplinary teacher organization occurs. Some years ago, for example, one new team in a junior high school (Walker Junior High School, Orlando, Florida) that had begun the reorganization process recognized the deficiencies of departmentalization: little or no correlation between and among the disciplines; territoriality; focus on the discipline rather than the student; and lack of flexibility. In an effort to establish a program that would remedy these deficiencies, a pilot interdisciplinary team was formed at the seventh grade level.

The pilot team at Walker Junior High School worked to interrelate the four academic disciplines represented on the team, in a successful effort to accommodate students coming from self-contained elementary school classrooms into a school requiring six changes of classrooms, six different teachers, and six different subjects. Their effort was described this way:

> As much as possible, the four teachers select a subject that all can emphasize, each in his own area. Unlike the traditional intermediate school where, for example, the metric system is taught exclusively by the math teacher, at Walker each teacher on the team teaches aspects of the metric system. In math, the students learn the various comparisons and conversions of the metric system. The English teacher emphasizes the spelling and proper use of the metric system terms within sentence structure. In science, students use the metric system in their lab and classwork. And, in social studies, the teacher emphasizes the historical background of metrics and its use in other parts of the world. In each academic area, the teachers function consistently in requiring the students to use correct grammar, spelling and usage while learning about the metric system.
>
> Another example of our efforts to correlate and interrelate the academic subjects comes from the period between Thanksgiving and Christmas. By taking advantage of a season that almost all students love, the team was able to capture the interest and motivation of the pupils by relating the curriculum to the season. The geography teacher emphasized the cross-cultural celebration of this season. The students decorated each of the classrooms in ways that emphasized the traditions of four continents. Students researched and presented oral reports of their research on how the season is celebrated elsewhere. Food that emphasized the customs and traditions of the various areas was prepared. In English classes, the students read from Dickens, from literature from other parts of Europe, and other continents. Vocabulary from the stories was inserted in the

curriculum of other subject areas. In science, some interest was focused on plant and animal life and how these things fit into the season. Math was difficult to correlate, but was worked in wherever it was possible to do so. (E. Hamil, personal communication, January 3, 1980)

A few exemplary middle schools have been able to move from this position to one which permits the frequent offering of interdisciplinary units throughout the school. Time, interpersonal skills, and planning skills are such that, in those schools, teams work together effectively and efficiently, offering an exciting thematic program to the students fortunate enough to be involved. The terms used to describe the typical effort at teamed instruction are many and varied: core, multidisciplinary, interdisciplinary, thematic, and so on. Most frequently, however, the process and the end product are quite similar, regardless of the name applied. Here, the term "teamed instruction" stands for all efforts of teachers from interdisciplinary groups who plan and teach together. (We discuss this effort further in the section on integrating the curriculum in Chapter 3.)

Given adequate time, and the interpersonal resources to carry on, the planning process becomes extremely important. One writer with considerable experience in the design and implementation of teamed instruction described a time-tested model to assist teachers in offering the type of teamed unit that most would prefer. Fox (1975) suggests, and we agree, that even under the most felicitous conditions, a team try only two to four such units in the first year, using a planning cycle of six weeks followed by implementation of the unit on the seventh week. Stressing the need to interpret the model flexibly, Fox identifies the following seven-step process:

1. Week One: Brainstorm possible interdisciplinary themes by combining objectives from state or local curriculum frameworks or other documents which present required content in a separate subject format.

2. Week Two: Spell out clearly the exact subject area objectives that will be covered in the unit and exchange all of these materials among the members of the team.

3. Week Three: Team members work independently, gathering resources and developing learning activities to match them.

4. Week Four: Team members meet to examine the activities and materials developed by each teacher, and to decide about the length of time to be set aside for the unit. A tentative schedule of events is produced at this meeting, tasks are divided, and the remainder of the week is spent in preparations related to these tasks.

5. Week Five: The final schedule for the unit is produced, with available resources, speakers, room schedules, student regrouping, and other details worked out.

6. Week Six: A meeting toward the end of the week helps teachers check on last-minute details and make emergency assignments and changes.

7. Week Seven: Implementation of the unit.

Considering the painstaking efforts required to develop and implement plans for teamed instruction that involve as many as five or more teachers and up to two hundred students, it is little wonder that there are only a few such units produced throughout a typical school year. We are aware, however, that many teachers in many schools seem to defy the laws of human effort in their determination to provide the best possible program for their students. Some schools (for example, Indiantown Middle School, Indiantown, Florida) have even produced thematic units that were planned and taught involving the entire school. More often, what emerges is the joint effort of the academic teachers on the team, supported and supplemented by specialists from other areas. One example of the hundreds of fine interdisciplinary units that take place in middle schools everywhere occurred on "W Team" at Lincoln Middle School, Gainesville, Florida:

> Following a discussion on the team of the need for greater team unity, the teachers decided to "build some bridges," which led eventually to the theme for an interdisciplinary unit titled "Bridges." The teachers identified three general goals for the unit, in addition to the need for greater unity: to offer students a different, yet meaningful experience in learning; to move team teaching from theory to practice on the team; to strengthen parental involvement. Since it was the first attempt of this team to produce such a unit, it was decided to limit it to one week's duration. Subsequent team meetings produced a series of learning objectives, and learning activities to match the objectives. Several of the teachers decided to venture into teaching areas other than their regular speciality. On the Saturday before the unit began, the team met at school to put up the props of the unit, and on Monday, following six weeks of intermittent planning, the unit was ready to go. To arouse student interest, the team posted riddles that hinted at the coming special unit. An advertisement in the school newspaper brought students to school on the first day of the unit at a peak of interest.
>
> A variety of objectives and learning activities were offered in several different subject areas: language arts, social studies, science, industrial arts and the advisor-advisee program. The language arts teacher worked on the understanding of the literal and symbolic meanings of the word *bridge*, upon exposure to "bridges" in different genres of literature, and in offering the opportunity for creative writing. The social studies students were involved in locating famous bridges, reading about them, reviewing the historical development of bridge design, and in an investigation of local bridges. In science, the teacher emphasized the physics of three types of bridge structures. In an exploratory model building class, the students worked in groups applying their knowledge and understanding of the physics of bridges to the construction of a model bridge. In the team's advisor-advisee groups during the week, an emphasis was placed on building interpersonal bridges, using activities such as one called "The

Friendship Bridge." One of the most exciting activities involved parents and students in the construction of a mural for each advisory group based on experiences that had "bridged the generation gap." (C. Hoy, personal communication, May, 1980)

As the reader might imagine, both teachers and students felt excited and revitalized by the unit described above. A follow-up survey revealed that 82 percent of the students had enjoyed the unit, and a similar number wanted another such unit sometime during the remainder of the year. Parent feedback was generous and plentiful. As the teachers said, "For one week teachers, students, and parents worked cooperatively towards a goal, but more importantly, we have laid a strong foundation for the bridges we have yet to build and cross."

Teams able to produce units like the one described above are often found in schools where the leadership has strongly encouraged teamed instruction and provided the training necessary for the fulfillment of the mandate to do so. Few systems, in the opinion of the authors, provide a more comprehensive approach to the systematic planning of middle school instruction, on both a team and schoolwide basis than does Individually Guided Education (IGE), the instructional program of the Institute for the Development of Educational Activities (IDEA), an offshoot of the Kettering Foundation's educational efforts.[2] The IGE program organizes the entire instructional program around the principles of democratic decision-making, individual responsibility and the worth of each person involved in the school. IGE offers a structure that includes: thorough interdisciplinary team teaching, balanced instruction, an advisory program for teachers and students, flexible student grouping, independent study, models for team and schoolwide decision making, strategies for self-improvement for teachers and teams and much more. Many of the exemplary middle schools cited in this volume have, as their organizational foundation, the IGE program.

The IGE program for middle schools is consistent with the basic premises of middle school education. It is more difficult to implement and maintain than some supporters of the IGE program would admit, but for educators looking for a comprehensive and systematic approach to planning instruction in the middle school, IGE is something that can be strongly recommended for study. In connection with teamed instruction, IGE provides a model for team planning and teaching that is unmatched in its comprehensiveness, solid structure, and ease of understanding for teachers.

The efforts at interdisciplinary instruction at Walker Junior High School, described earlier in this section, were successful and exceedingly important for the group of teachers and students there, so much so that the impact was felt beyond that team and their classrooms. These interdisciplinary efforts were such a dramatic departure from the previous patterns of instruction at that school,

---

[2]For additional information on IGE, write to the Institute, Suite 300, 5335 Far Hills Avenue, Dayton, Ohio 45429.

that the entire district was affected. Several other middle level schools in the district began to develop successful interdisciplinary approaches, and school district supervisors, impressed with what they saw, encouraged other teachers and administrators to move in this direction. Eventually, for many reasons in addition to these efforts, the district reorganized eighteen junior high schools into middle schools.

Hoping to replicate these instructional success stories in every new middle school, in 1987, the district mandated that every team of teachers design and implement a minimum of two interdisciplinary thematic units each year, beginning during the first year of the district's transition from junior high schools to middle school. Dozens of teams of teachers, in a majority of the schools in the district, attempted to do so. It did not last beyond the first year, if it endured beyond the first semester. Truly interdisciplinary teamed instruction of this sort, on a regular basis, in the context of today's middle schools, is simply a herculean effort, usually beyond the capacity of all but the most dedicated staff members.

James Beane (1990) argues that the creation of new curriculum of general education which rejects the separate-subject, departmentalized version of contemporary middle school curriculum should be at the top of the agenda of the national middle school movement. We agree. We are, however, rather pessimistic about the prospects for success in such an effort if the transformation of the curriculum becomes an additional task teams of teachers must undertake to design and implement under present conditions or the foreseeable future.

Instruction: Concluding Comments

There is much more that can be written about effective instruction in the middle school than can be included in a single chapter. There has been little reference here to the characteristics of effective middle school teachers, to middle school teacher education or certification. Nor has there been any provision for a look at teacher burnout or the effects of the school organization as an instructional phenomenon. Further, we have assumed that readers will not look to this volume for beginning instruction in the basics of lesson planning and the other characteristics of effective instruction at any level of schooling. This chapter has, instead, focused on major instructional strategies that have significance for all middle school teachers.

How are teachers to acquire such instructional competencies? Certainly, continuous staff development is critical, since, until recently, middle school teacher preservice preparation at the college and university level was virtually nonexistent. We believe, however, that the challenges of effective implementation of almost all aspects of the complete middle school program (advisories, the interdisciplinary team organization, an integrated curriculum, as well as new and more appropriate instructional strategies) ultimately depend on the spread of authentic middle school teacher education for their longevity.

Until quite recently, universities and colleges seemed unable or uninterested in developing teacher education programs that had as their goal the preparation of teachers specially trained to teach at the middle level (George & McEwin,1978). Where such programs did begin, efforts were often frustrated by the lack of supportive certification regulations. University educators discovered that prospective teachers would not enroll in large numbers for teacher education programs that offered either sharply restricted or nonexistent certification, and therefore severely limited employment opportunities. Pioneering efforts at the University of Florida, Appalachian State University, and the University of Georgia, have, however, now given way to fine programs at dozens of other colleges and universities in as many states. Nearly thirty-five states, we estimate, now have middle level certification requirements which support new and vigorous efforts for preservice teacher education. The National Middle School Association and the National Council for the Accreditation of Teacher Education have collaborated on guidelines for such preparatory programs.

Realizing that the large majority of teachers who will be practicing in the middle schools of the year 2000 are already teaching, however, makes the hope for a trained cadre of committed teachers emerging from our universities to infuse schools with new vigor and expertise a still doubtful prospect. The training necessary to produce effective middle school teachers will, in the years ahead, continue to occur as a process of inservice education and staff development. Declining enrollments in public schools seem likely to make this prediction even more certain, since fewer and fewer districts will have unfilled vacancies in which to place the teachers from the universities which do manage to install middle school teacher education programs. Public school people seem destined to be left with the task of identifying and training the staff of their programs, in addition to designing and implementing those programs.

Like the curriculum of the middle school, the topic of effective instruction for the middle school is complex, and in spite of such progress, it is as yet poorly researched and inadequately understood. It is likely that there will be more growth in our understanding of this topic than, perhaps, in any other aspect of the exemplary middle school. The more clearly we perceive the characteristics of our students, agree upon our purposes, and research the effects of our behavior, the more we will experience progress in the area of instructional strategies.

ADDITIONAL SUGGESTIONS FOR FURTHER STUDY

A. Books and Monographs

Bray, P. P. (1990). *Urchins and angels: Managing the middle school classroom.* Portland, ME: J. Weston Walch.

Callahan, J. F. & Clark, L. H. (1988). (3rd Ed.) *Teaching in the middle and secondary schools: Planning for competence.* New York: Macmillan.

Fusco, E. (1987). *Cognitive matched instruction in action.* Columbus, OH: National Middle School Association.

Johnson, D. W. & Johnson, R. T. (1989). *Cooperation and competition: Theory and research.* Edina, MN: Interaction Book Company.

Johnston, J. H. (1986). *What research says to the middle level practitioner.* Columbus, OH: National Middle School Association.

Joyce, B., Showers, B. & Weil, M. (1991). *Models of teaching.* Englewood Cliffs, NJ: Prentice-Hall.

Lounsbury, J. H. (1990). *Inside grade eight: From apathy to excitement.* Reston, VA: National Association of Secondary School Principals.

Pantiel, M. (1985). *The junior high computer connection: A guide to computers in the junior high and middle school.* Englewood Cliffs, NJ: Prentice-Hall.

Riedesel, C. A. & Clements, D. H. (1985). *Coping with computers in the elementary and middle schools.* Englewood Cliffs, NJ: Prentice-Hall.

Rottier, J. & Ogan, B. J. (1991). *Cooperative learning in middle-level schools.* Washington, DC: NEA Professional Library, National Education Association, c1991.

B. Periodicals

Baker, D. (& others). (1990). Teaching mathematics with technology. *Arithmetic Teacher, 38*(1), 38–40.

Barinaga, M. (1990). Bottom-up revolution in science teaching. *Science, 249*(4972), 978–79.

Becker, J. P. (& others). (1989). Some observations of mathematics teaching in Japanese elementary and junior high schools. *Arithmetic Teacher, 38*(2), 12–21.

Bidwell, S. M. (1990). Using drama to increase motivation, comprehension, and fluency. *Journal of Reading, 34*(1), 38–41.

Bosch, K. A. (1991). Cooperative learning: Instruction and procedures to assist middle school teachers. *Middle School Journal, 22*(3), 34–35.

Buckner, J. H. & Bickel, F. If you want to know about effective teaching, why not ask your middle school kids? *Middle School Journal, 22*(3), 26–29.

Bump, E. (1989). Utilizing cooperative learning to teach social studies in the middle school. *Social Science Record, 26*(4), 32–36.

Comber, G. (& others). (1988). The touchstones project: Discussion classes for students of all abilities. *Educational Leadership, 46*(6), 39–42.

Elder, C. L. & White, C. S. (1989). A world geography database project: Meeting thinking skills head-on. *Computing Teacher, 17*(3), 29–32.

Ferguson, P. (1989). Cooperative team learning: Theory into practice for the prospective middle school teacher. *Action in Teacher Education, 11*(4), 24–28.

Fields, S. (1988). Cooperative learning: A strategy for all students. *Science Scope, 12*(3), 12–14.

Goins, B. (1990). Effective teachers and teaching skills. *Childhood Education, 66*, 347–48.

Halas, J. M. (1991). Evaluating student feedback in physical education: An open approach. *Middle School Journal, 22*(3), 17–19.

Hubbard, C. (1989). Using the newspaper to teach geography. *Georgia Social Science Journal, 20*(2), 23–24.

Kierstead, J. (1985). Direct instruction and experimental approaches: Are they mutually exclusive? *Educational Leadership, 42*,(8) 25–30.

Kierstead, J. (1986). How teachers manage individual and small group work in active classrooms. *Educational Leadership, 44*,(2) 22–25.

Konet, R. J. (1991). Peer helpers in the middle school. *Middle School Journal, 23*(1), 13–15.

Manning, M. L. (1990). Contemporary studies of teaching behaviors. *Action in Teacher Education, 11*, 1–5.

McCarthy, B. (1991). Using the 4MAT System to bring learning styles to schools. *Educational Leadership, 48*(2), 31–37.

Reed, D. F. (1991). Effective classroom managers in the middle school. *Middle School Journal, 23*(1), 9–12.

Sharan, S. (1980). Cooperative learning in small groups: Recent methods and effects on achievement, attitudes, and ethnic relations. *Review of Educational Research, 50* (2), 241–271.

Snapp, J. C. & Glover, J. A. (1990). Advance organizers and study questions. *Journal of Educational Research, 83*(5), 266–271.

Strahan, D. B. (1990). From seminars to lessons: A middle school language arts teacher's reflections on instructional improvement. *Journal of Curriculum Studies, 22*(3), 233–251.

Wheatley, G. H. & Clements, D. H. (1990). Calculators and constructivism. *Arithmetic Teacher, 38*(2), 22–23.

Yager, R. E. (1989). The power of a current issue for making school programs more relevant. *Social Science Record, 26*(2), 42–43.

C. ERIC

Artzt, A. F. & Newman, C. M. (1990). *How to use cooperative learning in the mathematics class*. Reston, VA: National Council of Teachers of Mathematics, Inc. (ERIC Document Reproduction Service No. ED 322 006)

Eastman, S. T. (1989). Writing with computers: Accommodation, achievement, and attitudes. Paper presented at the Annual Meeting of the International Communication Association, San Francisco, CA. (ERIC Document Reproduction Service No. ED 315 778)

Epstein, J. L. & Salinas, K. C. (1990). *Promising practices in major academic subjects in the middle grades* (Report No. 4) Baltimore, MD: Center for Research on Effective Schooling for Disadvantaged Students. (ERIC Document Reproduction Service No. ED 324 121)

Land, W. (& others). (1987). *Effects of peer tutoring in middle school English classes*. Starkville, MS: Mississippi State Univ., Bureau of Educational Research and Evaluation. (ERIC Document Reproduction Service No. ED 290 143)

Lyman, L. & Foyle, H. C. (1989, February). *Cooperative learning in the middle school*. Paper presented at the Annual Kansas Symposium for Middle Level Education, Emporia, KS. (ERIC Document Reproduction Service No. ED 302 866)

Manning, Gary (& others). (1990). *Reading and writing in the middle grades: a whole language view*. Washington, DC: National Education Association. (ERIC Document Reproduction Service No. ED 314 731)

Morrow, J. (1990). *Keyboarding, word processing, and middle school language arts: a bibliography.* (ERIC Document Reproduction Service No. ED 315 782)

Potter, R. L. (1989). *Using microcomputers for teaching reading in the middle school.* Fastback 296. Bloomington, IN: Phi Delta Kappa Educational Foundation. (ERIC Document Reproduction Service No. ED 312 629)

Walker, B. A. & Klein, D. (Eds). (1988). *Infusing critical thinking skills into the middle school English classroom.* Brooklyn, NY: New York City Board of Education. (ERIC Document Reproduction Service No. ED 314 754)

Wikstrom, M. (1990, April). *Whole language for disabled readers.* Paper presented at the Annual Iowa Reading Conference, Des Moines, IA. (ERIC Document Reproduction Service No. ED 325 808)

Zarnowski, M. (1990). *Learning about biographies: A reading-and-writing approach for children.* Washington, DC: National Council for the Social Studies. (ERIC Document Reproduction Service No. ED 314 759)

D. Dissertations and Dissertation Abstracts

Dougherty, K. C. (1989). Effects of a social skills training program on the academic performance of underachieving adolescents (Doctoral dissertation, North Carolina State University, 1989). *Dissertation Abstracts International,* 50/06a, 1600.

Edwards, L. D. (1989). Children's learning in a computer microworld for transformation geometry (Doctoral dissertation, University Of California, Berkeley, 1989). *Dissertation Abstracts International,* 51/06a, 1943.

Fouts, C. B. (1985). *A peer facilitator-led study skills unit* (Doctoral dissertation, University of Florida, 1985).

Fulton, R. L. L. (1989). Assessing the effects of relationships between cognitive learning styles, cognitive abilities and teaching styles on gifted students. (Doctoral dissertation, University of Maryland, College Park, 1989). *Dissertation Abstracts International,* 51/03a, 726.

Harwood, D. E. (1988). An evaluation of the mastery learning math program at Ephraim Middle School (Utah). (Doctoral dissertation, Brigham Young University, 1988). *Dissertation Abstracts International,* 50/01a, 65.

Johnson, M. D. (1989). Organizational climate, discipline infractions, and student academic achievement. (Doctoral dissertation, Georgia State University, 1989). *Dissertation Abstracts International,* 51/01a, 38.

Lay, V. A. (1989). The effects of middle school mathematics practices upon student achievement (Doctoral dissertation, The University of Nebraska, Lincoln, 1989). *Dissertation Abstracts International,* 50/09a, 2817.

Levin, M. C. (1989). An experimental investigation of reciprocal teaching and informed strategies for learning taught to learning-disabled intermediate school students (Doctoral dissertation, Columbia University Teachers College, 1989). *Dissertation Abstracts International,* 50/08a, 2372.

Matthews, B. A. (1989). The effects of curriculum/instruction orientation on teacher beliefs and practices regarding student science project development (Doctoral dissertation, University of Louisville, 1989). *Dissertation Abstracts International,* 50/10a, 3143.

Rubin, R. L. (1989). Using a systematic modeling teaching strategy to promote the development of integrated science process skills and formal cognitive reasoning ability (reasoning). (Doctoral dissertation, Wayne State University, 1989). *Dissertation Abstracts International*, 50/11a, 3469.

Scherm, N. C. (1988). Factors influencing teacher content decisions when planning instruction of writing in middle schools of Georgia (Doctoral dissertation, University of Georgia, 1988). *Dissertation Abstracts International*, 49/09a, 2527.

Welker, W. A. (1989). The effects of conceptually oriented advance organizers on the learning and retention of short story prose by students in seventh-grade. (Doctoral dissertation, West Virginia University, 1989). *Dissertation Abstracts International*, 50/10a, 3146.

Wieland, S. J. (1988). Changes in students' perceptions of the writing process and themselves as writers in a middle school language arts classroom. (Doctoral dissertation, Indiana University of Pennsylvania, 1988). *Dissertation Abstracts International*, 49/08a, 2136.

Williams, W. V. L. (1989). A meta-analysis of the effects of instructional strategies delivered to the mathematically disadvantaged. (Doctoral dissertation, Peabody College for Teachers of Vanderbilt University, 1989). *Dissertation Abstracts International*, 51/02a, 443.

Yates, B. C. (1988). The computer as an instructional aid and problem solving tool: an experimental analysis of two instructional methods for teaching spatial skills to junior high school students. (Doctoral dissertation, University of Oregon, 1988). *Dissertation Abstracts International*, 49/12a, 3612.

CHAPTER 5

THE TEACHER AS ADVISOR

Guidance and Counseling in the Middle School

The position of counselor continues in middle schools much in the same role as in junior high schools. The counselor is a student service person working in a myriad of ways to help in personal, educational, social and other affairs of the students. Counselors are generally assigned duties that border on administration, with almost always too many students! Overall, guidance programs include attention to students' educational, personal, social, and career development. The guidance counselor is, in the best circumstances, concerned with the following factors identified by Melinda Young, counselor at Wakulla Middle School (Crawfordville, Florida):

1. individual and group counseling (problem-centered, preventative, and developmental)
2. classroom activities dealing with affective education and developmental guidance objectives
3. parent and teacher consultations
4. identification of individual differences, needs, and problems
5. working relationships of teachers, specialists, and administrators relative to students.

We consider their services sufficiently common in middle school and other levels, and sufficiently well treated in the literature of guidance and counseling to focus our attention on the unique aspects of guidance and counseling in the middle school: teacher guidance. In the description of teacher guidance services which follows, we indicate various helping roles for school counselors, but the primary focus is on the guidance activities of teachers as they work with individuals and small groups. Bushnell (1991) identifies four roles counselors must play for successful advisory programs to flourish:

1. *Cheerleader for advisement*   Counselors should "brag about things going well" in advisory programs. They should be visibly involved in the advisory program and encourage the school's administrators to do the same. Help organize schoolwide activities that come from advisory programs: door decorating contests, career fairs, etc. The counselor should be dedicated to protecting the advisory time from encroachment and interruption. She/He exhorts counselors to "above all else keep your advisement attitude positive and enthusiastic. Remember, the better job teachers do as advisors, the more time you will have to deal with the students who truly need your expertise."

2. *Advisor to the advisors*   Adopting the idea that advisors are the counselor's "advisees" is a healthy one. The strain of being both teacher and advisor may make it necessary for the counselor to employ listening skills, empathic understanding, and modeling appropriate behaviors for advisors.

3. *Teacher of advisory skills*   Counselors must help teachers develop a vision of what they want their classroom advisory program to be. The counselor must provide the staff development which teachers need to become better advisors. They may train peers as co-advisors.

4. *Supplier of resources*   The counselor knows more about materials, videos, books, and other resources on this topic than, perhaps, all of the teachers put together. The counselor must continually make this knowledge and these resources known to the advisors.

The Teacher-Student Relationship in the Middle School

Middle school educators often identify the teacher-student relationship in the middle school as the starting point of the entire program, proclaiming the middle school to be specially suited to the characteristics of this age learner. Among the list of characteristics which determine the uniqueness of the transescent, the need for a particular kind of teacher-student relationship is almost always placed at the top. Written philosophies from individual middle schools consistently strive to highlight the student-centered nature of the program, implying a concern for each student and a commitment to firm teacher-student bonds. The teacher-student relationship in the middle school, is however, different from the elementary school or high school model.

In the early years of the elementary school, the teacher-student affiliation has, perhaps, more significance than at any other time in the educational program. Young children, moving for the first time from the home to the public institution of the school, require a relationship with the adult teacher which very closely parallels the association experienced between parent and child. This relationship, in the past, took on the exclusive character of the parent-child affiliation, and was formalized by the legal system as in the Latin phrase "in loco parentis."

Teachers were expected to assume the care of young children, in at least a quasi-parental way, when the child came to school. Indeed, many of the activities of teachers in kindergarten and the primary school years today can scarcely be distinguished from those of parents. Young pupils, many educators believe, need an exclusive connection with one adult as they complete the move from the home to school, today as in years past. Following a decade or two of practices which weakened this association between the elementary school teacher and her pupils, many teachers and parents seem ready for a return to the conditions which permitted the strong relationship to develop. Even if such a reestablishment of the exclusive relationship experiences between teacher and student in the elementary school did not transpire, many would agree that this is the way it has always been, and still is, in the majority of elementary schools in this country. Some would argue that the practices which weakened the teacher-student relationship existed in only a few schools in only a few states, and never affected the majority of elementary schools.

Six-year-old children need a great deal more guidance and supervision, we would hope, than do high school students. The American high school has never acknowledged an obligation to establish formal teacher-student relationships. Not that high school educators were or are unconcerned about the nature of the relationships between teachers and students; they are, of course. Such relationships have, however, usually arisen from common subject matter interests, extracurricular pursuits, similar personality or style, and so on, rather than from an attempt on the part of the school to mandate such affiliations. Students who are close to the legal age of adulthood have been presumed to have the maturity to choose their own friends from among the professional adults in the school.

The middle school must find a way to weave together these two disparate patterns of teacher-student relationship, to assist students in moving from the exclusive association with one adult to the situation in which the student is equally responsible for establishing and maintaining the rapport. Most middle school students are beyond the need for the self-contained classroom and the relationships it provided, but are not yet ready to be completely on their own in a large school. The middle school attempts to help students move from one type of relationship to the other, while providing its own special brand of teacher-student affiliation along the way.

The teacher-student relationship in the middle school is often characterized by the term "advisor." Each middle school student is seen as needing to reach out and explore the world of adults, while maintaining a type of interpersonal haven until a new level of maturity permits him or her to function as a high school student. Middle school students are allowed to leave the sheltered atmosphere of an exclusive relationship with one adult behind, but are guarded from the impersonal anonymity that might characterize a large high school. Exemplary middle schools attempt to see to it that every middle school student interacts with more than one, and perhaps as many as a half dozen, adults during a day or week, while maintaining a special connection with one. Each student has a teacher in the school who will know him/her better and care about him/her more than most other adults in the school. Every student will have a teacher who is considered to be the school "expert" on that particular child. In this way, the middle school continues to supply a unique educational experience while providing for a smooth transition from the elementary to the high school.

In a survey of hundreds of parents of middle schoolers in the New England area, James Garvin (1987) learned that once parents knew that their child was safe at school, the concern shifted toward the availability of what might be called teacher guidance. Garvin found that parents were extremely eager for the presence in the middle school of a supportive adult that would be a sort of ombudsman for their child. In most districts, contacts from the elementary school to the home are frequent and supportive; this changes dramatically in many districts when the children move to a middle or secondary level. The once frequent communications often shrink to being virtually nonexistent, and this makes many parents uncomfortable and anxious about their child's programs and progress. Parents want their children to move beyond the dependence of childhood, but not more quickly than would be appropriate.

The middle school attempts to precipitate the student into just manageable difficulty. Extricating the student from the exclusive one-to-one situation of the early elementary years, the middle school encourages the development of meaningful contacts with several teachers. In the midst of these multiple contacts, however, the middle school permits the student to retain the refuge of one special teacher. Slowly but steadily the middle school student moves from dependency toward independence.

Many lists of objectives for education written to guide program development have, somewhere close to the top, an enthusiastic commitment to objectives which can best be summarized as affective. The middle school program for older children and early adolescents takes this commitment seriously, as every school philosophy proudly proclaims; and while there is a great deal more to affective education than the teacher-student guidance program, it is our position that such a program is the hub of affective education in the middle school (Doda, 1981).

Early surveys of middle school practices failed even to inquire about the existence of advisory programs, since such programs were so infrequently encountered. In recent years, however, the number of middle level schools implementing a formal teacher-based guidance or advisory program has risen dramatically. A recent national survey indicates that 39 percent of the responding schools had instituted regularly scheduled advisory programs (Alexander & McEwin, 1989). In our experience, more schools and districts implement such programs each year.

As defined here, the focal point of the teacher-student guidance program is what has come to be known as the advisor-advisee program. Although known by different names in different places (homebase, small group, fourth R, home-room), the faculty of almost every school that takes this commitment seriously is familiar with this term or recognizes its meaning immediately. Hence, for the remainder of this chapter, the teacher-student guidance program and the advisor-advisee program should be considered as one and the same, and the terms will be used interchangeably.

Purposes of the Advisor-Advisee Program

The fundamental purpose of the advisor-advisee program, regardless of its design in any particular school, is to promote involvement between a teacher and the students involved in the advisory group. Every student needs to have a relationship with at least one adult in the school which is characterized by warmth, concern, openness and understanding. Such a program focuses on what has been called the fourth R, relationships—interpersonal relationships which produce growth for everyone involved. Good middle schools can not be places where teacher and students pass by each other without recognition or attachment, like the stereotypical ships in the night.

> Teachers may need this type of involvement with students no less than the students do. While mature, stable adults, teachers still need to be involved with students who show that they respect and care for them. But more directly, from the teacher's perspective, the most relevant personal reason for the advisor-advisee program is that in a school of a thousand or more students, or on a team where the teacher meets as many as 150 students per day, it is frequently impossible to develop the kind of relationships with students that allow teachers to make a significant difference in their lives. Since most teachers really do seem to have a deeply felt need to make a significantly positive difference in the lives of their students, and the daily demands of the classroom often seem to make this difficult or impossible, the advisor-advisee program provides the teacher with an opportunity to get to know some manageable number of students in a meaningful way. In a middle school with an advisory program, there is "time available for teachers and students to become better acquainted and there are opportunities to build close working relationships which benefit both students and teachers." (Myrick, 1990, p. 14)

Education for personal and interpersonal competence is a closely related objective of the advisor-advisee program. Middle school students need models of effective interpersonal communication. They need an adult to whom they can look for assistance in their attempts to achieve success in school and out, an adult who is their school friend without being a peer. Middle school students do not arrive at the school door feeling as good about themselves as they might, or as able to use themselves as effectively as they should. The advisor-advisee program provides a forum for the exploration of these issues, and an adult who is committed to helping each advisee grow stronger and more positive about himself.

> The advisor-advisee program also attempts to offer an opportunity for social and emotional education. Students in the middle school are, perhaps, more concerned about social group difficulties than they are at any other time of their lives. The need for acceptance and approval by their peers is matched in its strength only by the frequent inadequacy of their efforts to secure this peer support. Consumed by the unquenchable need to belong, they are seemingly less able to satisfy this need than almost any other. New programs designed to assist students in developing more sophisticated social problem-solving skills fit well into the advisory programs now operating. (Elias, et. al., 1986)

Perhaps for the first time in their lives, middle school students are able to think about and analyze their emotions in a semisophisticated fashion. Sometimes experiencing amazing arrays of emotions in incredibly brief periods of time, middle school students need continuing assistance in comprehending, analyzing, and accepting the emotional components of their lives. Middle school students require aid in getting to know themselves, as well as the teacher. They need constant support in the struggle to master the requirements of successful living with peers, within and beyond the classroom and the school. (Carnegie, 1989)

In the early seventies, Vance Packard (1974) described our society as "a nation of strangers," and as we approach the twenty-first century, conditions seem very much the same. Middle school students need a sense of community now more than ever. With the demise of the neighborhood school, the attempt to build a "home base" within the larger school takes on considerably more meaning. Middle school students are simply too immature to function well as complete individuals in an anonymous, amorphous institution of from five hundred to one thousand or more people. The advisor-advisee program continues where the homeroom left off, to work for an educational milieu in which students and teachers feel part of a group which students experience as supportive, safe, and familiar. This atmosphere is simply impossible on the level of the total school, and it is often difficult to achieve in even the most reasonably-sized interdisciplinary teams.

The advisor-advisee program can also be a significant source of civic education. Since the advisor-advisee group is usually either a substitute for the homeroom or synonymous with it, decisions about student council representation, intramural competitions, and a host of related school issues can be discussed in a situation that brings the democratic process to a level that middle school students are capable of understanding. In schools where multiage grouping exists in the advisor-advisee groups, it is also possible that exposure to more mature moral reasoning over a period of several years will produce growth in this dimension that would otherwise not have occurred. The advisor-advisee group becomes somewhat of a model town meeting in microcosm.

The advisor-advisee program is a source of guidance for the student, different from that available from the school counselor. While the guidance provided by the student's advisor will never replace that of the school counselor, it is a crucially important supplement to it. Teachers who not only act as advisors to students, but who also teach those same students at least once each day (and possibly more often) have a knowledge of and a relationship with those students that school counselors, burdened as they are by a plethora of other duties, can never hope to have. Consequently, the advisor is likely to be aware of conditions in a student's life in or out of school which may influence his behavior and need to be handled. The advisor, as team teacher, will be well acquainted with the student's academic performance in every class. This knowledge of the students' lives, combined with the relationship which grows from the advisor-advisee program, and the repeated contact which they have with the students during each day, is likely to make the advisor the first source of guidance. Myrick suggests that "Good teaching is still, and always will be, the heart of good school guidance" (p. 5).

Teachers in middle schools report that their students turn to them for guidance in increasing increments under circumstances fed by an effective advisor-advisee program, if for no other reason, because the student's needs for guidance are often immediate and situation specific. Such needs must be dealt with at the time they occur. Waiting for an appointment with a counselor who may have more than 500 other students to deal with, or for a small group counseling session, is often ineffective and counterproductive. Teachers can provide on-the-spot assistance; thus, teachers and guidance counselors work together as a guidance team in schools where advisement is most effective.

Middle schools with effective advisor-advisee programs often report that classroom and school discipline situations improve as a result of the programs. Students who feel safe, accepted, and an important part of the school are much less likely to be disruptive. On numerous occasions, teachers have told us that students who have a place, time, and person to assist them in "centering" themselves, a situation which encourages the appropriate expression of feelings of frustration, hurt, and sorrow, are much less likely to be found venting these feelings in regular classrooms. Teachers who know students well, and who have developed friendly relationships with them, are more able to deal effectively with them in regular classroom situations, and to be a source of support and information to other teachers in the school when their advisees are involved in classroom discipline problems. The advisor-advisee group is, furthermore, a unique opportunity to teach the behaviors that students no longer seem to come to school already possessing, but which are essential to a productive school atmosphere. Teamwide advisor-advisee units which focus on issues like theft, responsibility, obeying rules, and so on, are excellent advisor-advisee activities that have productive consequences for individual classrooms.

The advisor-advisee group time is often used effectively as the organizational and informational hub of each team, and of the school. Announcements are made there. Field trips are organized around the advisor-advisee group as the unit of responsibility during travel. School activities and projects, intramurals, and other unifying operations are appropriately assigned to the advisor-advisee group. This is not only because it is efficient to do so, but because friendships form when people perform common day-to day activities with each other as well as when they are involved in discussions which promote self-disclosure. Adults develop friendships with people they work with, study with, play bridge with, go to church with, and so on; students and teachers become closer to each other as they participate in (and sometimes endure) the daily rituals and activities of the school.

"If it is true that middle grade years may be the last chance to significantly intervene in the positive cognitive and affective development of youth, as many middle school authorities suggest, then everyone needs to be involved to enhance programs that promote affective growth." Transescents "need both the advocacy of adults who care about them and planned programs which allow for social-emotional inquiry" in order to assist in the formation of healthy positive identities. This developmental task is too important to present and future successes to be left to chance (James, 1986, p. 4).

The most effective advisory programs are in schools where the staff has given a great deal of thought to the goals and rationale of the program. At Broomfield Heights Middle School, in Broomfield, Colorado, the staff has devoted as much, if not more, time to the advisory program than any other school known to us. In one faculty staff development session in 1990, years after the program began, the faculty reestablished these goals for their program, which has lasted more than a decade:

goals

The program emphasizes the role of the teacher as an advisor seeking to identify for the student, the teacher as a "significant other." The advisor serves as an advocate for the student's learning, a friend, and a resource to whom the student can turn for advice, caring, and understanding.

The REACH program also offers the student a "home base" while in the middle school, providing the necessary security and guidance that the transescent may need during the transitional years of the middle school.

The program emphasizes the worth and dignity of the student on an individual as well as a group basis.

The program assists in the recognition of personal interests and needs while participating in the educational environment of the school.

The program provides a secure place to learn and practice skills that assist in the social-emotional growth of the students.

The curriculum guidelines for the advisory program at Broomfield Heights Middle School also spell out the intended roles of both students and advisors. Role expectations stated for students included the hope that boys and girls will:

Get along better with others.
Respect the rights and opinions of others.
Appreciate the effort and contributions of others.
Practice simple kindnesses of everyday living.
Learn to assume responsibility.
Recognize that rules and standards are necessary for group living.
Participate in structured discussions.
Form a significant relationship with their REACH teacher.
Develop a positive self-esteem.

The role of the advisor was also articulated clearly. Advisors responsibilities included:

Meeting with their groups daily throughout the year.
Collecting and disseminating information for and about each REACH student.
Assisting students in recognizing their personal talents and interests through the
     facilitation of the personal development activities used within the program.
Serve as an in-school contact for all persons concerned with the student.
Establish a one-to-one relationship with the student.
Facilitate the REACH students' participation in all facets of the REACH pro-
     gram as well as their participation in the team and school.

At Broomfield Heights Middle, the role of the counselor in the advisory has also been clearly spelled out. The guidance counselor here, and in many productive advisory programs like it, has overall responsibility for the functioning of the program. At Broomfield Heights, this responsibility entails four major functions. Each counselor will:

Assume the responsibility for coordinating one grade level's participation in the
     program.
Facilitate the development of activities to be utilized by staff in the delivery of
     the program.
Provide orientation and delineation of the program for students.
Provide inservice, role-modeling facilitation skills, making guest speaker appear-
     ances, and providing other resources as needed.

In our experience, the best advisory experiences are in schools such as these and in the classrooms of teachers who have, individually, thought through the purposes of their individual classroom advisory programs and developed their own list of goals. One such list, developed by Terri Stahlman while she was a teacher at Lincoln Middle School in Gainesville, Florida, included the following objectives. To help students:

1. Make new friends in a new social setting.
2. Assess their own personal and academic strengths and weaknesses.
3. Make decisions in a logical, rational way.
4. Work cooperatively with others.
5. Develop a workable valuing process.
6. Understanding courtesy, manners, and fair play.
7. Develop effective study skills.
8. Communicate effectively.
9. Begin to build a philosophy of life; goals, attitudes, and efforts.
10. Develop self-understanding, self-acceptance, and self-discipline.

The above list should not be thought of as complete nor should it be adopted, without thought, by others. It is what one teacher set out to accomplish in her advisory program. Every teacher/advisor should attempt to establish his/her own goals.

Advisory programs are not unique to middle level schools in the United States. In Japan, many educators believe that early adolescents are at a unique point of readiness for learning about group involvement, loyalty, duty, responsibility, and citizenship. Indeed, it appears that the development of these qualities among students is one of the central goals of the Japanese junior high school (George, 1989). One of the authors was surprised and pleased to discover, during a two-month study of these schools, that the schedules of the Japanese junior high schools—the most highly academic institutions in the world—involve almost ten hours a week for activities and experiences designed to develop and enhance these attitudes and values. A dozen different sorts of activities were scheduled to involve "homeroom" students in community-building: group competitions, charity drives, cleaning the school, and so on.

Alternative Designs for Teacher-Student Guidance Programs

Middle school teacher-student guidance programs are of essentially two varieties: those that involve a daily meeting of the teacher with the same students and those that have a more variable schedule. The programs that emphasize a daily meeting involving the same teacher and group of students tend to underscore the sense of community ("groupness") that emerges, while those that do not involve a daily group meeting tend to stress the one-to-one relationship between the teacher and one student. Each has its advantages.

Daily Large Group Programs

A daily advisor-advisee program has been functioning in the middle schools of Alachua County, Florida for two decades. The advisor-advisee programs at all six schools are held first thing in the morning for about 25 minutes. Every certified teacher in the school has a group of advisees, and occasionally even the school counselor has a group. As soon as the student arrives at school, the first experience is the advisor-advisee program. Homeroom and advisory responsibilities are combined, so that after the morning announcements and homeroom business, teachers are left with about fifteen to twenty minutes for advisor-advisee activities. The four middle schools in Dothan, Alabama proceed similarly. We suspect that thousands of middle level schools now do the same.

At Stroudsburg Middle School in Stroudsburg, Pennsylvania, the daily advisor-advisee program adds up to about forty-five minutes, half an hour at the beginning of the day and fifteen minutes at the end. Homeroom and advisor-advisee activities have been combined here, too. At Stroudsburg, however, the morning time is divided into formal and informal time, giving teachers a chance to meet informally with students as they drift in to school. Then, when everyone has arrived, a formal advisor-advisee time is available. The quarter hour at the end of the day has also been intended as a formal advisor-advisee time, which is probably followed by another unscheduled informal advisor-advisee time as students leave school for home.

In mid-afternoon at New Smyrna Beach Middle School (Volusia County, Florida), core academic team teachers meet with a group of twenty-seven to thirty students from their team whom they have in class at least one other period of the day. Two days a week are devoted to structured advisement activities. One day, the advisors and advisees participate in intramural activities within the entire grade level house. The remaining two days include guided academic practice, where students set goals for that period and advisors confer with individual students about academic or personal concerns, as their classmates work on their stated goal for the period.

At Marshall Middle School (Marshall, Minnesota), the advisor-advisee program begins during the daily homeroom period, but extends in one way or another throughout the entire day. Teachers meet all their advisees in homeroom, but thereafter meet with each one on a weekly basis during a scheduled independent study time, during unscheduled time before school or at lunch time.

At Broomfield Heights Middle School (Broomfield, Colorado), the advisory period is the first thing that happens every day, lasting for about twenty-five minutes. Counselors prepare objectives and materials for monthly themes (e.g., decision-making) which are used in advisory groups two days each week. Teachers have the freedom to use the materials given to them by the counselors or to develop their own, but they must focus on the agreed-upon theme for the month during two days each week. A third day of advisory time is a "silent day" where students may read, write, or study silently, while the advisor uses the time to interact quietly with individual students. The other two advisory times of the week are up to the teacher and students to design. This advisory program has been operating under the supervision of principal Walt Grebing for nearly twenty years, a sign of the difference a commitment from the school leadership can make to the success of the program.

One-to-One Programs

At Rusk Middle School in Nacogdoches, Texas, a seven-period day permits the teachers in the school to have one planning period and one period of advisor-advisee time. Since the school is organized in interdisciplinary teams with common planning and advisor-advisee times, each team has its advisor-advisee period at a different time of the day. In addition, students on the teams are involved in physical education and unified arts during the time that teachers have the planning and advisor-advisee time. As a consequence, there is no attempt to build a sense of groupness as in the programs described immediately above. Instead, teachers are free to use the advisor-advisee time to focus on building strong one-to-one relationships with each of their advisees. Students are drawn out of either physical education or unified arts on whatever basis the advisor requires, but usually the teacher will work with one or two students at a time. This time is also scheduled for parent conferences, in which the teacher is assisted by the counselor. A unique feature of this program has been the effort of the school administration to secure the endorsement of the local chamber of commerce for the release of parents from work to attend a conference at the school.

Many middle schools, particularly those that follow this kind of schedule, use the advisor-advisee time for planning and conducting parent-student-teacher conferences. At Westbrook Junior High School in Omaha, Nebraska, the advisor assists in the conduct of such conferences on a quarterly basis as a substitute for the traditional report card. At Chaska Middle School (Chaska, Minnesota), the faculty has found that the conduct of such conferences, through the advisor-advisee program, has provided a ground-swell of parent support for that aspect of the program and for most other components of the school. Brookings Middle School (Brookings, South Dakota) was the first middle school in that state to use the advisory program for developmental parent-student-teacher conferences as well. As they are called at Brookings Middle, the "triad" conferences are held at the end of the first quarter, for the purpose of setting the student on a firm foundation for the remainder of the school year.

An advisor-advisee program with very special features has been operating in the six middle schools of Marion County, Florida for more than two decades. In what is called the "small group guidance" program at North Marion Middle School (Citra, Florida), for example, only the academic team teachers have advisees. Each team teacher has about forty advisees from the team. In much the same way as Rusk Middle in Nacogdoches, the teachers at North Marion are organized in teams and operate on a seven-period day. This means that here, too, the teachers have a planning period and an advisor-advisee period which happens at different times during the day, depending on the team one is on.

At North Marion, however, each teacher has a double planning period on Mondays, when all of the teacher's advisees go to physical education class. Then on Tuesday, during the time for advisor-advisee, most of each teacher's students go to physical education and only nine or ten remain in the classroom for the small group. On Wednesday, ten more students remain with the teacher while the majority are at physical education, and the same thing happens on Thursday and Friday. By the end of the week, then, the teacher has had a double planning period on Monday, and from Tuesday through Friday has seen each of his or her advisees in a very small group situation for an hour. Each student has had four periods of physical education and one period of small group guidance with his/her teacher.

The advisory program at Wakulla Middle School, (Crawfordville, Florida) also operates on this pattern, with one slight difference. Teachers have double planning periods on Fridays as well as Mondays, with advisory meetings on the three middle days of the week where they meet with about ten advisees each day.

This model allows teachers to experience relationships with a large number of students, but meet with them in unusually small groups. It also allows teachers to plan one activity for the week and repeat it often enough to minimize the burden on special planning for advisory programs. The program has lasted ten years in one district and twenty in another, and whenever an innovation manages to survive, even flourish, for that period of time, we believe there must be a substantial advantage. The staff members at these middle schools point to the double planning period each Monday (and possible Friday), to one period each Tuesday through Thursday or Friday during which the teacher has a very small group of students, and the lack of need for a new daily preparation as factors which make this program easy for and popular with teachers. Since the literature on effective advisors (Bushnell, 1992) has begun to stress the importance of the one-to-one relationship, organizational strategies such as those in Marion and Wakulla Counties take on additional attractiveness. The viability of this program, its endurance through difficult times in challenging situations, convinces us that school district planners who are interested in a relatively trouble-free and long-lived advisory program ought to look closely at the model operating in Marion and Wakulla middle schools.

Dozens of middle schools have experimented with an advisory program, without committing the school to a daily experience. At Noe Middle School in Louisville, Kentucky, the advisor-advisee program has occurred on a regular and frequent basis, but the scheduling is left to each individual team. Teachers on the team schedule the advisor-advisee time within the allotted but slightly expanded block of time for the basic subjects. Noe's teachers have committed themselves to a program that provides balance between the advisor-advisee program and the rest of the academic effort, and the principal and counselors help teachers follow through. Many of the other middle schools that have established advisor-advisee programs on a less than daily basis have decided to do so on an alternating basis with the unified arts area. At Coan Middle School in Atlanta,

Georgia, for example, students have had an advisory period twice a month for forty-five minutes, in addition to the fifteen-minute homeroom period that occurs on a daily basis. At Lego Middle School (Lego, North Carolina), students have had an advisor-advisee period three times per week alternating with a music program which involves all students. At Boyce Middle School (Upper St. Clair, Pennsylvania), students have advisor-advisee programs twice a week, alternating with an elective class that meets the other three days. Some schools expand the homeroom period when necessary or on a regular basis, providing the opportunity for the advisor-advisee time, but not requiring it on a daily basis.

A description of the program at Shoreham-Wading River Middle School in Shoreham, New York declares that the staff has "built its entire program around the concept of an advisory system, a system that emphasizes consistency, support, and advocacy for every child. The philosophy of the advisory system permeates the school day, influencing the children and the program at all times." The advisory arrangement is different than most places; it is a combination of small group and one-*on*-one advisement. Every morning, advisors and a small group of advisees meet for twelve minutes, much like the conventional program. But, later every day, the advisor meets with the group for another fifteen minutes during lunch. This is a time for catching up with the happenings of the morning, for discussing school issues, and so on. At Shoreham-Wading River, there is another component to the advisory program: all advisors have a conference period built into their schedules three days a week! This special period is held first thing in the morning, before school really gets underway, and is specifically for meeting with advisees on an individual basis, to build relationships as well as work on problems. On a fourth morning, the group of advisory teachers meets to discuss students. Advisors also meet with parents, formally, three times each year. Few schools, in our experience, stress the advisory role of the teacher more than Shoreham-Wading River Middle; few provide more opportunities for it to work.

Teacher Roles

The advisory role of the middle school teacher is complex and multifaceted, and since advisor-advisee programs tend to vary at least slightly from school to school, the roles teachers fill also vary. Many schools take great care in spelling out to teachers, students, and parents exactly what the roles played by the advisor in a specific school are likely to be. Combining the role descriptions of advisors provided by Marshall, Coan, Noe, New Smyrna, and Broomfield Heights Middle Schools, we summarize below potential duties and responsibilities for advisors.

Summary of Role Descriptions

The Advisor Is the Academic Expert on Each Advisee

As such the advisor:

- Assists the student in the planning of exploratory, extracurricular, independent study, and other academic choice activities. Keeps a record of electives chosen by each advisee
- Communicates information about facilities, materials, and personnel to students and parents
- Maintains and utilizes cumulative records, personal profile sheets, and other information-gathering options
- Prepares/distributes report cards
- Assists students in studying and learning how to study
- Assists students in the process of developing and clarifying special interests and aptitudes
- Identifies and considers any physical handicaps the student may have
- Identifies and considers the reading level of the student, and the mental and chronological ages of the student
- Contributes to the understanding of other staff members of the academic strengths, weaknesses, problems, and interests of each student
- Controls the student's overall academic schedule, assisting in decisions as to whom the student will study with, at what times, and in what groupings; the advisor will assist in determining the degree of responsible independence each student can assume, and what learning styles seem appropriate
- Prepares for and participates in parent conferences with reference to the student's academic progress

The Advisor Is the School Advocate and Guide for Each Student

As such the advisor:

- Attempts to build a relationship with each student that is characterized by caring, trust, and honesty
- Is, in general, an available buffer between student, general faculty, administration, parent, and community
- Attempts to see that each student acquires an increasingly positive self-image during his enrollment time at the school
- Knows each student and his background as thoroughly as possible
- Contributes to and supports the school guidance program, especially in referring advisees to the counselor when appropriate
- Contributes to the other staff members' understanding of the personal strengths, weaknesses, problems, and interests of each advisee

- Is aware of the attendance record of each of the advisees
- Is responsible for parent-school communication, and for participating in and planning for parent conferences concerning the personality and behavior of the advisee

The Advisor Assists with the Social and Emotional Education and Maturation of Advisees

As such the advisor:

- Attempts to create a sense of belonging and responsibility through participation in homebase activities
- Conducts activities during the advisor-advisee program which focus on increasing the social skills of advisees and on growth in personal and interpersonal understanding
- Assists students in clarifying their values and in developing more mature reasoning abilities
- Places increased emphasis on prevention of problems in the lives of the students
- Participates in outings, field trips, and after-school activities which promote opportunities for emotional and social education
- Helps students learn to work in a group and to realize the need for getting along with others in order to meet individual and group needs
- Assists students in the appreciation of individual differences
- Helps students develop appropriate attitudes toward competition and cooperation as the advisor-advisee group participates as a group in intraschool programs

Conducting an Advisor-Advisee Group

Designing a Program

Conducting a successful advisor-advisee group, from a teacher's point of view, depends in large measure upon how the program is designed at the school level. If the program is designed primarily as a daily meeting of the teacher with the same group of advisees, the advisor proceeds differently than if the program is designed to focus sharply on the development of strong one-to-one relationships between the teacher and each of the advisees. It is also important to remember that both practical objectives (group feeling and individual relationships) are important parts of each design, but that each program design fosters one of the objectives more easily than the other. In the daily group, teachers must work harder to build strong relationships with students, since their time is obligated to a group. In the situations where teachers do not meet with the same students on a daily basis, it is much more difficult to develop a sense of community, but easier to establish meaningful one-to-one relationships with students.

On the assumption that it is more difficult (but no less valuable) to function effectively in an advisor-advisee program which operates on the daily group design, and that many of the strategies a teacher pursues in this format can also be adapted to the one-to-one design, this section will focus on suggestions for successful operation of the daily program. It is also true that, as of the early 1990s, daily group advisory programs are far more numerous than those which focus on the one-to-one approach. It should be stressed, however, that we do not prefer one type of advisor-advisee program over another. Experience has not yet been broad enough to indicate whether either design (daily group or one-to-one) is superior.

Faced with the task of meeting with a group of advisees on a daily basis, for about a half hour each time, many teachers are initially quite apprehensive about beginning. Although almost every teacher in junior high school or middle school wants to be effective in this role, few feel confident in pursuing it without some special training. Counselors can provide inservice training in basic facilitative skills such as active listening, asking open-ended questions, and so on. In addition, teachers who are hard pressed to complete all the other assignments they are given in a new school situation often see the daily advisor-advisee group as an additional preparation they could do without, a burden they would rather not assume even if they believe themselves to be capable. Under these circumstances, it is important for teachers to see that they are not being asked to replace the school counselor, and that it is possible to operate an advisor-advisee group on a daily basis without rigorous preparations each night.

Teachers, remember, are not expected to be counselors or psychiatrists in order to be good advisors. Some districts, simply because of inexperience, have made the mistake of expecting teachers and middle school students to spend each day in intense encounter-like sensitivity sessions and, as a consequence, have had to endure a great deal of frustration from teachers, students, and parents. Teachers are not trained to conduct this type of activity, students are not ready for it, and parents will not support it. Advisor-advisee programs that insist on this type of format must expect to encounter serious difficulties in operation.

It is also true that teachers should not think of themselves, in their advisory capacity, as replacing the home or the church. Teachers do deal with values on a daily basis; humans can not interact in educational settings without being involved with values. It should be clear, however, that advisory programs are not established to compete with or usurp the values education students would, we hope, encounter in healthy homes and churches. Teachers as advisors do, nevertheless, deal with values. They do so, in successful programs which have the support of parents and community members, by focusing on school-oriented values, those attitudes and predispositions which are essential for student success in school. Such values as honesty, cleanliness, punctuality, tolerance, friendliness, endurance, loyalty—these are the values which are included in effective advisory programs. Rarely, in our experience, is the inculcation of such school-based values questioned by reasonable parents or community members or opposed by school board members.

Teachers are required, in their advisory role, only to be themselves. They must be able to display the same kind of characteristics that are found in good friendships, good teaching, and helping relationships in general. They must be able to accept the student and what he is experiencing and communicate that understanding clearly, without becoming a part of the problem or situation themselves to the extent that they need help too. They must be able to communicate clearly to the student, so that what they say matches what they think and feel inside. Teachers must exhibit, to the degree possible and appropriate in a school setting, the characteristics of unconditional positive regard, empathy, and honesty in their interactions with their advisees. They are not asked to possess advanced training in psychology or psychiatry, but merely to be a helping adult-school friend to the students they have in their advisor-advisee group (Connors, 1987).

Teachers need to develop plans for a schedule for their advisor-advisee program, plans which do not require continued daily replanning. Middle school students seem to accept a planned schedule of advisor-advisee activities quite readily, and are much less likely to balk at participating in an activity if it is what "we always do on Tuesdays." Middle school students, contrary to what an inexperienced lay person might believe, are often not ready to talk about themselves nor eager to engage in self-disclosing discussion without a great deal of encouragement, so a daily or weekly schedule helps. Teachers who are the most successful with advisor-advisee programs in exemplary middle schools almost always have a schedule which, while flexible, does provide structure and stability to the program and security to the students.

The advisor-advisee activity schedule should be well balanced, and it should proceed from a set of overall goals. Even though some middle schools provide teachers with a set of objectives for the advisor-advisee program on a schoolwide basis, the most effective advisors seem to give the program considerable additional thought, and design their own activities on the basis of the goals which they have established, perhaps with their students, for their individual groups. Most advisory group activities are of the type which can be done one day a week for the entire year, or for a week or so at a time without being repeated the remainder of the year. Beginning the year and the program with a schedule, modified by appropriate student input, will make the advisor-advisee time much more effective and much easier for the remainder of the year (Doda, 1981).

The activities that the advisor chooses to include in the program will have a great effect on the success of the program. Advisors need to balance their advisor-advisee schedule with activities that require little or no daily planning, mixed in with some that do require additional thought and planning. Activities which happen regularly without extra effort on the teacher's part will prevent the teacher from becoming exhausted, and occasional things which do require new teacher effort will keep the program from becoming too stultifying by injecting fresh and invigorating approaches.

Weekly Activities

Many teachers in exemplary middle schools, after five to ten years of experience in the advisor-advisee program, have developed a number of activities which students enjoy and which are relatively easy for the teacher to arrange. Here are just a few that we have observed being used on a once-a-week basis.

"Student of the Day/Week"   One day a week the teacher and the advisor-advisee group focus their attention on a different member of the group. Students, with pump-priming help from the teacher, ask the Student of the Day questions about his/her favorite teachers, subjects, foods, colors; questions about home and leisure time; and so forth. All of the discussion is focused on getting acquainted in an indepth way with one student, "stroking" that student, showing that he or she is important enough for the entire group to spend the whole advisor-advisee period listening to. Books on values clarification, guidance, and personal development are full of sample questions and discussion topics appropriate for this kind of activity. It should be easy to see that this activity and others like it can be used in the one-on-one situation as well.

In one teacher's class, this activity had a number of important steps. It began with the teacher taking pictures of all of the students in the advisory group. Each week, a different student's picture was placed on the special bulletin board used for this purpose. At the beginning of the period, the teacher asked each student to write at least twenty words describing positive attributes of the "Student of the Week." These positive statements were then placed in a hat, pulled out, and read by the student. The statements were then posted on the bulletin board by the picture. For the rest of the week, this student was the class "pet" with special privileges like running errands to the office, and so on. At the end of the week, the statements were removed from the bulletin board, placed in a stamped envelope and mailed to the student's parents. Such envelopes would be received, we would think, as a treasured piece of home-school communication.

Using this activity one day a week with, say twenty-eight advisees, will consume at least 20 percent of the total advisor-advisee time for the year with almost no additional preparation. Little teacher preparation with substantial positive outcomes: this is the most desirable combination for effective advisory programs.

"USSR/DEAR/SURF"   Many teachers, teams, and whole schools use an activity sometimes called Uninterrupted Sustained Silent Reading, in other places it might be called Drop Everything And Read or Silent Uninterrupted Reading for Fun. When used in conjunction with the advisor-advisee program, the teacher and all the advisees spend the greater part of the time reading silently and individually. At Lincoln Middle School in Gainesville, Florida, the students and teachers have been involved in USSR on Tuesdays and Thursdays, during the advisor-advisee period. The only real preparation required of teachers is to see that each student has something to read which, for nonreaders, may mean magazines to look at, if nothing else. When used on a schoolwide basis, everyone reads, even principals, secretaries, and custodians; visitors are simply not permitted. When teachers choose to do this individually, it must be planned carefully at the outset and the rules must be firmly in place. After that, it will, when implemented on a once-a-week basis, account for another 20 percent of the advisor-advisee time for the year.

Silent Writing   Many teachers have discovered that students will write about themselves in ways that they will not talk about publicly, with or without a group. Using a period each week in the advisor-advisee group to engage in journal writing is a very effective and appropriate use of student time together. There are several ways in which this can be done, apparently with equal success in middle school. Teachers can read and respond in writing to what the student produces, or they can choose not to do either. Some teachers have found that giving students the option to invite the teacher to read and respond or not is an effective practice. In New Smyrna Beach Middle School, students indicate that they do not want the advisor to read a specific journal entry by folding pages in half lengthwise and stapling these as private pages.

In another school, where advisors and advisees remain together for three years, the teachers have taken to the practice of retaining all three year's worth of journal entries for each advisee, and at the end of that period, binding the journals inexpensively and giving them back to the students as a going away present. We believe that these students are likely to keep this "autobiography of their transescence" for the rest of their lives. Even in schools where there is only a one-year advisory relationship, such a practice would be worthwhile. If the students knew that they would receive it all back, they might write all the more meaningfully.

At Wakulla Middle School (Crawfordville, Florida), silent writing in the advisory program also includes a pen pal program. Middle school students like to write to friends, and this sort of urge can be transformed into an effective advisory activity. It requires only that the advisor set parameters for selecting pals and topics and seeing that students produce appropriate products.

Once again, silent writing of this sort, done weekly, can account for 20 percent of the advisory year, with little or no preparation on the teacher's part. It might even be a good time for the teacher to do some journal writing. A year-long record of experience in a middle school would be a valuable keepsake in itself.

"Academic Advisory".   Since the teacher-advisor is equally concerned with the academic success of each of the advisees and their social and emotional maturation, if not more so, it is entirely appropriate and probably necessary for some of the advisory time to be used in an academic way. In what might seem like a glorified study hall at first, the advisor encourages all of the advisees to bring their problem work to the advisor-advisee group with them, say, on each Wednesday. During the advisor-advisee time the advisor circulates from one student to another, gathering information about one student, encouraging another, counseling with a third, working with as many as possible during the time allotted. In this way, the advisor is likely to discover the areas of the curriculum that individual students and groups are struggling with and can encourage team members to respond.

Short units on topics like "How to study" or "How to take standardized achievement tests" are very appropriate, and can even be done on a rotating basis throughout the team's advisor-advisee groups. Each teacher-advisor can design a part of the team's unit to teach to each other's advisor-advisee group. To do so would mean that a month's worth of advisor-advisee time would be used very effectively with the preparation that went into only one week. Certainly, many other topics can serve as themes of guidance units that teachers can cooperatively develop and work within the advisor-advisee program.

"Indoor/Outdoor Games"   There are many games which advisors can introduce into the advisor-advisee time; games which are fun for students, which can be used to teach group skills these students so desperately need, and which require very little preparation time from the teacher. Games like chess, checkers, the "Ungame", math puzzles, brain teasers, and other similar things allow teachers to move quietly from one student to another, and attend to a game in which a group is involved whenever it seems necessary or appropriate. One creative teacher reported a successful "paperwad basketball tournament" within her advisory group.

Many of today's middle school students need a great deal of help in interacting positively in intensely interpersonal situations. Ideas about fairness, tolerance, and sportsmanship are not inborn traits; they must be learned. Advisory groups in which students learn to play games (e.g., softball) together where such characteristics are likely to be further developed are important learning experiences for the next generation.

It is also important to make an observation about the nature of the process of developing friendships and the nurture of such relationships. People usually become close to one another as they participate in other things, rather than directly requesting that another person become one's friend. These games are the sort of situation in which common interests become shared and friendships develop. It is not a waste of time; and a game day once a week requires virtually no preparation at all.

"Story Time"   It is absolutely amazing how middle school students will become involved in listening to the teacher or to other students read aloud, if it is a story that has some relevance to their lives and the reader does the job well. Indeed, reading aloud has been brought back to the language arts classroom in the most modern approaches to reading and writing instruction at the middle level (Atwell, 1987). One very productive advisory time, therefore, is when the teacher does just that—selects and reads a story aloud to the students. Done on a once weekly basis, or for every day until the story is finished (e.g., the Christmas Carol read the week before vacation), this activity requires no more preparation than that involved in selecting a story and glancing at it prior to reading it so that one knows where the best dividing points are. Teachers who read stories to their students that contain values clarification issues and moral dilemmas report that talking about how a fictional character in a story handled a problem is relatively easy for middle school students and, consequently, often much more successful for teachers. Reading a story during the first four days of the advisory week, then involving students in a discussion of the issues on the last day is another commonly successful approach.

Many current videos are also available and can generate lively discussions. Each video requires previewing by the advisor for appropriateness and the development of follow-up discussion questions or related small group activities for processing the film's content. Many teachers praise a series like the *Degrassi Junior High School* programs for their usefulness in this area.

Media specialists and counselors are excellent sources for books that can be read aloud in lively ways and for videos that are appropriate for advisory groups. Some advisors discover that these resource people will also be happy to come to the advisory group and handle it all for the teacher for a short period of time, say a week.

"Career Exploration"   Another activity that fits with the nature of middle school students, and which requires just a little more teacher preparation than the preceding ideas, is the practice of devoting one advisory day each week to an investigation of adults and what careers they follow. Many states require some degree of career exploration as a part of the middle grades curriculum, and it can often be accomplished through advisory programs. All the teacher really has to do—and sometimes enlisting the students as assistants makes it even less— is identify and select the adults in the community who are willing and able to come to the class and talk about what they do and the significance it has for them. One good evening on the telephone or a Saturday in the car should allow the teacher to line up enough classroom visitors to last half the school year on a once weekly basis.

This sort of activity can also be done on a weekly basis once or twice a year. During the spring of 1991, for example, at Fort Clarke Middle School in Gainesville, Florida, the sixth grade team planned an advisory unit on career exploration that consisted primarily of speakers that the teachers or the students knew (One of the authors, for example). It lasted for most of the week in every advisory group in the sixth grade, and it was time which required little preparation for most of the advisors.

"Goal-Setting Day"   In some advisory groups, teachers use one day a week to help students take greater control of and responsibility for their lives; a popular task insofar as parents of middle schoolers are concerned. In one teacher's classroom observed by one of the authors, for example, the first thing the advisor did one Monday morning after taking attendance was to take out a filecard box and distribute the cards, by name, to the students in the advisory group. During the next ten minutes the teacher engaged the students in a fascinating discussion of the degree to which the students had met the goal that they had set for themselves the previous week. Goals were extremely varied, but most had to do with the student's lives at home or at school. If they had achieved their stated goal, why? If they had not, why not? The teacher vigorously worked at helping the students think it through in terms of their own responsibility for what happened and refused to let the students make excuses. This, as the reader may know, is not an easy task.

After this discussion, the teacher invited the students to formulate a new goal for the week, or reformulate the previous goal in a way that would make it more achievable. Then the students returned the cards to the filecard box, and the teacher put it in the closet. During the remainder of the week, when it occurred to her to do so, she talked with students about their progress toward their goals.

It took no more preparation than that—distributing and collecting file-cards—and it permitted the teacher to assist students toward increasingly greater degrees of self-discipline. Self-discipline is, after all, simply the capacity of the person to make a plan and stick to it; simple to say, not so simple to do. We believe that teachers who take 20 minutes a week to help students achieve more self-discipline will find parents as eager supporters of the effort!

"Organization Day"   In all six of the middle schools of Okaloosa County, Florida, the first day of the week in all advisory groups is "Organization Day." Advisors and students use a simple scheduling form to review the important tasks of the coming week. What tests are coming? What major projects may be due? What homework is already assigned? What special activities need to be noted? At the end of the first 25 minutes of the first morning of the week, every week, the students in all six of Okaloosa County's middle schools are as organized as their teachers can get them. Once again, an important advisory objective, supported by all the parents, achieved with little or no planning on the part of the teachers. Twenty percent of the advisory year is also used very effectively.

"Magic Circle"   Many skillful advisors report that simply arranging an opportunity for students to talk about what's on their minds results in powerfully important advisory time with little preparation required from the teacher. Such discussions, conducted in low-risk fashion on a once weekly basis, can lead to greater insights, for the advisor, into the interests and concerns of the students. There are any number of helpful books now available and these books contain an absolute plethora of activities that lead to productive discussions for an advisory group.

One teacher we know uses the technique of focusing on one word for the entire discussion, having the students begin by freely associating what comes to their minds. In one class we observed, for example, the word for the day was "mud." Eventually one student began by saying that she lived on a pig farm and told of the intensity of the meaning of mud in her life. Another student, a young boy, volunteered that his father often said "Your name will be mud . . . ." when he was in trouble, which turned out to be often. The discussion went on easily for about 20 minutes, with little preparation but lots of skill on the teacher's part.

These sessions can also be good times for problem solving, decision making, role playing, and so on. One teacher has adapted the concept of the "quality circle" from the corporate world for use in his class. Another uses the time for a weekly "Good news; bad news" discussion, where each student has to be ready to contribute one of each for the discussion.

It bears repeating, however, that many middle school students find these types of activities highly threatening and participate with great reluctance and with difficulty. Advisees should always be given the opportunity to pass if they are uncomfortable with the activity. It has been recommended to us by teachers we respect that such activities are moved into the advisory program with a great deal of preparation of the students. Individual teachers may find it easier, but many have found that by the spring of the year, students are more ready for this sort of discussion activity.

"Joke and Riddle Day"   Another teacher we know spends one day each week laughing and guffawing with his students over corny jokes and riddles they all contribute. Every Friday is "Joke Day" and everyone is required to bring a joke, a pun, a riddle, a story, or the like to contribute. They spend 20 minutes groaning together, but enjoying it. Such a weekly activity was primed by the purchase of a number of cheap joke books at the beginning of the year, and by the possession of a great sense of humor by the teacher. This is the same teacher who devotes one week each year with his advisory group to the celebration of Millard Fillmore's birthday. Decorating the classroom with Millard Filmore's pictures, singing Happy Birthday over the intercom, and so on become "camp" activities that capture students' interests. Middle school students, as the reader must know, greatly appreciate a teacher with a sense of humor.

Clubs   Many middle school educators have a negative feeling about clubs and early adolescents; it springs from the misuse of the practice in many earlier junior high schools. As we now know, early adolescence is often a time for exploration, and this is true in the area of leisure time interests and other club-oriented activities. Many a junior high teacher became discouraged about clubs when they had to try to maintain a high interest level in something for an entire year (e.g., model airplane building) when students lost interest after the first or second experience. Early adolescence is a time to try things, and the middle school ought to be a place to do them right.

Consequently, many exemplary middle schools have built club activities into their advisory programs, on a once-a-week basis. At Chinook Middle School, in the North Thurston School District (Lacey, Washington), students participate in clubs as an advisory activity. But the experience is well-suited to the characteristics of the students. The topics are contemporary: jogging, mountaineering, knots, basketball, cartooning, health food, card playing, baseball card club, computers, genealogy, macrame, foreign language, quiet reading, toymaking, gymnastics, volleyball, board games, movies, weight training, science-fiction films, aerobics, needlecraft, drama, breakdancing, mechanical drawing, head start helpers, rocket and kite club, sign language, and the school ensemble—this is one year's list. Students sign up for a club for nine weeks, although they can repeat if they wish. Advisors offer to work with the club of their choice, so everyone is interested. It makes a great, low preparation activity, and gives advisors an opportunity to connect with students with common interests. A visit to the school by one of the authors on club day confirmed the high interest level on nearly everyone's part.

Intramurals   Also at Chinook, one day a week is devoted to intramural activity as a part of the advisory program. Here, again, participation is spirited, unity is developed, and advisors have very little preparation required of them. In fact, all the advisor has to do is follow the students to the activity area and cheer them on; advisory participation is optional. Physical education teachers at Chinook are not advisors; their job is to make the intramural program go well. They offer, prepare for, and clean up after the following sorts of intramural advisory activities: nerf soccer, line basketball, volleyball, nerf kickball, and floor hockey. Advisory groups not scheduled (by the counselors) for intramurals may be scheduled to the board game competition area. The advisory packet distributed to all advisors at the beginning of the year contains detailed instructions for all of this, following a careful description of the nature and needs of young adolescents!

"Schoolwide Activity Day"   In the middle schools of Yakima, Washington, "Activity Day" is one of five weekly components. Its focus is "healthy schoolwide events and competitions" among advisory groups. Among the activities that have been offered during a four year period are: Punt, Pass, & Kick Tournament; "Hot

Shot Rules" (basketball free shooting); Jolly Volleyball (rules adjusted to make it easier and more fun); "Toss and Slide" (hoop toss, bottle bowling, and bean bag sliding); Cageball Soccer; Family Feud; Frisbee Golf; One Bounce Team Ball, and many others. All are designed to maximize fun interaction and group development. Each is coordinated by the physical education teachers with the cooperation of advisors.

There is a baker's dozen of advisory activities which can be highly effective uses of advisory time with very little preparation required by the teacher. We recommend a weekly schedule that incorporates as many of these as possible, so that teachers can see positive results from the program with as little effort on their part as possible.

Occasional Activities

The previous activities are samples of activities that can be used on a regular basis and which require little or no planning time on the part of the teacher. Educators who build such activities into an advisor-advisee schedule will find that the burden of planning they anticipated does not materialize to the extent expected. They may then find themselves willing to invest a little more time in planning activities which add a special flavor to the advisor-advisee group life. Here are a few activities that teachers have found to be worth the extra effort required.

Orientations   Teachers soon discover that a significant amount of their advisory time will often be consumed by activities which can best be described as orientation. Some schools schedule the first day of school as nothing more than advisor-advisee time, used in large part to introduce students to the school as it is organized for them that year, to explain course and class choices, to distribute schedules and locks, and to get acquainted with the team and its processes. Throughout the year, a teacher can expect that a number of advisor-advisee periods will be used to orient students to state and national assessment and testing programs, dental and physical examinations and treatments, and so on. Obviously, there is often very little a teacher has to do to prepare for such activities that would not have to be done anyway in some other context.

Special Meals   Americans make friends by sharing meals together; it is a tradition formed during the hard years on the frontier. Indeed, adult social life almost always includes something to eat! Advisory groups who get together for a simple breakfast snack, or who bring their lunch trays back to their advisory classroom, once a month or so, find that it does, indeed, leave students "with a good taste in their mouths."

Holiday Celebrations   Even in districts that sharply restrict the activities that can be conducted in the observance of religious holidays, or where teachers are concerned about the rights of religious minorities, there are literally dozens of secular holidays which can be a great deal of fun and which can produce both learning and community building opportunities. There are enough American patriotic holidays to fill the calendar, and one creative teacher, mentioned previously, is a member of the Millard Fillmore Society and regularly involves his students in the conduct of Millard Fillmore Week, which includes the celebration of a birthday and a great deal of other camp activity highly attractive to middle school students. Using a week to decorate the windows of a classroom, or to collect and display memorabilia associated with the lives of the students in the advisor-advisee group are just two examples of appropriate uses of the holiday periods. Looking through a Farmer's Almanac will amaze the inquirer at the number of official holidays—there's something to celebrate every week, if not every day.

Community Help Projects There are always projects in any community that need doing, for which there are few, if any, volunteers. A quick check with the service clubs in your home town and a contact or two with some homes for the aging or the disabled will turn up enough projects for an advisory group to do for years. This type of activity gives students a sense of contribution as well as helping develop an advisor-advisee spirit that does a great deal to foster the feeling that "we are proud of us." The recent Carnegie Report (1989), *Turning Points,* recommends that youth service be used to promote values for citizenship and also to reconnect schools with the community. Too many middle school students (especially majority culture, upper-middle-class students) have too few experiences in contributing to their community, or to anyone for that matter. Most take to it with vigor and enjoyment.

School Help Projects The same situation exists for the school. One middle school we know has, throughout the school year, a rotating Pride Week project. Each advisor-advisee group in the school has one week of the year to conduct activities or plan projects which have as their goal the fostering of pride in the school. An advisor-advisee group might, for example, redo the hallway bulletin boards or clean up and repaint a particularly unsightly part of the building.

In Japanese junior high schools, students in homerooms are organized into smaller groups of six or so, called "han." These small groups have regularly scheduled clean-up responsibilities, since there are no janitors in these schools. No maids follow them about cleaning up after them. The message is "This is your school; you are responsible for keeping it clean." And for about fifteen minutes a day, they do so. When Evan, the son of one of the author's, spent six weeks in a Japanese seventh grade, he was astonished to learn that his "han" was assigned to clean the boy's bathrooms, and that his job was to clean the urinals! Although he did not do so with joy, he gained a new respect for school property and for proper ways of using it.

With today's new spirit of volunteerism, many Americans have participated in "Adopt a Highway" programs. There is no reason why the same sort of activity can not be brought into advisory programs.

Field Trips   While few schools are scheduled in a way that permits advisor-advisee groups to take regular field trips to places around the community, it is possible to use the advisor-advisee group as the organizing center for such trips when taken by a whole team or part of a school. Walks to a local fast-food restaurant for a special lunch or breakfast are often popular in schools that are located near such spots.

Current Events   Advisor-advisee time is a very good time to be used to discuss current events, particularly if they are scheduled at the beginning of the day. Such an activity does require more preparation than other activities commonly do, but in schools where there is a great deal of stress on the basic skills of reading and mathematics, this becomes one very valid justification for the inclusion of the advisor-advisee time in the schedule of the day.

All of the above activities are just samples of the many different types of activities which are both possible and appropriate for the advisor-advisee period. The important thing to remember is that teachers may succeed best when they are able to design a schedule of activities, a schedule that is composed primarily of activities that require a minimum of extra planning on the part of the teachers involved.

Requirements for Successful Schoolwide Advisor-Advisee Programs

Teachers who have had success with the advisory role in the middle school offer a number of additional suggestions for teachers and others who are new to or are considering the adoption of such a program. The advisor should be sure to have a balance in the type of activity that is offered to the students during the advisor-advisee time. Seventeen straight days, let alone seventeen straight weeks, of having one's values clarified is very likely to be an unsuccessful advisor-advisee activity. Having the goals of the program clearly in mind as a teacher, and explaining the purpose of the advisor-advisee program to the students will be a very important part of the beginning of the program. Orienting parents to the activities conducted in each advisor-advisee group is an important step toward gathering parental support for the program. Sharing oneself in appropriate ways with the students at the beginning and throughout the year, adopting a non-moralizing attitude in which the teacher keeps from projecting what is believed to be correct onto student behavior, and doing lots of listening, are all correlates of success in the operation of individual advisor-advisee groups.

The advisor-advisee program is possibly the most attractive part of the entire middle school concept, but it seems to be the most difficult to implement successfully and carry out effectively over a period of years. Even after two decades of experience, in the 1990s many middle schools have begun with such programs only to find the idea scrapped after a year, sometimes in several months or even weeks. Schools which have managed to achieve some success with advisor-advisee programs report having learned a number of important lessons about doing it well. Here are some of the suggestions that have emerged from the last decade of experimentation and innovation.

First, and of crucial importance, is the provision of staff development in advance of and accompanying the implementation of the program. Because the role of teacher as affective guide is an attractive and appealing one, it can sometimes seduce teachers into thinking that they are better prepared than they really are. Often supervisors, administrators, and curriculum support people forget how much skill is required to operate such efforts effectively and, as a consequence, provide significantly less staff development than is necessary. Ironically, there is probably more staff development required for an effectively functioning advisor-advisee program than any other aspect of the middle school. If there is no staff development time available, it is probably better to put the program off until there is.

Staff development does not, however, guarantee effective implementation, even in the best of circumstances. In Orange County, Florida, the transition from junior high to middle school was accomplished unusually well, but even there staff development did not deliver an unblemished advisory program. Gene Pickler, Director of Secondary Operations for the School District of Orange County, Florida, observes:

> Although the staff development effort in Orange County was certainly as good as any other efforts with which I am familiar, I feel that the magnitude of change that would be required on the part of teachers and counselors was not fully appreciated.
>
> The staff development delivery model consisted of training school level teams of trainers, on the assumption that they would be able to go back to their schools and provide inservice for their faculties. Given the fact that these potential trainers, for the most part, had very limited experience in the use of facilitative teaching processes and literally no experience with an advisor-advisee program, their chance for success as trainers among their peers was in jeopardy from the start.
>
> Since the training was done in advance of the inaugural middle school year, certain assumptions about staffing levels were incorporated into the training and conveyed to the trainees. A model presuming teacher-student ratios of approximately 1:15 was described. This picture became indelibly etched into the minds of potential middle school teachers. As it turned out, the expectation that small advisory groups would be established was never realized. It is possible that such small groups may never be achieved. While this reality does not necessarily prevent refinement, redirection, and continuation of the program, it will probably continue to be a major weapon in the arsenal of teachers who are bent on its demise. (Pickler, 1991, p. 3)

In effective advisory staff development programs, it is made very clear that teachers are not being asked to engage in intense personal counseling and guidance with individual students. Staff development may, however, never be able to dispel fully the attitude (from teachers who wish to cling to it) that they are being asked to "be counselors." Sometimes staff developers say one thing, but the materials and activities which they distribute make it difficult for traditionally trained teachers to internalize the message. In Orange County, for example:

> Teachers developed a mind-set that it was a crisis centered guidance program and that they were not trained as guidance counselors. To this day, many teachers still use this argument for not attempting to use the scheduled IMPACT period in any constructive manner—even when they may have other members of their faculties who are making excellent use of the time. While common sense would lead thoughtful persons to conclude that conducting personal counseling sessions in a public classroom is an unreasonable expectation that was never intended, dedicated non-adopters continue to cite this "inherent program flaw." (Pickler, 1991, p. 3)

Organizing the program so that the maximum number of faculty members participate, leading to groups which are as small as possible, is often thought to be equally important. If a school is so understaffed that advisors are asked to work with a daily group of thirty-five to forty students, it is probably better to postpone the program until the numbers can be reduced. Sometimes certain faculty members are excused from having an advisor-advisee group in exchange for a school duty such as hall or cafeteria supervision. When this occurs, some of the best advisors (e.g., coaches) are lost to the program, groups are larger, and the morale of the other teachers in the program suffers because of the subtle message which says that the advisor-advisee responsibility is really a lower priority than officially announced. Involving everyone, however, does not always work perfectly either, as Pickler (1991, p. 4) continues:

> School personnel such as media specialists and counselors were expected to be involved in the program even to the point of being assigned to an advisory group. (This proposal was consistent with implementation models from other districts.) The negative feedback received from some such personnel, coupled with a personal knowledge of their motivation for securing non-teaching positions, led me to conclude that they felt as if they had earned the right not to have to interact with students. The middle school concept shattered that perception of their role in the school. Given this high concentration of concern at the personal level of the change process, I doubt that such personnel can be counted on to embrace the concept in the future.

We believe that if a faculty values a program, it will find its way into the schedule of that school in a way that announces the significance attached to the activity. When school staff say that, "Oh, yes, we act as advisors all day long," or "We do it in social studies," it is likely that there is actually very little of the type of activity described in this chapter being conducted in the school. Or when the comment, "We schedule it when necessary" appears, it is usually safe to guess that the need for the program appears very seldom. Schools which hope to develop any semblance of group feeling among their students need to think seriously about scheduling the activity on a daily basis. Schools that aim at the development of that special one-*to*-one relationship need to remember that this activity takes as much or more time to conduct.

There are some important factors to consider in the realm of when the advisor-advisee time is scheduled. Practice seems to be confirming the place of the advisor-advisee time at the beginning of the school day as best. In all the middle schools of Sarasota County, Florida, the advisory time is the first thirty minutes of the school day. In fact, a contest to name the program conducted among middle school teachers in the district resulted in the prize-winning "Prime Time" appellation. Slating the advisory program for the last period of the day is usually a reflection of the fact that it was barely scheduled on a daily basis at all, and enjoys the lowest priority of any regularly scheduled activity. Few schools have been able to maintain the health of the advisor-advisee programs scheduled then, since the message which teachers and students perceive is that this is probably just one more of the stream of innovations which will come and go. It is probably better to postpone an advisor-advisee program than to schedule it at the end of the day. While, obviously, something has to be scheduled then, one of the required aspects of the curriculum is likely to suffer less in this slot than will the advisor-advisee program.

Scheduling an advisor-advisee time at some time other than the first or last period of the day seems, for its success, to depend on how and why it is done. Filling a half hour before or after lunch, as a scheduling convenience, usually fails because students are either hungry or lethargic, depending on which schedule they have, and are in no mood to participate in advisor-advisee activities. It also conveys the only partly hidden message that placing the program thus was a device to fill the schedule and not really all that important; and teachers and students usually act accordingly. When schools are fortunate enough to have a regular period of the school day for the program, it does not seem to matter if a particular team has its advisor-advisee time during any special segment, as long as it is clear that this is an important piece of the school day and deserves equal treatment by teachers and students alike.

The length of time devoted to the advisory period is important, too. For programs where teachers meet daily with the same group of students, thirty minutes seems about right. Three quarters of an hour is too long for most of the activities that one would expect to be conducted during advisor-advisee programs, and less than twenty minutes seems too short and is likely to turn into a homeroom time where little else than attendance taking and announcements are accomplished.

It is becoming increasingly clear that teachers must be given a considerable amount of freedom in terms of the model of advisor which they attempt to emulate. Originally, many schools attempted to have each teacher follow a model which was almost identical to the Rogerian (or client-centered) therapy process, which should not be surprising since many of the people who were implementing the programs saw guidance in the traditional sense as the heart of the program. In a very short time following the beginning of those early programs, however, involved educators discovered that their expectations for teacher behavior were often incorrect. Given sharply restricted inservice education budgets—which prevented teachers from receiving the type of intense training that might have made at least a portion of them capable of and comfortable with the Rogerian model—supervisors realized that it was impossible to achieve this goal. What is more, they came to realize that the goal was not really appropriate. In a very real sense, a good advisory program is what the old junior high school homeroom was intended to be, and the interpersonal skills of the teacher are simply extended into that homeroom setting.

Just as there is no one right way to teach, there is no right way to operate an advisory group. So long as teachers have a stated goal and can demonstrate that they are making progress toward that goal with their advisees, they may make the most progress when permitted to pursue that goal in ways that are most comfortable for them. Many teachers are very comfortable and effective when using a great deal of their advisory time for small group affective discussion; but some are not. It is important to the success of the program that teachers see themselves as free to pursue their own activities in a mode that feels safe. It is, nonetheless, also important that teachers receive enough guidance in alternative methods of working with an advisor-advisee group that they actively pursue at least one model, and do not respond to the freedom to be themselves by doing less than they might, merely substituting more of what they always do in a regular class for their advisor-advisee activities.

Many times, in schools newly opened or reorganized as middle schools, the temptation is to move to an advisor-advisee program as the first step in implementing the new concept. This temptation is not difficult to understand: everyone knows and accepts the need for such a program, and organization and implementation seem simple. Not so. Schools which do not change from a departmentalized format, for example, but do implement an advisor-advisee program, will find themselves involved in a situation where teachers and students are together for that time, but may never see each other again during the day. Under such circumstances, the advisor-advisee program will work much less effectively, because of the absence of repeated face-to-face contact between advisors and their advisees, which they would normally receive during class later in the day. If teachers have students in their advisory groups whom they do not have in other classes, and the advisor-advisee group activity is not graded (as it should not be), there is often considerably more reluctance to participate fully in the activities of the group. Planners who fear the conflict that they believe will surround a change from departmentalized organization of teachers to an interdisciplinary framework, and who instead implement an advisor-advisee program in the hopes that this will satisfy the reorganization requirements, are often disappointed in the results, which usually include a failing advisor-advisee program.

The mutual support which the advisor-advisee program and the interdisciplinary organization of teachers offer to each other is another example of the synergy which operates in the middle school program. Implementing one part of the program without the others results in a loss of efficiency and effectiveness of considerable proportions. As the heart of the middle school program, the interdisciplinary team organization model, when present, will make the advisor-advisee program much more likely to succeed.

The exemplary middle school is a balance between an enriched curriculum possible only in large schools and the sense of community that holds people together. A good middle school is, as Figure 5.1 illustrates, a creation of smallness inside of bigness, what looks like concentric circles of unity or building blocks of community. When the interdisciplinary team block or level is missing, the advisory program is at risk. When advisory programs are absent, the team is on less sure footing in its work with individual students. Both need to be present for the full functioning of each.

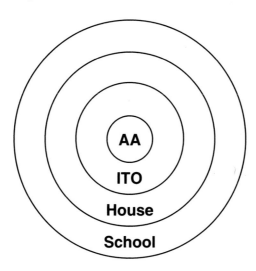

Figure 5.1

There are a number of other factors which contribute to the success of an advisor-advisee program. Some school districts, such as Sarasota, Okaloosa, and Alachua Counties in Florida, Fort Campbell Middle Schools in Kentucky, McCulloch Middle in Highland Park, Texas, and many others have found that preparing a handbook for teachers which explains the purposes of the program, offers suggestions for organizing one's group, and contains a package of effective advisor-advisee activities, is a very helpful project. A flexible but visible curriculum can add the right amount of structure to the program. The most comprehensive curriculum guide of this sort, prepared by a local school district, has been done, we think, by Putnam County Schools of Winfield, West Virginia. Several resource guides for classroom advisory programs are now also available commercially, and groups like Lions Club International have developed very effective and successfully structured programs ("Skills for Adolescence") requiring a firm commitment to staff development.[1]

The development of an advisory curriculum is not, however, an unmixed blessing. There is always the danger that teachers and others will stick to the book, regardless of the actual needs of a particular group of young adolescents. Gene Pickler found this to be the case. In order to prevent program failure and negative attitudes stemming from lack of a concrete basic resource, the district produced a three-volume (one for each grade level) advisory curriculum guide that "was equal in quality to similar resources from other school districts. In fact, it incorporated many refinements in format which made it considerably more "user friendly." The use of the guide did not produce uniformly positive results:

> It is my belief that there was an understandable reluctance on the part of many administrators and teachers to vary from the printed curriculum in the first year of implementation. At that point in the middle school conversion process, there was natural apprehension about public acceptance of the advisor-advisee concept. The "values clarification" and "secular humanism" paranoia syndrome can not be discounted. As a result, most schools took a "safe" route toward implementation. The norm quickly became a standardized, schoolwide utilization of the activities in the IMPACT book. Teachers were, in effect, protected from having to confront their responsibilities for implementing IMPACT. This practice continues to a large degree in some schools today. (Pickler, 1991, p. 2)

A number of middle schools organize schoolwide monthly topics for the advisory program. At New Smyrna Beach Middle School in Florida, staff members have found success in doing so. There, teams of teachers determine which specific activities to use in implementing the selected unit. At Chinook Middle School, Lacey, Washington, a group of teachers, counselors, and parents developed the following as monthly themes, with matching materials, for one school year:

September	"It's a Family Affair" (transition and unity)
October	"It's Not Just Talk" (communication skills)
November	"Is There Life Outside of Homework?" (life skills)
December	"Partnership: It's Your School and Community" (community involvement)

---

[1]See the "R.A.P." materials from Dale Seymour Publications, in Palo Alto, CA, and "Advisory," a product of the Incentive Publications Inc., in Nashville, TN; both developed in 1990. The Lions Quest Program is headquartered at 537 Jones Road, P.O.Box 566, Granville, Ohio, 43023-0566.

January	"Hour of Destiny" (goal setting)
February	"Caring Is for Everyone" (caring)
March	"What I Think of Myself Matters" (positive self-image)
April	"Look and Think Before You Leap" (decision making)
May	"Nobody Said It Was Easy" (coping skills)
June	"You Made It" (transition again)

At McCulloch Middle School, in Highland Park, Texas, a series of suggested (not required) themes for the 1991–92 year, matched by a packet of materials to use in developing them, looked like this:

Classroom Climate Strategies	September
Orientation/School Rules	September
Getting Acquainted	September
Study Skills/Time Management	October
Social Skills	October
School Spirit	October/November
Community Service	November/December
Holiday Themes	November/December
Decision Making	January
Self-Awareness	January
Goal Setting	February
Educational/Career Planning	February
Problem Ownership	March
Conflict Management	March
Accepting Responsibility	March
Communication	April
Community Service	April
Appreciating and Accepting Diversity	May

At East Grand Rapids Middle School (Grand Rapids, Michigan), the monthly themes for the 1990–91 year were as follows:

September	"What's Happening" (getting acquainted with my school)
October	"How Do I Fit In?" (establishing myself in the group)
November	"How Am I Doing as a Student?" (developing academic responsibility)
December	"How Can I Help Others?" (giving to others . . . a sense of community)

January	"Where Do I Go from Here?" (self-assessment and goal setting)
February	"How Do I Show I Care?" (getting along with others)
March	"Me? . . . Worry?" (stress management)
April/May	"Where Do I Stand?" (peer pressure and assertiveness skills)
May/June	"What's Ahead for the Summer?" (exploring summer opportunities)

In a similar fashion, the first monthly newsletter to parents from Broomfield Heights Middle School (Broomfield, Colorado) reminds parents that the month of September, during the REACH program, was devoted to "Getting to Know You" in all grades. Topics for October, 1991 were "What is a sixth grader?" for that grade, "Self-concept: Who am I?" for the seventh grade, and "What kind of a student am I?" for the eighth grade. Other monthly topics would also be announced to parents in advance in this way. In one recent year, eighth graders at BHMS dealt with the following monthly topics, keyed specifically to their age group:

September	Groups and Their Process
October	Ten Pressures and Social Situations
November	Let's See—How Do We Communicate?
December	The Holidays-Caring and Sharing
January	Soon High School—Then What?
February	Soon High School (continued)
March	Transitions: Who, Where, Why, When?
April	Career Awareness
May	Middle School is Over—Now What?

At the same time, the students in sixth and seventh grades at Broomfield Heights Middle School had monthly themes of their own, with some overlap:

Sixth Grade

September	Getting to Know Our School
October	On Becoming a Sixth Grader
November	Peers
December	Holidays
January	Safe in the Community
February	Self-Control and the Art of Refusal
March	"Let's Talk"
April	Deciding to Decide
May	"Services Sampling"

Seventh Grade

September	Who's Who in Your REACH: Group Building
October	Self-Concept
November	Who's on First . . . What's on Second . . . I Don't Know's on Third (communication skills)
December	Deck the Halls with Holiday Time
January	What's Happening around Me?
February	. . . Walk Beside Me and Be My Friend
March	Substance Abuse
April	How to Make Choices
May	How Time Flies when You're Having Fun— Welcome to the Eighth Grade

In a wise move calculated to defuse any misunderstanding of the value of the REACH curriculum, or official endorsement by the school board, the staff at Broomfield Heights Middle School also details, painstakingly, the manner in which the advisory curriculum is an integral part of the total middle school curriculum for the Boulder Valley School District. A full page in the advisory curriculum guide details the topics of the advisory program (e.g., friendship), the place of that topic in the regular curriculum (e.g., health, home economics, and physical education), the grade levels at which it is taught in the regular curriculum, and the districtwide curriculum objectives and belief statements (e.g., personalization, equity, pervasive caring) to which it is related.

Other school staffs have found that keeping the same advisor and advisees together over a period of years is an effective practice, as is the case in the middle schools in Yakima, Washington. They believe that the objectives of their advisory program are far more effectively accomplished when advisors and advisees (and their parents) establish and maintain a three-year relationship "unrelated to academic expectations." A considerable number of schools have used a parent orientation process at the beginning of every year, and found that to be very helpful. Parents can be remarkably receptive to the advisor-advisee program if they are given the information they need to understand it. Counselors do play an important role, perhaps the most important, in the success or failure of the advisor-advisee program. When counselors see their role as including the success of the advisor-advisee program, they act in ways which provide support and enthusiasm to teachers. They become the school's team leader for guidance, acting as if the teachers were, in a sense, in their advisor-advisee group. When counselors mistakenly view the advisor-advisee program as a rebuke, perhaps as a result of the failure attributed to their counseling efforts by others, they react defensively and act in ways which undercut and lessen the chances for a successful activity. Counselors must be given the responsibility for the success of the advisor-advisee program, and the freedom to accomplish the task. When counselors are used as assistant administrators, they will not have the time to fill other roles.

Nothing is more important, however, to the success of the advisor-advisee program than the understanding and support of the school principal and other administrators. When administrators are enthusiastically in favor of a program and are willing to put themselves forward in support of it, the chances for success are good. When they are not, teachers will soon get the message, and those who really are uncomfortable with the program will begin to lobby against it with the principal, neglect their own advisor-advisee groups, and generally seek to erode support for the program among other faculty members. Principals must be willing to treat teachers in the same way that they want teachers to respond to students. That is, they must explain the goals of the program, show the teachers how they may succeed, encourage them to try, and let them know that the program is an important part of their day and is not optional.

One school principal with a long record of success with advisory programs (Walt Grebing, of Broomfield Heights Middle School in Broomfield, Colorado) offers the following important suggestions for school leaders and the advisory program:

1. Be certain to reestablish the purpose and expectations of the advisory program, every year.

2. Provide "prime time" in the schedule for advisory.

3. Establish counselor and staff commitment to the program, especially with new staff members each year.

4. Be sure that advisory is not seen as an extra preparation for teachers.

5. Always be a role model of enthusiasm for the program: visit classes, attend staff development sessions, and so on.

6. Encourage continuous honest internal evaluation of the program.

7. Provide on-going staff development.

8. Share successes among the staff members.

9. Evaluate staff members on their effectiveness as advisors.

10. Constantly explain and advocate the program to the external community and to other school and district personnel.

Finally, the National Resource Center for Middle Grades, at the University of South Florida in Tampa, offers the following "Dos" and "Don'ts" for successful advisors. We endorse this list.

Do have a planned and regularly scheduled program.
Do inform your students why advisory is important.

Do share your own personal hopes, worries, and experiences when appropriate.

Do activities *with* the students, and not to them.

Do allow time for students to trust the program, the advisor, and each other.

Do lots of hands-on and interactive activities.

Do show your enthusiasm and commitment to the program.

Do initiate and maintain contact with your advisees' parents or guardians.

Do give advisees some ownership in the program through reasonable involvement in choices and decisions.

Do establish expected behavioral norms for advisory time.

Don't have unrealistic expectations.

Don't copy another district's program without customizing it to your students' needs.

Don't expect all students in your advisory group to like each other or you, especially at first.

Don't tolerate put-downs and "killer statements."

Don't forget to help other advisors be successful.

Don't cripple the program by complaining about it inappropriately.

Don't forget to have fun with your students.

The advisor-advisee program, properly organized and implemented, can be a bright place in the day of everyone involved. When all things were considered regarding the advisory program in Orange County, Florida, for example, the results were considered to be encouragingly positive. Pickler observed:

> Over the course of four years (1987–1991), interviews with interdisciplinary teams involved with IMPACT have revealed that teacher acceptance of and comfort with the concept is growing. More teachers report seeing value in the program and they are also able to cite more examples of ways in which they are personalizing the program to the needs of their students and engaging in collaborative efforts with their colleagues. This growth is admittedly slow, but after four years it is still evident. In schools where the leadership attaches significance to IMPACT and conveys expectations as to its implementation, acceptance has grown and the program has begun to find a niche in the total school program.
>
> It should also be noted that parents generally support the concept of IMPACT. The majority of parents responding to the middle school program evaluation parent survey feel that the program has been beneficial for their children. School level administrators who have taken the time to articulate the goals and intent of the program to parents report that they tend to agree as to the need for such an effort on the part of the school. (1991, p. 5)

Reflecting on the process of implementing effective advisory programs in his district, Pickler (1991, pp. 6–7) offers several important recommendations:

1. Make an all-out effort to dismiss publicly the perception that the advisory program is a crisis-centered psychotherapy program. Stress that it is intended to address the normal development that middle school students experience with or without adult guidance and direction. It is for mentally healthy children.

2. Accept the fact, from the beginning, that advisory groups will remain large and develop a program that is congruent with this reality.

3. Dedicate the district to providing continuing inservice to teachers and administrators regarding the purpose and redesign of the program. Point out that the district has its own ideas of what works and what doesn't and that much has been learned since the initial implementation of the program, when planners were dependent on what they could learn from other districts.

4. Provide regular opportunities for schools to share successful practices.

5. Place primary responsibility for the program with curriculum people in the district, thus playing down the guidance function.

6. Revise the role of the school guidance department to insure program involvement and support.

7. Keep the advisory program in the schools, no matter what. It belongs there. Many teachers are making good use of the time provided, and more can be encouraged to do so. "For those who staunchly refuse to do anything with it, it has its greater value in serving as a daily reminder to them that they may not be well suited for teaching at the middle school level."

When advisory programs are implemented incorrectly, it can be a glaring failure and a barrier to further progress. Educators who wish to implement the program, but who can not do so without risking its success, should consider postponing the program. The advisor-advisee program is an excellent addition to the interdisciplinary team foundation, but it ought not be built in the absence of that foundation without extreme care.

Research on the Advisory Program

During the spring of 1979, an evaluation of the advisory program at Lincoln Middle School was conducted by a research team from the University of Florida[2], as a part of a larger assessment of the affective components of the Lincoln program. A stratified random sampling procedure was used so that only one third of the 900 students were required to evaluate any one aspect of the program, yet the results were pertinent to all students within the school. The evaluation team worked with the principal and the faculty Program Improvement Council to specify the program's goals and objectives; they then developed instruments reflecting these goals and objectives. The instruments for both students and teachers were reviewed by a committee of teachers and modified as appropriate. To maximize the amount of information available to the school staff, the student data were analyzed by race, sex, team, and grade. The teacher data

[2]Then associate professors Afesa Bell-Nathaniel and Sandra B. Damico, along with their students Charles Green, Wendy McClosky, and Nancy McCowan, conducted the study. The assistance of Professors Bell-Nathaniel and Damico is gratefully acknowledged for providing this summary of the research.

were analyzed only by team. The design was such that the anonymity of all respondents was maintained.

Students were asked questions which examined their relationship with and perceptions of their advisor-teachers and the related activities. The teachers were asked questions on the centrality of advisor-advisee programs to a middle school experience and the amount of teacher preparation required for an effective effort. In brief, all students:

1. Perceived their advisory teachers as caring for them, and for the other students in their group.

2. Thought their group helped in their understanding of other people.

3. Differentiated between academic and personal problems. They indicated they would turn first to their advisor for help in solving an academic problem, but would also seek out the guidance counselor for assistance with a personal problem.

4. Felt the advisor-advisee group provided skills for problem solving.

5. Differentiated between most important and favorite activities: the most important AA activities were USSR (silent reading) and study hall; while favorite activities were talking with a friend and free time.

6. Frequently listed the advisor-teacher as their favorite teacher or the teacher they knew best.

7. Agreed that their advisor-teachers were fair.

Only a few significant differences emerged when the student data were analyzed by race, sex, team, and grade. These differences were:

1. African-American students were more likely than whites to believe that their advisors cared about them and other students; helped them understand other people; and helped them learn how to solve problems.

2. Females were more likely than males to believe that the advisory group helped them learn how to solve problems; they also identified more strongly with Lincoln Middle School than did the males.

3. There were no differences in responses among students by grade.

4. The only question on which there was a team difference was: "I feel like an outsider in my group." While a majority of students indicated a strong sense of belonging to their group, some of the students on three of the teams were less positive on this item than were students on the other three teams.

The teacher findings were:

1. Overwhelming endorsement for the advisory concept for middle schools.

2. Belief that teachers were prepared to function in the advisor role, although about one third of the teachers believed that they needed more training for this role.

3. Indicated that they had long-range goals for their advisory groups.

4. Perceived the guidance counselor as playing an active role in the program.

5. Half of the teachers indicated they prepared special activities for advisor-advisee time.

6. Slightly less than half of the teachers reported having a value clarification activity at least once a week.

An evaluation such as this provides useful information about a program to a faculty. Strengths and weaknesses are highlighted and directions derived for staff and program development. For instance, the advisory program was seen as an integral part of the school's program by both faculty and students. Of some concern, however, might be the less positive ratings given by the white male students; perhaps efforts should be made to identify and address their special needs. Although the teachers at Lincoln said that value clarification was important, neither they nor their students ranked it highly. This may reflect the fact that a significant minority of the teachers failed to include activities of this nature in their groups. Since many of the teachers expressed a need for additional training, value clarification and related activities might be a focus of an inservice education program at this particular school.

One of the concerns of program specialists, referred to earlier in this chapter, has been the role of the guidance counselor in an advisor-advisee program. Data collected in this evaluation indicated that both teachers and students perceived the guidance counselor as playing an important role in the school's program; thus, the advisor-advisee program has not eliminated the need for a counselor. There are so many other duties that counselors must perform in a middle school (for example, staffing students into special programs, guiding new students, assisting in quasi-administrative duties, and crisis intervention) that even the idea of eliminating or reducing their presence is unthinkable.

It is important to note that all students, regardless of grade level, felt an integral part of the school and their advisory group. Failure to find grade level differences is probably a reflection of the impact of multiage grouping at Lincoln, but additional information would need to be collected to insure this interpretation. Teachers at Lincoln Middle School should have been very pleased with the results of this evaluation. A critical step in developing an effective integrated school is for students to perceive their teachers as being fair and caring about them as individuals. This evaluation indicated that Lincoln had met this condition.

Another study of the advisor-advisee program at Lincoln Middle School was prompted by the Bell-Nathaniel and Damico study, and by some chance remarks made by some high school teachers who, at a district teacher's meeting, observed that students from Lincoln were more mature and easier to teach when they reached ninth grade than were students from several other schools in the district (Doda, 1979). After gathering considerable data from both questionnaires and interviews, Doda's analysis confirmed and extended the conclusions of the study by Bell-Nathaniel and Damico. Among the significant conclusions were the following:

1. Ninth grade students in the district's high schools felt good about their inter-personal relationships at school, and attributed some of their successes in this area to the advisor-advisee program at the middle school.

2. Students in the study believed that they understood themselves well and attributed this, in part, to the opportunities provided in the advisory program, particularly the extended relationships with a teacher who cared about them, and the chance to talk about personal matters with peers.

3. What might be called school survival skills appeared to be an area of weakness. Solving problems, using school time wisely, and meeting deadlines were perceived as unresolved difficulties by a significant portion of the students who had moved on to ninth grade.

4. There were no special activities that students pointed to as having been particularly helpful. A caring advisor and a special peer group were cited much more frequently as having been helpful.

5. Males seemed less prepared and less successful in ninth grade than females, African-American males in particular.

6. There was a small portion of youngsters who believed that the advisory program was of no help or value at all. They tended to remark, "We did nothing in AA."

Comprehensively, however, this study came to the same positive conclusions about the advisory program at Lincoln Middle School as did the first one.

Several more recent research projects have been reported widely. The "Rochester experiment" (Urbanski, 1991) indicates that, among the changes instituted in the wide-ranging reforms in that district, among the most successful has been the Home Base Guidance program in the new middle schools. Among the important outcomes in 1991, home contacts by teachers were at the point where 73 percent of the parents reported that they had direct contact with their child's advisor by the middle of the school year, and 82 percent of the parents who had been contacted said that such contacts were helpful. Such home contacts were up 45 percent over the previous year.

Putbrese (1989) surveyed 3,400 seventh grade students in middle and junior high schools with and without advisory programs. Of the forty-three statements included in the survey, twenty-nine were statistically significant in their results. From the data available, Putbrese drew the following conclusions. Advisory programs:

1. improve teacher-student relationships.
2. give students a feeling of more control over decisions.
3. promote an atmosphere of equality, especially according to girls.
4. provide opportunity for group work.
5. improve the sharing of feelings between students, especially girls. Three out of four boys refuse to share their deeper feelings with or without an advisory program.
6. help to maximize the altruistic nature of early adolescents.
7. reduce the incidence of smoking and alcohol use.
8. appear to make teachers more aware of or more attentive to student behavior, especially according to boys.

Putbrese concluded that "reports of research on affective education clearly support the concept that advisory programs are necessary for the middle level school. Early adolescents need to feel known and recognized. The advisory program has the potential for attending to this need" (p. 115).

Bergmann (1989) conducted a study of 115 boys and 66 girls, ages 11–16, in twenty middle-level schools in urban, suburban, and rural settings; students had all been identified by the principal as "at-risk" or having been frequently reported as discipline problems. Each was interviewed to determine the students' perceptions of discipline effectiveness, teaching strategies, and school climate. The overall purpose of the study was to identify instructional strategies which might assist such early adolescents in remaining in school. All students "mentioned that this was the first time anyone had asked them their opinion about anything" (p. 3). Also, "every student in the study mentioned at least once during the interview that they would like someone to listen to them . . . " (p. 6).

The author suggested that one of the ways to achieve such an objective would be to design an advisory program that:

1. trained teachers in skills for listening, group dynamics, and parent conferencing.
2. encouraged teachers to take time to teach skills associated with students decision making, problem solving, and responsibility.
3. included health information.
4. informed and involved parents whenever appropriate.

A study of 394 middle school students, by Buckner and Bickel (1990), reinforces the picture of desired personal qualities of teachers, especially as they act as advisors. The students indicated, again, that the most desirable were being respectful toward students, having an accepting attitude, and being easy to talk with. Students want teachers as advisors who are approachable and who, once approached, listen carefully, acceptingly, and respectfully to what the students say.

While such studies have been encouraging, there are still (in the early 1990s) too few well-designed studies of these programs to permit more than modest speculations about the ultimate value of the advisor-advisee program, from the point of view of educational research. More of this type of research needs to be conducted, and we hope that these studies are indicative of future efforts.

Peer Advisory Programs

Recent experience indicates that the advisement function can be extended to include students advising students. In the middle schools of Alachua County, Florida, and elsewhere, "Peer Facilitators" programs have been underway for several years. At Caddo Middle Magnet School (Shreveport, Louisiana), a "Peer Advocate Program" has been established. The Caddo program involves students helping students under close adult supervision. Thirty-five seventh and eighth graders (as a cross section of the student population) are selected each year by their peers and teachers. A five-week training program follows, in which students are taught the essentials of growth-producing interpersonal relationships and the skills of listening, support, and problem solving.

ADDITIONAL SUGGESTIONS FOR FURTHER STUDY

A. Books and Monographs

Beane, J. A. & Lipka, R. (1987). *When the kids come first: Enhancing self-esteem.* Columbus, OH (4807 Evanswood Dr., Columbus 43229): National Middle School Association.

George, P. S., Spreul, M. & Moorefield, J. (1987). *Long-term teacher student relationships: A middle school case study.* Columbus, OH: National Middle School Association.

James, M. (1986). *Adviser-advisee programs: Why, what, and how.* Columbus, OH: National Middle School Association.

Morganett, R. S. (1990). *Skills for living: Group counseling activities for young adolescents.* Champaign, IL: Research Press.

Purkey, W. W. & Strahan, D. B. (1986). *Positive discipline: A pocketful of ideas.* Columbus, OH: National Middle School Association.

B. Periodicals

Alexander, J. A. C. & Harman, R. L. (1988). One counselor's intervention in the aftermath of a middle school student's suicide: A case study. *Journal of Counseling and Development, 66*(6), 283–85.

Gerler, E. R., Jr. & Moorhead, S. (1988). Drug information: The facts about drugs and where to go for help. *Elementary School Guidance and Counseling, 23*(2), 139–45.

Hagborg, W. J. (1990). Enhancing middle-school-age students' knowledge of school counseling services. *Psychology in the Schools, 27*(3), 238–43.

Haynes, N. M. (1990). Influence of self-concept on school adjustment among middle-school students. *Journal of Social Psychology, 130*(2), 199–207.

Henderson, P. & La Forge, J. (1989). The role of the middle school counselor in teacher-advisor programs. *School Counselor, 36*(5), 348–51.

Hering, K. (1989). It's time schools considered the plight of the "latchkey parent." *PTA Today, 14*(5), 20–21.

Hubbard, R. L. (& others). (1988). Initiation of alcohol and drug abuse in the middle school years. *Elementary School Guidance and Counseling, 23*(2), 118–23.

Huff, J. A. (1988). Personalized behavior modification: An in-school suspension program that teaches students how to change. *School Counselor, 35*(3), 210–14.

Murphy, M. F. (1990). At issue: At-risk students. *Journal of Industrial Teacher Education, 27*(3), 72–74.

Peterman, F. P. (1990). Successful middle level schools and the development. *NASSP Bulletin, 74*(526), 62–65.

Prokop, M. S. (1990). Children of divorce: Relearning happiness. *Momentum, 21*(2), 72–73.

Remley, T. , Jr. & Albright, P. L. (1988). Expectations for middle school counselors: Views of students, teachers, principals, and parents. *School Counselor, 35*(4), 290–96.

Scales, P. C. (1991). Emotional fitness and the young adolescent. *PTA Today, 16*(3), 8–9.

Smith, P. B. (& others). (1989). Contraceptive and sexuality knowledge among inner-city middle school students from minority groups. *School Counselor, 37*(2), 103–08.

St. Clair, K. L. (1989). Middle school counseling research: A resource for school counselors. *Elementary School Guidance and Counseling, 23*(3), 219–26.

Sweeney, M. M. & Zionts, P. (1989). The "second skin": Perceptions of disturbed and nondisturbed early adolescents on clothing, self-concept, and body image. *Adolescence, 24*(94), 411–20.

Van Hoose, J. (Fall, 1991). *The ultimate goal: A/A across the day*. Midpoints: Occasional Papers. Vol 2, No. 1. Columbus: National Middle School Association.

C. ERIC

Austin, S. & Meister, G. (1990). *Responding to children at risk: A guide to recent reports*. Philadelphia, PA: Research for Better Schools, Inc. (ERIC Document Reproduction Service No. ED 322 271)

Becker, H. J. (1987). *Addressing the needs of different groups of early adolescents: Effects of varying school and classroom organizational practices on students from different social backgrounds and abilities* (Report No. 16). Baltimore, MD: Center for Research on Elementary and Middle Schools. (ERIC Document Reproduction Service No. ED 291 506)

Berla, N. (& others). (1989). *The middle school years: A parents' handbook.* Columbia, MD: National Committee for Citizens in Education. (ERIC Document Reproduction Service No. ED 316 310)

Bingaman, D. E. (1987). *Career counseling and development. Course of Study, Grades 6, 7, 8.* (ERIC Document Reproduction Service No. ED 319 985)

Gerler, E. R., Jr. (& others). (1990). The challenge of self discovery in early adolescence. In K. O'Rourke (Ed.)., *The challenge of counseling in middle schools.* Alexandria, VA: American Association for Counseling and Development; Ann Arbor, MI: ERIC Clearinghouse on Counseling and Personnel Services. (ERIC Document Reproduction Service No. ED 321 162)

Gerler, E. R., Jr. (& others). (1990). The challenge of family relationships in early adolescence. In K. O'Rourke (Ed.)., *The challenge of counseling in middle schools.* Alexandria, VA: American Association for Counseling and Development; Ann Arbor, MI: ERIC Clearinghouse on Counseling and Personnel Services. (ERIC Document Reproduction Service No. ED 321 163)

Gerler, E. R., Jr. (& others). (1990). The challenge of peer pressure and drug abuse in early adolescence. In K. O'Rourke (Ed.)., *The challenge of counseling in middle schools.* Alexandria, VA: American Association for Counseling and Development; Ann Arbor, MI: ERIC Clearinghouse on Counseling and Personnel Services. (ERIC Document Reproduction Service No. ED 321 164)

Gerler, E. R., Jr. (& others). (1990). The challenge of sexual maturation in early adolescence. In K. O'Rourke (Ed.)., *The challenge of counseling in middle schools.* Alexandria, VA: American Association for Counseling and Development; Ann Arbor, MI: ERIC Clearinghouse on Counseling and Personnel Services. (ERIC Document Reproduction Service No. ED 321 166)

Gerler, E. R., Jr. (& others). (1990). The challenge of stress and suicide in early adolescence. In K. O'Rourke (Ed.)., *The challenge of counseling in middle schools.* Alexandria, VA: American Association for Counseling and Development; Ann Arbor, MI: ERIC Clearinghouse on Counseling and Personnel Services. (ERIC Document Reproduction Service No. ED 321 165)

Hamburg, B. A. (1990). *Life skills training: Preventive interventions for young adolescents. Report of the Life Skills Training Working Group.* Washington, DC: Carnegie Council on Adolescent Development. (ERIC Document Reproduction Service No. ED 323 018)

Hamburg, D. A. (1989). *Early adolescence: A critical time for interventions in education and health.* New York: Carnegie Corp. of New York, NY. (ERIC Document Reproduction Service No. ED 323 453)

Haws, Z. & Lovell, N. (1988). *Support groups for identified "at risk" middle school/ junior high school students.* Odgen, UT: Weber County Dept. of Alcohol and Substance Abuse. (ERIC Document Reproduction Service No. ED 310 301)

Helge, D. (1989). *Report of pilot project regarding strategies for enhancing self-esteem of at-risk students.* Bellingham, WA: National Rural and Small Schools Consortium. (ERIC Document Reproduction Service No. ED 314 678)

Hendrickson, J. M. & Roth, J. (1990, March). *Challenging the high risk student—a model for after-school involvement of adolescents.* Paper presented at the Annual

National Dropout Prevention Conference, Nashville, TN. (ERIC Document Reproduction Service No. ED 321 207)

Lake, S. (1989). *Supporting middle level students through counseling and teacher advisor programs* (Practitioner's Monograph #4). Sacramento, CA: California League of Middle Schools.

Lockledge, A. (1988). *Social groups in the middle school.* (ERIC Document Reproduction Service No. ED 297 869)

Matthews, D. B. (1988). *A study of the effects of a stress management program on affective and cognitive measures of middle school children.* Orangeburg, SC: South Carolina State College. (ERIC Document Reproduction Service No. ED 303 747)

Millstein, S. G. (1988). *The potential of school-linked centers to promote adolescent health and development.* Working Paper. Washington, DC: Carnegie Council on Adolescent Development. (ERIC Document Reproduction Service No. ED 302 619)

Mitchell, S. (1988). *Evaluation of the Portland plan for drug free schools, October 1987–September 1988.* Portland, OR: Portland Public Schools, Research and Evaluation Dept. (ERIC Document Reproduction Service No. ED 300 519)

Morris, T. & Tadlock, M. (1990). *Extended day programs for latchkey children.* (ERIC Document Reproduction Service No. ED 327 299)

Myrick, R. D. (& others). (1990). *The teacher advisor program: An innovative approach to school guidance.* Ann Arbor, MI: ERIC Clearinghouse on Counseling and Personnel Services. (ERIC Document Reproduction Service No. ED 316 791)

National Center for Health Statistics (August 15, 1990). *Monthly Vital Statistics Report,* 39 (4) Supplement, U.S. Department of Health and Human Services, Centers for Disease Control.

O'Sullivan, R. G. (1989, March). *Identifying students for participation in a model middle school dropout prevention program.* Paper presented at the Annual Meeting of the American Educational Research Association, San Francisco, CA. (ERIC Document Reproduction Service No. ED 305 170)

Oxley, D. (& others). (1989). *Effective dropout prevention: The case for schoolwide reform.* New York, NY: Public Education Association. (ERIC Document Reproduction Service No. ED 298 225)

Sierer, T. M. & Winfield, L. F. (1988, April). *The concerns and attitude of early adolescent middle school students in transition.* Paper presented at the Annual Meeting of the American Educational Research Association, New Orleans, LA. (ERIC Document Reproduction Service No. ED 300 722)

Strodl, P. (1988, April). *Ethnic differences in dealing with experiences in multiethnic middle schools.* Paper presented at the Urban Educational Research Conference, Brooklyn, NY. (ERIC Document Reproduction Service No. ED 297 044)

Swanson, L. A. & Williams-Robertson, L. (1990). *School-community guidance center: An alternative education program for high-risk students, 1989–90* (Publication no. 89-28). Austin, TX: Austin Independent School District, Office of Research and Evaluation. (ERIC Document Reproduction Service No. ED 321 210)

Wheelock, A. & Dorman, G. (1988). *Before it's too late: Dropout prevention in the middle grades.* Boston: Advocacy Center; Center for Early Adolescence, Carrboro, NC. (ERIC Document Reproduction Service No. ED 301 355)

White, W. F. & Cass, M. (1988, November). *Motivation of middle school students*. Paper presented at the Annual Meeting of the Mid-South Educational Research Association, Louisville, KY. (ERIC Document Reproduction Service No. ED 303 495)

White, R. (1989). *Bibliotherapy and the reluctant student*. (ERIC Document Reproduction Service No. ED 309 390)

D. Dissertations and Dissertation Abstracts

Aiello, H. S. (1988). Assessment of a mentor program on self-concept and achievement variables of middle school underachievers (Doctoral dissertation, Virginia Polytechnic Institute and State University, 1988). *Dissertation Abstracts International*, 49/07a, 1699.

Bacon, C. S. (1988). Teacher goal structures and student responsibility for learning: a student perspective (Doctoral dissertation, University of California, Santa Barbara, 1988). *Dissertation Abstracts International*, 50/05a, 1269.

Bobbe, W. F. (1988). The development and validation of an advisement evaluation instrument. (Doctoral dissertation, University of Northern Colorado, 1988). *Dissertation Abstracts International*, 50/07a, 1856.

Connors, N. (1987). A case study to determine the essential components and effects of an advisor-advisee program in an exemplary middle school. *Dissertation Abstracts International*, 47, 2986A.

Smith, C. S. (1988). Teacher perceptions of computer-assisted counseling when applied in teacher-student interaction problems (Doctoral dissertation, United States International University, 1988). *Dissertation Abstracts International*, 49/10a, 2938.

Tighlman, W. S. (1988). The effect of peer counseling on lowering the rate of middle school suspensions (Doctoral dissertation, Florida Atlantic University, 1988). *Dissertation Abstracts International*, 49/08a, 2118.

CHAPTER 6

Interdisciplinary Team Organization

By the early 1990s, middle school educators seemed to have reached a consensus on the priority of the manner in which teachers and students are organized to learn. During the decade of the eighties, a number of national organizations (e.g., Carnegie, 1989) and hundreds, if not thousands, of school districts recognized that the interdisciplinary organization of teachers was the most distinguishing feature of the middle school, and the keystone of its structure. In the presence of a stable interdisciplinary team organization, other components of the middle school program function more smoothly. In the absence of the interdisciplinary team organization, they operate with considerably more difficulty, if they exist at all.

Sharing: The Basis for Organizing the Middle School Faculty

What teachers share with one another is the basis for how they are organized, at all three levels of American education. The degree to which teachers share in teaching the same subject, and the extent to which they share the same students determines, in most schools, the ways in which teachers are organized to deliver instruction. At each level, the phenomenon of teacher sharing has produced three distinct types of teacher organization for instruction.

In the elementary school, especially in the primary grades, the nature and needs of the students argue for very little sharing between and among teachers; students there need an almost exclusive relationship with one teacher.

Consequently, the self-contained classroom has been the predominant mode of elementary school faculty organization throughout the history of American education. Teachers share few students with other teachers, except specialists in music, physical education, and so on. They do not share the teaching of the same subject, since regular elementary level classroom teachers most often teach the basic academic program to their own students. In the nineties, however, it seems that, at least in the upper elementary years, teachers have begun to do more sharing of the same subjects and students. Perhaps, this is in recognition of the nature and needs of the students; perhaps not.

At the high school level, teachers share few students but are committed to sharing the teaching of the same subject. High school teachers rarely teach in more than one academic discipline. Often, they teach only one subject at one grade level; a teacher might, for example, teach only junior level American history, and never teach world history. Teachers see themselves as academic specialists, arguing that the sophistication of the subject matter at that level prohibits teachers from crossing disciplinary lines with ease. Released from a major concern with student relationships, the high school has maintained a steady focus on organizing in a way that facilitates the delivery of what they are committed to, the academic disciplines.

High school teachers are organized, therefore, into academic departments along the same lines as colleges and universities. Instead of one teacher generalist presenting virtually the whole world of knowledge to a specific group of small children, the high school teacher is usually responsible for an even smaller part (e.g., American history) of one of many areas (e.g., social studies). Instead of working alone, the high school teacher often interacts with other teachers, but with the common focus being the subject area they share.

The goal of the middle school is to contribute to the articulation between the elementary school and the high school by providing a program that ties the two together in a smooth and continuous way, while at the same time providing a unique experience for the education of older children and young adolescents; a middle-way between the elementary school self-contained classroom and the high school department. This middle-way has come to be known as the interdisciplinary team organization, an organization which focuses on teachers who share several very important components of the school program. The need for planned gradualism as the key to K–12 articulation (identified several decades ago) remains, and is met, in the exemplary middle school through the interdisciplinary team organization.

The Nature of the Interdisciplinary Team Organization

There is, in the nineties, considerably less misunderstanding and confusion about the meaning of terms used to describe the organization for instruction in middle schools. Numerous terms which had been used previously as synonyms (team teaching, interdisciplinary, intradisciplinary, multidisciplinary, cross-cur-riculum, and several others), have given way, generally, to the use of the term interdisciplinary team organization. Few educators now use team teaching and interdisciplinary team organization synonymously.

Three decades ago, in one of the few books ever written on the topic of teaming, the authors (Shaplin & Olds, 1964) defined team teaching as "a type of instructional organization, involving teaching personnel and the students assigned to them, in which two or more teachers are given responsibility, work-ing together, for all or a significant part of the instruction of the same group of students." With a few slight adjustments, this definition still works well for the exemplary middle school almost 30 years later.

Team teaching, as it was envisioned in the '60s, was basically a hierarchical gradation of faculty members' roles and titles wherein a master teacher had major responsibilities for planning and presenting lessons to large groups of students, who are then dispersed to small seminar-size groups, led by presum-ably less competent faculty, for discussion and review of the lesson presented by the master teacher. Quite naturally, the impression gained is one in which the essence of teaming is expressed in the act of instruction. Such a model may work well for high schools and colleges, but it rarely plays a major role in the exemplary middle school. In fact, it is our impression that the act of team teach-ing, as it was originally intended, is rarely practiced at any level of education.

By contrast, the term "organization" focuses on the structural requirements of the team. It highlights factors other than a particular style of large and small group instruction. Interdisciplinary team organization, the concept now endorsed not only by us but by the National Middle School Association and others, fits comfortably with Shaplin's definition cited earlier, but goes further. In this text, we use the term interdisciplinary team organization to define "a way of organizing the faculty so that a group of teachers share: (1) the same group of students; (2) the responsibility for planning, teaching, and evaluating curric-ulum and instruction in more than one academic area; (3) the same schedule; and (4) the same area of the building." These four factors are the necessary and sufficient elements of interdisciplinary teacher organization. When all four are present, nothing else is needed; when one or more elements is missing, the team organization is less than complete. Interdisciplinary team teaching is not a critical element of the exemplary middle school; interdisciplinary team organization is.

In describing the interdisciplinary team organization at Tenaya Middle School in Fresno, California, teacher Sharon Cook (personal communication, September 16, 1991) captured the essence of the concept:

> At Tenaya, we are formed into interdisciplinary teams, with four teachers to a team—English, science, history, and math. In some instances the teams are two or three teachers, due to student population, but all include the four subjects. Our special education (resource) students are integrated into one eighth and one seventh grade team, with the RSP teacher assigned to that team to work

with the team teachers. Each team has a common discipline plan, a team name, and treats the students as a family (we have close to 1,000 students, so this is an important concept—"family within a family"). This means field trips and assemblies together, joint parent-team teacher meetings to discuss student problems and lessons, team parties for special occasions and rewards, and shared detention sessions, in which the team teachers each take a day of the week. This is our fourth year with teams. We have had a lot of staff turnover in those four years, so our progress has been steady, but slow. I feel we are to the point now where each teacher really sees the value of the system and is beginning more and more to buy into it.

Four Phases of Interdisciplinary Team Life

Studies of the ways in which middle school teachers work together on teams (George, 1982; Plodzik & George, 1989) indicate that there appear to be four areas of middle school life in which teamwork is essential; four different ways exist in which teachers and students work together to accomplish the tasks of schooling more effectively and satisfactorily at the middle level. These areas of teamwork are: (1) organization; (2) community-building; (3) teamed instruction; and (4) governance.

Phase One: Organization

Teamwork is virtually impossible unless several critical conditions are met. First, of course, middle school teachers must share the same students, space, and schedule. Among the members of the team, at least two subjects must be taught. When these conditions exist, the interdisciplinary team organization is possible; when they are absent, teamwork is quite difficult.

Once these requirements are satisfied, teamwork begins, even without planning. Almost immediately, teachers on the team realize the power inherent in their acting together. Time between classes becomes more closely supervised, as teachers begin to use the phrase "our students" more and more frequently. Teachers almost always report that the job becomes more satisfying and more productive.

Students begin to notice that they are in classes with others who have the same teachers at the same and different times of the day. Students observe that they do not travel as widely from one part of the building to another as frequently as they may have under prior arrangements, if teachers had been organized in departments. They will discover that they are moving around the school more often, if they are moving up from the self-contained classroom of the primary grades. Teachers, students will notice, begin to share the same academic and behavioral expectations. Even if students have not been told by the teachers of the existence of the team, they will begin to feel its effects.

Teachers respond to the new opportunities they discover, and can take advantage of the new organization to design and implement common rules and procedures to govern student behavior. Time between classes can be shortened and more closely supervised. Team conferences with students, parents, and educational specialists become more productive. Teachers spend their common planning time discussing what they have in common—their students—so they end up knowing their students better, perhaps, than they ever have before.

Middle school teachers discover that there are a number of essential organizational tasks which must be performed in this phase of team life, if they are going to benefit from their work together. The teachers on the team must develop common team rules, which are consistently applied from one classroom to the next. Teachers can maintain their own individual classroom rules, but collaborate on those that are important enough to justify their cooperation. Developing common procedures (e.g., headings for papers, test day, etc.) can also simplify life for students while it is made easier for teachers. Conferences with parents, students, and specialists, once done individually, now should be done as a team; such meetings are almost always more satisfying for teachers when they work together on them. Finally, teachers can use their organizational time and skill to develop and redesign the schedules for their teams and for individual students on the team. Frequently, the block schedule permits teachers much greater latitude in such areas. Used properly, the interdisciplinary team organization affords teachers much greater leverage than they could possibly amass working independently.

Teachers on Team 6–N at Wakulla Middle School (Crawfordville, Florida) offered the following team rules in a letter home to parents in 1990:

6–N Rules

1. Show up on time.
2. Be prepared for class.
3. Complete all assignments.
4. Talk only at appropriate times.
5. Help keep the room and school clean.
6. Be considerate and respectful of others.
7. Gum and candy are not allowed at school.

The team rules were followed by a list of team consequences for breaking the rules, and rewards for following them. In addition, the teachers discussed positive aspects of team unity, special activities, and field trips. They expressed their hope that students and parents would realize that each student was a part of a team, no longer just an individual student on his/her own.

At Eggers Middle School in Hammond, Indiana, teams assume a substantial role in student discipline. They engage in the following:

1. Making phone calls and conducting parent conferences.

2. Making home visits where warranted.

3. Contacting parents when students accumulate three unexcused absences or tardies.

4. Notifying the principal of suspected "educational neglect" cases and filling out forms for all cases of potential abuse and neglect.

5. Developing and distributing Learning Community rules to all students, and explaining rules during advisory time.

6. Handling the punishment of all offenses other than: breaking specific school rules four or more times, fighting, verbal or physical threats to a teacher, possession of a weapon, or other similarly serious offenses.

7. Assuring that disciplinary action issued by the team is fair and consistent, with parental involvement a priority.

More and more evidence has accumulated indicating that middle schools are frequently incorporating the interdisciplinary team approach, and casting off the departmentalized organization. In a California survey, for example, Hough (1989) concluded that 6–8 middle schools were likely to feature "team teaching" while 7–9 junior high schools retained departmentalization. Many other studies (e.g., Cawelti, 1989; George & Oldaker, 1986) confirm this strong trend.

Phase Two: Community-Building

Once organized and operating somewhat collaboratively, teachers and students become more aware of the new arrangement, and a sense of community becomes possible. The experience of many middle level educators is that both teachers and students yearn for this group identity; but teamwork is necessary to make it happen. The need must be clearly recognized. Goals must be set for its realization. Activities must be conducted with zeal. With teamwork, this component of the team organization can be powerfully productive. Furtwengler (1991, p. 7) demonstrated that the authentic involvement of students in the creation of team cultures can be an important factor in improving the ethos of the school as a whole. One student leader, involved in a number of community-building activities, remarked that: "We blend in together now. Everyone has a say and works together. Our team members care about each other and they listen to what we have to say. Everyone, well not everyone, but most of the members of the team share the load, and we get the job done." Research (Mc-Partland, 1991) indicates that the potential of teams to build a sense of community, with a personal knowledge of students, is far greater than the high school-style department, but that in practice, this potential is, as yet, largely unrealized.

For teachers, the sense of community can be the redeeming virtue of the interdisciplinary team organization. Veteran educators frequently speak of the team arrangement as the factor that enabled them to continue teaching with a sense of joy and commitment that had long been absent from their lives in school. Students, of course, require this sense of community even more than the faculty. Older children and young adolescents are at a special time of readiness—ready to experience and learn the concepts of inclusion, group citizenship, responsibility, and duty. The team offers a turf to belong to and a group to join. Teamwork can make a major difference in the level of group feeling that exists on the team, and the benefits which result from that feeling.

Teamwork tasks which increase the feeling of community include:

1. Developing team names, colors, mottos, songs, T-shirts, and other visible common possessions.

2. Staging contests, special meals, meetings, field trips, intramurals, and a host of other group activities.

3. Planning interdisciplinary curriculum units involving the whole team.

4. Creating and working on a memo or newsletter which informs parents about the "learning community."

Team get-togethers, such as pot lunch dinners can broaden the base of support for the team concept and bring parents to school in ways that are satisfying and effective. At Broomfield Heights Middle School (Broomfield, Colorado), for example, staff members welcomed parents to the 1991–92 school year as the "Year of Team Spirit" and invited them to become Team Parent Representatives. The school's Citizen Advisory Council had even established the position of Team Parent Representative Coordinator. Schools that involve parents in team life, in this manner, find parental support of the school to be substantially greater than it otherwise might be.

Recent research indicates that proper use of the interdisciplinary team organization does, in fact, increase the sense of community experienced by middle school students. One careful study (Arhar, 1990, p. 19) concluded that "Interdisciplinary teaming does make a difference in student sense of social bonding to teachers and to school, and to a lesser extent, in student bonding to peers." Panama City, Florida, expresses its middle school organizational philosophy in a way that emphasizes the development of this sort of bonding into a school community:

> Each middle school is organized in a way to allow each student to be a part of a small unit within a large school. Schools have either a "School within a school" or a "House Plan." School within a school is a grouping strategy utilized to reduce the impact of large numbers of students, which divides students into sub-schools or little schools, each with its own faculty. The house plan is a kind

of organization in which the school is divided into units, with each house having an identity, and containing the various grades, and in large part its own faculty. The purpose is decentralization, close student-faculty relationships, and easier and more flexible team teaching arrangements. Each house or school is divided into interdisciplinary teams.

Phase Three: Teamed Instruction

When teamwork has been successful in the first two phases, and teams are well organized and have a sense of unity, they are able to move to a new phase, a phase some teachers think of first. Teamed instruction, better known as "team teaching" is, as we have discussed, only one aspect of teamwork in middle grades education. It is an important part, but only a part, of the interdisciplinary team organization.

Teamed instruction requires a great deal of teamwork, in addition to the completion of the first two phases. Teamed instruction requires, first and foremost, a predisposition toward working together, instructionally, on the part of teachers. A great deal of planning is required, using time that is a precious commodity in most middle schools. Teamed instruction also requires more sophisticated communication skills that are necessary to function effectively in an isolated classroom. Finally, teamed instruction requires a very different set of planning skills than are required for individual teaching situations. When the teamwork is moving smoothly, however, a number of exciting possibilities emerge:

1. Simple coordination. Teams plan so that tests and major assignments are not due on the same days, so that fieldtrips occur when they are most appropriate, and so on.

2. Parallel planning. Teachers make a serious effort to go further in their coordination of the curriculum, manipulating their individual plans so that topics that match, although they are from different subjects, are taught at the same time. Teams plan for instruction so that such topics match across classes from time to time, perhaps even including a few joint assignments.

3. On teams where coordination and parallel planning go well, where teachers have the time and energy, teamed instruction may enter an entirely new phase. Authentic interdisciplinary units may emerge when compatible people find the time available.

Phase Four: Governance

The evidence indicates that an additional phase of teamwork contributes greatly to the success of middle level education programs. Exemplary middle school programs are, we now know, far too complex to be handled unilaterally by one or two people in the front office. Even if this was possible, it would not be preferable. Shared decision making, in the team and across the school, is both the process and the product of fully-functioning interdisciplinary team organization. While we address this topic in substantial detail in the chapter on leadership, we address aspects of it here as well because it is so clearly and directly connected to the life of the interdisciplinary team organization.

Teachers, on teams, who successfully negotiate the first three phases of teamwork, frequently find themselves motivated to assume more responsibility for the decisions that affect their school lives and the school experiences of their students. Administrators who recognize the wisdom of a participative approach to leadership, and who possess the ego strength to implement it, help teams grow toward this area of teamwork.

Teamwork, in such situations, usually involves some form of representative government system. Often, each team has a team leader who represents the other team members at weekly or biweekly meetings of a schoolwide group, such as a Program Improvement Council. This group engages in teamwork for the whole school; it establishes policies, makes decisions, and solves problems that affect more than one team. This school team may wrestle with important issues like the master schedule, the budget, and promotion/retention issues, or with mundane but no less important issues like whether there will be a school assembly the last day before winter holidays.

Recent research indicates that the four phases described here do, in fact, appear in middle schools in more than one region of the country. But, of course, not all teams function fully. A study (Plodzik & George, 1989) including 159 middle school principals throughout New England, for example, concluded that the phases were observable in middle schools throughout that region, and that various stages of team development could be determined when viewed in terms of the four phase model.

Whether teams function fully, in all four areas, is determined by several factors. The availability of staff development for teachers was critical, as was the participation of the school principal in prior training in middle school education. The presence of effective teachers on a team was related to the degree to which teams became fully developed. Knowledge of procedures for grouping students for instruction and for interrelating curriculum also emerged as necessary skills for teachers functioning in well-developed teams. Interestingly, in the Plodzik study, the amount of common planning time for teachers on teams did not show a relationship with whether or not teams functioned fully. Clearly, further research is needed.

Characteristics of Highly Effective Teams

Knowing the phases of team life should make it easier to identify teams which are operating, in all of these phases, in the most exemplary ways. A recent study of "very best teams" (George & Stevenson, 1989) indicates that, while there is no one formula to determine the nature of highly effective teams, there are some distinctive trends which deserve the attention of those attempting to implement or improve an interdisciplinary team organization.

When asked to describe the most effective teams in their schools, principals of some of the nation's better middle schools agree on what might be called "team character." Teams that are identified as the best in the school, by the principal, tend to have the following attributes:

1. The team has an "elementary flavor." Even the most experienced secondary administrators describe the best teams as those that have a student-centered style. Such teams are far more likely to have members with elementary teacher certification and experience. Rarely are the "very best teams" identified by school principals staffed entirely by teachers with secondary certification.

2. The team, while it may be student-centered, is simultaneously committed to academic outcomes. The members of the team value academic achievement and are committed to the success of their students in those areas. Teachers see themselves as willing to do almost anything to help their students be more successful, academically and otherwise. Expectations are made clear to students and parents. Even small achievements were seen as worthy of recognition and reward. The team, as a whole, possessed what might be called a spirit of advocacy with regard to the students they shared.

3. Distinctive academic climates were matched by equally distinctive team policies in regard to behavioral expectations and climate. Team members worked out collaborative policies and established systems of operation and accountability. A formal plan with rules and rule-making procedures was often in place. Reinforcement and emphasis upon good citizenship through recognition and reward was as important as more punitive restrictions and punishments.

4. The team works hard to develop and maintain a sense of community among the teachers, students, and parents. Team names, mascots, logos, T-shirts, buttons, pins, colors—all were cited to signify belonging. The very best teams went beyond symbols, to specialized activities of an astounding number and variety, activities which built and nurtured the sense of community on the team: town meetings, award and recognition assemblies, student-of-the-month designations, camping trips, field days, competitions within and between teams, clubs, fairs, plays, musicals, parties, special suppers, and intramurals.

5. Exemplary teams develop unique and effective policies and procedures for communicating with parents. The striking thing is that good teams work not only to report their students' progress, but to involve parents in the educational processes that result in those progress reports. Teams use a variety of techniques with parents, including team newsletters and memos, progress reports, team dinners, and picnics. Most significantly, however, is that on these teams teachers saw themselves, as one principal described, as having a "customer orientation" and thought of themselves as providing a service to parents rather than doing them a favor.

6. It is this so-called proactive posture that is at the center of the nature of the very best teams. They do not wait to be told to contact parents. They initiate reward and recognition systems. They are willing to try something without being guaranteed ahead of time that it will be completely successful. They try, and when they fail, they examine their behavior rather than finding scapegoats.

7. With their peers, they attempt to remain "diverse but unified." Teachers on the team recognized and celebrated, even joked about, their differences rather than attempting to eliminate them. They were, however, wise enough to know that a sense of unity required the attention and effort of all of the members of the group. Principals described such teams as characterized by a "healthy give and take," "accepting each other's shortcomings," and as "close professional friends, but not necessarily close personal friends" (George & Stevenson, 1989).

Alternative Types of Interdisciplinary Team Organization

Although interdisciplinary team organization is essential to the exemplary middle school, it should not be assumed that there is only one acceptable model of such organization. Our study of exemplary middle schools reveals that there are a variety of ways of organizing teachers in an interdisciplinary fashion. In Chapter Seven, we describe, in detail, the variety of team designs which can emerge from a consideration of factors related to the characteristics and needs of the particular population of students in the school. While it is impossible, in practice, to separate the method of organizing the faculty for instruction from the method of grouping students for instruction, in order to be able to distinguish the essence of interdisciplinary team organization clearly, the discussion of student grouping will be delayed for the most part until the chapter on alternative forms of grouping. Here, we simply offer a variety of examples of the interdisciplinary team organization.

Teams vary in regard to size, roles and responsibilities of teachers, student composition, teacher autonomy, and the way time is structured for the team. All of these variations, however, fully satisfy the four conditions of the definition set forth previously. Interdisciplinary team organization in the exemplary middle school varies considerably in the number of teachers and students who comprise a separate team. The range of size commonly encountered extends from teams of two teachers and 40–60 students to teams of six teachers with 150–190 students.

History-making Boyce Middle School in Upper St. Clair, Pennsylvania was one of the very first middle schools in the country and, in the early nineties, continues to offer exemplary programs. Boyce, like many other exemplary middle school, offers small two-teacher teams to students in the fifth and sixth grades. As they described it in a bulletin in 1991:

> Because of our belief in nurturance, students are randomly placed in hetero-geneously grouped two-teacher teams. A student spends approximately three

hours a day with each academic teacher. This enables the teacher and student to develop a strong sense of bonding. One teacher is responsible for reading, language arts, and social studies. The other team member is responsible for math, science, and an exploratory component. Interdisciplinary teaming is strongly encouraged and, as a result, the team develops a strong sense of identity and pride. Because the skills and achievement levels of our learners are distributed across a broad continuum, different methods of instruction and strategies for grouping are used to adequately meet their academic needs. The homeroom size is approximately twenty-eight and instructional groups vary from discipline to discipline and from time to time.

The exploratory component provides the teacher with the time to guide learners into areas of the curriculum that are of special interest to individual students. This component is built upon the belief that the fifth and sixth grade learners are ready to see the interrelationships between various disciplines and can apply their knowledge and skills to solve real problems. An interdisciplinary unit, "Voyage of the Mimi" is taught during this time block. Although this is a part of the science program, its interdisciplinary potential extends to math, language arts, and social studies areas. This is also a time when students may pursue a personal interest. Teachers periodically survey their students and cooperatively plan their exploratory activities which include photography, visits to a planetarium, nature walks, and other activities which are a direct outgrowth of the curriculum.

In addition to the academic team, each student spends two and a half hours a week with a member of the expressive arts team which includes art, music, home economics, and industrial arts. Over the course of the year, each student will spend nine weeks of instruction in each of these disciplines.

None of the exemplary middle schools described in this text has teams of two teachers as the model for the entire school, however, and very few schools have teams of more than five teachers, except in what we describe in Chapter 7 as "grade-wide teams." A number of exemplary middle schools have teams of varying sizes.

The middle schools in High Point, North Carolina, for example, each have teams of varied sizes, with teams of two, three and four teachers with appropriate numbers of students. Two-teacher teams are placed in the sixth grades, three-teacher teams in the seventh, and four-teacher teams in the eighth. Educators in High Point believe that this progression provides incoming sixth graders with the supportive structure they need and gradually moves toward more and more teacher-subject specialization as the students near the transition to high school. West Middle School (Aurora, Colorado) has had teams of two, four, and five teachers, and MacDonald Middle School (East Lansing, Michigan) has had teams of two, three, and four teachers each, for much the same reason as the High Point design.

The new Donnegal Middle School in Mt. Joy, Pennsylvania, was designed to operate with teams of different sizes for each grade level (Lawrence, personal communication, October, 1991). In the sixth grade, there are self-contained classes for the first nine weeks, then teams of two teachers and their students are created for the remainder of each year. Each sixth grade teacher teaches English and reading, dividing the remainder of the curriculum in "an interdisciplinary fashion." In the seventh grade, there are two three-teacher teams, in which each teaches English and reading, dividing mathematics, science, and social studies among themselves. At the eighth grade level, two four-teacher teams exist, each teacher teaching one of the basic academic subjects, plus developmental reading through her/his own subject area.

Nipher Middle School (Kirkwood, Missouri) is an excellent example of a school that has offered a variety of team designs. Sixth-grade students and parents have been given this choice (within the limits of staff flexibility): a modified self-contained classroom where one teacher will be responsible for teaching students the four basic subjects; a two-teacher team where one teacher is responsible for language arts and social studies, and another for math and science; a four-teacher team, with students heterogeneously grouped and each teacher responsible for one subject; and, a two-teacher combined sixth and seventh grade team, multiage grouping, offering a two-year curriculum with a great deal of individualized instruction and student self-direction. Seventh grade students at Nipher have the same options, with the exception of the self-contained classroom, and eighth graders are all assigned to four-teacher teams. Nipher designs its teacher teams on the basis of student maturity, allowing for the greatest flexibility in the sixth grade and gradually moving toward the large four-teacher team for all students in the eighth grade.

Kinawa Middle School (Okomos, Michigan), another of the early middle schools in America, has had a special method for organizing the faculty in an essentially interdisciplinary way, but with opportunities for other emphases as well. For most of its history (it opened in 1969), the faculty at Kinawa has been organized into three different types of learning environments. As at Nipher, parents, students, and teachers have been given considerable latitude in choosing which academic environment they prefer.

Sixth grade students may opt for two-teacher teams, in which they are taught the four basic subjects, or they may choose the "Sixth, Seventh, and Eighth Grade House Program." At Kinawa, the House offers a "multilevel environment with a thematic-based approach to learning" (T. Tweedy, personal communication, October, 1991). The curriculum will be divided into major themes, each of which will include all curriculum areas. As principal Thomas Tweedy describes the process:

> Math, science, social studies, and language arts will be integrated and taught in theme units. Subjects will overlap so that reading and writing assignments, social studies and science topics, and math, where possible, will be coordinated and support each other rather than being viewed as separate, segregated subjects. Projects will be hands-on in nature with the emphasis on understanding,

practical use of concepts, and the students becoming actively involved in the world around them.

Seventh graders at Kinawa have the option of the 6–8 House, and also two other possibilities. They may join a regular interdisciplinary team where four teachers each assume responsibility for one subject, in what some might call a quasi-departmentalized format. Seventh graders may also choose the "7th Grade Block" which is also an interdisciplinary team, but less conventionally so. Four continuous periods "allow for varying lengths of classes depending upon need." Some of the goals of the block include "helping students become more self-directed (academically and socially), providing a variety of learning experiences and teaching techniques, and participating in interdisciplinary units." Eighth graders also have a range of options, including the 6–8 House, an eighth grade team limited to language arts and social studies, and a departmentalized option similar to that offered to seventh graders.

An organization of teachers, as it has been done at Kinawa, offers the maximum choice to everyone involved. It offers a situation that recognizes value in each person's preference for a learning environment. And, it permits the design of a variety of alternatives which are possible without a prohibitive amount of staff development time and expense. This offers some explanation for Kinawa's successful long-term operation over a twenty-year period.

At Parker Junior High School in Parker, Colorado, three very different designs are available. Within the same school, students may choose a traditional departmentalized option, or a conventional middle school-style interdisciplinary team organization. In addition, they may choose to participate in Parker's "intensified core program" where students learn in an interdisciplinary team context, but where they concentrate on learning one academic subject at a time, remaining with the same teacher four or five periods every day for up to six weeks at a time.

Often, the variance in the size or design of the team stems from the existence of unequal numbers of students in schools using chronological age-graded grouping. A school may, for example, have an unusually large group of seventh graders compared to the numbers in the sixth or eighth grades, making it impossible to have teams of equal size. It may also be the design of the building that dictates the size of teams within the school. The middle school may have inherited an old junior or senior high school building not designed for team organization. The building may have little or no pattern to the way in which regular classrooms are grouped; for example, three classrooms together on one end of the hall, two at the other end, four in the center. The possibilities for grouping classrooms offered by older buildings seem infinite, while regularity seems almost nonexistent. School principals often demonstrate considerable creativity in making the most of their buildings, and varied team sizes is a common response.

For whatever reasons the size of a team varies, it is the number of teachers on a team that usually sets limits on the number of different subjects each one teaches. The four basic subjects (language arts, social studies, science, math) are usually included, regardless of the number of teachers on the team. When two teachers form a team, as they do at Boyce, High Point, Wakulla, or in the sixth grades of all twelve of the middle schools in Volusia County, Florida, most often each teacher takes the major responsibility for planning and teaching at least two of the four basic academic subjects. Frequently, the teachers divide their responsibilities on the basis of personal preferences, desire for collaboration, or perceived subject matter compatibility, as well as certification requirements.

The most frequent combinations for two-teacher teams, quite possibly a common holdover from the days of the core curriculum in the junior and senior high schools, are social studies-language arts and math-science. But there are other possibilities, of course. Teachers could choose to share math and science and to assume individual responsibility for language arts and social studies. Teams can and do divide it differently: language arts-math and science-social studies. Interestingly, rarely do two-teacher teams at these schools opt to share all four of the basic academic subjects in a way that included each person teaching all of the four. There are many schools where this is done.

A number of middle schools have teams composed of three teachers. At Griffin Middle School in Smyrna, Georgia and in two middle schools in Dothan, Alabama (based partially on the model at Griffin), the three-teacher team is the norm. When a team of three teachers is assigned to teach the four basics (as is almost always the case) several possibilities for teaching responsibilities exist. Three teachers usually share the responsibilities for four subjects one of two ways: by having all three teachers teach all four subjects; or, by having each teacher responsible for one subject separately, while all three combine to teach the fourth.

Which path is chosen often depends on the number of elementary or secondary trained teachers on the team. In the sixth-grade teams, where elementary trained teachers predominate, the pattern often displays the three teachers commonly planning and teaching all four subjects in a coordinated and collaborative way. In the seventh-grade teams, teaching responsibilities seem split rather evenly between teams in which all teachers teach all subjects, and those in which each teaches two subjects, one separately and one in common. In the eighth-grade teams, it is the latter method which predominates.

In many teams of three teachers at the eighth-grade level, the teachers often plan and teach collaboratively those subjects that require their combined efforts to do well. An eighth-grade team might, for example, be composed of three secondary trained teachers, with certification in language arts, social studies and math, but not in science. Frequently, these teachers will choose to share the responsibility for science and teach the others individually. By pooling their expertise, they develop a science program that is respectable and maintain their individual specialties in the other areas. Schools which have opted for the three-teacher team have discovered that, by necessity, it produces a great deal of team planning in comparison with any other size team.

Teams composed of four teachers are by far the most common, probably because the basic academic curriculum is most commonly thought of as having four distinct elements. Even in schools which would describe themselves as far from being exemplary, the four-teacher unit is usually present. The four-teacher team organization is standard, but of course, not necessarily better than other possibilities.

The four-teacher situation usually finds one teacher having special responsibility for one subject area. Each teacher is a resource person for one of the four basic areas, with state certification or college preparation, or both, in that particular area. This special responsibility can be handled, however, in several different ways. Each of these different ways is acceptable in terms of the definition of team organization.

The most common division of responsibilities on the four-teacher team assigns almost total responsibility for one subject area to each teacher. At Fort King Middle School in Ocala, Florida, the team's math teacher plans and teaches all the math. The social studies, science, and language arts teachers each also plan and teach their individual subjects to the students on the team. Because they meet together regularly, however, teachers using this approach are likely to be aware of what is happening in the other academic areas, and may contribute suggestions for improvements even though their formal responsibilities do not extend to teaching these other subjects.

A second, far less frequently found method for assigning teacher responsibilities on four-teacher teams follows the model known as Individually Guided Education (IGE), developed by the Institute for the Development of Educational Activities (IDEA), a creation of the Kettering Foundation. This model usually identifies resource people in each of the special areas, but expands their teaching responsibilities to all four subjects.

At Spring Hill Middle School, High Springs, Florida, teachers successfully followed the IGE model for a decade. Each team had a resource teacher in each of the four areas. It was the task of the resource person in math, for example, to take the major role in planning the mathematics instruction for the students on the team. This involved many things: selecting objectives from the scope and sequence outlined in county and school curriculum guides; suggesting instructional activities; designing evaluative instruments; gathering materials and being certain that resources are ready; and many other activities. But, when the math unit was ready to be taught, all members of the team were involved in the instruction.

All four teachers taught math, but all four teachers were not likely to be teaching four identical math objectives. The teacher on the team least comfortable with math may, for instance, have taught remedial long division for six weeks, while two other teachers had different instructional assignments and the math resource teacher had the task of teaching the pre-algebra unit. The process was the same in the other three areas. All teachers on the team were involved in the planning and instruction of each unit, but in different ways. The same basic process has been followed, with some differences, at Oregon Middle School (Oregon, Wisconsin), Glen Ridge Middle School (Glen Ridge, New Jersey), and Trotwood-Madison Middle School (Trotwood, Ohio). We believe that, as middle school educators begin to search anew for more success in interdisciplinary curriculum work, that the IGE process may regain a measure of its former popularity.

With this in mind, a third possibility exists for the four-teacher team; but because of several persistent problems, it is often only partially implemented, even in the most exemplary middle schools. It is possible for the teachers to integrate the four subjects into truly interdisciplinary units, thematic curriculum plans that weave together the several disciplines into coherent wholes. Several middle schools identify such possibilities in what they describe as core programs. Montgomery Middle School (El Cajon, California) required that sixth graders experience a core program three periods a day, and seventh and eighth graders were involved in a two-period core. The core program is also a fundamental part of the interdisciplinary curriculum at Noe Middle School in Louisville, Kentucky. Typically, core at these schools and others involves the integration of language arts and social studies programs under the direction of one or two teachers on the team, but it may involve entire teams and up to four subjects.

Many schools have developed and taught thematic units without the formal designation of something like core. At Farnsworth Middle School (Guilderland, New York), teams taught these units: TETE (Total Education for the Total Environment), an interdisciplinary approach to the environment study on which all four basic subjects were involved; Anthropology (also involving all four subjects); Flow Charts (math and science); Earth Day (entire seventh grade); Drugs; and others. At Graveraet Middle School (Marquette, Michigan), this process produced thematic units like World War II, the Human Body, Japan, The Bicentennial, Russia, and a grade-wide unit on Camping. In the 1991–92 school year, one team (designated the "X Team") at Lincoln Middle School in Gainesville, Florida was organized as a third team at the sixth grade level because all of its members expressed a strong desire to integrate the curriculum through interdisciplinary unit teaching.

Thematic interdisciplinary units like those just described appear more or less frequently in almost all good middle school programs. However, few, if any, middle schools (no matter how exemplary) seem to be able to sustain the use of thematic units as the curriculum of the basic instructional program for a majority of the day over a long period of several years or more. This mode of teacher assignment on interdisciplinary teams remains largely at an aspirational rather than the actual level. (We discuss it more thoroughly in Chapter 3.)

A number of exemplary middle schools find themselves at the other end of the range in terms of size of team, with five-teacher teams relatively frequent, and teams of six and seven teachers less frequent. Teams composed of eight to twelve teachers are much less frequent and often can be described as gradewide teams, groups which then break into smaller, informal subject-oriented groups composed of teachers in the same discipline who often do a great deal of actual team teaching. The large teams (over six teachers) tend to subdivide, with each subdivision acting like a miniature subject-oriented department.

At Westwood and Fort Clarke Middle Schools in Gainesville, Florida, teachers operate on what we call "gradewide teams," meaning that there may be as many as a dozen teachers attempting to work together with all of the students at one grade level. In this situation, the teachers who teach the same subject do, indeed, operate as a miniature academic department. All of the teachers on the grade level do, however, have common planning time and often spend that time on grade level concerns and activities.

Teams of five teachers usually resemble the four-teacher team in that they assign one subject to each teacher for both planning and teaching. The extra member, as at Glen Ridge (New Jersey) Middle School, usually comes from the separation of reading from language arts, due to increased emphasis on reading skills now found in almost every school. At Glen Ridge, this works out to about forty-five minutes per day in each of the five subjects.

Lincoln Middle School (Gainesville, Florida), has differed, in some years, from this pattern, using four teachers to teach five basic subjects. Having separated reading from the remainder of the language arts program, the Lincoln staff found themselves still heavily committed to other aspects of their program (advisor-advisee and exploratory courses). This commitment resulted in a four-person academic team where one teacher had the responsibility for language arts, one for reading, one for math, and one teacher for both science and social studies. This means at Lincoln, when this model was used, that students received a half year of science and a half year of social studies.

Based on the definition of team organization offered earlier, all of the above descriptions are appropriate. In the exemplary middle school, interdisciplinary team organization seems to mean, most often, groups of from two to five teachers who share responsibility for planning and sometimes teaching curriculum in more than one academic area to the same group of students, with the same schedule, in the same part of the building. Teachers almost always represent a strength in one particular subject and they may teach only this subject to all the students on the team. Or, they may teach two, three, or four different subjects in various collaborative arrangements with their team members. Frequently in some schools, and occasionally in almost all schools, teachers from various academic perspectives will combine their areas in thematic units. All of these efforts fall in the range of interdisciplinary team organization, and while some are more extensive in the actual amount of teaming done by the teachers, the greatest benefits of the interdisciplinary team organization accrue to both teachers and students in all of the various models described here.

Roles and Responsibilities of Teams and Their Members
The Team

The roles and responsibilities of team members vary, depending upon the model of team organization followed. Virtually all exemplary middle schools, however, avoid complex hierarchical arrangements designating master teachers, regular teachers, and other less qualified members, and instead are much more likely to use a model that assumes a much greater degree of equality of expertise on the team. Team leaders are often chosen and relied upon, but rarely given enough extra prerequisites to make the tasks worthwhile simply in exchange for these extras. Most often, team leaders serve because they feel a sense of professional duty, or because they need the challenge of extra responsibility and the consequent opportunities for personal and professional growth. Almost always, team leaders work longer and harder than even they had believed possible.

Once organized, what must teams accomplish? When teams meet, what concerns are central? What decisions must be made? Members of a team in the exemplary middle school participate in decisions on many of the following:

Scheduling of classes and teacher assignments
student schedules
patterns of student grouping for instruction within the team
selection and development of curriculum plans and supportive materials
correlation of curriculum plans from different subject areas to insure maximum
    effectiveness
space allocation
budget disbursement
use of blocks of time for planning and instruction
team teaching
selection of new staff members
parent contacts
placing students in special programs
orientation of new students
evaluation and inservice staff development of team members
cooperation with special area teachers.

Some teacher responsibilities are more important than others, and few decisions can be made without taking the whole school into account.

Teaching Responsibilities

In many exemplary middle schools, the team decides on the teaching responsibilities for each member. The team must decide how many subjects each teacher will teach and what those subjects will be. Once the teams have been established, with the principal seeing to it that certification and related problems are resolved, the teams can be given the responsibility for staff-subject assignments. This is the case at Wakulla Middle School in Crawfordville, Florida. Here, once the teachers have been matched so that certification is properly covered, and the lunch and planning times have been established, teachers on teams are able to make the rest of the decisions as to what will be taught, by whom, when, and where.

Arranging the Physical Environment

Having been assigned the full complement of rooms or space in an appropriate area, the team must decide how these rooms should be used. Will space be assigned to individual teachers, in pairs, or some other combination? Will the space be assigned for the year, on a more temporary basis, or not at all? Will there be a planning room where each teacher will have a small space?

Structuring Academic Class Time

In most exemplary middle schools, teams are responsible for relatively large blocks of time to be devoted to instruction in the subjects for which the team has been given responsibility. Typically, the team is notified as to when their students will have certain activities such as lunch, physical education, and exploratory courses. Teams then decide what subjects will be taught at what times, and often how much time will be devoted to each subject or how frequently the subject will be studied each week. The teams are responsible for establishing, evaluating, and reestablishing a daily schedule for subjects, teachers, and students. At Sarasota Middle School (Sarasota, Florida), teams of teachers design virtually the total day, except for lunch, physical education, and unified arts.

Grouping Students

Often teams have some autonomy in the issue of student grouping for instruction within the team. The team may have to decide whether students will be grouped according to ability, and, if so, how they will be grouped. Some teams group heterogeneously in all classes, others group by ability for reading or math, or both. Teams frequently attempt to have social studies, science, and exploratory classes grouped without reference to ability. Typically, however, teams that find it necessary to group students according to ability for one or two subjects find it difficult to regroup heterogeneously for the other classes.

Scheduling Students

Principals of exemplary middle schools sometimes discover that teams can often do an outstanding job of scheduling students on their teams for their academic classes. Teachers quickly establish a method for assigning students to special programs like Chapter One and then parcel out students to different sections of academic subjects within the team. Teaming makes it possible for teachers to possess knowledge of students that enables them to decide which students should be grouped, which ones should be separated. Teachers also find it frequently necessary to change a student's schedule; when the team has this responsibility, the task can be accomplished much more efficiently. Having teachers make decisions about who studies what, with whom, and at what time also relieves the administrators of a tremendously time-consuming burden. This way, teachers appreciate having an important role to play in the decisions that have a daily effect on their lives, and administrators, sometimes counselors, are free for duties that they would otherwise be unable to perform.

One teacher from an exemplary middle school, experienced in the process of scheduling students, described the approach that worked in her school:

> During pre-planning, each team of teachers (usually four academic teachers and three support teachers) sits as a group to "hand schedule" reading, math, language arts, and science/social studies (we offer a half year of each). Our first considerations are to those classes or programs with the least flexibility; classes for emotionally handicapped, educably mentally retarded, learning disabled, and gifted students are scheduled first. These classes may only be offered two or three of the four possible times and therefore must be scheduled initially. Teachers of these specific classes present the teams with their time requirement for each individual student. Programs such as Chapter One and other compensatory classes are offered throughout the day and can be scheduled as are the regular academic classes.
>
> Once these restrictive considerations are negotiated, the team teachers then continue by scheduling their own academics. Each team has the option of grouping homogeneously for one or two classes. For instance, if reading and math are to be ability grouped by a specific team, those classes would be scheduled first. Reading and math levels for each student would be determined (results from standardized tests), the students grouped, and then assigned to a class section. A student might be high in reading and low in math, so he/she would fall in a high reading class and a lower math class. Classes do not rotate as complete sections from one teacher to another. Students will have a new group of classmates in each class with only a few students following similar schedules.
>
> Classes which are randomly grouped are scheduled last. In this case, numbers of students are balanced to give each class an appropriate load.
>
> Changes from day to day can be made at the team's discretion. Our administrators leave the responsibility of this process up to the teams, with the team leader reporting back all difficulties or problems, and final decisions regarding grouping.
>
> Our exploratory program rotates every twelve weeks and students may select the classes they want to take. Each student makes a first, second, and third choice. From this selection, the homeroom or advisory teacher assigns students to classes based on the students' choices and availability of classes. This same process repeats each time exploratories rotate.

Through this process of teachers scheduling their own students, the responsibility for developing appropriate learning activities and situations is left for teachers and teams to determine. We appreciate the opportunity of making these decisions and now perform this role automatically. (V. Childs, personal communication, March 4, 1980)

Selecting and Distributing Texts and Other Materials

Some middle schools follow a multitext approach to instruction which permits teams to select the texts which best suit their students, and the interests and teaching preferences of instructors. Almost all schools encourage team participation in decisions about texts or materials that the whole school must use. Some administrators turn over a portion of the operating budget of the school to each team. Teams at Fort Clarke Middle School (Gainesville, Florida), for example, are given a budget of $10.00 per student at the beginning of the year, which amounts to about $1,500 per team. The teams then apportion these funds as they determine their needs, but team budgets must include basic items such as photocopy and construction paper, chalk, film rentals, and other items such as field trips, materials for exploratory courses, and so on. This type of team budgeting enhances the teams' feelings of autonomy, and frees the principal from the tiresome and sometimes demeaning role of keeper of the purse, doling out sometimes large, other times minuscule, amounts of money, but each time requiring a form or a response to a request.

Teamed Instruction

When conditions are right (adequate planning time, planning skills, and communication skills) teams occasionally engage in actual teamed instruction. A few schools are able to offer thematic units on a regular basis, with a rare school or two actually offering such units on a schoolwide basis in which regular classes are suspended for a week or more in favor of a unit such as "Spanish Americans" where everyone teaches every subject area, but the subjects are not fused together as in the thematic units. Even more frequently, two or more members of a team will plan their instruction in a way that permits subject areas to be closely correlated in terms of skills and related concepts. Most teams, however, find fewer opportunities to team teach than the members of the team would like.

Other Student Matters

Teams often need to spend time meeting with a counselor for the purpose of placing students into a program for exceptional children. They also find themselves frequently occupied with students leaving school, or with new students transferring in from another school or, rarely, from another team in the same school. Teams also report a significant amount of time spent in conferences with parents of students on the team. The economy of time provided to parents by being able to speak with all their child's teachers at once makes this type of parent-team conference a very popular item with teams that encourage it. As this section should indicate, team consideration of the problems of an individual student is one of the major advantages of team organization.

Relating To Other Staff Members

Teams often need to act as a unit in collaboration with other school staff. There are, of course, many other times throughout the year when the principal or the assistant principal would meet with a particular team for a special purpose. In addition to these administrators, there are likely to be dozens of instances when teams confer with other staff members. Many exemplary middle schools have a person who acts as the curriculum coordinator. This person frequently works closely with the teams, often serving as a type of overall team leader and ombudsman dealing separately with each team on issues, inservice opportunities, curriculum development and so on. Just as often, teams meet with counselors, deans, or special education teachers regarding individual pupils or small groups of students from the team.

At Broomfield Heights Middle School (Broomfield, Colorado), each team spends one period each week in what they term their "Kid Meeting." Here, a team of teachers meets with the counselor, who brings a list of students who need special attention from the teachers on the team. A student may be having problems at home that teachers need to know about. Another student may have been tested in some special way and teachers need to know the results in order to do a better job with that student. Two students may be having real difficulty getting along. Whatever the multitude of reasons for bringing these students to the special attention of the teachers on the team, academic teachers swear that the weekly "Kid Meeting" is the "most important 45 minutes of the week."

Team Planning

Experience in some middle schools indicates that the energy of the team members is often consumed largely by matters related to the management of team affairs. While such a situation might seem, at first, to be less than ideal, it is important to point out that all working groups function this way. Such day-to-day interaction helps solidify the bonds that unite the team. Since agendas for team meetings reflect these concerns, an examination of what is discussed there should be instructive. One team had the following agenda for some of its meetings throughout one academic year:

October 11,
Field trip plans
Media Center policies
Parent welcome letters
Team discipline issues

November 14,
Bilingual children's needs
Speech problems
Summer school
Grading practices & particulars

November 28,
Retention policies & particulars
Christmas plans
Assemblies
Progress reports
Locker check for books

December 5,
Duty stations
Team honor roll
Coffee sharing

December 12,
Use of machines
Budget allocation
Team population enrollment
Program
Eighth-grade test scores
Teacher inservice workshop

January 4,
Schedules for new students
Parent conference plans
Involvement in Folk Arts
Library books due
Time out room

February 20,
Plans for desegregation workshop
Promotion and retention decisions
Hospitality
Reality Therapy Pilot Program

February 22,
Discussion of our goals
Professionalism
Schoolwide policies for new kids
Postschool planning
Intramural playoff plans

February 27,
MAT testing
Year-end field trips
Possible early dismissal
Title I problems

March 15,
Sex education plans
Fifth-grade orientation
Withdrawal forms

April 3,
Schedule for last 3 school days
Social Committee

April 19,
Field trips plans

April 26,
Counselor input
Special media center unit
Honor roll kids
Eighth-grade testing

May 1,
Special assembly plans
Money collection
Teachers appreciation week

Figure 6.1 illustrates the minutes from a sixth grade team (Frogtown), at Fort Clarke Middle School, Gainesville, Florida, on their May 14, 1991 meeting. The topics at the meeting ranged widely: welcoming a university visitor for a week, Southern Association of Colleges and Schools (SACS) report, teacher appreciation breakfast sponsored by parents, field trip details, Citizens of the Month, orientation visits to the school by members of elementary school fifth

FROGTOWN TEAM MINUTES

May 14, 1991

Members present: Paul Burdick, Bob Carroll, Paul George, Clyde Graham, Vic Harrell, Willie Jackson, Bev Jones, Nancy McMillin, Amanda Searle, Jill Walters, Elaine White, Sara Zemlo.

Members in class: Mike Gibson, Anne Knight, Sally Rist and Sarla Ramayya.

Team Notes ( ) :

1. Welcome to Dr. Paul George who is visiting with us this week. We hope you have a profitable stay in Frogtown.

2. The SACS report was very positive. The administration, faculty, and support staff were all mentioned as being exceptional! Dr. Dixon expressed his thanks to all who contributed to the success of this review.

3. Teacher Appreciation Breakfast this morning at 8:05 in the bandroom.

4. Today (Wednesday, May 15) is the final day for collection of field trip money. Use extreme discretion in granting any wavers to this date, and then only after consulting with Vic.

5. We established a list of eight potential "no-goes." See Bob or Vic if you have any questions.

6. The Frogtown Citizens of the Month are as follows:

March	Ko-Shin Wang
	Mya Brumfield
April	Jeff Berryhill
	Shu-Ping Shen
May	Wendy Carlson
	Mindy Freedman

1

FIGURE 6.1

If any of these students are in your AA, please inform them of this honor, and request a good photo of them to be used on the bulletin board up front.

7. The tadpoles will be here next Tuesday, Wednesday, and Thursday. Vic will have a schedule posted for us later this week.

8. We decided to ask our students to sign up in groups of four as a means of offering a bit more protection while in Busch Gardens. While they will ride with their AA classes, students will be expected to stay with their group throughout the remainder of the day. One student in each group will be responsible for submitting a complete list of all four students and their AA teachers. This should be completed by next Tuesday (May 21) so that we can begin compiling a master list.

9. Thanks for your cooperation with the Career Education speakers on Tuesday morning. We will do it again on Thursday!

"Well, next time you invoke the muses, don't mumble."

2/84

FIGURE 6.1 (continued)

graders ("tadpoles"), and a career education program that was conducted through the advisory program. "Frogtown" has been the name of this sixth grade team, by the way, for more than fifteen years.

At Deltona Middle School in Deltona, Florida, the minutes of the 7th grade "house" meeting for November 8, 1990, reflect the following:

1. Report Cards
2. Positive Recognition Forms
3. Championship Friday (intramural playoff day)
4. Conduct grades
5. Upcoming Goal Setting meeting for the entire faculty
6. Fundraisers
7. Newsletter articles
8. Candy Grams
9. Interdisciplinary unit-one per semester, per team
10. Team Notebooks due
11. Concerns

At Nock Middle School (Newburyport, Massachusetts), teams are provided with a set of guidelines for their meetings:

The time set aside for team planning each day should be used for that purpose. The meeting itself should take precedence over individual pursuits during that time.

1. Team members will assume the responsibility of designating a team leader. This could be done on a rotating basis.

2. Team leaders will organize and conduct the team meetings.

3. Teachers might use planning time to explain and show what work they have planned for their classes for the purpose of planning interdisciplinary activities.

4. Suggested topics for discussions:
   a. schedules and procedures
   b. youngsters with particular problems; what can be done to solve them
   c. re-grouping of students for teaching particular skills and concepts
   d. evaluation of learning
   e. making curriculum more appropriate
   f. efforts to individualize teaching and learning
   g. planning interdisciplinary ventures
   h. parent conferences

5. The House Coordinator will take part in team meetings on a regular basis.

At East Cobb Middle School in Marietta, Georgia, the two periods of team planning time came, as it does everywhere, at a high cost. In order to insure that this time is fully utilized, leaders at East Cobb Middle have developed what might be called specifications for monitoring planning to make sure it is "used to promote cognitive, behavioral, and affective growth of students." Team planning, at East Cobb, is expected to provide evidence that:

Plans are being made for individual student learning needs.
Plans are being made for individual student behavior needs.
Team spirit activities are planned.
Plans are made to improve student affective growth.
There is sharing of curriculum plans.
Interdisciplinary units are being implemented.
Learning and behavior goals are developed with and for the team as a whole
    and evaluated regularly.
Time is being used flexibly.
Grouping and regrouping is done appropriately.
Available test information is used appropriately for individuals and groups.
Parents are contacted as needed.
There is a sharing of instructional strategies and materials.
Conferences with other professionals are planned as needed.
There is evidence of teacher collegiality.

In August, 1989, Sharon Patterson, then principal of East Cobb Middle, distributed a "Team Planning Guide" to the teachers at the school. It introduced the expectation that teams of teachers, working together, would keep a "Team Log" which would be shared with the principal on a regular weekly basis. This would be the place where team's would record the minutes of their meetings and the decisions that were made during that time. Among the matters to be included in the log at the beginning of the year were the following items:

Team student academic and behavior management plan
Room preparation and hall decoration plans
Strategies for achieving schoolwide goals on the team
Strategies for improving student attendance
Strategies for emphasizing interdisciplinary teaching
Strategies for improving team and school spirit
Strategies for recognition of student success
A first day schedule for each team that will "make East Cobb the most inviting
    school in town"
Review of student grouping and scheduling to insure correct placement

At MacDonald Middle School in East Lansing, Michigan, teams are evaluated on a regular basis, including how they use their planning time, but also on a much broader scale. Comprehensive evaluations of intact teams occur every three years; new teams are evaluated within the first ten weeks of the school year, and then on a continuing basis. Detailed forms and procedures help to insure that the evaluation is done carefully. The "short form" of the team evaluation instrument asks team members to help evaluate twenty-six different factors in eight major areas: instruction, group composition, scheduling, expectations and rules, communications, support services, use of space, and miscellaneous. It should be extraordinarily clear to teachers on teams that planning and working together effectively, at MacDonald, is a high priority.

No middle school has been more specific in its detailing of the duties of team members than Olle Middle School (Alief, Texas). The agenda of team activities (Table 6.1) for the entire school year is introduced as follows:

Horizontal Grade Level Team Calendar
The suggested list of activities pertinent to team teaching are provided to give structure, continuity, and meaningfulness to our team meetings. While the list may seem formidable, it is in no way exhaustive.

This calendar, under the leadership and direction of the team captain is to be used as a guide and as a checklist. Actually circle each activity which you have accomplished according to the given suggestions during each of the report periods.

It is also recommended that some flexibility be maintained regarding your involvement with each activity during the marking periods. Do not hesitate to alter the sequence or extension of these activities or to suggest additions or deletions to this list.

TABLE 6.1   **Horizontal Team Activities***

1	2	3	QUARTERS
X			1. Select team captain, recorder, secretary and contact person.
X			2. Schedule students for English, social studies, math and science.
X			3. Team members review student orientation manual or handbook for new teachers on team prior to their use of the sequential material.
X			4. Obtain a schedule card for each section taught, and retain them in your classroom for your convenience in locating students.
X			5. Exchange copies of text books with other team members for teacher and student use in classroom discussions and correlating units of instruction.
X	X	X	6. Prior to conferences check file for "Team Conference Cards" for information obtained from student and parental interviews in the past.
X			7. Develop a technique for phoning parents, greeting them when they arrive, opening and closing the conference. Refer to teachers' manual on hints for conducting a conference. Get to the point early and remember that information is held in strict confidence.
X			8. In addition to formal orientation program for sixth graders and new students, develop a thorough explanation of academic policies and procedures in each classroom.
X			9. Distribute and explain the student handbook.

(continued)

TABLE 6.1   **Horizontal Team activities* (continued)**

X			10. Check to find whether cumulative record folders are up-to-date and available for each pupil.
X	X	X	11. Disseminate information about children with special problems to teachers who are not familiar with these problems and who now teach these children.
X	X	X	12. Review the statistical data provided for each child in your team. Make full use of anecdotal records in folders.
X	X	X	13. Acquaint yourself with all sixth grade pupils to see whether they are adjusting to middle school. Help other teachers to understand pupils' backgrounds, abilities and achievement. Let the students know that you are going to be interested in them, in the results of their tests, in their work habits, and in their overall academic and social progress.
X			14. Homeroom teachers should schedule individual conference with each student.
X	X	X	15. Initiate a card file for all conferences (parent and student) giving sufficient information on results.
X			16. Prepare for PTO open house meeting.
X	X	X	17. Meet with the librarian and become familiar with her services as a curriculum resource person. Brief her on your courses of study, needs and expectations as the year progresses.
X	X	X	18. Review the district M.B.O.'s and make preparations to meet the guidelines as stated.
X	X	X	19. When necessary, throughout the year discuss the merits of each student for resectioning purposes.
X	X	X	20. Throughout the year refer students who need individual counseling to guidance. Make referrals after the team has briefed the counselor on the need for such counsel.
X	X	X	21. Complete report cards.
X			22. Explain the reporting system to pupils.
X	X	X	23. Throughout the year acquaint nonteam teachers of areas covered by your team in classroom work.
X	X	X	24. Throughout the year check on transcripts of all new children for grades and other information. Designate one member to do this.
X	X	X	25. Coordinate the testing schedule so that pupils are not burdened with too many tests at one time.
X	X	X	26. Discuss the academic standards that will constitute achievement grades for each ability level. Try to arrive at some commonality within the team so that a particular grade has the same value of standards with each teacher.
X			27. Review guidance and discipline procedures in teachers' manual.
X	X	X	28. Review each pupil's disciplinary record and plan positive approaches to rectify this condition.
X	X	X	29. Compile lists of students not achieving at a reasonable level. Begin to confer with these students.

(continued)

TABLE 6.1   Horizontal Team Activities* (continued)

X	X	X	30. Prepare a list of those students who are having difficulties because of physical, social and emotional immaturity. Enlist the help of their teachers, and plan a program of counseling these students in conjunction with the guidance department. That these factors are passively understood is not sufficient. A planned program should be initiated.
X	X	X	31. Contact parents of children having academic, social or emotional difficulties for conferences with the team. Certify that the number of conferences required by M.B.O. has been met each quarter.
X	X	X	32. Confer with the art, music, industrial art and home economics teachers on correlating instruction in certain areas.
X	X	X	33. Exchange courses of study within the team to enable teachers to become familiar with the content of other subject areas. Give explanations to other team members.
X	X	X	34. Interview new students when they arrive.
X	X	X	35. Plan carefully for any large group-small group teaching and team or grade level assembly programs.
X	X	X	36. Distribute homework evenly.
X	X	X	37. Read and discuss current professional publications available in the media center.
X	X	X	38. Review grade distribution.
X	X	X	39. Prepare student progress reports.
X	X	X	40. Check with attendance office on reasons for excessive absenteeism. Enlist the aid of the office as patterns develop.
X	X	X	41. Confer with the Administration as trends in disciplinary incidents develop. Identify offenders and counsel them, or make referrals to the Guidance Department and Administration.
	X		42. Check your inventory and bulletins on future enrollment, and begin planning for preliminary budget considerations.
X	X	X	43. Continue to arrange parent conferences. Begin to conduct follow-up conferences when desirable. (Telephone, letter, note, personal, meeting, and so on)
X	X	X	44. Explore the opportunities for joint participation in testing, group teaching, audio-visual work, and so on.
X	X	X	45. Maintain close contact with children who have been resectioned. Aid them in their adjustments to the new group.
X	X	X	46. Team check on progress of students in Physical Education, Practical Arts, Art and Music.
	X		47. Counsel those students who are failing through the first quarter. Inform them of the dangers of nonpromotion and plan a course of action for successful achievement.
X	X	X	48. Check the condition of all textbooks. Notify students that they are responsible for materials issued and must pay for all damaged and lost books.
	X	X	49. Continue to conduct parent conferences. Encourage parents of well-adjusted, talented students to come in for a conference.
		X	50. Make final check to see that all transcripts on new students have been received.

(continued)

TABLE 6.1   **Horizontal Team Activities* (continued)**

X	51. Submit a list of failures to the Principal. A notification of each student's status will be given to the parent.
X	52. Organize team minutes in final form for the Principal.
X	53. Complete report cards, cumulative folders, and other closing-of-school tasks.
X	54. Begin final work on cumulative folders early in marking period.
X	55. Review student orientation for next year.
X	56. Check for lost and damaged books.
X	57. Adhere carefully to the schedule of responsibility in the closing-of-school bulletin.
X	58. Review with team personnel procedures for determining condition of textbooks and assessments for lost, damaged or misused books.

° From Olle Middle School, Alief, Texas. Columns 1, 2, 3 refer to marking periods.

The Team Leader

In most middle schools, team leaders are formally identified, and in others no formal leader is designated. We estimate that formally designated team leaders are present in about ten times as many cases. No school is known to offer both alternatives. Schools featuring team leaders seem to depend strongly upon them; those without formal team leaders are often equally adamant about the reasons why that way is best.

Valley Middle School (Rosemount, Minnesota), Twin Peaks Middle School (Poway, California), Stoughton Middle School (Stoughton, Wisconsin), and, Louisville Middle School (Louisville, Colorado) are four exemplary middle schools, out of many hundreds now, that have used a formal approach to team leadership. Each has had a clearly written definition of the duties of the team leader. Combining and editing the four lists yields a definition of a team leader's duties that reads like this:

1. Function as the liaison between the administration and the team; individually, teachers are encouraged, however, to keep open communication lines with the principal, avoiding any unnecessary hierarchical elevation of the team leader to something in-between teacher and administrator.

2. Program coordination within the team: this is, of course, a task of consuming proportions, including a role in every activity of the team as described above. Together, items one and two here comprise a majority of the responsibilities of the typical team leader.

Other more specific activities of the team leader spelled out in school materials, some of which fall within the scope of the first two above, include:

3. Coordinating between his or her team and other teams and teachers.

4. Serving on and appointing team members to various committees.

5. Scheduling and directing the utilization of teamwide criterion-referenced testing.

6. Preparing the team budget and requisitions, supplies, textbooks, work books, films, and equipment.

7. Familiarizing new teachers and substitute teachers with school programs and other pertinent information.

8. Responsibility for the development of new approaches from within the team by coordinating new schoolwide programs, soliciting creative ideas from other members, and actively contributing suggestions for new team programs.

9. Scheduling and conducting team meetings.

10. Assisting in the selection of new team personnel.

11. Directing aides assigned to the team.

12. Identifying and encouraging the use, for the team, of other school and district personnel.

13. Assisting in organizing volunteer and community resource activities.

14. Coordinating reporting procedures and parent-teacher conferences.

15. Promoting good home-school relationships.

16. Assisting (in some schools) in a positive program of supervision of team personnel.

17. Attempting to develop and maintain a high level of morale among team members.

18. Facilitating communication between team members.

19. Assuming responsibility for equipment, for instructional materials, and for their care and distribution.

20. Assuming responsibility for the supervision of the work of student teachers.

21. Recognizing and encouraging professional growth and initiative on the part of team members.

22. Serving as a first recourse for team members who encounter classroom problems.

23. Keeping abreast of trends and innovations in curriculum and instruction, and making recommendations to team members, principal, and other staff.

At Eggers Middle School in Hammond, Indiana, larger multiage-grouped "learning communities" of about 250 students and 10 teachers have two Learning Community Lead Teachers. Their primary function is to "provide leadership to students and staff within their community and to serve as a liaison to the administration on matters relating to their learning community." Each leader also serves as a member of the school's leadership council. The Lead Teachers share some responsibilities and also have individual duties.

The Lead Teacher for Instructional Development engages in these duties:

a. Coordinate teacher mentoring and peer networking within and among the communities.
b. Coordinate the development of interdisciplinary teaching units.
c. Supervise the planning of learning community field trips.
d. Coordinate testing.
e. Develop and coordinate staff development within the learning community.
f. Prepare a weekly instructional report for the principal.

The Lead Teacher for Pupil Personnel Services has these responsibilities:

a. Establish and maintain an accurate student file system, which includes records on discipline, attendance, parental contacts, and other pertinent information.
b. Develop class schedules for students who are new or who require a program change.
c. Coordinate special education referrals and intervention.
d. Coordinate textbook and supply orders and inventories.
e. Prepare a weekly pupil personnel service report for the principal.

The two Lead Teachers for each community share a number of responsibilities:

a. Serve as a contact regarding student schedules.
b. Handle special requests directed to the community from other school personnel.
c. Jointly facilitate the development and maintenance of the community's vision and goals.
d. Oversee students' discipline and attendance.
e. Coordinate student discipline with the Unified Arts team and the school administration.
f. Prepare the community master schedule.

g. Facilitate and coordinate parent-student conferences.
h. Attend community leader's meetings and other meetings as requested by the administration.
i. Coordinate activities related to student retention and placement.
j. Assist in the planning of all meetings of the community and other school affiliates including parent and community groups.
k. Coordinate celebration activities and other special events of the learning community.
l. Jointly engage in daily communication regarding team meetings and activities.

Six teachers at Lincoln Middle School in Gainesville, Florida, most of whom have been successful team leaders for more than a decade, described good and ineffective team leaders in a discussion held in November, 1990:

> **Good team leaders** have a number of important qualities. They are, first and foremost, good at organization and time management. They also possess excellent communication and interpersonal skills, since most of their power comes from the ability to influence and persuade their peers. They are able to keep their focus on the mission of the school and the team. They are skilled delegators, and also able to build and maintain the morale and cohesiveness of the team.
> **Ineffective team leaders** share a number of weaknesses. They are unable to represent the feelings of their team members in important school problem-solving discussions when the team's feelings are different from their own. They may feel, alternately, that "I have to do everything" or they are a "buck passer." Too often, the ineffective team leader "brings a negative approach to the table." They may not look for opportunities to build leadership skills in other members of their team. They may, lamentably, be unwilling or unable to invest "what it takes" to do the job.

These same team leaders also identified the ways in which regular team members perform their roles effectively, and thus support the team leader. Such team members:

Listen carefully and effectively
Take initiative appropriately
Compromise when the team needs a consensus
Support the team leader
Have a positive attitude
Support and implement the team's decisions
Use good verbal and nonverbal communication skills
Help make the team environment "livable"
Are unfailingly punctual
Give their undivided attention at meetings

Purposes and Possibilities of the Interdisciplinary Team Organization

Cecil Floyd, principal of McCulloch Middle School, Highland Park, Texas, described the advantages of the interdisciplinary team organization that have accrued to his school since the adoption of that organization in 1987:

> Rewards for teaming seem to multiply each year. Our discipline referrals have declined by 50 percent; teachers have closer relationships with students and increased communication with parents; and instruction has been enhanced by interdisciplinary planning and purpose. Team conferences with parents have resulted in early intervention with at-risk students. A unity of purpose develops and is nurtured by the important adults in the student's life. (C. Floyd, personal communication, December, 1990)

Advantages: Instructional

Now that the interdisciplinary team organization has been defined, an acceptable range of alternatives elaborated, roles and responsibilities delineated, and a number of examples shared, it should be more meaningful to discuss what might be called the rationale for this method of organizing faculty for instruction. The advantages of the interdisciplinary team organization, cited by teachers and administrators of exemplary middle schools, fall into several categories.

Many advantages of interdisciplinary team organization are claimed for the area of instruction, all of which emanate primarily from the combined knowledge, talents and abilities of the team members. One such advantage lies in the team's comprehensive knowledge of student needs, and the power this knowledge provides for educational planning of all kinds. The experience of the last two decades has convinced many middle school educators that increased knowledge of students leads directly to more positive feelings, among the teachers on a team, toward the students they share. These positive feelings, then, lead to the teachers' willingness to act more readily in ways intended to benefit their students. Knowledge leads to positive affect which, in turn, leads to advocacy.

Another advantage is the increased intellectual stimulation for teachers which results from the interaction of people with different academic perspectives and professional points of view. Certainly, teachers who develop trust in each other will learn new methods from one another, and this is particularly so in regard to the use of the team in the introduction and orientation of faculty new to the school or to the profession. Particularly in the now-rare open space schools, but not exclusively so, teacher-teacher interaction often leads to a knowledge of each other's teaching styles that produces improvement among less able or less enthusiastic teachers, or permits the more able teachers on the team to plan team operations in a way that minimizes the damage that might be done by the less skillful teacher. It is also true that teachers learn from working so closely together that even the most skillful and highly motivated teachers undergo periods of greater and lesser crises and stress, and the team organization permits colleagues to support each other with extra efforts during these periods.

Other instructional advantages of the interdisciplinary team organization deal with the group's ability to plan and evaluate the instructional program. The superiority of group problem-solving efforts and greater integration of the curriculum, even in the absence of actual team teaching, seem to be sufficient reason in themselves for the commitment to the interdisciplinary team organization. A more extensive evaluation of course content may also emerge from the interdisciplinary situation, encouraging, as it does, a variety of perspectives. The territoriality sometimes associated with the departmental structure finds little sustenance in the interdisciplinary team organization, and this lack of territoriality, in turn, is more likely to develop better coordination of the curriculum within and across grade levels. Teachers and administrators from exemplary middle schools remark about how dramatically the topics of discussion change, from the defense of a single subject and its place in the curriculum to a consideration of the students on the team and their varied curriculum needs, when teachers are organized in an interdisciplinary way rather than in departments. As might be expected, teachers talk about what they have in common, and when the teachers share the same students rather than the same academic discipline, the students are at the center of discussion and program planning.

Quite naturally, such a situation leads to a more balanced but comprehensive evaluation of individual student progress as well. Deficiencies a student may have in one area can become known to the total group almost immediately. Students experiencing difficulties in more than one academic area can be identified, diagnosed, and remedied much more accurately and efficiently when, in an interdisciplinary team setting, teachers in all the academic areas are present for discussions.

The interdisciplinary team organization also fits well and works synergistically with other elements of the middle school program, helping each component function more smoothly than it would alone. Advisor-advisee programs function much more effectively when the advisees of a particular teacher have an opportunity to interact with that teacher in a class situation another time in the day. When advisors work with the other teachers of each of their advisees, their knowledge of those students grows in a different way, and the teachers can share with their colleagues pertinent information about a particular child that only they, as advisors, may initially know.

Advantages: Affective and Behavioral

Teachers and administrators in exemplary middle schools refer much more frequently to the affective and behavioral potential of the interdisciplinary team organization, and identify at least as large a number of benefits in this area as in instruction. The majority of references focuses on some aspect of group processes.

Primary among the potentially positive group-oriented aspects of the interdisciplinary team organization is the contribution it seems to make to the development of what might be called a sense of community, with some models of the process going so far as to refer to teams as "learning communities." With dozens of scholars and quasi-scholars decrying the loss of this phenomenon in the larger society, the middle school, through the interdisciplinary team organization, does indeed attempt to move in the opposite direction.

Desmond Morris, author of *The Naked Ape,* has written of the agony produced in humans, essentially still tribal beings, by a modern society in which we are confronted by thousands of strangers masquerading as members of our tribe. Anonymity, amorphousness, and anomie seem to characterize contemporary society, and because the schools are in many ways a mirror of the society, these maladies infect the school as well.

The interdisciplinary team organization exercises an ameliorating effect on the degree to which these forces affect the middle school. Such organization has this effect first by limiting the number of people each student must learn with or from. Instead of an amorphous group of 1,500 students and as many as a dozen teachers to get to know, the exemplary middle school is designed in a way that permits students to be members of a team of 150 or less, often with a maximum of six teachers. The dimensions of the group that students must deal with are reduced dramatically, ninefold in this example. The team of students moves together, in various combinations, throughout most of the day. Further, the group spends most of the time in the same part of the building. As a consequence, both numbers and movements of students are reduced to appropriate levels, comfortably between the exclusivity of the self-contained classroom and departmentalized anonymity.

Rossman and Collins (1991) describe recent research clarifying the special advantages of the team in "lowering the threshold where students in difficulty were noticed by the teacher team, enhanced opportunities for informal, coordinated, and sensitive intervention with those students, and provided a formal organizational structure for coordination with other services, notably guidance and psychological services." Other researchers (e.g., Kramer and Colvin, 1991) point to the increased personalization of instruction, available through the interdisciplinary team approach, as particularly valuable for dealing with "at-risk" students.

Even Chrysler Corporation, which might be described as an "at risk" corporation, now recognizes the advantages of teamwork of this sort. In April, 1991, Chrysler announced (Maynard, 1991) that their automobiles will now be built by "platform teams" which will be "responsible for the start-to-finish process of creating, building, and selling large cars, small cars, trucks, and minivans." In the past, workers at Chrysler had specialized in tasks rather than on particular cars and it was "often unclear who had final authority, because no one shepherded a vehicle from beginning to end."

When advisor-advisee programs and multiage grouping are combined with the interdisciplinary team organization, the result is repeated face-to face inter-actions between and among the same teachers and students during the day, in several contexts, and over a period of several years. Identity of person, place, and time becomes possible. A student knows that he is a member of a specific team, even a specific advisory group; and these structures have dimensions that early adolescents can manage.

In a similar way the interdisciplinary team organization helps the middle school achieve a precarious but precious balance among the demands for a specialized, enriched curriculum and the need for in-depth, enriched interper-sonal knowledge among the teachers and students involved in the process of schooling. School size has been a perennial problem of American education. The burden of large schools has, in recent years, been large-scale anonymity. This has been contrasted with the blessing of size: an economy of scale permit-ting a stimulating and exciting range of course offerings sufficient to involve the most able students and support the least able. The challenge to the middle school is to develop an exciting array of curriculum plans within a context of schooling where students are known as persons and a sense of community exists.

Teams can identify and recognize individual students in ways that schools without teams simply can not. At Wassom Middle School in Fort Campbell, Kentucky, the Cosmic Kids team engages in a student-of-the-month program which has a real effect on student's feeling known and accepted. With six teams in a school, six times as many students can be so identified. A letter home from the principal will probably be kept, by someone, for a lifetime. Fortunately, such recognition activities are becoming more and more an integral part of life on such teams (see Figure 6.2 on page 286).

The junior high school emerged, originally, as at attempt to satisfy those two goals: a richer curriculum than the elementary school was able to offer, and a more personal atmosphere than the high school was able to develop, although it might be argued that the junior high school has failed to achieve the second. Educators in the middle school seem aware of the need to accomplish both. The interdisciplinary team organization can be the answer.

This sense of community can extend beyond the school, involving parents in new and different ways. The interdisciplinary team organization permits the middle school staff to assemble and present knowledge about students to parents in a comprehensive and efficient manner. Parent-teacher conferences take on a wholly different character when they become parent-team conferences, a situ-ation in which a lack of information, leading to misunderstanding, is rare. As time passes, parents begin to realize that students, rather than subjects, come first with teachers and, often, a new spirit of cooperation and understanding develops.

Cooperation and understanding are not restricted to relationships with par-ents. It seems clear that the interdisciplinary team organization develops an

WASSOM MIDDLE SCHOOL
Forrest and Gorgas Avenue
Fort Campbell, Kentucky 42223

February 13, 1990

Mr. and Mrs. Larry K. Fisher
4949-D Hammond Heights
Ft. Campbell, Kentucky 42223

Dear Mr. and Mrs. Fisher:

Your son has been chosen as one of the outstanding students of the month for February. Ronnie's teachers described his selection as follows:

The Cosmic Kid team has selected Ronnie Fisher as its Student of the Month for February.

Ronnie is well-mannered, cooperative, and always strives to do his best.

He has excelled in all academic areas, and the teachers are very proud that he has advanced to a higher reading level.

We are proud to have Ronnie as a member of the team!

We are proud of Ronnie's accomplishments. We know that it is your help and support that makes him an outstanding student.

Sincerely,

Carolyn C. Dove

rj

FIGURE 6.2

esprit de corps among teachers and the team as well. Teachers on teams evidence a higher morale, report greater job satisfaction, and go on to seek higher levels of professional responsibility than do teachers who work alone (Erb & Doda, 1989). In the last two decades, few teachers involved in an effective interdisciplinary team organization have chosen to return to the self-contained classroom or the departmental structure; and an amazingly few schools, having experienced the interdisciplinary team organization, depart from it.

Several years ago one of the authors sat in on a team meeting at a nearby middle school where he was on temporary assignment. The meeting was begun by the team leader, proudly, reading a letter that she had just received from a parent. It capsulizes the above discussion well:

> Dear "M" Team,
>
> Just wanted to let you all know how much I appreciate your efforts with Barry. His attitude towards learning is changing and I really believe it is due to your attitude toward teaching. Barry said "This is the best team I have ever been on; they don't just care about me, but they are friends with each other." I think this statement sums up what team teaching should be.
>
> Lucky will be the students that get on "M" Team next year.
>
> Sincerely,
>
> Delores Evans

Educators frequently report that the interdisciplinary team organization generally leads to an improved standard of student behavior. Certainly, the reduction in sense of individual anonymity and group amorphousness, with the consequent development of an increased sense of identity for students is a significant factor in improved student behavior.

Other educators point out that the interdisciplinary team organization, as opposed to the department, cuts back drastically on the amount of movement of students back and forth from one area of the building to the other. Since students remain in the same general area during their study of all four of the basic academic subjects, time and distance involved in movement are reduced by about half. Students have less time to encounter problems in the halls and they do not often find themselves in parts of the building where they are unfamiliar to teachers. Minutes gained from reduced passing time can be applied to advisory programs, special interest activities, or academics.

The cohesiveness of the teachers on the team also encourages the development of a degree of consensus about student behavior which leads to a more rational, well-planned and consistent set of rules for students on the team. This consistency itself, of course, makes even further behavior improvement likely. Too, team cohesiveness permits the development of a clearer and more complete picture of actual student behavior in response to rules than the solitary observations possible by teachers working alone.

The consistency of the rule making and enforcement process so essential to good classroom and school discipline is firmly reinforced by the interdisciplinary team organization. Students are more likely to know that they are cared about and that they have an opportunity to succeed. They can, therefore, accept rules more readily. The teachers on the team can determine whether a particular rule is reasonable by their collective awareness of whether most students follow the rule, whether the best students follow it, and whether the rule requires heavy enforcement to make it work.

The team teachers may also be able to model effective group behavior, encouraging imitation among the students. Early adolescents need to see adults working together cooperatively. If there is not interdisciplinary team organization in the school, young people may not witness collaborative relationships among adults at all. The team, functioning as a learning community, is also able to involve students in directly experiencing the group life, sharing in the decision-making process with teachers and their peers.

Such experience is, of course, only possible when the interdisciplinary team organization is functioning fully as a real learning community, and requires that the teachers have a measure of autonomy found only infrequently outside the interdisciplinary team organization. When school principals share power with teams, teams are free to share power among themselves and with the students on the team. A measure of professional autonomy is necessary to the success of the interdisciplinary team organization; and, interestingly, successful teams tend to produce even more autonomous behavior on the part of the teachers on the team. Teachers need to be given the opportunity to make some of the decisions about their team life, regarding the use of time, scheduling of students, distribution and use of funds, and a number of other issues. Working together, they can and will make these decisions and carry out such tasks effectively.

In July, 1991, a letter to one of the authors from a veteran team leader spelled out the advantages of the interdisciplinary team organization in detail:

> I think the team organization is "the only way to go." Of the thirteen years of teaching middle school reading, only the past two were in a team. Is there ever a difference! Without it I really think I'd be quitting. In fact, a teammate is sixty and was going to retire until she teamed up with the mighty Orca's—and she's staying on at least three more years now—a total of six beyond what she'd planned to do.
>
> Obviously teaming is better for *the child*—any child, whether gifted and talented or remedial. The communication among the teachers results in much better planning for all students. In our daily team meetings, we highlight *positives* for all of us to reinforce, and also target negatives that we'll all work to extinguish. Oh, I'm sure there are some teams somewhere who don't function as effectively, but for us it works miracles!
>
> A child's parents see an organized group of adults ready and willing to help. Parent conferences used to be a fiasco-time—a bunch of teachers blurting out the bad things the kid had done and none (or very few) offering solutions. Now *we* call the parents in most times, and we've already set up the agenda, with the emphasis on problem solving. Usually the counselor sits at the table and says little, and problems get solved. Most of our parents think we're the greatest things walking! We've structured several night activities—potlucks usually—for the parents and all their kids—sometimes with a talent(?)show and a "getting to know you" theme at the first of the year. We even did a Christmas play (guess

who directed) with a 7th grade team this past December, and presented it at night, with parents bringing desserts for afterward. It results in the parents knowing us better, us knowing the kids and their parents better, and all of us working together for the child's benefit. Does it take more time? Of course! But can we see rewards?? OF COURSE! When the environment is so positive (as it is in our team), you *almost* don't mind the extra work!

Finally, three very professional, previously very successful teachers have each other! Teaching in the public schools is lonely. You think you're the only one with problems; when you're down it seems others are anxious to see you crumble; but in a good working team, your mates boost you up, or shoulder part of your load if you're hurting. We inspire each other, add ideas to one another's projects—always causing more work, of course! When we began teaming we had a total of seventy or so years of successful experience, so we weren't new, or naively enthusiastic about any project. In fact, we were skeptical about our district's support—and with good reason! But we have weathered other teams' jealousy (lots of that), and a principal who on one hand would like to tell us to "rein in", but who doesn't dare because our parents are so happy about what's going on, and an assistant principal who is—well, an assistant principal!

If you didn't know me, you'd think this was just so much euphoric crap! But you know me! I work damned hard—and with the team I'm able to achieve far more with our students. I suspect that you even know that I'm not the easiest person in the world to work with—but all three of us on the Orca's are similar in those qualities—and somehow we haven't killed each other. In fact, we've grown closer, more efficient, and surely more effective.

Because it's summer and I'm trying not to give my district any free "mind time" until August, I just don't have specific examples on my brain. I'm sorry about that. But either come to our session in Louisville [NMSA Annual Conference, 1991], or have someone tape it for you—and you'll hear that it's not just me! We love it!!!

P.S. And I'm just as enthusiastic about teaching reading in the heterogeneous middle school classroom!

We bet she is.

Precautions

It would be a less than total exploration of the interdisciplinary team organization if there was no reference to the difficulties encountered by the staff of even exemplary middle schools as they attempt to establish workable interdisciplinary team operations. That the same difficulties appear in almost every situation should make caution considerably more important. There are several conditions that are crucial to the success of the interdisciplinary team organization, regardless of the particular model followed.

Early in the evolution of the contemporary middle school movement, one team leader in an exemplary middle school identified the factors she believed to be basic to the existence of authentic interdisciplinary teams (Doda, 1977).

In the nineties, these factors remain at the center of effective team organization. Balanced teacher and student populations—such that each team is a microcosm of the school—are crucial: teachers balanced according to complementing strengths, personal styles, instructional expertise and experience, as well as race, sex, and age; students balanced according to sex, achievement, race, exceptionalities, and age. Schools that have severely imbalanced teams in terms of the student membership will be likely to find the situation difficult to manage.

Other basics include the need for physical identity, having the members of the team housed in adjacent or nearly adjacent classroom areas. In this way each team has a separate and distinct territory. Without this closeness, teams may function only minimally, since teams of any kind (sports, academic, or otherwise) must play on the same field. Another aspect of the physical space needs has to do with the team planning room. Most advocates of the interdisciplinary team organization (Erb & Doda, 1989) see the planning room as highly desirable for effective planning, for the storing of materials, and for the maintenance of personal relationships.

In addition to place, time together is essential. Some time each week must be designated as team time, allowing regular team meetings and planning sessions to occur. Interdisciplinary team organization does take more teacher time, since teachers require the same amount of time for their individual efforts and additional time for whatever team activities require. Little wonder that early attempts at teaming were frequently disappointing, since team members were expected to teach together as well as work on teams together; the two were seen as synonymous, when, in fact, they are not. Teams that are asked to produce exciting thematic units or integrated lessons all day, every day, require at least 50 percent more planning time than teams which do not focus on actual team teaching. Fortunately, many of the benefits of team organization can be had without team teaching.

Recent experiences like Volusia, Orange, and Alachua County school districts, in the state of Florida, testify to the importance of planning time. In the early nineties, in these districts, two periods of planning time out of a seven-period day were recognized as the minimum for effective teaming and effective individual teaching. Teachers need a daily planning time to prepare for their own individual lessons, and to take a well earned break from time to time. If much is to be expected from the team organization, in terms of parent conferences, field trips, or other team activities, a second daily planning time is virtually essential.

This planning time was recognized as so essential and desirable that, at Westwood and Fort Clarke Middle Schools, both in Gainesville, Florida, teachers voted to achieve the two planning period situation by increasing the number of students in their other five classes. So, in these two schools, in the 1990–91 academic year, class sizes went from about twenty-five students per class to about thirty students. No one believed that it was good to increase class size by so much, but no one voted to eliminate it for the 1991–92 year either.

In addition to time, as mentioned earlier, teams need autonomy to function well. Given the opportunity, teams can and will assist the school principal with scheduling, budgeting, curriculum, evaluation, long-range planning, and dozens of other concerns vital to school progress. Administrators of exemplary middle schools find it essential to involve teams in participatory decision making (George & Stevenson, 1989). Given balance, time, place, and autonomy, most teams move forward. Without the proper skills and attitudes, however, forward movement will be minimal. The interdisciplinary team organization requires skills that are slightly different and considerably more sophisticated than those required by nonteaming teachers: planning skills and communication skills.

Teachers who do not know how to plan as a group will not do so. Teachers whose interpersonal communication skills are minimal will find their team functioning at a minimal level. Any group that is together regularly and intensely, as in an interdisciplinary team organization, soon discovers that it must devote almost as much time and effort to the interpersonal side of the process as it does to the more work-oriented tasks. This effort requires extra amounts of cooperative spirit and creativity.

In attempting to answer the question "What really makes a team work?" Erb & Doda identify a number of important ingredients: (1) establishing clear expectations among the members of the team; (2) careful attention to team meetings; (3) building team identity and spirit with team names, etc., fostered by regular spirit-building activities like projects, field trips, honor rolls, and special gatherings; (4) constant and effective team communication and conferences between and among teachers, students, parents, and administrators; (5) a team approach to discipline; and (6) when possible, a measure of totally teamed instruction. The teacher handbook of West Middle School (Aurora, Colorado) deals with team functions and describes the keys to success as:

1. These are our students—not my students.
2. There are many ways and not just my way.
3. There are goals to achieve and plans to implement the goals, including long-range as well as short-range plans and goals.
4. The team must evaluate what happened last week before planning for next week.
5. The team must be willing to change a plan if it appears to be going wrong.
6. Team members should remember that disagreements are normal, but can and should be resolved.

At Olle Middle School (Alief, Texas), the teachers' handbook included the following keys to successful interdisciplinary team teaching:

1. A tactful honesty and a willingness to work and plan together on an idea

2. A utilization of the differences, as well as the similarities, among team members

3. The ability to accept and recognize failure and a desire to try again

4. The realization on each teacher's part that his or her subject is of no more or less importance than the other subjects

5. A recognition of new and better avenues to a definite goal (Don't think "subject matter," just . . . THINK!)

6. An awareness of how student interest can be employed in teaching the required curriculum

7. A knowledge that students recognize "busy work" and respect work pertinent to the topic

8. The realization that ability grouping may not be compatible with interdisciplinary team teaching

9. A flexibility among team members in individual scheduling to meet a particular student's needs

10. A knowledge that interdisciplinary thinking compliments individual instruction

11. An interest in (not necessarily an understanding of) the other academic subjects

12. A sensitivity to the feelings of the other team members; an elimination of petty and/or personal "gripes" that may interfere with the primary objective . . . interdisciplinary team teaching!

13. The awareness that interdisciplinary topics may not include all four disciplines and may, in fact, encompass some electives

Ten Commandments of Teaming

During the period from 1981 through 1991, we have assembled the collective wisdom of hundreds of experienced middle school educators into what we might describe as the "ten commandments of interdisciplinary team organization at its very best." Here they are:

1. Interpersonal compatibility   Most school leaders of our acquaintance argue that interpersonal compatibility is more important than any other factor, even having team members' rooms in close proximity. Arranging teams so that members are comfortable with one another is critical. Using personality inventories like the Myers-Briggs Type Indicator, sociograms, and other methods of team design can be very helpful. Once achieved, however, team compatibility must constantly be nurtured.

2. Balance   In so many ways, balance is crucial to teamwork: subject strengths, personality style, ethnic background, sex, age, certification, and many others.

The key is to have teams balanced in as many ways as possible, both in terms of teachers and students on the team.

3. Planning time   Teamwork depends upon having the time to plan together, and using it effectively. At least one common planning time per day is required for full operation. Two planning periods (out of a seven period day) makes planning really possible, since team members can have their own time, and one period for teamwork.

4. Team leadership   Almost all effective teams have a skilled team leader. Whether selected by the team or the school principal, it is essential that the team leader be able to work with both teachers and administrators. The team leader coordinates team meetings, serves as liaison between the team and the school principal, and performs many other duties for the team. The good leader is "well-liked, trusted, efficient, and task-centered."

5. Personal characteristics of members   For teamwork at its best, individual members must like teaching at this level and enjoy their role as team member. They must be optimistic as persons, about themselves, their students, and the process of teamwork. Maturity, in terms of patience and tolerance, are high on the list.

6. Attitudes toward students   Effective teamwork grows from a pro-student attitude, where teachers are committed to their students' success; where team members explore every alternative to improve the educational process. On these teams the students aren't blamed. They even treat kids as "customers." Don't give up if the students are not properly appreciative, is the advice given by seasoned practitioners. Motivating students is part of the process.

7. Attitudes toward teammates   Teamwork depends on team members who fit the expression "diverse but unified." All good teams possess a variety of interests, values, and instructional styles that they recognize as potentially divisive. Good teams, however, accept these differences and work hard to preserve the team. They listen respectfully. They are willing to compromise. Agreement about school and team philosophy provides the foundation for resolving incidental disagreements. Team members do their best to show appreciation for each other on a regular basis, even to the point of institutionalizing certain team rituals like "Secret Santas," monthly breakfasts, and others. Effective teams welcome new members, regular and substitute.

8. Relative autonomy   Teamwork depends upon reasonable room for teams to create their own policies, schedules, activities, curriculum plans, systems for monitoring student behavior and academic performance, and for ensuring parent involvement. Teams are not, however, thrown into situations they are unable to handle.

9. Principal involvement   School principals must, in the language of one of them, "keep a tight grip on loose reins." They attend as many team meetings as possible, playing the role of observer and consultant—not chairperson. Principals help teamwork grow by listening to teams' ideas and focusing on teams' concerns, by modeling the behaviors expected in teacher's relationships with students and with each other. Encouraging innovation in teamwork also enhances team development. Walt Grebing, of Broomfield Heights Middle School, lists the following as central to the principal's involvement in team effectiveness:

a.   Develop individual team expectations and goals *with* teams each year.
b.   Allow *teams* to help in the selection of new members.
c.   Provide as much common planning time as possible.
d.   Require teams to make decisions.
e.   Provide *continuous* staff development for teams and team leaders.
f.   *Teach* flexibility in use of the block schedule.
g.   Encourage and expect interdisciplinary teaching.
h.   Give teams a budget.
i.   Require *all* staff members to be a member of a team.
j.   Evaluate teams on their effectiveness and the contributions which individual teachers make to the life of the team.

10. Continuing Education   Teacher and team involvement in inservice sessions aimed at their interests and concerns supports the refinement and extension of teamwork. When this education is the result of planning by the team, the team leader, and the principal, it can be most effective. Training in interpersonal communications skills and in the conduct of effective meetings are important topics, as well as the whole concept of interdisciplinary team organization, the nature of middle school students, and so on.

At Conway Middle School in Orlando, Florida, fifty teachers who have participated in the teaming process for several years gave the following suggestions in response to the question "What advice would you give the members of a brand new team?":

Keep the needs of the students first on your list when planning.
Go all out for your team identity.
Get to know one another and become friends.
Always be supportive of each other.
Work and plan together every day.
Share responsibilities.
Share the decision-making of the team.
Provide new members with training on the concept of the interdisciplinary team.

Know each other's personality types and capitalize on those strengths.
Develop a team discipline plan and be consistent.
Plan activities involving each other's curricula.
Plan advisory activities together.
Maintain a positive attitude and a sense of humor.
Be prepared to devote the time it takes to be a team.

Teams and Team Meetings: Problems to Avoid

Experience in the last several decades indicates that teams of teachers need to be able to function together effectively during team meetings in order for the work of the team to move smoothly. Teachers spend most of their days in their own rooms working with their students; this is what they know best and what they feel most comfortable continuing. Hence, when there are problems with team meetings, teams tend to have fewer of them, less is planned, less is accomplished, and teams feel a sense of failure and discouragement. There are several ways in which problems are likely to appear in connection with team meetings.[1]

Being aware of problems with team meetings may help team members avoid them. First, and most difficult, is the reluctance of one or more members to participate. Teachers assigned to teams, and unfamiliar or uncomfortable with working directly with other adults, may simply avoid team meetings if they can. Other teachers may not accept the need for teamwork, or may disagree with the goals of the team or even of the middle school concept. They may come late, if at all. They may come to the meeting, but spend the session on other tasks which they consider more important: grading their papers, chatting with other team members, or find other ways of sending the message that they don't want to be involved in the team's meetings. Faced with such lack of interest or open opposition, some team leaders are tempted to throw up their hands. This is a critical problem which can not be ignored and will not go away if it is. Once the team and its leader have exhausted all the efforts they can think of, including straightforward but skillful confrontation of the problem with the team member, it takes a real commitment from the principal, most often, to bring reluctant members into full participation with the team. Team leaders should not hesitate to ask for the help of the school administrator, if and when they have tried all they can think of to get the reluctant participant involved.

A lack of clarity or agreement on the agenda may cause team meetings to go awry. No agenda at all will bring a meeting's progress to a screeching halt. It is the task of the team leader to formulate the agenda for the team meetings and to be certain that it contains the items that are central to the goals of the team and its members.

---

[1]For a more in-depth treatment of team meetings, see Erb & Doda (1989). *Team organization.* Washington, DC: NEA.

Too much dependence on the leader can result in eventual team breakdown. Enthusiastic and energetic team leadership is important, but martyrdom is not. The burdens of teamwork must be shared by all its members. What the team leader does must be different but not more than what other members contribute, even in situations where team leaders are modestly compensated for their duties. We have never seen a team leader salary adjustment that adequately compensated them for what he or she contributes to the school.

Sloppy communication during the meeting can damage both the personal and pedagogical outcomes. Teachers on teams need training in listening, problem solving, assertiveness, and many other interpersonal and communication skills. It can not be left to chance, even though most middle school teachers demonstrate a remarkably high degree of skill in their interpersonal relationships.

Hidden feelings that surface only after the meeting, and outside it, can damage the trust between members, and the honesty and reality of the meeting itself. Negative reactions, unexpressed fears, jealousies—all of these feelings may result in a growing distance and unproductive formality between and among team members. One clue to the existence of such feelings is often the degree of formality in the way team members address each other and work together interpersonally. When team members who supposedly work together closely and intensely refer to each other in formal ways—as Mr. or Ms., for example, indicating that they either don't know each other's first names or are uncomfortable using them—not much trust, honesty, reality, and productivity is likely to be present in team meetings involving such "strangers."

Unclear decision-making procedures and the absence of action plans which throw too much weight on the team leader can also lead the "best laid plans" awry. Keeping notes of commitments of who, what, when, and how, regarding team plans and regularly reviewing those commitments at the beginning of meetings will help move plans toward fruition.

Principal Andre Trottier, of John F. Kennedy Middle School in Gallup, New Mexico, has developed and used an instrument to help teachers on teams in his school assess their effectiveness in group work (Trottier, personal communication, January, 1991).[2] The instrument helps teachers examine their team's strengths and weaknesses in three areas: group leadership, group processes (e.g., shared goals, sense of unity), and group tasks (e.g., consistent time and place for meetings). We think regular feedback and guidance using instruments of this sort can lead to improvements in the ways in which teachers work together in teams and, particularly, in the meetings they attend as they work together.

---

[2]For more information about the instrument, contact Dr. Andre Trottier, Kennedy Middle School, 600 South Boardman Avenue, Gallup, New Mexico, 87301.

Planning for an Interdisciplinary Team Organization in the New Middle School

Educators involved in or contemplating the move to an interdisciplinary team organization should look forward confidently to the outcome, given attention to several factors. Decisions need to be made regarding the size of teams, teaching assignments of each member, and the place in the school where each team will be located. Teachers new to this process should be helped to see that they will not be required to make major changes in the type of teaching they have always done. Unless there is a considerable amount of staff development money and time available, and an excess of planning time, teachers ought not be expected to produce any significant amount of actual team teaching. The effort required to make the team organization work will be considerable, and the results of effective teams reward enough. When provided with some tutoring in conducting team meetings and in the process of scheduling their own students, most teams will function quite smoothly, provided the interpersonal mix is right and the communication skills are what they should be. Combine this with a proper location and a comfortable division of teaching responsibilities and things should operate without major problems.

ADDITIONAL SUGGESTIONS FOR FURTHER STUDY

A. Books and Monographs

George, P. (1988). *Teamwork*. Gainesville, FL: Teacher Education Resources.

Vars, G. F. (1987). *Interdisciplinary teaching in the middle grades: Why & how*. Columbus, OH: National Middle School Association.

B. Periodicals

Bailey, D. B., Jr. (1984). A triaxial model of the interdisciplinary team and group process. *Exceptional Children, 51*(1), 17–25.

Erb, T. O. (1987). What team organization can do for teachers. *Middle School Journal, 18*, 3–6.

Hendrickson, J. M. (& others). (1988). The multidisciplinary team: Training educators to serve middle school students with special needs. *Clearing House, 62*(2), 84–86.

McKenna, B. (1989). Whatever happened to team teaching? *American Educator: The Professional Journal of the American Federation of Teachers, 13*(2), 15–19.

Preston, F. B. (1984). A behavior management plan for middle level students. *NASSP Bulletin, 68*(473), 39–41.

Smith, H. W. (1991). Guiding teaming development. *Middle School Journal, 22*(5), 21–23.

C. ERIC

Cangelosi, James S. (1990). *Cooperation in the classroom: Students and teachers together*. Analysis and Action Series (2nd Ed.). Washington, DC: National Education Association. (ERIC Document Reproduction Service No. ED 315 196)

George, P. S. & Stevenson, C. (1988). *Highly effective interdisciplinary teams: Perceptions of exemplary middle school principals*. (ERIC Document Reproduction Service No. ED 303 866)

Lake, S. (1989). Interdisciplinary team organization in the middle level school (Practitioner's Monograph #7). Sacramento, CA: California League of Middle Schools. (ERIC Document Reproduction Service No. ED 309 551)

Merenbloom, E. Y. (1986). *The team process in the middle school: A handbook for teachers* (2nd Ed.). Columbus, OH: National Middle School Association. (ERIC Document Reproduction Service No. ED 324 804)

D. Dissertations and Dissertation Abstracts

Ayalon, A. I. (1988). Teachers' perceptions of their working environment in departmental and interdisciplinary teaming organization in middle level schools (Doctoral dissertation, The University of Arizona, 1988). *Dissertation Abstracts International*, 50/01a, 30.

Bell, N. M. (1990). A case study of the implementation of interdisciplinary team organizations in a large school district (Doctoral dissertation, University of Florida, 1990).

Natvig, D. (1989). Interdisciplinary team development and job satisfaction of team members working with the mentally retarded (Masters thesis, University of Florida, 1989).

Plodzik, K. T. (1986). The middle school interdisciplinary team organization: an analysis of its life stages based on the perceptions of the principal. (Doctoral dissertation, Boston University, 1986). *Dissertation Abstracts International*, 47/04a, 1176.

Schumaker, R. C. (1986). Interdisciplinary team in the middle school. (Doctoral dissertation, University of Houston, 1986). *Dissertation Abstracts International*, 47/06a, 2011.

Walsh, K. J. (1984). Seventh and eighth grade interdisciplinary teaming and organizational climate. (Doctoral dissertation, Seton Hall University, School of Education, 1984). *Dissertation Abstracts International*, 46/12a, 3564.

CHAPTER 7

Grouping Students In The Middle School

Perhaps more than any other aspect of the exemplary middle school, strategies for grouping students are or should be strongly influenced by the characteristics of the learner. Variability and dissimilarity among students in the middle school, the central developmental features of this group of learners, require schools attempting to implement an effectively unique but transitional education program to consider a variety of alternative methods of student grouping. The special nature of the transescent is recognized most clearly by educators attempting to design ways of grouping students which accommodate this age group.

Organizing Students for Instruction

Orientation in Elementary and High School

Developmentally, students in the primary grades are strikingly similar. Most students in the first three or four grades will be at or below the stage of concrete mental operations in Piagetan terms. Most, if not all, will be sexually immature, not having experienced puberty. Few will have had to deal with the consequences of the early adolescent growth spurt. These elementary school pupils are children, in that they respond to peers, and to parents and other adults, in ways which do not yet reflect the changes they will experience as early adolescents. Mentally, sexually, physically, emotionally, socially, they are developmentally similar.

When chronological age is a reliable guide to the characteristics of the learners, as is the case in the primary grades, it is reasonable to have students grouped for instruction in a manner which reflects this. If six-year-olds are almost all alike developmentally, it makes good sense to group them in a way that capitalizes on this similarity.

Chronological age-grade grouping in the elementary school years appears to have considerable validity, particularly in the earliest years. Of course, flexibility is important even here. It is also true that, during the primary school years, similarity in academic achievement is at the highest level it will ever be. That is, during the first few years of school, students are more homogeneous in what they have achieved scholastically, than during any later period of school. Academically, as well as developmentally, relative similarity is the rule, so grouping students chronologically, by grades according to age, seems acceptable. Acceptable or not, this is the common practice.

We can think of students in the elementary school as being at a very early and vulnerable stage of development as learners. They have not established a record of success as students. In all too many instances, they come from homes and communities torn by poverty, divorce, crime, drug abuse, and other varieties of discord. They may enter schools which are immensely larger than any other setting they have ever been in. The responsibility of the elementary school has been, therefore, to provide great amounts of supportive interpersonal structure, usually in the form of an exclusive relationship with a warm and supportive teacher in a self-contained classroom. The nature of this supportive interpersonal structure, in the early years of the elementary school, was memorialized in the Latin phrase *in loco parentis*: the teacher takes the place of the parent.

At the high school, the developmental and academic characteristics of the learners also suggest strategies for grouping for instruction. Especially, in the later years of the high school, learners have matured as persons, they have established records of some academic success, or at least stability. Many less successful learners have dropped out. High school students are also returning to a position of developmental similarity, one to another, that parallels the situation in the early years of the elementary school. Many high school students have matured mentally, one hopes, to the stage of formal operations described by Piaget. Puberty has been negotiated. Physical size and strength reflect the experience of the growth spurt during early adolescence. Much of the stereotypical turmoil of the social and emotional changes is past. Developmentally, high school students are re-entering a position of considerable maturity and similarity.

Academically, however, the situation is quite different. By the high school years, the students who remain have reached a point where differences in academic achievement levels and areas of interest are at a maximum. As each year has passed, the differences have become more marked. Consequently, strategies for grouping students for instruction in high school reflect this developmental and academic situation.

Since variability among students is quite low developmentally, and quite high academically, the typical high school has responded by grouping students according to their interests in and their achievement of academic goals. Students, historically, select one of three subject matter pathways: general, academic college preparatory, or vocational. Students choose courses (for example, world history) with little regard to grade level, and it is common to find students from several ages and grade levels in a particular class. Grouping is accomplished primarily by the student's choice of or ability in a particular subject or group of subjects.

At the high school, because students select their programs in this way, and because they have achieved a substantial degree of developmental maturity, the amount of supportive interpersonal structure they require for academic success is likely to be much less than they needed as children in the early elementary grades. Consequently, at the high school, teachers are organized to deliver instruction in a way that is almost totally based on subject matter specialization. This results in the familiar departmental organization similar to that experienced in virtually all colleges and universities.

Organizing Students at the Middle Level

The exemplary middle school, too, attempts to group students for instruction in a way that accommodates the special developmental characteristics of the students it serves, but the situation is different in several ways. First, middle school students are dramatically different from both elementary school and high school students when development is considered. Developmental similarity has been replaced by great variability. Middle school students seem to have little in common with each other developmentally, except that they have so little in common. Rapid, pervasive, powerful, unpredictable, personal change is the rule, often so much so that it is almost impossible to describe a typical thirteen-year-old. They may be mature mentally; they may not. They may have already passed through puberty; they may not have yet begun. They may be six feet tall, or four. They may still act like children, they may often seem like adults, or they may range unpredictably from one end of the continuum to the other. Chronological age is frequently not a completely reliable guide to identifying the characteristics of such students and, hence, not the only guide to grouping students for instruction.

Academically, middle school students seem far more variable than their elementary school counterparts but less than they will be as high school students. They may, however, come to the middle school from very different academic experiences in the elementary school. Some will have been very successful. Some, unfortunately a rapidly growing number, must be characterized as abject failures. Others will be in between. In order that the experiences of the elementary school are not simply made permanent, especially in the case of those who are unsuccessful, the middle school staff must organize the students for learning in ways which supply the proper "positive structure" for success.

Organizing all students in middle schools according to subject matter choices, as if they were all ready for a high school-style learning experience, would be arbitrary, capricious, and contrary to the spirit of organizing the program on the basis of the developmental characteristics of the students. It would also be against the best interest of many of the students. Most middle school students need less supportive interpersonal structure than elementary students, but more than they will require when they reach the high school. In the same way, middle school students can benefit from a considerably greater degree of subject specialization on the part of their teachers, but much less so than is the case for high school students. Consequently, the balance of these factors must be different at the middle level that it is at either the elementary or the high school level.

If chronological age grouping and subject matter choices are not totally effective means of grouping middle school students for instruction, is there an organizational strategy which more closely considers the development and maturation of the students? Do exemplary middle schools often choose alternatives to the traditional organizational procedures? If, in fact, the middle school is unique in its attempt to focus on the special characteristics of the learners within, are there some methods which are more likely to be congruent with student development than others? As the middle school aims at a program that is different from that of the elementary school and the high school but leads smoothly in transition from one to the other, there must be a "middle way" with school organization and grouping, too.

For nearly a century, the evolving middle level concept has been based on the often fervently held conviction that middle school-age students, as a developmental age group, are unique in their characteristics and needs. Rarely will a meeting of any group of middle level educators pass without pointed references to the special nature of the students involved. There is some evidence that establishing and maintaining high quality middle schools depends, in several ways, on the recognition of the special qualities of these learners and the willingness to tailor programs to those needs (George & Anderson, 1989).

Just as in the case of the United States Post Office, therefore, the nature of specific school "addresses" should be determined by who lives there, educationally speaking. The nature and needs of the "residents" of a particular educational place should determine the specific design and operation of that individual program. The students and their developmental needs should determine more than just the general guidelines of generic middle level education. The specific needs of a single population of early adolescent learners should be the foundation upon which the unique features of any particular middle level school are constructed.

But which student development characteristics should be most carefully considered when designing the school and its program? Which features of the school program should be fine tuned to those developmental characteristics? These are subjects for contemporary discussions.

Student Development and School Organization[1]

Student developmental characteristics have always been a factor in school organization at all three levels. We have argued here that, organizationally speaking, the nature of the elementary school child requires a school organized with an emphasis on smallness and what might be called "supportive interpersonal structure" provided by teachers who specialize in a group of students instead of a particular subject. Teacher-subject specialization, in an academic department organization similar to that of universities, characterizes the large American comprehensive high school. This is congruent with the belief that high school students are far more developmentally mature. Because of their position between elementary and high school, middle level educators have struggled for almost a century to establish the single precise balancing point between supportive interpersonal structure (SIS) and teacher-subject specialization (TSS) which should characterize all middle level schools, with the corresponding expectation that all interdisciplinary teams ought to be identical.

This was a mistake. SIS and TSS are both important to every middle level school, but not in the same proportions or balance. We know that the interdisciplinary team organization is an important part, if not the most distinguishing characteristic, of the middle school "zip code." But it should not be exactly the same at every address; every interdisciplinary team organization should reflect the characteristics and needs of the students who live at that specific school. Every middle level school must balance SIS and TSS in the way that the needs of the particular student population require.

One fundamental question, then, facing those who seek to develop an exemplary middle level school, a school carefully tailored to fit the dimensions of those who inhabit it, is: "What do the developmental characteristics of *our particular* students suggest for the grouping of teachers and students in our school?" Another way of asking this question is "What special type of student grouping, within the context of the interdisciplinary team organization, will be right for *our* students?"

This is a question which must be asked in every individual middle level school. One answer will not do for all schools, or perhaps for all time in any one school; just like one address will not fit every family's needs. One size, in this case, does not fit all. The correct answer to such a question, asked in individual settings, will result in the appropriate balance of SIS and TSS, the combination

---

[1]Substantial portions of this section were first published in an earlier monograph: George, P. (Spring 1991). "Student development and middle level school organization," *Midpoints: Occasional Papers, 1,1.* Available from the National Middle School Association, Columbus, Ohio.

of the two which is most effective for the particular students in the school in question.

A Model of Student Development and School Organization

It is possible, we believe, to envision a model which integrates the factors of student development and middle school organization in such a way as to indicate more precisely the balance point of SIS and TSS which is appropriate for particular populations of early adolescent students. Such a model should be helpful in the design of new buildings and programs, in the reorganization of existing facilities and programs, in more effective deployment of teachers into various sorts of interdisciplinary collaboration, in the evaluation of middle level schools, and in prediction and solution of problems of the school which might be traceable to organizational roots.

The basic thesis which supports the model presented in Figure 7.1 is that the most effective grouping strategy for a particular population of students is dependent upon the specific characteristics and needs of the students in that school. Effective grouping (and teacher organization) is, in this model, defined as the appropriate balance of SIS and TSS. The higher the level of student development, the more the school organization can, theoretically, effectively emphasize teacher-subject specialization; the less highly developed the students in the school, the greater the amount of supportive interpersonal structure required to meet the goals of the school.

The apex of teacher-subject specialization in the public schools comes in the upper grades of the large comprehensive high school. Here, organized in academic departments, teachers specialize in teaching one small part of an academic discipline, usually at one grade level, and often to one ability level. A teacher might, for example, teach only ninth grade honors algebra; another might teach

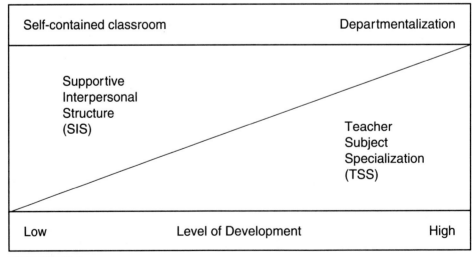

FIGURE 7.1

only Spanish Three, and so on. One teacher, teaching one small part of the world of knowledge to a small portion of the school population: this sort of assignment is, furthermore, often regarded as highly desirable.

Supportive interpersonal structure is most crisply illustrated, as one might expect, at the other end of the educational continuum. It is the hallmark of the elementary school. In the early years of the primary school—during children's first few years following their departure from the home—students need all the supportive interpersonal structure the school can provide. A further example can be found in the old one-room schoolhouse, where there was an exclusive relationship between one teacher and a group of students ranging from kindergarten to 8th grade. Typically, one teacher taught many subjects to one group of students, often over more than one grade level. In that one-room schoolhouse, and in the early years of primary school today, teacher-subject specialization is virtually absent and its encroachment down into the upper grades of the elementary school is often deplored by those not involved in what is called "departmentalization."

Middle school educators seek to balance these two factors when grouping students and teachers on teams and otherwise; each middle school must find the most appropriate "best fit" for its particular student population. It is the "best fit" (derived from a knowledge of the characteristics of the students) between SIS and TSS which determines, according to the model in Figure 7.1, the best grouping strategy for a particular middle level school. An important question, then, is what special characteristics and needs of the students are to be considered in arriving at the concept of best fit?

In a real sense, student development during the early adolescent years is hard to capture in generalities; these students are often described as having little in common other than the fact of changing development itself. Nevertheless, we believe it is possible to make useful generalizations about total school populations, as long as the tentative nature of this process is clear from the outset. Generalizations can be made about the age range of the students, their socioeconomic levels, their success in elementary school, or the extent of their heterogeneity as a group. It is also possible to make some accurate statements about the school environment: the size of the school, the distance students must travel, the attrition rates, the resources available to the school for the education of its youth, whether it is public or private, and so on.

Departmentalization

It is possible, for example, by putting together one composite of these factors, to recall the students in the once quite typical small town Midwestern junior high school. Such schools were often populated by students in grades 7–9; learners ranged from twelve to fifteen years in age. The students often came to junior high school having been quite successful in elementary school, we now nostalgically recall. Frequently, the students came from majority culture, middle or upper-middle income families, traditional in their makeup, stable in their structure. Many of these schools tended to be considerably smaller than their counterparts today. In comparison with today's typical middle-level schools, there were a number of important differences in student development.

Such a student population is defined here, according to the model, as "highly developed" or "mature." Such a population, we argue, is likely to be successful in reaching the goals of the school when learning within the traditional junior high school organizational model. This forerunner of today's middle level school, consequently, stressed a high degree of teacher-subject specialization and very little emphasis on supportive interpersonal structure.

Individual teachers in such schools, perhaps a majority of them, were known to care deeply about their students. But little formal attention was paid to structuring the school in any formal way intended to provide more interpersonal support. Teachers often saw themselves as subject matter specialists with little responsibility for the personal lives of their students. They might have argued, and perhaps accurately, that their students did not need such attention from them and that to organize in ways that would produce it might be counterproductive in terms of academic achievement. They may have been right—for that time and those students.

With these sorts of student development factors in mind, educators charged with organizing an effective learning environment might have been correct in their almost exclusive emphasis on TSS. Because the students were significantly younger than those in the high school, however, a few important adjustments were usually made. The junior high school was usually smaller than the high school. Competition may have been muted in comparison to the senior version. Teacher tolerance for their students' relative lack of maturity might have been higher. By and large, however, such schools were literally "junior" high schools.

There are still many such schools. In the upper-middle-class suburbs surrounding every major city in America, throughout New England, the Midwest, and the West, and in small cities and towns in every region of the nation, such schools abound. Compared to other school districts, student populations attending these schools today tend to be majority culture, middle- and upper-middle-class. These students have, on the whole, successful elementary school experiences, and the assumption is, at least until recently, that they come from stable and resilient home environments. State and national achievement tests support the belief that the schools they attend are productive, at least in terms of standardized tests.

Are these schools bad? Should they abandon their current grouping model for something else? When the faculties and administrations of such schools question the merits of alternatives for their students, are they wrong? It depends.

We would argue, on the basis of the model, that it depends on whether the students are achieving all three of the goals which the schools pursue. Is academic learning where it should be for these students? Are most students growing

The Middle School Zip Code

School A	School B	School C	School D	School E	School F	School G
Modified Core Program (MCP)	Develop-mental Age Grouping (DAG)	School-Within-A-School (SWS)	Long-Term Teams (LTT)	Grade-Level Team (GLT)	Grade-wide Teams (GWT)	Depart-menta-lized (DPT)

More Elementary   More Secondary

FIGURE 7.2

as persons, experiencing success, and feeling positive about themselves? Is the school capitalizing upon the natural early adolescent readiness for group involvement in positive and socially productive ways?

When a school is populated with "highly developed" students, organized to enable a high degree of teacher-subject specialization and a minimum of supportive interpersonal structure, and the students experience favorable outcomes in the achievement of goals, the organization must be considered effective. It is effective if it can supply valid and reliable evidence that it has, in fact, achieved all three goals.

For purposes of the model, let us identify one example of such schools as School G, and locate its appropriate "address" within the middle level zip code (see Figure 7.2). It is at the address we will call "Departmentalized." It would be placed just inside the middle level area, only a short distance from the high school zip code; its program, organization, and emphasis are very much oriented toward the secondary location: heavy emphasis on TSS, little SIS.

Gradewide Interdisciplinary Teams

Just one position further inside the middle level zip code, moving away from the high school area, one finds the address of schools which are organized into what might be called Gradewide Interdisciplinary Teams. In a school, such as School F, students tend to be high on the developmental criteria, but in grades six to eight, so they are younger than those in the traditional junior high school and, thus, need a bit more supportive structure. We have found, over the years, that such schools as these are also often located in upper-middle-class suburban areas, even though their population may be mixed as a result of busing to achieve racial balance.

Schools organized into gradewide teams usually use the terms "team" and "grade level" synonymously; terms such as "the 6th grade team" or "7th grade team" are commonly used. Teachers think of themselves as working with a team of other teachers who serve, in limited ways, the students from the entire grade level. As many as a dozen or more teachers may work with a grade level of three hundred or more students. Students may have a grade level mascot, colors, and so forth. The teachers and students will be organized by grade levels in different wings of the school, sixth grade occupying one wing, seventh another, and the eighth grade still another. Teachers design special activities of considerable variety, work together with parents when they have students in common, develop grade level rules and procedures, interact with school and district specialists, and perform many other activities and duties commonly associated with the interdisciplinary team organization concept. They enjoy their students and seek regular opportunities to support their development. They believe, however, that most students can succeed fairly well in school without further emphasis on supportive interpersonal structure and the teachers often see no need for and resist attempts to design smaller interdisciplinary teams where there would be only one teacher for each subject.

In this gradewide team grouping situation, however, one vital concept of the interdisciplinary team will be missing: most of the teachers will not share the same students. More often, teachers of the same subject, at the same grade level, will work together in what is, really, a small grade level department. Teacher planning will be focused, for the most part, on a single-subject curriculum, even when they work with other teachers. The emphasis will be on teacher-subject specialization, but not to the total exclusion of supportive interpersonal structure.

Core-Style Grouping

We turn now to the other end of the continuum of student development, to those students defined as the least highly developed, the least mature. Without going far in time or distance, it is possible for most educators to imagine such a school situation. For purposes of illustration, let us say that a particular school population contains students in grades 5–8, with ages ranging from ten to fourteen—50 percent younger as a school population, one might say, than those in the traditional junior high school. Let us also stipulate that the school is located in a large urban area, in an extremely multicultural situation. (We are familiar with one such school where ninety-seven languages and dialects are reported to be spoken in students' homes.) Let us further specify that the students come from predominantly lower-middle and lower-income homes, and that, in addition, their entrance into the middle level school is not often marked by measures of extreme success in the primary schools they attended. Let us, in fact, stipulate that the students, as a group, have experienced a great deal of what might be called delayed development, manifested in academic failure and low self-esteem, and that their cohesiveness as a group leaves much to be desired. Finally, let us indicate that it is a very large school for this age group—perhaps as large as 2,100 students at the same school site. (We know of two such schools just opening in one district.)

What would be the "best fit" between SIS and TSS for the organization of this school? What do these students need? Even though they attend a middle level school, should it be organized like School G? If it is, what is likely to happen to the academic achievement, personal development, and group citizenship goals of the school?

In an actual school very much like the composite one above (we will identify it as School A), the existing balance between SIS and TSS is very different. The staff believes that, for these students, the transition from primary to middle level school is an extremely vulnerable process for the students. They assert that the entry into the first year of the middle level school must be handled very carefully (i.e., with a great deal of supportive interpersonal structure). We will refer to this organizational address as the Modified Core Program.

At School A, the 5th grade is arrayed in predominantly self-contained classroom situations. Fifth grade students spend almost all day with their homeroom teacher and their peers in the homeroom group. Homeroom teachers are responsible for teaching all of the academic subjects. Students leave the homeroom only for lunch and one other period a day. The teacher-student interpersonal relationship is very highly structured; they spend almost all day, all year, together in a very small group much like an elementary class.

Fifth grade teachers' assignments at School A are the antithesis of subject specialization. Many fifth grade faculty members argue, however, that multiple lesson preparations in connection with a very small daily student load (e.g., twenty-five) are very different from teaching four or five subjects to as many as 150 students each day. Teachers with experience in such a situation argue that while such an assignment may not be easier than a more subject specialized one, it is often more satisfying in terms of relationships with students and parents.

At this school, the "best fit" emphasizes supportive interpersonal structure almost exclusively in the fifth grade. It permits the fifth grade teacher to concentrate on one group of students, rather than on one subject in the curriculum. Gradually, however, SIS and TSS strike different balances as the developmental level of the students at School A increases, especially in terms of age. In the sixth grade, the students still stay with their homeroom teacher for 70 percent of the day, moving out of the homeroom to one class with another sixth grade teacher on the interdisciplinary team (as they have defined it), and for an elective class. In the seventh grade, students spend 50 percent of the day with the homeroom teacher and group. In the eighth, the students spend 40 percent of their day with their homeroom teacher, and the remainder of the day with other teachers from the team and with elective teachers.

The faculty of this school believes that the developmental level of their students requires a very different mix of SIS and TSS than one would find in the traditional junior high school. Are they right? They are if they can demonstrate that they are more effective in reaching those three goals than they might otherwise be. What do you think might happen to academic achievement, personal development, and group citizenship if the school were organized with an exclusive emphasis on teacher-subject specialization as in School G? School A's placement is, most logically, near the border of the elementary zip code.

Middle schools in many districts approximate the grouping strategy employed in our composite example above. In the school district of Volusia County (Daytona Beach), Florida, for example, planners have been so concerned about the developmental immaturity of incoming 6th graders that they have organized all of the nearly one dozen middle schools so that 6th graders are in largely self-contained classroom settings. For most of the school day, the students learn from one teacher. In many of the middle schools of the state of Washington, all students in grades 6–8 are organized into what has come to be called a "block" program. This block program features extended daily relationships with one teacher, the homeroom teacher, balanced by learning from a much smaller number of other teachers who work together in interdisciplinary teams.

At Jefferson Middle School in Olympia, Washington, principal Kevin Evoy continues, in the 1990s, a grouping strategy developed in the early 1970s by Washington pioneer middle school educator Tom Eisenmann. At Jefferson Middle, every student is scheduled for a three-period daily block of time with his/her homeroom teacher—half of the student's instructional day. The teacher provides instruction in spelling, English, reading, social studies, and health during this extended period. Evoy believes, as do many other Washington State educators, that the intensive block program offers many benefits to all middle school students, not just those whose special needs require greater increments of supportive interpersonal structure. Washington middle school educators argue that all middle school students profit from this organization. Evoy states that students at Jefferson Middle achieve "greater concentration in the basic subjects, integration of subject matter," and develop a "student-teacher relationship similar to the elementary school setting" (K. Evoy, personal communication, November, 1990). The block program is, of course, in addition to the interdisciplinary team organization and a regular daily advisory program.

Between school grouping placements such as these (Schools A, F, & G), within the middle level zipcode, there are many, many special addresses, unique balance points of SIS and TSS. Theoretically, there are an infinite number of such points, each depending on the developmental level of the students. Only a few of the possibilities are now implemented in functioning middle level schools.

Grade Level Interdisciplinary Teams

By far, the most popular address in the middle level zip code is just two steps inside it, at the spot indicated by School E, with the gradewide team and the traditional junior high school separating it from the high school zip code. Alexander and McEwin (1989) estimate that approximately one third of all operating middle level schools organize teachers and students into what we will identify here as the conventional Grade Level Interdisciplinary Team program. A study by Connors and Gill (1991) reveals that upwards of 88 percent of middle schools identified as "Schools of Excellence" by the United States Department of Education organize in this interdisciplinary manner. Many of the exemplary middle schools cited in this textbook are organized in this basic grouping strategy.

Here at the "address" of School E, and at thousands of others, the "best fit" is determined to be at that point where one teacher teaches one subject to one grade level. Instead of being organized together with others who share that subject, as in the traditional junior high school program, however, the teachers are organized according to the students they have in common. This is the pattern which has been recommended as the most appropriate middle school address and has been adopted by increasingly greater numbers of school faculties.

Middle school educators now know that when teachers share the same students, schedule, building area, and responsibility for planning the majority of the academic subjects students study, the amount of SIS is often substantially increased in comparison to the tradtional junior high school. Frequently, it is the "best fit," balancing TSS and SIS in a way that permits teachers to concentrate on one or two teaching areas with a smaller group of other teachers who share the same students. In recent years educators have learned a great deal about the advantages of organizing middle level schools in this way (Erb & Doda, 1989). Teachers may teach what they have always taught, in the manner in which they have always taught it, if the subject and the teaching strategy made sense in the first place. They maintain a comfortable level of TSS. At the same time, by working closely with others who teach the same students, they can increase the consistency, the knowledge of students, and the degree of careful planning which permits them to reach middle school goals more effectively.

We believe that the conventional interdisciplinary grade level team organization (GLT) may be the most appropriate balance between SIS and TSS for many, perhaps for even the majority of middle level schools. But, we are now convinced that a consideration of the facts of student development at many middle level schools would indicate that important modifications might be necessary for the students to achieve the goals of the school. If the students in a particular middle level school are less highly developed along the lines described above, then some alteration of the standard team process will be important. The model suggests that under such circumstances, some new balance point would be appropriate, one which involves substantially more supportive interpersonal structure for the students. In the last two decades, several successful alternatives have emerged.

Long-Term Teams

At one such school (at the point for School D in the model), Lincoln Middle School in Gainesville, Florida, the level of student development suggests, according to the model, a significant need for more SIS in the school lives of the students. It is a school with grades 6–8, so that students are considerably younger than in the traditional junior high school, about one-third younger. The students at Lincoln are also much less successful in their elementary school experiences than one would wish. Most are from low-income homes; in 1991, 80 percent were on free or reduced lunch. Some of the students do, however, come from quite affluent homes. Minority culture students make up 60 percent of the school population; the school is also a district center for bilingual education, with twenty-one different languages spoken in the students' homes. The school serves, further, as the center for the education of middle school-age hearing-impaired students. Many educators would recognize that this student population is not typical of the traditional junior high school, but that it is becoming all too typical of today's middle level school.

Because many of the teachers at School D (Lincoln) are from secondary backgrounds, however, the staff prizes TSS at a much higher level than one might expect at a point like School A, where a majority of the teachers would have training in elementary education. The staff at Lincoln, nonetheless, recognizes that students need much more SIS in their school lives in order to be successful. So a unique address has been crafted: one teacher teaches one subject, to one grade level, *at a time*. For nearly twenty years, the staff at School D has been involved in one version or another of what might be called multi-year teams or "Long-Term Teams" (LTT).

Multiage Grouped Teams

At Lincoln, for the first ten years of its existence as a middle school, interdisciplinary teams were organized according to one variety of Long-Term Team called "Multiage Grouping" (MAG). The distinguishing feature of MAG is the fact that students remain not only in the same house or on the same team, but that they remain with the same team of students and teachers for three years; students almost always begin and end their MS careers on the same team.

Each of the six teams at Lincoln, when it opened in the early 1970s, for example, contained five teachers and approximately 150 students, 50 each from the 6th, 7th, and 8th grades. Each teacher taught one subject, but to students on the team from three grade levels. The teachers and students remained together for three years; each year, the eighth graders were replaced by a new group of 6th graders. Each team reflected the composition of the total school population; each team was a Lincoln in microcosm.

This long-term team process was relatively easy to operate at Lincoln. In mathematics, reading, and language arts, students were diagnosed, placed, and taught via a form of cross-grade ability grouping for the three years they were on the team. In social studies and science, a three-year cycle insured that every student received all three elements of the curriculum in each subject by the time he/she departed for the high school. At the same time, the cross-grade ability grouping worked so that teachers were confronted with a reasonable range on achievement levels in each of their classes. In fact, this appears to be one version of the few grouping processes which generally defy the negative outcomes to which most variations of tracking are prone (Slavin, 1987).

Concurrently, at Lincoln Middle, the school administration and staff were irrevocably committed to the interdisciplinary team model of teacher cooperation and collaboration. The staff also understood the tremendous need to belong felt by the great majority of early adolescents, so that the school was a model of "smallness within bigness." Students and teachers experienced three years of positive stability in their classroom relationships. Over time, individuals (staff and students alike) came to see themselves as important parts of an important group, with very positive consequences.

A number of barriers to the realization of appropriate school goals was lowered by the MAG process (George, 1987). Teams avoided problems associated with similar tracking and ability grouping systems elsewhere. Discipline inside and outside the classroom became much less of a problem when teachers and students maintained their relationships for three years; beginnings and endings of the year, in particular, were much smoother. Parent relationships and, thus, the conferences which they produced, were much more positive and productive. Interethnic relationships improved measurably. Teachers, students, parents, and administrators discovered that several dozen school processes were much more efficient and effective when the "promise of permanence" was introduced into the structure of interpersonal relationships in the school.

At Lincoln Middle School, the balance of SIS and TSS struck through multiage grouping appears to have fit the students and the faculty extremely well. To insist on the fit that worked for the traditional junior high school would have, we believe, been irresponsible folly. To force traditional secondary teachers to employ a process similar to that of School A would, most likely, have been unsuccessful. Multiage grouped teams were an important new and appropriate organizational pattern for the teachers and students at Lincoln.

Some curriculum adaptations are necessary for MAG to function smoothly, but MAG does not require that each teacher teach three different grade level lessons in each class each day. Some teachers recoil at the thought of being responsible for teaching world history, American history, and geography in the same class to three different groups. This is not what happens.

The basic academic program at Lincoln, and at most other schools which have implemented a similar grouping pattern, was modified in two ways. Mathematics, language arts, and reading were individualized so that students worked independently or in small ad hoc learning groups on specific objectives or tasks which were appropriate for them. Students moved from objective to objective or from skill to skill as they demonstrated mastery or completed a particular set of activities. So students could have joined a team in sixth grade, or at any other point, and moved along as quickly as possible from one year to the next.

In social studies and science, the curriculum was arranged on a three-year cycle. Based on the credible assumption that there is very little inherent sequence in learning either of these two subjects, entire teams of students studied a particular aspect of the curriculum during the same year, regardless of the age or grade of the students. In social studies, students on two teams might, for example, have studied American history during year A, world history during year B, and geography during year C of the cycle. Two other teams would study world history during year A, and the final two teams would study geography during year A. In science, the rotation of the cycle would be similar. Table 7.1 illustrates how the cycle revolves in these two areas.

It is important to note that, for new students, placement on a long-term team usually involves very little difficulty. Since everything major in the curriculum is always being taught on some team in the school, students are placed on the team which most nearly matches the program they had been following in their previous school. This situation also prevents excessive strain on library and other resources for any particular subject.

Mebane Middle School in Alachua, Florida may have been, at one point, the most flexibly grouped middle school in America. During most of the decade from 1975 to 1985, Mebane had approximately 460 students in grades 5 through 8. The school had three multiage grouped teams, each containing approximately 40 students from every grade level. Students remained on the team for four years. Thus, the student population on each team changed by one quarter each year. The eighth graders moved on to the high school, and new 4th graders moved up from the elementary school. The team or "learning community," as the faculty called it, remained about 75 percent whole each year. Within each team at Mebane, special grouping for instruction further accommodated the characteristics of the students on the team.

In reading and mathematics, students on the teams at Mebane were divided by ability into two large groups. One group was composed of middle to high ability students, the second contained middle to low ability students. Half of the students studied the basic skills in the morning, half in the afternoon. Since the grouping disregarded grade levels, it is common for students from at least three

TABLE 7.1   **Lincoln Middle School*—Three Year Curriculum Cycle**

TEAMS	B & C	D & M	T & W
Years			
A	American History Earth Science	World History Life Science	Geography Physical Science
B	Geography Physical Science	American History Earth Science	World History Life Science
C	World History Life Science	Geography Physical Science	American History Earth Science

* Gainesville, Florida

grade levels to be together in class. Such a program permitted regrouping for mathematics in much the same way grouping is done for reading.

In science and social studies, and in physical education and prevocational classes, the students were grouped without rigid ability or achievement level criteria, but with an attempt to reduce the instructional range. Within each team, students were grouped as follows: 5th and 6th graders together, 6th and 7th, 7th and 8th graders, and occasionally at least three grade levels are in class together if the student characteristics or needs suggested it. Curriculum units were repeated every other year, avoiding duplication for students. Mebane seemed to be able to combine both MAG and developmental age grouping into a very efficient and effective overall grouping strategy.

Eggers Middle School in Hammond, Indiana has utilized the MAG design since 1987. Having been organized into interdisciplinary teams since 1976, the Eggers staff moved to MAG, says the school principal, to assist in more effectively addressing the sociological, developmental, and academic needs of the early adolescent. Students are assigned to one of three heterogeneous "Learning Communities" for the length of the educational program through grades 6–8. Each Learning Community is identified by a color. Each has approximately two hundred and fifty students, and ten teachers (in the areas of language arts, reading, foreign language, math, science, social studies, and special education). Teams (Learning Communities) have block schedules which permit ninety minutes of daily planning, conferencing, and meetings. Much of this time is devoted to what the Eggers staff calls "community coordination."

Since each Learning Community at Eggers has the same students for three years, teachers tend to engage in considerably more "pupil personnel services." They use their "community coordination" time to:

Conduct conferences with students, parents, and school personnel
Make phone calls to parents and guardians
Handle discipline problems
Make referrals to special education, counselors, and administration
Develop interdisciplinary units and special instructional activities that address
    the specific learning needs of students
Engage in professional development activities conducted by peers

These activities are documented in a report to the principal each week.

In the spring of 1992, the faculty at Wassom Middle School in Fort Campbell, Kentucky began to plan for the implementation of MAG at their school. In a partial nod to the "schools of choice" phenomenon, parents on the post will be offered a number of organizational options. One will be a team of 6th–8th grade teachers and students who will focus much of their energies on the development of a truly interdisciplinary curriculum to match the innovative grouping arrangements. The first organizational teaching unit will focus on "China" since, as a military school, many teachers and students have contacts and friendships all over the world, and on this MAG team China just happens to present a good choice of relationships and resources.

Two exemplary Midwestern middle schools have used MAG in large schools and where only two grades are present. At Trotwood-Madison Junior High School (Trotwood, Ohio), 850 students have been divided into four teams, each containing an equal number of 7th and 8th graders. Each team has five teachers and an aide. At Brentwood Middle School (Greeley, Colorado), the school has been divided into six teams of between 100 and 140 6th and 7th grade students, with three to four teachers on each team. At Brentwood, the instructional groupings in the subject areas were based on diagnosed instructional need without regard to student age or ability. Thus, the sixth and seventh graders are mixed in all classes.

As the practice of MAG spreads, albeit much too slowly, a number of schools have found that offering this form of grouping in addition to the continued use of some chronological age grouping makes an effective transitional strategy. Choices may then be offered to parents, students, and teachers as to which style of grouping they prefer. Under such circumstances, all groups feel considered and well served, and a seemingly controversial grouping strategy is implemented with little or no turmoil.

Several varieties and styles of such combinations are in operation around the country. At Louisville Middle School (Louisville, Colorado), 5th and 6th graders have been combined for instruction in mathematics, language arts, reading, and exploratory options, but were taught by grade levels in science and physical education. Seventh and eighth graders worked together only in elective areas, except during the extensive activity period when students from grades 5 through 8 were grouped together. This method of interweaving MAG and chronological age grouping is likely to receive support from everyone concerned.

At Nipher Middle School (Kirkwood, Missouri), parents and students have been offered a variety of choices in a school containing grades 6 through 8. A self-contained sixth grade option is available, as well as two- and four-teacher teams; eighth graders all work in interdisciplinary teams. In between, there is an option of a two-year sixth to seventh grade multiage grouped situation. Materials distributed to parents by the principal explain that the sixth- to seventh-grade team is a two-year curriculum incorporating materials from both years and students would be expected to be on the team for two years.

At Noe Middle School (Louisville, Kentucky), the practice of MAG was introduced to the school gradually, one team at a time. Everyone involved, and particularly teachers, had a chance to become familiar with the concept of having sixth, seventh, and eighth graders on the same team. Initially, the students in the school were grouped entirely according to age and grade level. Then, a team of volunteer teachers and a selected group of students became a multiage grouped unit. After a year's successful operation, a second team switched to the multiage format, and the next year a third team changed over. By the 1979–80 year, there were three multiage and three graded teams at Noe. Eventually, all teams were multiage; then, over a period of years, changes again transpired such that, by 1992, multiage grouping operated on only one team.

Fairview Middle School in Tallahassee, Florida is another example of offering a choice between age level teams and MAG. In a school of 735 sixth, seventh, and eighth graders, three teams operated traditionally and three offered the multiage option. At Fairview, a cyclical curriculum operated on the multiage teams in much the same way as it has at Lincoln Middle School.

At Stoughton Middle School (Stoughton, Wisconsin), a "multi-level block program" operates successfully. Here, 880 6th, 7th, and 8th grade students are assigned to teams in which all teachers on each team teach all the basic subjects. The 6th and 7th graders on the team are in classes together for mathematics and language arts, with eighth graders grouped separately. In science and social studies, MAG is extensive.

It is important to point out that in several of the examples just discussed, the distinguishing feature of MAG was absent. The students and teachers did not develop a unit or community which lasted for the entire time the student was in the school. In this sense, some of the combination options appear to have more in common with developmental age grouping than with MAG as it is defined here.

Student-Teacher Progression (STP)

At Lincoln Middle School, after a decade of successful multiage grouping, the school board of the district (for other reasons having little to do with middle school) made a ruling which made it impossible for the staff to continue the process. The reaction of the faculty and administrators, as they realized the power of the long term team process, which they were about to lose, was to search for another version which the school board would permit. "Student-Teacher Progression" (STP) was born.

The faculty and staff of Lincoln, after considerable discussion, arrived at a consensus which brought them to reorganize their interdisciplinary teams so that three-year teams of a different sort emerged. For the next half dozen years or more, the teams were organized by grade level; two teams at each grade level, 6 through 8. Teams of teachers who began a year with sixth grade students stayed with that group of students for three years, through the end of the eighth grade, at which time they would rotate back to pick up a new cohort of sixth graders. This STP process, while less popular with the staff at Lincoln (School D) than multiage grouping, delivered many of the same benefits of multiage grouping. In the fall of 1991, one teacher from Lincoln recalled her last year there as "the pinnacle of my teaching career" because it coincided with the last year of the three-year cycle with the same students.

A number of other middle schools have implemented aspects of the Student-Teacher Progression model: Pittsford Middle School (Pittsford, New York),

Campbell Drive Middle School (Homestead, Florida), Westview Middle School (Longmont, Colorado), and Skowhegan Middle School (Skowhegan, Maine) are four dramatically different locations, with very different student demographics, where educators have decided that a version of long-term team (LTT) works for them and their students.

At Skowhegan Middle, containing only grades 7 and 8, there are five teams of teachers and students, each team stays together for the two years the students are in the school. Each team is heterogeneously grouped, and all special education and gifted students are completely mainstreamed on these teams. In an evaluation of the two-year relationship, the following conclusions were reported:

> Ninety-two percent of the staff agreed or strongly agreed that this approach results in our students receiving a better education.
>
> Ninety-six percent of the staff agreed or strongly agreed that this approach resulted in the team having a better understanding of the individual student.
>
> Ninety-six percent of the staff agreed or strongly agreed that this approach resulted in better parent communication and cooperation.
>
> Ninety-one percent of the staff agreed or strongly agreed that these organizational changes have made our students more enthusiastic about learning. (J. Lynch, 1990)

Westview Middle School may be the first school to implement STP in a brand new building and program, doing so during the 1991–92 school year. Bob Moderhak, principal of Westview, cites David and Roger Johnson (1989b, 4:24–26) for support for the STP program:

> School has to be more than a series of "ship-board romances" that last for only a semester or year.
>
> In this and a number of other ways schools act as if relationships are unimportant. Each semester or year, students get a new set of classmates and a new teacher. The assumption seems to be that classmates and teachers are replaceable parts and any classmate or any teacher will do. The result is that students have a temporary one-semester or one-year relationship with classmates and the teacher.
>
> Relationships do matter. Caring and committed relationships are a major key to school effectiveness, especially for at-risk students who often are alienated from their families and society . . . Classrooms and schools need to be caring communities in which students care about each other and are committed to each other's well being . . . Some of the relationships developed in school need to be permanent . . . When students know that they will spend several years within the same cooperative base group students know that they have to find ways to motivate and encourage their groupmates.
>
> Teacher relationships can also be permanent. If teachers followed students through the grades, continuity in learning and caring could be maintained. Better to be taught 9th grade English by a 7th-grade English teacher who knows and cares for the students than by an excellent 9th-grade English teacher who does not know and/or care about the students.

The meager evidence regarding the actual experience of teachers and students on multi-year teams indicates that it is a very positive experience for students and parents, but that some of the most influential and experienced teachers tend to resist moving from one grade level to another. Our experience is that this is particularly true in the case with eighth grade teachers, and especially 8th grade mathematics teachers who teach the advanced mathematics sections; it may be more challenging and difficult for them to move from a situation where they teach the most able and most mature students in the building, to teaching all ability levels of the youngest 6th grade students. If, however, the student population is such that increased supportive interpersonal structure is clearly a need in the school, we question the wisdom of permitting teachers the complete autonomy to choose a traditional organizational structure which emphasizes teacher-subject specialization.

During the 1990–91 school year, nearly twenty years after its first year as a middle school, Lincoln Middle School considered a third version of SIS/TSS balance based on a continuing interest in long-term relationships. In an effort to accommodate the needs of what the faculty perceived to be increasingly fragile groups of 6th graders, the staff discussed the wisdom of organizing smaller two-teacher teams at the 6th grade level. Each of the two teachers on the sixth grade teams would teach two or three subjects to a small group of fifty-five students during the day. At the end of the year, two separate teams of sixth grade students would be combined to form four-teacher 7th grade teams. Discussion whirled around whether the 7th grade teams would continue in STP fashion into the 8th grade or whether separate teams of 8th grade teachers and students would finish out the process. This variation, if implemented, would produce a different sort of SIS in the 6th grade, similar to the point of School A, and a continuation of STP in the seventh grade, and perhaps the 8th. Whether this is the "best fit" will depend on the progress students make toward achieving the goals of the middle school. To date, the discussion continues.

School-Within-A-School

At the point of School C in the model, the School-Within-A-School (SWS) approach to student grouping, usually retains the basic format of the conventional grade level teams, but adds a significant and increasingly popular organizational modification. In the SWS approach, each school is divided into "houses" or "villages," subschools which are representative of the larger school. A growing number of exemplary middle schools utilize this method of grouping students for instruction, and several objectives are cited by the staff members and students of schools using a SWS approach.

Wakulla Middle School, near Crawfordville, Florida, with a student population of almost 700 in grades 6–8, is comprised of a predominantly rural, majority culture, lower-middle-income group, characterized by a greater degree of respect for adult authority if not for education itself. These students require a different balance between SIS and TSS. Here, and at a growing number of middle schools across the nation, staff and students are organized according to what is being called the "School-Within-A-School" (SWS) process. Also a version of the interdisciplinary team process, SWS combines elements of several options.

Figure 7.3 is an illustration of the floor plan of Wakulla Middle School. The hallmark of the SWS process at Wakulla, and elsewhere, is that each so-called "house" contains an interdisciplinary team from each grade level, rather than organizing the school by subject departments as in the traditional junior high school or by grade level teams as in the conventional middle school. North House, for example, contains a team of teachers and students in each of the sixth, seventh, and eighth grades. Students spend three years in one house, but not with just one set of teachers. At Wakulla Middle, there are only eight academic classrooms on each wing. This would have been perfect for grade level wings, but Roger Stokely, the principal who designed and implemented the program in the early 1980s, was dedicated to the school-within-a-school approach. He adjusted to the number of classrooms by creating smaller teams of two and three teachers. This means that each house has all three grade levels, in smaller teams that would have been the case if the teachers and students had simply been placed in grade levels wings, one for each grade.

This simple alteration of the physical placement of teachers and the number of teachers and students on each team has had a tremendous impact on the culture of the school over the last decade, and leveraged the resulting popularity of the program in the district and the state. Smaller teams mean that teachers, students, and their parents have much more personal relationships. Teams of two and three teachers must work together to deliver the five-pronged curriculum. Teachers have more subjects to teach, but far fewer students to whom they must be taught. Teachers interact with 50 to 90 students daily, which is as much as 100 fewer students each day! The students' movement around the school is dramatically reduced by this arrangement, meaning that students spend almost all of their day in only two or three different classrooms, and almost all of their three years in one wing of the building. The placement of teams in houses, as it is done at Wakulla, means that incoming sixth graders quickly learn not only who their teachers are for the current year, but also who they will be for the next two years. Knowing this, do the sixth graders in North House pay closer attention to what the seventh and eighth grade teachers in that house say to them about their behavior? They certainly do. Do the seventh graders in a house care what sixth and eighth grade teachers think? Yes they do, because they had them last year or will have them next year.

There are many advantages to the SWS approach at Wakulla Middle School. Students know, from the beginning of their time at the school, almost exactly who their teachers will be for the next three years, and the teachers can, likewise, accurately forecast who will be in their classes one or two years hence. For example, members of 8th grade teams in each house (students and teachers alike) regularly inquire about members of 7th and 6th grade teams from their

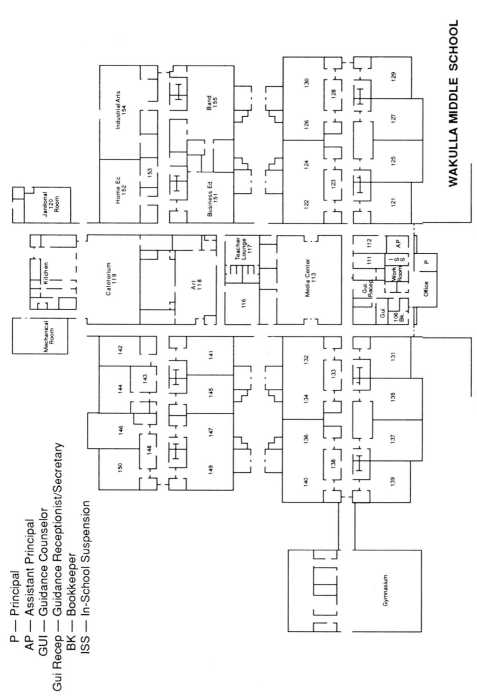

FIGURE 7.3   The Physical Plant of Wakulla Middle School

peers on those teams. Sixth grade students care what 8th grade teachers in their house have to say about behavior in the hallways. 8th grade students care what their former 6th grade teachers think of them. 7th graders have to look both ways on everything. It is a three-year positive structure without either the intensity or the complexity of the processes which have emerged at the point of School D (Lincoln Middle School) on the continuum balancing SIS and TSS. The school-within-a-school model also lacks the power of the three-year intensity, but the staff argues that the developmental level of the students at Wakulla Middle School does not require that sort of intensity.

At Wakulla Middle School, teachers may teach several subjects, but to only one grade level. This permits a comforting level of TSS for the secondary teachers on the staff, while deriving the benefits of more SIS for the students and parents. Wakulla Middle offers an example of a very highly successful version of SWS; a decade of experience there indicates a number of positive outcomes associated with fitting this model to th e corresponding degree of student development.

A school publication at pioneering Brookhaven Middle School (Decatur, Alabama), refers to the concern for the students' sense of identity which resulted, years ago, in the design for a school in a way that allowed the student to relate to a relatively small component of the total school. At Brookhaven, the staff believes that students' sense of security is fostered, and a spirit of loyalty and pride is developed in a situation small enough for middle school students. As one 8th grader at Brookhaven said, "I feel more loyal to Winter House than I am to the school."

Understanding the developmental level of most middle schoolers, this can be understood as a very positive statement. We now know that student loyalty to larger institutions such as total schools can result from a prior sense of belonging located in the smaller "house." School loyalty, the concern of many teachers and administrators, is not compromised by loyalty to the smaller group; it is enhanced.

Farnsworth Middle School of Guilderland, New York is now entering its third decade of excellence. There, the SWS approach is "an attempt at harmonizing the best of both worlds—one of which is small enough to foster a leveling of concern for the individual student, and one which is large enough to offer the varied resources necessary to meet the needs and interests of preadolescent and early adolescent youngsters."

The staff at Nock Middle School (Newburyport, Massachusetts) expressed well this important concept of balancing SIS and TSS, and the students must have come to understand its benefits early. Nearly a decade ago, in "Middle Unmuddle," as the student handbook was titled, students explained their conception of the SWS concept, concluding that it was designed "so that we students don't get lost in such a large school."

HOUSE, SWEET HOUSE

Our Middle School is divided into thirds. These divisions are referred to as the Red, White, and Blue Houses. Each house is, to some degree, a "school-within-a-school" and every effort has been made to give each house an identity so that we students don't get 'lost' in such a large school. The head of each house is the House Coordinator who is, in effect, the 'principal' of a school-within-a-school. In each house there are four teams of teachers. Each team of teachers works together to teach us all of our subjects. Sometimes we may have only one teacher in a class; at other times there may be several. Each of us is assigned to a certain house and within that house we are assigned to a certain team of teachers. Our basic subjects (language arts, social studies, science, and math) will be taught in a block of mods and then there will be other mods set aside for special subjects. This includes art, music, guidance, skill centers, and the SPARK block. The team to which we are assigned will decide what our schedule will be for each day during the basic block.

The SWS approach also attempts to assist in the process of articulation on a K–12 basis, as do all such efforts to balance SIS and TSS. The SWS permits students to enter the middle school from an elementary school and, depending upon developmental maturity, experience a range of options from self-contained classrooms to grade level teams. In the ensuing years, within the same house, students move smoothly and steadily to a more advanced interdisciplinary milieu which will help to prepare them for the first years of high school. Having students spend their entire middle school experience in the same house permits the house faculty to design each student's learning experience much more personally.

At Stroudsburg Middle School (Stroudsburg, Pennsylvania), 1,200 students are divided into two smaller houses, with 600 students in each. Both Mountain and Lake Houses contain students in grades 5 through 8, and while attempts are made to develop the separate identities of each house, grade level associations are also clearly maintained. This is done not only by locating each grade separately within each house, but by arranging the schedule so that, for example, eighth graders from both houses have the same basic schedule. Eighth graders appear on adjoining pages in the school memory book, arranged separately by house. Stroudsburg Middle School demonstrates an excellent balance of SIS and TSS, and between grade level identity and house identity.

At Nock Middle School, the house identity receives slightly more emphasis. Again, 1,200 students in grades 5 through 8 are divided into smaller units; this time there are three houses (Red, White, and Blue) of approximately 400 students each. Each house has its own educational leader, team coordinator or house director who, while a master teacher, also assists in the guidance function. Each house is encouraged to develop a feeling of uniqueness, and the design of the school (with specially colored carpeting for each house, for example) invites this feeling. Oaklea Middle School (Junction City, Oregon) operates in much the same way, identifying its houses by naming them each after a prominent river in Oregon.

Oak Park and Brookhaven Middle Schools, both in Decatur, Alabama, have had a long commitment to the SWS approach in grouping. Here, too, each of the three houses of both schools is appropriately named and color-coded to assist in the sense of a house of subschool identity. Brookhaven chose the names Fall, Winter, and Spring for its houses. Each house has its own student council, and since each house has its own counselor, students may also develop a three-year relationship with that professional. Brookhaven staff members have been particularly pleased with the cross-age groupings which are facilitated by the SWS design.

At Jamesville-Dewitt Middle School (Jamesville, New York), approximately 625 students are arranged into three houses (each including grades 5, 6, 7 and 8) of 210 students, about 55 students in each grade level. There are four grade level teams per house. Each house has twelve classrooms, a guidance suite and a team conference room. The students are randomly assigned to each house and heterogeneously grouped on each grade level team. Each house has a complement of academic teachers, with foreign language teachers, a counselor, and a secretary also serving the students of the house. At Jamesville-Dewitt Middle School the counselor also serves as the house educational leader; not so much as an administrator but, reflecting the school's child-centered philosophy, as counselor to the students, consultant to the house teachers, and coordinator and liaison between the house and other adults in and out of the school.

Farnsworth Middle School named its three houses Hiawatha, Mohawk, and Tawasentha (Indian tribes that once inhabited the area), achieving a measure of identity, vicarious distinction, and pride for its students. In this large school (1650 students in grades 5 through 8) each of the three houses contains approximately 550 students in four or five interdisciplinary team organizations of 110 to 115 students per team. While separate house identities are encouraged, every team and house is connected both physically and programmatically to the rest of the school. Houses are formed by random assignment of students, but within each house both homogeneous and heterogeneous ability grouping are found. At Farnsworth, each house is directed by its own principal/teacher, and in addition to the regular team teachers, each house has its own secretary, counselor, reading teacher, foreign language teachers, and "learning workshop teacher."

As an illustration of the way in which the SWS assists in articulation, the 5th grades in each house at Farnsworth Middle School are relatively self-contained. The house principal and the 5th grade teachers provide the close attention and counseling that they believe the 5th graders require. The house counselors, then, focus their efforts on the students in the 6th, 7th, and 8th grades, and assist the teachers who are working in the 5th grade. Because the students remain in the same minischool setting for the four years, the interpersonal knowledge required for truly supportive interpersonal structure is assured.

More and more versions of the SWS approach appear on the middle level scene as each new school year begins. In the fall of 1991, for example, Mandarin Middle School in Duval County, Florida opened with a capacity of 2,100 students. Recognizing the value of the SWS model, principal Walter Carr organized three houses of 700 students each, with two teams of each grade level in each house. More and more new buildings are being designed and constructed with the SWS concept in mind. It is, in our opinion, the most popular school-wide grouping concept in middle level education and promises to become even more so.

Developmental-Age Grouping

Donald H. Eichhorn (1966) has long advocated a strategy of grouping students based on selected developmental characteristics of the learner. First implemented at the middle level in 1969 in Boyce and Ft. Couch schools in Upper St. Clair, Pennsylvania, following an extensive medical and psychological analysis of the students in those schools, the process has come to be known as developmental or developmental-age grouping. Based on an index of social, physical, mental, and academic maturity, students were placed in three cross-age groups. The first group was composed largely of prepubescents, the second of pubescent youngsters, and the third of adolescents. The results have been substantial, yielding continued increases in academic achievement and self-esteem when compared with Upper St. Clair students from earlier years and with students from comparable districts in Pennsylvania. The procedure has continued there, with refinements, since that time. Perhaps because such a program appears to require a great deal of time and effort, few school districts have followed Upper St. Clair's lead.

This point on the continuum, illustrated by School B, offers yet another version of the interdisciplinary team organization, one which again shifts the balance away from TSS toward more SIS. The School B option, rare though it is, has also been practiced for over two decades at Spring Hill Middle School in High Springs, Florida. Here, students are developmentally far more mature than the traditional junior high school process demands. They are much younger; they are Southern rural and small town children from primarily middle- and lower-middle-income families; they are bimodally distributed in terms of their success in elementary school. About 20 percent of the students are from a minority culture. Consequently, for the entire history of the school, the staff has been committed to a much greater degree of SIS.

At the School B point on the grouping continuum, Spring Hill students from four grade levels are distributed onto three teams according to an index of developmental factors which adds chronological age to those originally identified by Eichhorn. Three interdisciplinary cross-grade teams each contain students from two grade levels. Unit One, for example, contains four teachers and 120 students ages 9–11 (90 from the fifth grade and 30 developmentally less mature students from the sixth). Unit Two contains and equal number of teachers and students from the sixth and seventh grades, ages 10–12 (60 of the more-mature 6th graders and 60 of the less-mature 7th graders). Unit Three contains 30 advanced 7th graders and 90 8th graders, ages 12–14 (see Table 7.2, below).

Teaching assignments at Spring Hill vary from unit to unit. Teachers in Unit One each teach all five basic academic subjects to some portion of the students on the team, grouped according to how the teachers feel most able to deliver instruction. Typically, there would be three sections of each subject from the 5th grade and one from the 6th. In Unit Two, each teacher teaches three academic subjects, and in Unit Three, each instructor is responsible for only one or two academic subjects. Students in each unit are grouped and regrouped by the teachers within the unit.

Since there are four grades in the school, but only three teams, each student must spend two years on one of the teams. Hence, students are also grouped each year according to the judgment of teachers, counselor, administrator, and parents, on the team which fits them best developmentally. Students receive the appropriate balance of SIS and TSS within the team.

Spring Hill Middle School found a way to make developmental-age grouping work well. Use of the Kettering Foundation's Individually Guided Education (IGE) curriculum planning model, at the beginning of the school in 1970, allowed the faculty, during most of the school's history, to design a curriculum that makes effective use of the flexibility offered by developmental-age grouping. In a self-study conducted a decade after the school's founding, the faculty identified as one of the school's major strengths, the "continuous learning cycle established for each student, unrestricted by chronological age or the number of years in school regardless of the Unit to which the student is assigned."

The unit planning process developed by IGE permits the faculty teams to fashion plans for curriculum and instruction that eliminate problems associated with having approximately thirty students on the team who were there the previous year. In reading, language arts, and mathematics, a great deal of pretesting and post-testing, and grouping and regrouping, accounts for the personalized curriculum. In social studies and science, a four-year curriculum plan is combined with a great deal of interteam coordination of what is taught each year, to whom, and to what extent or depth.

TABLE 7.2   **Grouping at Spring Hill Middle School—High Springs, Florida**

UNIT	ONE	TWO	THREE
GRADE LEVEL	5–6	6–7	7–8
STUDENT AGE	9,10,11	11,12,13	12–14
LEVEL OF DEVELOPMENT	Prepubescent	Pubescent	Adolescent

Spring Hill Middle School and the schools of Upper St. Clair are not alone in grouping students in this way, although there are only a comparatively few schools which have opted for this design. Another school which chose this process is Glen Ridge Middle School (Glen Ridge, New Jersey), which demonstrated that such a design can be implemented in a way that fits diverse school sizes. With a population of about 575 students, Glen Ridge is well over 50 percent larger than Spring Hill, but uses the same grouping strategy. The school has been arranged into five teams (compared with three in Spring Hill) of approximately 115 students, five teachers, and an aide. Each team at Glen Ridge includes two grade levels: two teams cover grades 5 and 6; one team contains grades 6 and 7; and two teams are composed of grades 7 and 8.

Glen Ridge also utilizes an IGE approach to a curriculum focusing on objectives and skills. Students move through the instructional program, within the team, as they master complete components of the curriculum in the various subjects. The flexibility of this program allows the school staff to offer equally flexible promotion and retention opportunities.

There are, of course, many other options and combinations of options which can be used to create special "addresses" on the continuum representing the middle school zip code. The precise placement of each one at some specific point would, of course, be somewhat arbitrary and arguable. Shelburne Middle School in Shelburne, Vermont, for example, has for twenty years offered students, parents, and teachers a multiage group team option. There, students from grades 5–8 may choose this multi-year, integrated curriculum option. The "Alpha Program" at Shelburne involves advisory groups, regular and frequent "community time" sessions in which all members of the team "share projects and writings, listen to a guest speaker, solve group problems, and participate in other group activities." Each week, a community time session becomes a "class meeting" where the group discusses and solves problems which face the Alpha community, a process modeled after the Vermont town meeting. Each June, the group takes a week-long camping trip; each year, the Alpha program participants produce their own musical "extravaganza," engaging in major interdisciplinary units and projects of a great variety. All of this is possible, Shelburne educators believe, at least in part because of the unusually lengthy (four year) teacher-student relationship.

Parker Intensive Core Program (ICP)

Another school, Parker Junior High School (Parker, Colorado) offers three different grouping possibilities to parents, teachers, and students. Within a large middle level school, Parker Junior High School (School P) offers a traditional junior high school option, a conventional interdisciplinary team option, and also what they call their Intensive Core Program (ICP). Every attempt is made to place students in the program that makes the most educational sense for them.

The Intensive Core Program at Parker is, we believe, unique. Within this version of the interdisciplinary team program, students concentrate on one academic subject each six weeks—only one—while teachers concentrate on teaching that subject to only one small group of students. Students take only one academic subject per day, for four periods of the day, for the entire six weeks of the grading period. A student might, for example, have social studies four periods a day for six weeks. The teacher would have only one group, perhaps twenty-five students, for six weeks, but still only one subject to prepare. At the end of the six weeks, students move to another subject, and the teacher repeats the six week plan to a new group of twenty-five students.

The staff at Parker has realized a number of advantages from this constellation of options. Parents are pleased to be able to choose the option they think best fits their individual child. Teachers also have some choice about the way in which they balance SIS and TSS in their own professional lives. Students are, theoretically, matched with the balance they need.

Within the Intensified Core Program, further advantages are found, say the staff members of "School P." Teachers can give far more attention to individual students where it is particularly needed; in mathematics, for example. Time restraints resulting from the ringing of the bell are forgotten, permitting a much more flexible use of instructional time. Passing time can be virtually eliminated. This, they say, results in much more of a thematic unit type of lesson planning. Parents and students have only one academic teacher to work with. Students never have homework or assignments in more than one academic subject. The last six weeks of the year is devoted to a regular schedule, with the traditional one period per day for each subject, permitting review and consolidation of the learning for the year. There are additional advantages, causing the staff to be quite enthusiastic about the long-term future of this option.

The way in which teachers and students at Parker are organized, can be modified and adapted in any number of ways. This is, of course, also true of virtually all varieties of the interdisciplinary organization, no matter what balance of SIS and TSS students may need or teachers may prefer. The Parker model, furthermore, certainly does not need to be the way in which students in all middle level schools are organized, nor should any other version be acceptable in all situations. That is the point of the model we have elaborated here.

The model of student development and school organization presented in this chapter asserts that there is no one right way to group all students in all middle level schools. The correct way to achieve a balance between SIS and TSS for a particular population of students depends on the developmental level of those students and no others. What is required for younger, less highly developed, diverse populations, in large urban schools, for example, may be very different from what makes pedagogical sense in a junior high school in a small Midwestern town.

In some schools, even today, an exceptionally high level of student development may indicate the effectiveness of a high degree of TSS, with little attention to SIS (However, we have not visited such a school.) In other schools, the opposite is likely to be the case. The "best fit" in any particular school should be determined by examining the developmental level of the students in the school, not solely by the strongly felt and firmly voiced preferences of some vocal portion of the faculty.

We believe that the experience of the last several decades of middle school education suggest that it is wholly undesirable to defer, in the organization of middle level schools, to the strongly-expressed preferences of a faculty or a segment of the community, for subject specialization, and to exclude a careful consideration of the needs of the students. Our belief is that a careful study and testing of the model presented here will indicate that errors in middle level school organization occur—far more often—in the omission of degrees of SIS that students need than in the inclusion of too little TSS.

All too often, this results in the failure of a substantial number of schools around the nation to achieve the goals to which middle level schools are dedicated. We believe that an exploration of the model will indicate that, generally, excessive reliance on TSS, to the exclusion of SIS, results in lower levels of academic achievement, less positive personal development, and less of a sense of group citizenship than the next generation needs.

Middle school educators have reached a point of widespread professional consensus, where there is considerable confidence about the existence of a middle level "zip code" (NMSA, 1992). The general concepts and practices of middle level education are often accepted as the most effective way for thousands of middle-level schools to achieve important goals in the education of millions of older children and early adolescents. This increased clarity in middle level education now enables educators to make important organizational decisions for individual middle-level schools more accurately, based on a knowledge of the development of the students within them. In Ann Arbor, Michigan, for example, the districtwide standards for the implementation of the middle school concept established the importance of "smallness within bigness" for all the middle level schools in that district; small teaching units or houses were a requirement. These standards were, however, designed so that "each middle school could develop a plan for program implementation. This permits site-based decisions about what serves each school community. Each school may determine the house structure appropriate for that school. This has resulted in schools with grade level houses and schools with multi-grade houses (6–8 in each of three houses)" (R. Williamson, personal communication, January, 1991). Here we have a district developing standards for all its middle schools based on the known generic needs of early adolescents, but making it possible for the educators in each school site to establish the organizational framework, to fine tune the structure of each school on the basis of the particular characteristics of the student populations of those schools.

We hope that the model of student development and school organization presented here, when adequately tested by research and the experiences of districts like Ann Arbor, will move middle level education further in the direction of conceptual clarity regarding how students should be grouped on interdisciplinary teams.

Advantages and Disadvantages of Alternatives to Age-Grade Grouping

Advantages

The thrust of this chapter might be described as the case for more flexible, learner-oriented methods of schoolwide grouping, balancing supportive interpersonal structure with the traditional teacher-subject specialization. It is not so much that the traditional process is bad, but that the alternatives seem so much better, in light of the changing demographic patterns with which we are all now so familiar.

Most important, of course, is that these alternatives more nearly satisfy the other twin criteria of offering a unique program to middle school learners and, at the same time, moving toward continuous progress from the elementary school through the middle grades on to the high school. But there are many more advantages than these.

Continuous Progress

These alternatives, from SWS through MAG, STP, and others, all offer increasing opportunities for continuous progress. Yet, each preserves the structure and accompanying economy, efficiency, and popularity of group (even grade level group) learning.

In the SWS situation, for example, teachers are familiar with their colleagues in the contiguous grade levels, and may consult with them frequently about the progress or problems of past, present, or future students. Records may often be kept in a common planning area. Counselors can serve the same students year after year. The scope and sequence of the curriculum and its development in each subject area can be carefully designed and scrutinized by "vertical committees" composed of in-house teachers who teach the same subject. The SWS retains all of the advantages of grade level grouping while providing significant opportunities for continuous progress for the students involved.

Conversely, MAG and STP provide maximum opportunities for continuous progress learning while permitting grade leveling to occur whenever necessary. Students may begin their studies at whatever point they are when they enter a MAG or STP situation and continue uninterrupted for two, three, or four years or until they move on to a high school situation. For as long as they are in the school, there are few, if any, important grade level barriers to learning. Both MAG and STP would seem to offer the advantages of both so well that it is rather astonishing that these practices are not widespread.

Community

All of these alternatives offer the promise of continuous progress and also deliver what continuous progress, as a single goal, would prevent—a strong sense of community. This sense of community, the feeling of membership, of ownership, may be the most important advantage of all. Middle school students, because of their nature and because of the character of contemporary society, need a place to belong, a place away from home that feels safe, accepting, and supportive.

The presence of a sense of community can be observed most dramatically in middle schools practicing extensive MAG and STP. Where teachers and students work together for up to four years, one teacher writes, important parts of the lives of each are invested in the others: "Powerful human bonds are formed and sealed."

In a society that has become, in Vance Packard's words, "a nation of strangers," stability and continuity in human relationships become more and more important in every endeavor. Schools are not exceptions. Loneliness and a feeling of disconnectedness drain the psychic energy from many of the society's efforts and the middle school suffers in direct proportion. As a poster on the wall of one middle school proclaimed, "True friendship is a plant of slow growth." Relationships that are growth producing do not develop overnight, and the results of such relationships can not be produced in their absence. There is no substitute for the human factor.

It has long been common knowledge that schools learn a great deal from the military, and that much that occurs in schools has been borrowed from the armed services. It is also the case in learning about the power of interpersonal relationships in human motivation. Long ago, the military learned that interpersonal bonds were a more important source of motivation than coercion. Men could be motivated to kill and die for their friends because of the incredibly powerful bonds that their common experiences had forged. The sense of community that this produced was more effective than the fear of death. If the armed forces have changed from force to relationships to accomplish their most difficult tasks, surely the schools can do no less. If interpersonal bonds can motivate grown men and women to risk their lives, the same kind of interpersonal power can motivate students to learn.

Discipline

The strength that derives from the sense of community produced by a group of teachers and students spending several years together is evidenced in a number of different spheres, but school discipline and classroom management appear to have significant benefits. In comparison to "single grade centers," which are the opposite end of the continuum from long-term relationships, statistics on factors such as vandalism, expulsions, suspensions, and office discipline referrals appear to be significantly lower. In the single grade center, there are often as many as 1,500 new students arriving in the fall, knowing almost no one, possessing no feelings of loyalty or school spirit. In the spring, these same students are all transferred to a new school, leaving the wreckage they have created behind, and 1,500 new students are delivered to finish the job the first group began.

It is a truism that effective discipline and classroom management depend in large measure upon a positive relationship between the teacher and the students. These relationships take time. In a middle school with MAG and STP, the time is readily available. At many middle schools utilizing STP, for example, at the beginning of each new school year, 95 percent of the students return from the previous year, and only a handful of the students are new. The entire first grading period of the year—so often wasted in other schools with rule setting, rule testing, and a host of other time-wasting activities—can be devoted to real academic effort. The teachers and students in STP schools have, by contrast, been together for as long as three years prior to the beginning of the year.

At the end of the year, the teachers and students in schools with MAG and STP find themselves, again, in a totally different situation. Rather than being desperately in need of release from one another, the eighth graders and their teachers discover that they have come to know and care about each other deeply over the preceding three or four years. Instead of yells of joy, an observer is often confounded by observing tears produced by the sorrow of separation in the eyes of both students and teachers. Other students in earlier grades, realizing that they will be returning to the same situation next year are much less likely to give up on the academics, and more frequently are found challenging themselves with their efforts to stay on task in spite of the heat. Teachers, also realizing that the large majority of their students from this year will be their students again next year, often find themselves possessed of considerably more creativity than might be typical at the end of the year in other school situations.

Based on our observations of MAG, STP, SWS and other models in action over a period of years, we believe that school discipline and classroom management problems are considerably reduced. Teachers and administrators from such schools confirm this belief.

Diagnosis and Prescription

Alternatives to traditional schoolwide grouping strategies considerably simplify the processes of diagnosis and prescription in the program of personalizing instruction, the ultimate goal of the middle school. Students who return to the same academic circumstances of the previous year(s) can begin where they left off. New students, because they may be a small fraction of the total team, can have their learning needs analyzed much more immediately, extensively, and carefully than would otherwise be possible. The efficiency benefits the students in more than one way. Because teachers can devote their attention and their energies to directing instruction, rather than to the seemingly endless routines of beginning and ending the year with new groups of students, much more time is likely to be spent in academically directed efforts.

Individualized Perception

In traditional circumstances, in a "worst case scenario," an individual teacher may face as many as 150 students a day, 300 a year, and up to as many as 900 in a three-year period. In such circumstances, the chances of being able to see students as individuals may be slight. New grouping alternatives, however, have the capacity to reduce the number of different students a teacher has to get to know and with whom they must develop positive and productive relationships substantially. Teachers may see 66 percent fewer students. With such a major reduction in numbers, it is reasonable to expect teachers to be able to get to know students and their needs in individual ways. Here are results from one study of students on a three-year team organized as STP. Note that as each year passed, the strength of students' responses increased. Nine hundred students responded to the following statements (George, 1987):

My teachers	6th	7th	8th
Believe in me	73	80	83
Care about me as a student	75	80	88
Care about me as a person	73	84	86
Trust me	69	89	90
Have patience with me	67	66	77
Expect more from me	—	80	81
I feel			
Pride in my team	72	78	82
Self-confident	65	67	75
I have more friends	74	78	77
I belong	70	81	80
I can be friends with all kinds of people	58	64	71

Parental Relationships

Not only do the years together strengthen the bonds between teachers and students, but between teachers and parents, and among the students as well. Teachers and parents have time to discover that both have the best interests of the students in mind. They have time to discover trust, empathy, and friendship. Barriers fall, and bonds grow.

Peer Relationships

As reflected in the data above, students also learn that their peers are okay—that older students need not be feared so terribly, that students from other ethnic groups can be valued friends, and that younger students are also tolerable.

Peer modeling and peer teaching are much more likely to occur in grouping situations where several ages and grade levels are combined in some way. Cross-age friendships, made possible by a grade-free grouping strategy, allow students to seek support from other students who are similar to them in development, regardless of age or grade level. In fact, teachers who have had experience with MAG, STP, and SWS report that often the older students seem less hurried in their attempts to act like high school students, and younger students are more likely to imitate the admirable traits of their older classmates than they are the less desirable ones. For some unknown reason, parents and other adults unfamiliar with alternatives to standard chronological age grouping often assume that putting older and younger students together will result in something socially undesirable. Experiences with these alternatives do not confirm these fears; the opposite is actually much more likely.

Synergism

One of the most important advantages of the alternative grouping strategies is that they act in a synergistic fashion, strengthening the other programs with which they interact. The advisor-advisee programs and the interdisciplinary team are both much more effective, for example, in combination with a grouping plan that extends the life of the team or the advisory group. When teacher and students remain in the same advisory group for two, three, or four years, all of the goals of the process become much more realizable. The interdisciplinary team, and all of the advantages connected with it, are significantly enhanced. Without this built-in increase in supportive interpersonal structure, these programs achieve significantly less than they might with the multiplier effect of the grouping strategy utilized.

Innovation

The grouping alternatives discussed here have a similar effect on innovation in curriculum and instruction. When teachers and students stay together for several years, repetition of the same units and instructional strategies becomes counterproductive, if not embarrassing. Teachers are, therefore, more frequently found in an innovative mode, searching for the most effective and most motivating instructional strategies and curriculum units. This innovative trend is most strikingly noticed during the spring. Weeks before the end of school, teachers, recognizing that many of the same students will be returning in the fall, implement plans that they hope will not only motivate the students for the remaining weeks, but bring them back with pleasant memories and eager anticipation in the new school year.

Teacher Investment in Students

Conventional wisdom holds that close interpersonal relationships are more likely to encourage one person to spend time and energy contributing to the welfare of another. Research in education in the area of school effectiveness, for example, indicates that academic achievement is related to the capacity of the teachers to make this kind of more intense investment in their students.[2] Within the context of long-term relationships, teachers more clearly recognize the special needs of particular students and, more importantly, are able to summon the psychic energy necessary to persist in attempting to meet those needs:

> Teachers believed that, because they knew students more thoroughly, they were likely to take their students' successes and failures more personally. The teachers were more likely to persist in working through problems with students rather than avoiding the problems or giving up as quickly as they might have had they not had three years to spend with the same students. (George, 1987, p. 12)

Academic Achievement

It is our belief that when all the above advantages pertain, increased academic achievement results. Furthermore, for individual students, failure and retention do not carry the social stigma that they might because, with these alternatives, students are frequently less aware of the grade other students are in, and since they were together last year, students often presume that it is normal that they should be together again. To date, however, the paucity of research in this area makes it impossible to substantiate such professional judgments.

Moral Reasoning

We believe that there is some logical support for the likelihood that the development of moral reasoning, as described by Lawrence Kohlberg (see Chapter 1), may be enhanced in situations where MAG or related practices are implemented. When students of varying maturity rates are together frequently enough to learn to value each other, exposure to more mature moral reasoning should enhance growth in these areas among less mature students. It also seems likely that the attachment to small groups like the advisory group and the team, strengthened over time by MAG, should encourage students in the first two stages of moral development to move continuously closer to stage three where they differentiate between right and wrong on the basis of the norms of the face-to-face groups to which they belong.

Disadvantages

In our opinion, the advantages of alternatives to chronological age grouping far outweigh the disadvantages, but no program is without trade-offs. Implementing some of these alternative grouping strategies requires a significant departure

---

[2]At the exact moment this section was being prepared, one of the authors received a "positive phone call home" from the high school advisor of one of his children. The advisor reported on how pleasant and productive he was, what a wonderful boy he is. Even for someone involved in this profession and with a history of encouraging this sort of thing from teachers, it was most heartwarming to hear it personally. The advisor and the student will be together for four years, a very long-term relationship in public education. We are convinced that the nature of this long-term commitment had something important to do with motivating that teacher to make that call.

from previous structure and some program disruption will occur, usually fading after the first year. Most frequently, some stress is experienced as a result of the curricular adjustments required when continuous progress or cyclical curriculum designs replace the graded program. Student turnover and teacher attrition can cause an erosion of the benefits of the program, to the extent that such turnover and attrition occur. In schools where teachers are already burdened by excessive demands coupled with insufficient funds, the flexibility and innovation required by multiage grouping and developmental-age grouping may demand more energy than teachers have to give. Finally, we believe that these alternatives to traditional schoolwide grouping strategies precipitate teachers into situations where they get to know and care more about their students; the teachers work harder because they know and care. Such work, unusually rewarding though it may be, is singularly exhausting.

Requirements for Success

With any new, alternative program, it is important for educators (in schools using an alternative program) to be able to explain it clearly to parents and other community members. In the area of middle school student grouping, this need appears to be doubly so, for while parents seem able to accept such practices in the elementary school or high school, they do not, strangely, appear to accept them with equal ease in the middle grades. Perhaps parents are anxious because they are witnessing their children changing into adolescents, and these changes indicate changes in their own lives they find difficult to accept. Perhaps it is only because they have enjoyed their children as children that they are reluctant to have them grouped with students who seem older and more mature. For whatever reason, patience and a willingness to take the necessary time to explain—and explain again—in simple and concrete language are absolute requirements. School leaders should be especially well-prepared to articulate clearly and with conviction the rationale behind the benefits to be received by such a plan. Parents will listen and be supportive if they believe that educators are competent and concerned. After planning carefully and providing ready explanations to new parents, most educators using grouping alternatives find the large majority of parents at ease and in full support of such practices.

Educators involved in grouping students differently must be thoroughly convinced of the validity of their own efforts when dealing with students in the same way as with parents. Initially, during the first year or two at the most, older students involved in a transition from chronological grades to an alternative may feel demoted. Students who were 7th graders in a junior high school, and become 8th graders in a new middle school where they are grouped with younger students may initially resent what has happened. After one year, however, when these students have moved on to the high school, there will be left only students who have known no other way and most of the complaints will have disappeared. Almost every school using an alternative form of grouping has experienced this pressure from older students but, having resisted it for at least a year, find the problem disappearing with their first group of graduates.

Staff development is, of course, as important here as in other aspects of the middle school program. But with grouping (in contrast to advisory, exploratory, or teaming components), the emphasis in staff development should be aimed primarily at curriculum development. As the school moves into its second, third, or fourth year, the benefits of the grouping plan will become increasingly obvious, as the need for curriculum adjustments becomes proportionately less.

Mainstreaming: Grouping Exceptional Students in the Middle School
Schoolwide Arrangements

The identification of exceptional students and the provision of special programs for those students has been an important theme in American education for decades. During the first half of the twentieth century, educators became increasingly aware of the inappropriateness of the continued exclusion of exceptional children from the schools. By the early 1960s, these children had been welcomed into the schools, and special classes had become the nearly universal method for educating exceptional students. Concurrently with the development of special classes, research was begun to assess its effectiveness and, by the middle of the '70s, the profession had concluded that this research did not conclusively support the special class process as being superior to other methods. Until November 1976, however, most middle school educators had only an academic interest in the question of the most appropriate method for educating exceptional children. When President Ford signed Public Law 94–142, at that time, professional interest became widespread and practical strategies became considerably more important.

Mainstreaming is the term most often used to describe the attempt to meet the mandates of Public Law 94–142. The term has been subject to widely varying interpretations and definitions. For purposes of considering its utility in the middle school, in this discussion it is intended to mean the educational placement closest to the normal classroom in which the child can succeed—the least restrictive educational environment. In the past, the placement options for the education of exceptional students were limited to the special classroom. Children were often diagnosed and placed in a special classroom out of the sight of, and out of the mind of, all but special education personnel. Today, Public Law 94–142 urges schools to use the regular school facilities and program, adapting them to the needs of exceptional students whenever this is possible.

Mainstreaming has several objectives. Special educators hope that moving the exceptional child into the regular program, when possible, will remove the stigma associated with special class placement, and that it will enhance the social status of the exceptional students among their more normal peers. Educators expect that mainstreaming will provide a more stimulating environment for cognitive growth, and that contact with the regular classroom will facilitate the modeling of appropriate behavior by their peers within it. Such an environment is intended to provide just manageable difficulty in areas and activities that must eventually be faced in out-of-school environments, such as competition and self-evaluation. Mainstreaming is touted as being more cost-effective, more flexible in terms of the delivery of services to students in need, and more acceptable to the parents of exceptional children. It is obvious from an examination of these objectives that mainstreaming is an ambitious and potentially far-reaching innovation in American education, and the exemplary middle school can not afford to dismiss it.

The Council for Exceptional Children (CEC), a professional organization for special educators, has identified four major components of mainstreaming:

1. Providing the most appropriate education for each child in the least restrictive setting.
2. Looking at the educational needs of children instead of clinical or diagnostic labels such as mentally handicapped, hearing impaired, or gifted.
3. Looking for and creating alternatives that will help general educators serve children with learning or adjustment problems in the regular setting. Some approaches being used to help achieve this are consulting teachers, methods and materials specialists, itinerant teachers, and resource room teachers.
4. Uniting the skills of general education and special education so that all children may have equal educational opportunity.

The CEC has also identified more common misinterpretations of mainstreaming. Mainstreaming is not:

1. Wholesale return of all exceptional children in special classes to regular classes.
2. Permitting children with special needs to remain in regular classrooms without the support services that they need.
3 Ignoring the needs of some children for a more specialized program than can be provided in the general education program.
4. Less costly than serving children in special self-contained classrooms. (West, Bates & Schmeil, 1979, pp. 8–10).

Middle school educators must deal effectively with the critical question of the students to be placed in these least restrictive environments. Public Law 94–142 defines the handicapped considered in the law (deaf, deaf-blind, hard of hearing, mentally retarded, multihandicapped, orthopedically impaired, other health impaired, seriously emotionally disturbed, specific learning disability, speech impaired, and visually handicapped), but special educators maintain that, all things equal, these students have far more in common with so-called normal students than they have differences. It is a matter of degree, since none of us is perfect. While there are some handicapped who need attention from, predominantly, specially trained teachers within exceptional environments, these are few in comparison to the numbers that can be served effectively in the general education system (Department of Special Education, 1975, p. 4).

A second question for middle school educators follows from the first. If much of mainstreaming is a matter of the degree of the handicap, what are the various degrees of least restrictive environments which are appropriate? Figure 7.4

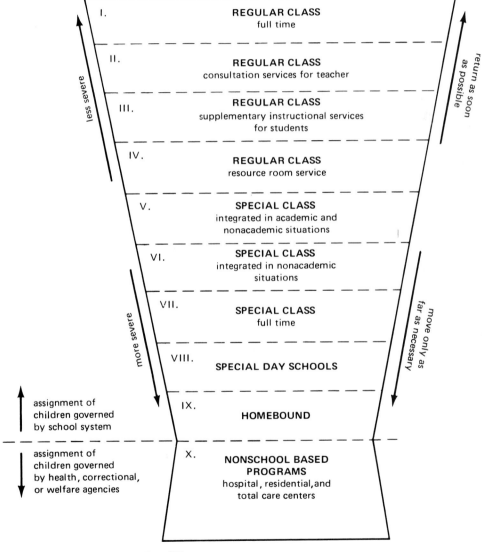

*Adapted from Reynolds p. 368.

FIGURE 7.4   **A Continuum of Instructional Settings**

represents a time-honored continuum of placement options that are now available in many school systems, and it has direct application in the middle school program. This chart, originally published in 1962, has been adapted and discussed in countless inquiries on the nature of effective placement of exceptional children since that time (Reynold, 1962). On the chart, the broken lines represent the importance of fluidity (versus rigidity) in classification and treatment of children in and between various levels of the continuum. In essence, children should only be moved as far down the continuum as necessary, and should be returned to a more normal environment whenever the child is prepared to function there.

Figure 7.4 illustrates that at one end of the continuum the regular classroom teacher is almost totally responsible for the education of all the children in the classroom, no matter what may be the degree of variation in exceptionality. From that point on, the amount of assistance to the classroom teacher increases until, at level seven, the students identified have little or no contact with regular classes. For most middle schools, when help is available to classroom teachers, functioning at levels one through six on the chart, it comes in increasing increments from special teachers, consultants, school counselors and school psychologists, nurses, social workers, and the principal.

For many middle schools, however, when mainstreaming is discussed, the major vehicle for implementation is the combination of resource room and regular classroom, students scheduled to attend the special education resource room on the basis of those skills, subjects, or situations which can be best handled there. Time spent in the resource room varies with the degree of exceptionality of the student and with the progress being made by the child; with some students spending as little as one hour per week in the resource room, while others spend as much as three quarters of each day there. The use of the resource room exemplifies the commitment of many middle schools that the needs of the individual student will take precedence over the convenience of the delivery system, as in the now outmoded special education classroom to which exceptional students were formerly exiled.

At Farnsworth Middle School (Guilderland, New York), the resource room becomes the Learning Workshop. Clearly committed to the integration of all children into the total school program, the school insures that each student, regardless of the handicap, is a member of a regular team with an assigned homeroom and is entitled to all services offered within the building. The Learning Workshop was developed to aid teachers in responding to as many individual differences among students as possible, drawing upon the services of four professional educators and seven teacher aides.

The majority of the students who are served by the Learning Workshop are divided into two general categories: those who are two to three years below their grade level, and those who are more than three years below their grade level. The Learning Workshop staff at Farnsworth has created two special programs for dealing with these youth. The Curriculum Adaptation Program provides students in the first category with the supplementary instruction, support, and materials that permit them to participate in almost all regular classroom tasks; adaptation, modification, and enrichment through alternative teaching methods designed for learning-handicapped children. Children who fall into the second category are generally guided to the Basic Skills Instruction program created by the staff of the resource room to provide intensive small group prescriptive instruction in language arts, mathematics, basic sight vocabulary, and occupational education.

The Learning Workshop staff at Farnsworth places special emphasis on occupational education in realistic settings. The program is aimed at developing positive work habits, personal responsibility, positive peer interactions, and exposure to as many areas of the world of work as possible. Many such opportunities exist within the school setting, involve community volunteers, and stress vocational skills in demand in the economy.

Each Learning Workshop teacher must work closely with the teaching teams. Weekly meetings occur with each team to discuss the progress of Learning Workshop students in each academic area, and joint plans are developed to encourage additional learning. Learning Workshop teachers are not assigned to homeroom tasks or other morning duties so that they will be free for consultation with individual teachers. Further assisting this cooperation with teams and within houses, resource room staff operate from small rooms located in each house, and utilize one other regular-size classroom for centralized functions. Table 7.3 (on page 342) illustrates a typical day for a Learning Workshop teacher at Farnsworth Middle School.

At Oaklea Middle School (Junction City, Oregon), the resource room functions in a similar way to meet the needs of handicapped learners. The stated goal of the Resource Center at Oaklea Middle is to continue and increase the student's enrollment in the regular program as much as possible, through instruction provided directly to the child, or indirectly through consultation with the teacher. The center also offers services such as program preparation and diagnostic testing; the center also provides services to middle school students who are functioning at least 1.5 years below grade level and who need special services to learn most effectively. The Resource Center, staffed by one full-time resource teacher for the retarded, one math teacher, two Title One reading teachers, and three full-time aides, provides intensive instruction to students after referral by regular classroom teachers.

At Oaklea, a special section of the Resource Center handles both remedial and gifted math students, and the staff at Oaklea are developing special programs for gifted students as well as those with deficiencies. Most middle schools do offer programs for the gifted, often structured in much the same way as the resource center for problem learners, except that the activities and

Table 7.3   **Model Learning Workshop Teacher Schedule***

	MOD TIME	CLASS	
1.	9:05– 9:30	Vince-Leon 8th grader's	
2.	9:30– 9:45	Stan-et al. curriculum assistance	
3.	9:45–10:00	Basic Skills Math Class	
4.	10:00–10:15	4 students	
5	10:15–10:30	Peter curriculum 6th	
6.	10:30–10:45	& assistance grader's Todd	
7.	10:45–11:00	Barry Red /Brian white	Silas-math
8.	11:00–11:15	Mark Day / Vince day	reinforcement
9.	11:15–11:30	/ Ed John curriculum assistance	
10.	11:30–11:45	LUNCH — teacher consultation	
11.	11:45–12:00		
12.	12:00–12:15	Basic Skills Math Class	
13.	12:15–12:30	4 students	
14.	12:30–12:45	Teacher (Team) Consultation Time	
15.	12:45– 1:00	(Guidance, Parents, etc.)	
16.	1:00– 1:15		
17.	1:15– 1:30	Todd Harvey	Harry-math
18.	1:30– 1:45	Gary	assistance
19.	1:45– 2:00	Peter Curriculum assistance	
20.	2:00– 2:15	Basic Skills Math Class	
21.	2:15– 2:30	5 students	
22.	2:30– 2:45	Team Consultation-8th grade	
			Don
23.	2:45– 3:00	Harry ⎫ Peter	Math assistance
24.	3:00– 3:15	Kevin ⎬ curriculum math	
25.	3:15– 3:30	Linda ⎭ assistance assistance	

* From Farnsworth Middle School, Guiderland, N.Y.

the curriculum are geared for acceleration, independence, and in-depth work. The referral procedure for the Resource Center at Oaklea Middle School seems fairly representative. The following nine steps are followed:

1. Teacher becomes aware of specific problem.

2. Teacher fills out top of referral form in as much detail as possible and notifies parents that child is being referred to Resource Center for individual testing.

3. Teacher places referral in the appropriate Resource teacher's box. Resource Center will get parental permission for individual testing.

4. Resource Center will do individual testing in specific skill areas and notify referring teacher of test results.

5. Resource Center teacher will set up time for staffing if test results indicate a skill deficiency.

6. Staffing will be held including resource teachers, referring teacher, counselor, and parent. Resource teachers will present program plan based on test results.

7. Recommendations will be made on the basis of the staffing.

8. If approved for entry in Resource Center, student will begin individual program.

9. If not approved, conference will be held with the referring teacher to determine alternative programs to be utilized in regular classroom.

Once the referral process is complete, for either a handicapped or gifted student, an individualized education plan, required by Public Law 94–142, is developed and implemented. Such plans are then subject to periodic review. Table 7.4 (on page 344) is an example of the form used at Oaklea Middle School to record the analysis of the plan.

At Steuben Middle School in Milwaukee, Wisconsin, a carefully planned program emerges in a way that demonstrates the centrality of the resource room strategy in mainstreaming at the exemplary middle school. At Steuben, two programs operate simultaneously, providing from one to four hours per day to students, depending upon their individual needs. One program (learning disabilities) is designed to work exclusively within a single team, making it possible for the exceptional education teacher to work closely with the four teachers on the team, an hour each day. This communication enables the faculty to assess a student's functioning in given classes on a daily basis, permits better communication with teachers, helps keep parents informed, and strengthens the role of the special education teacher as the fifth teacher on the team. As such, the special education teachers find themselves on an equal footing, no longer on the outside looking in at their students. This permits the planning of activities that will benefit not only the special students in the unit, but the more normal students as well. Since, therefore, more students view the special teacher as a member of the team, the resource room loses the stigma and mystery it once had. Within this model, exceptional students are mainstreamed for at least one regular academic class as well as for most speciality classes. Special education students are also included in regular teams for homeroom, lunch, field trips and other special events.

In 1990, the school district of Issaquah, Washington, developed a continuum of options for the integration of the concept of "least restrictive environment," a continuum which seems fairly common in middle schools across the country. In each option, a teacher with certification in special education is responsible for the students' IEP's and instruction:

Table 7.4 **Individualized Education Plan Review—Special Services***

			PERFORMANCE		Explain If Unmet					Action	
					Lack Pre-requisite Skill	Objective Too Difficult	Activity Inappropriate	Materials Unavailable	Other	Carry Over Objective	Drop Objective
STUDENT NAME:		**SCHOOL:**									
Annual Goal Code Number	Objective Number:	COMMENTS:	Met As Stated	Not Met As Stated							

RECOMMENDATIONS FOR FOLLOWING YEAR:

Teacher: _____   Parent: _____

_____   _____

_____   _____

_____   _____

_____   _____

TEACHER SIGNATURE   DATE   PARENT SIGNATURE   DATE

White: Permanent File   Yellow: Teacher   Pink: Parent

Consulting   One special education teacher works with regular education teachers. Eight to ten students, from each teacher, are seen directly by the special education teacher for twenty minutes per week. The regular education content is modified and delivered in the regular classroom by the regular teacher. Separate funds pay for the two different teachers.

Collegial   Three teachers, one of whom is special education, work directly with sixty to seventy students (ten to fifteen are special education). Regular classroom content is modified for learners. "Regular education pays for two teachers, special education pays for one."

Team Teaching   Two teachers, one of whom is special education, work with thirty to forty students (ten to twelve special education).

Integrated   One special education teacher works with twenty-five students, eight of whom will be identified special education students, with appropriate content modification for all learners.

Skills Classes   One special education teacher works with fifteen to nineteen students, including some special education students, in a specialized curriculum appropriate for all the students, in a traditional pull-out program.

Resource Room   One special education teacher works with ten to fifteen students, all of whom have been identified as exceptional students, in a specialized curriculum in a traditional pull-out option.

In Issaquah, a district special education team reviews the needs of students in the school and those projected to move up from the elementary school. A building level team then reviews the needs of the exceptional students in a particular building, and develops guidelines for scheduling students. Counselors and administrators develop a master schedule with these guidelines in mind. Finally, the school special education team leader and counselors fine tune the schedule for each exceptional student.

Mainstreaming and the Regular Teacher

Special educators stress that the methods which regular classroom teachers should use with the exceptional students who are mainstreamed into their classrooms for portions of the school day are actually the methods used by all efficient, well-trained teachers. There appears to be very little that separates the effective special education teacher and the effective regular classroom teacher. Again, it becomes a matter of degree. There are, nonetheless, several suggestions often cited as particularly important when considering students with special needs. Here is one such list:

- Accept the child as he comes to you. Guard against the formation of negative expectations based on appearance, smell, or verbal behavior.
- Realize that every child can do better than he/she is now doing.
- Learn as much as you can about the specific characteristics of the students who will be in your class.
- Survey your resources carefully, within and beyond the school.
- Respect the opinions of other professionals.
- Carefully determine the role and preparation of classroom assistants when available.
- Involve parents realistically.
- Offer a workable, practical curriculum broken down into subunits.
- Do not be overly rigid in your plans for grouping students for instruction.
- Make use of behavior modification and contingency management techniques. Be especially careful to function consistently with special students. Plan to reduce the child's dependence on you (Department of Special Education, 1975).

Other helpful hints for regular classroom teachers working with the "mildly handicapped" student in the regular classroom can be more concrete. Much of what seems to be recommended to the regular classroom teacher seems to be based on the primacy of attention deficits among such students. When these deficits are added to the makeup of the transescent student, in general, it seems clear that supportive *instructional* structure is also terribly important in the classroom lives of these students. Consider a few of the items on one such list of recommendations to the regular classroom teacher when mildly disabled students are present in some numbers (B. Commandy, personal communication, December, 1990):

Post a calendar on the front board for assignments, color-coded by class.

Provide monthly calendars to students for long-range planning.

Provide a weekly assignment sheet, for student's or parent's use in keeping up with assignments or results.

Write important, timely announcements on the board.

Post a homework chart somewhere in the room to record receipt of work.

Design opportunities for "breaks": pencil sharpening, trash deposits, passing papers; these build in "legal" opportunities for moving and talking.

Acquire a second set of textbooks, or permission to share for those who forget.

Develop tapes for poor readers.

Give two grades, one for content and one for spelling.

Give frequent quizzes rather than large examinations.

In math, color code steps, and use graph paper to keep columns and rows straight.

Give lots of extra credit.

Provide as many checklists as possible for students to use as guidelines (e.g., a
  proofreading checklist).

At least one comprehensive staff development program is now available for
training regular classroom teachers to work more effectively with the learning
disabled students in their classrooms: "Keymakers", a package available from
the Minnesota Association for Children and Adults with Learning Disabilities.[3]
The program helps teachers understand learning styles as they relate to the LD
student, curriculum modification, cooperative learning, motivation and behavior
management, "Precision Teaching" and "Teacher Assistance Teams." Educators
in the Orange County Florida, middle schools attest to its helpfulness in helping
implement the consultation and co-teaching process there.

In the broadest sense of the term, mainstreaming may be thought to apply
to more than those students who have been identified and staffed into exceptional education programs. Programs for "at-risk" students probably should be
considered under similar criteria. Programs such as Chapter One also deserve
to be considered when discussions of mainstreaming occur. In many school
districts, attempts are underway to weave students served by Chapter One programs back into the mainstream of the regular classroom. In Corning, New York,
for example, students at Northside Blodgett Middle School are involved in what
is known there as "Congruence Teaching," a program in which the Chapter One
teacher and the regular classroom teacher work together in consultation and co-
teaching procedures much like those described above.

Tracking and Ability Grouping: Which Way for the Middle School?

We believe that the practice of between-class ability grouping, arranging middle
school students in hierarchical groups according to a measure or ability or prior
achievement—known as tracking in its most rigid forms—is one of the most
controversial education issues of the 1990s. Not only is the practice of tracking
controversial, it is also a singularly widespread activity. In the last fifty years,
tracking has been the subject of more research studies (over 500) than almost
any other educational practice. And never have educational research and common school district practices been at greater variance; the great preponderance
of the evidence weighs against tracking, while the great majority of school districts utilize it comprehensively (Slavin, 1990). Tracking, certainly at the middle
level, may be the single most important unresolved issue in education.

Tracking seems like such a sensible idea; it ought to be possible to identify
and arrange students accurately by ability or achievement. Reducing class heterogeneity should then make it possible for teachers to target their instruction
to meet more students' needs more often. Students should learn better and feel

---

[3]For more information, contact MACALD, 1821 University Avenue, Suite 494-N, St. Paul,
MN 55104.

more positive about themselves as a consequence. Teachers should be able to accomplish their tasks with greater efficiency and ease. In practice, however, tracking does not seem to work out quite as sensibly, not for the great majority of the students.

Synthesis of Research on Ability Grouping

It appears to us that an enormous amount of evidence testifies to the failure of ability grouping to deliver the expected benefits. Oakes (1985) makes it clear that it is extremely difficult to identify students accurately and fairly; all too often, students are grouped so that it is income, social class, and race which are most highly correlated with the so-called ability groups. Recent reviews of research (Slavin, 1990, 1987; Gamoran & Berends, 1987; Hawley & Rosenholtz, 1987) indicate that the expected gains in academic achievement simply do not materialize. There is also good reason to believe that there are virtually no positive social or personal effects which are produced by between-class ability grouping at the middle level school (Good & Brophy, 1987).

Why Tracking and Ability Grouping Fail

Between-class ability grouping, or tracking, is supposed to reduce student heterogeneity so that teachers can plan and deliver lessons which more nearly match the needs of the class in terms of the pace and the level of the lesson. This practice is supposed to improve student self-esteem and increase academic achievement. But apparently it does so, if at all, only for the upper 10 percent in the elementary setting and for the college-bound in the high school. Why doesn't it work?

There may be several important reasons why ability grouping fails. First, there is the stigma which results from negative labels and placements. Second, when students are tracked for most or all of the day, the power of expectations acts on teachers and students in ways which lead both to settle for less for low-track classes. Third, students are exposed to dramatically different curriculum. Fourth, teaching assignments, in many middle level schools, are not made randomly and equitably; often, the more experienced teachers are assigned to high-track classes and unproven or inexpert teachers are given the low sections. Fifth, less successful students, continually placed together year after year become, at the middle level, like an "anti-school camp" (Gamoran & Berends, 1987).

In our minds, the most stinging indictment of ability grouping is that in many districts this process has resulted in the de facto racial and social class resegregation of what were intended to be integrated schools. In many such middle level schools, there are three schools in one building: a smaller honors or advanced track, of higher income, majority culture students who also comprise most of the students in the school's gifted and talented programs; an increasingly larger low track, comprised primarily of poor and minority culture students, who also have a higher number of students in remedial and special education programs; and a third group, of increasingly ignored regular class students whose educational experience is lacking in any special qualities. Even if ability grouping delivered tremendous benefits in academic achievement, it would be a practice educators would have to reject, if it resulted in the racial, ethnic, and social class segregation of the public schools.

Which Way for the Middle School?

Middle school educators like to think of themselves as both familiar and comfortable with the diversity of their students. Good middle school teachers are described as being student-centered, willing to meet their students where they are and carry the students forward as far as time and effort will permit. Exemplary middle schools are described as schools "willing to adapt all school practices to the individual differences in intellectual, biological, and social maturation of their students" (Lipsitz, 1984, p. 167). Such schools ought, hypothetically, to be places where the abuses of tracking and ability grouping are found far less frequently.

In fact, this appears to be so. The evidence suggests that schools identified as exemplary middle schools engage in considerably less tracking than other middle level schools (George, 1988). In a study of 154 of some of the nation's best middle schools, virtually all of the respondents indicated that schools were organized so that each student in the school was a member of a heterogeneously-grouped interdisciplinary team, with each team a microcosm of the school as a whole. Second, the survey indicated that fully one third of these exemplary middle schools rejected the practice of tracking, except insofar as they must serve students with identified special needs. Other schools grouped students on the teams for math or English, but rarely for more than two subjects. Most importantly, perhaps, the great majority of survey respondents indicated that they would like to move even further away from rigid between-class ability grouping.

The evidence indicates that ability grouping has little educational value at the middle level, that educators in exemplary middle schools already do substantially less such grouping than is practiced in other schools. But if middle level educators would like to move even further away from ability grouping, how should they proceed?

Educators at the McCulloch Middle School in Highland Park, Texas may, we think, represent a growing trend in middle school education. In 1988, the district formed the Committee on Ability Grouping in the Middle School. The committee met sixteen times, for a total of more than seventy hours, not including the far greater number of hours that individual members spent in reviewing the literature on the topic, speaking with experts, conversing with parents, meeting with teachers, and surveying other school districts and their practices. Members spent more than 2,000 hours in making an objective and comprehensive study (C. Floyd, personal communication, December, 1990). Based on their study, the thirteen members of the committee unanimously approved these recommendations, which were implemented by the school board:

> Beginning with the 1989–90 school year, the Academically Talented Program will be discontinued in favor of heterogeneous class groupings for all language arts, science, math, and social studies classes except for one accelerated math class in the 7th and 8th grades.
>
> All teachers in the middle school will receive training in instructional strategies for teaching heterogeneous classes, including cooperative learning, effective instruction, content modification, content enrichment, mentorship, challenging high achieving students, and use of team "blocks." It is expected that teachers will receive eight days of training prior to September implementation, but that the training program will be further developed and continued thereafter.
>
> A standing committee on Educational Excellence in the Middle School will be formed immediately. The purpose of the committee will be to monitor the implementation of the new program and to continue to promote educational excellence at the middle school.

Strategies for "Getting off the Track" in the Exemplary Middle School
1. Proceed with caution and a long-term plan.

Practitioners engaged in "detracking" argue that the grouping process has been deeply embedded in their schools for generations. It has a tremendous hold in the public schools; it is unlikely that tracking will wither tomorrow or next year, in spite of the seemingly overwhelming amount of evidence against its use or the most earnest efforts of those who seek to eliminate it. In order to protect the interests of everyone involved, and the success of the detracking effort itself, it will be best to engage in a strategic planning process which establishes a clearly desirable future state for the organization of the school or schools, identifies tactics required for success, and employs an action plan to achieve it all. Such a plan ought to involve a variety of efforts over a period of several years.

The worst possible results should be expected in situations where middle school leaders, even for the best of reasons, take unilateral and impulsive action to end tracking in their school or district. When this happens, practitioners with such experiences report that parents and policymakers in and outside the school react angrily and noisily. Many teachers will find such plans difficult to implement successfully and will feel frustrated and discontented. Such efforts rarely lead to complete success; more often the program, the participants, and the leadership suffer.

2. Secure widespread involvement and the representation of all groups of stakeholders.

Educational change of any sort is always at least partially political. In the case of tracking and ability grouping at the middle level, it is very political. The attempt to alter current grouping arrangements will surely go awry, practioners say, unless all of those affected are involved to some extent.

This may be particularly the case with two groups of parents: those who believe that the current situation benefits their children, and those who believe that it is inequitable. The first group must be persuaded that their children's educational experience will not be sacrificed on the alter of educational experimentation. They must be helped to see that educational excellence will not suffer as a result of capricious "social engineering." They must be assisted in learning that the research suggests that high-ability, high-achieving students do well academically in virtually any setting.

Parents are often already anxious about their children moving from the more protective, and often monocultural, atmosphere of the smaller elementary school to a larger, multicultural, and often far less personal middle level school. When this transition also includes the potential for heterogeneous classes, anxieties of middle class majority culture parents can reach a potentially explosive peak. These parents must be convinced that their children will be challenged academically but not threatened personally.

Other parents, initially less well-informed perhaps, must learn how important class placements are for the success of their children. They must come to see how important peer group influences are, especially for less successful learners. They must understand how important one teacher can be in the lives of their children, even at the middle level. They must be willing to speak out against what they believe to be unjust and unfair practices. They must be encouraged to insist on equity in the assignment of students, teachers, and school resources.

Policy-making school board members must become acquainted with the research. They must be shown that current arrangements may not meet the test of being fair or effective for all of the students in their schools, and that it can be politically safe to change.

Practitioners who have untracked successfully have frequently utilized a task force or steering committee comprised of educators, parents, community members, and representatives from the board. Such groups become informed, participate in the design of the alternative, and in doing so become more committed to the implementation of alternatives to the current practice.

3. Conduct a local self-study.

Practitioners say that research based on national studies is unlikely to convince the local professionals, parents, and policy-makers who most need to be persuaded. The national research must be reinforced with a study of the grouping practices in the local school or schools in question. The study must focus on real children known, at least in general, to those who will read the findings. One such study, conducted in a school on the east coast of Maryland sought answers to the following ten questions (H. Martin, personal communication, June 28, 1990):

a. How careful are we in the way we place students in ability grouped classes? Do we rely on a single measure? Do we use student behavior as an important criterion? Are all parents informed about the placement of their students in sufficient time for them to explore the ramifications? Can we be confident that students are placed accurately and fairly?

b. What are the results of our identification and placement processes? Are the high-track classes populated primarily by students from higher income home situations? Are minority group children underrepresented in high-track classes, or overrepresented in low-track classes?

c. What are the results in terms of academic achievement? Can we say with confidence that the results are not skewed in terms of ethnic group or family income? That is, do we have an "effective school" in the sense that no identifiable groups of students can be predicted to have either generally lower or higher academic achievement? Are the ranges of higher academic achievement the almost exclusive province of majority culture, upper-middle-class children? Are the bottom levels of achievement populated by predominantly children from families that are characterized as lower-income and minority culture?

d. How flexible are our grouping strategies? How much mobility do our plans permit, from day to day, and from year to year? Do students spend most of the day, most of the year, and most of their tenure in the school in one ability group?

e. How does the current situation affect students' perceptions of themselves? Do high-track students, for example, have an advantage in terms of self-concept? Might positive self-perceptions of high-track students be unjustifiably inflated, leading to an unreasonable sort of elitism? Do low-track students feel good about themselves and about school?

f. How do high-track and low-track students feel about school, and about each other? Is there a sense of community in the school such that students all enjoy being there? Do members of different ethnic and income groups evaluate school, and each other, positively? Is there a substantial amount of voluntary integration in terms of seating in classes and elsewhere, choice of friends, etc.?

g. Is there a relationship between track placement and student behavior in school? For example, do most of the referrals to the office, for discipline reasons, come from the lower-track students? Most of the suspensions? Do high-track students represent most of the participation in school extracurricular activities of an academic nature?

h. How do teachers respond to the current arrangements? Does faculty support for maintaining ability grouping come primarily from teachers assigned to high-track classes? Are such assignments made fairly? That is, do all teachers share in the teaching of both high- and low-track groups? Is the teaching "talent" in the school dispersed evenly over all ability groups? Given an opportunity, would most teachers honestly prefer to teach high-track classes?

i. Do teachers actually prepare different lessons for different ability groups, or do both groups get the same content with substantially different expectations for mastery? Do teachers actually use different instructional strategies with high- and low-track classes, or are both groups expected to learn the same way?

j. Does parental support of and involvement in school programs come from a broad spectrum of the school population, or is it primarily a middle-class, middle-income phenomenon?

If most of the answers to these questions result in a positive evaluation of the school organization as it is, there may be little need for the potentially upsetting changes which untracking might cause. If, however, the results of the self-study call the current situation into question, the data are likely to be much more persuasive than the results of national studies referenced by an outside expert.

4. Engage in a thorough effort in information dissemination before attempting any change.

The results of both national and local research efforts need to be widely publicized, and stakeholders need time to process the information. Practitioners assert that opposition to proposed changes, on the part of parents and board members, can be substantially allayed by reliance on data and logic.

One middle level principal evolved a strategy for the frequent one-on-one sessions with parents and policymakers in which he found himself prior to the decision to move to more heterogeneity in the social organization of the school which he led. Step one was to permit the concerned visitor a period of "ventilation" without interruption. Step two was to ask this question: "Do your concerns come from intuition or knowledge?" Inevitably, the answer given by the visitor was "intuition." Step three was this statement: "I'm using knowledge. Here are some of the resources and information I've been consulting. Please take it with you and read it carefully. Then let's talk again." According to this principal, there never was a need for a follow-up session.

Admittedly, the parents in this middle school population may have been exceptionally fair-minded and responsive to reason; other leaders may not be so fortunate. Efforts to alter the current grouping patterns will, however, be likely to proceed much more smoothly when there is a constant attempt to provide data where previously only "intuition" or bias prevailed.

Policymakers, responsible for all of the children in the district, must be helped to see the wisdom in John Dewey's remark that "What the best and wisest parents want for their children, that must the community want for all its children." It is the responsibility of the change-oriented practitioner to see that board members and others have all of the information they need for reasoned, balanced decisions, not just what they hear on the telephone from a smaller number of parents or others with more narrowly focused vested interests.

5. A number of practitioners have suggested that changing to heterogeneity in grouping is more successful when the changes are aimed at the lower grades in a school or district.

Thinking of changing the patterns in the whole district? The conventional wisdom suggests that the early years of elementary education are the place to begin. In a single school, try to change the 1st or 2nd grade in the school. In a 6–8 middle level situation, start in the 6th grade; in a 7–9 junior high school, practitioners advised others to attempt to change the 7th grade first.

Whether or not these suggestions are completely valid and reliable, there does seem to be a reasonable bit of folk wisdom involved. Our own experience with change in middle schools over the last quarter century squares with this contemporary advice. It is possible that organizations and hierarchies often naturally evolve to a point where, for one reason or another, those members most resistant to change are found in the higher grades of a school or upper school levels in a district.

6. Make no moves without carefully designed, effectively planned, comprehensive staff development for teachers.

Those who will be expected to implement successfully any proposed changes in the way students are grouped in a school or district must be prepared and confident. It is not enough to include teachers in the research and decision-making which result in proposals for change, although it is essential to do so. Teachers must be prepared to deal with a potentially different mix of learners.

Practitioners suggest that there are several important components to staff development programs which successfully prepare teachers for heterogeneous classrooms. Teachers must have an opportunity to think through the philosophical rationale which supports more flexibility in grouping. They must have a chance to study the research, both from the national and the local situations. These sessions will enable teachers to come to decisions about the moral issues involved, but more will be required for a successful transition to heterogeneous classes.

Teachers must be acquainted with the skills which are characteristic of their peers who are effective in managing and instructing such classes. Training and assistance in applying the strategies of effective classroom behavior management will be required. Techniques for giving in-class assistance to less successful students, and for challenging more successful students will need to be developed. Alternative models of grading, emphasizing individual progress, and de-emphasizing the normal curve must become part of the teacher's repetioire. Techniques for providing choice and diversity in homework and major assignments will be necessary. Every district has teachers who are or could quickly become effective in heterogeneous classrooms; staff development cadres can be comprised of these effective professionals.

Staff development in effective instructional strategies will be essential. Training in cooperative learning, for example, is both popular and potent. Other strategies also lend themselves to heterogeneous classes; mastery learning models and varieties of individualized instruction will help teachers cope successfully. We have dealt with two other important instructional strategies in the chapter on instruction: the reading/writing workshop approach, and consultation and co-teaching strategies.

As with the consultation and co-teaching strategy, educators trained to deal with exceptional students may have more to offer. Many middle level practitioners say that one high-quality, low-cost, staff development resource for helping regular classroom teachers enjoy the heterogeneous classroom are the special educators in the building. Inviting these teachers to provide staff development for their regular classroom peers (e.g., on how to deal effectively with LD students) may be credible, welcome, and inexpensive.

Some practitioners are using another strategy. These school building leaders are less than confident about being able to design and deliver adequate staff development to their teachers spontaneously, but are nevertheless feeling a sense of urgency to do something about tracking in their buildings. Their approach is to say to their teachers "Just do your best with the slow students." The school leader, in these situations, appears to be saying to the teachers "I know there's only so much you can do with the slower students. Do your best with them, but I won't expect you to accomplish miracles."

We believe this advice is based on the assumption, held by many middle school practitioners, that slower students moved out of basic or compensatory classes and integrated into higher sections will be likely to do no worse and perhaps considerably better on some criteria than they would have done in those ability-grouped lower level sections. Without probing into all the assumptions and implications of this sort of advice, and the outcomes to which they might lead, we think that, at the least, such statements might encourage some anxious teachers to agree to increasing the heterogeneity of their classes. As long as this temporary situation is followed by the sort of staff development that would permit the teacher to deal effectively with that heterogeneity, it seems to us a sensible stopgap measure.

7. More rigorously careful identification procedures should improve all grouping strategies, diverse or uniform.

Whether or not the school or district grouping strategies are amended, practitioners agree that virtually all procedures for the identification and placement of students into ability-grouped classes can profit from being closely examined and evaluated.

A number of suggestions apply here. Because of the nature and vulnerability of standardized instruments, educators in many districts are now reluctant to place students in any program on the basis of only one such test or evaluation. In other schools, placement procedures are careful to avoid placing students in low sections solely because of the classroom behavior they exhibit. In still others, educators take pains to explain the potential ramifications of placement to parents prior to actually finalizing the process. As more and more middle level educators move "off the track" during the nineties, new and improved strategies for doing so effectively should emerge.

Getting off the Track: Options and Alternatives

There are more than a dozen options and alternatives to rigid ability grouping currently being practiced in middle schools around the nation. Most appear to be congruent with research on tracking and ability grouping. Others seem promising and deserve to be implemented on a trial basis; careful evaluation of any attempt to "get off the track" should benefit all educators. All grouping patterns that attempt to account for differing abilities, however, should conform to the following characteristics (Slavin, 1987):

a. Students should spend most of their day in heterogeneous situations, being grouped only in specific skill areas that might benefit from such a sharp focus (e.g., reading or mathematics).

b. Grouped classes should be shaped on the basis of specific skills, not just on the basis of an IQ measurement or overall achievement.

c. Frequent reassessment of student placement should be a high priority.

d. Flexible reassignment should be an easy thing for teachers to accomplish.

e. Instruction should actually vary by pace and level to fit the real needs of the students in the groups.

f. Within classes, the number of smaller ability groups should be small.

1. Joplin-Style Plans

Grouping students for specific skills, across grade levels, appears to make instructional groups more manageable in terms of the range of achievement, but mitigate the worst effects of traditional ability grouping. Several real world examples are instructive.

For a decade (1972–1982), Lincoln Middle School in Gainesville, Florida engaged in what they defined as "multiage grouping." In this setting, each student became a member of one of six interdisciplinary teams in the school, to which the student belonged for three years, the entire tenure of their middle school education. Each team consisted of five teachers (specialists in reading, language arts, science, mathematics, social studies) and approximately 150 students, 50 each from the 6th, 7th, and 8th grades. Teams were mirror images of each other, heterogeneous in every possible way: age, race, sex, achievement, and neighborhood. Each team represented the characteristics of the school population as a whole.

Every spring, one third of the team's students moved onto the ninth grade; each fall a new group of sixth graders joined each team. Teachers and students knew each other and worked together in learning situations for three years instead of the customary nine months. A wholly different sense of community developed.

Grouping strategies followed the Joplin Plan. Students were grouped by achievement in reading and/or math without regard for grade level. A math class might have had ten 6th graders, seven 7th graders, and five 8th graders, or some other combination which would constitute a group of students who all needed the same math skills. In this way the range of ability levels which the teacher had to accommodate was much narrower, permitting the teacher to engage in much more large group, teacher-directed instruction and less time in arranging the traditional "three reading groups." Students were grouped and regrouped as time permitted, depending entirely on the progress they made in their respective classes.

There were and are a variety of possible positive outcomes from such a school organization, all of which are potentially related to academic achievement. The "three-year team" made diagnosis and placement of students, for example, a much more data-based process. Home-school connections became firm earlier and grew more positive as the years passed. Peer relationships were far more positive than the school demographics would have led one to expect. Time-on-task was easier to achieve in the fall of the year and sustain throughout the spring.

The advantages of this arrangement were so clear to the faculty and administration that, when the school board made decisions (unrelated to multiage grouping or the school in particular) which rendered multiage grouping impossible, the entire faculty protested. All of the members of the faculty and administration implored the board to make a policy exception which would allow them to continue multiage grouping, but they were unsuccessful in securing it. Consequently, the following year, the school was organized into another version of the three-year team: student-teacher progression (STP), where grade level teams stay together for three years. This STP organization remains in place. (We discuss this structure and its benefits earlier in this chapter.)

Similar designs have also been used, at different times and places, in elementary schools. Currently, the Success for All program (Slavin, Madden, Karweit, Livermon & Dolan, 1990) is attempting to establish a model for the reform of urban education which includes a substantial measure of Joplin-style school organization. Children in an inner-city elementary school are grouped for reading across grade levels one, two, and three. The students spend most of their day in grade level heterogeneous classes, but in reading they are grouped by skill level regardless of grade. This permits the teacher, once again, to utilize a great deal more teacher-directed large group instruction, since the range of achievement is much narrower. We are convinced that Joplin Plan organizational strategies which are combined with effective efforts to develop a real sense of community through team and school-within-a-school operations have a great deal to offer to middle level schools.

2. Partial Untracking

It may be politically unwise, pedagogically difficult, or possibly illegal to dismantle current grouping arrangements completely in many middle schools. State and national regulations may demand that certain identified student populations be served in narrowly prescribed patterns. Parents of certain students may exert intense pressure to maintain separate arrangements; advocacy groups may throw up barriers of various kinds. But it will almost always be possible to eliminate some of the levels of grouping or some of the subjects in which students are grouped.

If students in a particular middle school or district are grouped, shall we say, in five levels per subject, in five academic subjects, it may be possible to cut the number of levels to three, or the number of subjects in which students are grouped to two or three. Pressure from parents and teachers of students in gifted, honors, and advanced classes, for example, may make it impossible to eliminate those sections. So, say most middle level practitioners, don't touch them.

Practitioners argue that, instead of fighting an endless and costly battle to eliminate all tracking and ability grouping, cut back where it is easiest. Make a case to eliminate the lowest sections, or eliminate grouping totally in classes where the subject matter is anything but hierarchical (e.g., social studies). Eliminating a substantial degree of tracking may also be the path of greatest fairness, since the final "truth" may not yet be known on ability grouping, especially for the gifted and in subjects like mathematics and foreign language.

3. Teacher Autonomy

Many practitioners report that when they are unable to develop a consensus among the faculty for a major move away from ability grouping, another more moderate strategy is to empower teams of teachers to make the decisions. In any one school, it is possible to develop a policy on grouping which says, in effect, that in that school all students are taught in instructional configurations which represent the way in which their team of teachers believe that they can best deliver instruction to that student or group. In this way, the school leaders are in a positive position of being able to say that every student in the school is receiving instruction in the way that teachers believe they can be most effective.

There are a number of possibilities, depending on the level of the school. In the elementary school, for example, teachers who work in self-contained classrooms can often make major modifications in the degree of heterogeneity within learning groups. Small groups of teachers working as a grade level group can do the same for the students they have in common. At the middle school, teachers on interdisciplinary teams can agree to group students for achievement in a number of ways: for reading and math, or reading only, math only, all academic subjects, no ability grouping whatsoever. The strategies they choose need not affect any other teacher in the school if the schedule is done carefully.

4. Before and after School "Acceleration"

A number of middle school programs are being redesigned to shift funding for remedial programs away from the official school day to early morning, late afternoon, and Saturday sessions. This is combined with the elimination of compensatory or other bottom-rung basic sections which, in the opinion of many practitioners, are extremely ineffective as they are now operated.

Whether or not these changes will make a measurable difference is yet to be determined, but there is some precedent for feeling positive about them: the Japanese do it that way (George, 1989). Emphasizing effort rather than ability, the Japanese encourage those who are not being successful to try harder, study more, to "gambare" (endure with effort). In the Japanese junior high schools, contrary to many Americans' beliefs, there is very little ability grouping. The Japanese junior high schools are basically drawn from adjoining neighborhoods, and classroom groups are almost entirely heterogeneous. Students who are behind are encouraged to enroll in mostly private after-school remedial and acceleration programs called "juku." Many Japanese junior high school students spend one or two hours, one or two afternoons a week at such private schools. There appears to be no insurmountable reason why many American children could not do more of the same, especially if the costs are borne by the school system.

5. Split-Level Grouping (Winchester Plan)

Some middle schools are organizing both to maintain and minimize ability grouping in an attempt to get the best of both educational worlds. Although we have encountered this plan in several districts, we first became aware of it in Winchester, Kentucky, a small, forward-looking school district in the mid-South.

At Conkwright Junior High School, students and teachers are organized into grade level team-type groups, each of which contains about 125 students. All students on a team are placed into one of five ability levels (see Figure 7.5): low (K,H), low average (W,T), average (C,R), high average (N,G), and high (O,I). Then, each of these groups is further subdivided into two equal-size groups of twelve or thirteen students, yielding ten ability groups, two each at five levels. This grouping arrangement makes it possible for teachers to be assigned students from all five levels, but never to have more than two ability levels in class at any one time. More importantly, perhaps, is the fact that students travel with a group of peers of the same approximate ability, but never spend the whole day with any one ability group. All students mix with students of all ability groups throughout the day.

Let's look at a sample group of students, subgroup K. The students in this group begin their day with science, grouped with students from subgroup H, the other low group. Second period is completely heterogeneous, in elective and exploratory classes while the academic teachers have a common planning time. Then group K has reading, again with group H, followed by lunch and physical education (team planning), when students from group K are in mixed groups entirely. In math, during 6th period, they learn side-by-side with the students from group R, an average group. During the last period of the day they combine with group I, the highest group, for social studies.

The teachers' experience is similar. The greatest homogeneity may be in subjects where the subject matter is most hierarchical, but no teacher must endure an unreasonable range for much of the day. In fact, most of the day, the

Winchester Plan

CONK WRIGHT		MATH	ENGLISH	READING	SOCIAL STUDIES	SCIENCE
Low KH	1	CW	RT	OI	NG	KH
Low Average WT	2		ELECTIVE CLASSES/PLANNING			
	3	NG	OI	KH	CR	WT
Average CR	4		LUNCH			
High Average NG	5		TEAM PLANNING			
High OI	6	KR	NC	WT	OH	IG
	7	OI	KH	CG	WT	NR
	8	TH	WG	NR	IK	CO

FIGURE 7.5   **Winchester Plan**

groups are probably much more homogeneous than necessary. It would be possible, depending on the desires of the school or team, to inject far more mixture in the grouping. Teachers and administrators say that this process has passed the test of time with them.

6. Administrative or Student Choice

A number of middle level schools permit individuals to have their established placement altered for unofficial reasons. Some schools permit students to make the choice of the level or section they desire. Many middle level principals have been known to engage in "administrative placement" for a variety of reasons. Sometimes it is because of the power or persuasiveness of a parent, but in many schools it is because of the positive attitude and behavior of one or more students. These are students identified as "good bets," students who may not have the IQ or the test score but who seem to the administrator to be capable of success in a more advanced section or group.

In many parts of the country it is possible to alter substantially and constructively the racial and ethnic balances in school classrooms. By selecting as "good bets" minority group students whose re-placement will at least partially correct the imbalance in formerly all-majority culture classrooms, the resegregation of American schools inside the school building can be at least somewhat mitigated. In a school of 1,000 students, for example, identifying fifty students for administrative reassignment can make a big difference in the composition of high level classes. Most practitioners say that such reassignments are almost always successful.

7. Repackaging the Curriculum

One wily middle school administrator reports solving the honors math conundrum by requiring every student in the school to take regular grade level mathematics. Honors mathematics is placed on the exploratory wheel and may be chosen by students at every grade level, every year. This way, students get two periods of math a day, not an unpopular option with parents.

8. Consulting and Co-Teaching

In many school districts, practitioners are pleased with two other instructional delivery models: consultation and co-teaching. Here, teachers of exceptional children and general education teachers collaborate, to various degrees, to bring greater numbers of exceptional students and their regular classroom peers together for instruction. In the consultation model, the general education teacher consults with and is regularly coached by the teacher of exceptional education. In co-teaching situations, the two teachers may regularly work together in the same classroom with the same very heterogeneous group of students. Practitioners report increasing satisfaction with such efforts, with greater and greater numbers of students with learning disabilities being served effectively in the regular classroom. Educators with experience in this practice express their optimism but also stress that these procedures work only when they are voluntary, when careful training is a prerequisite, and when adequate common planning time is available.

Consultation and co-teaching models are primarily a consequence of the mainstreaming movement and focus most often on students with learning disabilities. Educators in increasing number of school districts are, however, discovering that the two models can work equally well when gifted and talented students are the focus. There seem to be little to prevent regular classroom teachers and teachers of the gifted from working closely together. Moving gifted and talented students back in to the regular classroom, where they can continue to have their specific needs met, ought, in our judgment, to assume a high priority in districts struggling to resolve the inequities and inefficiencies of rigid tracking and ability grouping.

We predict that the dialogue surrounding ability grouping, middle school concepts, and the effective education of the gifted and talented students will assume a position of increasingly greater significance among educators and parents as this decade continues. Advocates for gifted and talented programs will contend with those who support less emphasis on those programs in favor of more interdisciplinary and heterogeneous efforts (Robinson, 1991; Sicola, 1991). All children will suffer if adequate answers to these issues are not developed.

9. Pilot Programs

Many educators agree that there are, almost inevitably, a sizable number of teachers in every middle school who are willing to try virtually anything that they believe will improve the program. That is at least part of the secret of good middle level schools. Typically, practitioners assert, these same teachers usually possess the energy, dedication, and effectiveness to be successful at whatever they attempt. Consequently, many educators seeking alternatives to tracking are encouraging individuals and small groups of teachers to pilot heterogeneous grouping in one or more parts of a school.

Guidelines to successful pilot programs commonly suggest collecting benchmark data for later comparison purposes. Most practitioners have been satisfied that teacher responses are positive enough to persuade others in the building to consider doing the same, since the opinions of professional peers carry more weight than virtually anything else. Other data might also be helpful in attempts to encourage parents and policymakers to consider supporting further change: student responses, achievement scores, counts on school behavior problems like referrals to the office, and positive interaction between majority and minority culture students.

The evidence against tracking and between-class ability grouping continues to mount. The practices persist almost everywhere. Middle school educators must mount a determined effort to invent effective alternatives, proceed cautiously, and give each option a careful public trial. Only then will we be able to get American middle schools "off the track."

Good middle schools have often led the way, instructionally, in the last twenty-five years. With tracking, too, this appears to be the case. We know that among the very best middle schools, tracking is less often a part of the experience of teachers and students. Additional research ought to be able to tell us how these educators have resisted the use of tracking and the details of the effective alternatives which they do utilize. Which way for the middle school? Once again, middle school educators more often choose a different path.

ADDITIONAL SUGGESTIONS FOR FURTHER STUDY

A. Books and Monographs

Brady, M. P. (1988). *Middle school study of mainstreamed students dissemination report: A summary of year one findings and year two research activities.* Houston, TX: College of Education, University of Houston.

B. Periodicals

Campbell, A. (& others). (1983). Peer tutors help autistic students enter the mainstream. *Teaching Exceptional Children, 15*(2), 64–69.

Dunn, R. (& others). (1990). Grouping students for instruction: Effects of learning style on achievement and attitudes. *Journal of Social Psychology, 130* (4), 485–94.

Post, L. M. (1984). Individualizing instruction in the middle school: Modifications and adaptations in curriculum for the mainstreamed student. *Clearing House, 58* (2), 73–76.

Swank, P. R. (& others). (1989). Outcomes of grouping students in mainstreamed middle school classroom. *NASSP Bulletin, 73* (516), 62–66.

Truesdell, L. A. (1988). Mainstreaming in an urban middle school: Effects of school organization and climate. *Urban Review, 20*(1), 42–58.

C. ERIC

Braddock, J. H. (1990). *Tracking: implications for student race-ethnic subgroups* (Report No. 1). Baltimore, MD: Center for Research on Effective Schooling for Disadvantaged Students. (ERIC Document Reproduction Service No. ED 325 600)

Burke, A. M. (1987). *Making a big school smaller: The school-within-a-school arrangement for middle level schools.* (ERIC Document Reproduction Service No. ED 303 890)

Reuman, D. A. (1989, March). *Effects of between-classroom ability grouping in mathematics at the transition to junior high school.* Paper presented at the Annual Meeting of the American Educational Research Association, San Francisco, CA. (ERIC Document Reproduction Service No. ED 306 102)

Schatz, E. (1990). *Ability grouping for gifted learners as it relates to school reform and restructuring.* (ERIC Document Reproduction Service No. ED 327 047)

Spencer, C. & Allen, M. G. (1988). *Grouping students by ability: a review of the literature*. (ERIC Document Reproduction Service No. ED 302 326)

Toepfer, C. F., Jr. (1990). *Heterogeneous grouping in middle level schools: Leadership responsibilities for principals*. Reston, VA: National Association of Secondary School Principals (ERIC Document Reproduction Service No. ED 326 998)

D. Dissertations and Dissertation Abstracts

Hooper, S. R. (1989). The effects of cooperative group composition and a performance contingency on learning, interaction, and performance during computer-based instruction. (Doctoral dissertation, The Pennsylvania State University, 1989). *Dissertation Abstracts International*, 50/07a, 1918.

Rath, C. C. (1989). The integration of handicapped students in the middle school: The principal's view (Doctoral dissertation, Boston University, 1989). *Dissertation Abstracts International*, 50/05a, 1166.

Repman, J. L. (1989). Cognitive and affective outcomes of varying levels of structured collaboration in a computer-based learning environment (Doctoral dissertation, The Louisiana State University and Agricultural and Mechanical College, 1989). *Dissertation Abstracts International*, 51/02a, 485.

CHAPTER 8

Organizing Time and Space in the Middle School

School administrators and others charged with the responsibility for organizing and operating middle schools frequently discover that the successful implementation of an advisory program, exploratory curriculum, or interdisciplinary team organization largely depends on the effectiveness of the schedule and the creative use of the facility. Factors which, in the past, were often thought of as separate enterprises, are now recognized as intimately and systematically related. Few schools can overcome the barriers of ineffective schedules or restrictive environments, so this chapter focuses on the proper understanding of this interrelationship between program and the support of the program via schedule and space, and upon the effective organization and use of school time and space.

Organizing Time in the Middle School: The Middle School Schedule

Organizing time in the middle school follows the same mandate to provide a unique and transitional approach as does every other component of the exemplary middle school. Since the program of the elementary school and the high school differ from each other, and from the program in between, it should be no surprise that the methods of organizing the day differ as well. The middle school schedule attempts to lead from that of the elementary school to that of the high school, while reflecting the special program provided for the students in the middle grades. Figure 8.1 (page 366) illustrates the character of the three time frames.

In the elementary schools known to many of us, the self-contained classroom unit remains the predominant mode of teacher organization, with students allocated accordingly. The elementary classroom teacher often makes almost completely unilateral decisions as to what will be studied, when, by whom, under what circumstances, and with what processes. One teacher working alone makes the decisions which shape the day. As a consequence, time in the elementary school is organized to facilitate that model. Each teacher works with a large block of time, stretching from the beginning until the end of each day. With just a few interruptions from special teachers and a mandatory lunchtime, most elementary teachers are free to determine the day's schedule entirely on their own. Indeed, it is difficult to imagine a school organized around the model of the self-contained classroom that was not organized this way.

At the other end of the K–12 continuum, the high school has a very different program to schedule, with a completely different set of restraints. The high school program, organized around the departmentalized arrangement of teachers emphasizing specialization, is usually so large and so complex that efficiency and economy are prime objectives. With as many as several thousand students and teachers to account for, and an amazing array of specialized courses and electives to offer, the most efficient process for organizing time usually turns out to be one which requires centralized control. Individual teachers usually have very little to say about the schedule, since most of these decisions must come from the office. The result is that the school day is most often divided into equal or nearly equal segments called periods, controlled by the office, with student and teacher movement determined by the automatic ringing of bells. While some schools have experimented with modular schedules, featuring a widely varying schedule based on smaller units of time and different cycles, most high schools seem to have kept quite closely to the six-, seven- or eight-period day.

The middle school, attempting to accommodate a program which meets the needs of its students, offers a schedule that may be thought of as a compromise between the large single block of time in the elementary school and the smaller periods of the high school. In the exemplary middle school, the organization of

ELEMENTARY SCHOOL	MIDDLE SCHOOL	HIGH SCHOOL

Figure 8.1   **Organizing Time in Elementary, Middle and High Schools**

time attempts to facilitate the basic organizational framework of the school. And, since in the middle school this is the interdisciplinary team organization, it is the character of this component of the program that determines the nature of the scheduling process.

While there are several varieties of scheduling that are appropriate for the middle school, in order for the schedule to be congruent with the program it serves, it must accommodate the team organization. Not one teacher working alone and making all the decisions about scheduling his or her students; not a massive schedule determined by the office and operated by the bell without any teacher input. The middle school schedule is designed to be controlled by groups of teachers organized into teams in collaboration with the office, a unique and transitional type of schedule for a special type of program. Teachers from several different subject areas, working together to create and operate a comprehensive academic program for the students they serve, need a schedule with flexibility and structure. Any schedule which removes the team's ability to manipulate the daily time frame to suit the objectives of their planning is clearly inappropriate for the middle school.

The Eight Cardinal Principles of the Middle School Master Schedule

With the complexity of the exemplary middle school program in mind, many leaders believe, quite rightly, that effective scheduling is the *sine qua non* of the middle school; without that skill, all of the other efforts to design and implement a quality program will be for naught. Naturally, then, it becomes important to distill the experience of effective schedulers from the last decade or so. If one were to catalog a set of "cardinal principles" of master scheduling from the experiences of middle school leaders in the eighties and nineties, those which follow would compete for high priority in any set.

One: Scheduling is like budgeting; prioritizing is essential

A schedule is like a budget, used to maximize the opportunities for the balanced satisfaction of basic needs and luxury items. Just as few human beings are able to satisfy all their wants and needs in terms of the financial budget, it is often impossible to acquire enough time and to apportion it wisely enough to accomplish all of the possibilities a school program can muster. Choices must be made and priorities must be set.

First among the priorities is a schedule which molds itself to the other priorities set by the school staff, rather than forcing those items into a schedule designed for the high school. The school schedule is a means to an end, although for those given the responsibility of designing the master schedule, it may often seem like an end in itself. Unfortunately, because many of the administrators who become middle school principals have done their apprenticeships as assistant principals at high schools or have served as principals of traditional junior high schools prior to their designation as middle schools, these administrators frequently have little acquaintance with scheduling options other than the seven-period day as it is worked out in those junior and senior high schools. Consequently, the middle school sometimes has been forced into a schedule that is quite like the proverbial Procrustean bed, being stretched to fit an unnatural form.

The primary objective of the middle school schedule is to facilitate the operation of those school programs determined to be advantageous in the education of middle school students. Interdisciplinary team organization, exploratory curriculum plans, advisor-advisee programs, alternative forms of grouping students on a schoolwide basis—all these programs must be organized into an effective schedule. Sometimes priorities which are imposed from outside the school or the district make even the incorporation of these items seem like a luxury.

Priorities emerge from values, and values are the results of a philosophy, a sense of purpose, a commitment to a certain set of goals to be accomplished. Obviously, these will be different, in some way, in virtually every school, even though each middle level school ought to begin with a commitment to responding to the characteristics and needs of older children and early adolescents. At Broomfield Heights Middle School (Broomfield, Colorado) in the late 1980s, the priorities for consideration in the development of the master schedule were the following:

1. An advisory program will be held at least fifteen minutes daily.
2. Common planning time for teams of teachers will be allotted.
3. All teachers will be members of only one academic team.
4. There will be no more than 150 students per team.
5. Students will be able to choose exploratory classes.
6. A co-curricular program will exist.
7. Electives and academic classes will be scheduled on a trimester basis.
8. Multiage grouping will be permitted in electives.
9. There will be reasonable times for lunch periods.
10. A school-within-a-school model will be feasible.
11. The schedule will permit a pilot team of two grades, seven and eight.

The scheduling team at Broomfield Heights Middle School committed itself to attending to these priorities as the process of schedule development continued, and to achieving as many as possible, starting at the top of the list and working down. The best schedule for that year, at that school, would be the one which permitted the maximum number of priorities to be included. Of course, the priorities of any one school will be different from other schools, and priorities at a particular school will be different from year to year. Starting the scheduling process without a clear sense of the priorities, however, may introduce a fatal flaw at the outset. Just like an automobile tire which goes flat far down the road from the point at which the leak began, the scheduling process can suffer, in the end, from confused or conflicting priorities which were unresolved at the beginning of the process.

Just because scheduling priorities are not publicly listed as such does not mean that such priorities do not exist. Too often, we have worked with school administrators who have claimed to be unable to implement one program or another (e.g., pure interdisciplinary teams) because of "scheduling difficulties." In many cases, the difficulties experienced by these administrators are found to be tied to unannounced but very real scheduling priorities. When certain priority programs from earlier years are assumed to continue unchanged, and these assumptions are unspoken, the hidden priorities skew the scheduling process in very unsatisfying directions. When programs for special small groups, in particular, are allowed to assume priority in the curriculum, then they will also assume priority in the schedule. When gifted and talented programs, journalism, or athletic activities are placed at the top of the school philosophy, in a spoken or unspoken way, they must be satisfied first when it comes to scheduling.

Satisfactory scheduling processes depend upon the open, public, and honest discussion of school curriculum philosophy and the establishment of priorities in the same way. Schedules always reflect the school philosophy, the real school philosophy.

Table 8.1 (page 370) is an example of the schedule (1990–91) which emerged from the philosophical/programmatic consensus among the staff members of Broomfield Heights Middle School, a school of nearly 900 students, grades 6–8. Demographically, Broomfield is a suburban community located midway between Denver and Boulder. The school entered the 1990s with a firm philosophical consensus achieved by a combination of spirited leadership and dedicated professionalism in the classroom. That consensus at Broomfield Heights Middle School includes an advisory program, interdisciplinary teams, exploratory curriculum, a block schedule with common planning time, and a belief in heterogeneous grouping: the basic foundation components of an exemplary middle school design.

As one can see from studying the left side of the schedule, it is both a block schedule and a seven-period day, as are many schedules of exemplary middle schools. This combination offers stability and structure while preserving the flexibility so desirable when it is required. The day begins with a twenty-minute advisory time, called "Reach." Each grade level is divided into two interdisciplinary team organizations; each team is named (e.g., Blue Flames, Jetsons). The sixth grade academic block lasts from 8:19 a.m. until 12:52, with time out for lunch. Similar blocks are constructed for the seventh and eighth grade teams.

Not quite so obvious in the master schedule is the strong commitment to heterogeneous grouping at Broomfield Heights Middle School. In the sixth grade, where teacher-subject specialization is less, teachers can group and regroup their own students without much reference to the master schedule. In the seventh and eighth grades, the only ability grouping option included is one

Table 8.1   Broomfield Heights Middle School Master Schedule

Time	Pd.	6th grade: Blue Flame	6th grade: F-16 Fighting Falcons	7th grade: Thunderbolts	7th grade: Rolling Thunderbolts	7th grade: Phalanx	8th grade: Legal Eagles	8th grade: Jetsons
7:55–8:15	0	REACH Advisory Period						
8:19–9:07	1	Lang. Arts / Science / Reading / Social Studies / Math	Math	Lang. Arts / Science / Geography · Math · Elective	Lang. Arts / Science / Geography · Math · Elective	Lang. Arts / Science / Geography · Math · Elective	P.E./Health · Math · Elective	Science / Lang. Arts / American Studies · Math · Elective
9:11–9:55	2	Team	Science / Social Studies / Lang. Arts / Reading · Team	Math (H) · Math · Elective	Math · Elective	Math (H) · Elective	Lang. Arts / Science / American Studies · Math · Elective	P.E./Health
9:59–10:43	3	Team	Team	Math · Elective	Math · Elective	P.E./Health	Math (H) · Elective · Math · Elective	Math (H) · Elective · Math · Elective
10:47–11:17	Lunch	Lunch	Lunch	Team	Lunch	Team	Team	Team
11:21–12:04	4	Team	Team	Team	Team	Math · Elective · Math · Elective	Math · Elective · Math · Elective	Math · Elective · Math · Elective
11:34–12:04		Team	Team	Lunch	P.E./Health	Lunch	Lunch	Lunch
12:08–12:52	5	Team	Team	Team · P.E./Health	Team	Team	Team	Team
12:56–1:40	6	Art / Industrial Arts · P.E. · Mini-Society / Computing / Foreign Cultures · Music / Band	Music / Band / Orchestra	Team · Math (H) · Elective	Team · Math · Elective	Team · Math · Elective	Team · Math · Elective	Team · Math · Elective
1:44–2:30	7	Music / Band · P.E.	Mini-Society / Home Economics / Art / Computing / Foreign Cultures	Team · Math · Elective	Team · Math · Elective	Team · Math · Elective	Team · Math · Elective	Team · Math · Elective

high-level math group on each team (labeled H). This is achieved without grouping the students all day long by dividing each team into two groups of about 75 students. On the Rolling Thunderbolts, for example, one half of the team (seventy-five students) takes language arts, science, and geography, while the other half takes mathematics and two electives. This is reversed during the afternoon. A particular student might, if he/she was an able math student, have the following schedule on most days:

Period 1: Language Arts
Period 2: Science
Period 3: Geography
Period 4: Elective
Period 5: P.E./Health
Period 6: High Math
Period 7: Elective

Not all able mathematics students travel together all day; this one mathematics class is really the only time they are grouped for instruction.

Table 8.2 (page 372) provides another look at the schedule for Broomfield Heights Middle School for the 1990–91 year. Individual teacher assignments are obvious for those on interdisciplinary teams. Upper and Lower designations refer to upstairs and downstairs, not ability groups. Three teams eat lunch at once. The lower part of the figure reveals the planning time available for teams at each grade level. Table 8.3 (page 373) rounds out the scheduling picture, providing the individual schedules for teachers in physical education and exploratory areas.

Two: The objective of the middle school schedule is instructional responsiveness

In addition to accommodating the essentials of an effective middle school program, newer attempts at scheduling usually offer several other reasons for their use. Chief among these appeals is that the more flexible types of scheduling, those which allow teachers in teams to influence the process, avoid the necessity of giving equal time to unequal subjects. Within the acceptable options for middle school scheduling, all give teachers on the team the opportunity to make judgments about how much time should be given to each of the subjects under their jurisdiction, considering the characteristics of the students in their charge. The proper middle school schedule also allows school boards and other district policy setting groups to mandate greater time and attention to be given to certain subjects, like reading and mathematics, with the resulting lower priority to the others.

Effective middle school schedules permit teachers to vary the time given to different subjects on separate days. A team may decide, for example, to devote the first half of every day for an entire week to a review of basic math skills prior

Table 8.2 Broomfield Heights Middle School—1990–1991 Master Schedule

TEACHER SCHEDULE BY SUBJECT/TEAM

SUBJECTS: * A/B ■ LUNCH HOUR

	GRADE 6 ——— UPPER TEAM			GRADE 6 –LOWER				7TH GRADE — LOWER			7TH GRADE - UPPER			8TH GRADE — UPPER			8TH GRADE–LOWER		
	LA	SS	MAT-READ	LA	SCI	SS	READ	LA	SCI	GEOG MATH	LA	SCI	GEOG MATH	LA	SCI	SS	MATH	LA	SCI	SS
0 REACH	—	—	—	—	—	—	—	—	—	—	—	—	—	—	—	—	—	—	—	—
1	LA	SCI	HM	READ	TEAM PLANNING ————			LA	SCI	GEOG MATH	LA	SCI	GEOG MATH	PLAN	PLAN	PLAN	PLAN	LA	SCI	SS
2	PLAN	PLAN	PLAN	HM	HM	HM	HM	LA	SCI	GEOG MATH	PLAN	PLAN	PLAN	LA	SCI	SS	HM	LA	SCI	SS
3	LA	SCI	MAT-READ	LA	SCI	SS	READ	PLAN	PLAN	PLAN	LA	SCI	GEOG MATH	LA	SCI	SS	MAT-	LA	SCI	SS
4	LA	SCI	MAT-READ	LA	SCI	SS	READ	LA	SCI	GEOG MATH	LA	SCI	GEOG MATH	LA	SCI	SS	MATH	BASE	PLAN	BASE
A/B	AL	AL	AL	AL	AL	AL	AL	AL	AL	AL	BL	BL	BL	BL	BL	BL	BL	BL	BL	BL
5	LA	SCI	MAT-READ	LA	SCI	SS	READ	LA	SCI	GEOG MATH	LA	SCI	GEOG MATH	LA	SCI	SS	TEAM PLANNING			
6	LA	SCI	MAT-READ	PLAN	PLAN	PLAN	PLAN	LA	SCI	GEOG MATH	LA	SCI	GEOG MATH	LA	SCI	SS	MAT-	BASE	MAT- MATH	
7	TEAM PLANNING ————			LA	SCI	SS	READ	LA	SCI	GEOG HM	LA	SCI	GEOG HM	LA	SCI	SS	MAT-	BASE	MAT- MATH	

BLOCK SCHEDULE 1990–91

PER	6TH GRADE	7TH GRADE	8TH GRADE
0 REACH			
1	PLANNING		
2	PLANNING	PLANNING	PLANNING
3			
4			
5			
6	TEAM PLANNING	TEAM PLANNING	
7	TEAM PLANNING		

' OF STUDENTS ■   140   116   145   140   150   90

Table 8.3   Broomfield Heights Middle School Elective Schedule

SUBJECT: PERIOD	PE/HEALTH	ORCHESTRA	BAND	CHOIR	FOR. LANG.	ART	BUSINESS	COMPUTER	LIFE MGT.	IND. TECH.	DRAMA
ZERO	REACH		REACH	REACH	REACH	REACH	REACH	REACH	REACH	REACH	
ONE	8TH GRADE	ELEMENTARY	ELEMENTARY	X	6TH EXPLO	6TH EXPLO	6TH EXPLO	6TH EXPLO	PLAN	6TH EXPLO	HS
TWO	7TH GRADE	ELEMENTARY	ELEMENTARY	X	6TH EXPLO	6TH EXPLO	6TH EXPLO X	6TH EXPLO	6TH EXPLO	X	HS
THREE	7TH GRADE	HIGH SCHOOL	7TH – BAND I	PLAN	PLAN	X	PLAN	X	PLAN	X	HS
OUR	PLANNING	8TH ORCH	8TH –BAND II	CONCERT	X	PLAN	X	X	X	PLAN	PLAN
IVE	8TH GRADE	7TH ORCH	7TH – BAND	X	X	X	X	PLAN	X	X	X
IX	SIXTH GRADE	6TH ORCH	6TH – BAND	6TH EXPLO	X	X	X	X	X	X	X
EVEN	SIXTH GRADE	6TH ORCH	6TH – BAND		X	X	X	X	X	X	X

to the administering of standardized achievement tests. Another team might decide to teach a thematic unit that required a totally different schedule for as long as four to six weeks. Or, one teacher may simply request a few additional minutes to complete a lesson on a particular day. Good schedules, tuned to team decision making, permit these and many other modifications of the time assigned to each subject in the curriculum.

The school schedule, when designed effectively, permits the use of variable instructional strategies as well. Teams can manage their time to accommodate large group functions, laboratory experiments, individualized and independent study, or regular and small group classes. When a particular subject or skill requires a special method or grouping, the schedule permits it. The properly designed schedule can be thought of as an educational blueprint similar in many ways to the architect's work in preparation for the construction of a new building; it arranges for a variety of instructional opportunities but mandates none.

Schedules that offer a greater selection of academic opportunities to students, offer unstructured time when desired, increase teacher influence on school programs, and simply break the monotony of the traditional daily period schedule are now much more easily implemented. Since the middle school removes many of the objections raised by those who were threatened by a real or imagined challenge from the hourly requirements of the high school's Carnegie Unit, college preparation, and the standardization required for such accounting simply no longer govern the design of the middle school day. Having gone beyond the grip of the computerized schedule, many administrators are discovering that effective time-designing can happen with lower cost, fewer irrevocable errors, increased options, and greater flexibility.

The 1991 schedule at East Cobb Middle School in Marietta, Georgia (Table 8.4) is a variation of a schedule for the middle schools in that county which has operated effectively there since the early 1970s. In fact, educators in Cobb County were among the first known to us to implement comprehensive exemplary middle schools during those years. The continued excellence of the middle school program in Cobb County, twenty years later, is a testimony not only to the persistent commitment of middle school educators there, but to the effectiveness of the components as they implemented them, including the schedule. The East Cobb Middle schedule, with its blocks of time, provides much needed flexibility to teams of teachers. The schedule rotation each quarter (twelve weeks) is, we think, an ongoing feature in Cobb County that has been copied in too few other middle schools. Sixth graders spend their first twelve weeks with their academic time in the morning, and their physical education and exploratory time in the afternoon. This, educators there testify, provides a much smoother transition into the middle school for those young adolescents. By the end of the year, however, these students have had several changes, to which they adapt nicely after the first twelve weeks of introductions and orientations. The rotating schedule also gives every teacher and every student the best and

Table 8.4 East Cobb Middle School Rotation of Schedule

		1	2	3	4	5	6	7
FALL QUARTER	7	Reading	Academic	Lunch	Planning	-------	Academic	Academic
	6	Academic	Reading	Academic	Lunch	Academic	Planning	-------
	8	Planning	-------	Reading	Academic	Lunch	Academic	Academic
	EXPL	8th EXPL	-------	Lunch/Planning	7th EXPL	-------	6th EXPL	-------
WINTER QUARTER	7	Planning	-------	Reading	Academic	Lunch	Academic	Academic
	6	Reading	Academic	Lunch	Planning	-------	Academic	Academic
	8	Academic	Reading	Academic	Lunch	Academic	Planning	-------
	EXPL	7th EXPL	-------	Lunch/Planning	6th EXPL	-------	8th EXPL	-------
SPRING QUARTER	7	Academic	Reading	Academic	Lunch	Academic	Planning	-------
	6	Planning	-------	Reading	Academic	Lunch	Academic	Academic
	8	Reading	Academic	Lunch	Planning	-------	Academic	Academic
	EXPL	6th EXPL	-------	Lunch/Planning	8th EXPL	-------	7th EXPL	-------

worst of the schedule throughout the year; all have the best and the worst lunch-times, all have physical education in the morning and then in the afternoon. No one can complain about getting the least effective schedule, or boast about the best. All share equally in what the schedule has to offer; it has been working this way in Cobb County for twenty successful years.

Three: Beware of the war between the six- and the seven-period day

There is no right way to organize the middle school day, except insofar as the schedule facilitates or interferes with the program of the school. We believe that a seven-period day often can, if designed correctly, accommodate the programs of a middle school equally as well as a block or a modular schedule, and it is unnecessary for the staff of a school to feel either self-satisfied with one type of schedule or ashamed with another. The question is not "What kind of schedule is best?" The right question is "How can we schedule our day to facilitate the priorities we have established?" Misunderstanding this basic concept has led to scheduling "wars" that are bitter and divisive.

All schedules, no matter what variety, are arbitrary divisions of the total school day into smaller units. The only major differences are in the size of the smaller units and who influences or controls the manipulation of those units. In the middle school, the size of the unit is more varied than it often is in either the elementary school or the high school. Thinking of the division of time units on a continuum may help. The essence of scheduling wisdom is to manipulate some chosen series of units into a schedule that allows groups of teachers to operate in the most effective manner. As will be seen, blocks, periods, and modules are interchangeable. That is, modules can be used to construct blocks and periods of time, periods of time can be combined into blocks, and can be as small as a module, and so on. The idea that one of these varieties of schedules is, in and of itself, superior to the others is simply false.

Any way in which time is divided is arbitrary. Whether one chooses periods, modules, or blocks, the most important decisions will deal with assigning fixed times to the priorities which emerge in discussions of curriculum priorities. School-day time, in whatever pieces it is organized, must be divided between necessities and so-called luxuries. Even among the requirements, there are often more than a comfortable number of such necessities, each clamoring for its share of time during the day. Each luxury has its spirited advocates, enthusiastically claiming that the subject or topic is actually a necessity, and ought to be required of all middle school students on a daily basis. This shortage of time, compared to the plethora of possible subjects which might be included in the day, causes a number of serious conflicts for middle school leaders.

Among the first rough edges likely to abrade decision-makers in the nineties, when they confront the task of scheduling the new middle school program, is the squeeze which comes from attempting to combine the former elementary curriculum, in place in the sixth grades, with the traditional secondary one which has been used in the seventh and eighth grades. Elementary curriculum tends to include more subjects in the week than the secondary program, each for a relatively shorter period of time. The nature of requirements in the elementary school also tends to be different from the traditional secondary program; necessities in the curriculum tend to be described differently by the secondary specialists. When curriculum developers from each group sit down to develop the new middle school curriculum and to assign time frames to each component, the sparks begin to fly.

In particular, disagreements tend to arise around the perceptions of what are and what are not requirements, absolute necessities for daily instruction. In the elementary school, reading and physical education tend to be viewed as requirements. Reading, on a daily basis, often constitutes the greatest single use of time in the elementary school schedule. Physical education, on the other hand, tends to be required but to be offered less frequently during the week. Specialists in physical education may work with sixth grade students twice a week or so, with regular classroom teachers filling in with recess periods devoted primarily to exercise. Health education is also a factor in the elementary curriculum, although less clearly defined.

In many districts in the 1980s, the move to middle school meant that reading had been removed from the high priority it assumed in the elementary 6th grade program. This has been particularly likely to happen in districts that have maintained a six-period day in the middle school as a holdover from the former junior high school. Offering both reading and language arts as separate daily subjects, along with physical education, mathematics, social studies, and science, along with an exploratory course like band, adds up to seven separate subjects requiring seven separate time periods. Perhaps because there are almost always a full complement of tenured physical education teachers already on board in many new middle schools, the decision to eliminate reading as a separate subject often becomes the way to resolve the situation. Few school district decision makers, however, find appealing the prospect of having to admit, publicly, that the move to the middle school eliminated reading in the 6th grade, opening themselves to the charge that the move to middle school involved a softening of attention to the basics. Parents and community members, especially school board members, are unlikely to support the reasoning behind such a decision. Then why not move from a six period day to one having seven or eight periods, thus permitting the inclusion of all the desirable subjects? This option, it turns out, is more easily considered than implemented.

In the typical school district, changing from six to seven periods at the middle level means, for example, that the subjects previously taught in the junior high school would typically receive about twenty-five minutes less attention per week, or more than three weeks less of daily instruction than in the junior high school. Changing from a fifty-five minute period to a fifty minute period will do just that. To do this is to risk alienating the most content-oriented, and often the most influential teachers, in the junior high school, and to subject the new middle school organization to charges of being soft on academics, a situation not uncommon in dozens of school districts in the last decade. When the staff development programs are aimed at touting the advantages of the new middle school program, angry charges from the most content-oriented teachers can puncture the most effective training efforts.

Changing to seven periods a day also means that the teacher's day will be very different. It means, for example, that there will be twenty-five minutes less planning time for the average teacher, unless teachers are given two planning periods, out of seven, instead of the traditional (in many districts) one planning period in six. Hard-working teachers are unlikely to support the prospect of losing the equivalent of three weeks of planning time annually, in addition to having their class hours trimmed; it may prompt union-filed grievances.

Asking teachers to teach six shorter periods in place of five longer ones is a difficult proposition. One would expect that, in light of the attention span of early adolescent students, teachers would greet the prospect of shorter classes with glee. Not so. Some teachers argue instead that increasing the number of periods while shortening the average length still amounts to a considerable increase in the preparation and planning necessary to teach the added section. This is true, teachers stress, even with the same subject at the same grade level.

There are other objections. Some teachers believe that just getting a class going one additional time each day adds to the work load. Many teachers in special areas (e.g., industrial arts, science, home economics, physical education) also argue, with some merit we believe, that the reduced class time means that their students spend significantly less time in actual learning activity; the subject requires the same amount of set up and take down time, regardless of the length of the class period. Shortening the length of class periods has, potentially, an even more controversial correlation. At the risk of alienating some teachers, however, we believe that there is another reason why teachers often resist the change to shorter periods: It is easier to teach, less physically exhausting, when the class periods are fewer and longer. We believe observations in many middle grade schools would indicate that, as a rule, the longer the daily class period lasts, the more time many teachers spend doing something other than formally directing instruction. Longer periods increase the likelihood that teachers will devote class time to seatwork for students, while the teacher sits down behind the desk, resting, or otherwise occupied in other legitimate educational activity. In a school day comprised of thirty-minute class periods, there is absolutely no time to waste, and teachers must feel compelled to engage in instruction from the moment the students walk in the door to the moment they leave. Conversely, in schools where the periods are, say 55 minutes long, it is sometimes difficult for observers to find many classrooms in which teachers are standing up and engaged in instruction during the last 10–15 minutes of the period. The longer the period, the more time used for purposes other than formal instruction.

We do not believe that this is often the case because a middle or junior high school teacher is lazy. No one works much harder, not in the education world. Teaching for thirty minutes and then moving to an alternative activity may happen, in fact, because the teacher is tuned in to the nature of early adolescents and believes that it is difficult to go beyond a certain point without losing them. It is even possible that such ideas have been advanced at workshops we have conducted. But research on engaged learning time is very clear: seatwork is a very vulnerable activity and not nearly so likely to produce learning as is direct involvement in instruction with the teacher. So the result, whatever the reason, is likely to be less academic achievement for the students. If it is true that, when class periods are shorter, teachers actually spend a greater portion of class time engaged in instruction, this is surely a point in favor of a seven- or eight-period day. If it exhausts teachers, that argues for fewer and longer periods.

What if teachers had ninety minutes of planning time per day, instead of fifty? Changing to the seven period day, and avoiding the above problems by giving teachers at least two planning periods per day instead of one brings its own difficulties. First, it may cost several million dollars a year, in larger school districts, to hire the additional teachers who will be required. School boards may balk at that cost, and school district administrators, sensing the board's equivocation, may not be eager to engage in what could be a "career-limiting" activity by forcefully advocating such an expense.

The school board may be willing to devote a substantial increase in funds to providing a team planning period each day for academic teachers engaged in an interdisciplinary effort. In the eighties and nineties, many districts have done so—to their credit. Unfortunately, this leaves the other teachers in the building (physical education, exceptional education, and unified arts) asking serious questions about their value as professionals. Unequal amounts of planning time drives a terrible wedge into the unity of the school staff. The alternative to funding these additional teachers is to increase the average class size in the school significantly, so that teachers instruct the same number of students each day, but in five much larger class groups rather than six. The district contract may forbid it, and it is not a very popular idea in many faculty lounges.

Asking teachers to work together on interdisciplinary teams, for the increased benefit it brings to students, and to undertake all the additional planning and activity that comes with team organization, without any additional planning time takes a great deal of courage on the part of school district decision-makers. To ask it, and then to take away about a half hour of planning time a week (by asking them to teach six out of seven periods) can be foolhardy. Unfortunately, remaining with a six-period day is also likely to be less than fully satisfactory. Most American twelve-year-olds need the reading instruction that could be lost. Then, if the reading scores on subsequent standardized tests drop noticeably, school patrons may be very unhappy, and charges of neglecting the basics are sure to follow.

Retaining the six-period day may also penalize the most high-achieving students, and draw angry reactions from their often influential parents. Having successfully negotiated the basics, these students will be eagerly looking forward to options, choices, and exploration. Many will be talented musicians or artists, or those eager for an experience with a foreign language. A six-period day, presented as it usually is, leaves room for six subjects. Gifted and talented students may be dramatically restricted in the number of options they can exercise, causing their inquisitive parents to wonder about the wisdom of placing sixth graders in the middle school.

Retaining the six-period day also means that teachers on interdisciplinary teams will be torn between using the time to prepare well for their classes or meeting with their teammates for equally important but less pressing planning sessions. The team organization may suffer; it may not be able to demonstrate what it could deliver. Things may quickly end up being little different in the new middle schools than they were in the traditional secondary program. Or it may take a herculean (and short-lived) effort to make changes.

What to do? The move to a seven- or eight-period day, with funding levels which permit all professionals to have at least one period for their own lesson planning and a period for teamwide or schoolwide planning and duty, seems most reasonable. Some fortunate middle school staffs currently enjoy this arrangement, one period for planning and one period for schoolwide collaboration and responsibilities. Many secondary schools had arrangements like this years ago, and many high schools have them now. Unfortunately, what seems most reasonable may not be most reachable.

Four: Scheduling must be a collaborative effort

The above discussion should make clear that the process of time-budgeting which results in a school schedule is, in many ways, a process of prioritizing. Since it is extremely rare to be able to achieve all of the priorities of all of the constituents, if it is to be successful, prioritizing must be a collaborative process, a process of maximum involvement leading to a broad consensus. It should also be clear that the final schedule will require considerable compromise from a number of stakeholders. Willingness to compromise rarely comes from situations where decisions are announced as undebatable, from the district office or the school administrative suite.

There is at least one other reason why this process must be a collaborative effort: rarely is one person skilled enough to be able to produce unilaterally the most effective master schedule for a school of a thousand or more students and teachers. Rarely can one perspective, either teaching or administration, capture all of the important concerns that should shape a middle school schedule. In fact, some middle school educators argue that few persons are able to be effective in all the necessary areas of school leadership, and that, frequently, the ability to schedule is one skill missing from the repetioire. It is also true that experience in developing schedules for elementary, high school, and junior high contributes very little to one's skill at scheduling the middle school. It may even be counterproductive. So, a scheduling team made up of a variety of people possessing necessary skills and important insights is likely to produce the most satisfactory, long-lasting product, after numerous revisions have been attempted.

Five: The schedule must be a servant, not a master

Perhaps it should be called the "servant schedule" instead of the master schedule, since the purpose of the organization of time in a middle school is to facilitate the accomplishment of other components—team organization, advisory programs, curriculum plans, planning time, and others. Consequently, the schedule must mold itself to the other priorities identified by the staff and the district, and not the reverse.

This means, among other things, that the computer services and software packages available from the central office are unlikely to meet all the needs of a particular middle school. Such services are likely to have, as their priorities, the efficient packaging and movement of faceless masses across the entire district; not an unimportant task. But, every middle school schedule is unique, or should be. It is highly desirable, as well as highly improbable, that the developers of computer scheduling packages understand the priorities of the middle school program, in general, and the priorities of a particular school. It is much more likely that the standard computer scheduling services are driven by the needs of the larger schools in the district—the high schools. Course numbers seem, sometimes, to assume greater weight in such situations than the priorities of the school staff. The computer is, of course, not an evil thing. It is simply not the answer to every middle school scheduling need.

Jacquelyn Cake, Assistant Principal for Curriculum at Westwood Middle School, in Gainesville, Florida, like many other administrators with scheduling responsibilities, has found a way to utilize the district's computer services without dismantling the middle school concept in her own school. (Westwood Middle, as we describe it elsewhere, is organized into "gradewide teams," which tends to make scheduling an easier task, but also makes teaming more difficult.) Cake uses a registration and scheduling program called "SOLSTAR" from United Computer Services, in Charlotte, North Carolina. Her scheduling tasks take her through a process that involves six or seven steps.

First, the scheduler must determine the numbers of students at each grade level, and the curriculum needs for those students. How many students, for example, will want home economics in the seventh grade, and how many sixth graders want to be in band or in an "exploratory wheel" experience instead? A letter is usually sent to elementary schools to determine the number of rising sixth graders who will need each choice, especially some choices, like instrumental music, which may have to be "rationed." Cake recommends using a waiting list process for popular classes such as band, if necessary.

Second, the scheduler gets a printout of the registration form from the appropriate clerk or assistant principal. The students' choices are entered either individually or via "mass loading" (e.g., all 6th graders take PE first period). At Westwood, since there are eight periods and an advisory time, 900 students × eight courses are entered into the computer, by student name.

Third, the scheduler translates this information into the number of sections needed for each class, usually by a formula much like that used by Elaine Lane (in an upcoming section of this chapter) where the number of students is divided by the class size to determine the number of sections which will be needed for every required daily class. At this point, one must check this information against the number of teacher units available to teach these sections, to see if the teachers available match the student needs. The question is deceptively simple: "Do I have enough teachers?" Here the scheduler, together with others, will have to make decisions about classes with small numbers, like algebra and geometry, honors sections, or different sorts of band and orchestra. If there is no natural match, then school leaders will either find more teachers, crowd more students into existing classes, or operate on a first-come, first-served basis and deny some students enrollment in classes which are overenrolled. Here is where a knowledge of faculty preferences comes into play, since a teacher may say, "I'll take four large classes in Algebra One and regular math, if I get an Algebra Two class with eight kids in it!"

Fourth, only after these determinations have been made does one begin with the formal design of the master schedule. Here is the point where one runs what is known as a "conflict matrix", which determines the number of students whose schedules, if nothing is done, will be in conflict (they may be assigned to several "singleton" sections which are offered at the same time). The operative question, then, is "Where are my biggest conflicts?" Singletons and doubletons are scheduled first, with part time teachers and other known constraints dealt with now. As an example, if Algebra is going to be offered during the first and second periods, it will not work well to have the only section of Spanish One scheduled at the same time. Compensatory reading programs and compensatory math programs, for the same reason, can not easily be offered at the same period for the same grade level. Cake advises schedulers to work in the special compensatory classes as early as possible, although it will often be difficult to do so. Remember that, in a school of 900 students, during any one period, the scheduler must accommodate those 900 students, so naturally small classes have to be balanced with larger ones.

Once these difficulties have been dealt with, as successfully as possible, it is time to schedule the planning times for teachers on interdisciplinary teams. Actually, these planning times can often be kept constant from year to year, building the rest of the schedule around them. It is at this point, also where special features must be added. For example, in the 6th grade at Westwood Middle School, social studies and science classes are "blocked" so that all students in one teacher's social studies classes have the same teacher in science. This provides much flexibility for the teachers as they attempt to work together, integrate the curriculum, and so on. In the seventh grade at Westwood, another special feature is that language arts and reading are taught by one teacher to the same group of twenty-five to thirty students for a double period each day, providing a ninety-minute block of time which works remarkably better. The scheduler tells the computer to "tie" the two classes together to achieve the block of time. This is also necessary for semester classes that contain the same students, but in different semesters, like an exploratory class which lasts for one semester and is replaced by physical education for the same students the next semester (during the same period of the day).

Fifth, enter the master schedule into the computer. Put in the teachers and their numbers (e.g., social security, certification number, etc.). Then, for each period, put in course and number, plus the section number in a way that does not produce a duplication, since many state funding formulas are tied to student attendance and monitored through these registration data. Enter the maximum number of students in each section (whether it is a semester, a year-long course), identify the period, the room number, and the teacher number. For every teacher, there must be (at schools like Westwood) eight entries (their classes, including planning times). Every night, the computer program provides a "feedback run" which can be examined the next day to determine progress and difficulties remaining.

Sixth, build the data into a scheduling program which will schedule students into the classes you have designated according to the choices they have made. The computer program will provide a printout that tells you which students could not be scheduled and why (e.g., class load limits, conflict with a singleton, etc.). Transfer students, coming in from other schools, must also be anticipated, and experience in schools known to us indicates that transfer students who come to school for the first time on the first day of school are frequently remedial students who will need singleton compensatory sections. It is also at this step where teams of teachers can take over the task of scheduling the students on their team, rather than utilizing a computer scheduling program any further.

Now the schedule, and the needs of individual students and teachers, must again come to the fore. The schedule must be "massaged and massaged" says Cake, so that individual needs can be met. For example, in a school with a number of compensatory classes, it is good to spread out those classes through the day so that students don't experience so many back-to-back classes together that tracking becomes a worse problem than it already is. If ability groups are involved, Cake's advice is "always change kids up, when changing their place in the schedule, in terms of ability groups, rather than down, since they almost always do well and the higher sections can hold more students."

If a computer program is used, teachers and teams who want to change students—say, after the first week of school—must bring those changes to the scheduler for entry. This usually entails dozens of hours of rescheduling time, where the assistant principal or other scheduler works closely with teachers to move students who do not belong together, awkward imbalances in the size or demographics of classes, and so on, must be corrected individually, even with the use of a computer program for that purpose. Many hours of the first three weeks of school are used for this purpose and lamentably so, we think, since an assistant principal for curriculum ought to be able to be doing other things at this critical point of the year. Schools which are able to employ scheduling clerks may enjoy quite a luxury.

Six: Teachers can also make important scheduling decisions

The experience of the last twenty years indicates that teachers have the desire, and can learn the required skills, to exert a significant influence on the school schedules within which they must operate. Provided with a team of students and assignments for lunch, physical education, and exploratory times, teams of academic teachers can make fundamental decisions about how the remainder of the day should be organized.

At Sarasota Middle School in Sarasota, Florida (see Table 8.5), teachers on nine separate academic teams have assigned times for advisory periods (Prime Time, 9:00–9:30 for the entire school), lunch, physical education, and "Explo" (exploratory courses). Within these restrictions, the teams decide the design of the blocks of time remaining for "Basic Skills." A relatively large school of 1,200 students, the staff demonstrates that empowering teachers to make such decisions results in more effective instructional planning and feelings of greater efficacy among the teachers.

At Wakulla Middle School (Table 8.6 page 386) in Wakulla County, Florida, the school leadership places even more confidence in the teaching teams. After firmly fixing the times for physical education, lunch, and exploratory classes for each team, the principal empowers the teachers to decide when particular classes will be taught, how students will be grouped within the team, and which subjects will be taught by each teacher. Teachers at Wakulla Middle have the maximum amount of leverage in the decisions that affect their immediate professional lives at school, especially regarding the schedule.

At Wakulla Middle, the administration goes through a series of steps each year to make certain they deliver a balanced group to each team and house, making later scheduling easier for teachers and administrators. The process begins in the late spring when they receive the information about rising 6th graders from the elementary schools. Students are identified according to a number of criteria: ESE status, math and reading recommendations from 5th grade teachers, "alternative education" recommendations, retentions, teachers comments, special requests, and student identification by gender and race, and socioeconomic status. Each sixth grade team, and homerooms within the team, then is set up to receive the same number of students according to these criteria.

Table 8.5   Schedule Sarasota Middle School 1988-89

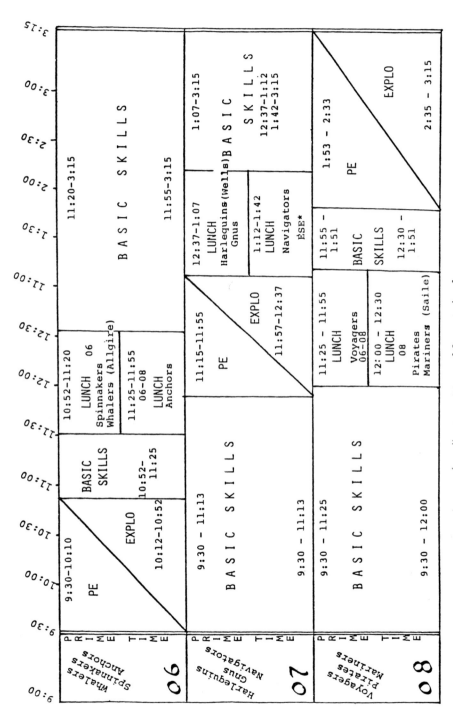

*ESE – LLD, EMH, SLD –self contained
            EH –self contained

Table 8.6   Wakulla Middle School Master Schedule 1989-90

First Bell - 7:40
Tardy Bell - 7:45
Homeroom - 7:45 - 8:00

HOMEROOM	1 (50)	2 (45)	3 (45)	4 (45)	5 (45)	LUNCH	6 (45)	7 (45)
	8:00	8:50	9:35	10:20	11:05	12:40	1:25	2:10
6N 122-Worrell 124-Williams	U.A.	P.E.	ACADEMICS	ACADEMICS	ACADEMICS	11:40-12:05	ACADEMICS	ACADEMICS
6E 131-Coyle 132-Allen 134-Rosser 6AE-Greene	P.E.	U.A.	ACADEMICS	ACADEMICS	ACADEMICS	11:40-12:05	ACADEMICS	ACADEMICS
6S 144-Douglas 145-Robbins	U.A.	P.E.	ACADEMICS	ACADEMICS	ACADEMICS	11:40-12:05 PETERSON	ACADEMICS	ACADEMICS
7N 125-Rodgers 126-Lashley 121-DuBois	ACADEMICS	ACADEMICS	P.E. (CHORUS)	U.A. (BAND)	ACADEMICS	12:10-12:35	ACADEMICS	ACADEMICS
7E 135-Hutchins 136-Freeman 140-Clemons	ACADEMICS	ACADEMICS	U.A. (CHORUS)	P.E. (BAND)	ACADEMICS	12:10-12:35	ACADEMICS	ACADEMICS
7S 146-Edwards 150-Scott	ACADEMICS	ACADEMICS	U.A./P.E. (CHORUS)	U.A/P.E (BAND)	ACADEMICS	12:10-12:35 SERVIES	ACADEMICS	ACADEMICS
8N 127-Zapata 130-Lemon 129-Whitesell	ACADEMICS	ACADEMICS	ACADEMICS	ACADEMICS	ACADEMICS	11:10-11:35	P.E. (CHORUS)	U.A. (BAND)
8E 137-Mitchell 139-Thornton	ACADEMICS	ACADEMICS	ACADEMICS	ACADEMICS	ACADEMICS	11:10-11:35	U.A. (CHORUS)	P.E. (BAND)
8S 147-Glisson 149-Thomas 8AE-Webster	ACADEMICS	ACADEMICS	ACADEMICS	ACADEMICS	ACADEMICS	11:10-11:35	U.A./P.E. (CHORUS)	U.A./P.E. (BAND)

Sixth grade teams are assigned a PE period, a Unified Arts period, and lunch; the rest is up to the team. For seventh and eighth graders, the process is much the same, except that compromises must be accepted in the assignment of band and chorus students. The teachers at Wakulla then decide how the responsibility for the curriculum will be divided among the teachers on the team; every teacher may teach every subject, or they may specialize according to their strengths and preferences. A schedule for academic instruction within the team is devised. Students are grouped in whatever configurations the teachers on that team believe will promote the most successful learning, for that particular team of students. Other teams in the same school may group students very differently, or arrange responsibilities for the curriculum in dissimilar ways. The professionals closest to the action—the teachers on the team—make these decisions.

A look at the master schedule for Wakulla Middle School (Table 8.6) will also illustrate another important point: the uselessness of advocating a particular way of organizing time in the middle level school. Would you describe the schedule at W.M.S. as a seven-period day, or as a block schedule? The answer is "Yes," just as it is at Broomfield Heights. It is both, depending upon the teachers and how they choose to arrange the time. Each subject can be arranged in its own period and taught unvaryingly through every day for the entire year. Or, the teachers can use their planning time to create interdisciplinary thematic units which last for days, weeks, or months. It's up to them, and the actual use of time tends to be a function of the planning time and the skills each team possesses.

The Sarasota Middle School block schedule (Table 8.5) also demonstrates the compromises necessary to arrive at a constellation of satisfactory priorities. Almost all teachers have approximately eighty minutes of planning time (when their students are being taught by others); more time than they had as junior high teachers, but less than the two planning periods (ninety minutes) that might be found in more financially fortunate districts. Class periods are shorter than in most middle level schools (forty minutes for separate classes), providing a challenge to special classes like physical education, science, home economics, and others. But because of teacher control, it is possible to save time between classes. At this school, this schedule reflects the consensus that has been developed through involvement and effort.

Mary Lou Moore, recently retired as principal of Sarasota Middle School, writes in the school handbook prepared for visitors and inquirers:

> Most principals have known the joys and frustrations of wrestling with the daily junior high . . . schedule. This typical 50- to 55-minute period schedule allows little flexibility and certainly causes conflict and arguments among those affected when students' choices do not fit the schedule.
>
> The effective use of time and space is the basis for the overall positive climate of the school. Use of the block schedule establishes an opportunity for flexibility, cooperation, and a more realistic view of the benefits of the middle school teaming concept.

The steps to building a block schedule center around time, space, goals, and curriculum offerings. The assumption is that many staff members work through this process with the principal. (Moore, 1988, p. 11)

Seven: Building the right master schedule is a systematic and methodical process

There are no two school schedules that are exactly alike. The most important steps in the scheduling process, it should now be obvious, are those which precede the actual design of the master schedule. Schedules are, in actuality, only a reflection of the decisions which have already been made with regard to curriculum and the instructional organization of teachers and students. Firm commitments to advisory programs, team organization, and to particular methods of grouping students will inevitably and irrevocably shape the schedule which eventually emerges.

Before launching into the final schedule development process, it should also be recognized that the outcomes will be predetermined by decisions already made about the curriculum. These curriculum decisions will influence the schedule almost as comprehensively as the decisions made about teacher and student organization. Since no school day can contain all the demands of parents, state departments of education, and so on, a considerable amount of the frustration in the final scheduling process is actually the result of pre-established curriculum priorities. Knowing how many curriculum components will comprise the basic day for each student is a crucial prerequisite to schedule development. Will reading and language arts be offered together or separately? Will there be daily physical education? Will there be an advisor-advisee program? What kind of exploratory emphasis will the curriculum offer? Will instrumental music be offered in a grade level format (e.g., sixth grade band) or skill levels (e.g., advanced band)? All of these questions, and many others, need to be answered before the final stages of developing the master schedule can begin.

Ideally, the school scheduling team will be able to make many of these decisions themselves, in collaboration with the rest of the staff. In practice, however, these decisions and many others come to the staff as givens, decided for them by others beyond the school. It may even be that the unit of time into which the school day is divided (module, block, or period) will have been previously determined along with the number of units in a daily schedule. Regardless of by whom these decisions are made, those who schedule must incorporate these data into the process. Additional decisions then will have to be made: How much passing time will be permitted between classes? What length of time will be required for each of the parts of the curriculum each day or week? Are there restrictions which arise from the nature of the school building? From the student-teacher ratio or other funding concerns? Answers to these questions, and others unique to each school, must be clearly known before scheduling can begin, otherwise barrier after barrier will arise during and after the construction of the schedule. Neophytes in the scheduling process may feel exhausted or discouraged in the face of all these prerequisites, even before they begin; but there is reason to believe that, in most situations, schedulers can emerge from the process with much of what they hoped for included in the final schedule.

Veteran schedule builders begin with equal amounts of humility and determination. Accepting that all of one's priorities can not be achieved is as important as the dogged determination to achieve them in spite of the impossible nature of the task. The objective of the scheduling process becomes the struggle to achieve as much as possible from the list of priorities with which one begins.

Building on these ideas, Mary Lou Moore followed four basic steps in constructing the master schedule at Sarasota Middle. The first, and most important step as we now see, is to establish a schoolwide philosophy which will guide the development of the schedule. At Sarasota, this distinctly student-centered philosophy is prominently displayed in the section of the handbook devoted to designing the block schedule, an important message to those who help develop the schedule and those who wish to know the rationale which supports the shape it eventually assumes. This philosophy is where the scheduling process begins.

The second step, building on the first, is to establish curriculum offerings. At Sarasota Middle School the curriculum emerges from a firm belief in the need to assist early adolescents in the process of exploration (see Table 8.5). Two separate exploratory "wheels" offer experiences in fine arts and vocational arts. In sixth and seventh grade, students are enrolled in a six-week rotation; in the eighth grade, semester and full-year electives are available. One third of the study day is comprised of physical education and exploratory classes. All students experience a daily time with their advisor and their homebase, "Prime Time," compatriots. The remainder of the academic day is devoted to basic skills. All of these priorities become embedded in the master schedule.

Step three is the establishment of teams: interdisciplinary, basic skills, exploratory, physical education, and exceptional education. This commitment to the interdisciplinary team process is exemplified in Mrs. Moore's description of the third step in the scheduling process (Moore, p. 12):

> The basic school relationship for a middle student is with his or her academic interdisciplinary team of teachers and fellow students. This team is their school family. This is where the students spend most of their school day.

The fourth step is the establishment of a room-use chart. Academic teams and others are placed so that teachers are closest to the other teachers who share the same students, rather than the same subject. This has often been true in exploratory areas, and now has become the preferred practice with academic teachers as well.

The last step at Sarasota Middle School is to establish the final block schedule. Moore cites the following advantages to the block schedule which finally emerges:

It permits advisory programs to begin the day.

All teachers have a common team planning time.

Every teacher has a lunchtime free of duties.

Physical education and exploratory classes can be shorter than basic skills classes.

Basic skills teams have the flexibility to schedule classes around the curriculum needs.

Students can be grouped and regrouped as needs change.

It allows for interdisciplinary units of study.

Moore argues that this process for designing the school master schedule is "an especially professional approach." Teams of professionals are given the opportunity to adjust for many types of activities. Time allotments can be expanded or shortened when teachers work together. The daily advisory program can be expanded or abbreviated. When teachers are empowered to control the time for instruction, "less duplication and better use of instructional time and space are possible." Time for planning is the key, says Moore.

Another gifted scheduler, Elaine Lane, former principal of Fort King Middle School in Ocala, Florida, followed a very similar methodology, successfully, for almost twenty years of developing workable middle school schedules. Lane began with the development of a school philosophy and with the establishment of curriculum priorities, just as Moore does. Priorities, at Fort King, translate into "required daily subjects."

Lane's first important determination, following the establishment of curriculum priorities, is the number of teachers needed to offer all of the required daily subjects. As a scheduling question it would be "How many teachers do I need for each subject?" The answer comes from dividing the number of students to be served by the number of students per class. This calculation gives the number of sections needed for each required class to be taught daily. The next step is to divide the number of sections by the number of periods that each teacher will teach. The result is the number of teachers required to serve the school's students in each of the daily required subjects.

These teachers are then formed into teams, configurations depending upon the number of students at each grade level. Teams may be different sizes at the same grade level, if the numbers of students are uneven. After teams are formed and the basic day of required subjects is determined, then and only then does Lane turn to adding the special features to the schedule. Special interest programs, advisory programs, schoolwide silent reading, and other special features take their place in the schedule at this point.

Fort King Middle is a large suburban school, built originally as a junior high school, now serving just over 700 students in grades 6, 7, and 8. The school funding situation in this part of the state is, perhaps, slightly below average for the nation. The master schedule at Fort King has always been prepared in accordance with the steps discussed above.

While the preparation of an actual schedule for a school of 700 students involves many smaller substeps that are impossible to include here, following the process of the major steps in the construction of the Fort King schedule should be helpful. As we discuss the steps, it will be helpful if you refer to Table 8.7 (page 392), a detailed version of the school's master schedule.

In step one, the number of students to be served at Fort King (716) is divided by the number of students per class (716 divided by 30 students per class equals approximately twenty-four sections of each class to be taught daily). Then the number of necessary sections (twenty-four) is divided by the number of periods per day each teacher is to teach (five). This yields the number of teachers required to serve the students in each subject (six). Fort King will need six teachers in each of the basic subjects: math, science, social studies and language arts; a total of twenty-four teachers for the academic group of subjects.

At the second step, Fort King has elected to offer an interdisciplinary team model which includes four teachers, one representing each of the basic subjects. This results in the construction of six teams. A glance at the extreme right side of the schedule indicates the room numbers for each teacher, showing how they are grouped together in the building. Opting for the standard version of chronological age grouping, this means two teams at each grade level.

Fort King divides the day into seven periods, approximately forty-five minutes per period. Notice, however, that the seven periods are most often conveniently grouped into two blocks, a five-period academic block and a two-period enrichment block. Teachers on each team can use this schedule flexibly. Only when the teams are organized, in place, and scheduled are the other attributes of the schedule built in.

Look at the sixth grades as an illustration. Each of the two 6th grade teams at Fort King is assigned approximately 125 students. Each 6th grade team has one teacher in each of the basics: language arts, mathematics, science, and social studies. In addition to those subjects, however, there are three or four other indicators of different activities: QST/RD, QST/CP, and EIP. This signifies that there are four subjects offered every day all year. In addition, 6th grade students receive nine weeks each of computer assisted instruction and reading. A special guidance-oriented program ("Quest," Skills for Adolescence) is provided to every 6th grader for eighteen weeks. An insider's knowledge of the schedule would also indicate that there is an advisor-advisee program also built into the daily schedule; EIP stands for "Extra Involvement Period."

So 6th graders on team 6A have a two-period block of academics first thing in the morning. This is followed by Quest, Reading, and Computer Assisted Instruction. The advisory program is fifth period for 6A students. During the fourth period, while their team teachers are planning, the students are placed in an exploratory expressive arts wheel, where they have five weeks each of home economics, art, band, chorus, agriculture, business education, and industrial arts. Students on 6A end their day with another two period academic block.

Table 8.7   Fort King Middle School, 1989–90

		Room	Subject	1	2	3	4	5	6	7	
6A	Douglass	P-1	Lang. Arts	L.A.	L.A.	QST/RD	PLAN	EIP	L.A.	L.A.	611
	**Avera	P-3	Math	Math	Math	QST/CP	PLAN	EIP	Math	Math	612
	Oldenburg	P-2	Science	Sci.	Sci.	QST/CP	PLAN	EIP	Sci.	Sci.	613
	Brennan	P-4	Soc. Studies	S.S.	S.S.	QST/RD	PLAN	EIP	S.S.	S.S.	614
				XXXXXXXXXXXXXXXXXXXXXXXXXXXXXXXXXXXXXXXXXXXXXXXXXXXXXXXXX							
6B	**Ellinor	P-18	Lang. Arts	L.A.	QST/RD	L.A.	EIP	PLAN	L.A.	L.A.	621
	Hill	P-10	Math	Math	QST/CP	Math	EIP	PLAN	Math	Math	622
	Ross	P-8	Science	Sci.	QST/CP	Sci.	EIP	PLAN	Sci.	Sci.	623
	R. Smith	P-7	Soc. Studies	S.S.	QST/RD	S.S.	EIP	PLAN	S.S.	S.S.	624
				XXXXXXXXXXXXXXXXXXXXXXXXXXXXXXXXXXXXXXXXXXXXXXXXXXXXXXXXX							
7A	Sickmon	81	Lang. Arts	L.A.	L.A.	L.A.	L.A.		PLAN	EIP	711
	Conklin	80	Math	Math	Math	Math	Math		PLAN	EIP	712
	Kelly	72	Science	Sci.	Sci.	Sci.	Sci.		PLAN	EIP	713
	**Shows	84	Soc. Studies	S.S.	S.S.	S.S.	S.S.		PLAN	EIP	714
				XXXXXXXXXXXXXXXXXXXXXXXXXXXXXXXXXXXXXXXXXXXXXXXXXXXXXXXXX							
7B	Almgren	64	Lang. Arts	L.A.	L.A.	L.A.	L.A.	L.A.	EIP	PLAN	721
	Mills	82	Math	Math	Math	Math	Math	Math	EIP	PLAN	722
	**Leslie	68	Science	Sci.	Sci.	Sci.	Sci.	Sci.	EIP	PLAN	723
	Saxon	83	Soc. Studies	S.S.	S.S.	S.S.	S.S.	S.S.	EIP	PLAN	724
	Richardson	86	Communication	Comm.	Comm.	Comm.	Comm.	Comm.	EIP	PLAN	731
				XXXXXXXXXXXXXXXXXXXXXXXXXXXXXXXXXXXXXXXXXXXXXXXXXXXXXXXXX							
8A	Orr	48	Lang. Arts	L.A.	PLAN	EIP	L.A.	L.A.	L.A.	L.A.	811
	Byrne	46	Math	Math	PLAN	EIP	Alg.	Math	Math	Math	812
	Trice	57	Science	Sci.	PLAN	EIP	Sci.	Sci.	Sci.	Sci.	813
	Cantrell	43	Soc. Studies	S.S.	PLAN	EIP	S.S.	S.S.	S.S.	S.S.	814
	**Hancock	13	Computer	CP	PLAN	EIP	CP	CP	CP	CP	815
				XXXXXXXXXXXXXXXXXXXXXXXXXXXXXXXXXXXXXXXXXXXXXXXXXXXXXXXXX							
8B	Barrett	47	Lang. Arts	L.A.	EIP	PLAN	L.A.	L.A.	L.A.	L.A.	821
	Willis	45	Math	Math	EIP	PLAN	Math	Math	Math	Math	822
	Myers	53	Science	Sci.	EIP	PLAN	Sci.	Sci.	Sci.	Sci.	823
	**Rizer	44	Soc. Studies	S.S.	EIP	PLAN	S.S.	S.S.	S.S.	S.S.	824
	Stanojevich	42	Reading	RD	EIP	PLAN	RD	RD	RD	RD	825
				XXXXXXXXXXXXXXXXXXXXXXXXXXXXXXXXXXXXXXXXXXXXXXXXXXXXXXXXX							
Cameron/Flett		Gym	Phys. Ed.	PLAN							921/922
Taylor/Morrison		Gym	Phys. Ed.	PLAN							923/924
Dosh		Gym	Phys. Ed.	SED/SC	SLD/SC	XXXXXXXXXXXXXXXXXXXXXXXXXXXXXXXXXXXXXXX					925
Summers		23	Art	PLAN	8	8	6	6	7	7	943
Collins		P-11	Chorus	PLAN	8	8	6	6	7	7	941
Fischer		26-2	Band	PLAN	8	8	6	6	7	7	942
Adams		P-16	Agriculture	PLAN	8	8	6	6	7	7	931
Atkins		17/20A	Home Ec.	PLAN	8	8	6	6	7	7	932
Furnish		27	Ind. Arts	PLAN	8	8	6	6	7	7	933
Ruth		27-2	Business Ed.	PLAN	8	8	6	6	7	7	934
Parker		P-12	Gifted	8	7	RISE	7	8	6	PLAN	911
Pledger		61	V.E.-Math	6	6	7	7	PLAN	8	8	912
Resor		41	V.E.-Sci./RD	7/Sc	7/Sc	6/Sc	8/Sc	7/RD	PLAN	6/RD	913
McKeever		85	V.E.-L.Arts	6	6	7	PLAN	7	8	8	914
Thurber		P-9	V.E.-SS/RD	7/SS	7/SS	6/RD	7-8/RD	8/SS	6/SS	PLAN	915
Allsopp		P-8	S.L.D./S.C.		PLAN						916
Lease		P-5	S.L.D./S.C.		PLAN						917
Cain		P-17	S.E.D./S.C	PLAN							918
Hope		P-6	R.I.S.E.			PLAN					951
Williams		65	T.O.P.S./6th	6/Sc	6/M	7/Sc	7/M	.7/CP	PLAN		952
J. Smith		62	T.O.P.S./7th	7/SS	7/LA	6/LA	PLAN		6/SS	QUEST	953
Hager		20	Counselor/6								961
Lynch		20	Counselor/8								962
Sorrells		20	Counselor/7								963
Rivers		Med.Cen.	Library Sci.								971
Maglio		Van	Speech								
Rawlins		13	Remediation								
Toms		13	Remediation								

Time Schedule: 6th, 7B, 8th	7:45–8:30	8:32–9:17	9:19–10:04	10:06–10:51	10:53–11:38	12:42–1:27	1:30–2:15
*1st Sem. (7A 2nd)	1st/1	2nd	3rd	4th	5th	6th	7th
7A House (7B 2nd Sem)	7:45–8:41	8:43–9:39	9:41–10:37	10:39–11:36		12:42–1:27	1:30–2:15

E. Lane, Principal
P. Miller, Asst. Prin., Curriculum
R. Pounds, Assistant Principal

**House Chairperson

ACTIVITY PERIOD/LUNCH: 11:38 a.m. – 12:40 p.m.

The enrichment period for team 6A appears where it says Plan, in the fourth period spot. At that time all students from the team are sent to the seven pre-vocational areas, providing a common planning time for the academic teachers on the team. During the fifth period, team 6A is involved in small group guidance and physical education. Each academic teacher works with ten advisees in a small group while the other thirty go to physical education. By the end of the week, each student has had four periods of physical education and one period in a small group with his advisor. (We discuss this advisory program model in depth in the chapter on Teacher as Advisor.)

The small group advisory program is an example of the implementation of the fourth step in planning the master schedule at Fort King. Having survived for more than ten years in this school district, this advisory program demonstrates the importance of proper scheduling to the life of an idea such as small group guidance.

Other special programs also are built into the schedule at this point. A special effort for at-risk learners in sixth and seventh grades (TOPS) has been implemented without disrupting the team organization. An in-school suspension program (RISE) has also been added. And, of course, important programs for exceptional students (gifted, LD, and others) are built into the schedule before it is finished.

Recognizing step five (the unfinished step) at Fort King means that while living with one schedule, the staff has already begun to consider changes for the following year. Because of the nature of the sixth grade students, the staff was considering a return to teams of two teachers each, with each teacher reponsible for two subject areas and a smaller group of students. And, in response to continuing pressures to shore up the basic skills area, the school staff discussed plans to exchange several teacher units so that two additional math lab teachers can be added. This would allow all students to spend twelve weeks each year in developmental reading, and almost all students to spend twelve weeks in the math lab. If implemented, students would receive the normal instruction in math and language arts daily for the entire year, but in addition, each student will receive social studies for twenty-four weeks, with math lab the final twelve.

Scheduling is, obviously, never finished at Fort King, nor will it be in any exemplary middle school. Those who schedule at Fort King emphasize the importance of flexibility and persistence. The schedule which we have analyzed here was the last in a series of five attempts for that year, all of which permitted the retention of the heterogeneous team concept, the common planning periods, and the small group guidance program. Many of the variations which appear from year to year are the result, simply, of the full utilization of whatever resources the faculty presents. This schedule is also an example of a basic schedule format which has been successfully used over and over again, year after year, for more than two decades in the middle schools of Marion County, Florida. As complex as this schedule is, and as time-consuming as the process to build it becomes, it is heartening to know that there are basic steps in the process which can be counted on to work not just once, but virtually forever.

Eight: The process of scheduling never ends

Master schedules are almost never finished. More often than not, the scheduling team simply reaches a point where they believe that the best possible schedule has been produced. It may be that the final product fails to accomplish a number of priorities that were established at the beginning of the process. In the real world of conflicting priorities, this often happens—it is impossible to have twice as much of everything. After you have done all that you can think of, and asked for assistance from others you respect, the schedule is probably as good as it can be. Keep in mind that if you designed the schedule to accommodate the inter-disciplinary team organization, teachers on the teams will be able to adjust their own schedules in ways that will make the ultimate fit of the schedule to the program even more acceptable.

Probably the very last step, and one which continues throughout the year, will be to do what is called "hand scheduling" for a small group of individual students. There are almost always students who just don't fit in easily to the regular schedule, but whose programs can be made to fit when done individually. Doing so also helps the parents of such students appreciate your efforts on their child's behalf. It will be worth the time.

Unfortunately, schedules, like life in general, must be lived in present time but can only be fully understood by looking back at what has transpired. In scheduling, one must live through a schedule in order to know well the advantages and disadvantages it offers. Developing a master schedule requires, of creators, both the courage to try something new and different, and the sense of humor to bear the slings and arrows which are flung from those who must live with the inevitable imperfections of any design.

As we said earlier, there are, in many schools, quiet priorities which sometimes confound the best attempts to establish a polished product at master scheduling time. The more so-called singletons (a class which is offered only once a day, to one group in the school) which one attempts to build into the curriculum (e.g., perhaps journalism, French, Algebra One, gifted groups, concert band, etc.), the more serious conflicts will develop in the scheduling process. When instrumental music, or some other important activity, dominates the scheduling process, it may yield groups of students on teams without the sort of demographic balance which is essential to success.

Here is where the school philosophy and the priorities which flow from it can be severely tested. In most school situations, where official priorities and traditional emphases may compete for space in the schedule, a great deal of final twisting and turning of time is usually done at the end of the entire process, by hand, for each individual student. The final product then becomes the rough draft for next year.

Fort Clarke Middle School (Gainesville, Florida) is an example of exemplary efforts in unending schedule development and modification based on changing needs, talents, and philosophies. Opened as a middle school in the mid-'70s, the staff at Fort Clarke continued in the 1990s to devote an incredible amount of attention to the scheduling process. The school has made use of many different schedules over the years. Not one of the schedules was perfect; each was designed for a particular year, confronting a unique set of contingencies. Faced with continually changing priorities derived from school board guidelines, teacher contracts, an open-space school where movement and noise were problems, a commitment to a brand of team organization, and several other complicating factors, the staff has responded creatively and practically to scheduling concerns.

While space limitations herein prevent a complete discussion of the scheduling process as it has evolved and changed over the last 15 years at Fort Clarke, a description of two different "stops along the way" will be helpful. The point is that not only is there no one right schedule for every school, there is no one right schedule that will fit even one school forever, or perhaps for even more than one year.

For virtually all of its history, Fort Clarke Middle School has served approximately 1,000 students in grades 6, 7, and 8. Teachers there have been organized into large single grade level teams since the beginning of the school, and continue as such into the 1990s. Each grade level has about three teachers for every basic subject. Until the 1991–92 school year, the students on each grade level/team were grouped for achievement in math and reading, throughout a three hundred-minute instructional day.

The typical junior high school would usually organize such a day into six fifty-minute periods. In the mid-1970s, the staff at Fort Clarke received a school board mandate, in response to the "back to the basics" movement of the time, which dictated that students at Fort Clarke should have extra amounts of reading and math (approximately twice that of science and social studies). The staff responded creatively, while maintaining their grade level/team configuration.

Table 8.8 illustrates the typical five-period day for the sixth grade prior to the school board mandate. Table 8.9 (page 396), however, represents a simple but profound modification of the basic student schedule that permitted the school to respond effectively to the board mandates. Each grade level team was

Table 8.8   Former Five-Period Schedule*

60	60	60	L U N C H	60	60

* **Fort Clarke Middle School, Gainesville, Florida**

Table 8.9   **Revised Sixth-Grade Schedule***

G R O U P A			L U N C H			
	75	75		50	50	50

G R O U P B			L U N C H			
	50	50	50		75	75

* Fort Clarke Middle School

Table 8.10   **Sample Sixth-Grade Student Schedule***

Language Arts Reading	Social Studies Science	L U N C H	Math	P.E.	Exploratory

* Fort Clarke Middle School

divided into two groups, roughly by ability and achievement, and given schedules that provided for seventy-five minutes of daily instruction in language arts/reading, and seventy-five minutes in a combined science/social studies program.

With this schedule, each student also received fifty minutes each of physical education, mathematics, and an exploratory course. Table 8.10 illustrates a typical day for the sixth grade students at Fort Clarke during those years: five periods of five subjects with the lengths of the periods modified according to the significance attached to a subject by school board members and parents. Half of the students begin the day with a seventy-five-minute period of language arts and reading, the balance between the two topics to be determined by the teachers based on the needs of the students. Next comes a seventy-five-minute period of either science or social studies, a half year of each. After lunch this half of the sixth graders had three successive fifty-minute periods of mathematics, physical education, and exploratory. The other half of the sixth grade team had a schedule that is basically the reverse. These other sixth graders have their math, physical education, and exploratory courses in the morning, followed by the two larger time blocks for language arts/reading and science/social studies in the afternoon. And it appears that the two groups could exchange schedules at mid-year with little difficulty. Similar schedules existed for seventh and eighth grade teams.

The teachers at Fort Clarke liked this design. For the mathematics, physical education, and exploratory teachers, the program was changed little from what had been—six fifty-minute periods with planning time before and after school. For the language arts/reading teachers and the science/social studies teachers, this design was very comfortable. None of them had more than four classes a day, with class sizes equal to the other teachers, since compensatory program students and other special and exceptional students were sent from the team for their special classes during these times. This design also provides for a great deal of teamed planning and instruction within these smaller mini-departments on each team.

Actually, this schedule seemed to work well for almost everyone at this particular school. The school board was satisfied and the teachers' union was content. The parents approved of the extra emphasis on reading and continuing attention to mathematics. The students did well on tests of academic achievement. The administration liked the situation where only a fraction of the students are changing classes at any one time, hand scheduling was simple, changes were uncomplicated, and the entire process (when one had all the information) seemed relatively traditional and rather easily understood.

It is crucially important, however, to point out that this schedule evolved to this form over a six-year period in response to the special characteristics of a particular school, in a particular place, at a particular time. The caution against the folly of attempting to impose a schedule from one school directly upon another can not be repeated too often. It can best be illustrated by a look at what the Fort Clarke schedule looked like a decade later.

At the beginning of the 1991–92 school year, a decade after the schedule described above had been implemented, many changes had occurred, and were reflected in parts of the schedule. Teachers and students were still organized into gradewide interdisciplinary teams. The school day had evolved to seven periods of forty-three minutes each, after years of improving test scores in reading and mathematics had mollified the school board. Other aspects of the consensus at Fort Clarke also required scheduling changes.

A new and deep concern for eliminating the worst abuses of ability grouping brought changes in both the curriculum and the schedule that facilitated and reflected it. In reading and language arts, for example, virtually all ability grouping had been eliminated by the 1991–92 school year. Utilization of the Reading/Writing Workshop approach, explained in the chapter on Instruction, permitted students to work on their own levels while remaining in the same classrooms. Table 8.11 (page 398) indicates a portion of the schedule for 6th and 7th grade language arts.

The right side of the schedule beginning with teacher Carroll, in room 315, reveals the details of this program. Carroll, Zemlo, Jones, and Shaughnessy share the duties of language arts/reading instruction for the sixth grade. Periods 1 and 2 represent a double block devoted to the Reading/Writing Workshop. This is

Table 8.11   **7th & 6th Reading/Language Arts**

	200 GODDARD 57	330 HONTZ 42	205 RICHARDSON 44	320 COAR 41	325	315 CARROLL 34	215 (SEE AIDES) ZEMLO 32	220 B JONES 31	335 SHAUGHNESSY 33
	0600020.100	0600020.100	0600020.100	0600020.100	0600020.100	0600010.100	0600010.100	0600010.100	0600010.100
AA	AA – 7	AA – 7	AA – 7	AA – 7	AA – 7	AA – 6	AA – 6	AA – 6	AA – 6
1	PLAN-7	PLAN-7	PLAN-7	PLAN-7	PLAN-7	1008010.000 6 READ	1008010.000 6 READ	1008010.000 6 READ	1008010.000 6 READ
2	PLAN	PLAN	PLAN	PLAN	1008010.000 6 READ W/	1001010.000 6 LA & FUNC* 1003000.000*	1001010.000 6 LA & FUNC* 1003000.000*	1001010.000 6 LA & FUNC* 1003000.000*	1001010.000 6 LA & FUNC* 1003000.000*
3	1001040.000 7 LANG ARTS	1001040.000 7 LANG ARTS	1001040.000 7 LANG ARTS	1001040.000 7 LANG ARTS W/C10	1001040.000 7 LA W/G2	PLAN	PLAN	PLAN	PLAN
4	1008040.000 7: READ	1008040.000 7: READ	1008040.000 7 READ	1008040.000 7 READ W/ 11	PLAN-6	PLAN-6	PLAN-6	PLAN-6	PLAN-6
5	7 READ W/ 9	7 READ W/ 10		7: READ W/C7	6 READ W/J6	6 READ W/S9	6 LA W/ 8	6 LA W/J9	6 LA W/S11
6	7 READ	7 READ	7 READ	7 READ	7 LA W/C9	6 LA & FUNC*	6 LA & FUNC*	6 LA & FUNC* W/ 5	6 LA & FUNC* W/C2
7	7 LA & FUNC* 1003030.000*	7 LA & FUNC* 1003030.000*	7 LA & FUNC* 1003030.000*	7 LA & FUNC* 1003030.000*	7 LA. W/H5	6 READ	6 READ	6 READ W/J10	6 READ W/S8

duplicated during periods 6 and 7. Each of the first three teachers works with approximately 25–28 students during each of these double blocks of time. The actual number of different students that each teacher meets during the day reaches about 90, significantly less than in the past at Fort Clarke.

Another curriculum feature helped shape this schedule: the emerging importance of computers as instructional tools. An eighteen-station Macintosh laboratory is available to support the Reading/Writing Workshop program in the 6th and 7th grades. A close study of the schedule for those teachers reveals that they are scheduled in such a way as to avoid overlapping use of the Mac lab. Seventh grade teachers have their two-period planning time (periods 1 and 2) just when the sixth grade teachers and students might be utilizing the computers for writing and reading work. The situation is reversed during periods 3 and 4.

A Consultation and Co-Teaching model furthered the goal of heterogeneous grouping in these grade level teams at Fort Clarke by identifying a special teacher who would serve about sixty to seventy students in what Florida calls its "Compensatory Program." Special funds are provided to schools and school districts for service to students who fall below a certain score on the California Achievement Test, but who are not identified for or served by other programs for exceptional students. These students are generally thought to be at risk. At Fort Clarke, these "Comp" students are, for the most part, no longer served in special classes. They are distributed throughout the classes of all teams on all grade levels, and served every period by a teacher whose only assignment is to work for the schoolwide success of these sixty to seventy students wherever they are in the school, coordinating all programs, services, and instruction for these students. Using the consultation and co-teaching processes, this teacher may work with ten to twelve students per period in regular classes, and still meet with every student every day. Special planning times permit this teacher to plan once each week with every team.

A lengthy advisory period also reflects changes in the Fort Clarke schedule for 1991–92. Every day will begin with a thirty-eight-minute period divided into three parts. Announcements and other details will occur during this time. A commercially produced TV news program will take up twelve minutes, and the teacher/advisor will have eighteen minutes of a structured advisory time.

Special Schedules

Experienced schedulers know that a master schedule can not be built to respond to every changing need of a school population. There are often special alternative schedules that are used, infrequently, whenever the special need requiring it arises. Some schools use floating period schedules to add an additional elective to an already full day. Others use a rotating schedule in which subjects appear at different times each day of the week. Many schools use a minimum day schedule which allows all classes to meet for something less than their regular allotment of time, permitting an early dismissal of students while the faculty remains for special activities such as inservice education or parent conferences.

Many schools use "A and B day" schedules which allow students to attend two different subjects (for example, physical education and unified arts) on an every-other-day basis. Even more schools follow a pattern similar to that at C.L. Jones Middle School (Minden, Nebraska) which designates one of the periods (usually the last) of the day as a special exploratory period. At Beck Middle School in Cherry Hill, New Jersey, the activity period is filled with difficult-to-schedule programs such as minicourses, intramurals, independent study, group guidance, study hall and so on. This type of schedule can also be used to offer special assemblies, to permit school field trips, and so on.

At the middle school level, however, stability and continuity are as important to the arrangement of the school day as are variety and change. Older high school students may be able to function effectively in a situation which manifests constant schedule changes controlled from the office. We believe, as do many educators from outstanding middle schools, that most needs for change and variety can be met within the structure of the interdisciplinary team organization, and met more effectively there than through some other mechanism. Once a school has found a team organization that works and a schedule that fits this process, fewer complicated special scheduling maneuvers are necessary or desirable.

Scheduling within the Schedule

Beyond the construction of the master schedule lies an entire world of time management. Effective master schedules permit teachers on teams to adapt time to the goals of the program of the team, and to accommodate the activities of the team to those of the larger school with a minimum of inconvenience. Moving students on the team to the unified arts program, scheduling students for academic learning within the team and arranging special whole-team learning programs are all important scheduling efforts that must be designed for individual teams.

At Beverlye Road Middle School (Dothan, Alabama), the design of an effectively simple master schedule in block form, permits the movement of students in and out of a fine unified arts program. Table 8.12 illustrates a master schedule at Beverlye. Based on the discussion earlier in the chapter, the reader should be able to identify a number of middle school program components within the schedule at Beverlye: interdisciplinary team organization (two teams at each grade level); an advisor-advisee time during the first period of the day (8:00–8:20 a.m.), and an extended time (ninety-five minutes) for exploratory experiences.

The middle schools of Dothan, Alabama, of which Beverlye is one, are committed to a strong exploratory emphasis in the unified arts and physical education. The schedule, hence, was designed to facilitate that program component without violating the interdisciplinary team organization. Table 8.13 illustrates the scheduling process for these curriculum areas that was built into the master schedule, but would not be obvious by looking at it. This is true, of course, of all master schedules (e.g., Fort King).

Table 8.12 **Beverlye Middle School, Winter Quarter**

SIXTH GRADE	SEVENTH GRADE	EIGHTH GRADE
8:00–8:20	Advisor/Advisee Period	
P.E./Exploratory Team Planning 8:30–9:55	8:30–11:30 A.M. Basics Content Area	8:30–10:05 Content Area
A.M. Basics Content Area 10:05–12:30	11:30–11:55 Lunch	P.E./Exploratory 10:05–11:40 Team Planning
Lunch 12:30–12:55	11:55–1:00 P.M. Basics	Lunch 11:40–12:05
P.M. Basics Content Area 1:00–2:35	1:00–2:35 Team Planning	P.M. Basics Content Area 12:05–2:35
2:35–2:45	HOME BASE	

2:45 Escort students to loading zone exit
Exploratory and physical education teachers will have their planning time and lunch period from 11:40 until 1:00
Team planning scheduled from 2:45 until 3:15

Table 8.13 **Beverlye Road Middle School, Sixth-Grade Exploratory Schedule**

* FIRST 47½	¼ 6A Art	¼ 6A H Ec	⅓ 6B-PE
			⅓ 6B-PE
	¼ 6A Ind. Arts	¼ 6A Music	⅓ 6B-PE
SECOND 47½	¼ 6B Art	¼ 6B H Ec	⅓ 6A-PE
			⅓ 6A-PE
	¼ 6B Ind. Arts	¼ 6B Music	⅓ 6A-PE

The 6th grade at Beverlye is used here for explanatory purposes; the 7th and 8th grades follow similar patterns. While the academic teachers have their planning periods, their students are involved in the exploratory programs. During the first half of the ninety-five-minute exploratory time, half of the 6th grade students are involved in an exploratory curriculum. One group is in art, home

Table 8.14 **Noe Middle School Master Schedule, 1977–78**

TEAM	TEAM DATA	TEAM SCHEDULE (ALL TEAMS WILL HAVE HOMEROOM FROM 7:30–7:40.)					
6:1		7:45–9:40 TEAM		9:45–10:40 UA	10:45–2:00 TEAM		
7:1		7:45–8:40 TEAM	8:45–9:40 UA	9:45–2:00 TEAM			
7:2		7:45–8:40 TEAM	8:45–9:40 UA	9:45–2:00 TEAM			
8:1		7:45–8:40 UA	8:45–2:00 TEAM				
MA		7:45–1:00 TEAM				1:05–2:00 UA	
Unified Arts		7:45–8:40 8:1	8:45–9:40 7:1–2	9:45–10:40 6:1	10:45–12:00 Cafe	12:05–1:00 Plan	1:05–2:00 MA

economics, industrial arts, or music. At the same time, the other half of the 6th grade is divided into three equal sections and sent to physical education. During the second half of the long period, the two halves of the 6th grade exchange places. This basic rotation can be modified to fit just about any local condition or demand, just about any division of the year into grading periods, and practically any type of curriculum offerings.

At Noe Middle School in Louisville, Kentucky, teachers have, historically, taken real advantage of the flexible schedule they have been given. Table 8.14 illustrates a schedule at Noe from the late 1970s, when there were six teams: one 6th, two 7th, one 8th, and one multiage grouped team.[1] The teachers on teams at Noe, as at many other middle schools utilizing block schedules (e.g., Sarasota Middle School) have the ability and responsibility for scheduling the advisory time within the extended periods of time allocated to them for their interdisciplinary use. Each team, therefore, structured the advisory time in a way which suited them best; a wise way to do things. One team, at the time, worked so well together that they often arranged the advisory time in a team fashion, using it to teach aspects of social and emotional education. Table 8.15 illustrates that team's plans for the advisory time over a period of three months. The column at the left indicated when the various topics will be covered; column

---

[1]Over the decade of the 1980s, Noe moved to a configuration where half of the students and academic teachers in the school were organized into multiage grouped teams; the other half remained in three chronological grade level teams. Toward the end of the 1980s, the school eliminated multiage grouping. For the 1991–92 year, one small multiage grouped team was reintroduced, for working with at-risk students. Changes such as these almost always reflect changing times and different leadership.

Table 8.15   **Advisor-Advisee Topics At Noe Middle School**

March	24–30	Values Clarification	Davis
	31–April 6	Decision Making	
April	7–13	Friendship Week	Sindalar
	14–20		
April	21–27	Development of Self-Confidence	McLaughlin
	28–May 4	and Identification of Strengths	
May	5–11	Development of Self-Awareness	Brakmeier
	12–18		
May	19–23	Interpersonal Relationships	Warner
May	24	Drug Day	All
May	25	Follow-up	All
May	26–June 2	Dating and Sex	All

two, the topics themselves; column three the teachers on the team who were responsible for the major planning of each separate unit. Scheduling the advisory time this way permits the team to deal with a wide range of important topics while it keeps individual teacher planning time to a minimum. It also builds in an important degree of accountability for each teacher, an important ingredient for successful advisory programs.

This same team of teachers utilized the maximum amount of schedule flexibility when designing the academic time for its students. Teams that take advantage of flexibility in one situation are likely to do so in others. During a week that included an interdisciplinary thematic unit on The West, the team utilized a scheduling procedure that reached what we believe to be the zenith of both flexibility and individual student choice within a teacher-designated structure that provided stability and continuity. Such creativity is, alas, all too rare.

The following illustrations and explanations clarify the set of steps through which the team and its students moved during the last week of the unit on The West, and some additional science and language arts activities. The process began with a series of team meetings during which teachers planned the activities and developed a schedule for each week to come. Table 8.16 (page 404) illustrates the activities for social studies, science, and language arts for the week. Math was not included in this unit, and was taught by team members at another time of the day. The list tells us what topics were dealt with, and the learning activities which were used for each subject. Science, for example, dealt with the use of the microscope, and involves discussions, laboratory activity, a review, and an exam. Social studies focused directly on the topic of The West and involved a series of learning stations, a movie, a guest speaker, and some group discussions. Language arts focused on skills and the application of these skills using the social studies topic The West. Table 8.17 (page 405) lists the topics in each of the three areas, the days they were offered, and the number of periods (or mods) that each student was required to take, even to the extent of assigning students to different language arts groups.

Table 8.16   **Topics and Activities—Unit on the West***

SOCIAL STUDIES		
Monday	Movie: "The Red West", narrated by Gary Cooper	2 Mods
Tuesday	Discussion of Life on an Indian Reservation	2 Mods
Wed.–Fri.	Stations on the "Old West"	6 Mods
Thursday	Guest Speaker, William Owl	2 Mods
LANGUAGE ARTS		
Monday and Thursday	Skills and Application (Groups A,B,C)	4 Mods
Tuesday	Skills and Application (Groups D,E,F)	2 Mods
SCIENCE		
Monday	Discussion on the Use of the Microscope	2 Mods
Tuesday	Lab Using the Microscope to View Prepared Slides	2 Mods
Wednesday	Lab Using the Microscope to Prepare and View Self-Made Slides	3 Mods
Thursday	Review of the Use of the Microscope	2 Mods
Friday	Test on the Microscope	2 Mods

* From Noe Middle School, Louisville, Kentucky.

Once the teachers completed their plans for the coming week, the entire team of teachers and students met during the last two academic periods of the week on Friday. Table 8.17 is the program that teachers distributed to the students at that time. Students were quickly able to see which activities were required and which were not, how many mods of each activity were needed and which teacher was in charge of each activity. The next step was to divide up into advisory groups for the actual choosing of activities for the next week.

Table 8.18 (page 406) illustrates the second planning form given to the students, on which they recorded their plan for learning. The upper square laid out the different mods during which these activities were to be offered for the week. Each mod contained the number of activities that were available at that time of day. Tuesday, at 11:05 a.m., for example, students could have chosen from among the microscope lab, learning stations on The West, discussion of life on an Indian reservation, a language arts group, and independent study. The bottom half of the form was initially blank, so that students could record their choices. Referring to the list of choices (Table 8.17), students worked out their own schedule for the week, within the limits and the structure which the teachers had built. Table 8.19 (page 406) illustrates the choices of one student on the team. Notice that many activities were offered at very limited times (for example, the planning for the following week, activity 17, is for everyone and must be scheduled from 12:15 to 12:55 on Friday). Nevertheless, it seems that most students experienced this opportunity for choice as a very positive experience,

Table 8.17

NUMBER	MODS	TOPICS FOR THE WEEK	GROUP	TEACHERS
1	2	Discussion-Use of the microscope		Brakmeier/ McLaughlin
2	2	Lab-Microscope techniques of viewing slides		''
3	3	Lab-Microscope-preparing and viewing self-made slides		''
4	2	Review-Microscope		''
5	2	Test-Microscope		''
6	2	Movie-"The Red West"		Sindelar
7	6	Stations-The West		Warner and/or Sindelar
8	2	Guest Speaker-William Owl, Cherokee Indian from North Carolina		Warner
9	2	Discussion-Life on an Indian Re-servation		Sindelar
10†	4	Literature skills & application	A	Davis
11†	4	'' '' '' ''	B	''
12†	4	'' '' '' ''	C	''
13†	2	'' '' '' ''	D	''
14†	2	'' '' '' ''	E	''
15†	2	'' '' '' ''	F	''
16	—	Independent Study		
17	2	Team Meeting-Plans for camping trip	A,B,C, D,E,F	

D,E,F-Critical Analysis Notebooks due in to Ms. Davis on Friday
All "Old West" Projects due in to Mrs. Warner or Mr. Sindelar Thursday
Special Arts Project students are to report to Mr. DeGiovanni at 12 noon Tuesday

* From Noe Middle School
† Language Arts Group attendance required.

and that students at Noe, and elsewhere, would gain in self-discipline and responsibility as a result of it.

The team planning and scheduling illustrated by one team at Noe exemplifies, in our judgment, the best uses of freedom and flexibility which well-designed master schedules offer. In the tight budget times of the 1990s, funds may not be regularly available to provide teachers with the planning time to engage in such complex efforts. Staff development may not be available to train them how to do it. Perhaps only the most effective middle school teachers could make this flexibility and student autonomy work smoothly. But one thing is certain: without the benefits of a schedule designed especially to encourage such activities, they could not occur even if the time and the skills were present.

Table 8.18   **Student Decision-Making Form—Schedule of Topics**

	MONDAY	TUESDAY	WEDNESDAY	THURSDAY	FRIDAY
10:45–11:05	1,6,7,10,16	2,7,9,13,16	3,7,16	4,7,8,12,16	5,7,16
11:05–11:25	1,6,7,10,16	2,7,9,13,16	3,7,16	4,7,8,12,16	5,7,16
11:30–11:50	1,6,7,11,16	2,7,9,14,16	3,7,16	4,7,8,10,16	5,7,16
11:50–12:10	1,6,7,11,16	2,7,9,14,16	3,7,16	4,7,8,10,16	5,7,16
12:15–12:35	1,6,7,12,16	2,7,9,15,16	3,7,16	4,7,8,11,16	17
12:35–12:55	1,6,7,12,16	2,7,9,15,16	3,7,16	4,7,8,11,16	17

	MONDAY	TUESDAY	WEDNESDAY	THURSDAY	FRIDAY

* From Noe Middle School

Table 8.19   **Student Decision-Making Form—Illustrative Choices***

	MONDAY	TUESDAY	WEDNESDAY	THURSDAY	FRIDAY
10:45–11:05	1,6,7,10,16	2,7,9,13,16	3,7,16	4,7,8,12,16	5,7,16
11:05–11:25	1,6,7,10,16	2,7,9,13,16	3,7,16	4,7,8,12,16	5,7,16
11:30–11:50	1,6,7,11,16	2,7,9,14,16	3,7,16	4,7,8,10,16	5,7,16
11:50–12:10	1,6,7,11,16	2,7,9,14,16	3,7,16	4,7,8,10,16	5,7,16
12:15–12:35	1,6,7,12,16	2,7,9,15,16	3,7,16	4,7,8,11,16	17
12:35–12:55	1,6,7,12,16	2,7,9,15,16	3,7,16	4,7,8,11,16	17

	MONDAY	TUESDAY	WEDNESDAY	THURSDAY	FRIDAY
10:45–11:05	1	2	7	4	16
11:05–11:25	1	2	7	4	16
11:30–11:50	6	14	7	8	5
11:50–12:10	6	14	3	8	5
12:15–12:35	7	9	3	7	17
12:35–12:55	7	9	3	16	17

* From Noe Middle School.

Scheduling in Perspective

Few aspects of the exemplary middle school are both as fraught with difficulties and as crucial to the success of the program as the process of scheduling. Most middle school administrators recognize that an effective schedule is the fulcrum upon which the remainder of the program is moved, yet the scheduling process has probably received less attention from research and development than any other item. Training in the skills necessary for effective schedule construction is still inadequate. Much remains to be done.

Organizing Space in the Middle School

The Middle School Building

The famous aphorism "We shape our buildings; thereafter, they shape us," attributed to Winston Churchill, applies directly to the discussion of middle school buildings. Often placed in the position of inheriting old high school or junior high school buildings, middle school educators find themselves in possession of a building designed for purposes and programs that are, at best, foreign to those the middle school advocates. With declining enrollments apparently likely to continue for some time, it seems possible that middle school educators who pin their hopes for a fully functioning school on the opportunity to design a new building to fit their program will often be disappointed. As this section of the chapter will demonstrate, however, exemplary middle schools can function beautifully in all kinds of physical plants.

Since, in architecture, form should follow function, comments on the most appropriate organization of space in middle schools must be accompanied by the familiar requirement to provide a unique and transitional approach. What the middle school building looks like and how it is organized should depend upon the type of program intended; the building should be designed to serve the program. Consequently, building construction should follow program design; organization of space in existing facilities which become the site of newly organized middle school programs should follow the acceptance of program changes. All too often, however, this does not happen.

Middle school buildings should be different from elementary and high school buildings. In the elementary school, where the emphasis is upon close relationships built in self-contained classrooms or those that are nearly so, where the curriculum focuses on skill development of the most basic kinds, and where teachers frequently work alone, the building is designed to accommodate this style. In spite of some recent changes in the construction of elementary schools, the building which focuses on single classrooms remains the model structure. Many elementary schools seem to be a series of single classrooms strung together for reasons that are difficult to determine. Because of the nature of the children they serve and the programs they offer, elementary schools tend to be smaller and less expensive than middle schools.

The high school building also reflects the program within it. Committed to the departmentalized organization of teachers, high schools are almost inevitably organized to reflect this design. The science department is housed in one wing, the mathematics department in another, the English department in a third, and so on. Subject specialization is the key to high school programs, and the building reflects it with a myriad of special rooms, equipment, and areas. High schools, because of this focus on specialization and the increased costs that accompany it, tend to be much larger and much more expensive than middle schools.

Middle schools serve a kind of student and offer a kind of program which fits somewhere between the elementary and secondary positions. Middle schools attempt to provide a middle way, balancing the twin goals of personalized climate and enriched curriculum, or what we have called supportive interpersonal structure and teacher-subject specialization. Most middle school students would be lost in buildings housing between 3,000 and 5,000 students, the size of some high schools. These same students would often be challenged less than optimally by the programs which very small schools can afford. The middle school building must be large enough to hold the number of students necessary to justify the inclusion of expensive special programs so essential for effective early adolescent education. The cost of computerized instruction, industrial arts, agriculture, music, art, home economics, and other expensive programs place them beyond the reach of the elementary school which, because of the young children involved, must remain small and connected with the neighborhoods it serves. The number of students required to offer high school programs, however, produces a school building and student body large enough to drown the average middle schooler in a sea of anonymity and amorphousness.

The challenge of the middle school building, thus, is to be large enough to hold a number of students which will justify the expenditure of funds necessary for the exploratory programs which educators believe these students require. At the same time, however, the middle school building must be organized in a manner which insures a sense of community and a personalized educational experience for each student. This is no simple task, designing smallness within bigness.

It is not an impossible task, however, even though it is made more difficult by the frequent need to implement middle school programs in buildings designed initially as elementary or high school facilities. Middle schools can be designed originally or modified later to accommodate: advisory programs; the interdisciplinary organization of teachers; just about any type of schoolwide student grouping pattern desired; enlarged library and media facilities; new programs in the unified arts; more complex and sophisticated opportunities for physical education and, if preferred, sports. These same schools can be organized in a way which permits the development of close personal relationships with teachers and a sense of community which leads students safely away from the protective atmosphere of the elementary school. Middle schools are the most effective way to educate older children and early adolescents, in part because they allow us to offer stimulating programs and enriched educational experiences without sacrificing the atmosphere most conducive to growth-producing interpersonal relationships. Neither program nor school climate needs to be subjugated to the other in an exemplary middle school.

Flexibility

There is no single type of physical facility which is required for the implementation of the middle school program, just as there is no one schedule appropriate for all. Programs are influenced by the buildings they inhabit, but they are not completely determined by those buildings. It is possible to reach the status of an exemplary program in an old motel-style high school building, a converted elementary school, a new open space school, or a structure built around pods of one kind or another. What one asks of a building matters most.

Much earlier in the life of the middle school movement, near the end of the 1960s, some educators seem to have been convinced that middle school and open-space facilities were synonymous, that open-space buildings were required for effective middle school programs. As a result, a great deal of public dissatisfaction with the way open-space schools were used in some school districts transferred to the middle school concept. Luckily, just as we seem to have realized that the middle school concept is not totally dependent on a particular instructional strategy (for example, individualized instruction), so, too, it seems that educators understand that many kinds of school buildings can be made to serve the middle school concept, and almost no building can totally prevent the concept from developing. Buildings without permanent walls offer the maximum amount of flexibility, but old high school buildings often present teachers and students with a great deal more space than might have been available if a new middle school building had been constructed. Almost every type of building has its strengths and weaknesses. The key to the use of the facility resides in being able to use the strengths of a particular building to enhance the program offered within.

No more effective demonstration of the truth of these comments could be found than the simple fact that of the many exemplary school programs described in this volume, no two are housed in facilities which are exactly alike. Outstanding programs are found in old buildings and new, large and small, open and conventional. Some of the schools had the buildings designed especially for the programs, others took old high school, junior high school, or elementary school buildings and modified them for new programs in highly effective ways. Equally true, in our opinion, is the observation that sterile, unimaginative, and ineffective programs can be found in buildings which were designed to accommodate much, much more than they do. A reasonably flexible school plant is necessary for a good program, but is far from being sufficient to guarantee that program.

With this latitude in the kind of building in mind, however, it is interesting to note that the schools described in this volume represent three different kinds of building style. Similar programs have evolved in three different sets of physical surroundings: older structures often inherited from previous occupants; new buildings focusing on flexible use of space and individualized programs; and, even newer facilities designed with the idea of smaller schools within the larger building.

Middle school buildings can be classified in one other way that is significant. Some buildings were designed with a sophisticated middle school program clearly in mind. Others inherited the building, or grew within it after it was built to highlight another purpose. In our experience, the number of middle school buildings seems to be divided unevenly; until the early 1990s, far fewer buildings have been designed specifically to incorporate all the components of the middle school. Those for whom the middle school was an afterthought, if it was a factor at all in the design of the building, are still far more numerous. The future will almost certainly include large numbers of middle schools that inhabit quarters designed to serve another student population. Both types of schools will, however, continue to offer exemplary programs for the remainder of this century.

Adapting Older Buildings

Perhaps because it may be easier to establish an exemplary middle school program in a new building designed specifically for that purpose, fewer schools which might be labeled exemplary are found, in our experience, in older buildings that have been adapted. This is certainly influenced by the likelihood of being able to assemble a new faculty, specially selected for the middle school program, whenever one opens a new middle school building. While it is, of course, possible for new faculties to be assigned to older buildings, it is almost mandatory in a new facility, since the staff has never been there before the building opened. Unless, that is, the faculty moved to the new building en masse from earlier quarters. Most middle school administrators in our acquaintance assert that it is many times more difficult to change from an existing junior high school to a middle school program than it is to begin a middle school program where no prior school existed. While the faculty makeup can be the most important factor, the building itself is quite important in determining the ease with which the new program is established. The simple fact that older buildings were almost always designed for other purposes and, therefore, require adaptations, creates a measure of additional difficulty.

Sometimes middle schools inherited their space from elementary schools, but more frequently the program moved into a plant that housed a high school, or even more frequently, a junior high school. In the relatively infrequent instances where the middle school took over space from an elementary school, the major problem stemmed from inadequate space and from facilities which did not contain areas or equipment to house the unified arts and other new programs which may have been in the planning. Since these enrichment areas were central to the middle school concept, their absence was serious. Accommodations for these programs usually came in the form of portable buildings or additions to the existing facilities, or they did not come at all. Schools fortunate enough to convince district planners to add the space had a new chance to excel; those who were refused were forced to accept severe limitations in the program they offered to their students.

Middle school programs that inherited their space from older secondary programs were more fortunate, or at least their problems were of a different nature. Moving into an older secondary school building usually meant that the enlarged library and media space was there, even if the books and the equipment were not. The areas where the unified arts had been offered were still there, even if the spaces looked like vacant airplane hangers. Inheriting a high school building has usually also meant that there would be more space of all kinds: offices, cafeteria, hallways, lockers, study areas, auditorium, laboratories, and larger classrooms. High schools, simply, were bigger, so, the problems were not connected with having enough space to put all the program components.

The major problem with inheriting the high school or junior high school building is related to the differing practices of organizing teachers for instruction. Most secondary schools have operated on the departmentalized model of curriculum and teacher organization. In addition, in the headlong rush to erect buildings large enough to offer expanded, comprehensive programs, consolidating (read eliminating) the smaller schools in the process, few architects or school planners seem to have given any thought at all to the need to design the new structures in a way that preserved the sense of community that existed in the smaller schools. New middle school programs in older secondary buildings, thus, found themselves with space that was often difficult to adapt to new needs.

Most older secondary school buildings were constructed so that classrooms were not grouped together in any type of recognizable pattern, except in the case of the science program. The department concept and, perhaps at the time, cost of construction, required the science laboratories to be grouped in the same area, and this simple construction decision has caused an endless round of difficulties for middle school planners as they have attempted to adapt the buildings to the pattern of interdisciplinary teacher organization. Finding convenient groups of classrooms, and surmounting the science department problem so that team members could be close to each other in the middle school, presents a major stumbling block to establishing effective new programs in old school buildings. Once these problems are solved, the rest seems to be relatively easy.

Consider the floor plans for Volusia County, Florida's Deland Junior High School for the school year 1986–87, and for the Middle School inheriting the same facility in the school year 1991–92. The organization of the building when it housed the junior high school program (Figure 8.2 page 412) illustrates the centrality of academic disciplines and electives. Figure 8.3 (page 413) demonstrates the challenge of reorganization: moving grade level teams into a school originally designed with a subject-centered facility. The location of the science labs, and thus, the science teachers, poses distinct challenges for the effective operation of interdisciplinary teams.

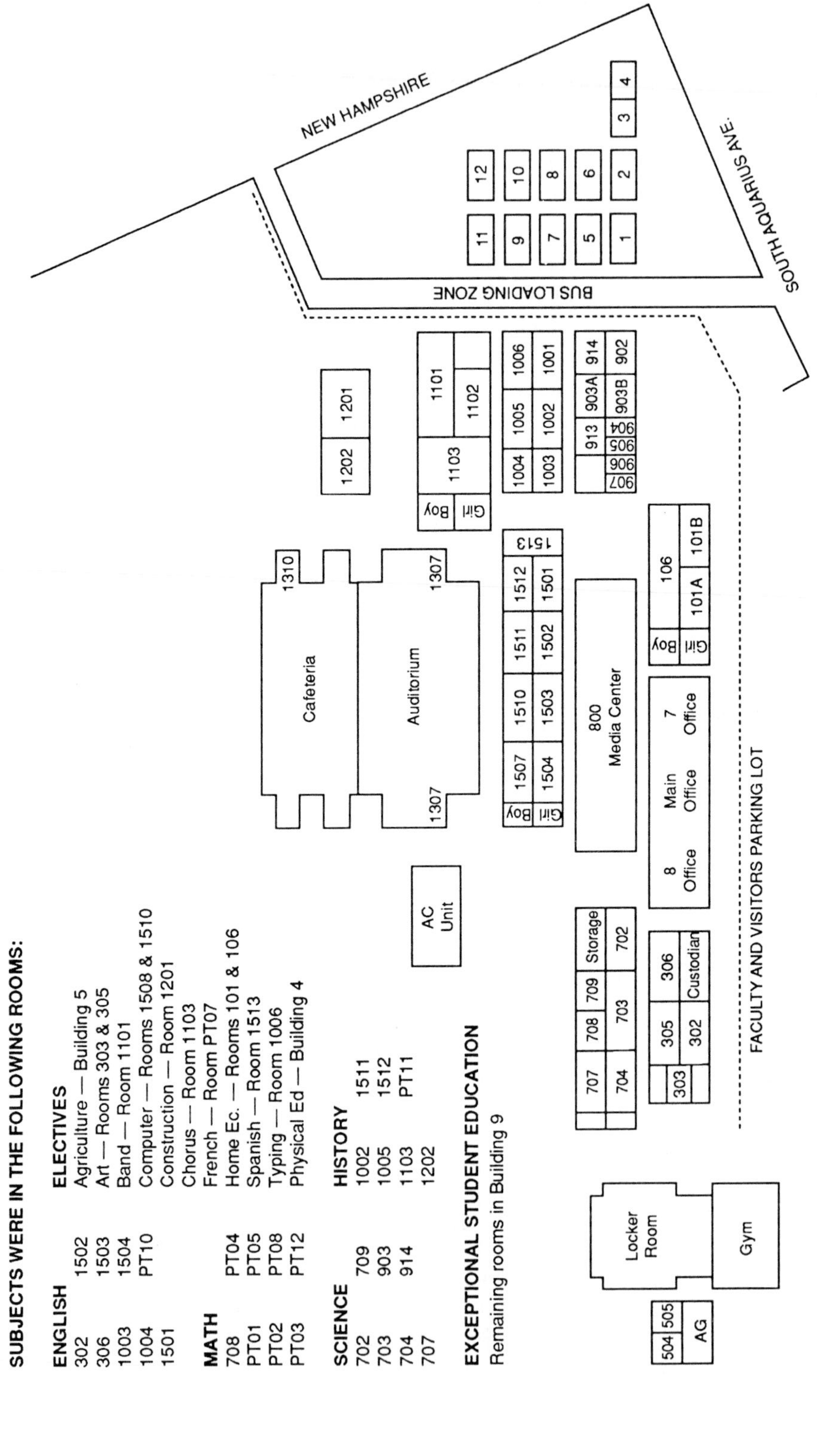

SUBJECTS WERE IN THE FOLLOWING ROOMS:

ENGLISH		ELECTIVES	
302	1502	Agriculture — Building 5
306	1503	Art — Rooms 303 & 305
1003	1504	Band — Room 1101
1004	PT10	Computer — Rooms 1508 & 1510
1501		Construction — Room 1201
		Chorus — Room 1103
MATH		French — Room PT07
708	PT04	Home Ec. — Rooms 101 & 106
PT01	PT05	Spanish — Room 1513
PT02	PT08	Typing — Room 1006
PT03	PT12	Physical Ed — Building 4

SCIENCE		HISTORY	
702	709	1002	1511
703	903	1005	1512
704	914	1103	PT11
707		1202	

EXCEPTIONAL STUDENT EDUCATION
Remaining rooms in Building 9

Figure 8.2   **DELAND JUNIOR HIGH SCHOOL / SCHOOL YEAR 1986–87**

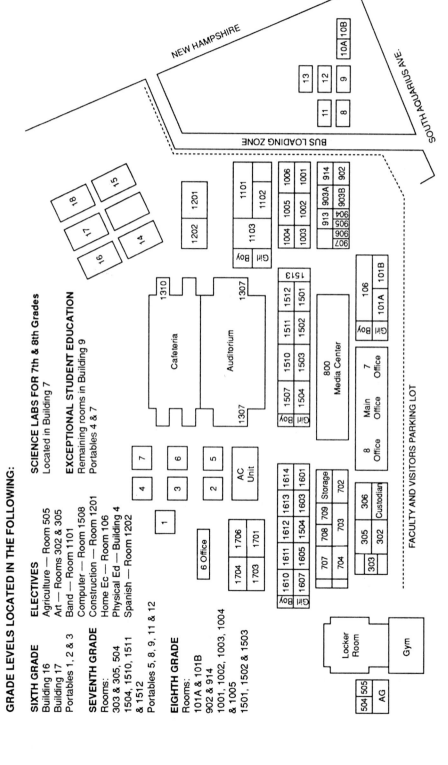

GRADE LEVELS LOCATED IN THE FOLLOWING:

SIXTH GRADE
Building 16
Building 17
Portables 1, 2 & 3

SEVENTH GRADE
Rooms:
303 & 305, 504
1504, 1510, 1511
& 1512
Portables 5, 8, 9, 11 & 12

EIGHTH GRADE
Rooms:
101A & 101B
902 & 914
1001, 1002, 1003, 1004
& 1005
1501, 1502 & 1503

ELECTIVES
Agriculture — Room 505
Art — Rooms 302 & 305
Band — Room 1101
Computer — Room 1508
Construction — Room 1201
Home Ec — Room 106
Physical Ed — Building 4
Spanish — Room 1202

SCIENCE LABS FOR 7th & 8th Grades
Located in Building 7

EXCEPTIONAL STUDENT EDUCATION
Remaining rooms in Building 9
Portables 4 & 7

Figure 8.3   **DELAND MIDDLE SCHOOL / SCHOOL YEAR 91–92**

Middle schools choose one of two or three ways to deal with the need to make the science area more flexible. Some planners organize the day and the teams so that teams are able to schedule the time in the available science laboratory areas, avoiding major conflicts. With some notable exceptions, many middle school science programs seem to be relatively independent of the need for constant access to a science laboratory, and being able to schedule special lab time when necessary often seems to be enough. Other schools have found that portable mini-labs or demonstration tables often suffice. Still others are able to arrange their teams in the space so that while the science teachers have their rooms in what was the science department, interdisciplinary groups are still quite close together. Some other schools have found themselves so stymied by the placement of the science rooms that they have had to resort to interdisciplinary teams composed of mathematics, social studies, and language arts teachers, leaving the science teachers together in a department. We believe that this is the least acceptable option, but that it is still considerably better than having the entire faculty remain in a departmentalized structure.

We also believe that, in almost every case, these science area problems can be resolved without sacrificing the interdisciplinary team concept. Faculties which find it difficult to do so may be philosophically resistant rather than spatially troubled. Since the experience of thirty years of middle school development from 1960–1990 so strongly affirms that the interdisciplinary team concept is central, and must come first in the development of an exemplary middle school, it is important to take the time to help the staff see the need to make both the philosophical and the territorial changes.

The new Galaxy Middle School (Figure 8.4), which opened in the fall of 1991, in Deltona, Florida, illustrates how a district (Volusia County) can respond with new facilities to match new middle school programs. Middle school interdisciplinary teams will operate with considerably greater ease, effectiveness, and efficiency in this building than in the older building for Deland Middle School in the same district, where adaptation is the rule.

One school that has done an outstanding job of adapting an older secondary school building to the middle school program is Lincoln Middle School (Gainesville, Florida). Lincoln inherited a building that had a history as a segregated high school for several decades, followed by a period of vacant idleness after schools in the district were integrated in 1970. Opened several years later as a vocational school, it was changed to a middle school in 1974. Figure 8.5 (page 416) is a floor plan of Lincoln drawn in 1973, prior to the opening of the middle school program there.

Lincoln houses approximately 1,000 students in a building intended to hold considerably more, when it was designed several decades earlier. A glance at the floor plan will show that the school was not intended as a middle school when built, but that the Lincoln staff did make the necessary adaptations to convert it to serve the team concept well. Believing that teams work better when

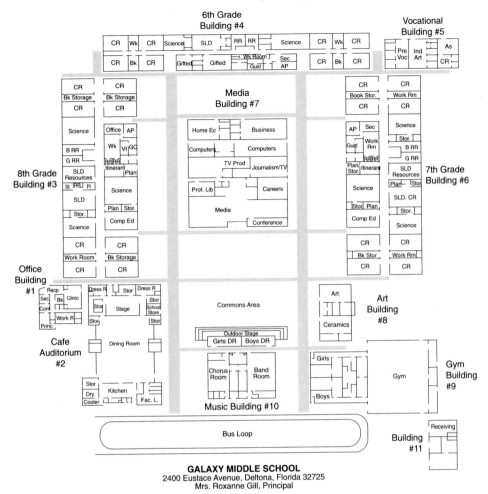

Figure 8.4   **Galaxy Middle School**

located in contiguous classrooms, and having inherited enough space to give each team a planning area, the school was organized, in 1974, along these lines. Each of the six teams at Lincoln were assigned to team areas: C Team was given rooms 25 to 28 as classrooms, and room 15 as a team planning space; B Team was given rooms 31 to 34 as classrooms, and room 13 as their planning area; D Team was given rooms 44 to 47 as classrooms and room 40 as a team room; W Team was housed in rooms 48 to 51, with 42 as a planning room; G Team had rooms 52 to 55 as teaching areas, with 56 as the planning room; M Team was located in rooms 87, 89, 90, and 91, with their planning space in room 88, which had been an automotive mechanics shop during the years the high school had been there. Six teams, six areas.

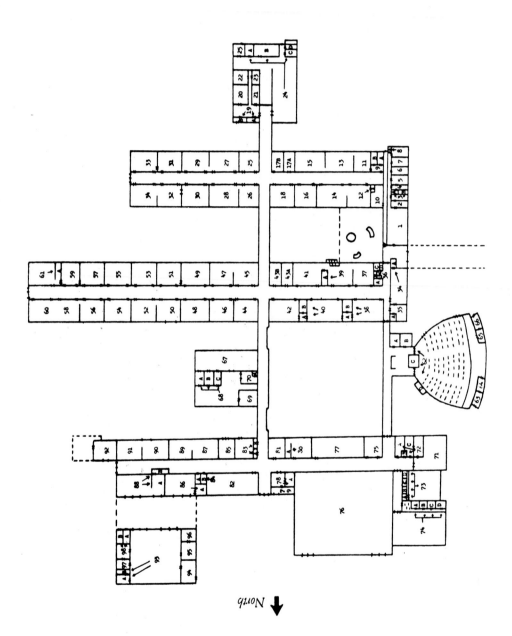

Figure 8.5   **Floor Plan, Lincoln Middle School, Gainesville, Florida**

Other rooms and areas in the school are used quite conventionally:

- Gymnasium—76
- Special Education—12 to 17
- Cafeteria—19 to 24
- Typing—18
- Auditorium—62
- Home Economics—39, 41
- Industrial Arts—93
- Offices—1 to 8
- Media Center—67 to 68

Since the opening of school that first year, many changes have occurred at Lincoln. New programs which affected the entire district, in areas like bilingual education, deaf education, and so on, have been located there. Enrollment fluctuations and other factors have required space to be adjusted, but the concept of team areas and planning spaces has been guarded jealously and sacrificed only when there was no other choice. Very much the result of this, in the early nineties, Lincoln is still an exemplary middle school, nearly two decades after it was opened. Separate team planning rooms have virtually disappeared as enrollment has grown and special science labs have been added to each team, but team organization and planning continues.

The simple fact of Lincoln Middle School's continued existence as one of the better middle schools in America should add confidence to those new to the concept, especially as they explore ways of adapting old buildings to new programs. The experience of most middle school educators, in the 1990s, is that it is leadership and professional commitment that sustain programs for decades, not buildings or money.

Many other middle schools have made creative adjustments of their inherited space in ways which have allowed them to develop and maintain outstanding programs. But some school districts, more than most others, seem to exemplify the ability to make creative programs develop and prosper in school settings of widely varying types. The district of Dothan, Alabama, is such a place.

In early 1974, the Dothan school district began to implement a well-planned project, with funding assistance from several sources, to close three junior high schools in the city and open four middle schools in the fall of 1977. Two of the four junior high school buildings were to be used as middle schools, and two new middle school buildings were to be built. The plan included a commitment to almost identical programs in each of the four middle schools, but the buildings that were intended to house these programs were radically different from one another. Two were to be brand new, flexibly spaced, pod-type structures. One was a relatively modern junior high school of conventional classroom design, built about twenty years previous to the middle school plan; and the fourth was a building that needed monumental renovation to make it acceptable to members of that community. Since the middle school plan also included a total reassignment of teachers throughout the district's middle level, the teachers had a vested interest in the building construction and renovation.

As it turned out, the programs for the four schools are, in fact, virtually indistinguishable from each other, with talented faculties operating within nearly identical team designs. Advisory programs function in each school, along with exploratory curriculum plans that should be the envy of neighboring districts. The most interesting thing about the program, in this respect, is that all four middle schools function with roughly identical schedules as well. The schedule for Beverlye Road Middle School is almost exactly like the schedules of sister middle schools Honeysuckle, Girard, and Carver regardless of the dramatic differences which exist in the facilities that house the programs.

Pod-Style and House-Type Middle School Facilities

The pod-style middle school building is the midpoint between the self-contained classroom school, which must adapt as described above, and the more completely open-space school designed to foster individualized instruction which were popular in the 1960s and 1970s. The pod-type construction seems particularly suited to the middle school program, accommodating the interdisciplinary team organization in a special way. In fact, the great majority of new middle school buildings opened during the period between 1981 and 1992 are pod-style facilities. We recognize that this is so because of the immense popularity of team organizations which utilize a school-within-a-school approach of some kind.

The building which contains the program for Wakulla Middle School demonstrates the profound interaction between building and program. (We discuss this in detail in Chapter 7 on grouping.) A review of this interaction, conducted by an architect ten years after the opening of the building (Peterson, 1991) examined the results and found that the building's design did, indeed, effectively enhance the implementation of the middle school concept. Peterson's conclusions (1991, p. 129) are fascinating:

> The Wakulla Middle School functions very successfully in its established framework of philosophies and curriculum concepts of a middle school. There has been an apparent commitment to those concepts by the faculty and staff since the inception. Most conflicts that have arisen over the ten years have been overcome through adaptation in policy or change in spacial usage. The optimum operation of a middle school as defined by the Wakulla facility demands a specific building type to support the curriculum concepts and organizational philosophies. Although the Wakulla Middle School was designed as such a building type, there are a number of aspects that have not proven optimum. The continued operational success is in large part attributable to the personnel and their goal commitment rather than the physical form.

An analysis of the floor plan (Figure 8.6 page 420) of the Tequesta Trace Middle School in Fort Lauderdale, Florida illustrates the features of the modern pod design. The Tequesta plant also illustrates the flexibility that permits a number of program modifications to be installed without major plant renovation. The design at Tequesta, for example, permits educators to organize teachers and students for instruction in a variety of ways. While the staff in Tequesta has decided to remain with the standard chronological grade level pattern, should there be a decision to move to a school-within-a-school program it could easily be accomplished with this building. Even a move to complete multiage grouping could be accommodated without plant modifications simply by establishing six or seven such teams.

Tequesta Trace Middle School houses approximately 1,700 students in grades 6 through 8, (we believe this is an uncomfortably high number of students, especially if they were housed in almost any other fashion). The program is almost identical to the program in the other twenty-eight middle schools in the Broward County school district, in spite of the radically different physical facilities of the separate schools. Broward County has, in fact, been pioneering the development of new middle school facilities for many years, having built some of the very first large open-space middle schools in the 1960s.

Tequesta obviously can offer an opportunity for an extensive exploratory program, with such a large number of students to support it, potentially including almost anything: physical education, vocal and instrumental music, drama, business education, home economics, arts and crafts, and industrial arts. The building, constructed in 1990, can accommodate these programs beautifully. The design of the building, with three major enclosed courtyard spaces, allows a gradual transition from the surrounding neighborhood.

The three courtyards at Tequesta function as circulation, congregating, outdoor assembly areas for teams, and as areas for overspill events. All student movements occur within the perimeter of the courtyards, enhancing security measures. Longitudinal corridors allow great visibility and help students and others become oriented quickly to the overall school space. The building was designed by architects (Donald Singer of Fort Lauderdale) as a prototype for a countywide system of new middle school buildings. According to principal Kim Flynn, the first year in the new building was wonderful.

Most important, however, is that the school was designed with a middle school program in mind, and with the realization that the interdisciplinary team organization was the heart of the program. The school building, therefore, is especially facilitative of the team and its community. At Tequesta, each grade level is housed in a separate pod. There can be two teams for each pod, with up to four teachers on each team, with a fourth pod for exceptional students and other classes. Or, as we said, the school can be organized in two houses, with grades 6–8 in each. In front of each grade level team is a smaller commons area for the grade level. The commons area radically expands the instructional

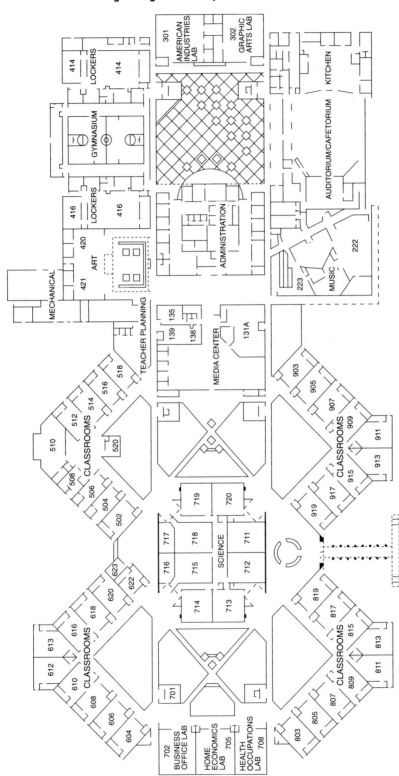

Figure 8.6   **Floor Plan of the Tequesta Trace Middle School.**

space available to teachers and, therefore, contributes a flexibility to the academic program that is far beyond the capacity of schools without this design.

The most exciting thing about this new building is its exceptional flexibility with regard to the science facilities. All science labs are contained in a science facility which, however, is located so centrally that it provides easy and equal access to science programs from every pod. This makes science much more likely to be a part of the interdisciplinary team process, yet permits central storage and use of materials and equipment.

The placement of this science area also allows for future changes in thinking about what is best in the organization of middle level teachers and students, or for taking into account the nature and needs of a particular school population, which is something the typical junior high school building never did. If, for some reason we can not currently imagine, the school staff believed that they were justified in reorganizing from an interdisciplinary organization into academic departments, this building would permit such a major change with ease. Had all middle level school buildings been constructed with this sort of flexibility for the last 50 years, the middle school movement would have been spared one of the major barriers to effectiveness and efficiency, and the team organization may have survived its earlier incarnation in many junior high school programs.

A new middle school for the school district of Lawrence Township, Indiana illustrates the power of new pod-style facilities to accommodate the needs of the middle school concept. The school is designed so that it can house three separate grade level pods, one of which is illustrated in Figure 8.7 (page 422), but it is flexible enough to be used in two other ways. First, the school could easily be organized to accommodate a school-within-a-school design, with a sixth, seventh, and eighth grade team in each of the three houses. It is also possible to return, at some future time, to a departmentalized approach in each pod, since the science facilities are located together. This is so even though each science room faces the rest of the classrooms of the interdisciplinary team of which it is a member. We find few designs to be more flexible and, simultaneously, more accommodating of middle school concepts.

A new middle school building in Leon County, Florida, provides a beautiful example of the use of a facility to teach. At Deerlake Middle School in Tallahassee, the school's buildings have been designated using the names of continents and major land areas to assist students in learning the geography of the world. Hallways are named after major waterways of the world. Homerooms and their advisories take on names of countries.

The new building (opened in 1991) for the Greene County Middle School in Snow Hill, North Carolina (Figure 8.8 page 423) is intended to serve a population of students very different demographically from those who attend Tequesta, but the designs of both buildings is very similar. This illustrates, we believe, the consensus, nationally, surrounding the essence of middle school programs and the nature of facilities that serve them well. Greene County

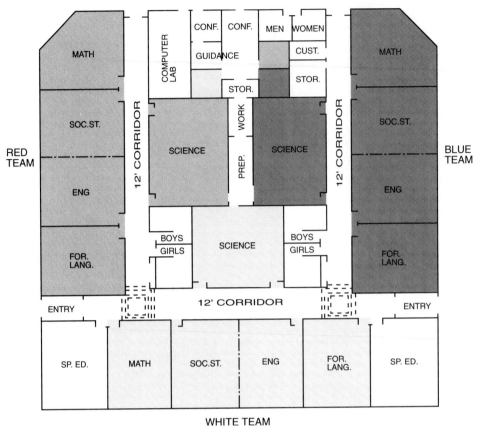

7TH GRADE

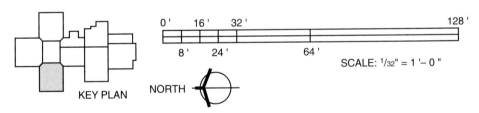

Figure 8.7

Middle School features the flexible placement of science laboratories, academic wings designed to hold two interdisciplinary teams at each grade level or three 6–8 schools-within-a-school, and a strong commitment to the unified arts and physical education, including the performing arts. Flexible partitions in academic wings facilitate innovative groupings or traditional classrooms.

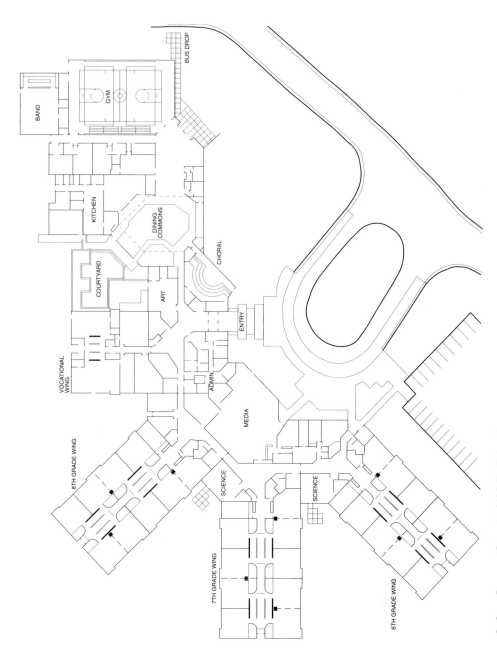

Figure 8.8   **Greene County Middle School**

Interestingly, the brochure describing the new school places a floor plan of the school next to a description of the instructional program which features advisory groups, interdisciplinary teams, block scheduling, exploration, and interest-based activities. The title of the brochure is "Greene County Middle School: A Transition," and we suspect that it is just that, in more than one way.

The Tequesta plant, Greene County Middle School, and other pod-style plants in schools elsewhere (for example, Beverlye Road Middle School, in Dothan, Alabama; Jamesville-DeWitt Middle School, Jamesville, New York; Nock Middle School, Newburyport, Massachusetts), offer the maximum flexibility to middle school programs. A number of schools described in this volume can, quite reasonably, be described as pod-type schools, even though their actual physical plant may or may not have been designed with this purpose initially in mind. Programs at schools such as Farnsworth Middle School, Guiderland, New York, are assisted by spaces that match the programs beautifully. Figure 8.9 and Figure 8.10 (page 426) illustrate both the first and second floors at Farnsworth, where each house extends over both levels. Designed to accommodate 1,650 students, each house consists of four or five interdisciplinary teams, from grades 6 through 8. The staff at Farnsworth express their commitment to "harmonizing the best of two worlds—one which is small enough to foster a feeling of concern for the individual student and one which is large enough to offer the varied resources necessary to meet the needs and interests of preadolescent and early adolescent youngsters."

Examining the floor plan at Farnsworth creates an excited expectation that this type of program is really possible there. One of the authors visited the school in the spring of 1991 to participate in the community celebration of twenty years of outstanding middle school education at Farnsworth. The design of the building has, in fact, contributed to that exemplary program for over two decades— a fact worth celebrating, indeed.

Figure 8.11 (page 427) illustrates the floor plan of Brookhaven Middle School in Decatur, Alabama, recognized since the late 1960s as an outstanding combination of program and plant. Notice the similar program potential in comparison to other schools described in this volume, and the flexibility to make changes in program without major building renovations. The strength of this type of building plan is a major factor in the ability of the school program to maintain a standard of excellence during more than a decade of challenges of all kinds. Figure 8.12 (page 428) shows the features of the building that houses another outstanding program of long duration, that of Olle Middle School, Alief, Texas. Olle illustrates a kind of facility that reaches out to bridge the gap between the pod-style school and the more sweeping open-space schools. Houses at Olle are clearly in evidence, but the program could also be easily modified to focus on an open-space individualized grade-level program.

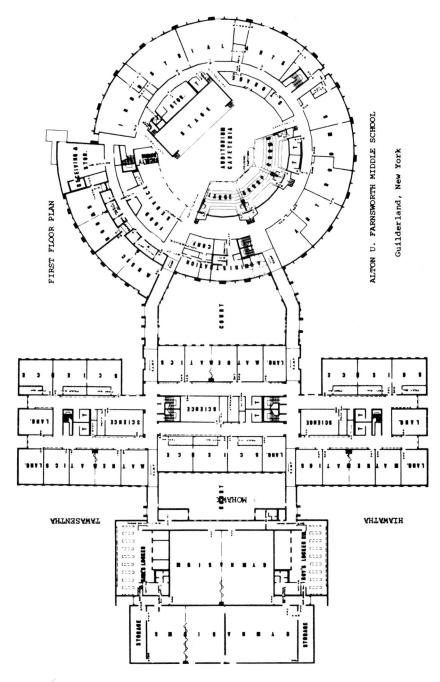

Figure 8.9   **First-Floor Plan, Farnsworth Middle School, Guiderland, New York**

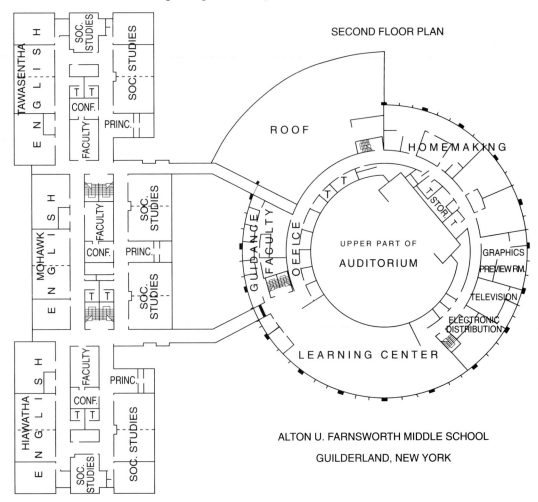

Figure 8.10   **Second-Floor Plan, Farnsworth Middle School, Guiderland, New York**

Open-Space Buildings

Many exemplary middle schools have been housed in what have been known as open-space facilities, originally designed to accommodate programs also described as open, featuring the centrality of individualized instruction and actual team teaching. Following two decades of sometimes painful illumination about the relationship between form and function, many open-space schools have been modified in major ways and have, therefore, come to be known more legitimately as flexibly spaced facilities. The use of movable walls has transformed rigidly open schools into schools where the faculties can shape the facility to fit the program they wish to offer there.

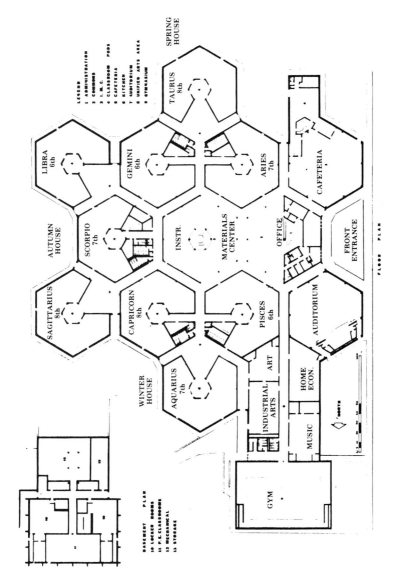

Figure 8.11   **Floor Plan, Brookhaven Middle School, Decatur, Alabama**

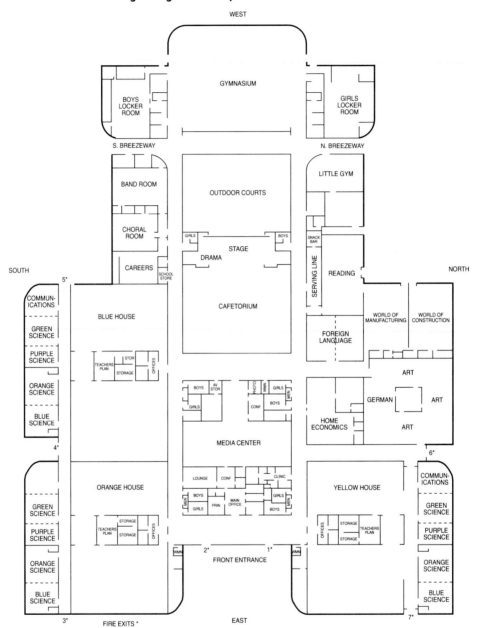

Figure 8.12   **Floor Plan, Olle Middle School, Alief, Texas**

North Marion Middle School in Citra, Florida offers an example of the wise design of flexible space. Figure 8.13 highlights the floor plan at North Marion. Simply stated, virtually all of the walls in the school are movable or removable. Classrooms in the sixth, seventh, and eighth grade team areas can be opened to feature one large space, closed to accommodate conventional classrooms, or arranged for varied sizes to fit almost any purpose. Notice the program reflected

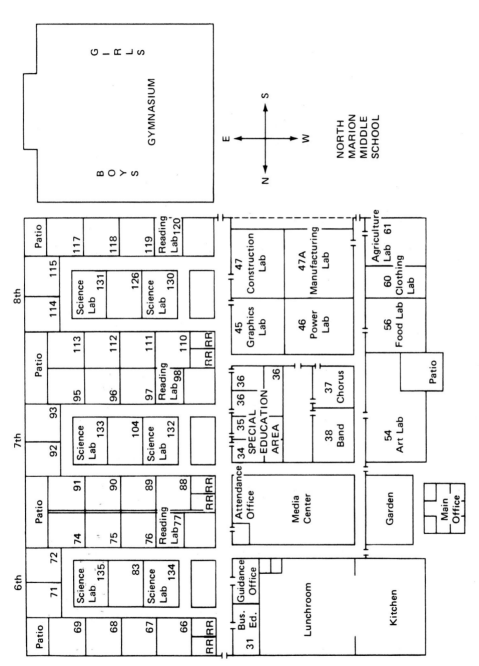

Figure 8.13   **Floor Plan, North Marion Middle School, Citra, Florida**

by the floor plan, and its emphasis on team areas, and exploratory curriculum opportunities. Teams of any size, reflecting the vicissitudes of shifting enrollment patterns in central Florida, can be fitted into each area.

Shellburne Middle School in Shellburne, Vermont exemplifies the effective use of the flexible open-space facility to strengthen the middle school program. Figure 8.14 shows the entire plant, housing 750 students in grades 5 through 8, with a special multiage grouped team as well. Team areas and exploratory spaces are clearly in evidence. Figure 8.15 details a classroom area, listing the advantages of this style: maximum flexibility in accommodating changes in teaching methods and curriculum; efficient use of classroom space to provide for teaching groups of various sizes; corridors utilized as part of the educational spaces; carpeting for acoustical treatment and a homelike atmosphere; completely accessible resource materials, stimulating their use by students; development of appropriate social attitudes based upon the increased awareness of other students; and the use of movable teaching aids, storage units, chalkboards, and tackboards for greater flexibility and increased use.

Many other middle schools have capitalized on the flexibility of the open space school to offer a challenging and stimulating middle school program. One

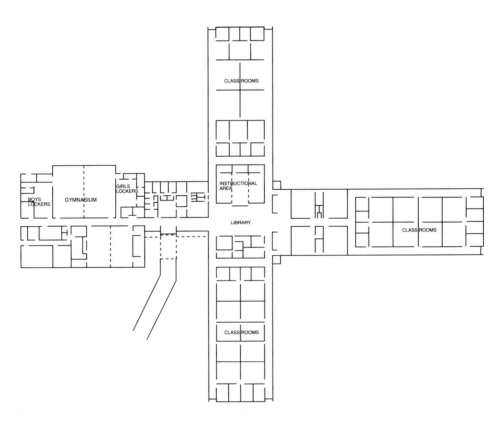

Figure 8.14　**First-Floor Plan, Shelburne Middle School, Shelburne, Vermont**

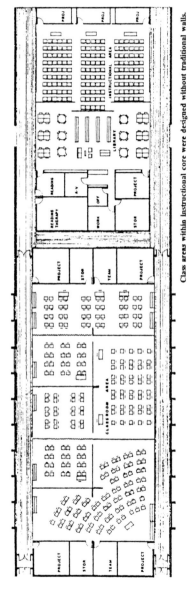

Class areas within instructional core were designed without traditional walls.

CONSTRUCTION STATISTICS

Grades 5–8
Designed Capacity 750
Site 30
Building Area ....85,500 sq. ft.
Cost of Construction (excluding
  land, landscaping, fees and
  furniture)......................$1,515,819.00
Construction Cost per sq. ft.. $ 17.73
Construction Cost per pupil .. $ 2,021.00

OPEN PLAN ADVANTAGES

Provides maximum flexibility for accommodating changes in teaching methods and curricula.

Efficient use of classroom space to provide for teaching groups of various sizes.

Corridors are utilized as part of the educational spaces.

Carpeting is used for acoustical treatment and homelike atmosphere.

Resource materials are completely accessible to stimulate their use by all the students.

Social attitudes are developed based upon the increased awareness of other students.

Teaching aids, storage units, chalkboards and tackboards can be movable for greater flexibility and increased use.

Figure 8.15   **Classroom and Core Plan, Shelburne Middle School, Shelburne, Vermont**

of the oldest and most successful is MacDonald Middle School of East Lansing, Michigan. Designed to accommodate 850 students in grades 6–8, MacDonald has been operating in this facility since 1968. The school has been recognized as a special facility and received a great deal of attention for its design. A number of journals (e.g., The American School Board Journal, Nation's Schools) offer numerous and detailed descriptions of new and different designs for use by school districts. Readers interested in an in-depth treatment of individual schools are encouraged to seek out examples in this part of the professional literature.

General Considerations for Specifications for New Buildings

Following two decades of adapting old buildings and erecting new buildings, most school leaders have come to agreement of several principles which should be considered by the next generation of middle school facility planners:

1. Size is an important factor. Schools with fewer than 800 students quickly become expensive propositions when planners attempt to build in a "full core" of opportunities beyond regular classrooms. Physical education facilities can not be "halved." Libraries and media centers can not be made so small that they make later expansion of the facilities difficult. On the other hand, schools substantially larger than 1,000 students quickly begin to lose the economy of scale which they gain by their size. This is true in terms of the physical facility, and also regarding the management of the program.

2. The larger the school, the more important it becomes to place assistant administrators and counselors in academic wings of the school, rather than in academic suites. Direct delivery of their services to teachers and students can be done much more efficiently. In small schools, where there are no assistants, this obviously can not be done.

3. Administrative and counseling areas should always be separated. Again, this is a result of considering who the counselor is serving. The recipient of counselor services, ideally, ought to be the students and not the school administrators. This separation is likely to enhance the services as they were intended.

4. In line with the mainstreaming movement, co-teaching, and other considerations for exceptional students, areas for these students should be dispersed throughout the academic wings, rather than being clustered together in the rear of the facility. This is particularly so in the case of learning disabled (LD) students, generally considered the best candidates for complete mainstreaming. But other exceptional students have a right to be considered a part of the school as a whole, and their placement should reflect it.

5. New schools should be designed to minimize student movement around the building, which recommends the house plan, or school-within-a-school

model where students remain in the same part of the building for the whole day, and for the whole tenure of their time in middle school. Schools like Wakulla, Tequesta, and Greene County are flexible enough to be used in this way, or in more traditional grade level wing groupings.

6. These schools also offer the sort of flexibility which is clearly desirable for the schools of the 21st century. Arranged as they are, they can be changed to reflect new insights into middle level education, changing demographics, or other factors which might influence the way in which a building should be used. The placement of the science facilities in buildings like Tequesta and Mandarin testify to the flexibility which a new generation may appreciate. Other plans should make future expansion a possibility.

7. Although it may seem trivial, the placement of driveways for parents and busses is also important. Experience indicates that there should be separate areas for parents and buses picking up students at the end of the day. And, it seems important to suggest that new facilities be planned so that the buses deposit students at an entrance near the cafeteria, since so many students now eat their breakfast at school.

8. Teachers on teams engage in an amazing number of parent conferences. Experienced middle school educators recommend that several larger conference rooms be placed near the entrance of the school to facilitate the efficient conduct of such conferences. This placement makes it unnecessary for parents to wonder through the school in search of a teacher planning room, or for administrators to accompany them to a distant destination.

9. Security of the school plant and school site should be considered in initial planning. Landscape designs should harmonize with building security, as in internal courtyards like Tequesta. Blind corners, dead end corridors and areas difficult to supervise should be excluded whenever possible. Smooth exterior areas, large glass panels, or other features which will provide for graffiti or other types of vandalism are not in the best interests of new middle schools. Adequate night lighting should plan for evening uses of the facility for community education programs and the like.

Time and Space in the Middle School: Concluding Comments

The effective use of time and space in the middle school is absolutely critical to the successful implementation of the other portions of the middle school program. If a component of the middle school program can not be scheduled, it can not be offered to the students. If there is no space which can be adapted to the use of a program part, that part will be unlikely to become a regular component of the program. In a sense, the organization of time and space stands as the ultimate restriction on the type of program possible in any particular middle school. But in the opposition sense, properly designed, these two factors represent a liberating opportunity for the expansion and enrichment of complex yet community-building school programs.

School planners interested in helping the staff of a middle school program get the most from the schedule and the building they use, must foster the development of several important skills. For administrators, a clear understanding of the program priorities and the knowledge of the steps involved in the construction of a master schedule to accommodate team organization are crucial. The ability and commitment to place teams together within the building seems almost as important. For teachers, directors of staff development programs will assist most directly when they help teachers learn how to use the schedule to their own advantage, to schedule their own students and special activities within the schedule, and to turn the design of the plant, however constructed, to the enhancement of the life of the interdisciplinary team.

ADDITIONAL SUGGESTIONS FOR FURTHER STUDY

A. Books and Monographs

Calhoun, F. S. (1983). *Organization of the middle grades: A summary of research.* Arlington, VA: Educational Research Service.

B. Periodicals

Alexander, W. M. (1988). Schools in the middle: Rhetoric and reality. *Social Education, 52*(2), 107–109.

Jung, P. W. & Gunn, R. M. (1990). Serving the educational and developmental needs of middle level students. *NASSP Bulletin, 74*(525), 73–79.

Koepke, M. (1990). Rebirth. *Teacher, 2*(2), 50–55.

C. ERIC

Braddock, J. H., II (& others). (1988). *School organization in the middle grades: National variations and effects.* (Report No. 24). Baltimore, MD: Center for Research on Elementary and Middle Schools. (ERIC Document Reproduction Service No. ED 301 320)

Daniel, L. G. (1990, January). *Operationalization of a frame of reference for studying organizational culture in middle schools.* Paper presented at the Annual Meeting of the Southwest Educational Research Association, Austin, TX. (ERIC Document Reproduction Service No. ED 315 452)

Hager, R. A. (1990). *Open education: A look at the subtleties. A guide for the unfamiliar observer of intermediate education* (Occasional Paper 90–1). Columbus, OH: National Middle School Institute. (ERIC Document Reproduction Service No. 322 567)

Lake, S. (1988). *Scheduling the middle level school: Philosophy into practice* (Practitioner's Monograph #1). Sacramento, CA: California League of Middle Schools. (ERIC Document Reproduction Service No. ED 300 920)

McGinley, N. J. (1988). *Middle school organization and scheduling*. Philadelphia, PA: Philadelphia School District, Office of Research and Evaluation. (ERIC Document Reproduction Service No. ED 309 530)

McPartland, J. M. (& others). (1987). *School structures and classroom practices in elementary, middle, and secondary schools*. (Report No. 14). (ERIC Document Reproduction Service No. ED 291 703)

D. Dissertations and Dissertation Abstracts

Doda, N. (1984). Teacher perspectives and practices in two organizationally different middle schools (Doctoral dissertation: University of Florida, 1984).

Green, R. P. (1989). The effect of classroom organizational structure on student relationships, staff cooperation and teaching practices in sixth-grade classrooms at the middle school level in Michigan (Doctoral dissertation, Michigan State University, 1989). *Dissertation Abstracts International*, 50/07a, 1867.

Lawrence, C. E. (1989). A study of eighth-grade student performance in two school organizational patterns (Doctoral dissertation, The University of Wisconsin–Milwaukee, 1989) *Dissertation Abstracts International*, 50/11a, 3433.

CHAPTER 9

Planning the New Middle School

Hundreds of school districts have reorganized their grade level configurations over the last twenty years. Some of these change projects have been managed in a way that has produced high-quality middle schools with programs in which that quality has been sustained until today. In many other districts, high-quality programs were either never established or, once established, quality quickly began to erode, so that few traces of those change efforts now remain, save for the changes in grade levels which accomplished other purposes for the district and were thus sustained for other reasons. The difference in these two experiences has a great deal to do, we believe, with the degree of understanding and skill (i.e., leadership) with which the reorganization effort was planned and managed.

Hundreds of additional school districts appear primed to launch reorganization efforts or are ready to install authentic middle school components in existing middle level schools. To do so effectively, we believe (based on our experiences) there are a number of important planning tasks which must be accomplished. We offer the steps and tasks described below as a relatively complete catalog of planning decisions which must be made during a district level reorganization. It is important to point out that the decisions we believe to be essential to the development and maintenance of quality middle school programs are also related to the recommendations of groups such as the National Middle School Association and the Carnegie Council on Adolescent Development.

Six-Step Middle School Implementation Plan

In our twenty-five years' experience working with school districts changing to middle school, we think we see, in the most ideal situations, what amounts to a six-step planning and implementation process. In the most ideal circumstances, each step is equivalent to a year. Even in districts where planners and implementers may not consciously employ a six-year model, it seems to evolve this way. Here we use the term "steps," although, regardless of however long the time period, the process is essentially the same.

Step One: Need. Planners determine that a move to middle school may meet one or more important needs manifested by students or schools in the district.

Step Two: Study. Planners study the middle school concept and its implications for the district.

Step Three: Plan. Specific guidelines, programs, and action plans are developed to translate the middle school concept into real school programs.

Step Four: Open. New middle school programs are implemented and evaluated formatively.

Step Five: Fix. Efforts are extended to make more certain that mistakes are corrected and revisions implemented to bring the original intentions to fruition.

Step Six: Evaluate. Summative evaluations determine the extent to which the new middle school programs produce the desired outcomes which manifested themselves as felt needs during the initial year.

Strategic Planning for Middle School Implementation

Plans will be made most knowledgeably and implemented most effectively throughout the entire implementation cycle when involvement of stakeholders is as complete as possible. Involvement is the key. Our experience has been that the process works best when a strategic planning model is followed carefully, including the in-depth and continuing involvement of the district superintendent, board members, parents, teachers, other school building leaders, and outside consultants. A steering committee representing these groups, and smaller task groups for each assignment, should study and develop a consensus on the following important questions. A carefully-written planning document, which will guide the implementation of exemplary middle schools should result from deliberations on fourteen very important planning areas.

(1) Middle school philosophy   Few exemplary middle schools are implemented without attention to developing a school or district middle school philosophy as a part of the initial planning process. The philosophy must spell out the district's beliefs about the characteristics and needs of their young adolescent students, based on an analysis of the specific demographics students present. Among questions for which planners need answers are these:

- How many students of what ages and grades are to be served?
- What are the characteristics of the school community to be served? Socio-economic status? Mobility/stability? Racial, religious, cultural backgrounds?
- What is the age/grade distribution of the population? What factors explain any unusual age variations (e.g., over-age students)?
- What data as to the distribution of mental ability are available? What do they show?
- What data as to academic achievement, especially reading levels, are available? What do they show?
- What generalizations can be made from available data regarding previous students in this school community as to such factors as: Continuation in high school? College attendance? Career choices?

Additional insight regarding the needs of the school community and the student population may be gained from examination of data that are available or can be gathered on such items as these:

Occupations of the parents of students who attend the school
Attitudes of parents toward schooling
Stability of families
Presence of both parents in the home

The second part of the middle school philosophy relates to affirmations about schools which are responsive to the needs of such students. This might include comments about the goals and objectives of the overall middle school program to be planned for students with the special characteristics that have been identified. Details of these program components will enter the plan at a later point, but the purpose of such components can be spelled out in the philosophical statement, alerting readers and planners that a different sort of school experience is intended.

This section of the planning document should also include a statement which clarifies the extent to which the district guidelines are to be interpreted flexibly by individual schools. If there are substantial differences in the demographic patterns for students attending middle schools in different areas of the same district, it will be important to include a statement encouraging flexibility in the implementation of the middle school plan. To do otherwise would abandon the commitment to build the school around the characteristics and needs of a specific group of students. In the real world of schools, many districts are characterized by schools in one area of the district serving majority culture, upper-middle-class students, while schools in another area of the same district serve primarily poor and minority children. To ignore such important differences in the implementation of middle schools is to ignore the uniqueness of each school population. This does not mean that there are no districtwide guidelines; it means that such guidelines should be implemented with specific groups of students in mind. All schools in the district, for example, might be committed to the interdisciplinary team organization without specifying exactly what sort of teams might be implemented in each school.

A middle school philosophy can also be sharpened into a mission statement. The "Mission Statement" for 1989 from Burlingame Intermediate School (Burlingame, California), is an example of a brief statement that is clear in its focus and appropriate for a school population of upper-middle-class, high-achieving, but multicultural students:

> Burlingame Intermediate School is a school where learning is truly celebrated, where each individual on campus is committed to excellence through a cooperative effort, and where there is a primary focus on academics. BIS is a safe, caring, friendly school where each individual is valued and respected. It is a school which meets the unique needs of students who are moving from childhood to adolescence. The total educational community works cooperatively for the successful completion of this mission.

Desert Sky Middle School of Glendale, Arizona was named one of the "top ten schools in Arizona" in 1990. The school's mission statement is clear and precise:

> The faculty and staff believe in the self-worth of each individual at Desert Sky Middle School. Our curriculum and instruction are organized to match the unique developmental characteristic of middle level students and to create a sense of belonging for all. Our focus is to integrate academic, explorative, and thematic learning. It is our emphasis to prepare our middle level students in cooperative and critical thinking skills to enhance their success in our informative society. Students at Desert Sky will possess a receptiveness for new learning and carry with them Thunderbolt Pride.

In the first edition of this textbook (Alexander & George, 1981), the statement of philosophy from MacDonald Middle School (East Lansing, Michigan) in the late 1970s was as follows:

> Regardless of the organizational structure, the ultimate goal of the MacDonald Middle School is in human relationships. Humanizing education can be accomplished when each person involved in the process recognizes and cares about the needs of each individual student. It is the goals of the middle school to help

transcents meet and effectively deal with the challenges confronting them. Thus, all personnel—students, teachers, administration, parents, community members, and other school related personnel—have responsibilities toward this end.

The mission statement at the same school, with the same leadership, twenty years later, is as follows (S. DiFranco, personal communication, December, 1990):

> The staff at MacDonald Middle School is committed to the belief that all children, regardless of gender, race, socio-economic status, or previous academic performance, can realize their potential. Our purpose is to teach skills, thinking processes, and concepts while fostering positive social and emotional growth. Therefore, we eagerly accept this obligation with the confidence that our combined efforts will prepare students to function as responsible and contributing members of society.

It is not necessary to omit student participation from this process. When Broomfield Heights Middle School (Broomfield, Colorado) was being established, the students were helped to develop a Student Philosophy which was permanently inscribed and displayed in the school foyer. The student philosophy stated that:

> Broomfield Heights Middle School is a good place to learn. It is a clean, bright, safe, comfortable, and peaceful place where we can learn and work. We will get a good education so we can go to high school while at the same time enjoying our school and its activities. [BHMS] is a place where we can:
> Work hard, be helpful, friendly, and meet new friends.
> Take basic subjects.
> Study new and different subjects, learn new things, and participate in different activities.
> Have many choices.
> Have many things going on so that learning will be done in many different ways.
> Develop personal pride and cooperate with the rules and standards of the school.
> Find out about careers and learn skills which may help us get a job.
> Have volunteers and parents in our school helping us.
> Have good todays and better tomorrows.

A faculty's philosophical statement can profit from a knowledge of what the students seek from their middle school experience.

(2) Organization of teachers and students for learning   In many ways, the uniqueness of the middle school concept, up to the nineties, relates to the way in which teachers and students are organized, not in how they teach or what they learn. District planners must develop two important plans: How will our teachers be organized to deliver instruction? How will our students be organized to receive it? Planners must use their knowledge of student needs to decide the degree of subject specialization that should enter into the way in which teachers are organized. Although there will be some variability among middle schools in large and diverse districts, the planning document must address the specific question of how many subjects teachers will be expected to teach and to how many students per day.

Planners will also want to highlight the importance of the teacher-student relationship in the district's schools, and the strategies that will be used to build those relationships. Questions about the amount of time that the same team of teachers and students should spend together each day must be answered. In many districts, long-term teacher-student relationships will be important, requiring the same group of teachers and students to stay together for more than one year; in other schools, this will not be nearly as important.

Balancing these two factors (subject specialization and teacher-student relationships) will yield information for planning the sort of interdisciplinary team organization that is implied for a particular school within the district, the particular "address" for a school within the middle school zipcode. Will the school(s) have gradewide teams, a school-within-a-school plan, student-teacher progression, or some other design?

(3) Curriculum   Planners will be required to outline the nature of the daily curriculum offered to middle school students. Plans must be made for both daily required subjects and additional curriculum opportunities which will be available in the form of exploratory, unified arts, or elective classes. The role that choice should play must be written.

(4) Co-Curriculum   Planners must arrange for an exciting array of activities in which all students can experience success. Planned policies must insure that middle school activities will be appropriate for young adolescents, and high school activities and experiences will be saved for high school. Controversies in these areas must be faced and resolved. (We discussed many of these issues in Chapter 3.)

(5) Advisory Programs   Plans must be laid so that every student will have at least one supportive adult in the school. Steps must be taken to insure that such a program will have the support of all members of the school and community. Okaloosa County, Florida did its level best to maximize community understanding and acceptance of the implementation of its advisory program in 1990 by involving church groups, community agencies, and parent representatives in the steering committee which reviewed the plans for the new advisory curriculum. Even then, fringe groups interested in advocating special positions on a very narrow range of issues found room to criticize it, much to the disappointment of hard-working planners.

(6) Instruction   A comprehensive plan for moving to middle school will include plans to move to instructional strategies which are the most appropriate and effective for the education of young adolescents. Methods of grouping for instruction within each classroom must be arranged. The most acceptable mix of heterogeneous and homogeneous grouping must be woven into the fabric of the new schools. It is with this issue, of course, that the most heated discussions will occur, even more so than those surrounding the advisory program. Planners must be well prepared if they want a positive response from parents. It can be done, even in the most difficult situations. In Ann Arbor, Michigan, for example, middle schools were successfully implemented in the early 1990s with a maximum amount of heterogeneous grouping due to the assiduous planning which preceded the transition.

(7) Schedule   Planners must arrive at the most effective time-design for implementation of the middle school program: Will it be a block schedule? Will teachers have the sort of planning time they need? A copious number of questions will have to be answered by school planners before individual school leaders will be able to implement an effective schedule. Every district must also be clear about the roles that will be played by the principal, the teacher teams, the central office, and, most notably, the computer services in the scheduling process.

(8) Leadership   Planners have, all too often, left leadership untouched in the last two decades of middle school development. New roles for teachers and accompanying staff development have been common, but little has been done to clarify new roles for leaders or to prepare leaders to acquire the knowledge, skills, and attitudes to go with those roles. Special roles must be developed for various school leaders: team leaders, subject area coordinators, committee chairs, etc. Processes for choosing and supporting such persons must be installed in the plans for the new schools. A preferred model of collaborative administrator-teacher decision making must be established in the district's middle schools.

(9) Special Programs   Plans must be drawn up which will insure that the needs of exceptional students will be attended to in the new middle schools. Such efforts must be coordinated with the new model of interdisciplinary team organization? Programs like those for the gifted and talented, foreign language, Chapter One, etc., must be accommodated in the new program.

(10) Staffing and Staff Development   The district must establish, as early as possible, a career mobility plan to insure that the new middle schools are staffed by the administrators and teachers most appropriate for that assignment. Staff members must have informed opportunities for making career choices which may involve moving from one school or school level to another. In Orange County, Florida, the career mobility plan included "job fairs" held several times during the 1986–87 school year, prior to the opening of the new schools the next fall. On several evenings, high school principals convened in a school library and interviewed any junior high teacher who wanted to transfer to high school rather than become a part of the new middle school. A parallel program was scheduled for elementary teachers who wished to move to the middle. As a result of these fairs, and other components of the career mobility plan, Orange County middle school planners were able to say that, on the day the new middle level schools opened, 98 percent of the teachers in Orange County were teaching at the school level they desired, and the others were on a waiting list for the first available openings at the level of their choice. Such results go a long way toward the sort of professional morale which leads to commitment to implement difficult new designs. Such staffing effectiveness lifts a considerable burden from the staff development needs.

Districts must, nevertheless, plan for training opportunities which insure that the staff that does come to the new middle schools possesses the appropriate knowledge, skills, and attitudes for launching and maintaining the new middle schools. Special training experiences will be required in knowledge of the characteristics of young adolescents, effective classroom strategies, working on and with interdisciplinary teams, acting as an advisor, and being a part of collaborative decision-making groups.

(11) Adjustments and Modifications to Buildings and Other Programs   The implementation of middle schools is not simply a middle level project. It is extremely critical to the success of district level reorganization that those responsible understand and act on the knowledge that *all* students and *every* school in the district will be effected by the reorganization effort. In one stroke, as we have said, virtually all of the schools in the district will become "younger." The elementary school will lose the older students, the middle level will be one third younger, and the high school will house a student body which will be 25 percent younger. This means that every administrator, teacher, student, and parent, in the district will be involved. "Business as usual" at any level, when the schools will have much younger student bodies, will court disaster. A task group must be assigned the responsibility for planning the communications tactics that will be pursued to inform both the internal and external publics of the purposes and programs associated with middle level reorganization. These planners must insure that teachers and administrators at the elementary and high school levels will be informed and involved, and that parents and community members will also be informed. The same group must confront the question of the adjustments in programs that will be necessary for the elementary and high schools in the district. They must figure out how the high school staff members will be involved in preparing for the changes which will be necessary to accommodate the arrival of ninth graders effectively. Failure to do so will cause substantial disappointment among ninth grade parents and frustration among the faculty and students. Plans must be made for adjustments to school buildings, at all three levels, to accommodate the new middle school programs, and the effects which new groups of students will have on high schools.

In New Hanover County, North Carolina, for example, planners implemented "Passport," a transition program which prepares students moving from fifth to sixth grade and from eighth to ninth grade. Developed by counselors at all grade levels, each spring students in the appropriate grade levels are involved in a program that is like going to a new country. Students receive "travel brochures," maps, travel kits, travel videos, penpals, and other items which orient them to their new school. Each spring, student "ambassadors" from the new schools travel with counselors to meet the rising groups.

In Panama City, Florida, the district has established districtwide articulation committees for elementary-middle transitions, and for middle-high school transitions. Videos of middle and high schools were developed for every school in the district. Students from middle and high schools return to their middle or elementary schools for visits in which they share their experiences and give advice. Each eighth grader in the district is given a booklet, "Into the Future," which helps him/her get registered in the correct high school programs.

In Randolph Township, New Jersey, planners established a "Passages and Transitions" program to deal with articulation between the middle and the elementary and high schools. The program includes more than 50 ideas for making these transitions smooth and effective: orientation visits of all types; contacts between teachers, administrators, and counselors at the three levels; evening programs for parents; summer mailings and social activities; joint meetings of the middle school and high school student governments; peer leader programs; and more. Perhaps the most interesting-sounding articulation program in Randolph Township, however, is the Project SMILE (Society for Making Incoming Learners at Ease), a peer leadership program focusing on the orientation process.

Redwood Middle School, in Napa, California, actually has a "Road Show," which is the name for the team of middle level educators that visits feeder elementary school faculty and parent meetings. The purpose of Road Show sessions is primarily to answer questions and dispel misconceptions. The district also holds "Teacher Transition Workshops" for teachers in the elementary schools to help them help their students get ready for middle school.

It may also be the case that the district is involved in programs or organizational strategies that, if not in direct conflict with the middle school concept, may make implementation of the middle school more difficult. The "Year-Round School" may be one such program. Educators in some districts have found that it is challenging to integrate the interdisciplinary team organization into a year-round school. At Cache County Public Schools in North Logan, Utah, for example, it has been difficult to bring both interdisciplinary teams and year-round school to fruition simultaneously. Difficult, but not impossible, since that district has made determined efforts to do just that. In the 1992–93 school year, each of four middle level schools was to be organized into four-teacher interdiscpli-nary teams. Even at this point, however, one "track" of students will always be out on vacation, so that teachers can never engage all students in team activities simultaneously. We see this as a minor complaint, and wager that the interdis-ciplinary team organization will become a more and more important part of year-round school efforts, especially at the middle school level. To do so most effectively, however, district planners must build in such intentions at the beginning.

(12) Communication Plans   The district must set out to inform all stakeholders of the concepts involved and the planning stages which the district will pass through. Communications must be targeted at both internal and external pub-lics, as soon as clarity can be assured, to quash any misinformation which might lead to misunderstanding and opposition. In Orange County, Florida, the com-munications plan involved a variety of strategies matching the stage of devel-opment of plans for the new middle schools. Early on, for example, bookmarks announcing "Coming August 1987—America's Best Middle Schools" were dis-tributed by the thousands. This simple message let everyone know that planners were convinced the change would be a positive one. Posters saying "6–7–8—Middle School Is Great" came later and appeared in all schools and all over the district. Students were given the opportunity to write letters to their middle level principals about concerns they might have about the new school; thousands of such letters were received. Parents received a letter from the superintendent and a middle school brochure. They read articles about middle schools published in school district and community newspapers. Dozens of orientations were held. An equally rigorous communications campaign focused on teachers and their concerns. All of these plans came out of the committee on Communications.

In Ann Arbor, Michigan, another district with a reputation for having accom-plished a difficult transition well, the communication plans were terribly impor-tant, because during "the early stages of the transition to middle schools there was not a broad base of community support" (R. Williamson, personal com-munication, January, 1991). The community information effort which resulted, in Ann Arbor, had three major components: surveying and gathering information from the staff and community; distribution of a newsletter to build a shared base of information; and, inclusion of all constituencies in the planning, including "known dissenters." We believe that this last strategy, including persons who are initially opposed to the transition, is as important as it is difficult. In districts where there is the courage to involve such opponents, the transition which even-tually takes place is almost always smoother. The temptation to attempt to exclude such dissenters, while appealing in the short term, is usually disastrous in the long haul. As Ron Williamson of Ann Arbor expressed it:

> Many school constituencies were included in the planning committees. The
> committees included staff, parents, community members without children in

the schools, senior citizens, an adolescent psychologist, business people, and others. This broad base of involvement contributed to our successful planning. One additional critical component was the inclusion of known "dissenters" on the planning committee. The district acknowledged their concern and recognized that the issues they raised would either be addressed during the planning or at a later date. It is particularly powerful when a known "dissenter" endorses the recommendations for a middle school program.

(13) Evaluation   Planners must identify which evaluation strategies are to be pursued, what data collected, in order for the district staff to be able to judge the extent to which the middle school program has been implemented as planned (formative evaluation). They must also identify the outcomes of the reorganization which should be measured to determine the degree to which the middle school program has improved the education of the district (summative evaluation).

(14) Action Plans   Ultimately, these subcommittees contribute recommendations which become a part of a school or district Action Plan for conversion to the middle school. Excellent examples of such plans abound and can easily be acquired from school districts mentioned in this textbook (especially valuable are those from Orange County, Florida; Ann Arbor, Michigan; and High Point, North Carolina) and from districts near one's own who have made a successful transition. The Middle School Action Plan from Orange County, Florida emerged from long months of careful study, and contained thirty-one basic standards, with matching activities which would guarantee the implementation of those program standards, persons responsible, and the date to be achieved. Each standard identified a component of the middle school concept that Orange County had chosen to implement. The plan became the guide which moved eighteen junior high schools toward a successful transition to middle schools, implementing all thirty-one standards, in 1988.

Individual schools must, of course, have their own action plans. And, as an indication of how far the middle school movement had spread by 1990, the Singapore American School Program Planning Guide, 1990–1991, serves as a good example of such a plan for an individual school. The action plan for the school identified eight basic steps in the transition process there, with accompanying assignments of personnel, start and due dates, and the date completed to be filled in. The major steps included:

1. development of a steering committee
2. needs assessment
3. development of questionnaires and surveys for research and study purposes
4. school visitations
5. inservice and staff development

6. establishment of a professional library
7. development of a written philosophy to be the driving force for program improvement
8. establishment of subcommittees for developing recommendations to the steering committee in the areas of academics, professional development, guidance and human relations, student evaluation, extracurricular activities, community awareness, and facilities.

The title of this overall action plan for the Singapore American School was "We will research, develop, and implement an exemplary middle school program." Indeed, the resolve to do so is now evident in many distant places, in American/international schools and Department of Defense Dependent Schools in many parts of Europe, Saudi Arabia, India, Japan, Indonesia, the Phillipines—virtually everywhere.

Strategic planning for school improvement at the middle level is not, of course, limited to changing from junior high to middle school or opening new middle schools. It can and should also happen when district or school leaders discover that existing middle schools are not attaining reasonable goals. Since so many middle schools were opened for reasons which, initially, had little to do with the actual rationale for middle level education, educators in many districts around the country are, in fact, discovering the need to create exemplary middle schools in buildings which had only changed their names or grade levels. In our opinion, this task is significantly more challenging than opening a new building or changing from a junior high school, but may be much more important.

In 1989, in Leon County, Florida (Tallahassee), educators there began an effort to reinstall an exemplary middle school program in a district which had an uninspiring 6–8 middle level configuration for many years. A new middle school philosophy was developed, with direct reference to the characteristics and needs of the students. Planning processes paralleled the recommendations of the Carnegie Council (1989) and the state of Florida's PRIME (Progress in Middle Level Education) legislation. Sixteen specific objectives emerged, with matching implementation strategies. An Action Plan stresses principal leadership in implementing the objectives over a period stretching from 1989 to 1994. The strategic plan for reinventing the middle school in Leon County also includes an "involvement plan" focusing on parents and community, and staff development and evaluation plans that are exceptionally detailed. We believe these efforts may represent the beginning of an important trend in districts around the country who now recognize that their middle level schools can be exemplary ones.

Assessing the odds for a successful conversion from junior high schools to middle schools, or in re-inventing existing ones, is an important part of planning. Gene Pickler, Senior Administrator for Secondary Operations, in Orange County, Florida, shares important questions which can help estimate the odds:

1. What is the history of middle level education in your district?
2. What is the real momentum behind your district's conversion plan?
3. Is there a district level commitment to the change process?
4. Is your district willing to commit its own resources (human, money, and time) toward your conversion process?
5. Does your conversion effort involve a broad base of participants?
6. What is your public relations plan?
7. How will you monitor your change process?
8. What is your staff development plan?
9. Will you convert all of your schools at the same time or in phases and pilots?
10. How will you staff your middle schools?
11. Is your superintendent elected or appointed?
12. Do you have any "good schools" in your district, those likely to resist change of any kind?
13. Will your contract permit you to begin pilot programs prior to implementation?
14. How will you evaluate your effort?

Staff Development: Guidelines and Roles

At its core, the middle school movement has been a reconceptualization and reorganization of the ways in which people work with each other to facilitate the learning process. As such, it is possible to interpret the failure of other attempts to meet the education needs of middle school students (i.e., some K–8 and 7–9 schools) as due to their failure to respond to the need to prepare people for this new way of being together professionally. Reorganization efforts that were stimulated solely by reasons essentially external to the mission of a school itself, however salutary (e.g., desegregation, efficient use of buildings), often achieved much less than might have been accomplished. We believe that effective staff development is the key to comprehensive program implementation. When this is acknowledged and planned, effective programs emerge; when it is not, little changes except the external elements that provoked the initial efforts. Even the most carefully designed multi-year implementation plan can not overcome the deficiencies imposed by inadequate staff development.

During the last twenty-five years, middle school educators have learned a great deal about effective staff development, but nothing more significant than that there are very important prerequisites to the entire inservice process. First, and long before the process of staff development formally begins, is the need for—the absolute necessity of—straightforward clarification and disclosure of the initiating circumstances for the move toward middle schools in the first place. The fact that most middle schools, by 1992, had still been opened as a concomitant to other fundamental changes is nothing to hide; it does not demean the middle school to have it born out of a need to meet other commitments. It has been our experience, however, that whenever staff development projects are undertaken without the real reasons for the move to middle school being fully clarified, elaborated, and discussed by all parties, enthusiasm for and willingness to participate fully in such projects is far less than desirable. When there is no choice for the professionals involved, there is all the more reason to surround the staff development process with the opportunity for questioning and discussion.

The school district of Columbia Heights, Minnesota offers a good example of the openness that permits a more objective investigation of the merits of moving to middle school. Faced with a drastically declining enrollment over the decade of the 1970s, the district entered 1980 with the unavoidable need to reorganize the K–12 school plan and develop a list of teachers who may eventually have had to be subject to the infamous "reduction in force." Under these circumstances, to have ballyhooed the implementation of the middle school as a quasi-cover-up for the real issue of declining enrollments would have been a terrible error. As it was, however, the district leaders faced the issue squarely and openly, and dealt fairly with all involved. Consequently, the bad feelings that might have blighted the move to the middle school did not develop. In Columbia Heights, the middle school plan was enthusiastically accepted.

Staff development efforts will, we believe, almost always be more successful when, as a second prerequisite, the commitment of the central administration to the middle school is clearly perceived and easily discussed by those who are asked to undergo the training to equip them for the move to the new school organization. Teachers and others at the school level have learned to measure the commitment of others "farther up" in the district hierarchy by, among other things, the amount of visible time that central office personnel and school administrators devote to participation in the fundamental efforts of retraining. People budget their time to projects they assign value to, and when central office staff are seldom seen at the staff development activities, or when teachers and others never have an opportunity to listen to these persons articulate their interest in or support for the reorganization effort, enthusiasm and effort wane. Modeling is an important tool for stimulating learning, even at such an advanced professional level.

In the school district of Okaloosa County, Florida, for example, over a two-year period of staff development leading to the implementation of middle school in 1990, rarely a single session went by without an appearance, even if just for a few minutes, by the district superintendent. The district had the highest test scores in the state, and the lowest dropout rate, in its junior high schools during most of the eighties, and highly popular junior high football programs. Consequently, many parents and patrons of the district were adamantly opposed to the middle school concept, and the transition could have been a very unpleasant and unsuccessful process. It was, on the contrary, highly successful, at least in part because of the willingness of several central office staff members to attend very frequent and time-consuming planning and staff development sessions.

Similarly, staff development efforts are enhanced whenever those involved have the opportunity to hear school board members demonstrate their understanding of and commitment to the reorganization effort. Early efforts to inform and advise the school board almost always, we believe, result in increased personal and financial support for professional staff development efforts when they become necessary. The adoption of a "wait and see" attitude by board members almost seems to guarantee less than optimal success in retraining the professional staff. In Okaloosa County, again, staff development time and funds were available in unprecedented amounts because of the direct involvement of school board members. Unpaid, after school inservice education was, therefore, held to a minimum. In the spring of 1990, consequently, a formative evaluation of the new middle school program there made it clear that the planned program had been effectively implemented.

A third prerequisite to effective staff development is the appointment of a coordinator for the retraining effort. One person must be the central figure responsible for the inservice education of those to be a part of the new middle schools. Spreading the responsibilities around will only dilute their power to change the schools. The coordinator should, ideally, have training and experience at both the elementary and secondary levels, in addition to an in-depth exposure to the middle school movement. Such a broad perspective is important to the design of appropriate components of the staff development program. Without such a broad background, it is all too likely that the staff development program will take on a character that reflects the narrower perspectives of an educator wearing professional blinders. It is only human to design programs, staff development or otherwise, that reflect one's own experience and training.

In Dothan, Alabama in the late seventies, and in Orange County, Florida in the late eighties, planning began three years prior to the implementation of middle schools in both districts, albeit a decade apart. A position for coordinator of middle school transition was created in each district almost at the time planning began. In Dothan, this position was filled by a person whose teaching and administrative experience had been exclusively at the middle school level in another district which had implemented middle schools years earlier. In Orange County, the position was filled doubly, by two people who had been teachers in the district for years and who had been involved in innovative pilot teaming programs. As the number of districts with middle schools increases, this opportunity has become commonplace, so that districts that do not select someone with this sort of experience are involved in glaring errors.

The design of a comprehensive staff development program is, however, too complex to be left entirely to one or two people. Therefore, another prerequisite to effective efforts is the presence of a broadly based staff development committee to assist the coordinator. There should be representatives from administration, curriculum, and the potential faculty of the school(s), ensuring a balance between organizational and programmatic concerns. Such a committee should find it possible to prepare an acceptable rationale for extensive staff development, and to articulate a sensible long-range plan of such activities, complete with timelines, learning experiences, funding requirements, and identification of participants. The committee should be able, further, to assist the district in escaping the trap of expecting too much too soon. Permanent change requires careful and realistic planning.

Effective staff development for a new middle school depends on the early identification of participants. Teachers, we believe, are not inherently opposed to change or even anxious to avoid extra duties. They are, however, likely to perceive the change to middle school as a positive one for them to the extent that they are provided with early opportunities for information and involvement. Kept in the dark about the future of the school, and especially about their own place in that future, teachers will find it difficult to concentrate on the purely professional aspects of the impending changes (Hall & Hord, 1987). Since the great majority of teachers care deeply about children, a great deal can be gained by extending to them the earliest possible opportunity to assimilate the meaning of the changes, and the chance to opt for inclusion or exclusion from any further participation. There seems to be, in our experience, a direct connection between voluntary participation in the change to middle school and the success of the staff development efforts that accompany it.

In Columbia Heights, Minnesota, the faculty of the middle school to come was selected and informed 18 months before the school was to open. Each faculty member was asked to give a first and second priority as to preferred level of teaching: elementary, middle, or high school. In all but a very few cases, even in a district with severely declining enrollments, teachers were given the choice they preferred. The faculty was, in addition, given a central role in the development of the local rationale and the unique components of the program to come. In Orange County, Florida, the process worked in virtually the same way, although it happened a decade later, in the late eighties, and in a district that was ten times larger!

Three Phases of Staff Development

Our experience with staff development programs leads us to conclude that there is a series of three phases into which the process of staff development flows. The first has to do with the encouragement of awareness and commitment among the potential members of the new or reorganized school. Since the success of any staff development effort is always dependent, in large part, upon the commitment, desire, and talents of the persons involved, significant portions of time and energy should be focused on the objective of creating excitement about the impending changes and commitment to the success of those changes. Teachers and administrators should be clear about the nature and the importance of the changes to come, or much of the staff development efforts that follow will be less successful than desired. An early understanding of and commitment to the entire reorganization effort is the fulcrum upon which all remaining staff development activities must move. Involvement, as in Columbia Heights, is the key.

The second phase of the staff development program focuses on a comprehensive understanding of the organizational components to be a part of a particular middle school plan, and the sharpening of the skills necessary for the successful implementation of those programs. If the first phase of staff development could be called resocialization, the second could be labeled re-education. And if implementation is jeopardized by teachers and administrators who are unwilling to perform the necessary roles, it is crippled by a staff who may be willing but unable to perform the proper duties. Everyone involved in the change effort must understand and be able to exhibit the requisite skills, or implementation will not occur.

The third phase of staff development coincides with the implementation of the middle school program. Much of what will be needed by way of insights and skills will not be clearly perceived until the program is underway. This phase actually extends throughout the existence of the reorganized program, since many exemplary middle schools discover the need for continuing staff development for new faculty, and for revitalizing experienced staff.

Successful Staff Development Strategies: Eight Recommendations

There are, of course, many more suggestions for effective inservice education than the eight to be discussed here. A great deal of research on the characteristics of successful staff development programs is now beginning to surface, and the cautious will review this literature carefully before embarking on any program of this nature. Indeed, the entire field of organizational development is quite relevant to the effort to reorganize the middle grades, under almost any circumstances. The few suggestions made here come primarily from the testing ground of experiences in middle school staff development efforts. With these disclaimers, here they are:

1. Operate on a 90/10 philosophy. That is, with the limited funds and time that almost inevitably accompany these activities, spend 90 percent of the funds available on 10 percent of the people. Permanent change comes when the staff is changed permanently, and this means that some of the faculty and administration must undergo a training experience that is sufficient to alter their ways of thinking and acting professionally forever. When the staff with the commitment, desire, and talent are also provided with the skills necessary to do the tasks required for implementation, we believe that these persons will train those with whom they work on a daily basis. A small cadre of expertly trained personnel can grow; a large group of confused and unskilled faculty members, no matter how professional in their attitude, can only grow smaller.

Spend 10 percent of the staff development money before the school is opened, and 90 percent afterward. Providing answers for questions that the staff does not yet have is a highly inefficient use of time and money, and the same amounts of time and money will bring much higher yields of understanding and skill development when applied as the needs become evident. Only the most alert and farsighted among us are able to suspend present needs in order to attend to issues we do not yet face, and most of this group is so highly professional that the training is almost unnecessary for them in the first place.

Another way of expressing this principle of expending staff development funds is to think in terms of pyramids. That is, when funds for inservice are limited, expend the funds with an inverted pyramid in mind; see that the majority of the opportunities are offered to those who will bear the greatest responsibilities when the reorganization arrives: school administrators, team leaders, and counselors, for example. When, in rare cases such as a special grant, a significantly greater amount of money is available, the luxury of making enriched staff development opportunities available for the majority of those who will be involved can be possible. In these instances, using the model of the pyramid (with the greatest effort at the base) becomes logical.

A unique approach to staff development utilizing this philosophy is employed by the Pittsburgh, Pennsylvania, Public Schools, in its Greenway Middle School Teacher Center.[1] Greenway Middle School is a functioning middle school, the educational home for 800 students, grades 6–8, in the city of Pittsburgh; it is also a unique staff development center geared specifically to the needs of middle school teachers. The school acts as a model middle school for the district, containing as much of an exemplary middle school program as possible. Greenway Middle is a two-house school, with grades 6–8 in each of the two houses. It features interdisciplinary teaming and advisory programs, as well as cooperative learning, shared decision making, special schedules, special programs for specific student groups, and a host of other attractive programs.

Over the life of the center, Pittsburgh educators say, it will offer special middle school staff development to over 500 teachers and administrators, each of whom will spend 5 1/2 weeks at Greenway Middle. Replacement teachers are used to teach the students of visiting teachers while the latter attend the Center's staff development program. Teachers develop personal action plans to guide their time there. Each visiting teacher is assigned to work closely with a Clinical Resident Teacher, who assists in planning the personalized staff development for the teacher. These resident teachers also act as observers and critics for the visiting teacher. Four separate but interrelated strands of staff development opportunities are available at the center: The Middle School Child, Middle School Programs, Instructional Practices, and Personal and Professional Enrichment. The program includes phases which begin before a teacher leaves the home middle school and continues with follow-through plans and new goals after they return. From our experience with such programs, we find them extremely effective.

---

[1]For more information, contact Dr. Richard Gutkind, Director, Greenway Middle School Teacher Center, 1400 Crucible Street, Pittsburgh, PA, 15205.

2. Be prepared to make difficult choices when it comes to deciding who will be included in the staff development activities. While it may sound somewhat Machiavellian, a person who has been designated as the coordinator of the middle school reorganization plan must develop leadership that will last, with the most efficient and economical expenditure of scarce resources. It may not even be too farfetched to suggest that coordinators take a page from the book of French battlefield medicine, investigating the usefulness of the concept of "triage" as applied to the development effort. Confronted with inadequate time and medical supplies, in the midst of a battle that would not stop, French physicians applied the concept of triage, which meant that the casualties were divided into three groups: those who would die regardless of the amount of help they received; those who would get well without help; and those who would recover only with help from the physician. The physician then spent the time and scarce supplies where they would do the most good, in essence applying the principle of the greatest good for the greatest number. It may behoove the middle school reorganization coordinator to think in similar ways. There are teachers and administrators who need little, if any, assistance in making the transition successfully, and many of these persons can be used to assist in the training of others less able or ready. There are teachers and administrators who, no matter what opportunities are afforded them, will never be able to make the adjustment, but who may make superb professionals at other levels; they should be helped to do so. There will be another larger group who will guarantee the success of the reorganization effort if they are able to receive the training opportunities that will allow them to develop the insights and skills that will be required. It is likely that concentrating a greater proportion of available opportunities for growth on this third group will result in the most effective deployment of meager staff development funds.

3. Develop a multi-year staff development plan. Based on the time-honored principle that spaced practice assists learning more effectively than does massed practice, it will be advantageous to have a long-term staff development plan that initiates different components at different times following the implementation of the middle school reorganization effort. A program component (for example, an advisor-advisee program) could be introduced one year, with a full-blown inservice effort, followed periodically during the next several years by supportive services that take new faculty into account and that solve new problems as they arise. Haste is the enemy of effective middle school staff development.

It is important to recognize that some elements of the middle school program appear to be prerequisites to others. It is our opinion that the firmly established interdisciplinary organization of teachers must come before other program changes are attempted. It also seems evident that the basic organizational effort, from departmental or self-contained to interdisciplinary, requires much less actual staff development than do other components of the new program. Teachers can be organized in an interdisciplinary fashion without being asked to perform dramatically new or different tasks. The teacher who, for example, has been teaching math for twenty years in a departmentalized junior high school can continue to do very much the same sort of thing in an interdisciplinary organization. Because it makes all the other programs easier to establish and maintain, and because it can be implemented with a minimum of staff development, interdisciplinary team organization should come first.

Consider arranging the remainder of the programs in terms of the difficulty of implementing them with a minimum of inservice education, so that the most difficult are last to be brought on line. Doing so would probably result in a decision to prioritize the grouping of students for learning in some way that would go beyond simple chronological age grouping, since only the most extreme forms of multiage grouping require a significant amount of retraining of the staff or redesigning of the curriculum. This might be followed, in a wisely designed staff development plan, by an attempt to structure the curriculum in a way that would permit the infusion of a more exploratory type of program. A more flexible schedule, if it emerges from the effort to regroup teachers and students, will follow naturally. Only when all of the above components of the program have been effectively planned and implemented will it be wise to implement an advisor-advisee program of teacher-student guidance, since this is a program that requires more staff development than possibly all of the others together. Changing from a completely tracked and rigidly grouped junior high departmentalized setup to a completely heterogeneous grouping plan requires phenomenal amounts of planning and staff development, and might be saved for last. All the components of the middle school program are not equal, in terms of the amount of staff development time and effort required for successful implementation, and it will be wise to plan carefully the sequence in which each is introduced.

Priorities sometimes also intervene in the planning of the staff development program in another way. Because the reorganization effort is, in many ways, a curriculum planning process, it is too frequently seen as a curriculum rewriting effort. That is, the middle school plan has sometimes been perceived too narrowly, especially during the years prior to 1990, as an adventure in rewriting the social studies, science, language arts, mathematics, and unified arts programs. When this happened, a great deal of activity centered around curriculum revisions, and committees wrote furiously, producing volumes which were very much like the curriculum of the junior high school, with the ninth grade removed and the sixth grade added on. Then, the crucial nature of the new organization arrangements was ignored. It is important that curriculum coordinators who become the motivating force for the new middle school remember that the curriculum plan goes far beyond a mere shuffling of the courses of study or a restatement of objectives in terms of observable skills. The middle school is also a new way of working and learning together and attention must be given, equally, to these new relationship patterns. We believe that, although authentic curriculum revision is a high priority in the nineties, organizational changes must still come first. It is easy to rewrite the curriculum; it is impossible, however, to change it.

4. Seek assistance in arranging and conducting the staff development program, but seek it very carefully. The first middle schools established during the 1960s and early 1970s were, primarily, on their own. A few guidelines had been suggested, but fewer school systems had actually established successful and long-running programs to which new middle school educators could turn. It was a time of experimentation and innovation in the middle grades, and, fortunately for middle school educators, for the nation in general. A plethora of new programs were attempted, some surviving, others failing. Since the middle school movement shows little sign of slackening, as we move toward the year 2000, it is fortunate indeed that more than 30 years of experimentation and innovation will now pay dividends in the coin of knowledge that can be relied upon. Whereas in 1960 there were few, if any, educators who could boast of years of experience in middle schools, this is no longer true. Educators seeking to establish a new program in the middle grades of their school systems can now reach out for assistance from hundreds of experienced educators who, remembering their own eager first efforts, are pleased to help in any way they can.

Consultant help can often be important to the success of a middle level reorganization effort. Chosen carefully, outside consultants can help a school district in the decision-making and planning phases of the move to a middle school. But, more often, consultants are needed to assist in the development of local expertise, leadership, and skills. Since it is in the area of leadership in the actual daily operation of middle schools that most districts need help, it is important to choose consultant help on the basis of demonstrated successful experience in the areas in question. Many districts report that the combination of university and public school personnel into a small consultant team leads to both a clear conceptualization of the needed skills and the credibility that makes the tasks acceptable to local teachers and faculty. The best clue to the potential effectiveness of any particular consultant would seem to be whether or not close proximity to and involvement with one or more exemplary middle schools is a prominent part of that person's regular professional experience. When districts are clear about the needs they have, and select a consultant on the basis of demonstrated experience with effective programs related to those needs, a satisfactory relationship is more likely to develop.

5. At all costs, develop and maintain a high degree of local leadership expertise. No consultant, regardless of how expert, can substitute for the existence of local school district employees who have developed a commitment to and the skills necessary for the implementation of an exemplary middle school program. The consultant's effectiveness depends in part upon the availability of an alter ego in the district or school who sets the stage and follows through, before and after the consultant. We believe that the performance of many programs depends in large part upon the emergence of strong local leadership.

Staff development efforts should begin at this point. If at all possible, these persons (curriculum coordinators, school principals, team leaders) should be given the opportunity to participate in a mini-internship in a middle school away from home, a school that has the characteristics which the local district wishes to build into its program. Hearing about the middle school concept, studying about it, even having participated in intensive workshops on how to do it are simply not enough for the development of exemplary programs that will last a decade or more.

In our experience, the most permanently successful programs are those that were built upon the resources that created an opportunity for direct involvement of the local leadership in fully functioning middle schools elsewhere. Implementing a middle school program guarantees that, no matter how well it is done, a great deal of anxiety, doubts, and new pressures will result. School leaders who have had an opportunity to experience a successful program directly will be much more likely to bear up under those pressures and see the program through to a successful future. Team leaders who have both seen it and made it happen elsewhere will be confident that it can happen in their own schools and will be able to bring it about. The funds required to provide such opportunities are so well spent that it seems impossible to mount an effective argument to the contrary. So many good middle schools are available for such assistance that it might be foolish to proceed without it.

The school districts of Alachua County, Florida, and Dothan, Alabama, offer convincing examples of the importance of this direct experience in other programs. Prior to the opening of Spring Hill and Mebane Middle Schools in 1970, the leadership (team leaders and principals) of both schools spent two weeks participating in schools in another state that had been identified as having the type of program that educators in Alachua County wished to implement. In 1992, twenty-two years later, these two schools continue to offer the same experience to educators from across the continent. Before implementing their own program, close ties were developed between the Dothan and Alachua County systems, resulting in having dozens of teachers and administrators from Dothan spending mini-internships in Alachua County schools. The exemplary nature of the Dothan middle schools is testimony to what was learned through this process. Since the Dothan schools are quite different from the schools in Alachua County, fears that one school system will be tempted to undertake the wholesale adoption of the program designed for another are obviously untenable.

6. Realize that changing an existing junior high school to a middle school plan is much more difficult than implementing a new middle school program where no previous junior high school existed. When a new faculty is being gathered, and perhaps a new school building being opened, innovative programs are much more readily implemented. When a faculty and building with a heritage remain and only the program is to be changed, one might be led to think that the tasks would be even easier, but such is not the case. Such transitions seem infinitely more difficult.

When faced with the task of changing the program with an existing faculty within a facility that will not be changed, the approach must be more deliberate, and will often be more costly. Interpersonal loyalties and differences, subject matter preferences, established ways of doing things and working together and pure inertia interact to make this sort of transition one of the most difficult processes in the educational profession. It is a task that ought not be taken on lightly. For those who find themselves involved in such a project, several factors are important for planning the staff development program:

Plan for the transition to take about twice as long as other reorganization efforts.
Plan for a staff development budget that will be about twice as much for each program component implemented as in the prior plan.
Plan to include, from the outset, those faculty members who are experienced and who have shown their leadership ability within the faculty over previous years. One real advantage to having a sizable number of experienced (in other words, over twenty years) teachers is that one can be certain that whatever they agree to implement will work and will last.
Plan to involve a great deal more visitations to exemplary schools, and to attend more conferences, and cut back drastically on the number of expert-led after-school workshops.

When staff development funds are minuscule compared to the needs, refuse to yield to the temptation to implement the programs without the inservice! Very little else will contaminate future change efforts more than the taint of badly managed present failures.

Be prepared to insist, however, that the change from departmentalized organization of teachers to an interdisciplinary grouping take place. Without this change, nothing else is likely to be successful for long. Teachers who have taught in one subject and in one grade level for many years may still do so with the interdisciplinary framework. It may be that several years of becoming accustomed to the interdisciplinary organization will be necessary before any additional program components can be easily brought on-line. Once comfortable with and acclimated to the interdisciplinary organization the faculty is likely to view other new programs much more favorably.

7. The concept of synergism is important when planning staff development activities. The programs of the middle school (for example, interdisciplinary organization, advisor-advisee, and so on) are complementary; the presence of one strengthens the others. So it is with staff development. Working on one component of the middle school program will contribute to the improvement of the others.

8. Tie staff development to state certification in middle school education whenever possible. An increasing number of states, perhaps as many as thirty-five, have middle level certification procedures. Staff development which delivers a new or broader license, enhancing a teacher's employment opportunities,

will be greeted with much more enthusiasm. Simply earning "points" for certificate renewal is better than nothing. In Florida, middle school certification has been available through district level inservice education for many years. New regulations in the early nineties both expanded the coverage under "middle grades" and increased the desirability of such certification by narrowing the elementary and high school certificates so that the middle level certificate was more necessary.

Some districts in Florida have carefully developed comprehensive inservice certification programs. Collier County (Naples, Florida), for example, now offers three separate courses in general middle school education. These courses concentrate on the nature of the learner, curriculum adaptations, and effective teaching strategies (including interdisciplinary teaming). Additional 60-clock-hour courses in academic subject area content, combined with the generic ones above, lead to a desirable subject area state certification in the middle grades:

Language Arts: American Literature, World Literature, Integrated Language Arts
Science: Middle/Junior Physical Science, Earth/Space Science for Middle Grades
Mathematics: Mathematics for the Middle Grades—Levels 1, 2, and 3
Social Studies: Characteristics of the Middle School Social Science and Economics Program, Characteristics of the Middle School World Cultures Program, Characteristics of the Middle School American Studies Program

The Focus of Middle School Staff Development: Skills

While it is very important to allow ample opportunity and time for the development of proper attitudes toward the change effort, behavioral psychologists have long maintained that changes in attitudes often follow changes in behavior. When behavior changes (in other words, when new skills are developed and used), changes in attitudes are close behind. With this in mind, staff development planners may be wise to focus on the new skills that will be required in the new organizational framework, on the assumption that once skills are mastered confidence and assurance will come, followed by increasingly positive attitudes toward the coming new programs. There are, of course, specific skills for both school administrators and for the faculty.

Staff development for school administrators will usually focus on two different areas: knowledge of the new program and organizational development expertise. Principals need to understand the team organization, the advisory program, the curriculum plan, the grouping strategies and other elements of the planned changes so that they can assist teachers in implementing those programs. The principal needs the knowledge so that he or she can effectively communicate the purposes and the structure of the program to parents and community members who will have dozens of questions that will need to be answered. Principals need this knowledge to bolster their own confidence in the efficacy of the proposed changes and to give them the courage to venture into areas that the district has not yet attempted.

Most of all, however, school principals need to know how to use the building and the daily schedule to accomplish the demands of the new program without placing unreasonable stress on the faculty and students. If a place in the building is not available for an activity, that activity will not occur. If there is no time in the schedule for the program, there will be no program. And, since many new middle school principals come from a secondary background, having often served successfully as an assistant principal in a high school, it can not be assumed that the necessary skills were learned prior to inheriting the leadership of the new middle school. It might be more likely that there will have to be some unlearning of certain skills that may actually lie at cross purposes with the new duties at the middle school.

In addition, because the middle school will be an adventure in new relationships of all kinds and in new patterns of teaching and learning, the school principal must be skilled at helping people solve the problems that these new patterns create. He or she must also be able to assist in the process of ongoing change and adjustment that any dynamic organization will encounter. And the principal must, whenever possible, represent an unwavering source of support and enthusiasm for the staff and for their involvement in decision making. These are behaviors that can be learned (Schmuck & Runkel, 1985).

Teachers, whether team leaders or not, will need dozens of new skills when the reorganization is complete, and most of these skills are spelled out in detail in other chapters. It is important, however, to underline several needs. First, in order to make the team organization function at its optimum, teachers need to be effective communicators and problem-solvers with each other. They also need help in planning and managing a program for a large group of students: ordering supplies, planning activities, conducting parent conferences, arranging student schedules, team budgeting, reporting pupil progress, and many other management activities. They need to learn how to schedule an advisor-advisee program so that they are not involved in making new lesson preparations for each new day of the week. They need help discovering activities for advisory programs that can be repeated on a once-weekly basis, and activities that require little or no teacher planning but which deliver considerable power to the advisor-advisee relationship. Teachers will require curriculum writing assistance if alternatives to chronological age grouping are implemented on a schoolwide basis. No one should consider eliminating ability grouping capriciously, without providing teachers with the training they require to diversify instruction. Exciting exploratory programs require creativity and high levels of energy from teachers, but assistance in learning how to develop and conduct an exploratory mini-course that students will enjoy can go a long way toward releasing that creativity and energy. Teachers must develop a repertoire of instructional skills and the knowledge of when each is effective. Above all, many would say, teachers must understand the characteristics and needs of the students they serve, and be able to respond to those needs in ways that are satisfying for both student and teacher.

The selection of effective school leaders and outstanding classroom teachers will all but guarantee the success of the new middle school program, but it is not sufficient. Staff development, even with the most outstanding recruits, is essential. Just as no corporation would introduce a major new product without assigning and carefully training some of its most talented staff, no school system can afford to introduce a major reorganization without a similar effort. Product knowledge is essential in private enterprise and in education. Remember, sooner or later every middle school takes on the characteristics of its leadership!

Special Planning Concerns
The Place of Exploratory Teachers

Many school district planners have discovered that, even after planning as carefully as possible, several unanticipated problems crop up. One of the most serious, in our judgment, is the situation which tends to develop with exploratory teachers, after the interdisciplinary teams begin functioning fully. Many exploratory teachers feel left out, like second class citizens, in the traditional junior high school; often, this changes very little during the transition to middle school. We believe that the place of the exploratory teacher in the modern middle level school is one of the most serious unresolved issues in middle school education.

In many middle schools, morale among exploratory teachers will be lower than it is for academic teachers in the same buildings teaching the same students. This has probably been the case since report card procedures, credit counting, and general school practices established a hierarchy in the earliest junior high schools. New efforts in interdisciplinary team organization frequently bring a new sense of unity and purpose to the academic staff, while exploratory teachers ask, "What about us?" Sometimes the academic teachers, as a consequence of their agreement to work as a team, receive an additional planning period during the day. When this happens, in some circumstances, exploratory teachers do not receive the additional planning time, and this sends their morale spiraling even lower.

Such a situation is particularly ironic, since, in many ways, exploration and enrichment were important reasons supporting the establishment of both the junior high school and the middle school. In a sense, the middle level school was created because of the exploratory teachers and their exciting new curriculum. The junior high was created in order to offer curriculum which went beyond the simple academic basics: to home economics and family studies; foreign language instruction; industrial arts; business and technology education; music education of all kinds; fine arts; and now, computer education. Small elementary schools, or one-room schools, simply did not have enough students to make the cost of such programs effective. In order to be able to afford such enrichment in the curriculum, larger schools were created. And, yet, as we approach the end of a century of middle level education, many exploratory teachers still feel pushed aside from the mainstream of the school into a curriculum backwater.

Many contemporary middle school leaders recognize the need to change this clearly undesirable situation, but few completely satisfactory arrangements have emerged. Virtually all middle level schools need some creative thinking in this area. What follows below is a list of ideas which some middle school educators have found useful—although not perfect—in narrowing the gap between exploratory teachers and their academic colleagues.

1. Have all exploratory teachers assigned as members of interdisciplinary teams. Each team would still have a "core" team, most likely, made up of academic teachers, and an "extended team," which would include the academic teachers and a representative of the exploratory teachers, special education teachers, and the physical education staff. Exploratory teachers would have advisees from that team, and would be a member of the team for school decision-making purposes.

2. Schedule weekly, biweekly, or monthly team meetings before students arrive for school, so that all teachers can attend their respective team meetings. When academic teachers have their planning session at the time their students are being taught by the exploratory teachers, it makes communication between the two groups of teachers virtually impossible, without a regular meeting held when students are not present.

3. Hold these team meetings in the exploratory areas of the building on a regular basis, so that exploratory teachers are not always the ones traveling to the meetings. No one should feel like they are always on foreign soil when they attend such meetings.

4. Rotate the responsibility for setting the agendas for the team meetings so that exploratory teachers have an equal opportunity to see their concerns discussed on a regular and equal basis. Academic teachers are often unaware of the perspective which exploratory teachers can add to their own. Similarly, they may be unaware of the concerns with which exploratory teachers are dealing.

5. Have the school administration monitor the agendas of team meetings and larger faculty meetings to make sure that the items to be discussed include the specific concerns of exploratory teachers. The school administrative team might also have exploratory teachers as advisors to their process.

6. Encourage each interdisciplinary team to create at least one truly thematic unit each year, a unit which would include exploratory teachers in the planning and teaching process. The sort of excitement which such units can contribute can be greatly enhanced by the participation of exploratory staff members.

7. Involve exploratory teachers, in a similar way, in the planning and conduct of field trips. Scheduling arrangements can often be made more efficiently if exploratory teachers are involved. In fact, academic teachers should never pull students out of exploratory classes for trips or any other purpose without first seeking the permission of the exploratory teachers in advance, or at least explaining in detail why such actions are necessary. The principal's permission is *not* sufficient.

8. Experiment with rotating the assignment of exploratory teachers from one team to another, according to grading periods, so that by the end of the year the exploratory teacher has been attached to every team in the school. Richview Middle School (Clarksville, Tennessee) has six interdisciplinary teams and six exploratory teachers, a not uncommon situation. At this school, the art teacher, teaches art to two sixth grade teams, for six weeks each. Then, the art teacher teaches art to two seventh grade teams, for six weeks each. The process is repeated for the eighth grade teams and, by the end of the year, the art teacher has been a member of every team, teaching only students from that team for the grading period. This pattern is followed at another school, King Middle in Portland, Maine, where music and computer teachers are each assigned to two sixth grade teams for one semester each, health and art teachers work with the seventh grade teams, and technology education and home economics teachers are members of eighth grade teams for a semester each.

9. Have exploratory teachers serve as team leaders whenever it is appropriate and can be organized effectively. Even though they may teach students from other teams, the process has worked in several schools which have tried it.

10. Articulate, on a regular basis, for all staff members, the purposes of the interdisciplinary team organization, and the extra work that it requires of academic teachers, so that all of this is clear to the exploratory teachers. Otherwise, it is natural for exploratory staff members to feel mistreated.

Special attention to the role and importance of exploratory teachers, in the planning stages, can save a great deal of difficulty in the first months and years of new middle level schools. Planners ignore such issues only to their peril.

Evaluation of the Middle School

Inevitably, schools are accountable for their results, and middle schools are no different. Perhaps the middle school movement ought to be more accountable, since the change to middle schools in America has involved many millions of dollars, an equivalent amount of human time and energy, and the adjustment of the school experiences of an entire generation. Patrons, parents, school board members, teachers, even students deserve to know that the money, time, energy, and adjustments involved were worth it. This sort of evaluation, the process whereby results are determined and judged, is a leadership responsibility.

Purposes and Scope of Evaluating Middle Schools

Two types of evaluation are common; both are applicable to the evaluation of middle school programs. Formative evaluation, in regard to middle school programs, is the process used to determine whether plans and intentions have been effectively implemented. It includes those processes that evaluate the school's progress in an ongoing program. Generally, formative data can serve as feedback for making corrections in faulty or incomplete plans as school life continues. Formative evaluation should be thought of as an important continuation of the planning process. Simply put, it answers the question of "Are we doing what we said we wanted to do in our new middle schools?"

Summative evaluation includes those processes involved in reaching a decision about the value of a program which has been implemented. It has to do with outcomes rather than implementation. Summative data are used to determine how well the new school programs have met expectations; it may make comparisons with earlier programs to determine if the changes made worked well enough to continue them. Summative evaluation of middle schools, done correctly, provides answers to the question "Is the middle school better?"

Generally, during the early years of the middle school movement, formative evaluation was done poorly and summative evaluation was not done at all. Many middle schools were opened, we now know, to accomplish other important goals such as school desegregation, effective use of school buildings, and so on. School leaders and policy makers could content themselves with observing the outcomes in those areas, and as long as the middle school program was not an unavoidable disaster, it could be safely ignored while other more urgent needs were attended to. And so it was.

Few districts devoted much in the way of resources, during the seventies and early eighties, to formative or summative evaluation. Consequently, middle school educators were often left without sufficient data to determine whether middle school programs which were planned were actually implemented. Nor did they know whether such programs, assuming they were functioning fully and effectively, actually performed as they had hoped. Such a state of affairs is understandable, but lamentable. We hope that the next generation of middle school educators improves upon the evaluation procedures of the last.

Evaluation Models

During the 1970s, embryonic emphases on evaluation and accountability did stimulate the development of new models of evaluation and the synthesis of new and old techniques into other systems and models. In their comprehensive chapter on curriculum evaluation, Saylor, Alexander, and Lewis (1981) described, with extensive citations of related sources, five evaluation models which they recommend for consideration in the development of an evaluation plan for a particular program or institution. These models are briefly identified in the following paragraphs with our suggestions as to the use of each in middle school evaluation processes.

1. *Behavioral Objectives Model* This model, widely used following its introduction by Bobbitt and Charters in the scientific management movement, and its further development by Tyler and such more recent advocates as Mager and Popham, can be effectively used in evaluating student progress, but should not be the only model used here.

2. *Decision-Making Model* This model, developed by a Phi Delta Kappa Committee chaired by Stufflebeam, emphasizes the use of evaluation data in decision making about a program. To us, it is a comprehensive approach that we recommend. We suggest some procedures in this section intended to fit the decision-making processes of middle school planning, evaluation, and improvement.

3. *Goal-Free Evaluation Model* This model, developed by Scriven to free an evaluator of the bias of the program developer, might be useful for evaluating particular innovations, but it is deficient in yielding formative data for purposes of program improvement.

4. *Accreditation Model* This model, characteristic of twentieth-century regional, state, and national (specialized higher education programs) accreditation, includes certain techniques such as use of criteria, self-study, and visiting-committee reviews that we include in this chapter as possibly desirable phases of middle school evaluation. Our view of the purpose, however, is continuing improvement of the school whether or not accreditation is involved.

5. *Responsive Model* Stake's evaluation model organizes evaluation procedures around issues or problems raised by students, teachers, parents, and administrators. It can constitute a comprehensive plan from which various interested parties can select data needed for school evaluation.

We see the foregoing models as useful systems of classification for evaluators, but believe that most readers of this book will be more concerned with specific evaluation procedures they can utilize in evaluation of student progress and of their middle schools. Those interested in further information can find full treatments of the models elsewhere.

Formative Evaluation of a Middle School

District and school leaders engage in formative evaluation of a middle school when they wish to know how well plans have been implemented and how fully the middle school concept is functioning. It is impossible to evaluate the outcomes of the change to middle school without first being able to demonstrate that the plans which were made for the middle school are actually in place and functioning as intended.

As a consequence of our experience with middle schools during the last 25 years, we have developed "Twenty Questions for Exemplary Middle Schools" (see Table 9.1), a combination of the concepts of the effective schools movement and the middle school concept (George, 1983). When we have been invited to participate in a district's formative evaluation of a middle school program, one version or another of this simple instrument has proven useful in guiding the

TABLE 9.1   **Twenty Questions for Exemplary Middle Schools**

Part One: Is there a vital philosophy which serves as the driving force behind the program of the school?

1. Is there evidence, written or otherwise, indicating the staff has developed a consensus regarding the proposed goals of the school?
2. Is there evidence that this mission relates directly to the characteristics and needs of early adolescent learners?
3. Is there evidence of a school learning climate which encourages increased academic achievement for all students? From the faculty? From the administration? From the students?

Part Two: Is there a curriculum alignment and assessment process which implements the school goals and objectives?

4. Are there written documents that clearly define specific course or grade level objectives that students are expected to accomplish with clear standards for mastery?
5. Are the curriculum documents easy for teachers to use in daily planning for instruction, with textbooks and other materials matched to the objectives of the school?
6. Is effective assessment of student achievement a central, regular, comprehensive, and public part of the process of curriculum implementation providing specific feedback for program improvements?

Part Three: Is classroom instruction congruent with the philosophy and the curriculum of the school?

7. Is there evidence that teachers hold high expectations for all students?
8. Can classroom climate be described as high in on-task behavior of students and low in teacher negative affect?
9. Are teachers clearly matching their classroom curriculum with the overall curriculum plan of the school?
10. Are students presented with instruction which can be characterized as active (both teacher and students) and varied?
11. Do most students spend the greater part of their school day learning in heterogeneous groupings?
12. Do the teachers plan whole class instruction on a unit basis, in a style that fits the teacher's and the learners' strengths, with opportunities for remediation and enrichment where needed?

Part Four: Is the school organized in a manner that maximizes opportunities for group involvement for both teachers and students?

13. Is there evidence that the members of the school staff recognize and support the need for group involvement, for a sense of unity and belonging, among the students?
14. Are there opportunities for smaller advisory groups to meet regularly and often?
15. Is the interdisciplinary team group the central organizing unit of the school?
16. Is the team process chosen by the school organized in an appropriate balance, for the needs of the particular students in the school, of teacher-subject specialization and supportive interpersonal structure?
17. Does the administration and faculty arrange for a maximum number of activities that enhance group involvement for students? For teachers?

Part Five: Is there evidence of the necessary balance between spirited leadership and faculty involvement in the governance of the school?

18. Is there evidence that school leaders are continuously engaged in the process of clarifying the mission of the middle school as a regular part of their school activity?
19. Is there evidence that the leaders in the school act in ways that can be described as "instructional leadership?"
20. Is there evidence that authentic, regular, and systematic shared decision making is the mode for school level problem solving and policy development?

process of data gathering and analysis. It can be useful to award five points to every question which evaluators consider to be answerable with a "confident positive" and withhold the points from questions which can not be so answered. The total points available add up to 100, yielding a very rough estimate of the degree to which a particular school is functioning in an exemplary way. It is an instrument to be used solely as formative evaluation, and we suggest that users modify and adapt the questions to fit their own particular middle school programs. We offer our version for whatever unofficial purposes readers may find it useful.

Another device which the authors have used in formative evaluation situations is what we have come to call the "Exemplary Middle School Checklist" (see Table 9.2). The checklist is a summary of what we believe to be the 15 most important attributes of a fully functioning exemplary middle school program. The items are not listed in any order of importance. Once again, it is a device which we offer for the reader's use in unofficial situations where formative evaluation of a middle school program is called for. We find it useful, also, in workshops and faculty meetings where staff members can be productively engaged in a review of the programs which comprise their school. Respondents can be asked to report their scores for a group total, or to work toward a consensus with another small group of two or three persons which then shares its consensus. An analysis of the findings of a complete faculty group can yield important formative data which will be useful in planning staff development and program improvement activities designed to bring the middle school closer to exemplary status.

A substantially more comprehensive approach to the evaluation of middle school programs has been undertaken in several regions of the nation. In Carrboro, North Carolina, at the Center for the Study of Early Adolescence, educators have developed the Middle Grades Assessment Program (MGAP) which has been used successfully in many parts of the country. The New England League of Middle Schools (NELMS) has also developed its own assessment guidelines. Based on ten core middle school concepts about which there is much national agreement, the NELMS program involves three major phases: consultation and school-generated reports; on-site visits by representatives of the NELMS group; and a post-evaluation audit based on another visit at a later time. The evaluation examines:

1. Educators knowledge and commitment to early adolescents.
2. Balanced curriculum based on the needs of early adolescents.
3. Organizational arrangements.
4. Instructional strategies.
5. Exploratory programs.
6. Advisory and counseling programs.
7. Evaluation procedures based on nature of early adolescents.

8. Cooperative planning.
9. Positive school climate.
10. Continuous progress for students.

TABLE 9.2   **Exemplary Middle School Checklist**

Directions: Each of the following items should be ranked in the following manner: (1) present and up to standard, (2) present but in need of substantial improvement, or (3) absent or in need of complete revision.

___ A. Flexible (perhaps block) scheduling within the classroom and across the school.
___ B. A real school philosophy firmly based on characteristics and needs of developing adolescents.
___ C. A building and facilities designed especially for the middle school program.
___ D. Flexible grouping strategies, primarily heterogeneous, within the classroom and across the school.
___ E. Active instruction based on the learning styles of developing adolescents.
___ F. A curriculum characterized by both a core academic focus and a broad range of exploratory opportunities.
___ G. A smooth and continuous program of staff development, renewal, and school improvement focused on the unique concerns of middle school education.
___ H. A smooth and continuous transition between the elementary and the high school program permitting uniqueness at the middle level.
___ I. A shared decision-making model which is formal, regular, systematic, providing authentic collaboration between and among teachers, administrators, parents, and students.
___ J. An extracurricular program based on the needs of early adolescents, providing regular success experiences for all students.
___ K. Teachers and administrators trained and selected especially for educating the developing adolescent.
___ L. Organizational arrangements which encourage long-term teacher-student relationships (e.g., multiage grouping, school-within-a-school, etc.).
___ M. A teacher-based guidance/homeroom program.
___ N. A school program focused on three overall goals: academic learning, personal development, and group citizenship.
___ O. An interdisciplinary team organization where teachers share students, space, and schedule.

Formative Evaluation of Specific Middle School Components

Most middle school educators believe that the interdisciplinary team organization is the heart of a good middle school, the single most important factor in distinguishing between an effective and an ineffective middle level school. It is, typically, also the component of the middle school program which receives the most attention at the time of middle school implementation. Consequently, formative evaluation of the middle school program often centers on the question of the successful implementation of the team organization. We offer, therefore, one additional checklist (see Table 9.3 page 470) for those interested in formative evaluation of the interdisciplinary team process. Answers to these questions will help the evaluator gauge how well the team process is working in a particular middle school. For each "Yes" answer, 5 points can be awarded. Adding up the number of points should give a "grade" to the team implementation process. If a school's teamwork scores an 85—which is a "B"—then the faculty will have a rough estimate of how well the teams are working. Answers which receive a "No" response will provide a set of goals for establishing more effective teamwork in the future, which is a central purpose of formative evaluation.

In Orange County, Florida, the formative evaluation following the implementation of middle schools was conducted over a two year period, from 1988–1990, and among other components of the extraordinarily comprehensive process was a series of interviews conducted with every interdisciplinary team in every one of the district's 18 middle schools! Interviews examined the extent to which the

TABLE 9.3   **Teamwork: Twenty Questions**

_____ 1. Are teams organized so that teachers share the same students, space in the school, and schedule?

_____ 2. Does the membership on the team represent all the basic academic subjects?

_____ 3. Does the team have some common rules, procedures, and expectations?

_____ 4. Do the students recognize and feel a sense of belonging to the team?

_____ 5. Do the teachers work together to develop and implement activities that heighten the students' sense of community?

_____ 6. Do the teachers on the team develop a sense of commitment to each other and draw professional and personal support from each other?

_____ 7. Do teams have frequent parent conferences and good home-school relationships?

_____ 8. Is there adequate planning time and a planning space used by the team members for their work?

_____ 9. Do the teachers on the team use the time and the place for teamwork?

_____10. Do teachers work on interrelating their separate subjects, coordinating major assignments, correlating major units, etc.?

_____11. Do the teachers provide, on the average, a special teamwide activity (e.g., a recognition assembly) during each grading period?

_____12. Do teachers take turns in assuming leadership for different activities within the team when appropriate to individual strengths and interests?

_____13. Do teachers meet at least weekly to discuss their students?

_____14. Do team teachers develop and carry out joint strategies in an attempt to resolve the problems identified in the weekly meeting?

_____15. Each time a substitute comes to a team, does one (or more) team member(s) talk with the sub about team expectations and encourage the substitute to contact the nearest team member for any assistance needed?

_____16. Do teams have carefully selected team leaders?

_____17. Do teams have at least some control over items like the schedule, the budget, and the curriculum?

_____18. Is there a formal group and process for shared decision making, composed of teacher, administrators, and others, which meets regularly and frequently?

_____19. Does the principal work with individual teams regularly and frequently?

_____20. Do team members, generally, feel a sense of success and satisfaction about their work together?

teams were functioning as they were intended: organizationally, developing a sense of community, and instructionally. The interviews also investigated the degree to which the district's advisory program had been effectively implemented. Information was collected by the middle school coordinators but analyzed and synthesized by the district's excellent Testing and Program Evaluation Section.

Other interview checklists and similar devices can easily be constructed for additional components of the middle school program which need to be subject to a formative evaluation. The advisory program stands out in this regard, but the curriculum, instructional practices, decision making, and even staff development practices can be evaluated formatively in the foregoing manner. Until such formative evaluation practices are conducted, as they were in Orange County, and leaders are satisfied that the planned program is in place as it was intended, summative evaluation will be relatively disappointing.

Summative Evaluation and the Middle School

Summative evaluation, as we have said, is an attempt to determine whether the middle school program has achieved the outcomes which were desired. When the desired outcomes are incidental to the central focus of the middle school concept (e.g., school desegregation, facility usage, conformity to state legislation), summative evaluation has rarely been conducted in any comprehensive manner. In the same way, if formative evaluation has failed to confirm the effective implementation of middle school components (which is usually the case), summative evaluation is frequently disappointing.

This is one reason why research regarding the middle school concept has been difficult to accumulate. Too often, poorly implemented programs have been compared with prior programs which also failed to be designed on the needs of young adolescents. Such research has, consequently, ended up comparing similar "treatments" and, thus, has failed to demonstrate any significant differences. During the seventies and eighties, misinterpretations of this sort of research led some to conclude that the middle school made no difference in the lives of learners. In the 1990s, fortunately, the situation has slowly begun to change. Reliable research can only be conducted where careful formative evaluation and descriptive studies have first demonstrated that substantially different programs have been successfully implemented.

District leaders may be pressed to present evidence to decision makers and policy makers that the move to the middle school, and away from some prior arrangement or design (e.g., junior high school), has been worth the investment of time and money. In such situations, the leader's first response should be to ask for a three year "grace" period to ensure the effective implementation of the program, to be followed by a formative evaluation. After conducting a careful formative evaluation and ascertaining that the implementation has been successful, it may be necessary, if not desirable, to engage in summative evaluation.

If a formative evaluation is rejected, or if the results are negative, leaders must have the courage to point out the frailties and inappropriateness of a summative evaluation. It may be, however, that a summative evaluation is either appropriate or unavoidable. Under those circumstances, we offer the following comments about summative evaluation of the middle school.

Use of Single Criteria

Evaluation of a middle school on the basis of achievement test results in a particular area such as reading or mathematics may occur. In fact, any use of achievement data for school evaluation is an example of the use of a single criterion. If this is the only criterion, it is an example also of the fallacy involved in judging a total program on the basis of only one criterion. Another example of the use of a single criterion is the evaluation of school personnel, or, better, of a single group of personnel, as teachers. And the evaluation of teachers may use single criteria also, such as the degrees attained, years of experience, rating of teachers by the principal, or achievement of students on a particular objective.

It is the use of a single criterion alone that can be least helpful in identifying strengths and weaknesses and needs for improvement of a school. Hence, our suggestion is that data regarding many specific criteria are needed and may be gathered singly or in combination as is feasible, but should be used in concert so that the school is not labeled good or bad on any single testing, opinion poll, visit of an evaluator, or other single aspect. Practice differs with this principle primarily in the use of achievement test data, although the state of the school building, the personality of the principal, the band program, or any other single item may also unduly weigh the general appraisal of the school by students, patrons, and visitors. Such weighting should be avoided or, at least, minimized by a comprehensive evaluation program employing a variety of criteria closely related to the goals of the school—all of them, not just one.

There are, nevertheless, exemplary school districts where the summative evaluation of the middle school conversion is done painstakingly and with positive results, even when focusing on the single variable of academic achievement. In Orange County, Florida, for example, in the spring of 1991, a memo from the director of testing and evaluation reported one part of the five-year evaluation of the middle school design (including many other components as well as the interviews described above): a longitudinal assessment of the results of student achievement on the California Test of Basic Skills (CTBS). The memo stated that:

> One conclusion which can be warranted is that the middle school cohort seems to have at least held its own and, in some cases, outperformed the junior high school cohorts.

Program developers and school board members in Orange County are pleased with these results. In central Florida in the early '90s, funds are low, new enrollments threaten to swamp the districts with new students, and social conditions are difficult. If the new middle schools had simply held their own in terms of achievement, it could be considered a victory. Under the circumstances faced by these educators, for achievement to rise substantially is something to be excited about, and they were.

Feedback Opportunities

"Feedback" is used, perhaps loosely, in educational evaluation to denote almost any type of reaction, formal or informal, made by a variety of individuals regarding one, many, or all aspects of a school. We ourselves believe it well to maintain a flexibility of definition in order to encourage the securing and use of reactions from appropriate sources. Thus, feedback includes not only formal opinion polls and systematically collected and organized data in a self-study program, but the informal comments of visitors and other persons. It is the latter type of feedback with which we are concerned at this point.

Middle school student feedback is immediate and direct. Student reaction to a person, an event, a class session, or a program of instruction is readily available, and indeed may get expressed too quickly without adequate thought on the student's part. But student feedback is highly relevant to almost all aspects of middle school education, and should be reviewed and evaluated as new elements in the school program or new groups of students in the school population make feedback timely.

Feedback is frequently all too obvious when parents come to school to discuss their children's problems, but more objective data are too infrequently sought. Every parent conference is an opportunity to secure feedback, as is every meeting of parents in parent-teacher organizations, advisory councils and other groups. In addition to the questionnaires and other polling instruments that may be used, informal, well-guided discussions can yield much information as to the reactions of those participating, to whatever aspects of the school program and issues therein are under discussion.

Perhaps the most insightful feedback can be secured from professional educators visiting an exemplary middle school, or one seeking to become exemplary. Middle schools, especially those in new buildings and those reported upon in professional journals and other publications, get visited by personnel from other middle schools, especially from schools in the process of reorganization or initial planning. These well-motivated visitors, frequently with some background information about desirable practice, form definite opinions about what they see. Some exemplary middle school personnel quite effectively invite the visitors' reactions in a final conversation before the visitors' departure.

Somewhat similarly, visitors from classes at nearby teacher education institutions are sometimes informed about middle school programs and practices, and may have worthwhile reactions. Some student teachers may lack experience but not self-confidence, and can and do offer with candor their opinions and

)

reactions; others may need to be urged to express theirs. The middle school principal or other representative conducting an informal feedback session can improve the flow of reactions and suggestions by avoiding argumentative and defensive statements, by indicating that all opinions and reactions are valued and will be considered, and by a generally courteous and grateful attitude, even in the face of undeserved criticisms.

Opinion Polls

An opinion poll is another form of feedback data: opinions of some group of people are sought through a written form or guided interviews or a combination of forms and interviews. In addition to the annual Gallup Poll on Education and the inclusion of questions on education in other national, state, and local polls, many school districts and individual schools use polls of their own to get opinions from many students, and also parents, that can be tabulated and interpreted. Teachers are also frequently included as a polling group.

Several issues must be dealt with in developing an opinion poll as an instrument to yield data for evaluation purposes. First, is opinion to be sought on a particular issue, outcome, or facet of the school program, or on many? Polls on specific controversial issues may secure more responses but be less useful for broad purposes of evaluation than polls on many questions. But if the issue is whether a new school program—course, activity, or service—is believed by the students to be helpful (or interesting or generally good), it may be easiest to use a very simple fill-in form on the program. If parent opinion is desired for reactions to several programs, a more comprehensive poll is indicated.

A second issue in the use of opinion polls is that of whose judgment is desired. Will the most reliable data come from students, teachers, parents, or citizens in general? And if comparable data are wanted from two or more groups, can the same instrument be used for both? An especially significant, related question is whether the poll is to be on a sample basis or to include the total population of the group to be polled. If only a sample is needed, is it to be random, representative, or of some other type? And what percentage of returns will be considered adequate? Resolution of these issues is beyond the scope of this book and should probably be done at the school or district level with the help of some research specialist. We would especially urge that the opinionnaire be carefully constructed. Some important precautions are suggested:

1. If the response may be influenced by the possibility that the respondent's identity is known, the poll should be made completely anonymous.

2. The respondents should be supplied with adequate background for expressing opinions.

3. All directions should be as clear and simple as possible.

4. The instrument should be tried out several times, with needed revisions made before its final use; the tryout should be on members of the group to be polled.

5. The questions and the responses should be constructed in such a way as to facilitate tabulation and summarization.

The accompanying parent questionnaire (see Table 9.4 page 476) from the Nipher Middle School (Kirkwood, Missouri) is illustrative of the many we have seen. The reader will note that several of the items on this instrument were definitely localized, as we believe they should be. The letter to a random sample of parents regarding the form asked for their help and stated that the parents need not sign their names. In view of the great importance of communication of parents and school personnel, the parent opinion poll is believed to have especial significance. It must be planned and constructed as above, and particular care must be given to the handling of it to get an adequate return. One procedure that may get good returns is a phone call requesting the parent to complete a form, followed by mailing the form to those agreeing to complete it. Of course, this procedure may be feasible only for a sample, although phone calls by teachers to their advisees' parents might be possible for the total population. Such general questions as these can be somewhat reliably answered when parent polls are used effectively:

1. Are parents satisfied or dissatisfied with the curriculum? To what extent and in what particulars?

2. What are parents' expectations regarding the middle school? Are the school's goals confirmed by parents? If not, what changes in goals need to be made?

3. How well do parents understand what the school is trying to do for their children? What problems in communication are indicated?

4. In what middle school curriculum areas do parents believe their children's experiences are adequate and inadequate?

5. What problems of the total middle school program and its individual aspects are indicated by the poll?

6. What suggestions for solving these problems (#5) are suggested by parents?

We should also note the utility of short opinion polls of appropriate groups on specific issues. The middle school beginning a new program does have early and serious need to determine student and parent reactions to the program. Even before beginning new programs, need for them may be assessed in part by polls. Especially when polls can be validated by samplings of interviews, the data from them may be highly significant formative evaluation data—data to help in modifying and improving a program.

Table 9.4   **Parent Questionnaire***

1. Nipher Middle School helped my child to develop effective study habits.
   A. Strongly Agree
   B. Agree
   C. Disagree
   D. Strongly Disagree
   E. No Opinion

2. Nipher Middle School encouraged my child to do his best.
   A. Strongly Agree
   B. Agree
   C. Disagree
   D. Strongly Disagree
   E. No Opinion

3. Nipher Middle School helped my child to become responsible.
   A. Strongly Agree
   B. Agree
   C. Disagree
   D. Strongly Disagree
   E. No Opinion

4. Nipher Middle School helped my child improve his basic skills.
   A. Strongly Agree
   B. Agree
   C. Disagree
   D. Strongly Disagree
   E. No Opinion

5. The exploratory courses—living arts, home economics, shop, vocal music, drama, creative writing, health and art were helpful.
   A. Strongly Agree
   B. Agree
   C. Disagree
   D. Strongly Disagree
   E. No Opinion

6. The instrumental music program at Nipher was helpful to my child. (Instrumental music parents only)
   A. Strongly Agree
   B. Agree
   C. Disagree
   D. Strongly Disagree
   E. No Opinion

7. The physical education program was helpful to my child.
   A. Strongly Agree
   B. Agree
   C. Disagree
   D. Strongly Disagree
   E. No Opinion

8. Nipher Middle School has helped my child to find ways to solve problems.
   A. Strongly Agree
   B. Agree
   C. Disagree
   D. Strongly Disagree
   E. No Opinion

9. Nipher Middle School's sixth-grade camping program was a good experience for my child.
   A. Strongly Agree
   B. Agree
   C. Disagree
   D. Strongly Disagree
   E. No Opinion

10. The Olympics were a good experience for my child.
    A. Strongly Agree
    B. Agree
    C. Disagree
    D. Strongly Disagree
    E. No Opinion

11. The twenty-three minute daily reading period was helpful.
    A. Strongly Agree
    B. Agree
    C. Disagree
    D. Strongly Disagree
    E. No Opinion

12. The total educational program at Nipher was helpful.
    A. Strongly Agree
    B. Agree
    C. Disagree
    D. Strongly Disagree
    E. No Opinion

13. Teachers gave too much homework.
    A. Strongly Agree
    B. Agree
    C. Disagree
    D. Strongly Disagree
    E. No Opinion

14. Teachers gave too little homework.
    A. Strongly Agree
    B. Agree
    C. Disagree
    D. Strongly Disagree
    E. No Opinion

15. My child enjoyed attending Nipher.
    A. Strongly Agree
    B. Agree
    C. Disagree

(continued)

Table 9.4   **Parent Questionnaire* (continued)**

D. Strongly Disagree
E. No Opinion

16. The curriculum at Nipher met the needs of my child.
    A. Strongly Agree
    B. Agree
    C. Disagree
    D. Strongly Disagree
    E. No Opinion

17. Reports from Nipher concerning my child were adequate.
    A. Strongly Agree
    B. Agree
    C. Disagree
    D. Strongly Disagree
    E. No Opinion

18. The co-curricular courses (mini-courses) were helpful for my child.
    A. Strongly Agree
    B. Agree
    C. Disagree
    D. Strongly Disagree
    E. No Opinion

19. Discipline in the school should have been more strict.
    A. Strongly Agree
    B. Agree
    C. Disagree
    D. Strongly Disagree
    E. No Opinion

20. The principals at Nipher were interested in helping the students.
    A. Strongly Agree
    B. Agree
    C. Disagree

D. Strongly Disagree
E. No Opinion

21. The teachers at Nipher were interested in helping the student.
    A. Strongly Agree
    B. Agree
    C. Disagree
    D. Strongly Disagree
    E. No Opinion

22. The counselors at Nipher were interested in helping the student.
    A. Strongly Agree
    B. Agree
    C. Disagree
    D. Strongly Disagree
    E. No Opinion

23. My child liked the cafeteria food.
    A. Strongly Agree
    B. Agree
    C. Disagree
    D. Strongly Disagree
    E. No Opinion

COMMENTS:

_____
_____
_____
_____
_____
_____
_____
_____
_____
_____

* From Nipher Middle School, Kirkwood, Missouri.

Unobtrusive Measures

Unobtrusive measures do not require the cooperation of the respondent and do not depend on the respondent's attitudes toward the interview or questionnaire. Questionnaires and interviews are, in a sense, obtrusive. We see tests also as examples of obtrusive measures, although wider use of other unobtrusive measures seems increasingly necessary to avoid the use of a single method (testing) and especially of one so influenced by individual differences in interest and ability.

Miller (1978) has suggested a long list of unobtrusive measures that can be used for gathering data in schools about the achievement of school goals. Several excerpts we consider illustrative of such measures for summatively evaluating a middle school follow:

Number of situations in which students are:

- Voluntarily remaining after school to chat with teachers
- Writing, rehearsing, and polishing their efforts
- Working independently

Data about students:

- What percentage of students skip each day?
- What percentage of students are tardy each day?
- How many students know the principal's name?
- How many students attend optional school events?

Number of situations in which teachers are:

- Complimenting students
- Attempting to measure student progress in other than academic areas
- Making positive remarks about students in the staff lounge
- Voluntarily staying after school to chat with pupils

Data about staff:

- What is the teacher absenteeism rate?
- What is the teacher tardiness rate?

Number of situations where administrators are:

- Involving staff, parents, students, and community in setting priorities, assessing progress, and reviewing rules
- Providing means whereby students can attend school at different hours, take different courses; where class periods are different lengths, etc.
- Listening to students

Data about administration:

- How many principals has the building had in the last three years?
- What percentage of the time in staff meetings are staff members talking?
- How many new courses or programs have been added this year?

Readers can undoubtedly add many such items that might be useful in their own schools. Obviously any school faculty using such measures in evaluating the school must be prepared to defend the validity of each item as a measure or indicator of school quality. It is important also to select items which are truly unobtrusive, that is, not requiring the cooperation or other involvement of students or other groups concerned. And note that most of the illustrative items we selected from Miller's list involve some type of quantitative data; this is to facilitate the collection and comparison of such data from time to time to provide a true measure of change.

Self-Study Programs

We turn now to a more frequent, comprehensive effort to evaluate a middle school, a self-study program. Self-study programs can be used for either formative or summative evaluation purposes. There are many types of such studies, ranging from a fairly cursory compilation of faculty responses to a questionnaire (such as those in the foregoing section on formative evaluation) or in a group evaluation session, to a complete analysis of each aspect of the school by the faculty followed by the review of a visiting team or committee. The complete review has most possibilities, we believe, for affecting program development and school quality, and we give it primary attention here. It should be noted that less comprehensive self-studies can be done for almost any aspect of the school by the designation of study committees and guides for the aspect(s) concerned, with the use of visiting individuals or committees also possible.

Purposes of the Self-Study Programs   Two overlapping purposes dominate self-study programs: (1) to evaluate the school in order to improve it, and (2) to satisfy accreditation requirements of the regional and/or state accrediting agency. These purposes should not conflict, since accrediting agencies require self-studies in order that the schools may improve; but it can happen that the immediate goal of accreditation overshadows the long-range goal of improvement.

Accreditation of a middle school by the state department of education or any agency designated by the state is essential for public schools, although the requirements for accreditation vary widely in the fifty states. The requirement of a periodic self-study program is a sensible means for the school to determine its status and maintain improvement, and an effective way for the agency to have data basic to accreditation. Regional accreditation is an option for the school; being accredited by the regional association is recognition for status purposes desired by some school boards, faculties, and patrons. Both purposes of the self-study program are stated in the following illustrative excerpts from the Superintendent's foreword to the 1990–91 self-study report of the Powell Middle School in Brooksville, FL:

> The self-study process afforded us an opportunity to critically re-examine our philosophy, mission, and goals. Our collective vision for our school is now more focused. With the completion of this report we have taken an introspective look

at our school and its program. We now have a better understanding of where we have been as well as a clearer picture of where we want to go.

Often, everyone involved in a Southern Association self-study benefits from the experience. The involvement required by self-evaluation can provide insight which will result in a stronger program and improved learning experiences for boys and girls.

A major problem in accreditation standards and processes for middle schools has been the tendency of accrediting agencies to expect the middle schools to use guidelines developed for secondary and/or elementary schools that may not provide for unique elements of the middle school. In the absence of applicable regional or state guidelines for middle school self-study programs, local districts may effectively develop their own guides for improvement. For example, middle schools in Alachua County, Florida have followed the same pattern of self-study as elementary schools, a pattern that does provide for considerable flexibility of programs and criteria. The purpose of the five-year review is stated as follows in the Alachua County guide:

> The review of a school's program should be viewed as a positive professional process. It provides the school's staff an opportunity to utilize self-study, peers, and other resource persons for a systematic comprehensive look at its programs every five years. The object of the review is to analyze the school's programs to ascertain strengths, weaknesses, and plans for improvement in terms of appropriate state, school board, and local school guidelines/criteria.

The Self-Study Phase   The period in which the school faculty carries on its own study of the school varies in length, although a major part of a year seems essential for a thorough study, carried on as it must be in addition to the regular school operation. The National Study of School Evaluation program, followed widely in high schools and junior high schools and in many middle schools, specifies that the self-study usually requires a minimum of one year and that the steering committee should be appointed a year before the evaluation is to be completed.

The process of the self-study generally encompasses the total school program and its personnel and facilities. The Evaluative Criteria of the National Study of School Evaluation, revised in 1985, includes these sections for junior high and middle schools, as revealed in the Powell Middle School Self-Study, for 1990–91:

Manual
School and Community
Philosophy and Goals
Major Educational Priorities
Design of Curriculum

Learning Areas
School Staff and Administration
Student Activities Program
Learning Media Services
Student Personnel Services
School Plant and Facilities

Most middle school self-study reports include the foregoing elements, although the terms and combinations may differ. The NSSE Evaluative Criteria follows for junior high and middle schools the basic pattern of the volume long guiding the accreditation self-studies of high schools throughout the United States. This guide has been regarded by many middle school educators as being more appropriate for secondary than middle schools. However, the 1985 edition of *Middle School/Junior High School Evaluative Criteria* has been made more relevant to middle schools than the prior edition, and we believe this can be helpful in middle school evaluations. Even in 1991, however, the central focus of the self-study, as guided by the regional accrediting association, appears to be dominated by concerns for a subject-centric school experience. Major new directions in which the faculty of the school was interested (advisory programs, heterogeneous grouping, etc.) seem somewhat crammed into the section on Major Educational Priorities. Certainly the group concerned should be free to eliminate inappropriate sections and to adapt the guide, which has considerable flexibility, to the local situation.

Schools using the NSSE Evaluative Criteria as the guide for their self-study may follow the form of this completely, having the report written into the fill-in spaces of its sections. Of course, schools not using this guide for accreditation purposes may also elect to use some sections and not others, or to follow another outline. Whatever the elements of the school studied, the general pattern of self-study is one by committees, primarily of the faculty, corresponding to the major sections of the study. Thus, if the Evaluative Criteria plan is utilized, there will be a committee responsible for each of the sections listed earlier, and usually multiple committees on the subject areas, one per broad field. Interdisciplinary organization was first recognized in the 1979 edition, but committees may need to develop a more suitable study guide. If the school has a departmental organization the department members may constitute the committee for their subject field. Each committee gathers the data required by the guidelines used, and works out the summarization, analysis, and presentation of the data for the report. The work is time-consuming and even tedious at times, but many middle school educators believe that the effort of a self-study is exceedingly well rewarded in the exchange of ideas, arrival at program changes, and improvement of school, faculty involvement, and student and faculty morale.

The Southern Association of Colleges and Schools has announced a new, alternative route to regional re-accreditation through self-study processes which will be available to schools in the early 1990s. A focus on "School Renewal," based on the work of John Goodlad (1984) will permit educators to engage in local school improvement in five areas: school climate; planning; staff development; curriculum and instruction; and communication. Each school faculty has the responsibility for setting its own agenda for improvement during a five-year period. In our judgment, this alternative has much to recommend it, and is much more likely to lead to evaluations focused on real change.

The aspect of the self-study that is most crucial is the setting of recommendations for improvement of the school. The recommendations may be made at several points: (1) preliminary ones based on first discussions of an element of the school that seem feasible for immediate implementation, at least on a trial basis; (2) recommendations based on the self-study prepared by the respective committees, and frequently reviewed and modified by steering committees and/or the total faculty; (3) recommendations made by the visiting committee; and (4) recommendations made by the school faculty and administration after reviewing the report of the self-study, and the report of the visiting committee. The latter two reports will be considered in later sections, but we should emphasize at this point the very great importance of carefully determined and stated recommendations of the faculty study groups. The following suggestions are offered as to the development and statement of recommendations in the report of the faculty self-study:

1. Each recommendation should clearly flow from the data presented in the self-study section immediately preceding the recommendation(s).

2. Each recommendation should be so clearly and fully stated that it can be understood by whomever is responsible for its approval and implementation.

3. Each recommendation should indicate clearly by what person or group it must be approved and implemented.

4. If the recommendation represents the judgment of persons other than the responsible committee—for example, the judgment of parents, students, community representatives, or educational consultants—this fact should be included in the statement of the recommendation.

5. Recommendations involving additional financial cost should include estimates as to the amount.

6. Recommendations involving the employment of additional personnel, and the reassignment of existing personnel, should include partial job descriptions of new positions or assignments.

7. Wherever feasible, the recommendation should include some statement of the time factor—when the recommendation should go into effect, for what period, and when any change involved should be evaluated.

The Visiting Committee   The prospective visit of a group of educators from out-side the school and, in some studies, from outside the district, is a focus of much planning, concern, and even trepidation for the faculty of the school involved in self-study. The visit takes on such overriding importance that some educators would like to minimize or eliminate this aspect of the school evaluation. The review of a faculty's self-study by an external group is so characteristic, however, of evaluations of high schools, colleges, and universities, and also of many ele-mentary schools, that this review is likely to be here to stay. Furthermore, the review can be of major importance in school improvement if it is carefully planned, executed, and followed up.

Local school districts usually have policies controlling the selection of visiting committee members. In our judgment, these policies should provide for select-ing a committee of persons experienced in good middle school education, includ-ing at least one specialist in each area or section of the self-study schedule and also one or more generalists. It is also important to include persons with special interests in elementary and high school education to help in the troublesome problems of articulation of the middle school with the schools below and above. Otherwise, usual criteria as to a balanced representation of the school population should assure an adequate committee.

The work of the visiting committee is detailed in the Manual Section of the *Evaluative Criteria,* and also well reflected in the reports of visiting committees available from exemplary middle schools. In general, regardless of the particular areas and sections under study, it is to be expected that the visiting committee will spend at least three days visiting the school, with some of this time devoted to meeting with school personnel and some to visiting classes and talking with students. Other time goes to meetings of the total committee and the various subcommittees, usually one for each major section of the self-study, and to the review of school materials and to the preparation of the committee report. Advance copies of the school self-study report and of various materials exhibiting the school program and operation are usually sent to the visiting committee members for study before the on-site visit.

The culmination of the visiting committee's work is the presentation of its report. In many instances, the visiting committee simply endorses or comments upon each section of the school self-study report and then adds other comments and/or recommendations; the report can be very brief if the endorsement-plus-comments route is followed. In other instances the visiting committee may pro-duce a report almost as long as the original self-study report. Usually, there is some oral reporting to the administration and faculty of the school before the visit is concluded, with a written report following in due time.

Reports and Plans. For purposes of continuing evaluation and planning, it is essential that written reports be made at each stage of the self-study program. First, there is the report of the faculty self-study which should be—and usually is—the basis for the work of the visiting committee, and the follow-up locally by the school and district. We have found that these reports necessarily run into many pages if they follow the *Evaluative Criteria* or some other complete guide, as they should for local credibility and utility. This basic document becomes a very important part of the continuing archives and the plans of the school—available as a benchmark for comparison from time to time, and especially for subsequent self-studies, as required by districts every three to five years, and by accrediting agencies, usually for five years with annual interim reports, or for ten years with periodic interim reports.

Examination of many self-study reports leads us to recommend that the local school have a clear-cut organization for this report, not only by the major sections of the self-study, but an internal organization of the sections that is easily followed by the writers and readers of the report. It is most disconcerting to read a self-study report that uses entirely different formats within its several sections. In general, the user of a self-study report wants to find in each section answers to these questions:

1. What is the role (or objectives) of this aspect of middle school education?

2. What evidence is available as to how well this role is being discharged (or these objectives realized)?

3. What factors seem to facilitate or hinder the achievement of this role (or these objectives)?

4. What plans or recommendations are made to improve the achievement of this role (or these objectives)?

As to the visiting committee report, we like the more succinct type that endorses or comments upon each self-study section and presents additional recommendations of the visiting committee. For example, a visiting committee report for the Amory (Mississippi) Middle School had for most sections of the self-study report these brief items: (1) commentary; (2) recommendations for school improvement; and (3) recommendations for meeting accreditation standards (generally none given since standards were met). A form used in Jefferson County, Kentucky middle school evaluations required for each section a rating, a listing of strengths, and a statement of specific recommendations for further study by the visiting team.

Some districts publish multiple self-study and visiting team reports. For example, an evaluation report of the four middle schools of District 6/Weld County, Colorado includes in one volume (166 mimeographed pages) data on the curriculum of the schools; a year-end summary by the principal and by the school advisory council; reports of opinion surveys of pupils, teachers, and parents of the four middle schools; and also some data for the two junior high schools. In the Decatur, Alabama schools, studies were reported separately of the Oak Park and Brookhaven Middle Schools, but a general statement by the visiting committee covering both schools was included in each report.

Another written post-evaluation report that may be prepared is the school's statement of recommendations or plans made as a result of the self-study and the visiting committee's evaluation. For example, the Alachua County, Florida five-year review plan provided that the school respond within one month to each of the recommendations of the visiting committee, with a final document for each school evaluation to include: (1) the report of the school's self-study; (2) the visiting committee's findings and recommendations; and (3) the school response. State and regional accreditation reports may include continued reports of progress made in compliance with recommendations of school evaluations, and plans for further improvement.

Long-Range Studies   A three-year study of the Brown Middle School in Hamilton County, Tennessee is suggestive of studies with a longer range than the usual one-year self-study. A report of this study published by Middle Tennessee State University (McGee, Krajewski & Keese, 1977) gave detailed information as to the hypotheses tested, the data gathered, and the conclusions and recommendations made in the course of this study, which was supported by a Title III, ESEA grant. Aspects of this study included: teacher attendance, attitudes, and turnover; student attendance, discipline, attitudes, and achievement; report card/student progress changes; parent evaluation; dissemination of program information; use of consultants; curriculum development activities; and others. An early progress report of the Webster Transitional School of Cedarburg, Wisconsin also included data for three years. This report included descriptive material regarding the development of the instructional program including school and instructional organization, instruction and curriculum, supporting services, and student effects in these categories: basic skills and academic concepts; independent learning; social skills and cultural understanding; self-discipline and responsibility; self-understanding and acceptance; and opinion polls of students, visitors to the school, parents, and teachers. Such reports should be of value not only to the schools and districts involved but to other middle schools interested in comprehensive evaluations as guides for continuing improvement.

Focus of Summative Evaluation

Eighteen hypotheses were proposed in the evaluation chapter of one of the first textbooks about middle school education, *The Emergent Middle School* (Alexander, et.al., 1969), as some of the possible bases for summative studies of and more formal research on middle schools. They are still valid in the 1990s:

1. Pupils in the middle school will become more self-directed learners than pupils in the control schools.

2. Pupils in the middle school will have fewer and/or less intense social and psychological problems than pupils in conventional schools.

3. Achievement of middle school pupils on standardized tests will equal or exceed that of pupils in conventional schools.

4. Middle school pupils will equal or exceed pupils in conventional schools on standard measures of physical fitness and health.

5. Pupils in the middle school will have more favorable attitudes towad school than will pupils in conventional schools.

6. Middle school pupils will hold more adequate self-concepts than will pupils in the conventional schools.

7. Social acceptance among middle school pupils will be higher than among those in conventional schools.

8. The average daily attendance of middle school pupils will exceed the attendance of pupils in conventional schools.

9. Measures of creativity among middle school pupils will show an increase, rather than a decrease, during middle school years.

10. Middle school graduates will compile better academic records in ninth grade than will ninth graders from the control schools.

11. Middle school graduates will drop out of senior high school less frequently than pupils who follow the traditional pattern.

12. Middle school teachers will more often use practices which experts generally recommend as superior.

13. Teachers in the middle school will experience a higher degree of professional fulfillment and self-satisfaction than teachers in conventional schools.

14. Teachers in the middle school will utilize a greater variety of learning media than will teachers in conventional schools.

15. Teacher turnover will be lower in the middle school than in conventional schools.

16. Teachers in the middle school will be more open to change.

17. Patrons of the middle school will hold more positive attitudes toward objectives and procedures of the school than patrons of conventional schools.

18. Principals of experimental and control schools will have similar operating patterns within each school system.

To our knowledge, no school district has attempted to test all of these hypotheses, nor did the authors of *The Emergent Middle School* suggest such a large-scale evaluation in a single district. Note this suggestion, which still seems to be very useful to school districts, and state and regional, even national, groups who might utilize it:

Obviously, a thorough evaluation in which even the hypotheses to be listed in this section were tested would strain or be beyond the resources of most school systems. However, with state or federal help, a single system could give evidence on many or most of the hypotheses. It would be better, however, from the standpoints of both economy and sound research, if a number of systems were to cooperate in testing these and perhaps additional hypotheses. If a dozen schools were involved, and if there were eighteen major hypotheses to be tested, then each school might test six of the eighteen. In this way, the opportunity to generalize results would be greatly increased, for each hypothesis would be tested four times in different schools. (Alexander, 1969, p. 139).

Many of these hypotheses have been at least partially tested singly or in some combination as self-studies, while other summative evaluations have collected and analyzed data relevant to the hypotheses. Some doctoral dissertations have used certain hypotheses for researching the effects of middle schools. The three-year study of the Brown School cited earlier in this chapter investigated many of the aspects concerned; the following hypotheses were posed and data collected and analyzed regarding them in this study:

1. That teacher attendance will be equal to or greater than attendance in a junior high school.

2. That average daily attendance of middle school pupils will be equal to or greater than attendance of junior high school students.

3. That student discipline cases will be equal to or fewer than pupil discipline cases in a junior high school.

4. That parent attitudes will be equal to or more favorable than parent attitudes toward a junior high school.

5. That student attitudes will be equal to or more favorable than student attitudes in a junior high school.

6. That student achievement on standardized test scores will be equal to or better than student achievement test scores in a junior high school.

7. That former middle school student grade point averages in the first semester of high school will be equal to or higher than grade point averages of students from junior high school.

8. That materials, activities, course and program development will be equal to or greater than that of a junior high school.

9. That program and school communications with the community, parents, feeder and receiver school will be equal to or greater than that of a junior high school.

10. That teacher attitudes toward school organizational design, programs, and students will be equal to or more favorable than teacher attitudes in a junior high school.

11. That curriculum expansion and flexibility will allow equal or greater individual student choices in the learning process than student choices in the junior high schools. (McGee, Krajewski & Keene, 1977, p. 6)

Although statistical data were inadequate for generalization on some hypotheses, the comparisons of the Brown Middle School over the three-year period with the predecessor junior high school were favorable toward the middle school. The design of this study should be of interest not only to school districts wishing comprehensive, longitudinal evaluations, but to research agencies and directors interested in comprehensive evaluations of the middle school.

In school districts approaching the transition to middle school education from some other organizational structure, decision makers are bound to want evidence that the process has desirable outcomes. In such cases, they are interested in research studies from other settings prior to approving the reorganization, but afterwards, they will be interested in outcomes in their own district. Wise planners will anticipate the need to respond to these concerns by capturing benchmark data from the years preceding the transition to middle school. In this way, presentations can be made to the school board, for example, comparing certain outcomes in the new middle schools to prior years and organizational formats. In our judgment, a number of factors will respond favorably to the change to middle school in documentable ways, if the transition is done in an exemplary way. We suggest that program developers in districts moving to middle school immediately capture benchmark data in the following areas:

1. Standardized test scores
2. School climate measures
3. Ethnic relationships
4. Suspension and expulsion rates
5. Faculty morale
6. High school performance in the 10th grade
7. Parent support and approval
8. Discipline referrals to the office
9. Attendance by students and teachers
10. Grade point average
11. High school dropout rate
12. Self-concept
13. Truancy

There may be other factors to look for. If the district has no data on the above items, planners will be in the uncomfortable position, a few years later, of being unable to prove the middle school is better than prior plans. If data on the above items are not now regularly collected, designing a few simple items to measure them with will be well worth the effort. At the very least, planners should be able to demonstrate, in later years, that important outcomes did not suffer as a result of moving to middle school. Even if things just stay the same, in the 1990s, with educational conditions becoming more challenging every week, holding steady is a victory of sorts!

Other Approaches to Middle School Evaluation

Several other approaches to evaluating a middle school that are recurrent in evaluation literature are briefly noted in this section.

Needs Assessment   Any needs assessment is a type of formative evaluation, and indeed any formative evaluation of a school yields needs assessments. The term is currently most frequently used to denote the process of identifying the discrepancy between where the program or program element under study is, and where the persons responsible wanted it to be. Thus, a repeated needs assessment, identifying the discrepancy at successive periods, evaluates progress or lack thereof on the element(s) studied. Any of the evaluation approaches discussed or combinations thereof could be used in the needs assessment process. A needs assessment is, in effect, a diagnostic evaluation; repeated needs assessments yield formative evaluation data, and various needs assessments can constitute a summative evaluation, as these terms were defined earlier in this chapter.

Shadow Studies   A historic report of the Association for Supervision and Curriculum Development on *The Junior High School We Saw: One Day in the Eighth Grade* (Lounsbury & Marani, 1964) was influential in revealing the inadequacies of the junior high school program at that time and also a significant application of the shadow study technique. Skilled curriculum workers followed ("shadowed") 102 eighth grade students in 98 schools in 26 states for one day, recording at ten-minute intervals the situation in which each student was working. The process has been repeated more recently (Lounsbury, Marani & Compton, 1980; Lounsbury & Johnston, 1985; Lounsbury & Johnston, 1988; Lounsbury & Clark, 1990) under the continuing direction of John Lounsbury, one of the shapers of the junior high school who has contributed equally to the emergence of middle school education. Such observations can now be more systematically made with observational procedures more recently developed. For evaluation of a particular school, it is important to have the shadowing done on a valid sampling basis and by trained observers using relatively identical procedures. This procedure can be used alone for a specific program element evaluation, or in combination with other procedures for comprehensive evaluation purposes. Use of the technique for more generalizable purposes requires district, state, or national samples, along the ASCD 1964 lines.

Employment of Evaluators   Consultants are frequently employed from other school districts, universities, or professional and/or commercial organizations to assist in various phases of evaluation involving local school and district personnel. They may also be employed to do the total evaluation job for particular purposes. The objectivity of the outside evaluator as well as the expertise presumably available support this practice, although there is the significant problem of how well school personnel will accept results and implement changes indicated from evaluations in which they have not been involved. We ourselves believe that internal evaluations, aided by consultants and other participants from outside, are most likely to effect continuing improvement.

Follow-Up Studies   Follow-up studies of high school and college graduates have been very valuable evaluation processes. Although generally somewhat more casual, follow-up conferences and reports of former middle school students' progress and behavior in the high schools are also used, and could be used more effectively for school evaluation and especially in planning for improved continuity of educational progress. For example, detailed data from the ninth grade as to former middle school students' status in continued learning skills such as use of library tools could influence instruction in these skills in both the middle and high school. Repeated assessment can yield information as to the results of changes made. Experimental studies using experimental and control groups from different schools or having different instructional systems can be very helpful in providing data for evaluating curriculum and instructional practices.

Annual Reports   The annual report is not an evaluation, of course, but it is an effective way of reporting evaluative data to the public. For example, an annual report of the Wakulla Middle School in Crawfordville, Florida reported for 1983–84 mental and achievement test score percentages within broad ranges: achievement of 3rd, 5th, and 8th grade students by percentages on each minimum performance standard, on the Florida Statewide Student Assessment Test; student attitude toward school from a statewide test; review team findings and recommendations in the self-study program; and the school enrollment and school budget. Other annual reports examined include similar data as available, and also results of opinion polls, and general statements as to school achievements, problems, and plans.

Comprehensive Evaluations   Earlier citations of long-term evaluation studies illustrated the use of combination procedures to yield continuing formative data as well as a summative profile on an individual school. Most efforts at significant school evaluations do use combination procedures including feedback of various types, opinion polls, self-study programs, student progress tests, and others. For example, a report from the Alief (Texas) Independent School District for 1978–79 on Management Objectives included detailed objectives for the total school district and a wide variety of data for the elementary, middle, and high school levels on many such objectives. Note an excerpt from the report on the objective that the "Students will feel a more personalized relationship with teachers and other employees":

1. 75 percent of high school students, 80 percent of middle school students, and 90 percent of the elementary students will indicate that most teachers take an interest in them (1977–78: H.S. 74 percent; M.S. 74 percent; Elem. 92 percent).

2. 70 percent of high school students, 75 percent of the middle school students, and 90 percent of the elementary school students will indicate that they can talk with at least one teacher on a personal basis (1977–78: H.S. 68 percent; M.S. 72 percent; Elem. 87 percent).

3. 85 percent of high school students, 85 percent of middle school students, and 90 percent of the elementary school students will indicate that teachers and support staff are courteous, friendly, and respectful to them (1977–78: H.S. 67 percent; M.S. 70 percent; Elem. 88 percent).

This report also included data regarding students' attitudes toward themselves and school, toward other students and student decision making and behavior, the provision of reports of student achievement and progress and plans for evaluation and reports thereof for all aspects of the school program and support elements.

Evaluating the Middle School Movement

Although statements are frequently made in journals and speeches about the success or failure of the middle school movement, there really is insufficient evidence available to support such statements. As we noted earlier, it is equally impossible and unwise to make any categorical assessment of the junior high school. Indeed, we know of no comprehensive study justifying categorical statements as to the efficacy of any one pattern of school unit organization—elementary, secondary, or otherwise. For one reason, it is very difficult, if not impossible, to control the other variables in experimental comparisons of different school organizations. Nevertheless, the middle school movement is a sufficient departure from the prior 8–4 and 6–3–3 school organizations as to need such critical examination if possible.

Several types of studies are possible, and a few have been attempted. Comparisons of the status of middle schools with regard to practices relevant to the goals of the movement can be made at different periods. We reviewed (in Chapter 3) several surveys that showed the numerical growth of middle schools, and through three of them (Alexander, 1967–68; Brooks, 1977–78; Alexander & McEwin, 1989), using some identical questions, gave some comparative data regarding program and organizational features of the middle schools. In addition to such repeated benchmark surveys, national collection and publication of local research studies and school evaluations (e.g., George & Oldaker, 1986) can help provide "state of the art" information and perhaps stimulate additional studies in neglected and critical areas. Also, statewide studies such as *Caught in the Middle* (Superintendent's Middle Grade Task Force, 1987) sponsored by leagues of middle schools or state agencies are useful as surveys and also comparisons of different school organizations in the state. It also seems desirable for networks or other organizations of middle schools to design, with appropriate consultant and financial help, large-scale studies seeking to control variables sufficiently to secure valid answers as to the relative effectiveness of middle school and other grade-age organizations serving the population of children moving from childhood to adolescence. Even more desirable, we believe, are studies minimizing the competitive nature of such organizations and maximizing the significant questions of what program and other features of their schools produce most effectively the results sought in student learning and behavior (e.g., Tittle, 1980). We believe that one very promising area of research which is often underutilized is that of dissertation research for the doctoral degree; hence, we include references to a few of the 1,200 such studies, completed between 1981 and 1992, which relate to middle school education. When and if basic research or full school evaluations can tell us how best to organize a school and provide a program therein that will tend to produce students with the most interests and skills in continued learning, then we can have full confidence in such a school. Even though we believe that the profession has drawn much closer to increased certainty about effective programs and practices (e.g., Epstein & MacIver, 1990), our own opinion is that such comprehensive and conclusive research studies and findings are as yet insufficient.

ADDITIONAL SUGGESTIONS FOR FURTHER STUDY

A. Books and Monographs

Fox, W. M. (1982). *A new proven procedure for problem-free problem solving*. Gainesville, FL: Graduate School of Business, University of Florida.

Fox, W. M. & Glaser, R. (1990). *Group problem solving without pressure*. King of Prussia, PA: Organizational Design and Development.

Guba, E. & Lincoln, Y. (1981). *Effective evaluation*. San Francisco: Jossey-Bass.

Knapp, M. S. & Shields, P. M. (1991). *Better schooling for the children of poverty*. Berkeley, CA: McCutchan Publishing Company.

Kohut, S. (1988). *The middle school: A bridge between elementary and high schools*. (2nd Ed.). Washington, DC: National Educational Association.

NASSP's Council on Middle Level Education (1988). *Assessing excellence: A guide for studying the middle level school*. Reston, VA: National Association of Secondary School Principals.

Williamson, R. (1991). *Planning for success: Successful implementation of middle level reorganization*. Reston, VA: National Association of Secondary School Principals.

B. Periodicals

Baer, V. E. (1988). Getting to know the neighbors: An information exchange between two middle schools. *Computing Teacher, 15*(8), 20–23.

Brown, D. S. (1988). Twelve middle-school teachers' planning. *Elementary School Journal, 89*(1), 69–87.

Jackson, B. (1988). A comparison between computer-based and traditional assessment tests, and their effects on pupil learning and scoring. *School Science Review, 69*(249), 809–15.

Jefferson, C. (& others). (1988). The evolving constitution: Middle school strategies. *Update on Law-Related Education, 12*(3), 42–46.

Merrill, A. B. (1991). Planning for the end of the year at a middle school. *Middle School Journal, 22*(5), 4–9.

Ramsey, E. (& others). (1989). Parent management practices and school adjustment. *School Psychology Review, 18*(4), 513–25.

Roach, P. B. (& others). (1990). The home-school link: New dimensions in the middle school preservice curriculum. *Action in Teacher Education, 11*(4), 14–17.

Schine, J. (1990). A rationale for youth community service. *Social Policy, 20*(4), 5–11.

Swank, P. R. (& others). (1989). Sensitivity of classroom observation systems: Measuring teacher effectiveness. *Journal of Experimental Education, 57*(2), 171–86.

C. ERIC

Baer, V. E. (1987, October). *An information and "cultural" exchange between two middle schools*. Paper presented at the Annual Meeting of the Rocky Mountain Educational Research Association, Tucson, AZ. (ERIC Document Reproduction Service No. ED 295 158)

California State Dept. of Education. (1989). *Quality criteria for middle grades: Planning, implementing, self-study, and program quality review*. Sacramento, CA: California State Dept. of Education, Office of School Improvement. (ERIC Document Reproduction Service No. ED 308 636)

Christie, S. (1989). *A report on opinion surveys of parents, students, and staff of four track year-round schools in Cajon Valley, 1987–1988*. (ERIC Document Reproduction Service No. ED 303 888)

Clark, T. A. (1989, April). *District-based and community-wide planning to address student dropout prevention: A discussion paper*. Paper presented at the annual meeting of the American Educational Research Association, Washington, DC. (ERIC Document Reproduction Service No. ED 302 596)

Dewalt, M. W. (& others). (1990, February). *Lunch at Sams: A cooperative community and school program*. Paper presented at the Annual Meeting of the Eastern Educational Research Association, Tampa, FL. (ERIC Document Reproduction Service No. ED 317 605)

Foody, M. (& others). (1990). *Developing a plan for multicultural education*. Syracuse, NY: Syracuse City School District. (ERIC Document Reproduction Service No. ED 327 605)

MacIver, D. J. (1990). *A national description of report card entries in the middle grades.* (Report No. 9). Baltimore, MD: Center for Research on Effective Schooling for Disadvantaged Students. (ERIC Document Reproduction Service No. ED 324 124)

Martinez, M. P. (1987). *Music program evaluation, 1985–1986.* Albuquerque, NM: Albuquerque Public Schools. (ERIC Document Reproduction Service No. ED 294 792)

Mitchell, S. & Hansen, J. B. (1989). *The use of evaluative data for instructional planning and decision making in the Portland public schools.* Portland, OR: Portland Public Schools, Research and Evaluation Dept. (ERIC Document Reproduction Service No. ED 312 275)

National Association of Elementary School Principals. (1990). *Standards for quality elementary and middle schools, kindergarten through eighth grade.* (Revised Ed.). Alexandria, VA. (ERIC Document Reproduction Service No. ED 322 639)

O'Sullivan, R. G. (1990, April). *Evaluating a model middle school dropout prevention program for at-risk students.* Paper presented at the Annual Meeting of the American Educational Research Association. (ERIC Document Reproduction Service No. ED 317 928)

Schine, J. (1989). *Young adolescents and community service.* Washington, DC: Carnegie Council on Adolescent Development. (ERIC Document Reproduction Service No. ED 325 206)

Shefelbine, J. (1990). *Parents sharing books: motivation and reading.* Bloomington: Indiana University, Family Literacy Center. (ERIC Document Reproduction Service No. ED 324 662)

Valencia, S. (& others). (1990) *Assessing reading and writing: Building a more complete picture for middle school assessment* (Technical Report No. 500). Bolt, Beranek and Newman, Inc., Cambridge, MA; Illinois Univ., Urbana: Center for the Study of Reading. (ERIC Document Reproduction Service No. ED 320 121)

Yager, R. E. (& others). (1988). *Assessing impact of STS instruction in 4–9 science in five domains.* (ERIC Document Reproduction Service No. ED 292 641)

D. Dissertations and Dissertation Abstracts

Burke, A. (1990). Junior high to middle school transition in Washington State: A survey and the case studies (Doctoral dissertation, University of Washington, 1990).

Coburn, T. A. W. (1989). The effects of diagnostic information on teacher planning and student achievement (Doctoral dissertation, Texas A&M University, 1989). *Dissertation Abstracts International, 51/01a, 65.*

Duthoy, R. J. (1989). An evaluation of middle school excellence by California school districts that have implemented a school program (Doctoral dissertation, United States International University, 1989). *Dissertation Abstracts International, 50/05a, 1152.*

Fine, R. (1989). A program evaluation of one school district's out of district placement program. (Doctoral dissertation, Rutgers, the State University of New Jersey, 1989). *Dissertation Abstracts International, 50/10a, 3117.*

Haboush, K. L. (1989). An evaluation of student learning outcomes under a critical thinking-social studies program (Doctoral dissertation, Rutgers, the State University of New Jersey, 1989). *Dissertation Abstracts International, 50/10a, 3185.*

Kane, C. C. (1988). Toward an expanded middle school philosophy: An analysis of philosophy and practice in middle level education (Doctoral dissertation, Florida State University, 1988). *Dissertation Abstracts International*, 49/12a, 3652.

Knight, R. W. (1989). Program evaluation as a catalyst for instructional change: A study of teachers evaluating the effects of a computer-assisted writing-to-learn initiative (Doctoral dissertation, University of Louisville, 1989). *Dissertation Abstracts International*, 51/04a, 1100.

Lee, Y. (1988). On the improvement of the middle school programs: The impact of north central association visiting team recommendations on junior high/middle schools in Iowa (Doctoral dissertation, University of Iowa, 1988). *Dissertation Abstracts International*, 50/04a, 865.

Smith, P. D. (1990). Planning, implementing, and maintaining a middle school program: A case study of excellence in a North Carolina school (Doctoral dissertation, North Carolina State University, 1990). *Dissertation Abstracts International*, 51/04a, 1076.

Twiest, M. M. (1988). Construction and validation of a test of basic process skills for the elementary and middle grades using different methods of test administration (Doctoral dissertation, University of Georgia, 1988). *Dissertation Abstracts International*, 50/02a, 423.

10

Middle School Leadership

Sooner or later every middle school takes on the characteristics of its leadership. In thirty years of observing and participating in middle school education, we find this statement to be as close to an absolute fact as can be found. Middle schools are affected by many factors as they seek to become exemplary, but none is more significant than the quality of their leadership. Theory, research, and experience all attest to the great importance of the leadership of the school principal and of the many other individuals who may at one time or another have roles as leaders. But since modern leadership theory tends to define leadership as a behavior or set of behaviors which contributes toward the mission of the organization, in this chapter we tend to emphasize important leadership behaviors rather than characteristics of persons. More specifically, we believe that effective middle school leadership is comprised of the following three sets of global behaviors:

1. Possessing a clear understanding of the characteristics and needs of young adolescents and translating that understanding into a vision of an appropriately organized and effective middle level school.

2. Planning the school program and developing effective implementation strategies in such a way as to create a unique and effective learning environment based on the characteristics of young adolescents, and evaluating the success of the school in achieving its objectives.

3. Engaging the stakeholders (teachers, parents, students, board members, central office staff) in a process of shared decision making which has, as its aim, the continued long-term maintenance and improvement of the school(s).

Because all of the foregoing chapters of the book deal with various aspects of item 2 above, in this chapter we focus on the concept of developing a vision for the middle school and on the leadership behaviors involved in maintaining exemplary middle schools. We believe that the carefully balanced presence of the other two factors—spirited leadership based on a clear vision and authentic involvement of all the stakeholders—is the catalyst leading to long-term survival of high-quality middle schools. Without spirited, visionary, leadership, there is no direction; without authentic involvement, there is no follow through.

Middle School Leadership and Vision

A study of the long-term survival of high-quality middle school programs (George & Anderson, 1989) did, in fact, link the longevity of commendable programs to a heightened sense of mission, and the resulting clarity of vision about the nature of the school, shared by the members of the school leadership team. That sense of mission, in order to contribute significantly to long-term effectiveness, had to be based on a familiarity with and an affinity for the characteristics and needs of older children and early adolescents. Understanding the purpose of the middle school, and the school's commitment to the personal and educational needs of youngsters from ten to fifteen, appears to play an important role, both prior to and following the implementation of quality programs at the middle level.

In that study, respondents identified:

> . . . the establishment of quality programs, and their continued existence over a long period of time, as resting on a bedrock of a leadership group which understands and demonstrates commitment to the needs of young adolescents. Exemplary programs are never established in the first place without this understanding; continued excellence in the education of early adolescents is impossible, say survey participants, when there is no clarity about or commitment to the needs of the early adolescent age group. (pp. 4–5)

Sometimes a written philosophical statement based on the nature and needs of the students is the filter through which successful program deliberations must pass. Constant reference to this written school philosophy when making decisions about curriculum, organization, schedule, and other program components can be more important than almost anything else in the preservation of high-quality middle schools. Written documents, of course, are worth very little unless they accurately reflect the degree of school leadership commitment to the needs of young adolescents and the extent to which that commitment is dispersed among the staff members of the school, the district, and its patrons. If, indeed, this student-centered mission is critical to the duration of superior programs, then careful selection of school leaders and their involvement in effective staff development programs seem to be crucial activities.

The proper process for moving effective persons into positions of middle school leadership is not clearly understood. One point does seem undisputed, however: the high school assistant principalship is not necessarily productive as a source of leaders who are able to commit themselves to the education of early adolescents as a comfortable career benchmark. High school administrative experiences were perceived as less than proper training for middle school leadership, whether or not the candidates had the required natural affinity for middle schoolers.

Candidates for leadership who emerge from the high school assistant principalship may sometimes be interested in the middle school primarily for its utility as a professional "roundhouse" which will permit them to return, as quickly as possible, to the high school as principals. Not only is there little to learn in that role which is directly related to the middle school concept, the training and experience received in the high school may be considerably counterproductive, in terms of producing effective middle school leaders. Yet, in many school districts, this is the unofficial career mobility route; it may be virtually impossible to arrive at the middle school principalship in any other way (e.g., from the principalship of an elementary school).

High school experience should not, of course, in and of itself, disqualify administrators for leadership at the middle level. In an inquiry into middle school leadership, as perceived by a sample of middle school principals (George, 1990), many respondents were confident about their ability to overcome the limitations of experience at other areas. One stated:

> Although my teaching background was working with high school students, through reading, research, observation, and listening, I was able to come to understand these kids and their needs. Knowing what they will face at the high school also impacted my understanding of their needs.

In the study identified above, 16 middle school principals were interviewed during their first year in that role. All 16 were administrators with prior experience at the secondary level; most had been principals of junior high schools. In answering a question about the reasons why they accepted the middle school position, only one talked about the characteristics of the students as having been a factor which attracted them to the post. In addition, these leaders, experienced with older students, expressed their reservations about the maturity levels of sixth graders and the difficulty which the students had in adjusting to the middle school, such as lockers, many different teachers, and dressing out for physical education. The principals were also concerned about their own ignorance of the curriculum of sixth grade programs. Some admitted that the energy level of the sixth grade students demanded an energy level from the principal that they found difficult to supply; the constant movement of the students, the noise—these were things secondary-oriented administrators had to accept, and it was difficult for them to do so.

It seems that it is also possible for a school leader to understand the intellectual needs of a young adolescent without understanding the other aspects of development—social, emotional, physical, moral. Such a limited understanding might, said one leader, cause the principal to "mistakenly place an exorbitant amount of emphasis on academics at the expense of the important socialization skills and self-concept needs of the preadolescent."

Career secondary administrators who had not developed a clear understanding of the characteristics and needs of younger adolescents expressed their doubts about the value of some changes in student activities (e.g., elimination of dances and tackle football) that had come with the middle school. Since successful coaching has, until recently, been one of the few ways in which leaders could demonstrate their readiness for responsibility, many experienced secondary school administrators have an understandable fondness for interscholastic athletic competition. Even though the departure of the ninth graders and the arrival of the sixth created a school that was, in effect, one third younger, many experienced secondary administrators had difficulty saying goodbye to programs and school activities that had been important parts of their lives. Focusing on the needs of younger adolescents and replacing inappropriate programs was not something they could easily do. We suspect that these findings have a wide application to many school districts changing from junior high to middle school.

Understanding the change to middle school means knowing that the school will be comprised of students who are substantially younger than the group who had inhabited the school when it was a junior high school. Successful leaders understand that "business as usual" is inappropriate at best, and may actually endanger the health and safety of the students. When athletic programs continue to emphasize tackle football, effective leaders understand that bodies are much more likely to be damaged, especially since the helmets do not fit well and the pants are too loose. When cheerleading tryouts remain a highly competitive, sometimes psychologically brutal, contest, a competent middle school leader knows that young hearts can be damaged in a different way. When positive structures, like teams and advisory programs fail to be installed because they are perceived as "too elementary", leaders grasp that all young adolescents are at risk. Successful middle school leadership is, indeed, based on an understanding of, and a caring for, older children and young adolescents. It is not soft-minded to be student-centered. "Philosophy and vision at the middle level is not 'fluff—it keeps us focused and gives us a point of reference from which the entire program and everything we do evolves," says one leader.

Effective middle school leaders are able to translate their understanding of and commitment to the development of early adolescents into a vision of the school which grows out of an understanding of the needs of those students. Such a vision, at its most galvanizing best, should be convincingly clear, should be possessed by more than the leadership group, should be compelling, and it should unblock creativity. The sort of vision that leads to longevity in good middle schools should represent shared values, should imply risk, should lead to growth and development for professionals in the school, should lead to further empowerment of those individuals, and should provide a roadmap for program implementation, evaluation and revision. Little wonder that discussions of leadership vision and sense of mission receive so much attention in the literature of today's schools.

One school principal described the need to communicate the vision this way:

> In the beginning (6 years ago) this skill was highly necessary, with all these groups, to the point where I developed a "stump speech" that could be given to any group at a moment's notice. Now, teachers, parents, and central office staff members use our program as a shining star, where before it was a millstone. My job has gotten much easier in this area now because we have developed so many "true believers." (George, 1990)

In an important study of effective middle schools (Lipsitz, 1984, p. 167), Lipsitz concluded that the leaders of those schools possessed a driving vision which helped everything make sense. "The leaders of these schools are ideologues. They have a vision of what school should be for the age group" (p. 174). Staff members in the exemplary schools she studied were guided by a vision which led to the "willingness and ability to adapt all school practices to the individual differences in intellectual, biological, and social maturation of their students." Struck by the centrality of this vision to all that was said and done in these schools, Lipsitz concluded:

> A central weakness in most schools for young adolescents is a widespread failure to reconsider each school practice in terms of developmental needs in order either to incorporate responsibility for meeting them into the school's academic and social goals or to keep them from being barriers to attaining those goals. The four schools [in the study] begin with an understanding of early adolescent development that is not tangential to but rather helps form the school's central set of purposes. Decisions about governance, curriculum, and school organization, while different in each school, flow from this sensitivity to the age group. Given massive individual differences in development during early adolescence, it is doubtful that a school for the age group could be successful without this sensitivity. (p. 168)

Lamenting the general confusion about the purposes of middle school education and the ignorance about the nature of early adolescence as a developmental stage of life, Lipsitz (p. 171) determined that, in the exemplary schools of her study, the staff members "had achieved an unusual clarity about the purposes of intermediate schooling and the students they teach. These schools had reached consensus about primary purpose." She went on to say:

> The schools make powerful statements, both in word and in practice, about their purpose. There is little disagreement between what they say they are doing and what they actually do. As a result, everyone can articulate what the schools stand for. School staff, parents, students, and community leaders tend to use the same vocabulary in discussing their school. While this achievement is in part a result of the principal's superb community relations skills, it is also a reflection of clarity of purpose. (p. 172)

And finally, Lipsitz concluded:

> Most of the principals, three of whom have elementary-school backgrounds, and most of the teachers, identify their schools as more elementary than secondary. Because these are such coherent schools, there is greater consensus about this issue than in most middle schools. (p. 173)

Bringing the vision to reality also depends, in a substantial way, in the ability of school leaders to attract to the staff, and keep, the most effective teachers available. One principal expressed it this way:

> Staff selection is a critical skill. Principals must select teachers who are, first, child-centered; second, team players; and third, have teaching skills and methods which stress hands-on, while utilizing a variety of methods. . . . Content knowledge is important, but not as important as those [other factors]. Content can be learned by a teacher; child-centeredness and caring disposition [can not]. Principals must be able to recognize a teacher who has child-centered qualities. (George, 1990)

Selecting the best teachers for middle schools is substantially easier when the vision of the school is known and shared by the existing school staff. Finding the best ways to select the "right staff" has begun to assume an increasingly more central position in the essential activities for middle school leaders (Carnegie Commission, 1989). Targeted selection processes, structured interviews, and other devices which will help future leaders select staff more effectively are just now beginning to appear on the scene. Most of today's leaders must, however, still rely on their ability to articulate the vision for the school and their intuitive sense of whether the teacher has that elusive "child-centeredness" mentioned above.

Maintaining the Middle School: Shared Decision Making

Establishing an exemplary middle school is a wonderful thing, but maintaining an exemplary program for two decades or more has been extremely arduous. At this point in the middle school movement, however, we believe that it is the long-term maintenance of high-quality programs that should most concern us, since educators already know how to begin them. The profession seems to know a great deal less about how to maintain an exemplary middle school, and this may be the most important leadership aspect of all.

There are many leadership factors which contribute to the extended health of an exemplary middle school. A study of these factors cited at the beginning of the chapter (George & Anderson, 1989) identified as many as a dozen. Among the more significant were:

1. the support of the central office and of colleagues in other schools
2. a focus on continuing improvement

3. establishing the most exemplary program possible at the start
4. carefully planned staff development, without the expection of miracles.

Assuming the establishment of an exemplary program to start with, and the firm and continuing support of central office staff members (which is sometimes, we admit, a great deal to assume), planning for continuing school improvement seems to be a crucial factor to the maintenance of an exemplary school. It is the responsibility of the school leadership to establish the mindset in staff members which leads them to expect to work on continuing school improvement as an important regular aspect of their professional lives. No school is ever "finished," and this is certainly true of middle schools, especially since the concept itself is still evolving. Annual goals, with specific objectives, activities, completion dates, assignments, and assessment plans are part of school improvement of this sort.

At Broomfield Heights Middle School (Broomfield, Colorado), for example, the School Improvement Plan for the 1990–91 school year focused on academic achievement gains. Having firmly established advisory programs, interdisciplinary teams, and rich exploratory and special interest programs, school leaders decided it was time to focus directly on academic achievement. The four major goals, and accompanying objectives, of the plan were:

I. Improve educational achievement at BHMS
   A. Students will demonstrate an increase in being prepared for learning. Student's level of motivation/attitude toward learning will improve.
   B. Identify students whose achievement is below 39 percent on CAT areas and develop auxiliary components to address under-achievement areas and groups.
   C. School CAT scores will increase 3–5 percent in all areas.
II. Enhance Boulder Valley School District philosophy of curriculum and instruction
   A. Examine and improve effective teaching.
   B. Re-focus on middle level education philosophy.
   C. Enhance affective learning of student.
III. Maintain current middle school attendance rate above state guidelines of 95 percent
   A. Provide a positive, secure school climate that empowers student attendance.
   B. Provide experiences that meet the needs of the adolescent.
IV. Maintain current middle school graduation rates above state level requirements of 90 percent
   A. Maintain information follow-up on all school attendees.
   B. Use of auxiliary components/program to encourage continued attendance of students.

At Fort Campbell, Kentucky, two exemplary middle schools established in the 1980s continue to grow through school improvement efforts, and maintain their exemplary nature at the same time. In 1990, educators in the schools engaged themselves in a comprehensive "effective schools" assessment and improvement project. An Assessment Questionnaire was developed around the five most common correlates identified with the effective schools concept: safe and orderly environment; clear school mission; high expectations; instructional leadership; and careful monitoring of student progress. Data generated from the assessment were used during the following years to improve the program in these specific areas, while strengthening the middle school program since there is no conflict between the effective schools movement and the middle school concept (George, 1983).

Beyond such efforts as these, there seem to be two factors which explain a great deal more of the long-term survival of exceptional middle schools. First, a schoolwide vision built solidly on a compassionate understanding of the characteristics and needs of young adolescents, as detailed above. The second factor is at least as important as the first, if not more so. It seems that few middle school programs achieve exemplary status and fewer still are able to maintain that status for long periods of time in the absence of a regular, honest, systematic, frequent, problem-solving, decision-making, policy-setting, collaborative group which brings together leaders from the administration, the classroom, and other areas of the school community. Without real shared decision making, exemplary middle school programs do not appear to be viable for long periods of time.

We believe that the very best middle schools (and of this number, those that last) are characterized, truly, by a dynamic tension between spirited, visionary leadership and authentic, effective involvement of as many members of the school community as possible. Without leadership of this sort, there is no direction, no mission; without involvement, there is no continuing comprehensive momentum toward completion. How does this involvement come about in the exemplary middle school?

The Program Improvement Council

It has been our experience that viable exemplary middle school programs are so complex, and their mission so challenging, that they require constant "mid-course corrections" to help them continue toward the realization of important goals. Authoritarian, control-oriented leadership has been shown to have a negative effect on the ways in which teachers and administrators work toward maintaining an exemplary middle school (Blase, 1990). Spirited, visionary leadership is necessary and critical, but not sufficient. Some broader, schoolwide group of leaders, by whatever name, must be the locus of control for the decisions which provide the continuing momentum to the school program. This is achieved by shared decision making.

Such groups have had many names in many places, but we believe that when the shared decision-making process works effectively, the process is the same, regardless of the name of the group. Many middle schools have adopted the

Program Improvement Council (PIC) plan included in the Individually Guided Education (IGE) program of the Kettering Foundation's IDEA organization. Defined in this program as "a decision-making body especially concerned with schoolwide policies and operational procedures," the PIC group was further described as follows in an IGE publication:

> With the principal as its chairman, it establishes schoolwide policy and oversees the many wide-ranging aspects of the total program. LC [team] leaders who make up the balance of the PIC's membership have teaching and advising, as well as administrative, duties in their Learning Communities [teams]. They combine a thorough understanding of LC operations and problems with an overall appreciation of the task of implementing IGE successfully throughout the school. (Coakley, 1975, p. 45)

The middle schools of Alachua County, Florida were established more than 20 years ago, in the late 1960s and early 1970s. In the early 1990s, the middle schools in that district are still viable, still growing and developing, still refining the concept of middle school for their students, and providing leadership for the state and the nation. Times have changed, early leaders have moved on to other responsibilities, and new leaders with new visions have taken their places. Intense pressures of all kinds have been endured, and the mantle of "lighthouse middle school" in the district has moved from one school to another. None of the schools is perfect. But, as a district, the middle schools of Alachua County have been as fully functioning, as complete, for longer periods, as any other set of middle schools in the nation. Why? As long-time close observers of this program, we believe that it is because of the propitious combination of leadership and involvement of which we write here.

The middle schools of Alachua County (and, of course, elsewhere in the state and nation) have adapted the Program Improvement Council to meet the needs of their middle school programs. It is a practical and effective way to combine leadership and involvement in a way to provide continuing energy and enthusiasm to middle school education. The way it works in Alachua County's middle school need not be exactly the way it works everywhere, but it has proven itself to be both effective and hardy in the form it is utilized there.

Typically, the process begins on Monday morning, on a weekly or biweekly basis, when the principal posts the tentative agenda for the PIC meeting to be held that afternoon, after the students have departed. Posted near the faculty sign-in area, anyone can add an item to the tentative agenda. Sometime near mid-morning the principal takes down the tentative agenda, goes back to the office and makes out the final agenda for the afternoon meeting. Then at, say 2:55 p.m., all of the staff members who wish to attend the PIC meeting move to the library, where the meetings are always held.

PIC has regular members. All of the team leaders in the school are members, as are the members of the school administration. In addition, there are representatives from unified arts, P.E., and special education. A counselor will also be a member. In some schools, in other districts, parents and students also have representatives. Only regular members can vote, if a vote becomes necessary.

Any staff member can attend, and all are encouraged to do so, even if they can not vote. Sometimes teachers come to advocate a particular position or to ask for special permission for an activity that will affect the whole school. At certain times, issues may be so important to the life of the school that a substantial number of staff will attend just to "fishbowl," to observe the deliberations closely. New staff members are encouraged to attend PIC meetings for staff development purposes, since this is the closest one can get to the heartbeat of the school culture and new staff members can get in touch with the mission of the school in record time.

At PIC, decisions are made openly and with authentic shared decision making, but school leaders do not "give the store away." This means that the items which are brought up for discussion and decision are carefully planned and selected, and widely known. In fact, when the process is done correctly, school leaders know ahead of the meeting that they can live with whatever decision is made. This does not mean, however, that decisions are foregone conclusions and that the PIC group is simply a rubber stamp for the principal. It means that the substance of the PIC group's deliberations are recognized as concerns that require everyone's input and commitment to decide correctly and implement effectively.

Items for discussion and decision making at PIC are, consequently, selected from a very specific, albeit wide-ranging, area. PIC members do not discuss items beyond their control, like the total monies allocated to the school, or changes they would like to see in the school board contract or state legislature. They do not discuss items like teacher evaluations or problems within one team, nor do they discuss the myriad items which bore teachers to death during traditional faculty meetings and which administrators can manage with their knowledge and permission but without their involvement. PIC agendas are composed of the schoolwide issues, problems, and decisions which most concern the staff as a whole. Here are the items which appeared on the November 26, 1990 agenda for the PIC meeting at Lincoln Middle School:

1. "Steppers" (a singing and dancing group) will be out Monday, December 10, at the Village Retirement Home. They will also be out Thursday and Friday. All work must be made up. If this does not happen, let Hannah know.

2. Sixth grade chorus students will be out Friday, December 14, at Alley Katz, as a reward for performing two shows.

3. Be careful of scheduling parent conferences during special activity time.

4. Dance Party video? Too many concerns and not enough support. Not this year.

5. Teacher-student football game.

6. C Team teachers will provide a special "hospitality time" for the rest of the faculty on Wednesday morning at 8:00 a.m.

7. The Recycling Program.

8. Christmas Party at Don's house.

9. Monday night's School Advisory Council.

10. Report Cards.

11. Alachua County Council of Middle School Educators meeting.

12. IBM workshop for reading and writing teachers.

13. Comments for D, F, or U grades on interim reports.

Nothing is done carelessly regarding PIC; even the physical setup is carefully designed. The meeting takes place in public, not in the privacy of the principal's office where everything is expected to go one way. Participants sit in a circle, and seats change every week so that cliques do not form. The moderator's role changes on a regular basis. The recorder's role also rotates.

At the end of each meeting, it is the task of the recorder to copy the minutes of the meeting and place them in each staff member's mailbox. At 7:45 a.m. the next morning, the first information each faculty member receives is the record of what happened at PIC the previous afternoon. At 7:50, each staff member reports to one of the team meetings which are scheduled at that time, with the school administrators circulating from meeting to meeting to insure that all are present and that the meetings are moving along as intended.

The first item on the agenda of every weekly team meeting in the school is the record from PIC, so that there is instant schoolwide communication about the concerns about which the faculty cares most. Faculty members react to the decisions and decide how they will be implemented on their team; but they may also tell their team leader that they just can't live with a particular PIC decision and why. In such a case the team leader would bring this feedback to the next PIC meeting and at least ask for a reconsideration of the issue.

Life in urban schools like those in Dade County, Florida can be challenging, and even the PIC concept can be difficult to implement smoothly. At Campbell Drive Middle School, the PIC process reflects both the high profile of the teachers' union (United Teachers of Dade) and the district's commitment to school-based management. The members of the faculty and administration worked out and agreed to a carefully designed "PIC Contract." Among the provisions of the contract are the following:

1. Attendance is mandatory to vote. One must have attended the previous meeting in order to vote at a current one, and must be present the entire meeting.

2. Meetings will follow a formal written agenda; late items will be placed on subsequent agendas.

3. Length of the meetings, to be held after school twice monthly, will be determined by the agenda.

4. The chairperson of the group will be determined by majority vote.

5. The principal has one vote, and no veto—only the right to table a motion.

The process can work beautifully, but not simply or easily. When the process is in place, increased ownership of decisions is frequent. Effectiveness and consistency of implementation is common. Morale improves. Working with early adolescents, a consummately challenging task, takes on a more positive momentum. But, of course, it can be faked, and it can be fumbled. Authentic, effective, shared decision making takes both commitment and skill on the part of the leaders and other participants involved (Spindler & George, 1984).

Bright Ideas

Shared decision making, of the sort that makes program improvement councils work, is most effective when it is pursued through the use of a systematic problem-solving process. Using a systematic process encourages confidence among participants that it is the authentic problem-solving process which will prevail in important questions and not arbitrary and unilateral decisions. Use of a systematic process also permits participants to review their decision-making and problem-solving work to see where they might have gone wrong, omitted a step, or otherwise misused the process and, therefore, made a poor decision or failed to solve a problem.

We recommend a systematic problem-solving process, for use in school-based management, shared decision-making settings, which is really a simple modification of the traditional "scientific method" with which almost all American school children become familiar at one time or another. The components of this model have been utilized in literally thousands of similar problem-solving situations, in organizations of all types, for many, many years.

To adapt it to the middle school situation, we have borrowed from and adapted the problem-solving model of the American Management Association (Marshall, 1986). The process, as we have reshaped it here, revolves around six steps, and we have used the acronym BRIGHT IDEAS to describe it, an appropriate acronym for a problem-solving method if there ever was one.

Step One: Build a Climate for Collaboration   The first step in the effective problem-solving process is to build a climate of trust, meaning, and dignity, conducive to consensus and collaboration among the members of the middle school staff. The sort of problem solving which permits high-quality middle school programs to emerge and to exist for a decade or more is simply not possible in a climate of interpersonal distance, formality, hierarchy, and mistrust. Collaborating with people we do not know well or have not come to trust is much like trying to borrow money from a total stranger; satisfactory agreements are usually very difficult to reach (Reck & Long, 1985). In such situations, it is natural to keep one's guard up, to react defensively, and to remain as non-committal as possible. People must spend time together in order to get to know and trust one another, to share the same goals and objectives.

The typical middle school day is usually not conducive to this sort of professional interaction, so conscious attention to what is called "team building" will be necessary. The team building process might start with having some fun together, since fun is essential to both individual and group strength and health, and it is possible to "work at team building while enjoying it" (George, 1987). Because having fun together is one of the most effective ways of building bridges and bonds between people, there are almost as many ways of having fun as there are different groups. Consider some of these methods for building a climate for collaboration:

1. Sharing meals together. All the way back to the frontier days, when sharing meager foodstuffs with others was a way to show trust and warmth, Americans have used shared meals to build group unity. It still works today. It can be as simple as bringing in donuts, or it can be a monthly breakfast. If your group can't find ways to share meals together, or doesn't see the need for it, it may be time to assess the unity and spirit in the organization.

2. Shared laughter and special ceremonies are two other team builders that create understanding and empathy. Simple techniques work well, such as a joke or humorous quote for the day or week. Cartoons, pictures, or other items posted in conspicuous places (bulletin boards, sign-in sheets) can prompt healthy, happy laughter. Humorous ceremonies and rituals, such as roasts and awards ceremonies, also build bridges through laughter—a lesson the Japanese have learned well. One school we know conducts such an awards program for the faculty every spring. The "Mario Andretti Award," given (in fun) to the faculty member who most often gets out of the parking lot in record time, is typical of what happens there. Another school enjoys the tradition of "Secret Santa" just prior to the winter holiday every year when names are exchanged for inexpensive and humorous gifts.

Special recognition for weddings, births, and birthdays, from brief acknowledgements to being a special guest at lunch, is another way to build good feeling. Occasions that generate great personal meaning can be acknowledged on a regular basis without detracting from the power they add to the individual's life outside the school. Furthermore, many school staff members want to share the highlights of their lives with those they work with and they want to stay informed on at least the highlights of their peers' home lives.

Sometimes school leaders, intent on the organizational and managerial duties which surround them, forget how important it is to attend to the process of human interaction in these ways. It is a mistake to believe that attention to such matters is either unnecessary or a waste of time.

3. It is often well worth the money to send people off together on a professional trip of one kind or another. Attending conferences and workshops together often builds strong, positive, and appropriate bonds among members of a middle school staff. Find out about state, regional, and national meetings that members can attend.

4. Eliminate unnatural and unnecessary signs of institutional hierarchy and administrative privilege. The concepts of teamwork and collaboration are undermined by conspicuous inequality. One of the most obvious and, we believe, unnecessary symbols of this sort is the arrangements sometimes made to have special parking places set aside for the administration and the office staff. If someone must have a reserved spot, why not have it be the "teacher of the year?" Make it clear that everyone is on the same team, valued for the contribution they make, different though it may be. Administrators who argue that the convenience of having a personal parking spot right in front of the school is more important than the message it sends and the collaboration it prevents are not likely to engage in authentic consensus-based problem solving.

5. Perhaps the most effective way to build a climate of trust and collaboration is for the leaders to model the behaviors, to encourage by example. Self-disclosure by the leader who reveals important information about ideas and feelings relevant to the work of the staff, in appropriate ways and circumstances, encourages others to do the same. In addition to self-disclosure, leaders must demonstrate honesty in dealing with the staff (e.g., by keeping all the promises they make). It is this type of interpersonal sharing that builds the bonds necessary for true collaboration.

There may be many other ways to build the sort of culture conducive to collaboration (e.g., specially structured small-group training experiences), but there are no substitutes for the time and energy required to bring a group of middle school staff members to the point of being able to trust each other enough to engage in authentically open and non-defensive problem solving. Such relationships go several steps farther than the typical casual relationships usually shared by school staff members. The climate of trust necessary for shared decision making is consciously designed with the intent of having all of the members of the staff feeling relaxed, open, and comfortable in dealing with each other. These are relationships in which staff members enter with the expectations for mutual benefit as a result. Shared decision making will not proceed, and exemplary middle school programs will not last long without it.

Reck and Long (1985, p. 55) summarize the process of building a climate for collaboration in three steps:

1. Plan and conduct a series of activities which allow positive personal relationships to develop among the members of the faculty and between the faculty and the administration.

2. Cultivate a sense of mutual trust.

3. Allow the relationship to develop fully before attempting to engage in really serious or difficult shared decision-making projects.

Step Two: Recognize and Define the Problem or the Situation   There is a decades-old adage that "a problem well-defined is a problem half-solved." Often, difficulties in the organization and operation of middle schools, complex institutions that they are, arise from the failure to define or to agree on the definition of exactly what the problems are. Disagreements and competing solutions may arise simply, and often, because people are attempting to solve different or competing problems without recognizing that this is what is occurring. Begin a problem-solving session by devoting the necessary time and energy to bringing clarity to the nature of the problem and agreement to pursue solutions to one problem at a time. The American Management Association (Marshall, 1986) says that "as individuals or groups struggle to define a problem, sometimes they solve the problem or come close to solving it. Sometimes the problem seems to solve itself." Problems which do not disappear quickly, when they are examined, tend to be complex and difficult, requiring careful handling.

When this is the case, it is important to distinguish between the substantive and the emotional aspects of problems and the problem-solving process. All problems and conflicts, and most important decisions have both emotional and substantive components, and a purely rational approach rarely works satisfactorily when emotions are running high. "When feelings are strong, it is usually a sound strategy to deal with the emotional aspects of the conflict first" (Bolton, 1979, p. 217). Ignoring the emotional charge will usually only prolong the conflict; plus, it may damage the degree of trust and harmony which has been laboriously constructed.

This juncture in the problem-solving process must be handled as carefully as any other, if not more so. A strictly positive structure must govern the interactions at this point. Participants must be aware that they are entering a point in the process where emotional components are being explored. They must be able to recognize the potential damage which may be done to the trust level if feelings are not vented with care. Blaming, moralizing, threatening, judging, and ridiculing are forbidden (Gordon, 1977). Participants in the process must be encouraged to point out and reject such behavior when it intrudes into middle school shared decision making.

To extinguish these anger-driven responses which destroy trust and harmony, Bolton (1979) recommends strict adherence to three important steps. First, treat the other persons with respect at all times. Second, listen until you "experience the other sides." Third, briefly and calmly state your own views, needs, and feelings. Leaders of effective middle school shared decision-making groups will introduce these guidelines at the beginning of every year, insist on adherence to them, and periodically reinforce them, especially if the climate for collaboration is in jeopardy.

When the council group has assembled, asking "What appears to be the problem?" should open the floor to teachers and others stating what they think and how they feel about the problem. This question will, especially when trust levels are high, encourage members to speak about aspects of the problem about which they feel most strongly.

Eventually, when emotions have receded, it will be possible to move forward to a rational and logical consideration of the substantive aspects of the problem. When members of the group verbalize brief definitions of the problem, the leader and others may be able to distinguish between symptoms of the problem and the problem itself. Focusing only on the symptoms instead of the problem may permit the group to eliminate the symptoms, at least temporarily, but since the problem itself is not resolved, new and different (and perhaps more difficult) symptoms may appear. Asking "Why does the problem exist?" will help focus on the real problem instead of on the symptoms of the problem.

Stating the problem simply makes the problem easier to solve. Simple, however, does not mean simplistic. It means clear and agreed upon. The problem itself may be complicated, and arriving at solutions may be difficult, but the statement of the problem should be simple and succinct.

At this point, it is especially important to define the problem, and to resist making and accepting suggestions that are intended to solve the problem. Otherwise, groups may end up dealing with symptoms of the problem, or with something other than the actual problem. A lot of time can be wasted solving the wrong problem.

Identifying the problem as a situation and then describing the desired situation may also help clarify the problem and lead to a clear statement. "Can someone describe the current situation clearly?" is often a useful question at this juncture, followed shortly by "Can someone describe the desired situation clearly?" Here, it is important to distinguish between needs which must be attended to and potential solutions to the problem which the needs create.

It is often helpful to use a flipchart to record the discussion leading to a definition of the problem as it is defined. Some experienced problem-solvers are adamant about the utility of such flipcharts in group problem solving. They argue that flipcharts control problem definition, through such a record and visible reference point. Doing so helps control the urge to digress, or to offer solutions prematurely, before the problem is defined. The choice of the person to record the solution on the flipchart is especially important. The permanence and visibility of the flipchart also renders it superior to the chalkboard, the overhead projector, or a leader's notes.

Eventually, someone should say "How does this sound as a definition of the problem?" If there is a consensus on the definition offered, it will be appropriate to move forward to step three. It may take some time to arrive at this point, and that is as it should be, since ordinarily not enough time is taken to define a problem clearly before moving ahead to attempt solutions. Time spent here can save considerable time, bad feelings, and even expense later. The final problem statement should evolve from the group's discussions, and often will not be the first or the second definition offered.

Step Three: Inform the Group about the Problem and Its Consequences　Collect as many facts as possible, related to the clearly defined problem. This is the point to examine how the situation arose, the causes of the problem. It is also the time to identify the dimensions of the problem—the difficulties the problem situation causes for members of the group and those whom they represent. It may also be appropriate to invite members of the group to talk about their feelings associated with the situation, if such a ventilating time can clear the air without blame and recriminations which might damage the level of trust in the group. It is a good time to involve those people who might have a tendency to digress during other steps in the process, but it may be necessary to limit the amount of time devoted to this step and to abide by a series of ground rules which help to limit any bad feelings which might otherwise result.

It is still not a time to suggest or discuss solutions, not until the members of the group know and agree on how the problem came about and the effects of the problem which are being experienced by members of the staff. This knowledge will help in the evaluation of potential solutions when they are eventually made.

Step Four: Generate Alternative Solutions or Actions　This is, finally, the point at which alternative solutions are proposed. Social psychologists and negotiators stress that it should, first, be a search for possible solutions, not the best or final solution. The most effective solutions are found when the group creatively explores as many alternatives as the members can develop.

The time-tested process of brainstorming is very useful in generating a large number of potentially useful alternative solutions, developing a list of ideas from which an eventual solution can be chosen or fashioned. Brainstorm rhymes with "rainstorm," and the objective is also similar—to precipitate an outpouring of ideas, as fast as they can be recorded, without attempting to elaborate, praise, or criticize. Sometimes an imposed time limit, of say five minutes, adds to the appeal and effectiveness of the process. The process works well in groups which have the size of the typical middle school council and builds upon the trust level, permitting members to suggest creative or unusual options which they might otherwise not have the courage to mention.

One easily remembered model for the brainstorming process is that offered by the American Management Association (1986). This group uses the acronym IDEAS to summarize the process. The five aspects of brainstorming include:

1. Ideas are recorded for later reference.
2. Delay discussing, agreeing, or disagreeing with ideas.

3. Expand and hitchhike on one another's ideas.
4. Abbreviate thoughts to record ideas quickly.
5. Strive for quantity of ideas; quality can come later.

Brainstorming sessions based on these steps are likely to succeed more frequently. Be certain to record ideas without any discussion *whatsoever*, without even clarification, let alone criticism or approval. Give each suggestion a number, so that discussion of alternatives, later, can be done more quickly. Since brainstorming is likely to produce a lot of incomplete ideas, it is effective to expand on each other's ideas; some of the best solutions will result from combinations of other ideas, or adding to an existing suggestion. Skillful abbreviation and quick recording are essential for the person working at the flipchart. It is also important to avoid attaching specific people's names to ideas or listing each person's ideas separately. This is the point to strive for quantity of ideas, not quality, and following these suggestions will virtually guarantee more ideas than would otherwise be produced.

It is important to stress that the group facilitator or leader will almost certainly have to interrupt, gently but firmly, to insist that ideas not be critiqued one at a time while they are being generated. If this is permitted, many valuable potential solutions will be lost.

Step Five : Hold off the Decision until All the Alternatives Have Been Analyzed   This is the point at which the group identifies the solution or combination of solutions which will best meet the needs of the group. If clarification of earlier suggested ideas is needed, this is the time to do it, before discussing the merits or demerits of solutions. Evaluations must wait, especially since it will be tempting for many groups to jump on what appears to be the most popular solution, or to vote for the solution made by status leaders in the group. Failing to evaluate potential alternatives increases the likelihood of adopting a less than satisfactory one as the final solution.

Several strategies may add to the effectiveness of the analysis. First, don't feel a need to evaluate every single suggestion one by one; this will consume far too much time, and generate impatience and frustration with the problem-solving process. Instead, begin by eliminating a large group of alternatives, those which are unlikely to meet the needs of the group because they are flawed in some way (e.g., lacking in fairness; costly; difficult to implement; wouldn't really solve the problem). Then, combine the remaining ideas which fit together well. Eventually, ask "Which alternatives look best to you?" Be sure to identify the alternatives which most appeal to you. Finally, see if one or more of the choices coincide, and jointly choose one or a combination of alternatives.

It is critical to the problem-solving process, and to shared decision making in the middle school, that the solution be a joint one. Insisting on reaching consensus is important. "Majority vote, parliamentary procedures, adherence to

Roberts's Rules of Order—these are not used in collaborative problem solving" (Bolton, 1979, p. 246). Consensus decisions require that the process of discussion continue until everyone's point of view has been heard, and a sincere attempt has been made to incorporate those differing perspectives into the final solution. All members, but especially the leader, must be willing to say, gently, "I just can't live with that," when a proposed solution is simply not acceptable. The alternative which is finally agreed upon may not be perfect, but since it does not violate any member's deepest convictions, it can be agreed upon by all, including the leaders.

Arriving at conclusions by consensus is not fast or easy; it is just better than any other way, since decisions tend to "stay decided" and problems tend to stay solved. It requires mutual commitment to implement the solution. It demands that this mutual commitment be reached without pressure, powerful persuasion, or coercion of any kind. Mutual commitments, freely arrived at, are indeed difficult, but they are also the agreements most likely to be carried out, and this is, after all, the objective of the process. Successful implementation, not having one's own idea voted upon favorably, is the goal.

Step Six: Take Action and Follow Up   At this point, everyone in the group has contributed to and agreed upon the chosen solution. Now, there are two final moves to make—taking action and following up. This is the point to work out the "nuts and bolts" details of the solution, before relaxing in the afterglow of having achieved a solution, since no solution can be more effective than its implementation. An action plan must be developed, and appropriate individuals outside the decision-making group may need to be informed about the plan.

The action plan should be detailed, precise, written—without being lengthy—and widely distributed; one or two pages in checklist fashion works well. Such plans become what, in the corporate world, is called a "memo of understanding"— who will do what, where, and by when. Staff members must understand how the action will be documented, that is, the evidence that will demonstrate that the action has been taken. Since many people are sometimes forgetful, and deadlines have a way of slipping by, such an action plan can be the salvation of an elegant solution.

The last part of the problem-solving process is to determine whether or not the solution has been implemented effectively and if it is solving the problem. This is the evaluation phase, and since not all solutions turn out to be the best, it is always important. Sometimes staff members will simply not complete actions which they were assigned. At other times, the solution will demonstrate weaknesses which were simply not obvious when the alternative was chosen. Or, group members may overcommit themselves as they attempt to demonstrate their willingness to be cooperative. The problem may have to be re-examined and solved again, or simple adjustments may be all that is necessary. As a final check, ask "Have we solved the problem?"

The Generative School

Recent research in the application of systems theory in the world of organizational behavior (Senge, 1990) indicates that schools, as organizations, may come in three types. The Reactive School is a place without spirited leadership and limited vision or involvement—a place where staff members have no direction or capacity to deal with problems in a systematic way. In difficult periods, life in such schools may be a process of hurtling from crisis to crisis. Principals and teachers feel as if they have no control over their professional lives. Eventually, many, especially those who are deeply committed to education, burn out. Cynicism pervades the Reactive School.

In the Responsive School, a visionary leader may help the school's ability to respond more positively because of the leader's capacity to see causes and effects, or because the leader can help the school respond to emerging trends. In such schools, the climate is less reactive, life is less crisis-oriented. But there are limits to the school's capacity to respond—limits imposed by the lack of involvement, the lack of commitment on the part of the staff as a whole. Or, a Responsive School may be a place where there is a systematic approach to solving problems, with a high degree of involvement of teachers and administrators working together collaboratively, but without the sense of mission produced by a driving vision of a school truly based on the characteristics and needs of young adolescents. In such Responsive Schools, problems are solved, but the solutions are likely to be short-term. Goals may atrophy. Direction is imposed from outside the school. In such situations, certainly more positive than in a Reactive School, faculties may feel less failure, but also experience little real success. Cynicism may not be all-pervasive, but authentic professional satisfaction may also be elusive.

In a truly Generative School, spirited, visionary leadership combines with authentic involvement to produce a possible future for the school, and for the individuals within it, that draws all staff members toward it. Administrators and teachers possess a shared vision and the skills to make the continuous adjustments and improvements required to make progress toward the goals of the school. They feel pride in their short-term accomplishments, energized by their progress, and satisfaction with their achievements. The work is hard, the tasks are exhausting, the challenges daunting; but everyone knows they are involved in an endeavor that gives meaning and purpose to their lives as educators. This is the exemplary middle school.

Additional Suggestions for Further Study

A. Books and Monographs

Berla, N. (1989). *The middle school years: A parents' handbook*. Columbia, MD: National Committee for Citizens in Education.

Glatthorn, A. A. (1986). *Middle school/junior high principal's handbook: A practical guide for developing better schools*. Englewood Cliffs, NJ: Prentice-Hall.

Merenbloom, E. Y. (1988). *Developing effective middle schools through faculty participation*. (2nd Ed.). Columbus, OH: National Middle School Association.

Myers, J. W. (1985). *Involving parents in middle level education*. Columbus, OH: National Middle School Association.

The Research-Based Training for School Administrators Project. (1987). *Effective middle schools: Project leadership presenter's guide*. Eugene, OR: Center for Educational Policy and Management, College of Education, University of Oregon.

B. Periodicals

Armstrong, J. D. (1988). A change of leaders—a case study in instructional leadership. *NASSP Bulletin, 72*(510), 11–16.

Aronstein, L. W. (& others). (1990). Detours on the road to site-based management. *Educational Leadership, 47*(7), 61–63.

Bauch, J. P. (1989). The transparent school model: New technology for parent involvement. *Educational Leadership, 47*(2), 32–34.

George, P. S. (1990). From junior high to middle school—principals' perspectives. *NASSP Bulletin, 74*(523), 86–94.

Parkay, F. W. & Damico, S.B. (1989). Empowering teachers for change through faculty-driven school improvement. *Journal of Staff Development, 10*(2), 8–14.

Stronge, J. H. & Jones, C. W. (1991). Middle school climate: The principal's role in influencing effectiveness. *Middle School Journal, 22*(5), 41–46.

C. ERIC

Dauber, S. L. & Epstein, J. L. (1989). *Parent attitudes and practices of parent involvement in inner-city elementary and middle schools*. (Report No. 33). Baltimore, MD: Center for Research on Elementary and Middle Schools. (ERIC Document Reproduction Service No. ED 314 152)

Doud, J. L. (1989). *The K–8 principal in 1988: A ten-year study*. Alexandria, VA: National Association of Elementary School Principals. (ERIC Document Reproduction Service No. ED 319 134)

Epstein, J. L. & Dauber, S. L. (1989). *Teacher attitudes and practices of parent involvement in inner-city elementary and middle schools*. (Report No. 32). Baltimore, MD: Center for Research on Elementary and Middle Schools. (ERIC Document Reproduction Service No. ED 314 151)

Melenyzer, B. J. (1990, November). *Teacher empowerment: The discourse, meanings and social actions of teachers*. Paper presented at the Annual Conference of the National Council of States on Inservice Education 15th, Orlando, FL. (ERIC Document Reproduction Service No. ED 327 496)

Merenbloom, E. Y. (1988). *Developing effective middle schools through faculty participation.* (2nd. Ed.) Columbus, OH.: National Middle School Association. (ERIC Document Reproduction Service No. ED 325 909)

Osterman, K. F. (1989, March). *Supervision and shared authority: A study of principal and teacher control in six urban middle schools.* Paper presented at the Annual Meeting of the American Educational Research Association, San Francisco, CA. (ERIC Document Reproduction Service No. ED 307 678)

D. Dissertations and Dissertation Abstracts

Beard, J. E. (1988). A study of leadership styles and their relationship to management effectiveness among middle school principals in the state of Maryland. (Doctoral dissertation, The George Washington University, 1988). *Dissertation Abstracts International*, 49/09a, 2460.

Campbell, G. B. (1989). Staff development through dialogue: A case study in educational problem solving. (Doctoral dissertation, University of Pennsylvania, 1989). *Dissertation Abstracts Internatioal*, 51/02a, 352.

Cheponis, I. M. (1990). *An analysis of leadership styles of first-year middle school principals* (Doctoral dissertation, University of Florida, 1990).

Connelly, M G. (1990). Perceptions of middle school principals about shared decision making in Los Angeles Unified School District (Doctoral dissertation, University of Southern California, 1990) *Dissertation Abstracts International* 51/05a, 1455.

Contreras, W. J. (1989). Professional development and Massachusetts middle school principals. (Doctoral dissertation, Boston University, 1989). *Dissertation Abstracts International*, 50/05a, 1149.

Gamble, M. L. M. (1990). Teachers' participation in school-based curriculum decision-making and their perceptions of school climate: An investigation of identified and non-identified schools in the Georgia schools of excellence recognition program (Doctoral dissertation, Georgia State University, 1990). *Dissertation Abstracts International*, 51/04a, 1098.

Hanke, R. E. (1988). A national comparative study of principals pf exemplary junior high/middle schools and principals of other junior high/middle schools on selected instructional leadership tasks. (Doctoral dissertation, Northern Illinois University, 1988). *Dissertation Abstracts International*, 50/06a, 1503.

Harris, G. K. (1989). Similarities between leadership characteristics of managers of successful business corporations and principals of schools cited for excellence. (Doctoral dissertation, Boston College, 1989). *Dissertation Abstracts International*, 51/01a, 35.

Hilton, J. C. (1989). The middle school principal's role as it exists, and should ideally exist, as perceived by superintendents and middle school principals. (Doctoral dissertation, Boston College, 1989). *Dissertation Abstracts International*, 50/07a, 1869.

Holt, S. L. (1989). Staff development and teacher change (Doctoral dissertation, Arizona State University, 1989). *Dissertation Abstracts International*, 51/02a, 396.

Kelly, J. H. (1988). The perceptions of Huntsville, Alabama, standard metropolitan statistical area principals toward their role in staff development. (Doctoral dissertation, The University of Alabama, 1988). *Dissertation Abstracts International*, 49/08a, 2047.

Kshensky, M. (1990). Principal power and school effectiveness: A study of urban public middle schools (Doctoral dissertation, Fordham University, 1990). *Dissertation Abstracts International*, 51/06a, 1852.

McPherson, N. F. (1989). The attitudes of Georgia principals towards systems of evaluation. (Doctoral dissertation, Georgia State University, 1989). *Dissertation Abstracts International*, 51/01a, 41.

Nakaoka, B. (1989). International leadership of the middle/junior principal. (Doctoral dissertation, University of La Verne, 1989). *Dissertation Abstracts International*, 51/01a, 43.

Pagano, R. J. (1989). Middle school principal: the relationship between perceived leadership style and the implementation of selected middle school characteristics. (Doctoral dissertation, University of Akron, 1989). *Dissertation Abstracts International*, 50/01a, 44.

Palermo, R. J. (1990). Parents and middle schools; A sudy of the views of parents from two communities (Doctoral dissertation, Boston University, 1990). *Dissertation Abstracts International*, 51/04a. 1071.

Rivas, E. R. (1989). Application of quality circles in junior high/middle schools: Job satisfaction, rapport among teachers, community support and community pressures (participative management). (Doctoral dissertation, University of Miami, 1989). *Dissertation Abstracts International*, 51/02a, 372.

Shelor, L. G. (1989). Empowering teachers: An ethnographic account of reform activities in a middle school (Doctoral dissertation, University of Louisville, 1989). *Dissertation Abstracts International*, 50/10a, 3112.

Vass, L. J. (1989). An analysis of princpals' work behavior. (Doctoral dissertation, Northern Illinios University, 1989). *Dissertation Abstracts International*, 50/09a, 2745.

Wright, M. K. (1987). Staff development impact on teachers and students (Doctoral dissertation, University of San Francisco, 1987). *Dissertation Abstracts International*, 49/07a, 1664.

REFERENCES

Adelson, J. (1983). The growth of thought in adolescence. *Educational Horizons, 61,* 156–162.

Alachua County Schools. (1972). *Report of the middle school task team.* Gainesville, FL: Alachua County Public Schools.

Alexander, W. (1964). The junior high school: A changing view. *NASSP Bulletin, 48,* 22.

Alexander, W. (1968). *A survey of organizational patterns of reorganized middle schools.* Washington, DC: United States Office of Education, Cooperative Research Project No. 7-D–026.

Alexander, W., Hines, V. & Associates. (1967). *Independent study in secondary schools.* New York: Holt, Rinehart and Winston.

Alexander, W. & McEwin, C. (1989). *Earmarks of schools in the middle: A research report.* Boone, NC: Appalachian State University.

Alexander, W. & McEwin, C.K. (1989). *Schools in the middle: Status and progress.* Columbus, OH: National Middle School Association.

Alexander, W. & Williams, E. (1965). Schools for the middle school years. *Educational Leadership, 23,* 217–223.

Alexander, W., Williams, E., Compton, M., Hines, V. & Prescott, D. (1968). *The emergent middle school.* New York: Holt, Rinehart and Winston.

Allan, J. & Dyck, P. (1984). Transition: Childhood to adolescence. *Elementary School Guidance and Counseling, 18,* 277–286.

Andrus, E. & Joiner, D. (1989). The community needs H.U.G.S.S. too! *Middle School Journal,* May, 8–11.

Arhar, J. (1990). *The effects of interdisciplinary teaming on social bonding of middle level students.* Unpublished manuscript. See also, Arhar, J. The effects of teaming on students. *Middle School Journal, 20,* July 24–27.

Arnold, J. (1990). *Visions of teaching and learning: Exemplary middle school projects.* Columbus, OH: National Middle School Association.

Arth, A. A. (1990). Moving into middle school: Concerns of transescent students. *Educational Horizons, 68,* 105–106.

Association for Supervision and Curriculum Development. (1954). *Developing programs for young adolescents.* Washington, DC: ASCD.

Atwell, N. (1987). *In the middle: Writing, reading, and learning with adolescents.* Portsmouth, NH: Boynton/Cook Publishers.

Beane, J. (1975). The case for core in the middle school. *Middle School Journal, 6,* 33–34, 38.

Beane, J. (1990). *A middle school curriculum: From rhetoric to reality.* Columbus, OH: National Middle School Association.

Bell, L. & Schniedewind, N. (1989). Realizing the promise of humanistic education: A reconstructed pedagogy for personal and social change. *Journal of Humanistic Psychology, 29,* 200–223.

Bennett, D. & King, T. (1991). The Saturn School of Tomorrow. *Educational Leadership, 48,* 41–44.

Bergin, D. A. (1991, April). *Mastery versus competitive learning situations: Two experimental studies.* Paper presented at the meeting of the American Educational Research Association, Chicago, IL.

Bergmann, S. (1989). *Discipline and guidance: A thin line in the middle level school.* Reston, VA : Naitonal Association of Secondary School Principals.

Blase, J. (1990). Some negative effects of principal's control-oriented and protective political behavior. *American Educational Research Journal, 27,* 727–753.

Bloom, B. S. (1984). The search for methods of group instruction as effective as one-to-one tutoring. *Educational Leadership, 41,* 4–17.

Bolton, R. (1979). *People skills.* Englewood Cliffs, NJ: Prentice-Hall.

Booth, R. Personal communication. December 7, 1989.

Borg, W. (1979, March). Time and school learning. *BTES Newsletter.* Sacramento, CA: The Commission on Teacher Preparation and Licensing, pp. 2–7.

Briggs, T. (1984). *The junior high school.* Boston: Houghton, Mifflin.

Bronfenbrenner, U. (1973). *Two worlds of childhood.* New York: Pocket Books.

Brooks, K. & Edwards, F. (1978). *The middle school in transition: A research report on the status of the middle school movement.* Lexington, KY: College of Education, University of Kentucky.

Brooks-Gunn, J. & Warren, M. P. (1989). Biological and social contributions to negative affect in young adolescent girls. *Child Development, 60,* 40–55.

Brophy, J. (1979). Teacher behavior and student learning. *Educational Leadership, 37,* 33–38.

Brophy, J. & Alleman, J. (1991). Activities as instructional tools: A framework for analysis and evaluation. *Educational Researcher, 20,* 9–23.

Brophy, J. & Good, T. Teacher behavior and student achievement. (1986). In Wittrock, M., *Handbook of research on teaching, Third Edition.* New York: Macmillan.

Brown, T. Personal communication. December 4, 1989.

Buckner, J. & Brickel, F. (1990). *Teaching in the middle: Given'em what they want while providing what they need.* Paper presented at the annual conference of the National Middle School Association, Long Beach, CA.

Burns, R. B. (1979). Master learning: Does it work? *Educational Leadership, 37,* 110–111.

Bushnell, D. (1991). The middle school counselor's role in advisement. *Florida School Counselor's Newsletter, 8,* 8–9.

Bushnell, D. (1992). *Middle school teachers as effective advisors: Student and teacher perceptions.* Unpublished doctoral dissertation, University of Florida, Gainesville.

Carnegie Council on Adolescent Development (1989). *Turning points: Preparing youth for the 21st century.* New York: Carnegie Corporation of New York.

Caswell, H. (1978). Persistent curriculum problems. *Educational Forum, 43,* 100–101.

Cawelti, G. (1988). Middle schools a better match with early adolescent needs, ASCD survey finds. *Curriculum Update,* 1–12.

Cawelti, G. (1989). Designing high schools for the future. *Educational Leadership, 47,* 30–35.

City School District. (1988). *Guidelines for school-based planning.* Rochester, NY: City School District.

Coakley, J. (1975). *The School.* Dayton, OH: Institute for Development of Educational Activities, Inc.

Coleman, J. C. (1980). *The nature of adolescence.* New York: Methuen.

Commission on Secondary Curriculum. (1961). *The junior high school we need.* Washington, DC: Association for Supervision and Curriculum Development.

Compton, M. (1976). The middle school: A status report. *Middle School Journal, 7,* 3–5.

Connors, N. (1987). A case study to determine the essential components and effects of an advisor-advisee program in an exemplary middle school. *Dissertation Abstracts International, 47,* 2986A. University Microfilms No. DET 86–26791.

Connors, N. & Gill, J. (1991). Middle-schoolness and the federal school recognition program. *T.E.A.M.: The early adolescent magazine. 4,* March/April, 44–48.

Cotton, N. (1985). The development of self-esteem and self-esteem regulation. In J. Mack and S. Ablon (Eds.). *The development and sustaining of self-esteem in childhood.* New York: International Universities Press, pp. 122–150.

Council on College-Level Services. (1991). *Advanced placement pre-high school initiative committee summary and recommendations.* New York: The College Board.

Cuff, W. (1967). Middle schools on the march. *NASSP Bulletin, 51,* 82–86.

Curry, L. (1990). A critique of the research on learning styles. *Educational Leadership, 48,* 50–52, 54–56.

Department of Special Education. (1975). *Instructional settings for exceptional children: A continuum of services.* Unpublished manuscript. University of Florida, Gainesville.

de Rosenroll, D. A. (1987). Early adolescent egocentrism: A review of six articles. *Adolescence, 22,* 791–802.

Dickson, D. & Knarr, T. (1989). *The school improvement process: An explanation of the history and concept of this process in Hammond.* Hammond, IN: Hammond Public Schools.

DiVirgillio, J. (1973). Why the middle school curriculum vacuum? *Educational Leadership, 31,* pp. 225–227.

Division of Public Schools. (1991). *Florida multi-agency middle school program directory.* Tallahasee, FL: Department of Education.

Doda, N. (1976). Teacher to teacher, *Middle School Journal, 7,* 9.

Doda, N. (1979). *Advisor-advisee and high school preparation: An evaluation report on student perceptions.* The University of Florida, Gainesville. Mimeograph.

Doda, N. (1981). *Teacher to teacher.* Columbus, OH: National Middle School Association.

Dorman, G., Lipsitz, J. & Verner, P. (1985). Improving schools for young adolescents. *Educational Leadership, 42*(6), 4–49.

Duke, B. (1986). *The Japanese school.* New York: Praeger.

Dunn, R. (1991). Rita Dunn answers questions on learning styles. *Educational Leadership, 48,* 15–19.

Educational Research Service. (1969). *Middle Schools in Action. ERS Circular No. 2.* Washington, DC: The Service.

Educational Research Service. (1983). *Organization of the Middle Grades: A Summary of Research.* Washington, DC: The Service.

Eichhorn, D. (1966). *The middle school.* New York: The Center for Applied Research in Education, Inc.

Eichhorn, D. (1972). The emerging adolescent school of the future—now. In Saylor, J. G. (Ed.), *The school of the future—now.* Washington, DC: Association for Supervision and Curriculum Development. p. 35–52.

Elias, M., Gara, M., Ubriaco, M., Rothbaum, P., Clabby, J. & Schuyler, T. (1986). Impact of a preventive social problem solving intervention on children's coping with middle school stressors. *American Journal of Community Pscyhology, 14,* 259–275.

Elkind, D. (1967). Egocentrism in adolescence. *Child Development, 38,* 1025–1034.

Elkind, D. (1981). *The hurried child.* Reading, MA: Addison-Wesley Publishing Company.

Elkind, D. (1985). *All grown up and no place to go.* Reading, MA: Addision-Wesley Publishing Company.

Epstein, H. & Toepfer, C. (1978). A neuroscience basis for reorganizing middle grades education. *Educational Leadership, 35,* 656–658, 660.

Epstein, J. & McIver, D. (1990). *Education in the middle grades: Overview of national practices and trends.* Columbus, OH: National Middle School Assocation.

Epstein, J. L. (1990). What matters in the middle grades—grade span or practices? *Phi Delta Kappan, 71* (6), 438–444.

Erb, T. & Doda, N. (1989). *Team organization: Promise—practices and possibilities.* Washington, DC: NEA.

Erikson, E. H. (1963). *Childhood and society.* New York: W.W. Norton and Company.

Eson, M. E. & Wolmsky, S. A. (1980). Promoting cognitive and psycholinguistic development. In Johnson, M. (Ed.). *Toward adolescence: The middle school years. 79th Yearbook of the National Society for the Study of Education. Part One.* Chicago: The University of Chicago Press.

Etzioni, A. (1983). *Rebuilding America for the 21st century: An immodest agenda.* New York: McGraw-Hill.

Faulkenberry, J. R., Vincent, M., James, A. & Johnson, W. (1987). Coital behaviors, attitudes, and knowledge of students who experience early coitus. *Adolescence, 22,* 321–332.

Feldman, S. & Elliott, G. (Eds.). (1990). *At the threshold: The developing adolescent.* Cambridge, MA: Harvard University Press.

Fitts, M. B. Personal communication. January 30, 1990.

Florida State Department of Education. (January, 1989). *Florida's teachers as advisors program: Guide for implementation. First draft.* Tallahassee: Florida State Department of Education.

Foshay, A. (1978). Editorial: It could work better. *Educational Leadership, 36,* 164.

Fox, J. (1975). Planning interdisciplinary units within a team structure. *Middle School Journal, 5,* 49–51.

Frisancho, A. R. (1981). *Human adaptation: A functional interpretation.* Ann Arbor: The University of Michigan Press.

Furtwengler, W. (1991). *Reducing student misbehavior through student involvment in school restructuring processes.* Paper presented at the conference of the American Educational Research Association, Chicago, IL.

Gage, N. (1979, May). Address to the seminar on teacher effectiveness. Gainesville, Florida.

Gamoran, A., & Berends, M. (1987). The effect of stratification in secondary schools: Synthesis of survey and ethnographic research. *Review of Educational Research, 57,* 415–435.

Garbarino, J. (1980). Some thoughts on school size and its effects on adolescent development. *Journal of Youth and Adolescence, 9,* 19–31.

Garvin, J. (1987). What do parents expect from middle level schools? *Middle School Journal, 19,* 3–4.

George, P. (1980, November). Discipline, moral development, and levels of schooling. *Educational Forum,* 57–67.

George, P. (1982). Interdisciplinary team organization: Four operational phases. *Middle School Journal, 13,* 10–13.

George, P. (1983). *The theory z school.* Columbus, OH: National Middle School Association.

George, P. (1984). Middle school instructional organization: An emerging consensus. In Lounsbury, J. (Ed.). *Perspectives: Middle school education, 1964–1984.* Columbus, OH: National Middle School Association, 52–67.

George, P. (1987). Teambuilding without tears. *Personnel Journal, 66,* 122–129.

George, P. (1988). *Teamwork.* Gainesville, FL: Teacher Education Resources.

George, P. (1989). *The Japanese junior high school.* Columbus, OH: National Middle School Association.

George, P. (1990). From junior high to middle school—principals' perspectives. *NASSP Bulletin, 74,* 86–94.

George, P. & Anderson, W. G. (1989). Maintaining the middle school: A national survey. *NASSP Bulletin, 73,* 67–74.

George, P., George, R., Martinello, M. & Kinzer, S. (1973). *Learning centers.* Gainesville, FL: Florida Educational Research and Development Council.

George, P. & McEwin, K. (1978). Middle school teacher education: A progress report. *Journal of Teacher Education, 29,* 13–16.

George. P. & Oldaker, L. L. (1985). *Evidence for the middle school.* Columbus, OH: National Middle School Association.

George, P. & Oldaker, L. (1986). A national survey of middle school effectiveness. *Educational Leadership, 43,* 79–85.

George, P. & Stevenson, C. (1989). The "very best teams" in the "very best" middle schools as described by middle school principals. *TEAM, 3,* 6–17.

George, P., Stevenson, C., Thomason, J. & Beane, J. (1992). *The middle school: And beyond.* Alexandria, VA: Association for Supervision and Curriculum Development.

Golay, K. (1982). *Learning patterns and temperament styles.* Fullerton, CA: Manas-Systems.

Good, T. & Brophy, J. (1990). *Educational psychology: A realistic approach.* (4th ed.). New York: Longman.

Goodlad, J. (1984). *A place called school.* New York: McGraw-Hill.

Gordon, T. (1977). *Leadership effectiveness training.* New York: Bantam Books.

Greeson, L. E. & Williams, R. A. (1986). Social implications of music videos for youth. *Youth and Society, 18,* 177–189.

Groover-Leak, E. Personal communication. December 4, 1989.

Gruhn, W. & Douglas, H. (1971). *The modern junior high school.* (3rd ed.). New York: The Ronald Press.

Guillard, O. Personal communication. October 19, 1989.

Gullotta, T. P. (1983). Early adolescence, alienation, and education. *Theory into Practice, 22,* 151–154.

Guskey, T. R. (1985). *Implementing mastery learning.* Belmont, CA: Wadsworth Publishing Company.

Guskey, T. R. (1988). Response to Slavin: Who defines best? *Educational Leadership, 46, 26–27.*

Guskey, T. R. (1991, April). *Using mastery learning in the regular classroom to help learning disabled and at-risk students.* Paper presented at the meeting of the American Educational Research Association, Chicago, IL.

Guskey, T. & Pigott, T. (1988). Research on group-based mastery learning programs: A meta-analysis. *Journal of Educational Research, 81,* 197–216.

Hall, J. A. (1987). Parent-adolescent conflict: An empirical review. *Adolescence, 22,* 767–789.

Hall, G. & Hord, S. (1987). *Change in schools: Facilitating the process.* Albany, NY: State University Press.

Hopfenberg. W., Levin, H., Meister, G. & Rogers, J. (1990). *Toward accelerated middle schools.* Stanford, CA: Stanford University School of Education.

Holland, A. & Andre, T. (1987). Participation in extracurricular activities in secondary school: What is known, what needs to be known? *Review of Educational Research, 57,* 437–466.

Honig, W. (1987). "Foreword", in *Caught in the Middle.* Sacramento, CA: California State Department of Public Instruction, Bill.

Hough, D. (1989). *Middle level education practices in California.* Riverside, CA: California Educational Research Cooperative.

Howard, A. & Stoumbis, G. (1970). *The junior high and middle school: Issues and practices.* Toronto: Intext Educational Publishers.

Hughes, K. & Martray, C. (1991, April). *Motivation training with preadolescents.* Paper presented at the annual meeting of the American Educational Research Association, Chicago, IL.

Huyett, W. Personal communication. December 7, 1989.

Ianni, F. A. J. (1989). Providing a structure for adolescent development. *Phi Delta Kappan, 70,* 673–682.

Irvin, J. (1990). *Coming of age: The impact of PRIME legislation of middle level schools in Florida.* Tallahassee: Florida Department of Education.

Isberg, R. S., Hauser, S. T., Jacobson, A. M., Powers, S., Noam, G., Weiss-Perry, B. & Follansbee, D. (1989). Parental contexts of adolescent self-esteem: A developmental perspective. *Journal of Youth and Adolescence, 18,* 1–23.

Jackson, M. A. (1987). The LD adolescent at risk: Developmental tasks, social competence, and communication effectiveness. *Journal of Reading, Writing, and Learning Disabilities International, 3,* 241–257.

James, M. (1986). *Adviser-advisee programs: Why, what, and how.* Columbus, OH: National Middle School Association.

Jenkins, J. (Ed.). (February, 1988). *Teachers as advisors program: Evaluation report.* Tallahassee: Florida State Department of Education.

Johnson, D. & Johnson, R. (1989a). *Cooperation and competition: Theory and research.* Edina, MN: Interaction Book Company.

Johnson, D. & Johnson, R. (1989b). *Leading the cooperative school.* Edina, MN: Interaction Book Company.

Johnson, D. W., Johnson, R. T. & Holubec, E. J. (1991). *Cooperation in the classroom.* Edina, MN: Interaction Book Company.

Johnson, M. (1962). School in the middle—Junior high: Education's problem child, *Saturday Review, 45,* 40–42, 56.

Jones, G. (1990, November). *The impact of middle school organizational changes on science classroom instruction.* Paper presented at the annual conference of the National Middle School Association, Long Beach, CA.

Joyce, B., Showers, B. & Weil, M. (1991). *Models of teaching.* Englewood Cliffs, NJ: Prentice-Hall.

Kealy, R. (1970) The middle school movement, 1969–70. *National Elementary School Principal, 51,* 20–25.

Klausmeier, H. & Daresh, J. (April, 1979). *A description of Webster Transitional School, 1977–78.* Madison, WI: Wisconsin Research and Development Center for Individualized Schooling.

Knapp, M. S. & Shields, P. M. (1991). *Better schooling for the children of poverty.* Berkeley, CA: McCutchan Publishing Company.

Kohlberg, L. (1981). *The philosophy of moral development: Moral stages and the idea of justice.* San Francisco: Harper & Row.

Kohn, A. (1986). *No contest: The case against competition.* Boston: Houghton, Mifflin.

Kolb, D. C. (1988). Self-esteem change and mandatory experiential education. *The Journal of Experiential Education, 11*(3), 31–37.

Kozol, J. (1991). *Savage inequalities: Children in America's schools.* New York: Crown Publishers.

Kramer, L. & Colvin, C. (1991). *Rules, responsibility, and respect: The school lives of marginal students.* Paper presented at the annual meeting of the American Educational Research Association, Chicago, IL.

Kroger, J. (1989). *Identity in adolescence.* New York: Routledge.

Kulik, C-L., Kulik, J. & Bangert-Drowns, R. (1990). Effectiveness of mastery learning programs: A meta-analysis. *Review of Educational Research, 60,* 265–299.

Lambert, B. G., Rothschild, B. F., Altland, R. & Green, L. B. (1972). *Adolescence: Transition from childhood to maturity.* Monterey, CA: Brooks/Cole.

Lawrence, C., Galloway, A. & Lawrence, G. (1988). *The practicum centers approach to seatwork: A handbook.* New York: McKenzie Press.

Lawrence, G. (1982). *People types and tiger stripes.* (2nd edition). Gainesville, FL: Center for Application of Psychological Type.

Lawson, E. Personal communication. May, 1989.

Lipsitz, J. (1980). The age group. In M. Johnson (Ed.), *Toward adolescence: The middle school years, Seventy-ninth Yearbook of the National Society for the Study of Education, Part 1.* Chicago: University of Chicago Press.

Lipsitz, J. (1984). *Successful schools for young adolescents.* New Brunswick, NJ: Transaction Books.

Lounsbury, J. (1960). How the junior high school came to be. *Educational Leadership, 18,* 145–147.

Lounsbury, J. & Clark, D. (1990). *Inside grade eight: From apathy to excitement.* Reston, VA: National Association of Secondary School Principals.

Lounsbury, J. & Johnston, H. (1988). *Life in three sixth grades.* Reston, VA: National Associaton of Secondary School Principals.

Lounsbury, J. & Johnston, H. (1985). *How fares the ninth grade?* Reston, VA: National Association of Secondary School Principals.

Lounsbury, J., & Marani, J. (1964). *The junior high school we saw: One day in the eighth grade.* Washington, DC: Association for Supervision and Curriculum Development.

Lounsbury, J., Marani, J. & Compton, M. (1980). *The middle school in profile: A day in the seventh grade.* Columbus, OH: National Middle School Association.

Lounsbury, J. & Vars, G. (1978). *A curriculum for the middle school years.* New York: Harper and Row.

Luker, R., & Johnston, J. (1988). TV and teens: Television in adolescent social development. *Social Education, 52,* 350–353.

Lynch, J. (1990). *Evaluation report for Skowhegan Area Middle School.* Skowhegan, ME: School District #54.

McDonald, F. (1976). Report on phase II of the Beginning Teacher Evaluation Study. *Journal of Teacher Education, 27,* 39–42.

MacIver, D. (1990). Meeting the needs of young adolescents: Advisory groups, interdisciplinary teaching teams, and school transition programs. *Phi Delta Kappan, 71,* 458–464.

MacIver, D. (1990, August). *Effects of report card and recognition practices on the achievement of early adolescents who have fallen behind or learn more slowly.* Paper presented at the convention of the American Psychological Association, Boston, MA.

Maerhoff, G. (1988). Withered hopes, stillborn dreams: The dismal panorama of urban schools. *Phi Delta Kappan, 69,* 632–638.

Manfredonia, W. Personal communication. December 6, 1989.

Manning, M. L. (1988). Erikson's psychosocial theories help explain early adolescence. *NASSP Bulletin, 72* (509), 95–100.

Marshall, J. (1986). *Dealing with difficult behavior. Workbook.* New York: American Management Association.

Maynard, M. (April 19, 1991). Chrysler builds team spirit. *USA Today.* p. 11.

McCarthy, B. (1991). Using the 4MAT System to bring learning styles to schools. *Educational Leadership, 48,* 31–37.

McEwin, C. K. & Alexander, W. (1990). *Middle level programs and practices in elementary schools.* Columbus, OH: National Middle School Association.

McGee, J., Krajewski, R. & Keese, E. (1977). *A three-year study of Brown Middle School, 1974–77.* Murfreesboro, TN: Middle Tennessee State University.

McKenry, P. C., Everett, J. E., Ramseur, H. P. & Carter, C. J. (1989). Research on black adolescents: A legacy of cultural bias. *Journal of Adolescent Research, 4,* 254–264.

McPartland, J. (1991). *How departmentalized staffing and interdisciplinary teaming combine for effects on middle grades students.* Paper presented at the annual conference of the American Educational Research Association, Chicago, IL.

McWalters, P. (1989). *Superintendent's proposal to the board of education. Position paper on the redesign of public education in Rochester.* Rochester, NY; Rochester City School District.

Meyer, L., Harootunian, B. & Williams, D. (1991, April). *Inclusive middle schooling practices: Shifting from deficit to support models.* Paper presented at the annual conference of the American Educational Research Association, Chicago, IL.

Middle Grade Task Force. (1987). *Caught in the middle: The task of educational reform for young adolescents in California schools.* Sacramento, CA: California State Department of Education.

Middle Grades Task Force. (1991). *Last best chance.* Raleigh, NC: North Carolina Department of Public Instruction.

Mijuskovic, B. (1988). Loneliness and adolescent alcoholism. *Adolescence, 23,* 503–516.

Miller, B. (1980). *Achievement of ninth grade students in science curricula emphasizing concrete and formal reasoning.* Unpublished doctoral dissertation, Gainesville, FL: The University of Florida.

Miller, W. (1978). Unobtrusive measure can help in assessing growth. *Educational Leadership, 35,* 264–269.

Mills, G. (1961). The how and why of public schools. *Nation's Schools, 68,* 6.

Mills, R. C., Dunham, R. G. & Alpert, G. P. (1988). Working with high-risk youth in prevention and early intervention programs: Toward a comprehensive wellness model. *Adolescence, 23,* 643–660.

Mizell, H. & Gonzalez, E. (1991). *Disadvantaged youth. Program update.* New York: Edna McConnell Clark Foundation.

Moeller, T. Personal communication, December, 1989.

Montemayor, R., Adams, G. R. & Gullotta, T. P. (Eds.). (1990). *From childhood to adolescence: A transitional period?* Newbury Park, CA: Sage.

Moody, M. Personal communication, October, 1988.

Morgan, L. (1987). *Freeport high school advisor handbook.* Freeport, FL: School Board of Walton County.

Morris, D. (1969). *The naked ape.* New York: Dell Publishing Company.

Murphy, J. (1965). *Middle schools.* New York: Educational Facilities Laboratories.

Muuss, R. E. (1988). Carol Gilligan's theory of sex differences in the development of moral reasoning during adolescence. *Adolescence, 23,* 229–243.

Myrick, R. & Myrick, L. (1990). *The teacher advisor program.* Ann Arbor, MI: ERIC Counseling and Personnel Services Clearinghouse.

National AIDS Information Clearinghouse (October, 1990). Phone correspondence. Service of U.S. Department of Health and Human Services, Public Health Service, Centers for Disease Control.

National Association of Secondary School Principals. (n.d.). *An agenda for excellence at the middle level.* Reston, VA: Author.

National Center for Health Statistics (August 15, 1990). *Monthly Vital Statistics Report,* 39 (4) Supplement, U.S. Department of Health and Human Services, Centers for Disease Control.

National Commission on Excellence in Education. (1983, April 27). An open letter to the American people. A nation at risk: The imperative for educational reform. *Education Week.*

National Council for Teachers of Mathematics Working Group.(1989). *Curriculum standards for school mathematics.* Reston, VA: The Council.

National Middle School Association. (1977). Report of the NMSA Committee on Future Goals and Directions. *Middle School Journal, 8,* 16.

National Middle School Association. (1990). Resolutions 1989–1990. *Middle School Journal, 21,* 56.

National Middle School Association. (1991). *Position statement. Preliminary draft.* Columbus, OH: The Association.

National Middle School Association. (1992). *This we believe.* Columbus, OH: The Association.

Needham, N. (1989). We've got the time to teach. *NEA Today.* September, pp. 4–5.

Newman, J. (1985). Adolescents: Why they can be so obnoxious. *Adolescence, 20,* 635–646.

Newman, P. R. & Newman, B. M. (1988). Differences between childhood and adulthood: The identity watershed. *Adolescence, 23,* 551–557.

Oetting, E. R. & Beauvais, F. (1987). Peer cluster theory, socialization characteristics, and adolescent drug use: A path analysis. *Journal of Counseling Psychology, 34,* 205–213.

Office of the Superintendent (March, 1979). *The plan for the two year transition to the middle school.* Milwaukee, WI: Milwaukee Public Schools.

Oliner, P. M. (1986). Legitimating and implementing prosocial education. *Humboldt Journal of Social Relations, 13,* 391–410.

O'Neil, J. (1991). Making sense of style. *Educational Leadership, 48,* 4–9.

Palmer, A. (1985, October). Paper presented at the meeting of the Florida Association of Children with Learning Disabilities, Orlando, FL.

Petersen, A. C. & Crockett, L. (1985). Pubertal timing and grade effects on adjustment. *Journal of Youth and Adolescence, 14,* 191–206.

Peterson, J. (1991). *A post occupancy evaluation: Wakulla Middle School.* Master's project for the Florida A & M University School of Architecture. Tallahassee, FL.

Piaget, J. (1977). *The essential Piaget.* New York: Basic Books.

Pickler, G. (1991). *IMPACT: The Orange County middle school advisement program.* Unpublished manuscript.

Porter, A. C. & Brophy, J. (1988). Synthesis of research on good teaching: Insights from the work of the institute for research on teaching. *Educational Leadership, 45,* 74–85.

Plodzik, K. & George, P. (1989). Interdisciplinary team organization. *Middle School Journal, 20,* 15–19.

Proefrock, D. W. (1981). Adolescence: Social fact and psychological concept. *Adolescence, 16,* 851–858.

Putbrese, L. (1989). Advisory programs at the middle level—the student's response. *National Association of Secondary School Principals Bulletin, 73,* 514.

Reck, R. & Long, B. (1985). The win-win negotiator. Escondido, CA: Blanchard Training and Development, Inc.

Reeves, B. (1974). *Implementation guide, IDEA change program for individually guided education, ages 10–15.* Dayton, OH: Institute for Development of Educational Activities.

Resolutions Committee. (1989). National Middle School Association 1988–89 resolutions. *Middle School Journal, 20,* 18–20.

Reynolds, M. (1962). A framework for considering some issues in special education. *Exceptional Children, 28,* 368.

Riemke, C. (1988) All must play—the only way. *Middle School Journal, 19,* 8–9.

Robinson, A. (1991). Cooperation or exploitation? The argument against cooperative learning for talented students. *Journal for the Education of the Gifted, 14,* 9–27.

Robinson, S. A. (1991). Collaborative consultation. In Wong, B.Y.L. (Ed.), *Learning about learning disabilities.* San Diego: Academic Press.

Romano, N. & Timmers, N. (1978). Middle school athletics—intramurals or interscholastics. *Middle School Journal, 9,* 16.

Rosenshine, B. & Stevens, R. (1986). Teaching functions. In Wittrock, M. *Handbook of research on teaching, 3rd edition,* pp. 376–391. New York: Macmillan.

Rossman, G. & Collins, P. (1991). *Restructuring to support students in the middle school: "Teaming" to create enhanced identification of at-risk youth.* Paper presented at the annual meeting of the American Educational Research Association, Chicago, IL.

Savin-Williams, R. C. & Demo, D. H. (1983). Conceiving or misconceiving the self: issues in adolescent self-esteem. *Journal of Early Adolescence, 3,* 121–140.

Saylor, J., Alexander, W. & Lewis, A. (1981). *Curriculum planning: For better teaching and learning.* New York: Holt, Rinehart and Winston.

Scheidlinger, S. (1984). The adolescent peer group revisited: Turbulence or adaptation? *Small Group Behavior, 15,* 387–397.

Schmuck, R. & Runkel, P. (1985). *The handbook of organization development in schools, 3rd Ed.* Prospect Heights, IL: Waveland Press.

Schreck, W. (1969). Cited in Frank Brunetti, "The School in the Middle—A Search for New Direction," *SPL Reports,* June, 1969, p. 2.

Schwartz, G., Merten, D. & Bursik, R. J., Jr. (1987). Teaching styles and performance values in junior high school: The impersonal, nonpersonal, and personal. *American Journal of Education, 95,* 346–370.

Senge, P. (1990). *The fifth discipline: The art and practice of the learning organization.* New York: Doubleday.

Shaplin, J. & Olds, H. (Eds.). (1964). *Team teaching.* New York: Harper & Row.

Shave, D. & Shave, B. (1989). *Early adolescence and the search for self: A developmental perspective.* New York: Praeger.

Sicola, P. K. (1991). Where do gifted students fit? An examination of middle school philosophy as it relates to ability grouping and the gifted learner. *Journal for the Education of the Gifted, 14,* 37–49.

Simmons, R. G. & Blyth, D. A. (1987). *Moving into adolescence.* New York: Aldine de Gruyter.

Slater, J. (1990). *Middle grades reform in California: Auspicious beginnings and high expectations. Executive summary and recommendations: Interim evaluation.* Sacramento, CA: California State Department of Education.

Slavin, R. E. (1987). Mastery learning reconsidered. *Review of Educational Research, 57,* 175–213.

Slavin, R. E. (1989). On mastery learning and mastery teaching. *Educational Leadership, 46,* 77–79.

Slavin, R. E. (1990a). Research on cooperative learning: Consensus and controversy. *Educational Leadership, 47,* 52–55.

Slavin, R. E. (1990b). Achievement effects of ability grouping in secondary schools: A best-evidence synthesis. *Review of Educational Research, 60,* 471–500.

Slavin, R. E. (1991a). Synthesis of research on cooperative learning. *Educational Leadership, 48,* 71–82.

Slavin, R. E. (1991b). Ability grouping, cooperative learning and the gifted. *Journal for the Education of the Gifted, 14,* 3–6.

Slavin, R. E. & Madden, N. A. (1989). What works for students at risk: A research synthesis. *Educational Leadership, 46,* 4–13.

Slavin, R., Madden, N., Karweit, N., Livermon, B., & Dolan, L (1990). Success for All: First year outcomes of a comprehensive plan for reforming American education. *American Educational Research Journal, 27,* 255–278.

Smith, L. (1980). A model for cross-age tutoring. *Middle School Journal, 9,* 26–27.

Speaker's Task Force. (1984). *The forgotten years: Report of the speaker's task force on middle childhood education.* Tallahassee: Florida House of Representatives.

Spindler, J. & George, P. (1984). Participatory leadership in the middle school. *The Clearing House, 57,* 293–295.

Staff. (1990, Winter/Spring). Adolescence: Path to a productive life or a diminished future. *Carnegie Quarterly,* p. 1.

Steinberg, L. & Silverberg, S. B. (1986). The vicissitudes of autonomy in early adolescence. *Child Development, 57,* 841–851.

Streitmatter, J. L. & Pate, G. S. (1989). Identity status development and cognitive prejudice in early adolescents. *Journal of Early Adolescence, 9,* 142–152.

Stevens, R. (1990a). *Student team reading: A brief overview.* Unpublished manuscript.

Stevens, R. (1990b). *Student team writing: A brief overview.* Unpublished manuscript.

Storeygard, J., LeBaron, E. & Shippen, N. (1991). The development of the reading/writing workshop course. *Middle School Journal, 22,* 33–35.

Summer Seminar. (1972). *Report of the middle school task force.* Gainesville, FL: Alachua County Schools.

Superintendent's Middle Grade Task Force. (1987). *Caught in the middle: Educational reform for young adolescents in California public schools.* Sacramento: California State Department of Education.

Syropoulos, M. (1990). *Efficacy: The middle school program. Evaluation report, 1989–1990.* Detroit, MI: Detroit Public Schools, Division of Management Effectiveness.

Taba, H. (1963). *Curriculum development: Theory and practice.* New York: Harcourt Brace & World, Inc. *The Middle School.* (1971). Chestertown, MD: Kent County Public Schools.

Thompson, E. (1971). *The middle school.* Atlanta, GA: Instructional Division, Atlanta Public Schools.

Thomas, R., Pickler, G. & Sevick, M. J. (1990). *Middle school instructional practices scale.* Unublished manuscript. Orlando, FL: Orange County Public Schools.

Thornburg, H. D. (1980). Early adolescents: Their developmental characteristics. *The High School Journal, 63,* 216.

Thornburg, H. D. (1983). Is early adolescence really a stage of development? *Theory into Practice, 22,* 79–84.

Tierno, M. J. (1983). Responding to self-concept disturbance among early adolescents: A psychosocial view for educators. *Adolescence, 18,* 577–584.

Tittle, C. (1980). Evaluative studies. In Johnson, M. (Ed.) *Toward adolescence: The middle school years, Seventy-Ninth Yearbook of the National Society for the Study of Education,* Part I. Chicago, IL: University of Chicago Press.

Toepfer, C. F., Jr. (1980). Brain growth periodization data: Some suggestions for reorganizing middle grades education. *The High School Journal, 63,* 224–226.

Tye, K. (1985). *The junior high: School in search of a mission.* New York: University Press of America.

Urbanski, A. (1991, October 25). Real change is real hard: Lessons learned in Rochester. *Education Week,* p. 29.

Uribe, V. M. (1986). Adolescents: Their special physical, social and metapsychologic needs. *Adolescence, 21,* 667–673.

Usiskin, Z., et.al. (1990). *Transition mathematics: Teacher's edition.* Glenview, IL: Scott, Foresman and Company.

Van Til, W., Vars, G. & Lounsbury, J. (1961). *Modern education for the junior high school years.* Indianapolis, IN: Bobbs-Merrill.

Waber, D. P., Mann, M. B., Merola, J. & Moylan, P. M. (1985). Physical maturation rate and cognitive performance in early adolescence: A longitudinal examination. *Developmental Psychology, 21,* 666–681.

Wagner, J. A. (1987). Formal operations and ego identity in adolescence. *Adolescence, 22,* 23–35.

Wagner, J. H. (1978). *Peer teaching in spelling: An experimental study in selected Seventh Day Adventist High Schools.* Unpublished doctoral dissertation, University of Florida, Gainesville.

Walberg. H. (1986). Synthesis of research on teaching. In Wittrock, M., *Handbook of research on teaching, 3rd Edition.* New York: Macmillan.

Walberg, H. (1990). Productive teaching and instruction: Assessing the knowledge base. *Phi Delta Kappan, 71,* 470–478.

Warren, R., Good, G. & Velten, E. (1984). Measurement of social-evaluative anxiety in junior high school students. *Adolescence, 19,* 643–648.

Waxman, H. C. & Walberg, H. J. (1991). *Effective teaching: Current research.* Berkeley, CA: McCutchan Publishing Company.

West, T., Bates, P. & Schmeil, R. (1979). *Mainstreaming: Problems, potentials, and perspectives.* Minneapolis, MN: National Support Systems Project.

Winton, J. (1989). *Shelburne middle school.* Unpublished manuscript.

Wittig, M. A. (1983). Sex role development in early adolescence. *Theory into Practice, 22,* 105–111.

Working Group on the Emerging Adolescent Learner. (1975). *The middle school we need.* Washington, DC: Association for Supervision and Curriculum Development.

Zerlin, F. Personal communication. June 20, 1989.

Zorfass, J., Remz, A. & Persky, S. (1991). A technology integration model for middle schools. *T.H.E. Journal,* 69–71.

Taylor Middle School
850 Taylor Blvd.
Milbrae, CA 94030

Tenaya Middle School
1239 W. Mesa
Fresno, CA 93711

Colorado

Angevine Middle School
1150 S. Boulder Road
Lafayette, CO 80026

Broomfield Heights Middle School
1555 Daphne St.
Broomfield Heights, CO 80020

Challenger Middle School
10215 Lexington Drive
Colorado Springs, CO 80920

East Middle School
830 Gunnison Ave.
Grand Junction, CO 81501

Estes Park Middle School
Box 1140
Estes Park, CO 80517

Heaton Middle School
38 Robertson Road
Pueblo, CO 81001

Laredo Middle School
5000 Laredo St.
Denver, CO 80232

Louisville Middle School
1341 Main St.
Louisville, CO 80027

Panorama Middle School
2145 S. Chelton
Colorado Springs, CO 80916

Parker Junior High School
6651 Pine Lane Ave.
Parker, CO 80134

Westview Middle School
11651 N. 85th St.
Longmont, CO 80503

Connecticut

Killingsly Intermediate School
1629 Upper Maple St.
Dayville, CT 06214

Quirk Middle School
85 Edwards St.
Hartford, CT 06120

Delaware

Shue Middle School
1500 Capitol Trail
Newark, DE 19711

Florida

Azalea Middle School
7855 22nd Ave. North
St. Petersburg, FL 33710

Brookside Middle School
3636 S. Shade Ave.
Sarasota, FL 33579

Campbell Drive Middle School
900 NE 23rd Ave.
Homestead, FL 33033

Conway Middle School
4600 Anderson Road
Orlando, FL 32806

Coral Springs Middle School
10300 W. Wiles Road
Coral Springs, FL 33076

DeLand Middle School
1400 S. Aquarius Ave.
DeLand, FL 32724

Deltona Middle School
250 Enterprise Road
Deltona, FL 32725

Fort Clarke Middle School
9301 NW 23rd Blvd.
Gainesville, FL 32606

Fort King Middle School
545 NE 17th Ave.
Ocala, FL 32670

Glenridge Middle School
2616 Westminster Terr.
Oviedo, FL 32765

Howard Bishop Middle School
NE 9th St.
Gainesville, FL 32601

Jackson Heights Middle School
141 Academy Drive
Oviedo, FL 32765

Jackson Middle School
6000 Stonewall Jackson Road
Orlando, FL 32807

Lakeview Middle School
1200 W. Bay St.
Winter Garden, FL 34787

Lincoln Middle School
1001 SE 12th St.
Gainesville, FL 32601

Lockhart Middle School
3411 Dr. Love Road
Orlando, FL 32810

Logger's Run Middle School
11584 West Palmetto Park Road
Boca Raton, FL 33428

Mandarin Middle School
5100 Hood Road
Jacksonville, FL 32257

McIntosh Middle School
701 S. McIntosh Road
Sarasota, FL 34232

Meadowbrook Middle School
6000 North Lane
Orlando, FL 32808

Mebane Middle School
Rte 1, Box 4
Alachua, FL 32615

Nautilus Middle School
21211 NE 23rd Ave.
North Miami Beach, FL 33180

New Smyrna Beach Middle School
1200 S. Myrtle Ave.
New Smyrna Beach, FL 32069

Norland Middle School
1235 NW 192nd Terr.
Miami, FL 33169

Ormond Beach Middle School
151 Domicilio Ave.
Ormond Beach, FL 32174

Sarasota Middle School
1001 School Ave.
Sarasota, FL 33577

Silver Sands Middle School
1300 Herbert St.
Port Orange, FL 32119

Southside Fundamental Middle School
1701 10th St. South
St. Petersburg, FL 33750

Southwest Middle School
3834 Appleton Way
Orlando, FL 32806

Spring Hill Middle School
Box 907
High Springs, FL 32643

Tequesta Middle School
1800 Indian Trace
Fort Lauderdale, FL 33326

Wakulla County Middle School
Rte 2, Box 526
Crawfordville, FL 32327

Walker Middle School
150 Amidon Lane
Orlando, FL 32809

Westwood Middle School
3215 NW 15th Ave.
Gainesville, FL 32605

Georgia

Bunche Middle School
1925 Niskey Lane Road SW
Atlanta, GA 30331

East Cobb Middle School
380 Holt Road
Marietta, GA 30065

Sandy Springs Middle School
227 Sandy Springs Place
Atlanta, GA 30328

Trickum Middle School
948 Cole Drive
Lilburn, GA 30247

Illinois

Batavia Middle School
10 S. Batavia Ave.
Batavia, IL 60510

Gregory Middle School
2621 Springdale Circle
Naperville, IL 60564

Jefferson Middle School
1115 Crescent Drive
Champaign, IL 61821

Indiana

Crispus Attucks Middle School
13th & M.L. King
Indianapolis, IN 46202

D.W. Dennis Middle School
222 NW 7th St.
Richmond, IN 47374

Henry W. Eggers Middle School
5825 Blaine Avenue
Hammond, IN 46320

Jennings County Middle School
820 W. Walnut St.
North Vernon, IN 46265

Navarre Middle School
4702 W. Ford
South Bend, IN 46619

Kansas

Blue Valley Middle School
7500 W. 149th Terr.
Overland Park, KS 66223

Leawood Middle School
2410 W. 123rd St.
Leawood, KS 66209

Kentucky

Clark Middle School
2105 Mt. Sterling Road
Winchester, KY 40391

Conkwright Middle School
360 Mt. Sterling Road
Winchester, KY 40391

Graham Brown Middle School
546 1st St.
Louisville, KY 40202

Lassiter Middle School
820 Candleworth Drive
Louisville, KY 40213

Noe Middle School
121 W. Lee St.
Louisville, KY 40208

Oldham County Middle School
P.O. Box 157
Buckner, KY 40010

South Oldham Middle School
6403 W. Highway 146
Crestwood, KY 40014

Southern Middle School
4530 Bellvue Ave.
Louisville, KY 40215

Thomas Jefferson Middle School
4401 Rangeland Road
Louisville, KY 40219

Wassom Middle School
Forrest Road and Gorgas Ave.
Fort Campbell, KY 42223–5000

Western Middle School
2201 W. Main St.
Louisville, KY 40212

Louisiana

Caddo Middle Magnet School
7635 Cornelius Drive
Shreveport, LA 71106

Maine

King Middle School
92 Deering Ave.
Portland, ME 04102

Middle School of the Kennebunks
87 Fletcher St.
Kennebunk, ME 04043

Skowhegan Middle School
Willow St.
Skowhegan, ME 04976

Wells Junior High School
P.O. Box 130
Wells, ME 04090

Maryland

Hoover Middle School
8810 Postoak Road
Rockville, MD 20845

Mayfield Woods Middle School
10782 Green Mountain Circle
Columbia, MD 21044

Owen Brown Middle School
6700 Cradlerock Way
Columbia, MD 21055

Patapsco Middle School
8885 Old Frederick Road
Ellicott City, MD 21403

Pikesville Middle School
77012 Seven Mile Lane
Baltimore, MD 21208

Westminster West Middle School
60 Monroe St.
Westminster, MD 21157

Wilde Lake Middle School
10481 Cross Fox Lane
Columbia, MD 21044

Massachusetts

Lynnfield Middle School
505 N. Main St.
Lynnfield, MA 01940

Nock Middle School
Low Street
Newburyport, MA 01950

Powder Mill Middle School
94 Powder Mill Road
Southwick, MA 01077

Shrewsbury Middle School
Sherwood Ave.
Shrewsbury, MA 01545

Winthrop Middle School
Pauline St.
Winthrop, MA 02152

Michigan

East Grand Rapids Middle School
2425 Lake Drive SE
Grand Rapids, MI 49506

Kinawa Middle School
1900 Kinawa Drive
Okemos, MI 48864

L'Anse Creuse Middle School North
46201 Fairchild Ave.
Mt. Clemens, MI 48045

L'Anse Creuse Middle School South
34641 Jefferson
Mt. Clemens, MI 48045

MacDonald Middle School
1601 Burcham Drive
East Lansing, MI 48823

Marshall Middle School
100 E. Green
Marshall, MI 49068

Tappan Middle School
2251 E. Stadium Blvd.
Ann Arbor, MI 48104

West Hills Middle School
2601 Lone Pine Road
West Bloomfield, MI 48323

Minnesota

Chaska Middle School
1750 Chestnut St.
Chaska, MN 55318

Marshall Middle School
207 N. 4th St.
Marshall, MN 56268

Missouri

Antioch Middle School
2100 NE 65th St.
Kansas City, MO 64118

Cross Keys Middle School
14205 Cougar Drive
Florissant, MO 63033

Nipher Middle School
700 S. Kirkwood Road
Kirkwood, MO 63122

Montana

Frank Brattin Middle School
215 Olive St.
Colstrip, MT 59323

Paris Gibson Middle School
2400 Central Ave.
Great Falls, MT 59401

Nebraska

Millard North Middle School
2828 S. 139th Place
Omaha, NE 68144

New Hampshire

Amherst Middle School
P.O. Box 966
Amherst, NH 03031

New Jersey

Russell Brackman Middle School
25 Birdsall St.
Barnegat, NJ 08005

West Windsor-Plainsboro Middle School
55 Grovers Mill Road
Plainsboro, NJ 08536

New Mexico
John F. Kennedy Middle School
600 S. Boardman Ave.
Gallup, NM 87301

Vista Middle School
301 W. Amador
Las Cruces, NM 88005

New York
Amherst Middle School
55 Kings Highway
Snyder, NY 14226

Bay Shore Middle School
393 Brooke Ave.
Bay Shore, NY 11706

Canandaigua Middle School
Granger St.
Canandaigua, NY 14424

Churchville-Chili Middle School
139 Fairbanks Road
Churchville, NY 14428

Farnsworth Middle School
State Farm Road
Guilderland, NY 12084

Iroquois Middle School
2495 Rosendale Ave.
Niskayuna, NY 12309

Jamesville-DeWitt Middle School
Randall Rd.
Jamesville, NY 13078

Louis Armstrong Middle School
3202 Junction Blvd.
East Elmhurst, NY 11369

J. MacArthur Burr Middle School
143 Church St.
Nanuet, NY 10954

Newark Middle School
316 W. Miller St.
Newark, NY 14513

Salamanca Middle School
50 Iroquois Drive
Salamanca, NY 14779

Shoreham-Wading River Middle School
Randall Road
Shoreham, NY 11786–9745

Wantagh Middle School
Beltagh Ave.
Wantagh, NY 11793

North Carolina
Brewster Middle School
Bldg. 40, MCB
Camp LeJeune, NC 28542

Charlotte County Day Middle School
5936 Green Rea Road
Charlotte, NC 28226

Griffin Middle School
E. Washington Drive
High Point, NC 27260

Piedmont Open Middle School
1241 E. 10th St.
Charlotte, NC 28204

Western Middle School
Eldon Drive
Elon College, NC 27244

Ohio
Dublin Middle School
150 W. Bridge St.
Dublin, OH 44107

Ford Middle School
17001 Holland Road
Brook Park, OH 44142

Johnny Appleseed Middle School
314 Cline Ave.
Mansfield, OH 44907

Lee Burneson Middle School
2240 Dover Center Road
Westlake, OH 44145

Trotwood-Madison Junior High
3594 Snyder Road
Trotwood, OH 45426

Oklahoma
Summit Middle School
1703 NW 150th St.
Edmond, OK 73013

Oregon
Oaklea Middle School
1515 Rose St.
Junction City, OR 97448

Roosevelt Middle School
680 E. 24th
Eugene, OR 97405

Pennsylvania
Boyce Middle School
1500 Boyce Road
Upper St. Clair, PA 15241

Fort Couch Middle School
3326 Elmdale Drive
Bethel Park, PA 15102

Greenway Middle School Teacher Center
1400 Crucible St.
Pittsburgh, PA 15205

Stroudsburg Middle
Chipperfield Drive
Stroudsburg, PA 18360

Tennessee
John Sevier Middle School
1200 Watere St.
Kingsport, TN 37660

Texas
Andrews Middle School
405 NW 3rd St.
Andrews, TX 79714

Canyon Vista Middle School
8455 Spicewood Springs Road
Austin, TX 78759

Chisholm Trail Middle School
500 Oakridge
Round Rock, TX 78681

McCulloch Middle School
3520 Normandy
Dallas, TX 75205

Olle Middle School
9200 Boone Road
Alief, TX 77099

Rusk Middle School
411 N. Mound
Nacogdoches, TX 75961

Ysleta Middle School
8691 Independence St.
El Paso, TX 79907

Utah
Bear River Middle School
900 N. 400 East
Tremonton, UT 84337

Vermont
Missisquoi Valley Union School
R.R. 2, Box 268
Swanton, VT 05488

Shelburne Middle School
Harbor Road
Shelburne, VT 05482

Virginia
Northside Middle School
8720 Granby St.
Norfolk, VA 23503

William Byrd Middle School
2910 Washington Ave.
Vinton, VA 24179

Woodbridge Middle School
2201 York Drive
Woodbridge, VA 22191

Washington
Chinook Middle School
4301 NE 6th Ave.
Lacey, WA 98506

College Place Middle School
7501 208th St. SW
Lynnwood, WA 98036

Franklin Middle School
410 S. 19th Ave.
Yakima, WA 98902

Islander Middle School
8225 SE 72nd
Mercer Island, WA 98040

Jefferson Middle School
2200 Conger
Olympia, WA 98502

Odle Middle School
14401 NE 8th
Bellevue, WA 98007

Wisconsin
Oregon Middle School
200 N. Main St.
Oregon, WI 53575–1499

Steuben Middle School
2360 N. 52nd St.
Milwaukee, WI 53210–2796

Stoughton Middle School
220 North St.
Stoughton, WI 53589

Webster Transitional School
Wauwatosa Road
Cedarburg, WI 53012

Wyoming

Douglas Middle School
801 W. Richards
Douglas, WY 82633

Monroe Middle School
250 Monroe Ave.
Green River, WY 82953

Singapore

Singapore American Middle School
60 King's Road
Singapore 1026

Canada

Cosburn Middle School
520 Cosburn Ave.
Toronto, ONT M4J 2P1

Valley Park Middle School
130 Overlea Blvd.
Don Mills, ON, T M3C 1B2

AUTHOR INDEX

SUBJECT INDEX

A

Accreditation of middle schools, 480–482
Activities programs, 204, 215–224
    guidance, and, 215–224
Accelerated Schools Project, 18
    Administration of middle schools, grouping
    students (*see* Grouping students in middle
    schools) leadership as function of (*see*
    Leadership for middle schools) scheduling
    activities (*see* Scheduling classes and activities in
    middle schools) staff development plans, 450
Adolescense, early, 1
    characteristics of, 2, 5
        intellectual, 7–8
        physical, 5–7
        psychosocial, 11–12
    group citizenship, 11
    importance of, 3
    needs, 4
    variability, as outstanding characteristic, 4
AIDS, 5
All Grown Up and No Place To Go, 91
American Association of School Administrators, 513
A Plan for Action, 35
Assistant principals, 499
Association for Supervision and Curriculum
    development, 3, 39, 40
At-risk middle school students, 15–20

B

BRIGHT IDEAS, 508–515
Buildings (*see* Facilities for middle schools)

C

Career education, 76
Carnegie Council on Adolescent Development, 3,
    163
Carnegie Task Force on Education of Young
    Adolescents, 3–4
Caught in the Middle, 33–34, 45
Center for the Study of Moral Education, 10
Chrysler Corporation, 284
Civic Achievement Award Program (CAAP), 11
Civic education, 202
College Board, 19
Cognitive Style Mapping, 173
Computers, 103–105, 174–175
    individualized instruction programs, 163
    scheduling, and, 381–384
Core curriculum (*see* Curriculum of the middle
    schools, design of)
Council on Middle Level Education, 39
Council For Exceptional Children (CEC), 38
Counseling (*see* Guidance)
Curriculum of the middle school, 55–140
    arts, unified programs, 73–77

basic skills programs, 92–100
C.L.A.S.S. program, 112
design of, 62–67
    core and block plans, 64–66, 112
    domains, as basis for, 67
    communications and learning skills as a, 91–
        104
    illustrated, 68
    knowledge as a, 105–112
    personal development as a, 68–91
    interdisciplinary, types of (*see* Inrerdisciplinary
        programs and teams)
    needs and interests, as basis for, 66–67
    problem-solving as basis for, 104–105
    subjects, as basis for, 64
exceptional students, planning for, (*see* Grouping
    students in middle schools, exceptional students)
goals for (*see* Middle schools, goals of)
implementation of (*see* Instruction in middle
    schools)
minicourses, as part of, 78
PALS program, as part of, 79
planning of, 55–62
    citizens' participation in, 62
    department's role in, 59–60
    district's role in, 61–62
    external agencies, participation in, 61–62
    school council, role in, 58–59
    at school level, 57–60
    teacher's role in, 61
    by teams, 60–61, 65
SEARCH program, as part of, 79
SEEK program, 79
seminars, included in, 81–82
SPARK program, as part of, 78–79
subjects in (*see* Subjects in middle schools)

D

Discipline and guidance, 204
"Discourse System", 102
Domains (*see* Curriculum of the middle school,
    design, domains)
Drop-out prevention programs, 19

E

Early Adolescent Health Program, 77
Edna McConnell Clark Foundation, 18
Educational Zip Code, 45–51, 307, 329
Educational Research Service, 38
Effective Parenting Information for Children
    (EPIC), 18
Effective Schools Movement, 504
Elementary Schools,
    grouping plans in, 299–300
    guidance in, 198–199
    instruction in, 247–248